IN PLAIN SIGHT

IN PLAIN SIGHT

THE LIFE AND LIES OF JIMMY SAVILE

Dan Davies

Quercus

First published in Great Britain in 2014 by

Quercus Editions Ltd
55 Baker Street
Seventh Floor, South Block
London
W1U 8EW

A CIP catalogue record for this book is available
from the British Library

HB ISBN 978 1 78206 743 6
TPB ISBN 978 1 78206 744 3
EBOOK ISBN 978 1 78206 745 0

10 9 8 7 6 5 4 3 2 1

Text designed and typeset by Ed Pickford
Printed and bound in Great Britain by Clays Ltd, St Ives plc

Picture credits: p. 99, © Getty Images; p. 171, © DobsonAgency.co.uk; p. 263,
© Mirrorpix; p. 347, © Stanley Franklin/The Sun/News Syndication;
p. 447, © James Leighton-Burns

CONTENTS

PART ONE

1. Apocalypse now then   3
2. Frisk him   12
3. Not again child   20
4. The first brick   31
5. The world was completely black   40
6. Specialist subject: 'Jimmy Savile'   46
7. They felt they were in control   50
8. The power of oddness   59
9. Old and infirm   69
10. 'Power' is the wrong word   80
11. I didn't ask   85
12. Look up, you bastard   94

PART TWO

13. Oscar 'The Duke'   101
14. Smokescreen   109
15. Didn't die, very good   116
16. All front and no back   120
17. Scumbags and slags   127
18. *Sonderkommandos*   137
19. Someone the kids could look up to   141
20. Little slaves   148
21. A lot worse if it was true   158
22. Project DJ   161

PART THREE

23. Nostalgic memories   173
24. The only punter you can recognise from the back   179
25. Let 'em think   184
26. A cross between a Beatle and an Aldwych farce curate   193
27. A dead straight pull time   201
28. Out of the mouths of babes and sucklings   206
29. An old man even then   214
30. TCP tonight   224
31. Good enough to eat   236
32. They know I'm honest   243
33. *Eins, zwei, drei* in the sky   251
34. More insidious than filth   254

PART FOUR

35. Young crumpet that would knock your eyes out   265
36. A bloody saint   274
37. It's obscene   281
38. The best five days of my life   285
39. Pied Piper   292
40. The only thing you can expect from pigs   299
41. We always line our artists up   302
42. A particularly religious moment   310
43. The 1976 temptation   318
44. Your porter hurt me   327
45. Am I saved?   338

PART FIVE

46. Rewriting history   349
47. Sir James   355
48. All sorts of trouble   365

49. I wouldn't let the side down 371
50. Like a Stradivarius 380
51. SOS – Same Old Shit 389
52. I am the boss – it's as simple as that 393
53. 50 million, give or take a few quid 407
54. Runners are junkies 410
55. Off the hook 421
56. And a bit of leg-over and chips 430
57. Ultimate freedom 433
58. A void 444

PART SIX

59. The wrong idea forever 449
60. Operation Ornament 463
61. The policy 472
62. Piss and shite 482
63. Mistakes were made 487
64. Two 16-year-old girls from the Ukraine 495
65. The last great gimmick 499
66. In the palm of his hand 511
67. No local connection 523
68. All that remains 532

Endnotes 547
Select Bibliography 564
Acknowledgements 568
Index 570

PART ONE

S hortly before midnight, on a hill overlooking the North Yorkshire seaside town of Scarborough, the wrought-iron gates of Woodlands Cemetery were locked shut. Police officers took up position outside, while beyond, in the darkness and at the highest point of the burial ground, undertaker Robert Morphet and his men removed tools from their truck. Little was said as portable floodlights were assembled and attached to the generator they had brought with them from the Bradford head-quarters of Joseph A. Hey & Sons, funeral directors.

The plan had been to arrive early the next morning but public and media interest was so great that Morphet had decided to discuss arrangements again with Scarborough Council. It was agreed to get the job completed as quickly as possible; in the dead of night, safe from prying eyes, telescopic lenses and those with possible vengeance on their minds.

The mood was sombre as the men set about their task with hammers, chisels, wedges, long bars and drills. Removing a six-foot wide, four-foot high triple headstone in black, polished granite was hard, physical and, in this case, demoralising work. For the headstone had taken Robert Morphet and his men eight months to complete, being inscribed both front and back with pictures of the man buried beneath, poems written by his friends, a short biog-raphy, a list of charities he'd supported and an epitaph in flowing script along the base: 'It was good while it lasted.'

Three separate slabs of granite, a base and fourteen hundred letters in total, each one finished in gold; Joseph A. Hey & Sons'

3

bill was in excess of £4,000. The headstone had been fixed to its concrete foundation stone only three weeks before.

The placing of the headstone, which was wide enough to cover three plots, should have been the concluding act in the biggest funeral ever arranged in the 130-year history of the firm. It had been a national funeral, a celebration of a remarkable life that had drawn crowds to the streets and been reported extensively in news bulletins and papers across Britain.

Morphet had told reporters that he considered it an honour when his firm was contacted soon after Saturday, 29 October 2011, when the body of an 84-year-old man had been discovered by the caretaker of a block of flats bordering Roundhay Park in Leeds. The man had been found lying in bed. There was a smile on his face and his fingers were crossed.[1] The police confirmed there were no suspicious circumstances; he was old and had been unwell for some time. The last two months of his life had seen him cut short a round-Britain cruise through illness, and he'd been in and out of hospital. Morphet considered it an honour because he knew of the man; the whole country did.

Reaction to the news of his death had been widespread. On Twitter, comedian Ricky Gervais hailed the deceased as 'a proper British eccentric', while author and newspaper columnist Tony Parsons described him as 'a sort of Wolfman Jack for Woolworths'. BBC Radio and TV presenter Nicky Campbell went further, saying he was 'so unique, a character so extraordinary, a personality so fascinating yet impenetrable. You could not have made him up.'

The following morning, his familiar face dominated the front pages of almost every Sunday newspaper in the land, while on the inside pages the great and good lined up to pay their respects. A spokesman for Prince Charles, who he had mentored and served as a trusted confidant, said he was 'saddened by the loss'. Louis Theroux, maker of a memorable film twelve years earlier, described him as 'a hero'. BBC Director General Mark Thompson said, 'Like millions of viewers and listeners we shall miss him greatly.'

Even I was interviewed. The *Mail on Sunday* asked me to sum up his character and share a few stories from the times I had spent with him over the previous seven years.

Reporters called up former colleagues from his long career in radio to add their voices to the growing chorus. Curiously, none professed to have any great insight. David Hamilton talked of a 'very remote figure' that didn't mingle much. Tony Blackburn suggested he was lonely and didn't have many friends. Dave Lee Travis, who had known him for close on fifty years, revealed in all that time they'd never had a meaningful chat. 'He kept himself to himself and put a shield up,' said Travis. Broadcaster Stuart Hall told BBC Radio Five Live that he was 'unique' but 'a loner'.[2]

As a child, Robert Morphet had written to the man whose funeral he was about to arrange. It was at a time when he was a huge national star, possibly Britain's biggest, famous for his charity work and for hosting a hit television show that made children's dreams come true. The young Robert Morphet had written in asking to become an undertaker for the day. Like the thousands of other British children who wrote letters in the course of the show's 19-year run, he had not received a reply. His wish had come true anyway.

Decades on, the funeral director acted on the instructions from the dead man's family and arranged for the body to be dressed in a favourite tracksuit fashioned from Lochaber tartan, a white T-shirt bearing the emblem of the Red Arrows, running shorts, socks and trainers. An honorary Marine Commando Green Beret was placed in one hand and his mother's silver rosary in the other; his Marine Commando medal was hung around his neck. Once dressed, the body was placed in an American-style coffin made of 18-gauge galvanised steel and finished in brushed gold satin, along with a single cigar and a small bottle of whisky.

For the first day of the funeral proceedings, the gold coffin was driven to a hotel in the centre of Leeds. There, in the foyer, it was placed carefully on a plinth draped in gold-tasselled blue velvet and adorned with cascades of white roses. When the doors of the hotel opened the next morning, people were already queuing outside to pay their final respects. Thousands more followed over the course of the day. I was among them.

The following morning, the coffin was opened for close family and friends to say their goodbyes. Make-up had been applied to the man's face, something he had always refused during his lifetime. He'd always maintained that wearing make-up was like lying.

Two hearses and five black limousines pulled up outside the hotel, and as crowds gathered on the pavement, the gold coffin was loaded before members of the man's family climbed into the vehicles for a final tour of the city. The cortège slowed in front of the man's childhood home and the hospital where he had worked as a volunteer for more than half a century. Outside, hospital porters formed a guard of honour in the rain.

From there, the fleet of black limousines proceeded to St Anne's Roman Catholic Cathedral where cheering crowds lined the approach. Six Royal Marines in full ceremonial uniform waited at the front steps to carry the seven-foot long casket from the hearse. At the doors, the Bishop of Leeds, the Right Reverend Arthur Roche, sprinkled holy water on the lid before it was shouldered to the altar.

I joined the 700 people occupying every available seat inside the cathedral for the requiem mass. Loudspeakers broadcast the service to the many thousands outside, among them television news crews and reporters from across Britain.

Bishop Arthur Roche spoke and reminded those present that this cathedral was where the man had been baptised in 1926. He went on to give thanks for his 'colourful and charitable life'. It was a life that Monsignor Kieran Heskin later described as 'an epic of giving' before concluding that now he would surely be given 'the ultimate reward – a place in Heaven'.

Friends of the man gave eulogies. One talked of how he had recently told medical staff at a local hospital he had 'absolutely no fear of dying' because 'he had done it all, seen it all and got it all'. The same friend recalled the man's 'courage, nobility and trust', but still touched on the rumours that had surrounded him: 'He many times answered the question about what he might be hiding in his private life by saying that the really great secret was . . . that there was no great secret.'

The third and final day of the funeral saw the gold coffin transported to Scarborough. The cortège began on the Esplanade, outside the dead man's seafront flat, before stopping briefly in front of the Grand Hotel where another of the company's funeral directors led the procession on foot along the Foreshore.

Then it was on to Woodlands Cemetery on a hill overlooking the town. In accordance with the dead man's final wishes, Morphet had arranged for a plot at the highest point and a grave to be dug at a 45-degree angle. It had taken two days to complete and required a laser device to get it exactly right.

I was among the few hundred onlookers that joined the man's family and friends inside the cemetery. As the coffin was lowered into the grave, coming to rest on a cement ramp at the bottom of the shaft, some moved forward to take photographs down into the hole. I did not require a photograph of the gold coffin, a coffin that would be encased in reinforced concrete once we had all left.

In the weeks and months after the funeral, the BBC aired tribute shows to the man on national television and radio. Up and down the country, committees were formed to discuss how best to acknowledge his contribution to society, most conspicuously the £40 million he was believed to have raised for a variety of good causes.

The following summer, an all-day auction took place of the man's belongings. It was hosted in a large function hall in Leeds that had been named in his honour, and raised more than £300,000 for the two charitable trusts bearing his name.

And yet at a little after 1 a.m. on the morning of Wednesday, 10 October, 2012, less than a year on from the fanfare of the funeral, Robert Morphet and the men of Joseph A. Hey & Sons could be found packing away their tools and taking down their floodlights. Behind them they had left only a rectangular patch of bare soil.

Across the turned earth were four bedraggled bunches of flowers in cellophane, two still with ink-smudged cards attached; a single white Yorkshire rose at one end and a spray of red carnations at the other.

These damp, wilting stems were all that remained from the small family ceremony less than three weeks before to mark the placement of the headstone. Afterwards, a plaque had been unveiled outside the man's house on the Esplanade at which Roger Foster, the nephew who had helped to organise the lavish funeral, talked about his hopes that the headstone might become a tourist attraction.

'He was just an ordinary bloke from the back streets of Leeds but everyone loved him and wants to pay their respects,' said Foster.[3] He added that he wouldn't be surprised in the future to find an ice-cream stall selling refreshments to fans that had travelled to enjoy the headstone and to offer thanks for the life of his uncle.

Just a few short weeks later, dawn broke over a rectangular patch of bare soil to reveal an unmarked grave and a ruined reputation.

The three 18-inch thick slabs of dark granite it had taken eight months to craft and to polish and to inscribe had been taken to a yard in Leeds where the fourteen hundred letters were ground down and the black granite smashed into tiny pieces for landfill. Nothing was to be left of the headstone and nothing was to be left to mark the spot where the coffin was buried beneath the earth. It was good while it lasted.

The events leading up to the nocturnal dismantling had been driven by a television documentary. The announcement of the film's transmission date, its airing on national television a week earlier and the deluge of newspaper revelations that followed in its wake purported to expose what the man had been hiding all along. Like the headstone, the notion of 'the great secret' was now smashed into tiny pieces and consigned to a skip.

Just over eleven months after his death, the man had become the biggest story and the most reviled figure in the land. His fall from grace was as sudden as it was shocking.

All across Britain traces of his life were now being systematically erased. At a leisure centre in Glasgow, staff removed a likeness of the man in carved wood. 'Given the controversy and the seriousness of the allegations, we thought it appropriate to move the statue at this time,' explained a spokesman for the company that operated the centre.[4]

The gold-coloured memorial plaque unveiled outside the man's home in Scarborough was taken down after being defaced. Soon afterwards, the council removed a footpath sign commemorating his place in the town's life. It had been installed only weeks before.

In Leeds, his name was deleted from a wall commemorating celebrated citizens in the Civic Hall. The chief executive of the city council said it was the appropriate course of action in light of the 'very serious allegations'.[5]

In London, Scotland Yard's response to the aftershocks caused by the television documentary was to assemble a special team of 10 officers to review the numerous allegations, and to process the calls now flooding in from members of the public. Operation Yewtree was the codename given to their investigation. One hundred and twenty lines of inquiry were already being pursued involving as many as thirty victims. Specially trained staff had been seconded from the NSPCC, which itself had reported fielding numerous calls in the first five days after the documentary aired. Twenty-four of these calls had been referred to the police, of which seventeen were directly related to the dead man.

Eight criminal allegations had been formally and posthumously recorded against him – two of rape and six of indecent assault. Details emerged; the majority of the alleged offences had been committed on females aged between 13 and 16. From those who had come forward, there were reports of sexual abuse taking place on the premises of the BBC, at hospitals, at a children's home in Jersey and in an approved school for girls in Surrey.

Commander Peter Spindler, head of Scotland Yard's Specialist Crime investigations, described the man as a 'predatory sex offender' and said that his pattern of offending appeared to 'be on a national scale'.[6]

But the man was dead and could not defend himself. Spindler was asked whether he felt sure of his guilt. 'I think the facts speak for themselves,' he replied, 'as does the number of women who have come forward and spoken of his behaviour and his predilection for teenage girls.'

By the time Prime Minister David Cameron appeared on breakfast television to make his views known, the firestorm was blazing through the Roman Catholic Church, which had announced that it was to consider stripping the man of the papal knighthood it awarded him in 1981, and through parliament. The BBC, meanwhile, appeared in danger of being totally engulfed by the flames. After bearing the brunt of the media's outrage, the national broadcaster finally declared that it would be launching an inquiry of its own.

'These stories are deeply, deeply troubling,' said Mr Cameron of the revelations and victims' testimonies that now dominated the news. 'I hope that every organisation that has responsibilities will have a proper investigation into what happened, and if these things did happen, how they were allowed to happen. And then of course everyone has to take their responsibilities.'[7] He added that he was looking into whether the man could be posthumously stripped of the knighthood he'd received in the Queen's Birthday Honours List in 1990.

And it was at this point that a bottle was thrown at the six-foot wide, four-foot high triple headstone in black, polished granite. Security was immediately stepped up at Woodlands Cemetery but relations of those buried in neighbouring plots expressed their concerns about possible damage to the final resting places of their loved ones.

So, shortly after contacting Morphet to ask that he return to Woodlands Cemetery, the relations of a man who had been acclaimed as a 'latter-day saint' less than 12 months earlier, released a statement of their own. '[We] are deeply aware of the impact that the stone remaining there could have on the dignity and sanctity of the cemetery. Out of respect to public opinion, to those who are buried there, and to those who tend their graves and visit there, we have decided to remove it.'[8]

Among the last people to see the headstone before it was removed was a woman who had worked at the same Leeds hospital where the man had famously volunteered as a porter. She said she had always thought he was odd. In 1969, she explained he had volunteered to drive a friend to her wedding in his Rolls-Royce. The man had turned up sitting in the back, with a chauffeur in the driver's seat. The friend had told her he had tried to grope her all the way to the registry office and that she'd been forced to fight him off.[9]

There was now only one person left who was unaffected by the tumultuous revelations; revelations that had seen a nation question itself and re-examine its past, and many of its biggest institutions turn on and against themselves. That one person was where he had always been: bricked in and beyond reach.

Friday, 12 March 2004. The taxi turned into West Avenue and continued a few hundred yards up a gentle incline before dropping me off outside Lake View Court, a modern block of apartments that would have been considered the height of chic in the Sixties. I pressed the intercom button marked 'Penthouse' and after a short pause, a voice: 'Morning.' The sound of the Yorkshire Dalek was unmistakable. The door buzzed, I pushed against it and took a seat in a small lobby that smelled of pot-pourri.

Two or three minutes later, I heard voices coming from the lift shaft. Then the wooden doors of the lift slid open, releasing a cloud of smoke and two large, unsmiling men in their fifties. 'Frisk him,' barked Jimmy Savile, who had stepped out of the lift behind them and was wearing a blue shell suit with chevrons of red and white on the shoulders.

I was pinned to the wall and searched before Savile finally called them off. He chuckled, extended his hand and introduced the two men as Mick Starkey, a West Yorkshire Police inspector, and Jim 'The Pill' Cardus, a retired pharmacist. 'Meet the Friday Morning Club,' he trumpeted before ushering the men out of the front door to the flats.

He showed me into the lift, which was cramped and stank of cigars. The doors shut and to my surprise, I felt quite calm about being up this close to a man I had spent so many years wondering about, looking into, talking about and hating. He looked at me and raised his eyebrows. His lips stretched into a thin, toothless grin. Silver chest hair poked through the garish French tricolour string vest, a spider's web of broken veins covered his nose.

I had not seen Jimmy Savile in the flesh for 24 years, not since an early evening in the autumn of 1980 when, as a treat, my mother took me, my best friend and my younger brother to watch an episode of *Jim'll Fix It* being recorded at a television theatre in Shepherd's Bush, west London. I was nine years old at the time and *Jim'll Fix It* was one of Britain's biggest family shows.

Since 1975 its winning formula had cast Jimmy Savile, madcap disc jockey, *Top of the Pops* presenter, confirmed bachelor and charity fund-raiser extraordinaire, as a real-life Santa Claus, only one with the power to make Christmas Day come round every Saturday evening. Children wrote letters in the hundreds of thousands, and for the lucky few, Jimmy Savile made their dreams come true. Those who were picked got to fly with the Red Arrows, blow up water towers or sing with The Osmonds. One boy even got to visit the place where baby Jesus was born. Millions tuned in to watch and the bizarre-looking man with the big cigars, odd catchphrases and helmet of white hair became a national institution.

I can still remember sitting in the red velvet seats of the auditorium, and the excitement when the lights finally went down and the floor manager waved his clipboard as the signal for us to clap and cheer. Savile emerged from the wings in a grey three-piece suit with flared trousers, which was relatively subdued attire for him. With Jimmy Savile, you never knew what to expect. One week he might appear in a tracksuit, the next he could be dressed as a pharaoh or in the tiniest of running shorts or as an adult cub scout. The only constant was his refusal to ever make reference to what he wore.

To children, he was a mysterious, Wizard of Oz-like figure. He possessed the power to dispense happiness and silver 'Jim Fixed It for Me' medallions from a chair with drawers and compartments that emerged robotically from the arms. Jimmy Savile was quite simply the man who could do anything.

The *Jim'll Fix It* theme tune played out of speakers above our heads: *'Jim'll Fix It for you and you and you.'*

Like every other child in the audience that evening, I had gone expecting to witness magic. What we were presented with instead was the unvarnished reality of pre-recorded television: packages played back to us on monitors, cameras blocking the view, a messy tangle of leads and numerous stressed-looking adults corralling a procession of insanely grinning 'Fix Its' to go for their chat with Jimmy Savile who finished by rewarding them with those magical red-ribboned badges.

My overriding memory of that evening, however, was not of the boy in the wheelchair doing a dance routine in the studio with Legs & Co., the troupe of saucy dancers from *Top of the Pops*. It was of leaving the theatre feeling ambivalent about Jimmy Savile. In his gruff manner there seemed to be a suggestion of menace. For someone we all felt that we knew so well, there was something remote and cold and untouchable beyond the façade. I spent the car journey home in silence.

The troubling experience of those couple of hours in the BBC Television theatre in Shepherd's Bush might have remained nothing more than a flicker in the recesses of a child's subconscious, had it not been for the accidental discovery some years later of a copy of *As It Happens*, Jimmy Savile's autobiography. The cover photograph alone was enough to reopen the box: Savile in a pinstripe suit and adorned with jewellery, his snow-coloured hair hanging like that of a medieval peasant. He was leaning forward in his chair, his right hand raised to his mouth as though about to call out. The eyes were blank and unsmiling. On the back cover was a picture of his elderly mother proudly cradling a framed portrait of her famous son.

I was in my mid-teens at the time, by then too old to be interested in writing to *Jim'll Fix It* but very possibly looking for something or someone to rail against. The book, published in 1974, was read in one sitting. But rather than guffawing at Savile's capers as a child drummer in a wartime band, Bevin Boy miner, racing cyclist, dancehall manager, pioneering deejay and pop personality, I was struck by his evangelical zeal, his fascination with death, his all-consuming obsession with money and his frequent references to teenage girls, inevitably followed by cheerful accounts of how he had made narrow escapes from suspicious parents.

Furthermore, there was his evident pride in lacking normal human emotions, the recurring subtext of violence and the highly unusual relationship with his mother, a woman he described as his 'only true love'. Looking back, *As It Happens* was my Rosetta stone, a text that reawakened and then put flesh onto the skeleton of a dormant bogeyman.

From that point on he was fixed in my mind. I began collecting Jimmy Savile's increasingly odd pronouncements on all facets of life. These were initially unearthed in newspapers, magazines and in old *Top of the Pops* and *Jim'll Fix It* annuals found in car boot sales and charity shops. From this limited source material I learned that he didn't much like children, boasted about being known as 'the Godfather' in his younger days and, inexplicably, enjoyed the ear of prime ministers, princes and popes.

God'll Fix It, a thin volume first published in 1978, was the next major milestone on my journey to the real Jimmy Savile. Intended as an accessible overview of his views on religion and presented as a series of wide-ranging discussions, to me it provided a window onto his disturbing opinions on sex and 'sins of the flesh'. He talked of trussing up troublemakers at his dancehalls and also of walking alone in the wilderness in the Holy Land before admitting that he viewed his good works as credits to offset the debit column of his many transgressions.

As a child of the Seventies and Eighties, I had heard the play-ground rumours about Britain's favourite uncle; we all had. Jimmy Savile was a weirdo and possibly worse; a poofter, a necrophiliac or a child molester.

Friends thought I was kidding when I spoke of my 'Jimmy Savile Dossier' and how I was going to use it to one day to bring him down. My parents' generation dismissed such talk, reminding me that Jimmy Savile was a clever, wealthy, self-made man who had done an awful lot of good in his life. He was, after all, nationally celebrated for raising many millions of pounds for charity and rebuilding an entire hospital unit.

As the years passed and the internet afforded greater access to information, my Jimmy Savile Dossier grew, and its contents became reliable dinner party fodder. It seemed I wasn't the only one with misgivings. In 1990, the respected broadsheet interviewer Lynn Barber probed Savile about the uncommonly close relationship he had with his late mother, sex, and the rumours that he had a 'thing' for young girls.

A year later, the well-known psychiatrist Anthony Clare tried to get to the bottom of why Jimmy Savile had become so fixated with death, so fearful of attachment and so determined not to show or share his feelings. 'There is something chilling about this twentieth-century "saint" which still intrigues me to this day,' concluded Clare.

In 1999, five years after the final episode of *Jim'll Fix It*, Savile appeared on *Have I Got News for You*. He insisted on smoking a cigar and cut a somewhat tragic figure, a relic of a bygone age who was unable to tap into the vibe and whose humour felt dated and out of step.

Not long afterwards, a transcript of an off-air exchange that was alleged to have taken place between Savile and Paul Merton, the opposing team captain, appeared on various internet sites. In it, Merton goaded Savile about an underage girl he'd threatened with violence when she said she'd go public about their relationship. Savile's lawyers intervened, and websites carrying the transcript, which was later proved to have been a hoax, were forced to remove the offending material.

Jimmy Savile suddenly seemed at odds with the modern world, a decline that was most famously captured by the documentary maker Louis Theroux. *When Louis Met Jimmy* went out on national television in September 2000 and trained a beam of light on what a strange old man Jimmy Savile really was. After 40 years at the forefront of popular culture, he was seen leading a sad, lonely and peripatetic existence; a tracksuited, cigar-chomping dinosaur. And in keeping with the tenor of interviews conducted since Savile's celebrity status had waned, Theroux quizzed him about the dark rumours. The film became an instant talking point. It was entertaining, bleak and surreal in equal measure, but I refused to accept it had got to the bottom of who Jimmy Savile was.

By 2004, the editor of *Jack*, the magazine I was working for, decided he'd heard enough of my conspiracy theories about the powerful cliques Jimmy Savile moved between and influenced. The editor was from Scarborough, the holiday town on the North Yorkshire coast that Jimmy Savile had visited all his life – more regularly after moving the Duchess into a flat on the Esplanade in the Sixties. He decided it was time that I went and put my years of Jimmy Savile study to the test.

The lift opened directly into a wood-panelled vestibule adorned with plaques from Royal Navy ships and army regiments. A cascade of woolly hats and thick, quilted coats of the type more commonly worn by football managers clung to a row of hooks; beneath them, a row of running shoes. This cramped entrance hall opened right into a long, rectangular living room with electric blue shagpile carpet and floor-to-ceiling windows on two sides.

The clutter of the room's time-warp interior was in stark contrast to the panoramic views of Roundhay Park and the hills beyond. An ancient-looking exercise bike, a low sideboard with two *This is Your Life* books lying open on the top and a free-standing glass-fronted cabinet stuffed with what looked like cups, medals, plaques and various awards from his career in entertainment dominated the first half of the room. A low wooden shelving unit against the far wall accommodated a stack of videotapes and a pair of extravagant lamps with white bases fashioned as cherubs holding the bough of a tree. At the far end was a black swivel reclining chair, an L-shaped white leatherette sofa and a coffee table cluttered with ashtrays, pens, brochures and assorted pieces of paper. Perched on the top of a modest black stack hi-fi system was a framed photograph of Jimmy Savile in a field. He was wearing a kilt and struggling under the weight of a 15-foot caber. Above it was another framed shot: Jimmy Savile standing with Prince Charles and Princess Diana. In the corner, a set of sliding doors led out onto a small outdoor terrace covered in green Astroturf.

Savile showed me through to his kitchen, decorated in tiles of pink and brown, or 'The colour of sex' as he put it. He asked me what was missing but I already knew the answer: it didn't contain a cooker. He liked to boast that none of his many homes had one. 'It would give women the wrong idea – and that would only lead to brain damage,' he said. The 'brain damage' caused by conventional relationships was something he had discussed with Theroux. He opened the fridge to reveal a spartan range of assorted chocolate wafers, a half-finished box of After Eights and pallet of long-life milk cartons held together with gaffer tape. He filled the kettle, flicked the switch and encouraged me to snoop around.

On the walls of the long living room in his penthouse apartment there were framed gold and silver discs and a black and white photograph of Savile squashed together on a sofa with The Beatles. He told me it was taken during the five weeks he spent compèring The Beatles' Christmas Show at the Hammersmith Odeon in 1964, a time when Beatlemania was erupting across the world.

Coffee made, he shuffled into the front room and sank into his black recliner which allowed him to lean back at a 45-degree angle. Lighting one of the three giant Bolivar cigars I had bought him – one of his conditions for granting the interview – he took a couple of puffs and announced that we could now begin.

Sir James Wilson Vincent Savile, OBE; Knight of Malta, Knight of the Vatican, 'Special' Friend of Israel; Honorary Royal Marines Green Beret, Honorary Doctor of Law and Honorary Assistant Entertainment Officer at Broadmoor maximum security psychiatric hospital; miner, scrap metal merchant, inventor of the disco; racing cyclist, wrestler and marathon runner; pop Svengali, radio DJ and *Top of the Pops* presenter; charity fund-raiser, highly paid business consultant, hospital administrator; confidant of prime ministers and princes. Most famously, though, Jimmy Savile – fixer of things.

There was so much I wanted to ask him even though I was already familiar with many of his stories thanks to the steady growth of my Savile Dossier. What I really wanted to find out, though – over and beyond whether he genuinely hated children, why he never married and if his relentless charity work was a bid for atonement for some awful sin in his past – was where the border existed between the public persona and the private man. The latter appeared to be someone few, if anyone, really knew.

In other words, what or who lay beneath the shell suit, the jewellery and the cigar smoke? And where better to start than at the beginning.

Jimmy Savile was always old, it seems; even as a child. 'I was the youngest of seven, which with hindsight was phenomenal, because you are never a kid. I didn't have a childhood.' This was the very first thing he told me about himself. He leant back in his chair and cackled, blowing a self-satisfied plume of cigar smoke into the cloud hovering at head height in his living room in Leeds.

'You can't be left at home if you are the youngest of seven,' he continued. 'You have to be taken everywhere. I grew up with adults, which meant I didn't have anything to say. So I finished up with big ears, listening to everything, and big eyes, watching everything, and a brain that wondered why grown-ups did what they did.'

James Wilson Vincent Savile was born on 31 October 1926. His parents, Agnes and Vince Savile, had already produced six children in fifteen years of marriage: Mary, Marjory, Vincent, John Henry, Joan and Christina. This Halloween baby, arriving nearly five years after their last, was an unwanted early birthday present for its mother: Agnes turned forty the very next day.

Jimmy Savile was what he always called a 'Not again child'. As he told me at that first meeting, 'When the Duchess told the neighbours she was up the tub, the neighbours said "Not again."' The unplanned youngest of seven, scrapping for attention and trying to survive in a large, working-class family living on the breadline in a northern city during the Depression: this was the foundation stone for the mythology he'd constructed around himself.

Leeds celebrated its 300th anniversary in the summer of 1926. An historical pageant was staged in Roundhay Park. The realities of life, however, were less vibrant: soot-darkened skies glowering over cobbles and chimneys and endless terraces of squalid back-to-backs. By late October, when Agnes gave birth to little Jim, as she called him, the city's miners had only just been forced back to the pits having remained defiant long after the end of the General Strike.

The city Jimmy Savile was born into was one in which daily life saw packed trams ferrying workers to and from the engineering plants at Hunslet and the mills at Armley and Wortley. At Montague Burton's tailoring factory on Hudson Road more than fifteen hundred men, women and children toiled side by side. But Leeds had also become somewhat notorious for its thriving black market, prostitution rackets and easy access to illegal gambling. It was a reputation that prompted one newspaper to describe it as 'the City of Sin', a label that Jimmy Savile always relished.

Savile's father, Vince, held down regular if poorly paid employment with Jim Windsor, a bookmaker who took a certain pride in defying the law by accepting wagers from the working men of Leeds – off-course betting was illegal up until 1960. Operating out of a 'blower room' above a parade of shops on Vicar Lane, Vince Savile took such bets and issued handwritten slips through a small hole in the door. Outside, a lookout kept watch for the Black Marias that would periodically cart off those caught in the act. The punters were not the only ones to fall foul of the local constabulary; in later life, Jim Windsor boasted to one newspaper that he was arrested once a year for 20 years.[1]

Vince met Agnes Kelly before he had turned to illegal gambling. He was working at a small railway station in rural Yorkshire that she passed every day on the way to her first job as a supply teacher and child minder. Twenty-three years old and venturing beyond the pit villages of the north-east for the first time in her life, Agnes was tiny, fair and spirited; the opposite of the tall, awkward and softly spoken young man who passed the long hours he spent alone by training birds to take breadcrumbs from his hand. Despite their manifest differences, they were married in Lanchester, County Durham in March 1911.

The newly-weds moved in temporarily with Vince's parents in Leeds, and just over a year later Agnes gave birth to their first child, Mary. Vince dabbled briefly with the idea of following his father into the assurance business but it seems that he was not designed for hard graft. When war broke out in 1914 an army medical revealed a condition that exempted him from duty.

Money was tight, and the family had to get by on Vince's meagre earnings and the little that Agnes brought in as a supply teacher. And yet they still managed to maintain the payments on a larger than usual house situated only a short walk from the city centre. For Jimmy Savile, though, the memories of childhood that he shared with me all contained a common thread, that of being penniless in a time and place where opportunity simply didn't exist. 'I was forged in the crucible of want,' was one typically florid description of his predicament.[2]

Added to the family's relative poverty, Jim Savile was a small, undernourished and sickly child, the latter a legacy of the mysterious illness that struck him down as an infant. He consistently refused to elaborate on the nature of this illness, sticking instead to the well-worn line, 'When you were poor, you got ill and generally died.'

According to Savile's version of events, the situation was so dire that a doctor was called to the family home. After making his examination, the doctor shook his head gravely and wrote out a death certificate to 'save himself a return journey'. With all hope seemingly gone, the local priest was duly summoned to administer the last rites.

As a devout Catholic, Agnes Savile decided to seek refuge in St Anne's Cathedral in the city centre, leaving her mother to tend to the child in what seemed certain to be his final hours. While she was there, Agnes picked up a leaflet on a little-known Scottish nun, Sister Margaret Sinclair, who had died just a few years earlier. Sinclair had been posthumously credited with a series of miraculous intercessions, so Agnes closed her eyes and prayed to Sister Margaret for help.

In the very first chapter of his autobiography, Jimmy Savile wrote that as his grandmother lowered a mirror over his mouth expecting to collect his dying breath, she received instead 'a right eyeful of involuntary, well-aimed pee'.[3]

Agnes Savile's account was significantly different, however. In 1970, aged 84, she recalled the 'illness' struck when Jimmy was two and a half. 'My eldest daughter had him out in the pram and stopped at a shop leaving Jimmy outside,' she said. 'He was strapped in, but jumped about so much that the pram overturned and the hood caught the back of his neck and severed one of the muscles.'[4]

The muscle refused to heal, Agnes explained. 'He could not sit up, he could not even shut his eyes to sleep, and in fact slept staring up at the ceiling. He would go into spasms in which his face would turn round over his neck till he was looking over his back.'

After six months, she took her spasmodic and perpetually staring child to the hospital. He was admitted but after 10 days the doctors were still at a loss to diagnose the infant's condition, concluding that their only option was to perform an exploratory operation. Agnes refused, saying she would rather take her youngest son home.

The child's prospects looked bleak. 'My mother was with me at the time,' Agnes recalled. 'She persuaded me to go to my husband's office and bring him back. The office was near the cathedral. Seeing the door open, I went in – more because I didn't want to get to the office before three than any particular wish to pray. I had been praying for so long, it was as though I had spiritual indigestion and could not pray any more.'

When Vince and Agnes got home later that day, they were expecting the worst. When Agnes's mother announced the child had gone to sleep, they thought he was dead because his eyes were closed for the first time in months. It was then that they noticed his regular breathing.

Agnes Savile claimed that when Jim woke up that evening he was 'perfectly cured'. The doctor was called back, but she made no

23

mention of a death certificate. When the reporter asked Agnes what had happened, she replied: 'We prayed for him to be cured, and our prayers were answered.'

Following her son's startling and inexplicable recovery, Agnes wrote letters to her local priest and joined the campaign for the beatification of Margaret Sinclair. From 1965, when the Margaret Sinclair Centre opened in Rosewell, Scotland, Agnes embarked on the annual pilgrimage to give thanks.

This seemingly miraculous intercession was hugely significant to Jimmy Savile. 'I was dying,' he wrote in the very first page of his autobiography. 'The Master, or one of his minders, hearing of this imminent addition to his heavenly host, sent in the nick of time a miracle cure.'[5] It was not just how he saw himself, it was something the whole family believed, as his sister Joan Johnson confirmed many years later: 'Someone up there listened and realized that the world needed [him], which of course it did.'[6]

So, rather than the downtrodden image of the 'Not again child' that he peddled in so many interviews over the course of his life, a different picture emerges of how Jimmy Savile regarded himself from the very beginning; a miracle child, the chosen one.

The one surviving photograph of all nine members of the Savile family was taken in a photographer's studio on Burley Road at the outbreak of World War II. It was displayed in Jimmy Savile's flats in Leeds and Scarborough. Flanking the group are Jimmy's two older brothers, Vince and John Henry, both in their Royal Navy uniforms. Mary and Marjory, the eldest girls, stand at the back, while Christina and Joan, who smiles shyly from behind her father's elbow, are to one side. Jimmy, who was twelve at the time but looked considerably younger, beams from the front.

Agnes is in the centre of the group, with Vince, a balding, slightly stooped figure at her side. It was a position she was accustomed to for she was the hub of the household, as well as for Jimmy being the sun that he orbited.

Diminutive and determined, Agnes managed the family's

finances skilfully, ensuring there was food on the table and just about enough money left over for her and Vince to attend the weekly dance and make a small contribution to the collection plate after church on Sunday. Her seven children were all made to attend church with her. 'She was an old-fashioned *religioso*,' Savile said. 'She went to mass because she had a guilty conscience.'

Jimmy Savile described his mother as 'ferocious', albeit affectionately. He said it was her decision that the family moved into the three-storey, five-bedroomed terraced house on Consort Terrace, a house that was technically beyond their means. They had plenty of room, he recalled, but little in the way of furniture. With only enough for coal for the fireplace in the parlour, it was Agnes who kept the family entertained by playing a cheap upright piano.

'The house had lots of steps and corridors,' he remembered. 'We had a bathroom with an old Victorian bath and an inside toilet. There was a cellar where the fuses were fitted . . . [and] an apostle clock on the wall. When it used to strike every hour, figures of the twelve apostles appeared above the face. I don't know how my mother got that. She was very good at organizing and, suddenly, things would appear.'[7]

Joan maintained that it was from their mother that her younger brother inherited his drive. It was not the only personality trait they shared: 'He's very like her,' she once said, 'dominant, likes to get his own way.'[8]

If Agnes wanted the best for her family, she was generally frustrated by her husband's lackadaisical approach to money. 'She was never happy because she couldn't provide what she really wanted,' Savile maintained. 'She was ground down by the wheel of life. It knocked bits off her.'

While his mother looms large in his story, there is not much more than the family portrait and one faded black and white snap of his father taken during his time as the stationmaster from which to gain a sense of Vince Savile. Jimmy Savile remained reluctant to talk about his father, to the extent that he even refused to tell me when he died.

Records show that Vincent Joseph Marie Savile was born in Salford in 1886, and by the age of 15 was working as a butcher's assistant. His father, John Henry Savile, had been an estate agent in Leeds before becoming a superintendent in an assurance agent's office.

According to Savile, Vince's chief gift in life was a flair for arithmetic. He rose at 11 each day because the horse racing didn't start until 12, meaning the children had to tiptoe around the house before school. He also introduced his youngest son to cigars when he was seven, offering him a drag one Christmas thinking it would make him violently ill and put him off forever.

'He was a lovely, line of least resistance, *mañana*, never got excited fella,' Savile told me. 'That's what he was.' It was about all that he did confess of his father. But was theirs a close relationship? On one rare occasion, Jimmy Savile did reveal a bit more: 'As close as you could be. At that age you don't understand closeness . . . you only understand closeness when you haven't got it . . . He demanded nothing from me. I demanded nothing from him.'[9]

Whether Jimmy Savile actually cheated death as a child or not, whether the family was as impoverished as he maintained, and whatever the truth about his relationship with his father, he was unquestionably the runt of the litter. He was so 'skint', as he put it, that he qualified for subsidised canvas sandshoes, and was given free milk and spoonfuls of malt each day at school to stave off rickets.

A photograph of his class at St Anne's Elementary School on the day of their first Holy Communion shows the pencil-thin Jim Savile sitting at the front. He is not wearing socks. Joan admitted that her brother had fewer opportunities than the other children in the family: 'We all went to college but when it came to [his] turn the money had run out.'

And yet the few people who did remember Jimmy Savile as a child recalled him as bright and his mother as a warm, welcoming figure who was well known in the Woodhouse area of Leeds.[10]

At Christmas, Savile maintained his big treat was being taken to Lewis's department store in the centre of Leeds to look at the toys. He also reminisced with me about days out to Scarborough organised for the children of the poor and of a holiday camp in the Yorkshire Dales where he was made to bed down on a wooden floor. He recalled standing outside and looking at the stars: 'I'd come from a back street in Leeds in the days before clear air, when everywhere was smoky and dirty. It was so magical I stood there for ages.'[11]

One of his favourite stories was about coming home from school to find the house empty. A tin of baked beans and an egg would be waiting for him in the kitchen, which he'd heat up on the stove and eat out of the tin. He said it was like his mother had gone on strike but insisted this was an arrangement which suited him down to the ground.

Here was a solitary child who did not spend much time playing with kids his own age. Sometimes he would head into town to the cinema but more often than not he whiled away the hours outside school in the corridors and wards of the St Joseph's Home for the Aged across the road from the house. Vince Savile was a trustee of the home which was run by the Little Sisters of the Poor, an order of nuns that Jimmy Savile continued fund-raising for long after they had been forced from their premises on Consort Terrace.

St Joseph's, I suspect, was where the seeds of his fixation with death were sown. 'They were always dying,' he said of the elderly residents in our first interview. 'I'd ask, "Where's Mrs so and so?" and one of the nuns would tell me that she'd died. Then they'd say, "Why don't you go downstairs and say goodbye to her?"' He claimed to have enjoyed getting to ride in the hearse for the funerals.

He talked of smuggling in bottles of stout for the elderly residents and stated that his desire to help others stemmed from the example set by his parents, both of whom were active members of the community. 'My earliest recollections are of having strange people in my house playing cards, and going to whist drives, beetle

27

drives, socials and dances,' he said.[12] 'I made the realisation even in the early days, and bearing in mind I was only six or seven years old, that doing things for people isn't a bad idea. People smile at you and they patted you on the head and they were pleased to see you. And at that age it was quite easy to be a pain in the arse.'

When she accompanied her son to Buckingham Palace to collect his OBE in 1972, Agnes Savile remembered how as a little boy 'her Jimmy' made a habit of helping old ladies with their parcels when they stepped off the trams. When I asked him about where the desire to do philanthropic works had come from, he replied, 'When you're born in the circus, you stay in the circus.'

Her little brother might have been a frail and oddly self-contained boy but Joan also recalled that he possessed a markedly different outlook on life to the other Savile kids. 'Maybe it was because he was a delicate child,' she offered. 'Maybe it's because children who have been snatched from the jaws of death lead a charmed life.'[13]

She also said that by the age of 14, they were expected to fend for themselves. 'We were out there on our own. It were up to us,' she claimed. 'We used to get smacked many a time, but it never did us any harm. Mum were a great believer in self-help, but if we were ever in dire straits we knew she was there.'

In later life, Jimmy Savile steadfastly refused to elaborate on his relationships with his brothers and sisters. During that first meeting in Leeds he did reveal, though, that the trials and tribulations of his siblings' various relationships had stoked his own fear of emotional attachment. He spoke of the excitement on the street when one of them announced they were getting married, the trestle tables and tablecloths and women making sandwiches. 'And then,' he said with a well-practised look of incredulity on his face, 'the women cried in the ceremony.'

He maintained that he could never work out why they cried: 'I thought it was very strange. And anything from six months to two years later the participants wanted to kill each other. I thought this was amazing . . . It gave me a lop-sided view of partnerships because they started off as idyllic but invariably for some reason went wrong.'

Beyond the lessons he learned from them about the pitfalls of romance, Savile's two brothers and four sisters appeared only in brief cameos in his anecdotes. It seems that most came to enjoy his fame and occasional largesse, although the few newspaper clippings on John Henry, or Johnnie as he was known, suggest that he for one was jealous not only of his younger brother's success but his status as their mother's favourite.

In interviews, Jimmy Savile would get prickly when pressed about his childhood. 'I don't believe all this psychological stuff that says you're a bastard because you got frightened by a snake as a child,' he told one reporter. 'That's a cop out.'[14]

In 1990, Lynn Barber reported that Savile became 'seriously annoyed' when she probed him about his formative years. 'We had no time for psychological hang-ups,' he'd snapped at her. 'We were just survivors, all of us. None of that, "Oh, I was ignored as a child" – what a load of cobblers. All I know is that nothing particular wrong happened and I had a good time.'[15]

After the memorable 1991 interview for his *In the Psychiatrist's Chair* series on Radio 4, Anthony Clare remembered Jimmy Savile being 'exceedingly wary, edgy, like a prize-fighter on his toes, anticipating a flurry of hooks to the head.'[16] Clare later wrote that he was particularly struck by his interviewee's recurring 'emphasis on money and a denial of feelings'.

Despite Savile's reluctance, or inability, to open up, Clare picked up hints that being the 'not again' pregnancy, the seventh of seven in a household that was 'skint', 'may have left the young Jimmy not merely materially deprived but emotionally deprived too'.

In conclusion, Clare pondered what made him 'project into [Savile] a foreboding that his solitary, shifting life is but a manifestation of a profound psychological malaise with its roots in that materially deprived, emotionally somewhat indifferent childhood which he so flatly describes'.

In the light of what we now know both of Jimmy Savile and how common it is for those who abuse to have been abused themselves, it is a question mark that coils, unfurls and hangs in the air like cigar smoke.

Meirion Jones told me that he has vivid recollections of the summer garden parties at Duncroft Approved School for Girls. As both a child and a teenager, he had attended the events with his parents. His aunt Margaret Jones was the headmistress of the school and, since 1970, she had shared a house in the expansive grounds with her mother, Meirion Jones's grandmother. 'Imagine a stately home with a huge gravel drive littered with posh cars,' Jones replied when asked to describe the spectacle. He spoke of the lines of trestle tables with 'amazing food laid out on them by the girls', and guests that included minor royals – Princess Marina (the Duchess of Kent) and Princess Alexandra; fading film stars such as James Robertson Justice, who starred in the *Doctor in the House* films, John Gregson, who was in a number of big British war movies, and Ian Carmichael, who played Bertie Wooster in a big BBC TV series in the Sixties. Another visitor was Dick Haymes, an actor and crooner who was famous in the Forties and Fifties and who was married six times, once briefly to Rita Hayworth. Jones described his aunt 'swanning around as the grand dame of the event, with a celeb on each arm'.

'It was a really strange scene,' he said of the half Jacobean, half Georgian hall that had been transformed into a secure facility for troubled and criminally minded girls of above average intelligence. All of which meant that when, in the early 1970s, Jimmy Savile drove through the gates in his convertible Rolls-Royce, and started making regular visits to the school thereafter, 'it didn't seem all that weird'.

Duncroft occupied an unusual space on the outer edges of the care system. As well as its celebrity guest list, it had a high-profile patron in Lady Norman, widow of Lord Montagu Norman, the celebrated wartime governor of the Bank of England. Lady Norman was an enthusiastic advocate for mental health issues and had two buildings named after her at Duncroft, one a hostel for girls over the age of 16 and the other the house that Margaret Jones and her mother lived in.

The school was regarded as something of an experiment, one that was using psychotherapy to correct the behavioural defects of the girls placed in its care. In an era that witnessed the rise of social services and a school of thought that argued vulnerable, damaged youngsters were better off being looked after by the state, Duncroft was considered to be at the cutting edge.

Evidence of Duncroft's place within the care system can be found in a Royal Society of Medicine article from 1953,[1] in which Dr Christofer Lack, consultant psychiatrist at King Edward Memorial Hospital in Ealing, wrote about the role of psychotherapy in approved schools. He stated, 'certain types of girl are found unsuitable for psychotherapy at Duncroft. The mentally dull girl . . . does not respond.' Lack concluded that throughout the approved school system, girls of poor intelligence should be kept together 'so that their sense of inadequacy is minimised'.

Dr Lack also revealed that each year, of the 300 or so girls sent by the courts to approved schools in the southern half of England, 'only about 12' went to Duncroft. The school was, therefore, a small community with a deliberately selective intake. Among the girls at Duncroft were daughters of ambassadors, surgeons and well-known producers at the BBC, as well as others from less white-collar backgrounds. The common factors were they had transgressed and all possessed high IQs. Margaret Jones viewed them as 'her chosen ones'.[2]

Girls were sent to Duncroft for a variety of misdemeanours. One girl, who arrived at the school as a 14-year-old in 1972, insisted years later that 'half the girls were there as punishment for being the victims of sexual abuse – the "crime" of having sex under age, as we thought it'.[3] Others were put in Margaret Jones's care for dabbling with drugs, anorexia, attempting suicide or for running away from children's homes or abusive parents.

According to another girl who was sent to the school in 1965, Margaret Jones was passionate about proving to the Home Office, under whose jurisdiction Duncroft fell, that the girls' lives could be turned around given the chance to continue their education and live in a decent environment. The headmistress was, as this woman remembers her, 'a messiah on the subject'.[4]

Meirion Jones describes his aunt as a complex woman. He believes she had been 'shaped by the fact she was running this very strange institution'. He has clear memories of the photographs of Margaret posing with the celebrities who visited Duncroft. Jimmy Savile was among them.

'She had a strange view of what the world was like,' explains Jones. 'She was very bright, very focused and interested in celebrity, which is why you ended up with all these film stars and, eventually, Savile. I think she thought she was doing right by the kids, by opening things up to them and letting them see another life.'

In November 2012, Margaret Jones, then 91, told a newspaper that she had been 'hoodwinked by Jimmy Savile'[5], who she allowed to occasionally sleep overnight at Duncroft. She explained he had been introduced by the mother of one of her pupils, and that no complaints were made about him.

Duncroft was nothing if not a curious set of contradictions: on the one hand was its bucolic Surrey setting and garden party guest list; on the other was its barred windows and staff carrying large bunches of keys. It was 'a stately home crossed with a prison,' said Meirion Jones, and as such, it doesn't hold happy memories for many of those who were sent there.

The school was run primarily by single women, most of whom, like Margaret Jones, were in their forties and fifties. Discipline was enforced through chores – endless cleaning of corridor floors, tidying staff quarters or working in the kitchens – and a rewards system of cigarettes (40 a week if a girl behaved, down to 10 a week if she didn't). Days were filled with lessons in typing, short-hand and home economics, or sessions with the psychiatrist who, according to Margaret Jones, had the authority to put girls in the padded isolation unit. During their time off, girls lounged in a common room where they smoked incessantly, gossiped about the staff and listened to records.

Life behind the eight-foot high walls surrounding the estate was also subject to the scrutiny and curiosity of regular visiting parties of trainee psychiatrists, social workers and Home Office officials.

But by the early Seventies, fears were expressed that the experiment was beginning to founder. Duncroft was placed in the hands of social services, and as such became known as a community home school. This reclassification makes it sound cosier but the reality experienced by some of those inside does not tally. The recollections of some former Duncroft girls, published online, speak of emotional abuse and staff cruelty. Other girls, however, have warmer memories of their time there, and its staff. From 1970 to 1974, Meirion Jones says he visited Duncroft School 'very regularly' with his parents, chiefly to visit his grandmother. 'The normal thing we'd do is drive over to the school where my aunt would be finishing up stuff. We'd go and have a chat with her, leave the car there and then and wander through the grounds to my aunt's house.'

From 1971 onwards, Jones recounts that he saw Jimmy Savile at Duncroft 'on at least half a dozen occasions', and spotted his Rolls-Royce parked on the gravel drive on numerous others. Jones was in his teens by this point and his memories of Savile are clear: 'He was full of banter, though had no real conversation as such. I had a feeling that he was somebody with whom you didn't really know what was going on. There was somebody hidden behind who you couldn't see.'

On one occasion, Jones saw Jimmy Savile drive off the premises with three Duncroft girls in his dark convertible. He says his parents, who both had backgrounds in teaching, confronted Margaret Jones about it. 'They would say to my aunt, "He's a 50-year-old guy and these are underage girls. What are you doing?" And she would say, "He's a friend of the school."'

'[Savile] said, "I'll take them for a run,"' admitted Margaret Jones. 'I had no reason to doubt him. Please remember, my staff were always on watch. Except when they were off in his car, which I allowed stupidly.'[6]

Margaret Jones claims she considered Savile to be an 'oddball'. Her nephew insists she thought Savile 'was fantastic', and his invitation to her to take a holiday in one his homes on the south coast provided further conversation on the drive home.

Meirion Jones was suspicious of Jimmy Savile from that day on, as were his parents. His grandmother had altogether more serious misgivings about the famous visitor in their midst. 'She hated him,' Jones says. 'She thought he was creepy.'

In October 1978, Meirion Jones's mother had dropped in to Duncroft to visit her mother-in-law when Savile arrived at the house unannounced and demanded to be cooked a meal. 'It was all very awkward and ended up in a row,' he recalls his mother telling him. She also said that she had found him to be 'quite intimidating'. Meirion Jones is sure of the dates, as is his mother, because his sister had just gone to university and his grandmother died the following month.

By this stage, Meirion had left London to attend university in Cardiff, where he went on to edit the student newspaper. After graduating, he worked as a print journalist before landing a job at BBC Radio in 1988. Seven years later, he moved into television and a job with BBC2's *Newsnight* where he would establish a reputation as one of Britain's leading investigative journalists.

'I always had my ears open,' Jones says of the suspicions aroused by what he'd witnessed of Jimmy Savile at Duncroft. 'I didn't hear anything at first but when I moved into telly at the BBC, I started to hear the odd story. I'd try to track down where the story had come from but it always ended up as a conversation in a green room, or something like that. There was never anyone who was a witness or who knew a victim or anything like that. Cameramen would say he had underage girls in his caravan but I could never get to the bottom of any of that.'

Jones also heard Jimmy Savile's name mentioned in the course of his investigations into paedophile priests within the Catholic Church. Having looked on websites such as Friends Reunited for references to Duncroft, he had found hints but nothing concrete. Something did grab his attention, though: mentions of a police investigation having taken place at some stage.[7]

In late 2008, a 50-year-old woman named Keri began writing her biography.[8] The project was suggested by her counsellor as part of her therapy following a mental breakdown. Keri had suffered with chronic anxiety and depression since spending an abusive childhood in and out of care homes and approved schools.

She had gone on to marry three times, and had seven children by five different fathers. 'Due to my background of abuse, I was entirely unaware of how to have, or hold onto, any kind of intimate relationship with a man,' Keri explained. Three of her children had been taken into care as babies, and another as a 10-year-old. In 1982, while she was pregnant with her fourth child, she spent a year in prison for deception.

Keri had never known her natural father and claimed to have been abused by her stepfather. At the age of 12 she was sent to Garfield House in Norfolk where, she alleged to the local police in 1999, a care worker had sexually molested her. Two years later, in late 1972, she was transferred to Duncroft. She was 14 at the time.

In late 2009 and throughout 2010, Keri began publishing online chapters from the second instalment of her biography, *Keri-Karin Part 1*. They covered her time at Duncroft. In one chapter, she wrote about typing classes, being taught dressmaking and the screams she heard coming from the padded room. More pertinently, she referred to the first time she witnessed a celebrity visit to the school, by a man she referred to only as 'JS'.

Keri reported that the 'girls flocked to gain attention' from JS and a small group was tasked with cleaning and polishing his car. He brought with him records and cartons of duty-free cigarettes, which he distributed among the girls as gifts. She also wrote that he would spend hours with Margaret Jones, chatting and laughing in her office. 'I always looked forward to JS visiting,' Keri recorded, 'because it meant pleasant food, rides down the lane in his sports car and extra cigarettes.'

In the very next paragraph, she spelled out the price of such perks. 'Sadly, it also meant one had to put up with being mauled and groped when he pulled into a lay-by some five miles along the road. I wasn't the only girl that JS favoured with this either. In fact, he often tried to press me to 'go further' than simply fondling him and allowing him to grope inside my knickers and at my partly formed breasts. He promised me all manner of good things if I would give him oral sex.' [9]

One of these inducements was the promise of a trip to see him record one of his television shows at the BBC. Keri acquiesced. Afterwards, she said she gagged and JS leaned across her and flung open the car door, telling her 'Not in the car. Not in the car.' He was good to his word, though, and the first of a number of trips to the BBC was arranged.

In the summer of 2011, Meirion Jones found the website on which Keri had published her biography. 'It was absolutely clear cut,' he says of his reaction to what she had written. 'I recognised everything she was saying about Duncroft, whereas most journalists would have probably seen it as a fantasy world with all these celebs and these girls being locked up in this stately home and being on drugs the whole time. Going out to Television Centre or Shepherds Bush Empire? Yeah, I knew they did that. Most of that world knew. And as soon as I saw "JS", it was obvious who that was.'

Jones was working on a film with Mark Williams-Thomas, a former Surrey Police officer who specialised in major crime and child abuse. They were collaborating on an investigation into how paedophiles can be tracked down. While carrying out research together at Interpol in Lyon, Jones had 'a long chat' with Williams-Thomas about Jimmy Savile, his own memories of Duncroft and what Keri had written about hers. He thought Williams-Thomas might have heard about the Savile investigation, given his Surrey connections. Williams-Thomas, who left Surrey Police in 2000, had not.

Williams-Thomas was immediately interested, recalls Jones, 'but the libel situation was such there was no chance [of doing anything while Savile was alive]'. In any case, Jones, who also discussed Savile with his *Newsnight* colleague Liz MacKean, was fully committed to other investigations.

When news broke of Jimmy Savile's death on 29 October 2011, Meirion Jones knew it was time to make his move. On the morning of Monday, 31 October, he spoke to his boss at *Newsnight*, the programme's editor Peter Rippon. He also fired off an email to Tom Giles, the editor at *Panorama*, writing: 'This may not be up *Panorama*'s street but when I was little my aunt ran a bizarre approved school in a stately home and we would go and visit and Jimmy Saville [sic] would turn up and charitably take the 14-year-old girls on unescorted outings to TVC [BBC Television Centre] and the like and then molest them with his friends. Some of the girls are now prepared to talk about this . . . and of course he's dead so he can't sue.'[10]

It was not the first time at the BBC in which aspersions had been cast on the previously good name of Sir Jimmy Savile OBE. In May 2010, it was brought to the attention of senior executives at the corporation that Savile was gravely ill. Nick Vaughan-Barratt, a senior executive, emailed George Entwistle, then the BBC Controller of Knowledge Commissioning, to inform him that the BBC had no obituary prepared. At the end of the email, Vaughan-Barratt added, 'I am not sure we would want one . . . I have a personal interest here: my first job in TV was on a JS show – I know him well and saw the complex and sometimes conflicting nature of the man at first hand.' He concluded by adding, 'I'd feel v queasy about an obit. I saw the real truth!!!'[11]

On 1 November 2011, a day after the announcement of Jimmy Savile's death, Vaughan-Barratt, by then the BBC's head of Events, sent another email. This one was addressed to Jan Younghusband, Commissioning Editor for BBC Music and Events, and contained the reasons why no obituary had been prepared in advance. 'We decided the dark side to Jim (I worked with him for 10 years) would make it impossible to make an honest film that could be shown close to death.'[12] Younghusband followed up by sending an email of her own to Entwistle, agreeing 'something celebrating a particular part of [Savile's] TV career is probably better than the [life] story as there are aspects of this which are hard to tell'.[13]

When later questioned about what he meant by 'the dark side', Vaughan-Barratt explained that he had worked with Savile on regional BBC programmes in Leeds in the 1970s, and heard rumours 'about him abusing his position at Stoke Mandeville . . . there were accusations that he was having sexual relations with patients.'[14] He stated, however, that he never heard anything about 'illegal activity . . . with underage girls'.

Younghusband claimed that she didn't know what was meant by 'the darker side' of Jimmy Savile, although she had heard rumours that he 'mishandled charity money' and knew there was speculation about his sex life.[15] George Entwistle would later claim that he did not read Younghusband's email and did not believe it was sent as a warning about Savile.[16]

J immy Savile's school career was coming to an end in 1939 when, like all other schoolchildren in Leeds and other major cities across Britain, he was issued with a gas mask. It came in a small cardboard box with a length of string knotted to each end that allowed it to be worn over a shoulder or across the back.

That summer, children were given forms for their parents to sign, giving consent for evacuation in the event that war was declared. In August, as hopes for peace dimmed in mainland Europe, the Department of Education outlined the requirements for each child in the event of evacuation: one full change of clothing including an extra pair of shoes, toothbrush and towel, three St Ivel triangular cheeses, six cream crackers and two ounces of barley sugar sweets.

On 1 September, more than 18,000 children left Leeds Central Station on 51 trains. The 12-year-old Jimmy Savile was among them, heading to a temporary home with a family in Gainsborough. He would describe his time in the flat, open expanses of Lincolnshire as a widescreen experience after the leaden skies and grime of Leeds.

This rural idyll was not destined to last long. When his parents cadged a lift off a neighbour to visit their youngest in his strange new surroundings, Agnes Savile discovered that he was living in the shadow of some prominent gasometers. She decided there and then to take him home, figuring if he was going to be killed by a German bomb it might as well be in Leeds. He was back at Consort Terrace before Hitler's Panzers had rumbled into France.

Despite what Savile later claimed about how badly Leeds suffered in the war, the city was getting off lightly in comparison to Grimsby and Hull to the east, Sheffield to the south and Manchester and Liverpool to the west. The low throb of enemy aircraft engines rarely presaged anything more serious than a few incendiary bombs that were advanced on by fire wardens wielding dustbin lids and broom handles like amateur lion tamers.

Of course this was not how Jimmy Savile remembered it. 'There were no lights from windows, no street lights,' he recalled wistfully at our first meeting in Leeds. 'You got a visit from the air raid warden if there was a chink of light from any of the curtains. The whole world was completely black.'

In fact, the fledgling Jimmy Savile was faring better than most. 'We were all in the racket business,' he said of a period in which the city's black market went into overdrive. He claimed to have learned much from the city's growing Jewish population, many of whom were first-generation Jews who had fled the Third Reich. 'They used to fascinate me,' he said of watching the newcomers carving out their living on the markets. 'All they knew about was being successful.'

His other fascination was the local dancehall. His parents were regulars at the Mecca Locarno ballroom situated in the County Arcade, and Savile told me about being trailed along in his Sunday best and being made to sit on the balcony while Vince and Agnes glided across the dance floor under the coloured spotlights. He said he was always intrigued by how the dancehall became a temporary escape from the rigours of life outside and how people were transformed once the music played.

The Mecca Locarno in County Arcade also afforded the young Jimmy Savile access to the more disreputable elements within society. As he memorably put it in his autobiography, he became 'the confidant of murderers, whores, black marketeers, crooks of every trade – and often the innocent victims they preyed on'. He recounted how the body of a regular female patron was found in several plastic bags in a ditch, reflecting, 'It was all part of the strange adult world that I never tried to understand.'[1] It was here, under the lights and amid the spit and sawdust that Savile claimed to have received his formal education.

He liked to talk about how he was effectively invisible during this period in his life. 'I was a tiny kid, about as thick as my finger. I was like a chair or a table. People used to talk in front of me because I didn't exist. Anybody who had done anything wrong, I knew who had done it. But nobody ever asked me.' He was, as he liked to put it, a child with big eyes, big ears and the good sense to keep his mouth shut.

While the young men of Leeds, his two older brothers included, were off at war, Jimmy Savile wangled himself a job in the dancehall as a stand-in percussionist. He accompanied the pianist who normally played with Pauline Grey and Her All-Girl Band. Finishing school at four o'clock, he ran down to the Mecca for the afternoon session, returning for a further half-hour spot in the evenings during the band's break. He said he earned 10 shillings a week, an income he'd supplement by scavenging for cigarettes under the seats.

From an early age, he was pulled by the twin sirens of money and sex. The shortage of adult males was something he turned to his advantage; he claimed to have scored his first date at the age of twelve.[2] She was about 20 and worked in the dancehall box office. He said he took her to the cinema where, in the darkness, he discovered a salient fact about the opposite sex, namely the '90 per cent you can't see is just as important as the 10 per cent you can'.

Not long afterwards, Jimmy Savile lost his virginity to a young woman who, he maintained, picked him up in the dancehall. He said she asked him to take her home to Horsforth. In his autobiography, he described his feelings as 'terror mixed with embarrassment'[3] when the woman slipped her hand into his trousers before attempting to have sex with him on a train. He said she eventually succeeded in getting what she wanted in a bush at the back of her house.

*

In June 1940, the evacuations from Dunkirk brought ragged columns of tired and filthy British troops to the centre of Leeds. Pouring from trains, they marched along Wellington Street to the Majestic Cinema where they were fed and able to rest up for a short time. 'We had to go down and cop for as many as we could take to come and live with us,' Savile told me. 'We got two soldiers . . . It was totally, totally bizarre.'

Vince and Agnes stepped up their charitable endeavours as Leeds became one of the first cities to embark on a programme of civic fund-raising for the war effort. A wooden 'cashometer' was assembled in City Square, and during 'War Weapons Week' enough was collected to fund the production of 250 bombers, a source of great pride to the local population. Speeches were made and a march-past of troops took place outside the town hall.

More than 50 years later, Savile talked to me about his brothers serving in the Royal Navy and how their infrequent letters home were pored over by the family because nobody knew whether they would ever return. Vincent had been trapped during the siege of Malta, making Agnes Savile all the more proud of the message she received thanking her for the money she'd raised to help buy a bomber for the island.

'In war living and dying is part and parcel of breathing,' Savile explained. He talked of the dread fear of the postman coming up the front path with a telegram in his hand. Many refused to open them, he said, and asked neighbours to do it instead. 'In the street where I lived I opened two or three telegrams,' Savile added with a certain relish.

Even then, as a child, he talked of himself as being strangely devoid of normal human emotions: 'I wondered why people wept during the war when their relatives had been killed. I didn't even know what killed was. I was much more enquiring than I was affected.'

Soon after turning 14, Jimmy Savile left school and it was only thanks to his mother's skills of persuasion that he was able to land a job as an office boy with Clarkson Brothers, an Irish company manufacturing threads used in the production of military uniforms. He started at 8.30 in the morning, finished at six and was paid 13 shillings and 9 pence a week, most of which went to his 'Mama' for his board and lodging. Any shortfall was comfortably made up through his dealings in the black market.

Not long afterwards, Leeds experienced its worst two days of bombing. At 9 p.m. on 14 March 1941, air raid sirens wailed around the city. Jimmy Savile and his mother were walking home along Great George Street when Luftwaffe explosives began raining down around them and they were forced to take shelter in a doorway.

A policeman standing nearby was killed that night, blown clean across the road as a bomb detonated. When the raid was over, Savile claimed that he stepped out into the street and picked up a black leather glove only to find it still contained a hand. It is a morbid detail and one that Savile savoured.

Consort Terrace was fortunate to emerge unscathed from the raid, with bombs landing on houses in nearby Burley Road, Wellington Street and Hanover Square. In neighbouring Willow Street and Willow Grove, a block of eight houses was completely destroyed. One of the bombs contained a timing device that detonated two minutes after the 'all clear' had sounded, killing an elderly woman and seriously injuring several others. Some of those left homeless by the destruction were taken in and housed by Vince and Agnes Savile.

Jimmy Savile spoke of the war as a time of great excitement. The cinemas reopened, the BBC resumed its broadcasts of dance bands on the wireless and a wave of popular massed dances swept through the ballrooms. After successfully adapting 'The Lambeth Walk', Carl Heimann of the Mecca organisation introduced 'The Siegfried Line', which involved dancers simulating hanging out their washing on the German line. Heimann, who would go on to play a pivotal role in Jimmy Savile's career, was regarded as the king of the dancehalls, which increasingly became focal points for the community.

The war years also represented opportunity, especially for a young man with a single-minded approach to getting what he wanted. Jimmy Savile landed a new job, this one at a large company handling vital foodstuffs such as currants, raisins and yeast. Agnes approved wholeheartedly, particularly when her son arrived home with his pockets stuffed full of produce. His passion for bike riding took him to the Yorkshire coast and Scotland for the first time, and when his four years of training with the Air Training Corps' 168 Squadron came to an end, Savile braced himself for what he imagined would be a call-up to the RAF. Or at least that's how he liked to tell it.

6. SPECIALIST SUBJECT: 'JIMMY SAVILE'

I was standing at one end of Jimmy Savile's front room in Leeds, looking at a large, wooden, free-standing unit of shelves and cabinets. It was packed with framed photographs, trophies, ornaments and boxes that looked like they contained medals and awards. We were midway through the third of our by now regular summits, meetings that would last for whole days at a time and generally involve me staying over at one of his flats.

Eighteen months after our first encounter, I had gone to interview him for *Maxim* magazine, this time at his flat in Scarborough. I'd ended up staying two days. Although I was still no closer to understanding what or who lay behind the familiar façade of the shell suit and the mist of white hair, the ever-present cigar and jewellery hanging from every appendage – I was now more intrigued than ever. My fascination had also become tinged with a certain, guarded affection. After spending my youth telling anyone who listened that he was evil incarnate, Jimmy Savile had succeeded in persuading me away from the belligerence of my younger self.

The room was by now thick with smoke. We had been at it for hours and I was in need of a break; he had talked me into submission – again. The phone rang.

'Not only alive but also here . . . How are things with the empire? Really? . . . Really? . . . Yeah . . . Yeah . . . Yeah. How's the baby? Have you got a date for the wedding yet? . . . I'll send you a card . . . Weddings and funerals is not my kick . . . I'll consider it . . . You won't have time to be offended . . . You'll go before me, that's for sure . . . I'll consider it . . . You'll have to bribe me . . . That's the way it is . . . I'm always ready for bribing . . . Alright then . . .

'Have you seen poor old Gordon has been given the elbow by Madame Tussauds? That's terrible, isn't it? . . . Wonderful . . . I've just had the call from Downing Street this week. His missus wants to come and see me at Stoke . . . I said the best thing is to wait until you get to Chequers . . . Yes . . . Yes . . . Yes . . . Trouble is, he's only a charismatic leader when he's gone. He wasn't a charismatic leader when he was there . . . The big deal is that he's got a few quid but she earns plenty . . . Margaret was getting a quarter a million a lunch . . . Yeah . . . Yeah . . . Yeah . . .

'So listen, I've got to go now because I've got a young lady here with no clothes on and she's getting a bit cold now . . . She's not doing anything with the Hoover . . . Bye.'

Savile put the phone down, rose from his chair and joined me at the cabinet. He was wearing a black shell suit. 'See that there,' he said pointing to a particularly ancient-looking black and white photograph. 'That's P.T. Barnum. When I first went to Granada TV it was nothing more than a series of huts, and that picture was on the wall everywhere. It was Sidney Bernstein, who owned Granada, who insisted on the picture as he didn't want us to ever forget what sort of business we're in.' He explained that he got Bernstein to sign a copy of the Barnum photo in return for 'a favour'.

A little further along was another signed photograph. It was of Savile's hero, Winston Churchill. One of Savile's friends later told me that the way he held his cigar was directly copied from Churchill. In 1965, Savile had queued up for hours to see the body of the great wartime leader lying in state at Westminster.

'This one here is one of the only pictures of Winston Churchill that's signed by him,' he said proudly. 'Now, his daughter Mary wanted me to do her a favour and I said, "OK, get me a signed photo of your Dad." She said he didn't sign anything so I said, "Tough. No favour." She said, "Leave it with me".'

He opened the glass door of the cabinet and removed the small, signed photograph. 'Look what it says on the back. "Jimmy Savile.

From Mary Soames. My thanks and in memory of someone we both admired.'" He put the frame back in the cabinet and closed the door. He looked pleased with himself. 'That's worth a lot of money, especially in America.'

Lower down was a photograph of Vince Savile, his father. He was pictured with a bird on his arm. Savile confirmed it was taken at the one-man station in Yorkshire where he'd first met the woman who would become his wife. Then, pointing to what looked like a small coin, he said, 'That's my first communion medal from about a million years ago.' Next to it was a tiny silver trophy: 'This here is the first thing I ever won, for playing the drums in a talent contest in 1939.'

There were other more impressive trophies, too: 'These are the bronze, silver and gold Mecca Cups. I won everything there was to win when I worked for Mecca.'

'What's this?' I asked, pointing to a seven-branched, silver candelabra. 'It's a Menorah, a Jewish sacred object,' he said. 'I did the Jews a favour in London and so they got special permission from the Chief Rabbi to give me something.' He picked it up and read the inscription: 'Presented to Jimmy Savile Esq, in apprecia-tion and esteem.'

When I asked him what the favour was, he barked 'Forget that' and moved straight to the next item. 'This one is the Variety Club of Great Britain Show Business Personality Award, and this,' he said, picking up what looked like a small mat, 'is the only booby prize anyone ever won on *Mastermind*.' I asked him what his specialist subject was: 'Jimmy Savile – 1926–2008.'

Below the cabinets were two shelves crammed with boxes. He told me they contained his papal knighthood, 'the Queen's knight-hood' and his knighthood of Malta. Next to them was a Doctor of Law certificate and a picture of Savile with his mother and another man outside Buckingham Palace. 'That's when I got my OBE,' he said. 'That's Joe, one of the porters I worked with for years at Leeds General Infirmary.'

From the table, he picked up the older of his two *This is Your Life* books. The cover was brown rather than red. Disappointingly, it was a shoddily put together album of out-of-focus pictures. 'In those days there were no videos or anything like that so the back page is an LP of the soundtrack of the show,' explained Savile. 'That's my brother Vince and that's John. That's the girl who used to do my hair. That's Davy Jones out of The Monkees. That's my sister Mary from Australia.

'In that second one there's a great letter at the back,' Savile pointed out. He settled back into his chair and waited for me to read it aloud. 'The last time Jimmy was seen going through the gates of Downing Street he was dressed for the occasion. He was dressed in running shoes and puffing away on a cigar. He has quite the most distinctive approach to fitness training, some might even say it was a little eccentric, but then so many great Britons have had a touch of eccentricity about them and Jimmy is truly a great Briton. He is a stunning example of opportunity Britain, a dynamic example of enterprise Britain and an inspiring example of responsible Britain at Leeds General Infirmary, Stoke Mandeville and Broadmoor, to name only three institutions which have benefitted from his charity compassion. Miner, wrestler, dancehall manager, disc jockey, hospital porter, fund raiser, performer of good works, Officer of the Most Excellent Order of the British Empire, Knight of the Realm, Jimmy, I and millions more salute you. God bless you.'

It was signed 'Margaret Thatcher'.

7. THEY FELT THEY WERE IN CONTROL

Over the 10 years and more Liz MacKean worked as a general reporter on *Newsnight*, she became good friends with Meirion Jones. They had regularly collaborated on investigations and she says they enjoyed a 'very healthy working relationship' in which she tended to be 'a balancing factor': he was more bullish in his approach; she was more circumspect. In 2010 they won a Daniel Pearl Award for their investigation into Trafigura's dumping of toxic waste in Africa.

Immediately after Savile's death, and in a climate that saw his face adorning the pages of newspapers across Britain, Liz MacKean was Jones's immediate choice as reporter on an investigation he planned to produce.

Newsnight's editor Peter Rippon had been emailed extracts from the web memoir written by Keri. He had subsequently been told by Jones, who had been following chatter on the Duncroft pages of the Friends Reunited website, that there was more than one Duncroft girl involved in Jimmy Savile's abuse. Also significant was the rumour the police had investigated Savile when he was alive. Rippon agreed that Jones should press ahead.

On 3 November 2011, Rippon emailed MacKean to tell her that he wanted her to prioritise work on Meirion Jones's story. Among her specialist areas were social affairs and domestic coverage, so she was an obvious candidate to work on the investigation.

The first priority was to find Keri and get her to agree to an interview. It would form the central plank of *Newsnight*'s report, and Meirion Jones knew he was in a unique position to persuade her.

'I thought I was probably the only person who could because of my knowledge of Duncroft,' says Jones. 'She was nervous and hostile at first but I told her how much I recognised from her account of Duncroft, which reassured her. I recognised the staff from her descriptions and I'd even seen Savile taking girls out on one occasion and I remembered Margaret [Jones, his aunt] telling us about trips to the BBC to see Savile.

'She trusted me because I knew that the most unlikely elements of her story were true. The old manor house out of *The Avengers*, the celebrity parties, Jimmy Savile and the trips to the BBC would all have seemed improbable to most journalists but I knew that was so. The only further step I had to take was believe what she was saying about what Savile had done to her and the other girls.' Jones reveals that although Keri had gradually opened up to him, she remained extremely sceptical that he would even interview her, let alone that it would be broadcast on the BBC.

Jones was in America working on a separate report for the first half of November, so MacKean would be responsible for much of the initial leg work, supported by a Glasgow-based BBC trainee Hannah Livingston, who was on attachment to *Newsnight* at the time.

They began by emailing the 60 or so ex-Duncroft girls active within the Friends Reunited online community, and Livingston was immediately contacted by one who said she had received a letter from Surrey Police asking her for information. As this exchange was taking place, Jimmy Savile's nephew and niece were speaking to the press outside their late uncle's flat in Leeds. They announced details of how he would be buried: holding his Marine Commando Green Beret and wearing his Help for Heroes bracelet and laid to rest at a 45-degree angle. 'It was his last wish that he be buried like this,' explained Amanda McKenna, 'so he could see the sea.' She added that his flat would be left untouched for the time being, even down to his last, unfinished cigar in the ashtray.

A spokesman for the Catholic diocese of the city encouraged members of the public to go and pay their respects when the coffin went on display at the Queens Hotel, saying, 'He is Our Jimmy, our main man in Leeds.'[1] A bandwagon was also now rolling to erect a permanent tribute to Jimmy Savile in his hometown. The deputy leader of Leeds City Council, Judith Blake, was confident she was speaking for the local population when she said, 'We want [any memorial] to be a tremendous celebration of his life and everything he contributed. He had that ability to reach people and connect with them.'[2]

The connections Liz MacKean and Hannah Livingston were now making, however, produced a very different portrait to the one being admired by the nation at large. MacKean, in particular, had gone into the investigation needing to be convinced and felt strongly that Keri's testimony was not enough on its own. Her opening pitch to the women who had been at Duncroft between the late 1960s and the late 1970s was that she was investigating a story about a celebrity visitor to the approved school. Jimmy Savile's name wasn't even mentioned.

MacKean told me she believes the blanket coverage of Savile's death and his impending funeral worked to her advantage. 'Their motivation [for talking], and this includes [Keri], was they were so furious at the way [Savile] was being eulogised and admired. They knew the truth.

'A lot of them had put it behind them. Some of them hadn't told their families. With a couple of them, no one knew they had been at Duncroft, so it was a source of embarrassment. They were never in a position to raise their heads above the parapet. But they were being driven to distraction by what was being said about Savile, not least by the BBC, which made a huge song and dance about his funeral . . . People wanted to talk, they were willing to say, not on the record most of them, but they wanted it out there and they were willing to share what had happened to them on the basis of confidentiality.'

Evidence began to point firmly to a police investigation into

Jimmy Savile taking place not long before his death. Livingston heard various accounts of a letter from Surrey Police suggesting that no charges were pressed due to his age. Keri had made no mention of this in her online memoir, and professed no knowledge of the police looking into Savile, and therefore it represented an intriguing new strand to the story. Meirion Jones felt that Mark Williams-Thomas, as a former Surrey Police officer, might be able to help them get to the truth of what the police's involvement had been, and emailed him stating that he was 'very keen' for him to be involved in the story as a consultant and expert.[3]

MacKean and Livingston were in constant touch via telephone and email, exchanging information, impressions and questions for each other. Of the sixty women they contacted, ten had come back with useful information, of whom five claimed to have been sexually abused by Jimmy Savile during their time at Duncroft. One also reported that her sister had been abused during a visit to Stoke Mandeville Hospital.

A pattern started to emerge, and with it MacKean's doubts quickly evaporated. 'There were certain things that made me believe they're telling the truth,' she says. 'It was the fact there was a lot of commonality in the stories they told but their stories weren't identical . . . Some of them said immediately, "It didn't happen to me but we knew it happened to other girls. We basically knew that when Savile came some of them would cluster round him because they knew they would get things from him."' MacKean says girls such as these knew there might be a price for any transaction with their celebrity visitor, and some were willing to pay it.

'Their accounts collectively seemed to tell me a lot about the institution they were in,' she continues. 'And explain a lot about why Savile targeted them, how he insinuated his way in and how, even by the standards of the time, he had what was most unusual access. Meirion, who was a bystander at the time, thought it was odd; his parents thought it was odd; but his aunt was bamboozled and charmed. That's how he managed it.'

Some of the women were terrified about being exposed. As was the case with many who had been at Duncroft, the lack of trust in authority figures represented a serious issue for the *Newsnight* investigators. 'I had to persuade them that I wouldn't reveal their names or give away any identifying features,' explains MacKean.

'Their stories fitted the trend. We were able to build up a pattern of Savile's offending behaviour,' she says. 'At one end, the most extreme end, it was lifts in his car and blowjobs. And at the other end was this constant sticking his tongue down [their] throats, shoving his hands up skirts, pushing people up against the wall and groping them. He was very open and did it in front of the other girls. None of the abuse that was described to us fell outside those goalposts, if you like.

'I believed it and I believed them,' she continues. 'I respected and understood their reasons for not wanting to be seen on camera, not wanting their names out there, but also their willingness and their desire that their quotes would be used to help.'

Three of the women Liz MacKean, Meirion Jones and Hannah Livingston spoke to talked about abuse taking place on BBC premises. They described the opportunity to get out of Duncroft and be a part of one of his TV programmes as Savile's 'ultimate calling card'.

On 9 November, inside St Anne's Cathedral in Leeds, Professor Alistair Hall was revealing to those packed inside and out that a new hospital institute was to be created using a bequest from Jimmy Savile's will. He said the Savile Institute in the city would help those with cardiovascular disease and pioneer research into heart disease.

On the same day, a meeting took place in the *Newsnight* offices attended by Liz MacKean, Peter Rippon and Liz Gibbons, one of the programme's deputy editors. At this meeting, Gibbons voiced her objection to the story 'on grounds of taste' and because of how recently Savile had died.[4] In a subsequent email to a friend, she wrote, 'Personally I wouldn't have gone near it in the first place and I was very supportive of the decision to drop it, for a host of reasons.' MacKean says she was able to talk her around, in light of the new line of inquiry on a possible police investigation, and because there was 'a clear public interest'[5] in exposing the fact that Jimmy Savile was a very different man to the one whose life was being celebrated in the media. She also says that both Gibbons and Rippon expressed concerns about the credibility of the witnesses.

'It is always, as everyone knows, a real issue with these old cases,' MacKean told the Pollard inquiry[6], the independent review commissioned by the BBC into the management of the *Newsnight* investigation into the allegations of sexual abuse of children by Jimmy Savile. 'Claims are generally made by people who don't expect to be believed and tend not to be. Certainly in the case of these women . . . [they] had a chequered history, some of them very much so. But despite what Peter said [in a subsequent email], they didn't all have criminal records. That's why in my mind, from the get-go it was very important to talk to a lot of people.'

In the days that followed, MacKean and Livingston continued to gather more evidence and pursue the twin strands of whether there had been a police investigation and whether the police had sent a letter saying no further action would be taken against Jimmy Savile because of his age. On the latter, both Meirion Jones and Liz MacKean were in firm agreement that proof of the letter's existence was not essential to the story making it to air.

News of the investigation was now spreading within the BBC. On 11 November, a day after Jimmy Savile was lowered into his grave, a member of the BBC's 'Impact Team' emailed a colleague of Stephen Mitchell, the deputy head of news and Peter Rippon's line manager, to say that he had heard about *Newsnight*'s 'Jimmy Savile expose'.[7] The Impact Team ensures big BBC news stories are covered across the network, and it was suggested the report might need to be on the Managed Risk Programme List (MRPL), a management tool that alerts senior figures within the organisation to upcoming controversial or potentially risky programmes. An email was sent back that same day confirming that the story was on *Newsnight*'s MRPL.[8]

That evening, a tribute programme to Jimmy Savile aired on BBC Television. *As It Happened* opened with Chris Evans's voiceover and footage of Jimmy Savile standing among gyrating teenagers in the *Top of the Pops* studios. 'He was a pop pioneer . . .' boomed Evans, 'and a multi-million pound charity fund-raiser . . . For 60 years Jimmy Savile has been part of our lives, a great British eccentric.' A host of British celebrities appeared as talking heads, offering up their views on his peculiar appeal. Nicky Campbell, who succeeded Savile on Radio 1, donated his £250 fee to the National Association of People Abused in Childhood when he found out about Savile's offending.

Keri's teenage memories of Jimmy Savile were markedly different from the madcap capers depicted in the first of the BBC's tributes. Three days later, on 14 November, Meirion Jones, Liz MacKean, Hannah Livingston and a cameraman travelled to Oswestry to interview Keri in her home. Liz MacKean conducted the interview and says that she was in no doubt that Keri was telling the truth. 'We just knew,' she says. 'She wasn't pretending to know more than she did. She wasn't pretending that her memory was perfect. She was a woman telling the truth.'

Keri was about to have major surgery for bowel cancer. She was doubtful about surviving the ordeal, which meant she was even more determined her story should be told. 'She was weary, she was bloody cynical,' recalls MacKean, 'but by then I'd had so many conversations with people who'd been at this school, she fitted the type.'

In the interview, Keri spoke at length about Jimmy Savile's visits to Duncroft, and how the girls universally considered him to be 'a creep'. She says they were not frightened of him as such, but recognised they could get things from him: cigarettes, perfume, records, better food on the days he visited, even trips away from Duncroft to see his television shows being recorded at Television Centre.

'That was one of my striking impressions, and it really helped me get the bit between my teeth,' says MacKean. 'It is clear [the girls] were compromised and as such that was how he reeled them in and why it was so difficult for them ever to pipe up. A lot of them were difficult teenagers; that's why they were there. Their parents couldn't handle them, they had been in trouble with the police or mentally they were disturbed. But they were all highly intelligent and therefore I think they felt they were in control. Savile allowed them to feel in control and that is the subtlety of his grooming process as it applied to them . . . He hooked them so that they felt complicit, and they had to pay the price. They [felt they] deserved what came to them . . . He recruited them to be the agents of the abuse.'

MacKean reveals that Keri spoke frankly about not feeling any sense of shame at the time about what she had to do to secure such treats from Savile. A few of the ex-Duncroft girls told MacKean that as they got older and had children themselves, their view of what went on had changed. 'That is when they felt the anger,' she confirms, 'much more anger towards Jimmy Savile than what they appeared to feel at the time because of this subtle process that went on.'

If Savile was regarded as a lecherous old man, albeit one who bestowed occasional benefits, Keri had very different recollections of Gary Glitter, who she met during a visit to the BBC Television Centre to watch an episode of *Clunk Click* being recorded in early 1974. A forerunner to *Jim'll Fix It*, the show featured Jimmy Savile talking to a variety of studio guests, with filmed segments in between. Children from a number of institutions Jimmy Savile was involved with sat on beanbags on the set, including, on occasion, girls from Duncroft.

Keri told MacKean that Glitter made them feel uncomfortable, and none of them wanted to be left alone in a room with him.

In her evidence to the Pollard inquiry, MacKean also revealed that she had been told the singer had offered the girls 'a safe house'[9] if they were ever in trouble with the police or had run away from Duncroft. 'They entirely mistrusted his motives,' she said. They felt there was 'something dangerous about him'.

The filmed interview with Keri was a turning point in the *Newsnight* investigation. 'By the end of it we were all convinced that [Keri] was genuine, that what she was saying was overwhelmingly true,' says Meirion Jones. 'As I left she told me that she didn't believe the BBC would broadcast it – they'd cover it up. I assured her that once we found some corroboration – which we did with the *Clunk Click* footage and the other girls' accounts – we would run with the story. There would be no cover-up.'

On the drive back to London that evening, Jones, MacKean and Livingston were in buoyant mood. It was then that they heard the news that the BBC were planning to broadcast a Christmas Special of *Jim'll Fix It*, to be presented by Shane Ritchie.

'We were in the car, hearing it on the radio and almost giggling,' recalls MacKean. 'We were going, "Oh my God, they're going to have to cancel [it]. That's awkward; we're making it awkward for the BBC." It was perfectly obvious what had to be done,' she says. 'To us, it was always one or the other. And then it seemed that the whole weight was against us and for the tributes.'

I n late October 1944, Jimmy Savile turned 18 and received his call-up papers. In his autobiography, he wrote about an interval in the war when for him 'the question was, what to join'.[1] He said he couldn't join the Royal Navy like his brothers because he couldn't swim; he was unsuited to the army because he was too weak; and his hopes of joining the RAF were thwarted by failing a sight test. Instead, Ernest Bevin, the minister of labour and national service in Winston Churchill's wartime coalition government, made the choice for him: the last digit on his national service papers corresponded with the number drawn out in the fortnightly ballot and, like one in 10 men aged between 18 and 25, he was ordered to report to the coalmines.

During his time as a conscript miner, or 'Bevin Boy', Savile claimed to have realised that opportunities existed in being different, or as he liked to put it, he recognised 'the power of oddness'. And like the hardships he endured as a 'Not again child' during the depression in Leeds, his experiences in the deep mines of the Yorkshire coalfields can only have contributed to the man he became. Unfortunately, the details remain equally elusive.

As in other areas of his life, he steadfastly refused to allow a chronology to be established for this phase in his development. His standard response whenever I asked for clarification on the specifics of date or place was, 'How the fuck should I know? 1642.' It was a tactic he employed often: obfuscation – occasionally coupled with menace – that erected a dead end for channels of enquiry he didn't much care for.

Up until this point, the war hadn't caused Jimmy Savile too much additional discomfort, and though he always protested that he loved mining and would have remained at the pit had he not been injured, the experience can only have been the most brutal introduction to the realities of physical labour. He preferred to describe the period as one in which he learned about himself and, ironically for one who was confined to dark, sweaty tunnels a mile underground, about the world beyond his native Yorkshire.

As far as it's possible to tell, Savile worked at three Yorkshire collieries. The first, the Prince of Wales Colliery in Pontefract, was a training centre for new conscripts, one of 13 in the country. South Kirkby Colliery in South Elmsall was where he was posted after completing his basic training, and was one of a string of mines in the area north of Barnsley, Rotherham and Sheffield. Waterloo Main at Temple Newsam in Leeds was his third and final posting, and the scene of the accident he claimed finished his mining career.

Pontefract was a bleak, unforgiving place: a racecourse, pit and not much besides. Like Savile, Herbert A. Purnell was a Leeds boy who had trained with the Air Training Corps from the age of 15, been called up as a Bevin Boy and sent for training at Pontefract in late 1944. 'A lot of the lads there lived in a hostel because they were from all over the country,' he remembered. It chimes with what Savile wrote in his autobiography about his fellow recruits being the 'most incredible and bizarre types'. Among his intake, he said, were 'doctors, auctioneers, farmers, officer cadets, clerks'.

On their first day, the conscripts were kitted out at the stores with a pair of sturdy boots with steel toecaps, a safety helmet and a belt from which to hang a safety lamp. Four weeks later, at the end of 'Stage A' training, the rookie miners were then sent underground for the first time.

For many, memories of the first 'big drop' remained vivid. 'You went into the cage with trepidation,' remembered Warwick Taylor who was put to work at a coalmine in Wales and later became chairman of the Bevin Boys Association. 'It was supposed to descend at 30 foot per second, but they let it go at 70 foot per second . . . The pressure on the eardrums was intense. Some of the lads got nosebleeds on the way down. Most of us couldn't wait to get out.' At the end of his first drop, Jimmy Savile remembered, 'Twenty-five white, wobbly-legged flowers of British youth emerged like cattle to the abattoir.'[2]

Stage B Training took place at the mines the recruits were assigned to. Savile was sent 20 miles away to South Kirkby Colliery, known for containing the finest steam raising coal in Yorkshire and being the deepest mine in the county. He and his childhood friend Joe Baker were initially billeted in a temporary miners' hostel in Featherstone, where they received orders to present themselves in work clothes at the pithead baths no later than 6 a.m.

On a normal day, a miner's shift began with undressing and placing his everyday clothes in a locker. He would then be given a bar of soap, scrubbing brush and towel and told to move naked along a short corridor, past the shower room and into the dirty area containing further lockers containing work clothes. Once changed, he'd move on to the lamp room where a 'tally', one of two numbered brass discs, was exchanged for a freshly charged hand lamp. Each tally was placed on a hook in the lamp room and served as proof that a miner was in the pit.

But rather than join the queue for the cage, Jimmy Savile claimed to have been put to work at the pithead. This was a noisy, brutal arena in which the incessant din was created by shunting engines, hammers on steel and giant spoil buckets tipping muck that piled up into an ugly scar across the surrounding countryside.

Savile was assigned to the screens, the long, steam engine-powered steel trays that shunted backward and forward allowing graded lumps to fall through into railway trucks below. It was a common posting for new Bevin Boys who took up position alongside elderly or disabled miners on either side of the conveyor belt.

For all his later claims that he was unlike the other recruits because he actually enjoyed being a miner, even Savile admitted working on the screens was 'a job reserved for the young, the old and the damned . . . The noise, the dark and dust and the torn fingers created an impression of Hell that I will carry to the grave.'[3]

In time, he secured work underground but only because it was a job that nobody else wanted. The pit bottom at South Kirkby was a subterranean cathedral from which roadways, or maingates, took the men to the various mining districts. Savile's new job was in one of these tunnels, working for the Corporal, the man in charge of all haulage work in the mine.

'There was no doubt I was odd,' he told me during our first meeting in Leeds. 'I was always odd. People would say, "You're a funny one, you are lad."' And the job he was given reflected that. He was stationed two miles from the pit bottom and a mile and a half from the face. Forced to perch on a narrow bench in a manhole chiselled into the wall of the tunnel, he spent his eight-hour shift alone. His task was to lever coal trucks back onto the tracks whenever they derailed. 'The job used to drive everyone bonkers – no lad would do it,' he said. 'They would imagine ghosts and all sorts. I loved it.'

He told me about the pocket he had stitched into his coat and smuggling in books on astronomy, languages, people and travel. 'I learned down South Kirkby colliery,' he explained. 'You can't get a better learning place in the world than a pitch dark hole underground with only a lantern for company.' He said he remained 'King of the Corner' for three and a half years.

Hemsworth and the surrounding villages of South Kirkby, South Emsall, Fitzwilliam and Kinsey were home to tough, tight-knit communities that looked after their own and in which favours were rife. Jimmy Savile said he did not fit in: 'I'd never go to the pub for a drink with the lads, it wasn't my scene. I was quite prepared to go home and sit and think.'[4]

He pinpointed one day when 'they drew apart from me and I started to draw apart from the normal world'.[5] He arrived late for work, still dressed in his blue suit, white shirt, navy tie and suede shoes from the night before. There was no time to go through the bathhouse and change into his work gear so as he came skidding into the yard, he just managed to exchange his tally for a lamp before squeezing into the cage. He was still dressed in his Sunday best and clutching a newspaper.

Ignoring the looks and comments from the other miners, Savile said he smiled and looked ahead as if nothing was out of place. 'The deputy sat at the bottom to check the lamps,' he recalled. 'When I turned up in a sharp suit, he checked the lamp and his eyes went up the suit. It freaked him.'

He talked of feeling the eyes on him as he walked off in his suit to his position on the dark bend in the tunnel. Once at his manhole, he took off his shirt, jacket and trousers, folded them up in the newspaper and settled down to read his latest book, occasionally stopping to shoulder a wayward tub back onto the rails. He said he worked naked and saved enough water from his canteen to wash down his face and hands at the end of the shift. Then, when the eight hours were up, he unfolded the paper and climbed gingerly back into his folded suit and shirt and headed back to the pit bottom. He claimed that he arrived looking as immaculate as when he had left: 'The effect was electric.'

This was a story he told on many, many occasions, and it was the same ending every time: 'In the history of coalmining nobody ever went to work at the coal face in an immaculate suit and came back clean,' he claimed. He insisted the other miners didn't want to stand next to him in the cage. Miners were superstitious by nature, and in the queue someone had said he was a witch. Jimmy Savile didn't care. For the first time in his life he realised being odd had an effect on people.

'I wasn't sure what it did but it did develop my out-of-the-box thinking,' he told me 60 years later. 'I didn't do it for any reason, I just realised that going back clean would freak people out, and it did. Underneath the clothes I was as black as night. But I realised that being a bit odd meant that there could be a payday.'

When victory over the Germans was declared in September 1945 there was a sharp rise in absenteeism among the Bevin Boys.[6] The country still needed coal but there was little motivation for the conscripts to return to work when they could see servicemen being welcomed home as heroes. Under the terms of the Emergency Act, however, periods of extended leave or absence still had to be registered with both the pit and the labour exchange.

Savile had been mining for less than a year and, I strongly suspect, had become a repeat absconder by this time. For example, he claimed to have been one of the first tourists to cycle through France after the war, obtaining a transit visa that allowed him to travel by train to Switzerland via France. He said he spent his first night in France 'in a shelter with 300 homeless people' before setting off for Le Touquet, the fashionable seaside resort some 40 miles away. There, he found beautiful villas with furniture smashed to smithereens inside. 'No birds flew about it and the feeling of unreal macabre was overwhelming,' he said.[7]

When he returned from France, stocked up with spare bike parts he intended to sell on at a tidy profit, Jimmy Savile discovered he had been transferred to Waterloo Main colliery in Leeds. In his autobiography, he stated that by this time he had done 'nearly four years at South Kirkby' which would have made it late 1948, some months after the last of the Bevin Boys had been demobbed.

On my last visit to see him at his Scarborough flat, he had on display his miner's lamp, a snap tin used for food and a thick slab of coal mounted on a wooden plinth that was presented to him when he returned to South Kirkby in the 1980s. As one of the most famous men to be recruited under Bevin's scheme, his photograph had dominated a display at the National Mining Museum of England in Wakefield. It hung in a glass case above the items now arranged on his mantelpiece.

I asked him how he felt about going back underground once the war had been won and troops were returning home. 'I'd learned enough not to necessarily go down the pit,' he replied, hinting at the wheeling and dealing he was doing on the side. 'I knew I could always get a quid or two one way or another. But unfortunately you didn't get a ration book. I had to go down the pit to get a ration book to eat, so of course I went.' He also admitted that he was put on night shifts as punishment for going AWOL.

The upside to be being assigned to Waterloo was that he could move back in to Consort Terrace. Each morning, he said he'd rise at 3 a.m. and walk for half an hour in his clogs to catch the train that took him to the pit. But rather than being left alone with his books on a quiet stretch of tunnel, he spoke of Waterloo teaching him to 'enjoy the delights of manual labour'. Such delights were to indirectly lead to the accident that resulted in him leaving the mines; another significant brick in the facade of his mythology.

He said he was lying on his side in an eighteen-inch high tunnel, shovelling dust off the belt between shifts. He was working alone and should have had his safety lamp placed in a position so its light shone down the coalface to let others know he was there. Instead, when the shot-firer looked down the face and saw nothing, he detonated his charges. A split second later, the roof of the tunnel came crashing down on the concealed figure up ahead. 'There was no sound,' Savile recalled, 'just a localised "WHUMP".'

Concussed and covered in debris, including one large piece of stone that had fallen onto his back, he said he called out and was pulled clear by his fellow miners. He remembered being totally unmarked, 'but my legs moved in a funny sort of way.'[8] At the surface, he was told to lie on a pile of coal until the end of the shift.

During the next few days he recalled that his aches and pains gradually disappeared, all except for the one in his back. He went to Leeds Infirmary where neither X-rays nor a physiotherapist could locate the source of the problem. As a last resort, heated electrical pads were placed on his thighs.

Savile maintained that as the pain got worse, he kept returning to the hospital for regular check-ups. He was eventually fitted with a surgical webbing corset fortified by steel rods, which left him incapable of lifting his feet more than an inch. When he asked what his prospects were, a nurse is supposed to have taken his name card from a filing cabinet and coldly informed him that he would never walk again without sticks.

He was signed off on sick pay: 'two walking sticks were added to my survival kit and hey presto I was released into the free world, after seven event-filled years underground.'[9] Of course, seven years underground would make it 1951 or 1952, a period in which Jimmy Savile was making a name for himself as a racing cyclist rather than as a shuffling invalid.

Trying to confirm the dates when he was mining is like trying to nail smoke. In 1994, Savile showed a reporter the rudimentary surgical support jacket he once wore. 'I keep this . . . as a reminder of an accident that changed, and nearly wrecked, my life,' he explained. 'I was 24 and had been working in the pits for six years when I was blown up underground . . . I was like a zombie for three years, with two sticks and that boned jacket.'[10]

According to this timeline the accident must have happened in 1950, or more probably early 1951. But if his recovery did indeed take three years, one small but rather significant fact is ignored: in August of 1951, he took part in the very first Tour of Britain cycle race. And in the official race brochure he was listed as 'Oscar "The Duke" Saville' [sic], a 'company director'.

In 2008, over lunch at the Athenaeum Club, the story changed again. He told me, 'I did seven years as a Bevin Boy, two extra than I was meant to have done.' The most plausible timeline was given to a newspaper 30 years previously: 'So there I was, a young man just turned twenty with two sticks and about half a mile an hour as top speed.'[11] If he'd just turned 20, the accident would have happened in late 1946 or early 1947.

But even if Jimmy Savile was signed off sick in 1947, the speed of his recovery can have been nothing short of miraculous. Why? Because in the spring of 1948 a young and extremely fit Jimmy Savile appeared as an extra in the British film, *A Boy, a Girl and a Bike* starring Diana Dors and Honor Blackman. The story is based around a fictional cycling club, and Savile and a pal landed work and moved into digs in Grassington as the production moved between locations. The film climaxes in a prestigious Yorkshire road race, in which, for a second or two, the unmistakable figure of a 21-year-old Jimmy Savile can be seen. He looks lean and healthy, and is pedalling his racing bike like the elite competitor that he surely was at the time.

The dates are not the only inconsistencies in his story, however. During the miners' strike of the 1980s, Savile gave an interview to the *Sun* in which he expressed his sadness at the state of the industry. The article stated: 'In 1948, Jimmy was finally allowed to leave the pits when a chest cold showed up on X-ray.'[12]

More perplexing still is a throwaway quote from a 1981 newspaper article in which he hit back at critics who accused him of being too hungry for publicity: 'When I was James Wilson working down the pits for £2 a week for six shifts, it didn't matter to anyone,' he retorted.[13]

It is unlikely that this was a typo, given that Wilson was one of Jimmy Savile's middle names. So why did he refer to himself as James Wilson, and was it an uncharacteristic slip of the tongue? He once told me that he was named after a cousin, Jimmy Wilson, who died in a car crash at the age of 22. Could it be that Jimmy Wilson died much later than this and Jimmy Savile was using his late cousin's papers to evade work? Unfortunately, records of the Bevin Boys were destroyed in a fire in 1950 and only around 500 members of the Bevin Boys Association are alive today, making corroboration of any of this impossible.

The Bevin Boys were, as the title of Warwick Taylor's memoir attests, *The Forgotten Conscripts*. They had to wait more than 50 years before being presented at the Cenotaph on Remembrance Day. Taylor's long campaign for public recognition finally came to fruition in 2008 when he led a delegation of former Bevin Boys to 10 Downing Street to receive medals from Prime Minister Gordon Brown. 'This is wonderful news for a brave group of men who have been forgotten and shelved for years,' said Taylor afterwards. 'We have finally surfaced in the national consciousness.'[14]

I met Jimmy Savile that very morning outside the Athenaeum Club before he joined the former Bevin Boys at Downing Street.

But as Taylor later explained to me, the association had not invited Savile. Jimmy Savile was invited by Downing Street. Taylor recalled that a member of Downing Street staff had told him to 'think of the publicity' that his presence would generate.

Taylor also told me that he'd approached Jimmy Savile at the reception and invited him along to one of their regular get-togethers. He did not get the response he had expected: 'Savile said nothing and just walked away from me,' recalled Taylor. 'He didn't want to get involved.'

Taylor's theory is that Jimmy Savile wasn't a Bevin Boy at all. He said that he knew of no other conscripted miners who had been sent to work at South Kirkby or Waterloo. While the terminology Savile used when describing his mining career, and Joe Baker's confirmation that he trained with him at Pontefract and worked with him at South Kirkby would seem to suggest otherwise, it is very unlikely that he was a Bevin Boy for as long as he variously claimed. The possibility that he was using another man's identity papers in order to dodge work and further his career on the edges of the black market is, of course, another intriguing alternative.

This period in Jimmy Savile's life remains as murky as the environment he claimed to have worked in. Most of the pits where the Bevin Boys served have long since closed. The gates of South Kirkby colliery were padlocked in 1988 and it was demolished soon afterwards, while golfers now roam the landscaped grounds where Waterloo Main Colliery once stood. Among the 164,000 and more records stored by the Coal Mining History Resource Centre, I could find no evidence of a shot-firing accident at Waterloo Main between 1944 and 1950 although, as Warwick Taylor pointed out, one miner was killed every six hours and another was seriously injured every six minutes. 'It's unlikely the accident would have been reported,' he conceded.

Attitudes towards the Jimmy Savile investigation within the *Newsnight* offices seemed more positive in the wake of the successful interview with Keri, even if the spectre of the planned *Jim'll Fix It* tribute show at Christmas remained a background worry for those working on the story. The BBC received more than 12,000 applications for tickets for the recording of the show, though Jones and MacKean didn't know this at the time. Jones was concerned enough, however, to voice his reservations about the scheduling of the tribute to *Newsnight*'s editor and their executive editor on the Savile report, Peter Rippon.

Keri had given the team a potential lead on the identity of the Duncroft girl who encountered Gary Glitter in Jimmy Savile's changing room in 1974, and Hannah Livingston, who had by now established that the programme was *Clunk Click*, continued to follow up. By 17 November, Liz MacKean had emailed Jones and Livingston to say that she had heard from six ex-Duncroft girls but was still no nearer to being able to confirm whether there had been a police investigation and if so, whether letters existed explaining why it had been dropped.

Jones contacted Mark Williams-Thomas to give him an update on the police angle, confirming that most of the women spoken to believed they had been interviewed by the police around 2009, before receiving a letter that confirmed the Crown Prosecution Service had declined to proceed on the grounds that the individual was too old and infirm. Jimmy Savile's name was not said to have appeared on the letters.

If the Savile investigation was to be broadcast it would have had wider implications for the corporation, particularly for BBC Television which George Entwistle ran as director of Vision.

On 21 November, Rippon had a meeting with his line manager Stephen Mitchell in which they discussed the implications of the investigation for the Christmas *Jim'll Fix It* tribute programme. Mitchell told Rippon it was not an issue and that he should 'follow the evidence'[1] on his story.

Following this conversation, the Jimmy Savile report was taken off the *Newsnight* Managed Risk Programmes List at Mitchell's behest, although he could later provide no adequate reason for his decision.

One plausible reason is that Mitchell believed Peter Rippon had grasped the meaning of his oblique language regarding the 'Vision issues'.[2] It was the same term Liz Gibbons, who was responsible for the Managed Risk Programmes List for *Newsnight*, had used in a contemporaneous email. Contrary to what the Pollard inquiry concluded, 'Vision issues' could have conceivably meant the potential awkwardness of the clash with tributes to Jimmy Savile that had already been scheduled.

Later that day, Rippon also met in his office with Helen Boaden, the BBC's director of news. She described it at the inquiry as a 'very short conversation'[3] in which she was told about the Savile investigation and the allegations involving sexual abuse of underage girls. What Rippon failed to tell Boaden was that there were allegations of abuse on BBC premises.

In this meeting, Rippon is recorded as asking Boaden whether the story was a potential problem in terms of embarrassment for the BBC, to which Boaden replied it was not. She told him to be 'guided by the evidence'[4] and that taste was not an issue. The main thing Rippon recalls of the conversation is '[Boaden] talking about . . . the funeral and the "climate in which he would be making his judgement". He agreed with her assessment that the story needed to reach a "reasonable threshold of certainty."'[5]

Curiously, given what she said about this being a 'a five- to ten-minute conversation,'[6] the discussion with Peter Rippon led Helen Boaden to miss the prestigious Reuters Memorial Lecture at Oxford. When asked when the meeting took place with Rippon, she replied it was the 21st and 'the reason I remember it is that looking through the diary I know I was meant to go to Oxford to do a lecture or attend a lecture, and the meeting overran so I literally didn't have enough time to get on the train and get there'.[7]

The lecture she missed was given by Baroness O'Neill who, ironically, spoke on the subject of press freedom. It was followed by a high-powered panel discussion chaired by Lord Patten, Chairman of the BBC Trust.

Two days later, Boaden met up with her deputy Stephen Mitchell, who told her that she ought to tell George Entwistle, director of Vision, about the Savile investigation as he might need to change the Christmas schedules.

On 24 November, Hannah Livingston made a breakthrough in finding the relevant episode of *Clunk Click* featuring Gary Glitter. The episode in question closes with Jimmy Savile inviting the glam rocker onto the beanbags where the teenagers are sitting. As he's invited to sit between two girls, Glitter remarks, 'I get two?'

'You get two,' replies Savile, who mock sighs: 'I should be giving girls away.' He then walks further down the line and sits between two other girls.

MacKean says, 'It's as plain as day: the tight gripping of the girls [on the beanbags], the embracing. And you see the discomfort of the girls.'

A day later, the investigating team received another major boost when Mark Williams-Thomas told Meirion Jones that a very well-placed contact had confirmed off the record that Surrey Police had investigated Jimmy Savile. This was proof that the police had taken the allegations seriously, as well as underlining the credibility of the accounts of the ex-Duncroft girls.

Rippon's response was his most enthusiastic to date: 'Excellent,' he wrote, before advising that planning should now commence for a transmission date. A Rolls-Royce convertible, like Savile's, was hired to film reconstructions around Duncroft and the film was scheduled to be broadcast on Thursday, 8 December.

Liz MacKean had by now set up a filmed, on the record interview with Rochelle Shepherd, who was at Duncroft in the late 1970s, after Keri had left. Meirion Jones was to do the interview. '[Shepherd] did not present herself as a victim,' says MacKean, 'but she saw the groping, the tongues down the throat. She corroborated and added to the general picture. [We now had] these other vital quotes and testimonies from other victims and witnesses, and when you put it all together with the footage of *Clunk Click* and the fact we did get confirmation of a police investigation, we had a really cracking story.'

What's more, the team had also received an account that related to abuse at Stoke Mandeville, the hospital Jimmy Savile had worked at as a volunteer before leading the fund-raising drive to rebuild the National Spinal Injuries Centre, which opened in 1983.

'We'd heard a rumour about Broadmoor [another hospital Savile was closely associated with] but we hadn't gone anywhere with it,' says MacKean. 'And we knew, because of the photograph in the *Sun* [in 2008], that he was at Haut de la Garenne [the Jersey children's home at the centre of an abuse scandal]. So we were thinking, "Hang on, if we know this now about Duncroft . . . we are building up a picture and there could be a lot more [victims] out there".' Meirion Jones predicted that there might be as many as one hundred. It was an estimate that turned out to be conservative in the extreme.

On 27 November, less than three weeks after Jimmy Savile's funeral had taken place amid rapturous national coverage, Meirion Jones began drafting a preliminary script that would be read as the 'cue' for the report. This is what he wrote:

'When Jimmy Savile died in October, Prince Charles led the tributes to a national treasure. But there was a darker side to the star of *Jim'll Fix It*. *Newsnight* has learnt that he was investigated by police for sexual assaults on minors but the Crown Prosecution Service decided in 2009? [the question mark is included because they were still waiting for confirmation from the police and the CPS] that he was too old and infirm to face trial. Now some of the girls who say they were assaulted by him in the 1970s when they were 13, 14 and 15 have talked to *Newsnight*. They say Savile was an evil man who should rot in hell and that his charity work gave him cover to get young girls. They even claim some of his abuse took place after BBC recordings and involved other celebrity paedophiles who appeared on Savile's shows such as Gary Glitter. Liz MacKean investigates . . .'[8]

MacKean was also working on a first draft of the script proper, and parallel discussions were taking place about what Mark Williams-Thomas could add as an expert in child sex abuse cases. A copy of the first draft was sent to Peter Rippon, Liz Gibbons, who was responsible for booking editing suites at the BBC, and Roger Law, a BBC lawyer. On the same day, the Impact Team began gathering information in order to prepare versions of the story that could be rolled out across the BBC network. 'It is safe to assume there will be a huge amount of interest in the story, I would expect all domestic outlets to want versions,' said a member of the team in an email to Rippon.[9]

Liz Gibbons's reluctance to have anything to do with the story was again underlined when she emailed Rippon to confirm that he would be the executive producer on the report.[10]

At lunchtime on 29 November, Rippon emailed Stephen Mitchell, who was in Belfast, with a positive-sounding update on the state of the *Newsnight* report on Jimmy Savile. Seven victims of sexual assault from Duncroft Approved School had been spoken to, Surrey Police had carried out an extensive investigation, which was recent even though the offences took place in the 1970s, and the women were credible. He added that Sky were also chasing the story so it would be prudent not to 'sit on it'.[11] It is a telling detail, given that Sky's interest made it more likely that the story would come out one way or the other.

Mitchell replied 18 minutes later, enquiring as to whether the headmistress of the school had been spoken to, and whether the girls had approached any of the staff. Rippon answered the questions and sent some cut and pasted sections from the script. That evening, Rippon emailed Mitchell again stating that he would send a script after speaking to Meirion Jones, who was due to interview Rochelle Shepherd the next day. A telephone conversation is then understood to have taken place between Rippon and Mitchell though neither could recall details for Pollard.

Suddenly, on the morning of 30 November, the course of the investigation shifted decisively. MacKean's background fears about the 'alternative reality' within the BBC over the tribute show that had aired and the *Jim'll Fix It* special planned for Christmas suddenly emerged front and centre when she received an email from Meirion Jones. It was forwarding a message from Rippon in which he stated he now wanted to establish that the Crown Prosecution Service had decided not to press charges because Jimmy Savile was too old and infirm. To Jones, MacKean and Livingston, this represented a 'journalistic bar' that had never previously existed. Rippon's attitude to the story had changed overnight.

In his later statement to the Pollard inquiry, Rippon set out his thinking at the time: 'The extent to which we had to rely on the testimony from [Keri] was stark. She was the only victim in vision we had and would be the face of our allegations and I remained concerned about how well her testimony would stand up to the scrutiny it would get.[12]

'I was also concerned with the way we collected the additional evidence from other victims and witnesses. The women were to remain anonymous. The interviews had all been done on the telephone. Some of them were done by a junior researcher who was with us on work experience who I had never worked with. I was also concerned that the evidence could be potentially undermined because some of the women had already discussed the claims amongst themselves via a social networking site. In my personal experience, the strongest testimony from victims of alleged child sexual abuse has to be collected individually, face to face, on neutral territory, with trained interviewers used to not asking leading questions. This was a long way from what we had done.

'For these reasons I emailed Meirion on 30th November saying I wanted to pursue the CPS angle on the story to its end before finally deciding on publishing.'

Rippon had previously expressed doubts about the women's credibility and his desire for the CPS angle to be explored, but his sudden volte-face came as a total shock to the report team. The non-appearance of the letter from the police had suddenly become a major problem. I asked Liz MacKean whether she now thinks the letter ever existed.

'I don't know but I have to question whether it did,' she says. 'I really wanted to find that letter because clearly it would have been signed, sealed and delivered in terms of persuading *Newsnight*. I believed it did exist, although not necessarily as people were describing it to us. We were led on a complete goose chase [by one former Duncroft girl]. She was the one account that we had the greatest disagreements about.'

This particular woman assured MacKean she had emailed the letter for her to see. On another occasion, MacKean offered to drive to the woman's house to collect it in person. When the letter didn't materialise, she began to suspect that the woman was enjoying rather too much the power she had in the whole investigation.

Looking back, Meirion Jones agrees: 'When you actually got down to people who said they actually had a letter from the police it was only one person. From what we know of the procedure, they would have got letters but the letters wouldn't have said anything like [Jimmy Savile was too old and infirm]. I think, very likely, that whoever was dealing with them, the police officer or whoever, would ring them up and soften it by saying, "It's not that you're a bad witness but he's very old and he'll probably be dead by the time we got him to trial", softening chit-chat so they don't feel that they've just been trampled on.'

MacKean remains in no doubt, however, that the police letter and the CPS line were mere side issues. 'It didn't make any difference. The really important thing was that people like [Keri] and others we'd spoken to had never been to the police. So the police letter was only a very narrow context, it wasn't the single thing that made or broke the story because Meirion and I had more than the police. So whether the CPS dropped [the case] because he was too old and infirm, which they were never going to admit and what was being claimed, or whether it was dropped through lack of evidence, which is the usual thing, we still had more than the police.'

She says they knew the tide was running hard against them when Rippon announced his overnight change of mind. 'We knew he wasn't getting much support on the programme and we knew there was this view among some senior people, like Liz Gibbons, who thought it was in bad taste. We knew it didn't take much to raise the white flag.'[13] Indeed, when Jones and MacKean confronted him on the day of his turnaround, Rippon is reported to have given the surrender sign and said that he 'was not willing to go to the wall on this one'.

Jones told his editor that if the story was pulled and word got out, the BBC would be accused of a cover-up to protect the Christmas tribute shows and the BBC's reputation. MacKean says she felt Rippon was unwilling to challenge his bosses if they had concerns about the Savile report.

On the morning of 1 December, Jones sent himself what he calls his 'Red Flag email', setting out in detail his thoughts on why the story should run and the serious consequences to the BBC if it did not. He felt the journalistic bar suddenly put in place by Rippon was illogical and unnecessary. MacKean urged him to send it to Helen Boaden, partly because she knew Rippon had spoken to her. Jones demurred.

Later that day, Jones received an email from Rippon enquiring again about the letter from the police: 'I think we should stop working on other elements until we know for sure what we are likely to get from them because we don't really have a strong enough story without it.' Rippon added that he'd cancel the editing suite that had been booked for the report.

Jones went into Rippon's office and reiterated he was putting an artificial bar on the report and that if the CPS had dropped the case, they were hardly likely to risk embarrassment by saying anything other than it being through lack of evidence. He listed the confirmation the police had taken the allegations seriously enough to investigate and pass a file to the CPS as being hugely significant, as was the fact that they had more evidence than the police because Keri had never been spoken to. He finished by saying it was a story that would make the front pages of every national newspaper and they would be accused of a cover-up if any of the victims went to the press, which he thought very likely.

The artificial bar of the CPS line and the police letter, if indeed it ever existed, is what MacKean describes as Peter Rippon's 'fig leaf'. 'I just thought, "This is wrong," she says. 'It's as simple as that. We had more than the CPS, we bypassed them, and we had more than the police had. We had wider testimonies.'

Despite ongoing conversations and protestations of the strength of what they had, MacKean says she was by this stage resigned to the fact the story would never see the light of day. 'It was the definition of futile,' she recalls. 'There was no way we could go back to it after the tributes [had run]. How could the BBC then go back and say, "We could have revealed this"? Plus the victims knew and we thought it was only a matter of time before they told other journalists.'

On Friday, 2 December, while Meirion Jones was filming reconstructions for the Savile report with a rented Rolls-Royce at Duncroft, a group of senior BBC executives, among them Peter Rippon, Stephen Mitchell, Helen Boaden and George Entwistle, sat down for lunch at an event to honour Women in Film and Television.

The director general, Mark Thompson, was soon to leave the BBC, and Boaden and Entwistle were the favourites for the top job. The testimonies given to the Pollard Review by Boaden, Mitchell and Entwistle are conflicting on whether at that point it was considered likely the report would go to air.[14] But at some point during the lunch, and some nine days after being advised to do so by Stephen Mitchell, Helen Boaden mentioned *Newsnight*'s investigation into Jimmy Savile to George Entwistle, and referred to how it might impact on his Christmas schedules. She told Pollard this was the first opportunity she had had to speak to Entwistle, having been away on holiday and then missed him 'at least twice'[15] when she called by his office.

Mr Entwistle's account to Pollard was that he could not even recall asking Boaden what the *Newsnight* investigation was about.[16]

The bitter irony of them being at an event to celebrate women while the women of Duncroft remained unheard, is not lost on MacKean. 'A 10- or 12-second conversation is a disgrace. These people had big careers. For one of them it was about to get a lot bigger with the Director General contest.'

'It was that, I think, that created the huge embarrassment. And it's why they were at pains to emphasise[17] that they were investigating Surrey Police. It seemed to let down the sort of people the BBC should surely be there to represent. A 10-second conversation? How is that remotely adequate? And I do think a lot of the BBC's subsequent chaos did come down to that essential embarrassment that they'd taken their eye off the ball.'

Three days after that lunch, Surrey Police issued a formal statement confirming they had investigated Jimmy Savile over 'a historic allegation of indecent assault . . . alleged to have occurred at a children's home in Staines in the 1970s.' Meirion Jones responded with some further questions, to which they replied with the information, 'the case had been referred to the CPS and it was the CPS who decided not to take it any further'.

Further conversations with Rippon took place, including one on 5 December in which he is alleged to have pointed out that the girls in question were 'not the youngest' and 'it wasn't the worst kind of abuse'.[18] MacKean was shocked, and pointed out it was exactly this sort of attitude that persuaded victims of historic abuse not to come forward. Rippon also told her he had not warned the controller of BBC1, Danny Cohen, about the story. It seems clear that by this stage *Newsnight*'s editor wanted to see the back of the story. Meirion Jones and Liz MacKean sat and fumed.[19]

On 9 December, the Crown Prosecution Service provided Meirion Jones with a statement: 'Following the investigation by [Surrey] Police, the CPS reviewing lawyer advised the police that no further action should be taken due to lack of evidence . . . As this is the case, it would not be correct to say that his age and frailty was the reason for no further action being taken.'[20]

Jones immediately forwarded the email to Rippon and they spoke shortly afterwards. Rippon then emailed Mitchell with the news, adding, 'As a result Meirion has accepted my view and agreed not to pursue anymore.' To which Mitchell replied, 'Fair enough'.[21]

I asked MacKean how the news was relayed to the ex-Duncroft girls, none of whom had asked for payment of any kind to tell their stories. 'It was very difficult,' she says. 'Meirion and I had a conversation about how to tell [Keri] and Rochelle. We didn't because we didn't know how to say it. It just felt that we were in a hopeless position and therefore we didn't do what we'd normally do in this situation. What were we supposed to say? We just felt that our hands were tied. It was very uncomfortable indeed.'

Jones says he suspected strongly at the time that Peter Rippon had been leant on from 'on high'. 'I think Helen [Boaden] raised the bar,' he later told the Pollard inquiry. 'And I think [Rippon] took that as . . . an indication about what he should or shouldn't do. So, yes, I do think he was leant on . . . that was the impression I got.'[22] This impression was not shared by Nick Pollard, the former Head of Sky News who led the inquiry, however: 'I have not concluded that any inappropriate managerial pressure affected Mr Rippon's decision-making process.'

10. 'POWER' IS THE WRONG WORD

'We didn't think he'd walk again,' said Jimmy Savile's sister Joan. 'But he were up on his bike, in plaster from hip to shoulder, leaning flat over the bar. You had to admire his guts.'[1] If the period after the war witnessed a second miraculous recovery from the 'chosen one', it also saw the first stirrings of the persona that would transport him to national fame – and ultimately, infamy. Again, it is one in which detail and dates swirl like smoke.

Signed off on 16 shillings a week sick pay, Savile said he spent his convalescence in the downstairs front room at Consort Terrace. For inspiration, he tore a picture of a Rolls-Royce from a magazine and pinned it on the inside of the cupboard door. The long days and weeks spent on his back were passed looking at the picture, thinking about how he might one day be able to own a Rolls-Royce. He also listened to new music on the American Forces Network thanks to a long antenna lead trailed from an upstairs window. 'A bed, a radio, super parents who were poor in pocket but rich in understanding: it was all quiet, peaceful and lovely really,' he later wrote.[2]

He claimed that it was his mother who provided the motivation for beating the hospital's dire prognosis. One day, he was hobbling to the bus stop when he caught sight of an old man's reflection in a shop window. The man was on crutches and trying to overtake him. 'I suddenly realised the shambling figure was me,' he said. 'Then I saw my mother, the Duchess, coming across the road. She had one of those faces that lit up when she saw someone she loved.

That day her face was sad, and I knew that she'd seen that old man, too.'[3] [4]

Having survived as the latchkey kid, vied with his older brothers and sisters for his mother's attention, and finally got her to himself, Jimmy Savile became more desperate than ever for her approval. Her look of sorrow and resignation at his predicament would have cut him like a knife.

The time spent at home recovering from his back injury represented the point when Savile began claiming Agnes for himself. By this stage, his father had been written off as a malingerer when in fact his body was riddled with cancer. Savile said he saved up to send his father on a holiday to Scarborough while he tagged along with his mother, who generally visited her relations in South Shields.

So as he struggled to prove to his mother that he could make himself better through sheer force of will, not to mention many hours spent on his bike, he also began stepping into the space vacated by his father, looking after Agnes and, when he could, treating her with the profits of his various moneymaking schemes. In one, he created plaster of Paris ladies' brooches and sold them on the markets. In another, he told me that he and a partner collected and sold the milled steel wire binding the giant bales of wool that arrived at local mills from Australia and New Zealand. In an early interview in a national paper, he claimed to have been earning £60 a week from scrap metal – a small fortune at the time – before his partner was killed.

As his back improved and his confidence grew, Jimmy Savile exhibited his resolve to prove his physical prowess. He became known locally for his ability on a bike, and particularly for his bloody-minded approach to tackling the steepest inclines offered by the Yorkshire Dales. He also joined the government-backed 'Lend A Hand on the Land' scheme, supplementing his income by working in the fields at summer farming camps around the county.

It was on one such camp that he said he discovered his talent for hypnotism, surprising himself and those watching by persuading an unsuspecting female victim out of her clothes. 'A sign of the unpermissive [sic] times was that room emptied in a second,' he wrote.[5]

If this is when he began to understand how his eccentric behaviour and unusual mannerisms impacted on those around him, his all-consuming obsession with money ensured he remained vigilant for possible angles to exploit.

Again, it was his mother he had to thank for the opportunity that would change the course of his life. According to him, she had heard of a lad in the neighbourhood who had come up with a novel invention. Savile wasted no time in acting on the tip-off. 'I shuffled round to his house because by then I was walking on two sticks,' he explained, 'and there this was this amazing thing.'[6]

He was referring to a wind-up gramophone in a flat box that had been modified with a pick-up attached to a valve radio. Rather than the sound coming out of a small aperture in the gramophone box, it came out of the radio which resulted in significantly increased amplification.

Immediately recognising its potential, Savile struck a deal with the contraption's inventor, Dave Dalmour, offering fifty-fifty on what he'd already decided would be called a 'Grand Record Dance'. He borrowed a dozen 78s by big band leaders such as Caruso, Geraldo, Harry James and Glen Miller and hired an upstairs room at a Catholic social club near his home. Agnes was even persuaded to make tea and sandwiches. Jimmy Savile claimed that twelve tickets were sold to friends for a shilling each.

When the evening arrived, the equipment was installed on top of a grand piano. But once plugged in, the tangle of wires coming out of the back glowed red-hot and charred the lid. To make matters worse, the modified box also gave off electric shocks to anyone who touched it. By nine o'clock, it had overheated to the extent that a fuse was blown, plunging the room at the Belle Vue branch of the Loyal Order of Shepherds into total darkness. Agnes was called in from the refreshments room to play the piano but was put off by the lingering smell of burnt wood varnish and melted gramophone.

Despite these technical hitches, Savile said he and Dalmour pocketed five shillings and sixpence each. 'If nothing else in life, at least I've had the ability to recognise an opportunity,' he later reflected. 'Even then, as I stood there and played the records, I felt this amazing ... "power" is the wrong word. "Control" is the wrong word. "Effect" could be nearer. What I was doing was causing twelve people to do something. I thought, "I can make them dance quick, I can make them dance slow or I can make them stop." That one person – me – was doing something to all these people. And that's really the thing that triggered me off and sustained me for the rest of my days.'[7]

Before the truth emerged about Jimmy Savile, readers might have been forgiven for thinking he was referring to how music set him on the path to fame and riches. But I believe he was talking about control, which was far more important to him than any record. He was transfixed by his newfound ability to get people do as he pleased, and it was this rather than the idea of making punters dance that lit the fire.

Dalmour was asked to produce a more robust and portable version of the device, this one consisting of an electric gramophone turntable attached to a two and a half inch speaker.

While dancing to amplified records was a novelty in the late 1940s and early 1950s, there was no indication these disc dances were set to make Jimmy Savile his fortune. He was nothing more than a small-time local grifter with slicked-back hair, two sticks and plenty to say for himself, not to mention the hired help of his father Vince and brother-in-law Ron. On one occasion, he said he staged a record dance in a barn but did a runner when the audience went round the corner for fish and chips during the interval.

In the late 1940s, Savile met John Swale. They had both been offered some easy money to move a couple of chicken houses in Otley, a market town just five miles from Leeds. It suggests that Savile's back had healed by this time. The two young men hit it off and briefly joined forces on the scrap metal earner, as well as a series of other entrepreneurial activities. 'We'd get a band on at the

[Otley] Civic Centre and James would be the MC and do the patter while I'd be on the door,' Swale explained soon after Savile's death.[8]

In 1951, Swale recalled they were asked to put on a 21st birthday party in Otley but couldn't afford to hire a band. Savile suggested an alternative and the girl 'quite liked the idea of having this jig around to a guy playing records'. Their fee was to be two pounds and ten shillings.

The upstairs room at the Wharfedale Café in Market Place was secured, and Swale then set about building a version of the contraption that his friend had first used in Leeds: 'I went to Neil's Secondhand Bicycle and Radio Store and bought two old wirelesses and the innards of a gramophone, screwed lampholders onto a board and wired it all together so the lights flashed to the music.'[9]

The evening got off to a bad start when they connected the amplifier incorrectly, causing an ear-splitting shriek to erupt from the tiny speaker. Savile told me that things soon improved: 'I wore my best suit, two sticks, pulled a bird for later'.

The dates for these first record dances, or disc nights, further muddy the mystery of Jimmy Savile's mining career and the accident that curtailed it. In 2003, he claimed the Loyal Order of Shepherds record dance took place in 1943 or '44: 'I'd be just 18. At the time I'd been rendered hors de combat by the explosion.'[10] He gave an almost identical timeline to Anthony Clare in their 1991 interview.

Even the key building blocks in his story – in this case, the moment he stumbled onto the power and financial potential of playing records for people to dance to – prompt confusion. If he was still walking on sticks by 1951, when Swale claimed they staged the birthday party in Otley, how was it that he came to be on the start line for the first Tour of Britain cycle race, which took place in August that year?

G iven the widely held belief that there had never been a regular woman in his life, in death the opposite suddenly seemed true. In the days before his funeral, Janet Cope, Jimmy Savile's secretary for 28 years at Stoke Mandeville Hospital, became the first to break cover and share her memories of the 'eccentric whose life wasn't always quite what it seemed'.[1]

The 70-year-old recalled that the pair had met in 1971 when Savile began doing voluntary work at the hospital. As the medical records officer in the National Spinal Injuries Centre, Cope said she agreed to type a letter for him, and the relationship snowballed from there, to the extent where she dealt with all his correspondence during the three-year national appeal to rebuild the unit, and was available to him on the phone at all hours of the day. In 1990, she perceived their relationship was such that she asked him to give her away at her second wedding. She recalled spending the night before the service ironing his white shell suit.

After driving her to the ceremony in his white Rolls-Royce, Janet Rowe, as she was, reported that Savile took centre stage. 'When the ceremony started he lay down across four chairs so people would look at him rather than us. Later he gave a speech which outlasted the best man's.'[2]

Cope claimed that working for Savile was a 'non-stop, seven days a week' commitment, particularly during the period of intensive fund-raising. In the course of administering the hospital's Jimmy Savile Charitable Trust and attending to his every whim, Cope claimed to have glimpsed the private man beneath the familiar façade. 'He never talked about women and nobody asked,' she said. 'People knew he was a bit different.' Interestingly, she added that she saw no evidence 'he had any other proclivities.'

According to Cope, Jimmy Savile was a man who loved to be alone and yet lived for the adoration of the public. When he embarked on a round-the-world cruise in 1992, he made her promise to call him at every port. 'I'd chat to him about what post he'd had, but I think speaking to me was really a reminder he hadn't been forgotten,' she said. 'A lot of the people on the ship were American and they wouldn't have known who he was, which was hard for him.'

It is clear that Janet Cope doted on Jimmy Savile, and from her tales of cooking for him, doing his washing, polishing his jewellery and even allowing him to dominate her wedding, a picture emerges of a man who found such emotional entanglement a bind. Theirs was a one-way relationship, to the extent that she gamely went on answering his letters even while she lay in a hospital bed recovering from a mastectomy that caused her to temporarily lose the use of one arm. Savile's response was to buy her an electric typewriter.

He took pleasure in irritating her with his smoking, his unwillingness to take his shoes off in a house that she kept fastidiously tidy, and his refusal to thank her for all that she did for him. 'I could tell that I annoyed him sometimes but he never lost his temper with me,' she explained. 'I didn't mind the way he could sometimes be because there was a lot about him I admired.'

She also believed he was terrified of getting old, which was why he wore the tracksuits and liked to be photographed with women much younger than himself. 'He was fearful of the day he wouldn't be famous anymore,' was how she put it.

In 1999, Jimmy Savile decided to cut back on the costs of running his charities and dispensed with Janet Cope's services. She said it was 'like a marriage coming to an end' and told me that she cried for weeks.

'Everybody in the hospital thought it was my fault,' Cope told me in April 2014. 'I clearly remember Jim saying to me, "Do not go back in that hospital." He was frightened of what the staff were going to say to me. He did not want people saying things about him to me that he had no control over . . . He was quite lethal in lots of ways.'

The Jimmy Savile that Janet described in the days after his death was a man who always needed be in control. It was, she believed, why he discharged himself from hospital in his final days so that he could die at home, on his terms. 'I bet he has written his own eulogy,' said Cope a few days before his funeral, which she did not attend. 'He'll want to be in control until he passes through those Pearly Gates.'[3]

Less than a month later, Sue Hymns, a glamorous 61-year-old former PA, decided it was time to tell her story. It was printed under the banner headline: 'I Was Jimmy Savile's Secret Lover.'[4]

Hymns told the *Daily Mail* they had met for the first time at Leeds General Infirmary in September of 1968. She was 18 years old and on her way to a doctor's appointment; Savile was 41 and on one of his regular stints as a volunteer hospital porter. Interestingly, on the day before his funeral, the *Yorkshire Evening Post* had run a short interview with Sue Hymns in which she claimed she was 17 when she had met him in a lift.[5]

This could easily have been a mistake, but it could also say something about why she decided, or was urged, to break her silence on a relationship that lasted over 40 years. 'After much soul-searching,' wrote reporter Natalie Clarke, '[Sue] has concluded it would serve Savile's memory better to "set the record straight" rather than allow unkind rumour to tarnish his memory.'

Hymns's motives for telling her story show that while Meirion Jones and Liz MacKean were battling to get their story on air, Jimmy Savile's close friends and family were closing ranks as a darker picture began to emerge, one that contradicted the glowing tributes in the period after his death. Hymns's decision to go public and lift the lid on their unconventional life together was a clear attempt to redress the balance. 'Our relationship was private for so long,' she explained. 'But so much rubbish has been said about him that I think people should know the truth.'

Despite the age difference, Hymns said she was initially bowled over by Savile's fame and largesse. He took her to dinner at the Queens Hotel in Leeds, and to the InTime nightclub in the city. She told the *Yorkshire Evening Post* that one evening Savile collected her from the family home in his E-Type Jaguar, and her father had confronted him about the unusual garb he wore on television. 'Don't you feel like a bit of an idiot wearing a suit with bananas on it on the telly?' he'd said. Savile's reply was trademark: 'What's in your bank account, Reg?'

Hymns revealed that they would meet up in a café opposite Leeds General Infirmary or she'd stay with him in a cheap hotel in London when he was filming *Top of the Pops*. On one occasion, he invited her along to a photocall for the opening of the new offices for the *Yorkshire Evening Post*. Sue and a friend were persuaded to wear miniskirts and boots. 'I think he even had his hand up my skirt,' she admitted. The 22-year-old Prince Charles, who was guest of honour, seemed to find the whole thing hilarious.

The relationship petered out in 1970 when Sue Hymns moved to Munich. Three years later, she returned to Britain and settled in London where she met the man she would go on to marry. It was not until 1991, by which time she had divorced and moved back to Leeds, that their paths crossed again. The relationship was swiftly resumed, although if anyone ever inquired whether she was his girlfriend, Savile would reply that she was his cleaner or that he'd found her in a homeless hostel. She said he was frugal and not given to romantic gestures, although he did pay for dinner and regularly filled her car up with petrol.

Hymns insisted it never bothered her that she was kept in the shadows; she actually enjoyed the fact they lived apart. He had told her long ago that marriage and children would never work in tandem with his showbiz lifestyle. It was a life that saw him group his friends 'into boxes', she said. And as someone placed firmly in the Leeds box she learned not to ask questions of the others: 'There may have been other women,' she remarked. 'I didn't ask.'

Trying to discuss feelings with him was pointless. 'Jim did have emotions, but he couldn't show them,' she said, although he was upset when she moved to London in 2004 to be closer to her daughter. Despite his desire to be seen as a flirtatious single man, kissing up the arms of strangers and being photographed with 'dolly birds' on his arm whenever the opportunity arose, he was said to have been 'grumpy' about her decision.

On their last night together, at Savile's favourite pizza restaurant near his flat in Leeds, a member of staff offered to take their photograph. When the woman joked that they should look lovingly at each other, he whispered, 'I don't know what it would be like to be loved.' Sue Hymns replied that she loved him, to which he said, 'Yeah, I know you do.'

The popular image of Jimmy Savile as a famously private man with a regular, if larger than usual, sexual appetite was further underpinned less than two weeks after the *Daily Mail* article appeared, albeit in a manner that infuriated Roger Foster and Amanda McKenna, the relations who had assumed the roles of Savile family spokespeople in the aftermath of his death. In a story splashed across the front page of the *Sun*, Georgina Ray, a 40-year-old blonde divorcée from Cannock in Staffordshire claimed to be Jimmy Savile's 'love child'.

Ray insisted she was the result of a brief fling in 1970 between Savile and her mother, at the time a 19-year-old waitress in a greasy spoon café on the A5. She recalled her mother telling her that Jimmy had come in, made her laugh and carried her out across his shoulder and into his motor caravan. The fling lasted two weeks and her mother apparently made no secret of the fact Jimmy Savile was Georgina's biological father.

In 2010, Georgina Ray defied the wishes of her mother and tried to contact Jimmy Savile. She wrote him a letter but heard nothing. Then, in early 2011, she travelled to Leeds and rang the bell of his flat. She told reporters that they spoke on the intercom but Savile pretended not to be in, shouting, 'He's away.' She returned to Leeds to visit his coffin as it lay in state at the Queens Hotel.

Georgina Ray did not consider herself to be a gold-digger, although she was now pressing for a DNA test in order to be able to stake her claim to a share of Savile's personal fortune, estimated at around £6 million.

On the same day, 16 December 2011, it emerged that Jimmy had in fact left £5.2 million, split between the Jimmy Savile Charitable Trust and the Jimmy Savile Stoke Mandeville Hospital Trust. The executors of his will, the National Westminster Bank, were still collating his assets and possessions. Roger Foster was reported to be furious: 'For [Georgina Ray] to say this is outrageous. Her only reason must be money.'[6]

Six months later, in a joint television interview with Sue Hymns to rebut still more sinister rumours emerging about her late uncle, Amanda McKenna offered her view of what had happened with Georgina Ray. 'I first found out about [her] in the newspapers, which isn't a great way to find out,' she said. 'I've got 31 cousins anyway, we're an enormous family, [so I initially thought], "Great, that's another cousin and it's fabulous that my uncle Jimmy's got a child." Before I'd had any opportunity to make contact with her, the next minute there's legal letters coming through and then she was contesting his estate. I do have very strong feelings about that because all that money is earmarked for charity.'[7]

Five days before Christmas, Mark Thompson, the director general of the BBC, hosted a drinks party. In attendance was Caroline Hawley, a BBC World Affairs correspondent. Hawley had just heard about the shelved *Newsnight* report and as Thompson worked the room, she took her opportunity, commenting that he 'must be worried about the *Newsnight* investigation into Jimmy Savile'.[8] Thompson's response was non-committal; it was a decision and an investigation he professed to know nothing about.

The following day, freelance journalist Miles Goslett contacted the BBC to inform them he had information about the *Newsnight* report. His allegations were that the BBC had covered up misconduct on its own premises and axed the Savile investigation to save the Christmas tribute programmes.

Goslett's approach was dealt with by press officer Helen Deller, who knew about the Savile story. If the report had not been pulled, she was the person who would have written the press release explaining *Newsnight* had exposed Jimmy Savile as a paedophile. Indeed, just over a year before, Deller had written an email to Peter Rippon and Meirion Jones saying she understood the story was about Savile and focused 'on allegations of abuse with victims willing to go on the record'. She had also warned, 'we may have to do a bit of managing around this – despite such rumours circulating in the media for years.'[9]

Helen Deller contacted, among others, Peter Rippon to suggest a press response stating, 'the angle we were pursuing could not be substantiated'.[10]

With the help of managers, including Peter Rippon, she now set about drafting their version of what had happened. Peter Rippon briefed her: 'yes we did interview an individual about Saville [sic] with a view to pursuing a story involving the CPS and Police. We had been led to believe there had been a recent investigation into the allegations but these were dropped. However we could not gain sufficient information to stand this up.'[11]

Peter Rippon was at home on his Christmas break when he responded to Deller's email. His minor correction was ambiguous as it suggested the woman who had alleged the CPS did not press charges due to Jimmy Savile's age and infirmity was the same woman who had alleged that abuse took place on BBC premises. This was not the case. As Nick Pollard would later conclude in his report into the affair, 'This elision of the two women's accounts was extremely unfortunate and the consequences of the error were profound and resonated for months to come.'[12]

A final wording was quickly agreed between Deller and Rippon that emphasised *Newsnight*'s inquiries had been into the police/CPS investigation and why it was not ultimately pursued. It made no reference to the fact it had been launched because of Jimmy Savile's years of abuse at Duncroft, the new testimonies obtained by MacKean, Livingston and Jones or that abuse was alleged to have taken place on BBC property.[13]

Neither Meirion Jones nor Liz MacKean were consulted about the official line the BBC had now adopted.

Sometime over the next 48 hours, Mark Thompson claims that he discussed the story with BBC News. He cannot remember whether it was in person or on the phone, or whether he spoke to Helen Boaden or her deputy Stephen Mitchell, but the details he received on the matter of what Caroline Hawley had said to him at the drinks party were as follows: 'Oh well, they were doing an investigation into Jimmy Savile . . . but the programme themselves decided not to proceed with it for editorial or journalistic reasons.'[14] He maintains that he did not learn any specifics of the investigation or the fact it was into allegations of sexual abuse. The transcript of a recorded telephone conversation between the journalist Miles Goslett and Nick Pollard would appear to suggest otherwise. The dialogue, which took place eleven months after the publication of Pollard's report, and was released by a Tory MP, included Pollard making an off the record acknowledgement that it might have been a 'mistake' to omit from his report a piece of evidence that would appear to cast doubt on Thompson's assertion that he knew little or nothing of the nature of the allegations against Savile until after he left the BBC. The piece of evidence in question, which Pollard received before publishing his findings in December 2012, was a letter from Helen Boaden's lawyer that explicitly stated in December 2011 she had told Thompson that the BBC had investigated Jimmy Savile over allegations of sex abuse.

'I think the truth is that I sort of overlooked [the letter]. I didn't see there was a particular significance in it,' Pollard told Goslett. 'Partly because Mark Thompson had said "No [Boaden] didn't tell me about it. It was an open question. She might have done or she didn't."'[15]

A subsequent statement by Pollard's lawyers maintained that the 'letter was given full and proper consideration and the Review stands by its conclusions on this issue'.[16] Namely, Pollard found 'no reason to doubt' Thompson's version of events.[17]

Whatever former Director General Mark Thompson knew, on 1 October 2012, less than two weeks after he'd left office, BBC executives faced spiralling outrage over Savile and the national broadcaster's handling of the situation.

Its response was to turn on itself. Helen Deller, believing that Jones was the source of the leaking of material to the media, sent an email to Peter Rippon, Stephen Mitchell and Paddy Feeny, the head of communications. It is an accusation Jones has consistently denied, and all the journalists involved confirm that he was not the source of the story.

'No excuse. No more discussions with him,' wrote Deller, referring to Meirion Jones. She then suggested 'a discreet conversation with HR to establish options' about the *Newsnight* reporter's employment at the BBC.[18]

'Have you got anything with four wheels?' Jimmy Savile was on the phone to a local cab company. 'Well now. We'd like to go to Helmand province, Afghanistan.'

The radio controller had clearly heard this one before because Savile didn't even have to give an address. He rang off, put the portable phone down on the footrest and left the sitting room. Morning light streamed through the floor to ceiling windows. Beyond the glass, fast-moving clouds cast shadows on the North Sea and across the ruins of Scarborough Castle on the horizon.

When Savile returned he was wearing a quilted black Adidas jacket over his regulation shell suit, this one in electric blue with red and green detailing. The woolly hat was the last bit of what he called 'the disguise'. He loved Scarborough and wanted to show me some of it before we headed back up towards his flat for breakfast at his favourite café.

Five minutes later, the minicab pulled up below. Savile was standing in the window looking down at the driver. He was stock still, offering a double thumbs-up. The thumbs were no more than 20 centimetres apart and facing inwards. It was an inward double thumbs-up, a style that was briefly popular in the Seventies.

After he'd been holding the pose for about 30 seconds I decided to break the impasse and ask him whether I should go ahead and let the driver know we were on our way. Savile ignored me and continued to hold the pose, readjusting his feet and gently flexing his knees to take a more solid stance.

'Come on, yer twat.' He tapped the window with one hand before resuming his inward-facing double thumbs-up. I stood back, willing the driver to look up at the window and wave or smile or better still, both. It had been at least a minute now, maybe more, and it was getting uncomfortable. 'Look up, you bastard,' Savile hissed.

Having finally been prised from the window, he carried on as if nothing had happened. Locking the door to his flat behind him, he rustled along the landing and descended two flights of communal stairs sideways, rather than straight on. He said that if I knew how many of his patients in Stoke Mandeville wound up there after falling down the stairs, I would be doing the same thing.

Savile instructed the driver to take us through Scarborough's impressive boulevards before heading down towards the arcades, seafood stalls and fish and chip emporia along the pleasure beach. This was once the domain of two of his friends: Jimmy Corrigan, whom he had mentioned in his autobiography, had his amusement arcade empire, and Peter Jaconelli, the former mayor, who had crowned himself the 'Ice-Cream King' of the town.

We passed by the lifeboat shed and the small fishing port to our right. Savile pointed out a boat, the *Corona*, which had seen service at Dunkirk. As we rounded the headland, he said something about the road being engineered to move in order to withstand the tide. He liked to describe himself as a cork on the waves, someone who ebbed and flowed with the current. He stared out of the window, his mouth set in a grimace.

His mood seemed to brighten when he recalled the day the QE2 arrived in Scarborough on its last round-Britain voyage. As a publicity stunt, he had boarded it in high seas from a fishing boat. It was touch and go whether he'd make it. Were it not for the strength he had acquired as a wrestler, marathon runner and long-distance cyclist, he said he would have fallen and drowned.

'That's enough,' he suddenly barked, and he told the driver to turn around and head back the way we came.

Later, we were sat opposite each other in a cramped wooden booth in the Francis Café near his flat. The café used to be a hairdresser's and retained many of the original fixtures. We were talking about his days as a professional wrestler. I told him I had just finished reading the memoirs of Jackie Pallo, Savile's regular tag team partner in the late 1960s. Like Savile, he dyed his hair blond (although Savile insisted he never dyed it; he bleached out all the natural colour), and like Savile, he was an acquired taste. He was what they called in wrestling circles, a 'heel', and crowds booed him.

In his book, Pallo had been quite open about the sexual shenanigans that went on backstage, but insisted the wrestlers abided by a strict set of rules.

'Wrestlers have their own code about females,' he wrote. 'For instance, it is strictly taboo to take a girl out who is under 16, even if she looks – and claims to be – a lot older. The lads reckon it's up to a bloke to make sure, and if anybody breaks the rule, he gets a very heavy sorting out from the others, sometimes for several weeks. Wrestlers really loathe men who attack children, rape young girls, and beat, mug and rape the old and defenceless.'[1]

I put it to Savile that this was an odd thing to say, given that surely the vast majority of people loathed men who attack children, rape young girls, and beat, mug and rape the old and defenceless. 'Well there you go,' he said, shrugging his shoulders and focusing on his food.

Pallo also said the bachelors among the wrestling fraternity never had to go looking for girls. 'The Ring Rats – wrestling's equivalent to the pop world's groupies – go after them,' he claimed. 'In the 60s, hundreds of girls used to shriek at the violence and drool over rippling muscles and bulging trunks.' At some venues, he insisted, grapplers had to step over 'undulating bodies' on their way to and from the ring.

I asked Savile whether this was the case. 'Ooh there was,' he said, egg yolk dripping from his chin, 'but that happened in the pop business too. All the lads would be out pulling a bird and bringing them into the changing room. In those days sex wasn't important. Newspapers have made it important by scandalising it.

In those days it was entirely consensual, it just happened and there was never any scandal chat in the papers about people having sex like there is now. They've made it into something else.'

He had been flirting persistently with a rather flustered looking teenage waitress and just as I was thinking about why he had offered this odd caveat about the newspapers and their 'scandal chat', all the lights in the café suddenly went out. 'Give us all yer money,' barked Savile, jumping to his feet and making pistols with his fingers.

When the lights came back on a few seconds later, Jimmy Savile announced he no longer wanted to talk about wrestling. And he certainly didn't want to talk about sex.

PART TWO

13. OSCAR 'THE DUKE'

Jimmy Savile often told stories of the marathon rides that he embarked on as a young man. It was during one such cycling trip to Scotland that he first clapped eyes on the remote Glencoe bothy he would buy half a century later.

He had been a keen cyclist since the age of 11 when his mother had bought him his first bike. She hoped it would build up his strength after what had been a sickly childhood. But if the bike made him fitter, it also gave him independence; from the moment he first wobbled down the cobbled slope of Consort Terrace, he regarded his bicycle as his 'passport to freedom'.

After pedalling his way back to fitness following the accident at Waterloo Main Colliery, Jimmy Savile became well known within Yorkshire's burgeoning cycling community. Except he wasn't known as Jimmy Savile at all, but Oscar Savile, thanks to the rare Oscar Egg frame on his bike.

'At the time it was one of the top lightweight frames,' confirmed Ken Russell, a Bradford rider who was one of the county's leading cyclists at the time. 'They were quite expensive.'

I tracked Russell down in the months before Savile's death, and he had fond memories. '[Savile] was supposed to be a company director. At one time he was into scrap metal but I don't know much of the detail. He was always quite flashy, even then.'

Cycling was going through a boom period and Jimmy Savile made a lasting impression on his fellow riders. 'We used to meet in Otley nearly every Sunday night with the other clubs and the other cyclists,' recalled Russell. 'We'd have a general chinwag and he was nearly always there. He was the life and soul of the party. We used to think he was a bit of a buffoon really, but I could tell he wasn't. I could see that years before he became well known.'

By 1950, Savile said he was racing competitively on a regular basis. Records show he achieved a second place finish in that year's Edinburgh–Newcastle race and looked set to go one better in an event in Skipton after pulling clear of the chasing pack alongside his friend Dave Dalmour, who decades later would run with him in marathons and become a regular at his Friday Morning Club meetings.

'It looked like we were going to win it,' Savile told me, 'but then we saw this grass verge with two girls having a picnic.' Not for the first time, his libido overruled all other considerations. They slammed on the brakes, threw down their bikes and joined the girls. By the time they reached Skipton, Savile said the race was long finished.

'He was a good rider, but he was never a great rider,' said Russell. 'He was a real character, however. Some of the other riders thought he was a bloody fool, and he was a buffoon at times. But he was just one of the bike riders. He wasn't important and nobody thought that he would ever become famous.'

Jimmy Savile was desperate to take part in the first Tour of Britain, organised as part of the Festival of Britain celebrations and sponsored by the *Daily Express*. A race of twelve stages covering 1,403 miles over 14 days, it would take riders from London to Brighton, along the south coast and into the West Country, up into Wales, the north-west and the Lake District, before arriving at its most northerly stop in Glasgow. From there, it would head back south to Newcastle, on down the eastern side of England and finish in London. The prize fund totalled a princely £1,000.

A place in the four-man team representing Yorkshire could only be secured with a strong performance in one of the major stage races leading up to the Tour. The inaugural Butlins Holiday Camps 7-Day race, which saw competitors racing between camps in the north, was significant not only because it was where Jimmy Savile earned his ride in the Tour of Britain but also as the moment he chose to unleash his brand of jack-the-lad showmanship on an unsuspecting public. 'Even though I was nobody at the time nationally, I worked by instinct,' is how he described it to me.

'In the Butlins Race, he would get to the start dressed in a tuxedo,' said Ken Russell some 60 years later. 'And then he would arrange for somebody to come with a tray and mirror and a brushing comb.' Doug Petty, a young bike builder, gave exactly the same account of Savile's bizarre antics. So, while the other riders were stretching their legs and going through their final preparations, 'Oscar' Savile was prancing around in his best suit and preening for the crowds.

Petty's memories of the Newcastle–Ayr stage in that race suggest that Savile revelled in his role as two-wheeled eccentric. 'Oscar was Oscar – he had his cigars and his flash clothes,' he said. 'He always used to ride with a five-pound note pinned inside his jersey. It was the old fiver, the big white thing.

'We were going through this village in Scotland and everybody was knackered and we saw Jimmy, who was a bit in front, going into this Co-op, selling sweets and everything. We knew he had money so we dived in after him and this woman behind the counter said, "Is this a hold up?" And we said, "No love, we're road racing but we're all starving hungry and we've got no money. But he has and he'll pay for it."' Petty said Savile dutifully unpinned the fiver, paid for his rivals' refreshments and then got back on his bike.

On the next stage, 'Oscar' Savile secured his place in the Tour of Britain by crossing the finish line third in Carlisle. He also finished the race with a new nickname: 'The very first national picture I had was on the front page of the *Daily Express* with a cigar in my mouth,' he told me, although I searched and could find nothing. 'It said 'Oscar "The Duke" rides in the Tour.' He also claimed that a picture of Winston Churchill posing with a cigar was relegated to page five.

'I was forever with the gimmicks, before gimmicks had even been invented,' he continued, insisting not for the first time 'the common denominator was fun'. 'Not fun at anyone's expense,' he said, 'it wasn't fun belittling anyone, it wasn't fun cheating. It was straightforward fun.'

Honest, clean fun at nobody else's expense: it was, he claimed, his philosophy for life.

On 15 August 1951, 49 cyclists representing thirteen teams assembled at 'the Cockpit' in Hyde Park. Among them were outfits consisting of professional riders from France, Ireland and Scotland; semi-professionals racing in the colours of British bike manufacturers such as Dayton, ITP, Viking and Pennine; and a mixture of amateurs and independents representing the various regions.

In the race programme, rider number 48 was listed as 'Oscar Savile, a company director also known as "The Duke".' The picture showed him grinning, jaw jutting forward and dark hair slicked back to his head. His Yorkshire teammates were Don Wilson, a 24-year-old cycle frame builder from Bradford, Jim Wilson, a bike dealer from Sheffield, and 20-year-old Douglas Petty.

At 9.30 a.m., the peloton rode out of London under orders, spare tyres tied to their bodies in a figure of eight and fruit stuffed into pouches in their jerseys. A convoy of vehicles followed in their wake: the commentary van with its pair of giant horn speakers fixed to the roof, support cars for the various teams and a swarm of fun cyclists and kids who wanted to ride alongside the competitors.

The race started at noon from Farnborough Common in Kent and after flying through Sevenoaks and Tonbridge, 'Oscar' Savile decided to make his move at St John's Cross. His break was brief and unsuccessful; the first stage was won by Frenchman Gabriel Audemard, who passed the finishing line on Brighton's Madeira Drive in front of thousands of cheering fans.

Savile seemed to be more focused on making headlines than he was on the race. On the second stage to Bournemouth, he trailed in last but promptly changed into his suit and joined the winners, race officials and local dignitaries at the civic reception in the town that evening. There, he got up on stage, thanked the crowds for turning out and got a big laugh when he said while the other riders had been timed by stopwatch, he was being timed by calendar.

The race certainly earned its epitaph as the 'Hard Luck Tour'; the weather was appalling throughout, and little was laid on for the riders. On their way out of Plymouth and riding as a group, Savile told me the competitors pulled alongside an open-backed truck carrying groceries.

'We were all pirates in those days because nobody had any money,' he said. 'So I went up to the front and talked to the driver while the lads at the back were knocking off all the gear – grapes and fruit and this, that and the other. That was how we ate.'

He admitted his 'strokes', as he called them, were designed to get him into the pages of race sponsors the *Daily Express*. 'They were always looking for stories,' he said.

He duly gave them one in Weston-super-Mare: 'Cyclist wins by a neck' pronounced the headline above an item about race leader Dave Bedwell, a cycle mechanic from Romford who had used his day off to go for a 20-mile practice ride. 'Before that,' wrote the *Express* reporter, 'he had been challenged to a race, had accepted and had been beaten. The challenger, and the winner by a neck – was cigar-smoking Oscar Saville [sic], otherwise known as "The Duke". The race was on donkeys.'[1]

The item went on to say that Oscar then missed the boat ferrying competitors across the Bristol Channel to the start of the fifth stage in Cardiff. Savile told me the whole thing was a set-up: 'I'd pulled a bird who was staying at the same hotel I was staying at – oh, thank you very much indeed!'

Not wanting to leave for Cardiff at six o'clock that evening with the rest of the competitors, he made arrangements to spend the night with his 'bird'. 'One of the officials had one of the early Jaguar SK120s, so I said to him "Why don't I miss the ferry and you can drive me round to the start?" That was the story: Oscar has missed the ferry. I hadn't missed the ferry; the ferry hadn't gone by that time.'

'I was a known character,' he said as we looked through a replica programme from the 1951 race one afternoon in Scarborough. 'They didn't bother that I didn't win anything. I was part of the Yorkshire team because I'd flash the team out. I had more front than Brighton and Blackpool put together.'

Doug Petty, who was faring significantly better in the race than his teammate, agreed: 'I don't think some of the other riders appreciated how good he was on a bike. But they all loved him, oh yeah. Some dismissed him as a bit weird, you know, but he was marvellous at appealing to the crowds.'

And among the crowds there were plenty of willing young women. 'I remember one of the stages and there were thousands of people there as we were lining up to start,' said Petty. 'This bunch of girls came up and said, 'Can we have your autograph? And do you mind if we take your photo?' Well of course it had to be a snogging session photo. When I looked up the race had gone. They went without me. I had to chase like buggery.'

The 160-mile stage between Morecambe and Glasgow turned out to be Savile's undoing, although in his autobiography he claimed his demise was caused by doing a good deed for a fellow rider whose finances were running low.

The plan hatched was for Savile to make a break from the peloton, a break that nobody would take seriously, and Derek Buttle, a 25-year-old former Thames lighterman, would give chase. They figured that by building up a big enough gap between the rider and the pack, they could ensure Buttle claimed the £10 prize for being first to the top of the 1300-ft Shap Fell.

By Kendal, they were seven minutes in the lead. Buttle was first to the top and won the £10 but Savile was physically spent and soon afterwards he climbed off his bike and collapsed beside the road. 'I tell you where he packed,' said Ken Russell. 'It was at Penrith. I always remember the PA van coming past and saying that he's packed.' Oscar had paid the price for his late-night carousing.

His retirement from the race proved to be a blessing in disguise. So taken were the organisers with this oddball in their midst that they forbade him from cycling home to Leeds and summoned a second loudspeaker car instead. 'Oscar' was invited to become a race commentator: 'It turned out that I was a natural ad-lib broadcaster and finished up entertaining crowds up to 50,000 without turning a hair,' he wrote in his autobiography. 'This lurking ability sealed my racing fate. My chat was more valuable than my legs.'[2]

Without a race to get in the way, he gave his undivided attention to courting publicity. In Scarborough, on only the second rest day of the Tour, he persuaded Doug Petty to join him in a fishing boat off the front. And when the race resumed its progress down the east coast, he enjoyed the buzz of hurtling into towns and villages ahead of the riders to inform the waiting crowds what was happening. And in an age when announcers generally spoke in the cut-glass diction normally heard on the BBC, Savile's Yorkshire accent and quick-fire patter represented a genuine novelty. 'I'd keep the crowd well entertained,' he told me. 'The *Daily Express* loved that. They thought it was the greatest thing in the world.'

Thirty-three of the 49 riders who started the race succeeded in making it all the way back to London. At the finish, huge crowds again braved the wind and rain to hear Jimmy Savile's unusual commentary describing the closing stages. Scotland's Ian Steel was presented with the trophy but Jimmy Savile had glimpsed the future, and it did not involve hawking scrap metal or pedalling up hills. 'A former teammate said to me, "He's a right idiot",' Ken Russell said. 'I said, "If he meets the right people, he'll really go the top". I was proved right.'

Russell would go on to win the very next Tour of Britain, a race for which the *Daily Express* retained Jimmy Savile's services as race commentator. 'I think they paid him very well,' said Russell. 'When the *Daily Express* stopped sponsoring the Tour of Britain, which would have been about 1954, I remember seeing him on television maybe a year or two afterwards. The BBC was showing Silverstone motor racing and who should be there but Jimmy

Savile; it was sponsored by the *Daily Express*. I often think that's what made him, really. I think the *Daily Express* really helped him, they kind of adopted him.'

Russell offered a final footnote from the aftermath of his victory in the second Tour of Britain. He was back at work at Ellis Briggs bike builders in Shipley when Jimmy Savile walked into the shop carrying a briefcase. 'I used to pull his leg a bit,' Russell recalled. 'I said to him, "Now then, Jim, let's have a look at what's in your briefcase," because he used to play the part of the suave businessman. He opened his briefcase and all that was in there was his handkerchief.'

I n January 2012, Helen Deller in the BBC press office was alerted to the fact the *Sunday Mirror* was preparing a story on the axed *Newsnight* investigation into Jimmy Savile. She tried and failed to dissuade the paper from printing it,[1] and the article appeared on Sunday the 8th. '*Newsnight* probe into sex claims against national treasure Sir Jimmy axed by BBC bosses' blared the headline. Underneath: 'Programme is scrapped days before Christmas TV tributes'.

The opening ten paragraphs laid out the bald facts of what had happened, although there was no mention of all the ex-Duncroft girls who had been spoken to by *Newsnight*'s reporters. The story then alluded to 'new reports' that had surfaced since Savile's death suggesting he was a recluse who couldn't stand to be around children.

The article quoted a 'BBC source' who had told the *Sunday Mirror* that by interviewing the three women, *Newsnight* hoped to establish the truth of the claims about and details of a 2007 police investigation. 'But senior BBC executives then halted the investigation,' it continued. 'Our source said *Newsnight* reporters were told to scrap it. It clashed with a Boxing Day *Jim'll Fix It* tribute show hosted by the actor Shane Richie.'

On the day before the story was published, 'a BBC aide' also told the *Sunday Mirror* that '*Newsnight* were investigating alleged failings within the CPS, and the programme was canned because they did not have enough proof to run the story.' The lie was now in the public domain.

The full-page story concluded with a further closing of ranks by those close to the dead star. Janet Humble, Savile's niece, was quoted as saying, 'It looks like muck-raking. As a family we just wish Sir Jim could be left to rest in peace. He did more good than bad in his life and how many celebrities can say that?' Stephen Purdew, owner of Champney's Health Farm and friend for more than 30 years, weighed in with his own rebuttal: 'Sir Jim was a great man, a legend who should be remembered for all the wonderful things he did for other people.'

That afternoon, Meirion Jones emailed Peter Rippon to say that it sounded like the BBC source was someone who thought they shouldn't have done the investigation in the first place. The BBC press office was of a different opinion; in other words, that Jones himself was the leak. James Hardy, head of communications for BBC News, seemed to sum up management's suspicions about *Newsnight*'s investigative reporter when he emailed Deller to say that he was unconcerned by the newspaper story but given the opportunity he would 'drip poison about Meirion's suspected role'.[2]

The day after the piece ran, I emailed Peter Rippon to say that I had information that could be useful to the *Newsnight* investigation into Jimmy Savile – I had started to find people who had seen and heard of his offending behaviour. He forwarded my email to Meirion Jones with the message: 'Do you want to have a chat with him? I guess we should stick to just public domain help.' This email would appear to suggest Rippon was comfortable about Jones speaking to a journalist, even though senior figures within the BBC, including Helen Boaden and Stephen Mitchell, had not sat down with him to get his version of events. This was for the simple reason they considered him to be 'untrustworthy'.[3]

Meirion Jones was still privately furious about Rippon's decision when I met with him for the first time in February 2012. It was soon after the publication of a story in the *Oldie* by Miles Goslett which revealed the *Newsnight* report contained evidence that Savile abused minors on BBC premises and allegations that

Mark Thompson knew about what a contentious report it was. The story significantly increased what was in the public domain, but Jones still categorically refused to go into the reasons for the report being pulled.

Liz MacKean, it transpires, was equally angry. 'The BBC immediately began lying, suggesting the story was about the CPS and we'd not stood it up, and not about the thing it was about,' she says. 'I challenged Rippon on that. I was thinking that I had contacted 60 people, and I've told them we were investigating a story about a celebrity visitor to Duncroft and was there anything they wanted to tell us.

'But if the BBC is then saying that it was about the police or the CPS, depending on which press office put it out, that makes me a liar, right? It was just outrageous. I was so aware of what [the women] would think. Would they think I was pulling the wool over their eyes? Probably not. [Keri] obviously knew exactly what was happening but it was a very difficult position to be in. The people who make these decisions don't go out and meet people, they don't talk to victims, they don't have anything on the line in terms of trust and that is exactly what they were jeopardising.'

MacKean says she had a 'very uncomfortable' conversation with Peter Rippon after the *Sunday Mirror* article ran. 'His eyes glazed over,' she says. 'It was very awkward.'

On 16 January, Miles Goslett had contacted the BBC press office again, this time to ask who had made the decision to axe the report, and when Director General Mark Thompson and the controller of BBC2 had been made aware of it. The BBC refused to comment.

In early February, having tried and failed to get the story picked up by the nationals, Goslett's piece for the *Oldie* appeared to nail the myth that *Newsnight*'s investigation had been into the police and CPS rather than Jimmy Savile's activities at Duncroft School and in his dressing room at the BBC. Goslett went on to say that a 'BBC source' had told him that the line about it being stopped for editorial reasons was 'a smokescreen'. The real reasons were it would compromise the Christmas tribute show. Questions were also asked about whether *Newsnight* had uncovered evidence unknown to the police, and if that evidence had been passed on. 'The BBC has serious questions to answer,' Goslett concluded, before warning 'that the matter is not at an end.'

Peter Rippon's response did not betray any great anxiety. He emailed Stephen Mitchell and Helen Deller to say, 'The evidence about BBC premises was anecdotal, second hand and forty years old.'[4] When the *Daily Telegraph* followed up by contacting Mark Thompson's office for comment about whether he was aware of the investigation, Paul Mylrea, the BBC's director of communications, told them it was being passed to the press office for a response.

After the *Oldie* article was published on 9 February, a number of national newspapers followed up with stories of their own. It was at this point the BBC press office decided it would be helpful to get an official response from Peter Rippon, as *Newsnight*'s editor. 'The allegations are personally damaging for your credibility as an editor,' warned Stephen Mitchell. 'So [it would be] good to put your name [behind] the denial.'[5]

Rippon emailed Meirion Jones to say he was considering making a formal statement denying the allegations that *Newsnight* had withheld information from the police. He also asked for clarification on whether everything they had was from the same women that had spoken to Surrey Police during its investigation into Savile. Jones replied that it was not: Keri's testimony was information the police did not have in 2007.

On 10 February, Rippon supplied the BBC press office with a personal statement. 'It is absolutely untrue that the *Newsnight* investigation was dropped for anything other than editorial reasons. We have been very clear from the start that the piece was not broadcast because we could not establish enough facts to make it a *Newsnight* story. To say otherwise is false and very damaging to the BBC and individuals. To allege that we are withholding evidence from the police is also damaging and false. I note that a number of newspapers are using the fact we did not broadcast something to put the allegations into the public domain themselves.'

Stephen Mitchell recommended the last line be dropped.

'I was very mistrustful of the reasons for dropping [the investigation],' states Liz MacKean, who confronted Rippon again after the *Oldie* ran its story. 'What I thought was, they don't care; they're not interested.'

Soon afterwards, a member of the public contacted Meirion Jones via an email address listed on the *Newsnight* website. The woman explained she was a former BBC employee in the north of England who had witnessed sexual activity between Jimmy Savile and a girl of around 13 or 14 in a BBC dressing room in Yorkshire. Meirion Jones forwarded the email to Mark Williams-Thomas, the freelance child-protection expert who had decided to take on the investigation and was in the process of attempting to get a documentary commissioned by ITV.

MacKean was convinced it was now a case of when, not if, the truth came out. 'It was obvious that it would come out for no other reason than perhaps [Keri] or one of the others would come forward,' she argues. 'We knew . . . that Mark Williams-Thomas was going to take it elsewhere, with our blessing, because this was a story that needed to be told and the people that wanted to tell it deserved to have it out there.

'My feelings were variously dismay, anger and resignation. I was very aware of this breach of trust. [It] made me feel extremely uncomfortable. It was obvious to me and Meirion we were the lonely voices. There was a them and us situation.'

Jones and MacKean continued to discuss their grievances in private. 'I remember saying to [Meirion], "There will be a reckoning." What's happened is wrong, particularly in relation to pretending we weren't looking at what we really were looking at. I don't know when it will happen, but this is not something that can be kept quiet.' Meirion Jones agreed. He was very clear about how it would look.

Within a month, however, the initial furore surrounding the *Newsnight* investigation into Jimmy Savile had died down. By mid-March, details emerged of how the dead disc jockey had arranged to dispose of his personal fortune. His last will and testament, dated July 2006, put the gross value of his estate at £4,366,178, of which around £3.6 million was earmarked for charity. It was a story that got unanimously positive coverage.

The rest was to be shared out among his family and friends. Eight people, including two couples, were to benefit from the annual interest on a £600,000 trust fund. They included Savile's nephew Roger Foster and niece Amanda McKenna; Sylvia Nicol, a member of his original fund-raising team at Stoke Mandeville Hospital; Mavis Price, who got to know him through Leeds General Infirmary and went on to manage the Jimmy Savile Charitable Trust; Donald Bennett, the former transport manager at Broadmoor Hospital, and his wife Josie; and Roddy and Julie Ferguson, the latter being someone he had befriended in Fort William in 1969 when she was 15.

Julie Ferguson, who wrote the poems on Jimmy Savile's headstone, recalled first encountering Savile when he climbed Ben Nevis to test a tent in Arctic conditions. She and a friend were invited back to his hotel for a Coca-Cola. She said he was very strict and had high morals when it came to girls: 'He had a zero tolerance to women behaving badly.'[6]

Savile also made provision of £1,000 each for a further 18 people in his will. They included members of his Friday Morning Club, trustees of his charitable trusts, his cleaner, two cardiologists from Leeds, companions from his marathon-running days and Sue Hymns. His possessions would be auctioned off for charity at a later date.

'I am very pleased that the bulk of Jimmy's fortune will go to his charities,' said Roger Foster, to whom Savile had also bequeathed his parents' weddings rings. 'I was aware [I was getting them] as Jimmy had lost them and I found them,' Foster revealed. 'Jimmy always insisted that it was the Duchess who, from heaven, guided me where to look and as such, when he was no longer here, she would want me to have them.'[7]

These two tiny gold bands would be about all he did get.

We ventured outside into the salty air. Savile was wearing his green woolly hat, the 'disguise', although he seemed more upset when the disguise worked and people passed him by without a second look.

Progress was slow. He was busy telling me that the experience of watching his brothers and sisters going through the emotional ups and downs of relationships and marriage had soured him for life. 'If you have a dog you've got to walk it; if you have a cat you've got to give it a litter to have a shite in; even if you have a plant you've got to water it,' he said. 'Those are all things that live. If you don't have anything that lives, 99 per cent of your problems are gone.

'Imagine taking a human being in,' he continued. 'Wow! You have to dedicate 50 per cent of your life to them and they've got to dedicate 50 per cent of their time to you. In the old days, mothers looked after their sons; ironed their shirts, mended the holes in their socks. I remember 60 years ago a lad talking to me about how his marriage had gone wrong. He said, "She wouldn't even clean my shoes." Now that was because his mother cleaned his shoes and he was taking a female into his life. You can't blame him for thinking that. What that lad said to me was just one snowflake making up a big snowball.'

It was a curious mental association: marriage and his mother. And the way he had segued from things that don't live to holes in socks left me confused. This didn't bother him, he simply launched into the now familiar story about coming home from school to find nobody in the house. As we stopped at some railings beside the beach and looked out at the sludgy waves of the North Sea, I mentioned my brother and his wife who were sailing across the world in a small boat at the time. I told him about the fears my family harboured about them being out at sea.

'Living and dying is part of life,' he snapped. 'If you live you're lucky, and if you die, big deal. There's a lot of it about. When I work in the hospitals 20 die every night.'

I asked him whether he feared death or whether the formative experience of kissing corpses in the old people's home across the road from his house in Leeds had given him a different perspective. 'I'm not entirely sure,' he said, somewhat surprisingly. Jimmy Savile was never less than sure about anything that passed his lips.

'I prefer to feel my way and it could be that all that has made my attitude to living and dying what it is,' he added. This was a rare glimpse of something beneath, perhaps a hitherto unseen ability to question himself and on occasion to be surprised by the answers. 'I have faced death several times,' he continued. 'I didn't even know that I faced death when I was ill as a small child. And then there was down the mine when the shaft collapsed.'

He gestured ahead, to where a few lone souls on the sand were bent against the wind. 'I came across here, 50 feet from where we are now, in the back seat of a Buccaneer with the Police Air Arm. We just missed the Grand Hotel; took two windows out. We were supposed to refuel in the air but the tanker couldn't take off. So we ran out of fuel. I'm sitting strapped into this bloody amazing thing.'

He explained the jet had to divert to RAF Honiton. 'They told us they would put the arrester wires out and we'd see if we could pull those bloody great concrete blocks out of the ground. We hit the ground at 350 miles per hour, because we had no fuel left, and the thing caught on the arrester wire, and the next minute you're standing still.' He laughed.

'It's all a bit of fun. You're gonna die, you didn't die, very good. I had plenty of time to think about it because I was up in the air when we ran out of fuel. It didn't bother me because I'm a bit odd. One minute you're here, the next minute you're not.'

We continued along the Foreshore. Pensioners huddled on benches eating chips from card boxes or leaned against the railings in macs, caps and scarves. Beyond the tired façade of the Futurist Theatre, the flashing lights and bleeps of amusement arcades: Olympia, Gilly's, Casino, Silver Dollar and Henry Marshall.

We met a man who Savile introduced as the owner of some of the biggest arcades. 'You see all this stuff here,' he said, waving an arm at the gaudy seafront, 'this kid owns all that. Like me, he is shy, retiring, self-demeaning.'

The man smiled and shuffled his feet. 'Unlike me, he doesn't have any way to disguise it because he's worn all the girls out and now he's married.' Savile explained that he was close to the man's late father, Jimmy Corrigan, the slot machine king of Scarborough.

Did he ever want to start an empire, I asked. 'That was the exact opposite of what I wanted to do,' he hooted, seemingly delighted at the opportunity to confound any theories I might be working on. 'In the 42 years of working in the hospitals I have come across so many people who have suffered and died because they didn't understand the meaning of the word "enough". They didn't think they had enough money or booze or silly white powder you stick up your nose. I learned very early on the meaning of the word "enough". As soon as I had enough of anything I decided to take things easy for a bit.

'An empire gives you aggravation. If you've got enough without that why should you be greedy and want for more? When I wake up in the morning I have got more money than when I went to sleep the night before.'

He proceeded to tell me about 'a geezer' who 'did the empire bit'. One day, the man went into his garage and found his son hanging by the neck. 'He wished then that he could turn the clock back and spend less time getting far more than he needed in the first place,' Savile said. 'Some people are empire builders but as an individual it wasn't the path that I chose.'

We entered a coffee shop and sat down at a table with a Formica top. In the window was a sign with the word 'PACE'. Savile called the owner over and made a comment about it being a 'Paki shop'. It was a toe-curling attempt at humour. I felt embarrassed and asked her how she put up with him. 'It does wear a bit thin,' she replied. 'I don't know what we're going to do with you,' she sighed, addressing Jimmy directly.

'Is there much room in the back?' he gurgled, and took a loud slurp from his mug of tea.

Why would Jimmy Savile choose to give up the freedom of self-employment, which, he claimed, saw him earning what would have been the very considerable sum of £60 a week from his scrap metal business, as well as his regular bike races and occasional record dances, in return for the £8 and 10 shillings he was offered as assistant manager at the Mecca Locarno dancehall in Leeds? It was something he never adequately explained.

On another occasion, he spoke of having an epiphany while riding his bike across the Yorkshire Moors. What he never elaborated on, though, was the mysterious death of his business partner in the scrap metal business.

I now believe that this sudden change in direction, and precipitous fall in income, was prompted by the death of his father in April 1953. Vince Savile was 67 and riddled with cancer having been misdiagnosed on a number of occasions. I also suspect that his father was his business partner.

On the walk from the Queens Hotel to St Anne's Cathedral for Jimmy Savile's requiem mass, Alistair Hall, a cardiac specialist who delivered one of the eulogies, explained that Savile had confided in him that he'd used whatever money he had to get second opinions on his father's condition and to pay for better treatment.

The very last time we spoke, Savile, who wore his father's wedding ring on the little finger of one hand, offered a rare insight into his mind-set at the time: 'It was time to stop playing games and start thinking about what you were going to do tomorrow.'

He talked many times about lying in the downstairs room in Consort Terrace and compiling lists of all the things he enjoyed in life and whether there was any way they could be combined in a job. His list of priorities included a late start to the working day, warmth, coloured lights, carpets, music and, most importantly, girls.

One day, as he perused the situations vacant pages in the local paper, he spotted an ad for a job at the same dancehall where he had earned his first pay packet during the war. He told me that he marched straight into town, entered the County Arcade and presented himself to the Mecca manager as his new assistant. John Swale, for his part, insists that it was he who persuaded his friend to seek a job with Mecca.[1]

'The daily routine nearly broke my spirit,' Savile wrote of his first few weeks working at the dancehall.[2] He described how his job consisted of dealing with 'drunken bums' at the door, lost property in the cloakroom and the ever-present threat of violence. He also said he moved out of the family home, which seems like an odd decision considering his beloved mother would be alone.

At first, he chose to sleep in the dancehall's cloakroom under a pile of coats. Then he moved into an old lifeboat moored near a weir on the canal that ran through the city centre. These floating lodgings were accessed via a builder's yard, a plank onto a rotting barge and then a short jump over a gap between the vessels.

When I asked him why he left the comfort of Consort Terrace, he said, 'You can kid to mothers and that can be fatal. You can then start to kid to yourself.' A more likely reason is that unlike his mother's house, he was able to take girls back to his barge – very young girls, according to some.[3]

If he swaggered into the Mecca feeling like 'Jack the Lad' on the grounds he'd put on dances in country halls and cafés, Jimmy Savile soon recognised he had a lot to learn: 'I realised there was a lot more to it than just being a Flash Harry . . . All I was before was like a Hollywood film set: all front and no back.'

The dancehall was a regimented place, managed locally but centrally controlled by Mecca Ltd, which ran its chain of venues from offices in London. Staff had to be smartly attired and there was no alcohol on sale, except for over 18s who could buy drinks in the Tudor Club bar on the balcony overlooking the dance floor.

Steve Martin, a Leeds contemporary, remembered the Mecca in County Arcade as something of a dive. 'I must admit it was always our third choice,' he told me. 'Dancehalls filled up very quickly in those days and queues would form before opening time. Our routine was to go to the Capitol in Meanwood. If it was full we would go to the Astoria in Harehills and if we were stymied again we would go to the Mecca.' Martin said Reg Parks, a Leeds native who was crowned Mr Universe in 1951, was a regular at the Mecca on Saturdays, 'but he was too muscle-bound to dance'.

Mavis Simpson, an 18-year-old in the early Fifties, recalled things a little differently: 'We were allowed to go to the Mecca Locarno because the standard of behaviour was good. There was no bopping or jiving, and if you or your partner tried to do anything other than strict tempo dancing, you were asked to leave the dance floor.'

Even back then, Jimmy Savile was bending the rules. '[He] was the young manager,' said Simpson. 'He wore clothes that were completely different to the usual suit, white shirt and tie. He made it more exciting. During the interval when the band had its rest periods he introduced dancing to records and that was a real magnet for jitterbug fans.'

Savile told me he badgered the manager into letting him try out his record sessions idea. Although not hugely successful, they did manage to stimulate interest and business at a struggling provincial dancehall. Neither of which went unnoticed. Two hundred miles away, Mecca Ltd joint chairman Carl Heimann was made aware of the livewire young assistant manager working at one of his joints in the north.

As a result, in the summer of 1955, Jimmy Savile was offered a promotion – and a major change of scene. Mecca Ltd asked him to take over the Ilford Palais-de-Danse, a struggling concern at the furthest reaches of London's East End.

His tenure as a rookie manager got off to a slow start. Business was sluggish, and Savile said that he was called into the company's Dean Street offices for a meeting with Heimann, to do, as he described it, 'some explaining'.[4]

Heimann was a Dane who had moved to England at the age of 16, beginning his career at a waiter before becoming a catering manager with Ye Mecca Cafés. His chief skill had been in recognising the potential for public dancing during the 1920s and then persuading the company to invest in a string of ballrooms. By 1934, Heimann was general manager of Mecca Dancing, an offshoot from the café company. A year later, he joined forces with Alan Fairley, a Scot with interests in the leisure industry north of the border, to form the Mecca Agency, which by the end of the decade controlled virtually all aspects of the company's dancehall business. In 1946, Heimann and Fairley became joint chairmen of the new Mecca Ltd, and under their stewardship, Mecca's dance-halls became not only a place to foxtrot, waltz and tango, but social glue for communities across Britain.

Eric Morley was variously Mecca's publicity director, general manager of its dancing division and a director. During his long service with the company, he devised *Come Dancing* for the BBC and organised the first Miss World contest as part of the Festival of Britain celebrations. He witnessed first-hand what an astute judge Heimann was. 'He could "read" a dance floor as could no other man in the country,' said Morley. 'He could tell within sixteen bars whether a dance orchestra was any good and he was right, with uncanny accuracy.'[5]

Everything within the Mecca empire flowed downwards from Heimann and Fairley. The company's ballrooms were all decorated in the same way. From the teacups and the light bulbs to the staff uniforms and dance bands that played, everything was organised and supplied centrally. The programme for the week was dominated by old-fashioned ballroom dancing, with two nights usually set aside for private hire functions that ranged from fund-raising whist drives of the type that Agnes and Vince Savile organised, to works social nights or local beauty pageants. Sunday was the only day off.

On the way to the Mecca offices in Soho, Jimmy Savile mulled over new ideas for drumming up business. He wanted to suggest a record dance to Heimann but was wary due to the low-key response they had met with in Leeds. He recalled 'the big man' sitting at his impressive desk with his chin in his hands and saying something quite out of the blue: 'What about a record session, Savile? All night for a shilling and we'll call it "Off the Record".' The young manager was stunned. 'The secret of pop success is starting the right craze at the right time,' he later said, 'and the genius of this principle is undoubtedly Carl Heimann.'[6]

In his own words, Jimmy Savile was about to become 'the man'. After the years of lugging his rudimentary contraptions around small venues in Yorkshire, he now had a ballroom and, most importantly, the blessing of a dancehall guru. On a more practical level, he was given access to Westrex, the company that supplied Mecca with the microphones for its dancehalls.

Westrex also made turntables, so Savile called up and placed an order. A few days later, he said he walked into the Palais to find an electrician fitting a record deck in the box from which the lighting was operated. He told the man that he wanted two turntables, and for them to be installed on the stage, one next to the other. It was, he claimed, the first twin turntable system in history.

Posters were put up advertising an 'Off the Record' disc dance night for the following week, with revellers invited to bring their own 78s for the simple reason the dancehall manager didn't have any of his own. Savile also decided to deviate from Heimann's plan in one significant detail: admission would be free.

'The week before we'd had 24 people in, long leg dancing,' he claimed. 'But at about ten to eight we had 600 people turn up. It was like locusts. The bloody place was heaving. I was ankle deep in records on the stage. Didn't know what the bloody hell they were. If anything worked I played it three times. From that day on I was the guvnor.'[7]

The triumph of this first record session in Ilford put Jimmy Savile on the map with Mecca Ltd. But being a fast-talking Yorkshireman with 'more front than Blackpool', as he put it, meant that he needed backup, especially in an alien city like London. Partly for self-preservation and partly for what it would do for his image, he took to walking around his dancehall flanked by a team of large and mean-looking bouncers.

It earned him a reputation as someone not to be messed with, even if he rarely if ever got his hands dirty. 'One of our local lads was described to me in terms that would have got him a place in a mafia family,' he wrote years later. 'In the two years I enjoyed the area's hospitality he never struck a blow or pulled a job but still enjoyed his Joe Bananas reputation to the day I left.'[8]

Another plausible explanation for wanting protection is the attention he was by now attracting among the local teenagers who flocked to his Monday record nights, and the consternation this must have caused among some of their parents. As Kathy Kirby, who would go on to become one of Britain's most successful singers in the Sixties, revealed, even back then, Jimmy Savile liked to get what he wanted.

Kirby was just 16 when she began attending the Palais with her younger sister, Patricia. She said that Jimmy Savile, who was 28 at the time, pursued them both from the beginning, and that they both turned him down.

In the summer of 1956, Kathy was still a virgin when she got up on stage at the Palais to perform a number with the famous bandleader Bert Ambrose. Ambrose was sufficiently impressed to invite her on tour with him. Kirby fell hard for the renowned taskmaster and ladies' man, who was forty years her senior, but Ambrose rejected her advances, telling her she needed to 'get some experience'.[9]

On returning to the Ilford Palais for a singing engagement, Kathy Kirby decided to do just that. So, when Jimmy Savile came into her dressing room and began making his customary over-tures, she locked the door behind him. According to her biographer, she said 'Savile hemmed her in and then it happened.'[10]

Seven years later, in 1963, Jimmy Savile recalled Kathy Kirby in his weekly newspaper column on pop music. He wrote, 'She has a knockout family which includes a darling sister.'[11]

In 1978, Savile gave a series of interviews that were collated in the book, *God'll Fix It*. 'In my early years I can tell you I did a lot of things that need a bit of forgiveness,' he said. 'I was in a business that was fraught with temptations. Temptations of the flesh are all about. So in my early days, I was a great "abuser" of things, and bodies, and people.'[12]

He had only just begun.

The Plaza was located on the first floor of a squat, three-storey building next door to the Odeon on Oxford Street, the hub of Manchester's burgeoning nightlife. Like many venues for dancing in the late 1950s, it was not licensed to sell alcohol. Beyond the cash booth, a café area selling cakes displayed on glass shelves, as well as tea, coffee and glasses of milk, led into a cavernous, low ceilinged arena with a small stage with red velvet curtains at one end. Members of the house trio would soon discover that their time on this stage would be limited, for the focal point was to shift decisively to the sprung wooden dance floor in the centre of the room.

Across the country, teenagers were being swept up in the fast-running tide of rock and roll flowing out of America. In Manchester, about the only way young people could hear this new music was by either hanging out in the coffee bars with jukeboxes that were springing up across the city, or by climbing the flight of stairs from the Plaza's entrance before passing its manager, an odd-looking figure with pale skin, a long nose and dark hair Brylcreamed tight to his head. He was a man who seemed to possess an intuitive understanding of what it was they wanted, and the impression he made on them with his tight-fitting black trousers, black suede shoes and see-through shirt, was only enhanced by the suited heavies he had positioned at each elbow.

Securing a move to Manchester, Jimmy Savile told me, was the next best thing to a return to his beloved Yorkshire. He'd been homesick in London's East End and pleaded with his bosses at Mecca to be transferred back to the north.

On Tuesday evenings, he began running a talent contest. 'It was a golden age because everyone wanted to express themselves,' he explained. 'At three o'clock in the afternoon you could buy an acoustic guitar for £3 and by eight o'clock at night you could be on stage at the Plaza.'

Lonnie Donegan's 1956 hit 'Rock Island Line' had been responsible for an explosion in skiffle music. Scores of local outfits cut their teeth on cheap acoustic guitars, snare drums and a bass fashioned from old tea chests. 'You could win the talent contest and become a superstar in the locality,' Savile declared. 'There was one duo that came in and I had to tell them that they could only enter once a month, because they would have won every week. They were called The Four-Tones and went on to become The Hollies.'

John Mepham was a teenage member of The Four-Tones and recalls wistfully the impact the new sound made. 'Up until then, there was no such thing as a teenager,' he says. 'You were just kids and then adults. You wore the same clothes as your father and the girls wore the same clothes as your mother. All of a sudden with skiffle, big blokes had open-necked shirts and didn't wear ties or suits. Then they started wearing jeans, and that was it; every lad in this country got a guitar for their 16th or 17th birthday. We were very successful. We were only together 18 months, but everywhere we went there were girls screaming – like you see on the old films.'

These talent nights became hugely popular, and before long the Plaza was pulling in the same numbers on a Tuesday as it did on a Saturday, traditionally the busiest night of the week. 'It was amazing,' Savile said. 'Everything I touched turned to gold.'

One teenage entrant to the Plaza's weekly contest recalled winning and being presented with a five-pound note as his prize. 'It blew my mind,' he said. 'At the end people clapped and went wild. It wasn't about the fiver. It was . . . people liking me for doing something. And this guy, Jimmy Savile, was great.'

The talent nights were just a starter. Savile's subsequent decision to open the dancehall on weekday lunch-times not only transformed the fortunes of a failing venue that had previously been associated with trouble, it also radically changed the lives of young people in the city. Under his stewardship, the Plaza quickly became a magnet for teenagers who were soon to be found pouring out of local offices, shops and schools to dance, chat and flirt for an hour or two.

Sixth-formers arrived in their uniforms, changed in the toilets and stashed their tunics or blazers in the cloakroom. Office secretaries and factory workers headed down in their lunch breaks with their sandwiches wrapped in brown paper. Even the city's famed footballers caught the bus into town to stand around and gawp at the spectacle unfolding on the dance floor.

The success of these lunchtime sessions was built on the manager's novel record-only slots in the breaks between old-style ballroom dancing numbers performed by the house band. Using the twin turntable set-up he'd pioneered in Ilford, Jimmy Savile seamlessly blended slower swing records such as 'Cinnamon Sinner' by Tiddy Gibbs and The Beat Boys, 'Fire Down Below' by Peggy Lee, and 'Smoke Gets in Your Eyes' by Vic Damone and The Diamonds with newer, uptempo discs coming out of the US from the likes of Bill Haley, Elvis Presley, Buddy Holly, Bobby Darin and Little Richard.

He devised a winning formula, part of which involved taking to the microphone at regular intervals to announce 'smooch time': 'Now then,' he'd bark, 'it's time for belly dancing. So put your belly against someone of the opposite sex.' The tempo of the music suddenly dropped, the dance floor was plunged into darkness and a single arc light on the ceiling was directed at a giant spinning glitter ball sending a cascade of white stars onto everything and everyone below.

'He was creating something that had never happened before,' said one regular. 'He was giving teenagers the chance to get together. [Smooch time] was separate from the jiving. Teenagers had the chance to hug each other and fall in love . . . It was a romantic, fantastic time: sandwich, cup of tea in the bar and a dance. It was the start of Jimmy Savile in Manchester.'

As the cash register kept ringing so the buzz around the Plaza continued to build. Word quickly got around too about the venue's outrageous new manager who took pride in the fact local headmasters complained bitterly about their pupils returning late to school. Businesses in the area weren't too impressed either: 'Bosses used to write to me telling me I was knackering them,' Savile boasted to me. 'But my bosses couldn't argue because of the money we were taking and because I was a law unto myself.'

He began to dress more flamboyantly, too. In the breast pocket of his favourite see-through shirt he kept what looked like a thick roll of banknotes. In fact, the bankroll was a couple of twenties wrapped around a tight ball of newspaper. When asked why he did this, Savile replied, 'Because if anyone nicks it they only get the two twenty-pound notes.'

The larger-than-life, oddball persona that Jimmy Savile became famous for was fast taking shape. He invested in a Rolls-Royce – or, more accurately, an old Bentley saloon to which he had welded a Rolls-Royce radiator grill and hubcaps bought from a scrap yard. This hybrid status symbol was parked outside the Plaza, much to the consternation of his bosses at Mecca, who felt sure he must be on the fiddle.

Bruce Mitchell, a local musician at the time, remembered the rumours about Savile's spell at the Plaza. As he told Dave Haslam, author of the excellent book *Manchester, England*, 'the management couldn't work out why this twenty pound a week club manager was driving about in a white Rolls Royce. It's pretty certain that he was playing piano with the till to an outrageous degree . . . they [Mecca] suspected him, but they didn't want to lose him.'[1]

According to a man who worked at the Plaza for a short time, the fake rolls – both kinds – had the desired effect because girls were soon queuing up for 'a chat with Jim'. In the manager's walnut-clad office at the back of the dancehall was a large couch that Savile insisted was for resting on but saw frequent action in more energetic pursuits. 'He always used to say, "I'm going to interview this young lady for a job." That's all he'd say. I don't know what went on behind those doors but I do know he was a man.'

Savile basked in the kudos that came with the success of the Plaza. Suddenly, he was known around town, not least among the seemingly inexhaustible supply of Manchester's teenage girls.

'In them days it was hard to say who was a paedophile,' says Jimmy Donnelly, who was 16 when he first went to the Plaza. 'We didn't have the word paedophile in them days. We had the word weirdo, and [Savile] was a weirdo. He always had the bobby sox girls, the young girls, in his cars. He'd always pull up with the girls in his car, and going home he'd always have the girls in his car.'

As important to Savile as the steady stream of girls coming through his doors were the piles of cash he now had access to. He spent some on clothes and on taking his 'Mama' out for lunches with her friends, but the secret to maintaining his newly acquired state of prosperity was to remain as frugal as he'd been when he'd worked as a miner or lived on an abandoned vessel on a Leeds canal while still adopting the trappings of a millionaire. For all the flash clothes and cars, Savile ate at cheap cafés frequented by taxi drivers, took cheap lodgings with a German widow in Broughton and tried every trick he knew to avoid paying his minders and DJs.

In surrounding himself with adoring teenagers, and specifically teenage girls, Jimmy Savile was also astute enough to recognise that he needed a tight circle of trusted, older allies. One of them was Jack Binks, his regional boss at Mecca, who was based at the Ritz, around the corner from the Plaza.

When Savile began putting up posters locally advertising 'Saturday night is crumpet night' at the Plaza, Binks was furious. After a dressing-down, Savile simply changed the wording to 'Saturday for Kife', Yiddish slang for much the same thing. But if Binks occasionally despaired of his younger colleague's antics, he was comforted by the knowledge that between them they were successfully carving up the business in the city. As the Plaza filled with jiving teenagers, the older crowd migrated to the Ritz, which stuck resolutely to the tried and tested format of ballroom dancing.

Outside the dancehall, Inspector Lewis Harper of Manchester City Police served as Jimmy Savile's eyes and ears. Known as 'The Lion', Harper was chief superintendent of A Division, which was responsible for the city centre, from 1950 to 1961. Harper understood the dynamics of his beat, its characters and their con tricks intimately. He was a regular visitor to Jimmy Savile's office at the Plaza.

Ian Skidmore, who was night editor of the *Daily Mirror* in Manchester at the time, recalls Harper, who was awarded an MBE in 1960, as being head of the Vice Squad. He also claims that when he died, Harper left more in his will than he earned during his entire service in the police force.[2]

Whether Harper worked in vice or not, he would have certainly been familiar with Jimmy Savile's best friend, a bearded behemoth by the name of Bill Benny. An 18-stone slab of a man, Benny made his name as a wrestler better known as 'Man Mountain'. He was a particular favourite at Belle Vue's Kings Hall where he roared at the top of his voice and incited the crowd.

This lisping, hare-lipped Henry VIII lookalike owned the Cabaret Club and Casino opposite the Plaza, and also ran Manchester's main gambling and wrestling venues, as well as prostitutes working around Oxford Street.

In his memoirs, George Melly, the jazz and blues singer, wrote of being entertained by Benny at one of his venues, the Stork Club, which was located in a dark court off Cross Street. Benny, he recalled, 'was a fund of unsolicited but useful information about his hostesses. "They're no good," he'd tell us as two of them swayed past on their way to the ladies. "Strictly platers."'[3] Plating was a slang term in the 1960s for oral sex.

Jimmy Donnelly, who went on to become a founder member of Manchester's infamous 'Quality Street Gang', confirms that Benny was 'a pudding eater', or pimp. He also suggests that Savile 'stuck to' Benny because he was a 'face in the town'.

With his trio of matching powder blue Jaguar Mark 10s – number plates BB1, BB2 and BB3 – parked bumper to bumper on Oxford Street, and cash to match his considerable flash, it's not surprising that Benny inspired a rare level of admiration from his neighbour across the street.

Manchester's nightlife was booming in the late 1950s. It was a city of spielers and speakeasies with spy holes in the doors, illegal gambling dens and striptease joints serving cheap bottles of Chianti, and working men's clubs offering cabaret acts and wrestling shows for the family.

The gangs of Teddy boys that roamed the streets were a visible reminder of the violent flipside to the city's many pleasures. Savile's response to the threat they posed saw him go to the local paper, as he'd done when he first pulled up outside the Plaza in his fake Rolls-Royce. He wanted to publicise his zero tolerance policy with anyone wanting to come into his dancehall wearing crepe-soled shoes, drape coats or sideboards. It was a PR stunt that saw him keep a razor in the cash box so sideboards could be shaved off at the door, and he was duly photographed clutching the cutthroat and flanked by two of his heavies.

'Jimmy was like a headmaster with the way he dealt with [troublemakers],' said another of the men who had worked with Savile at the Plaza. 'He would explain to them that there are two ways of doing things, one right and one wrong. "If you do the right thing," he said, "you'll have a great time with us. And if you do the wrong thing," he said, "we'll have a great time with you."' The latter, the man explained, meant heads being used as a battering ram on the exit doors.

According to this man Savile told his bouncers to be careful not to mark their victims because he was wary of the police. 'It was illegal to give someone a battering. But on the way out, whoever it was . . . you'd hear a clunk when their head opened the first set of fire doors and then they'd be dragged down the stairs by the doormen and you'd hear another clunk when their head opened the outside door downstairs.'

In Louis Theroux's film, one memorable scene captured Savile up late, enjoying a medicinal dram and regaling the cameraman with tales of his dancehall days. During the conversation he admitted his hard-line approach brought him into regular contact with the law. 'I couldn't care less,' he bragged. 'Tied them up, put them down in the boiler house until I was ready for them. They'd plead to get out. Nobody ever used to get out of my place . . . I was judge, jury and executioner.'

On one occasion, as we trudged back to his flat on the Esplanade in Scarborough, Savile revealed that he sometimes went too far. 'The only time I ever got in bother was because I was too heavy-handed with some of the villains,' he said. 'People knew there was never, ever any trouble in my place because they knew they would get a spanking, and two, they would never get in again, ever. With me, if you were barred you were dead.'

On other occasions he admitted the police came in to inquire why there were so many young girls on the premises. His account of what he told them was typical of his tactic of making everyone feel a degree of complicity with what he was doing: 'I said to the police chief, "You do know that your 16-year-old daughter comes in here, don't you? Would you rather she was safe here with me or being preyed on by all those scumbags and slags?"'

For all Savile's boasts about zero tolerance and brutal bouncers, Donnelly scoffs when asked whether the upstart dancehall manager was a major player in the Manchester underworld of the late 1950s. 'He wasn't a worry to anyone,' he spat. 'Fucking hell, you'd knock him over. At one time everyone thought he was a poof, thought he was gay. That was his persona, and that's why I think nobody worried about him with the young birds.'

*

The polio scare of the mid-Fifties had led to much hand wringing in government circles. Children left crippled by the disease were commonplace, and more than 3,000 died in the epidemic of 1952. Six years later, in 1958, when a vaccination programme was finally approved, a national information campaign was launched to quell the public's fears. Mecca Ltd decided to offer its support by offering to make injection facilities available at each of its dancehalls. Jimmy Savile told me he placed a trestle table on the middle of the dance floor at the Plaza so people could be inoculated while the dancing continued all around them.

Studio chiefs at Granada Television, located within walking distance of the Plaza, were on the lookout at the time for someone who regularly engaged with the younger generation who could talk on camera about the vaccination programme. When the call came, Jimmy Savile jumped.

'I didn't have a television set, I didn't even know what a camera looked like,' he explained. 'I got showed in and sat down at a desk with a geezer. I was giving him the crack and all of a sudden two big barn doors opened at the end and about eight geezers rushed in and said, "That was terrific." I said, "What was?" They said, "You've been on television. Can you come back next week?"'

At six o'clock that night, an hour before the doors to the Plaza opened, Jimmy Savile claimed to have walked back up Oxford Street to find queues of people outside. When he asked what was up, they told him they'd been seen him on television. 'Being conscious of body language, when I walked around I could see them all fall back a bit,' he said. 'There was this great difference because I had been on television and I thought, "Fucking hell, this is like having the keys to the Bank of England."'

Granada asked him back, hiring him to do a regular series of book reviews on a youth-orientated show. Savile claimed he was sacked after only a few weeks. The reason for his dismissal gives an insight not only into what was on his mind at the time, but also into how in later life he seemed to get a kick from hinting at his secrets. As he told the *Guardian* in April 2000, 'I said [to Granada],

"I want to expose a book. It's for children and it's dreadful; there's this girl who's well underage and she takes up with a geezer who's yonks old and eventually they schlep off together . . ." Now bear in mind this was live TV, and I'm saying personally, I don't think it's a good thing because I don't think an underage girl should be exhorted by her parents to strike up a relationship with a guy five, six, seven times older than she is."[4]

The book he was referring to was *Peter Pan*, and the journalist from the *Guardian* reported that when Jimmy Savile finished his story, he laughed himself silly.

I t was November 2009 and in the fug of Jimmy Savile's front room in Scarborough we were now onto the fourth 90-minute cassette of the first day. In the time I'd been with him he had regaled me about cycling, wrestling, and run at least three marathons. And that didn't take into account the two length-of-Britain epics – one a walk from John O'Groats to Land's End and the other a cycle trip in the opposite direction.

He'd just finished rebuilding an entire hospital wing and described how he lent his name, and his time, to the 'I'm Backing Britain' campaign of the late 1960s. And yet despite these considerable endeavours, he never once stopped smoking his cigar. At 83, he didn't look in the slightest fatigued.

It was time to take a detour from his long list of sporting and charitable achievements and cross over into some darker, more intriguing territory. We returned to Manchester of the 1950s. I told him I had read that Bill Benny was known as a bit of a gangster and wanted to know more.

'Between us we were an unbeatable pair,' Savile said, which was a relief because if he didn't like a subject he'd feel no compunction at chopping it off at the knees. 'We struck up this strange relationship stroke friendship. We'd look like Laurel and Hardy because he was this big, hulking geezer and I was a slim geezer and we developed into being a couple of local characters as a pair. We were characters individually but as a pair we were even bigger characters. I copped for the lord mayor and he copped for the mafia.'

Savile explained that Benny had a reputation as the meanest man in Manchester – a title he was keen to wrestle off him. To settle the matter, he said they went on holiday together to the south of France. The bet was that both would take £50 spending money and the winner would be the one who returned home with the most.

Savile claimed they were level pegging as they arrived at Nice airport to catch the return flight. At this point, he said, Benny suddenly disappeared. 'I thought he was going for a piss until I thought, "Hang on, he went for a piss when we left the hotel." Ah ha, now then. Sure enough . . .

'What you need to know about grossly fat people,' he continued, warming to his task, 'is they freak out over perfume and after-shave. Their body odour is such that they think they are worse than everyone else. Bill is standing at this perfume counter and because he has no neck, he can't turn his head. So I went up behind him and said, "That's a nice one over there." And he realised I had sussed him. He didn't turn round, he just said, "You dirty, mean, tight-fisted, oyster-faced bastard." The whole of Manchester was hanging on this thing . . . And from then on Bill Benny called me "Oyster" because I was so tight.'

I wanted him to tell me how the doors were run on Oxford Street, and whether the success he cultivated at the Plaza made him a target for extortionists, racketeers and mobsters. We were talking about an era when chucking-out time was regularly accompanied by a mass punch-up and the blare of police sirens.

'Not with me,' he said. 'I knew 'em. I knew the west coast mafia, they were friends of Frank Sinatra's and they wouldn't touch me. They left me alone.'

So nobody was going to mess with you, then?

'Nobody messed with me because I didn't upset anybody. If they wanted to at least I was half prepared for it, you know. If you start wrestling with somebody in the street you could finish up pegging it.'

What about the hoodlums and heavies in London, Manchester and Leeds?

'The English mafia was the Kray twins,' he replied. 'The Kray twins influenced the whole thing. They operated from east London but such was their reputation that they influenced the whole country. All the gangsters wanted to be like the Kray twins. Ronnie was my patient for 11 years [at Broadmoor]. Ain't nobody was going to mess with me because if I complained to Ron . . . ,' – he was now laughing slowly – 'that would be it. I was the man leaning on the gate as far as Ron was concerned and I could make life hard or easy for him. We got on dead well. Nobody bothered me. Half of the people that worked for them [the Krays] worked for me. It's about reputation. If you have a reputation that you know and employ these people . . . none of my lads ever, ever had to fight anybody, it was the reputation.

'I brought three Hungarian lads who worked in the concentration camps in Germany – they pulled the dead bodies out and burnt them and things like that. For some reason, they finished up in Britain and I heard about them and sent for them.

'They had dead white faces. They were Hungarians who had been pressed into service by the Nazis. They were called *Sonderkommandos*. They were not Nazis but they did Nazi work. And they worked for me. To them, life and death was a strange non-event. They'd pulled hundreds and thousands of bodies out of the gas chambers.

'So what I did was for five pounds each I bought them a black evening dress suit, with a white shirt and a black tie. Every now and then I'd put on a bit of a party after the dance in honour of the saints where they came from.' He cackled, the sound dampened against the thick Cuban cigar clamped in the centre of his mouth.

'Well these guys, all I'd need to do was ask and they'd go and knock someone off, that was all there was to it. Nobody could talk to them because they didn't understand the nuances of the English language. They never smiled, they had dead white faces and they were completely besotted with me.'

Savile let out a low, menacing gurgle of pleasure. 'One of my minders in Leeds weighed 36 stone. He was the fattest kid you ever saw. He was a good-looking lad and he had slicked back hair. He was giant, giant, giant. His name was Bernard. If someone called him a fat bastard . . . ' By way of illustration he explained that back then Coca-Cola was sold in bottles with metal caps. Bernard, he says, would pick up the cap, put it between his ring finger and his little finger and flatten it.

'Nobody ever fronted me up. They realised it was a job that didn't carry any bonuses. I had these people – so it was reputation.'

19. SOMEONE THE KIDS COULD LOOK UP TO

Those early television appearances released the genie of Jimmy Savile's ambition. And yet not long afterwards, Mecca took the decision to remove him from the Plaza. As Bruce Mitchell correctly stated, even if he was fiddling the takings he was worth too much to the company to lose. The company's chief, Carl Heimann, also saw something of himself in the lippy young hustler doing brisk business at previously failing venues.

It was decided to make him area manager for the north. He was informed he would be returning to Leeds where he was to apply his Midas touch to the ballroom that had nurtured him during the war.

Jimmy Savile was in his early thirties when he returned to the Mecca Locarno in Leeds. The dancehall still seemed an incongruous addition to the genteel emporiums, mahogany and marble of County Arcade, one of architect Frank Matcham's trio of matching glass-roofed shopping emporiums and a hymn to Victorian ambition. When he stood outside the front doors, the Mecca's new manager could look straight down Cross Arcade to Queen Victoria Street and the very first branch of Marks & Spencer, smiling at the thought that he was now a neighbour of one of the city's other great exports.

The Mecca was a very different proposition to the ballroom he left behind. Originally opened as a grand teahouse at the end of the nineteenth century, it was far larger than the Plaza. With its entrance off the arcade, the main space was accessed through a set of double doors beyond the pay kiosk. There was no seating in the ballroom area, but down a small flight of stairs was a café area named the Del Rio. It was decorated in Hawaiian-style bamboos and served snacks and soft drinks, and its most famous resident was a large and foul-mouthed African parrot named Jackie that lived in a cage in one corner.

Situated off a balcony offering views onto the dance floor, the Tudor Club resembled an old-fashioned pub, with dark wood, chandeliers and furnishings in gold and red. It had its own small cocktail bar called the Pompadour and was popular with the local villains. Savile maintained that once he got going most of its regulars voted with their feet and joined the throng in the main dancehall.

Further along the balcony was the manager's office, which proved to be more popular with the Mecca's younger female customers. On the instructions of Mecca top brass, its previous occupant had already started running the lunchtime teen disc sessions that Jimmy Savile had initiated in Manchester.

Spinning the records on stage at these sessions was a young man named Jeffrey Collins. Known as 'Little Jeff' because he needed to stand on a crate to be able to see over the turntables, Collins was a hit with the crowd. But as he soon discovered, there was only ever going to be room enough for one star turn at the Mecca.

Jimmy Savile immediately set about pulling the strokes that would get him, and less importantly, the Mecca, noticed. An exotic American saloon and a bubble car were added to the sham Rolls, although he found less extravagant modes of transport to be every bit as effective when it came to publicity. He took to cycling into work dressed in a red, white and blue tracksuit topped off with a big hat, pink glasses and gold shoes. A flag with the words 'Mecca Dance Hall' was fixed to the back of his bike and he insisted on doing two complete laps of the city centre before freewheeling down through County Arcade.

Before the scandal broke, Brian Thomas, a Mecca regular in the late 1950s and early 1960s, explained that a whole social scene sprang up around Jimmy Savile. On Sundays, he said, it was not unusual for as many as 40 cyclists to set off with him to Bridlington,

Scarborough or Filey. He also encouraged teenagers to enter dancing competitions, driving his 'team' to Manchester for heats in a minibus. 'I think that's how he made his name – becoming involved with the kids,' said Thomas. 'He made it into more of a club than a dancehall really. He was big character, with his cigar and so on. He was someone the kids could look up to and speak to.'

Early on in his tenure at Leeds, and still sporting dark, slicked-back hair, Savile accepted the offer of a free haircut from a group of young female hairdressers who attended his record nights. Arriving at Muriel Smith's, a salon in Leeds, he surprised the staff by requesting that his hair should be dyed blond. It was the moment that perhaps the most defining aspect of his singular image took shape.

'The next time I went into my dancehall it brought the place to a grinding halt,' he told me. 'One of my disc jockeys didn't recognise me and told me to get off the stage. When they realised it was me there was a stampede of a thousand people to see or touch this weird thing with blond hair. I realised at that moment that I had stumbled on something.'

Naturally, he was straight on the phone to the local paper and a photographer was despatched to capture the new Mecca manager with his extraordinary 'mother of pearl' hairstyle.

Those who witnessed it still remember the impact it made. Tony Marshall was another Mecca regular who saw nothing that gave him cause for concern. He recalled walking through County Arcade and seeing Jimmy Savile standing outside the dancehall. 'By this time his zany personality had come through,' he explained. 'One side of his clothing would be all black and the other side would be all white: he'd have one black shoe on and one white shoe. His hair would be dyed black on one side and white on the other. Or everything he wore would be tartan and he'd have his hair sprayed tartan as well. He was a fantastic publicity figure.'

Alan Simpson was a teenager working part-time at the Wakefield Locarno when he came across Savile for the first time. He said he regularly dropped in to pay a visit or to borrow something. 'He used to dye his hair every colour under the sun,' confirmed Simpson, shortly before Savile's death. 'You don't realise how radical that was at the time. Managers were expected to be flamboyant, but collar and tie flamboyant. Savile used to get away with murder. Some people said he was a tartan-haired idiot.'

Simpson acknowledged that Jimmy Savile was very far from being an idiot. His new programme for the Mecca – based on more records, less band – paid instant dividends. But his most dramatic change was to decree that the lunchtime hops would now run from Monday to Saturday. The Mecca would also be opened on Sundays for another record-only session, the Sunday Dance Club, aimed exclusively at the teen market he had exploited at the Plaza.

Savile trained up a team of young disc jockeys to help him, and to cover when he was off talking to girls, leading them up to his office or taking care of his expanding number of 'outside interests'. One of the DJs would not last much longer, however. At the Wednesday night talent contents, 'Little Jeff's' impersonations of Jerry Lee Lewis and Little Richard had started to get a little too much attention for the manager's liking.

'He used to do it to their records with a piano as a prop,' remembered Peter Jackson, who regularly attended the Mecca, where he met the woman he's now been married to for more than 50 years. 'He always ended up bare-chested, so frantic was his performance. We all thought he was brilliant.'

'I had a following when Jimmy arrived,' confirmed Collins from his home in America. 'When Jimmy saw me he didn't want me there because he was a personality himself. He wasn't nasty to me, or anything like that, but he said, "Look, I will get you gigs in Scotland." So I went up to Scotland with him and he put me in the Locarno in Glasgow and then he put me in Edinburgh.'

Jimmy Savile's reputation was still intact when I spoke to Collins. 'It would be a great compliment if he saw me as competition,' he added. 'Between you and I, I think he did. He was a bigger personality than I was and he was the manager, he could do whatever he wanted, when he wanted, how he wanted.'

Savile once told me about the strict rules he put in place for his DJs. 'Number one, if you're going to say something to the people, let them hear what you've got to say . . . Number two, when you are on stage you will be the object of affection of many of the girls in the place. Don't touch one of them, don't even put a friendly hand on their shoulder because you don't know whether that girl has a very irate boyfriend who will want to chin you afterwards. Talk to them but don't touch any of them.'

It was clearly not a rule that applied to him. In each one of our lengthy discussions, I quizzed Savile about his thoughts on sex and the rumours he liked young girls, and he served up a variety of evasive answers. His version of how he regarded his opportunities at the dancehall, however, demonstrated that he applied the bald laws of economics to every area of his life.

'I would stand on the stage with the record player with a thousand people in the room for four or five hours,' he explained. 'Of the thousand people 700 were girls. If half of them can't stand you that leaves 350 who can stand you. If half of them are not too keen on you at all, then the other half is; that's 125 people. If half of them don't actually fancy you that leaves around 65 girls that might want to go off with you. You don't have to be a brain surgeon to work out that you're never going to be short of ladies' company.'

He said he often let the girls in free because he knew they would be good for business. He also claimed to have 'loved them all' before immediately adding, 'it never occurred to me to take a liberty with them'.

Alan Simpson insisted this anomalous caveat contradicted what his older colleagues were saying at the time. 'One of the biggest laughs we had with [Jimmy] was either he was going to be a huge success or in prison for screwing 14-year-old girls,' he told me. 'Everyone knew about it. It was wink, wink, nod, nod. It was never made public. It was a different world. If he could get away with it – wink, wink, nod, nod – good luck to him.'

It was something Jeffrey Collins corroborated: 'He was a naughty man, a naughty man. He'd go with teenagers . . . I don't know how he got away with it but he got away with it. Maybe it was because he was Jimmy Savile.' When I asked Collins whether these underage girls were picked up in his dancehall, he confirmed this was indeed the case: '"Go up to my office, I'll be up there later." That sort of thing.'

Savile had moved back in with his mother on Consort Terrace, but often stayed at a flat owned by Mecca on St Martin's Terrace. Avril Harris, who went on to have a relationship with him in later life, lived opposite and remembers Savile and his friends wolf-whistling at her when she was just 13.

'I lived with my parents,' she told Alison Bellamy, a reporter on the *Yorkshire Evening Post* who wrote a posthumous biography of Jimmy Savile that was endorsed by his family. 'They strictly forbade me to go the wild parties in the house Jimmy and his friends shared. They would invite all the girls in the street, but my mother's techni-colour threats on such matters put me in an emotional straitjacket and she won. I remember them calling out to us as we walked past, inviting us in. We knew it was wrong, but when you are that age attention from older boys is very flattering.'[1]

Jimmy Savile was not an older boy by this stage, he was a fully grown man. 'In those days nobody gave a shit,' Simpson argued. 'In those days, if you had a 14-year-old, nobody would bat an eyelid; "She's a bit young for you, 'int she?", nod, nod, wink, wink. In the Sixties, the band had their pick of the girls, some under 16.'

Collins agreed: 'It was completely different than it is today. It was free love, free sex. In those days sex was so free and easy.'

In one episode in his autobiography, Jimmy Savile recalled 'a high ranking lady police officer' coming into his place to warn him to keep a lookout for an attractive young girl who had escaped from a remand home. He recalled telling her that if he found her he would keep her for one night as his reward. 'The law lady, new to the area, was nonplussed,' he wrote. 'Back at the station she asked "Is he serious?"'[2]

He went on to explain that the girl did come in and he advised her not to run. He also claimed that it was agreed that he would hand her over if she was allowed to stay at the dance before going home with him, and that he would promise to see her when she was released.

At 11.30 the next morning, Savile said he presented the fugitive girl to 'an astounded lady of the law'. He added, 'The officeress was dissuaded from bringing charges against me by her colleagues, for it was well known that were I to go I would probably take half the station with me.'

One of Jimmy Savile's doormen at the Mecca, Dennis Lemmon, is now in his eighties. He recalls that his boss zeroed in on groups of 15 and 16-year-old girls. One day, he says, Savile arrived for work in a foul mood and when Lemmon asked a colleague what was wrong, he was told that the boss was due in court the following day for 'messing about with a couple of girls'. When the doorman later enquired what had happened with the case, he was told charges had been dropped because '[Savile] did what he did last time – he paid them off'. As Lemmon adds, 'Apparently that wasn't the first time either.'[3]

News of Jimmy Savile was spreading. In late 1959 he received a call inviting him to appear on a new television programme on the BBC hosted by David Jacobs. *Jukebox Jury* saw four panellists asked to judge whether a new record was going to be a 'hit' or 'miss'. It was filmed at Lime Grove studios in London on a Saturday evening. At that time, it was unheard of for a dancehall manager to be away on the busiest night of the week. But having already experienced the mysterious power of television, Jimmy Savile chose to go anyway.

He was determined to make an impact, and settled on an outfit of clashing colours, even though the show was filmed in black and white: a light biscuit-coloured suit, gold bowtie, bright green patent shoes and a pink shirt. During the broadcast he never once made any reference to his attire, figuring it better to let the public make up its own mind about why he'd dressed as he did. It was the same policy he adopted when wearing his Sunday best in the cage on the way to the coalface.

When Mecca head office learned of his Saturday night foray, Savile was given a sharp dressing-down, although not from the one person whose opinion really mattered to him: 'The top man Carl Heimann, he could see it and he sent me a cheque for £25.' Better still, a music paper ran four pictures of the curiously garbed Yorkshire dancehall boss.

Savile decided to strike while the iron was hot. He wrote a letter to the BBC in Manchester, asking whether there were any opportunities 'panel-wise or teenage programme-wise'[1] and followed up with a letter, also enclosing the cutting from the music paper, to George and Alfred Black, the owners of Tyne Tees Television. He told them that he would be in Newcastle the following Thursday. A couple of days later he got the call to say they wanted to meet him.

So, on his one day off in the week, Jimmy Savile drove up to Newcastle in his Rolls-Royce, making sure he parked it right outside the Tyne Tees building. 'I had a camel hair overcoat on and a collar and tie,' he told me, 'but my hair was slightly pink in shade. I walked into George Black's office and he said, "Yes, so you were on *Jukebox Jury*." Then he looked up and noticed the curious figure standing before him had pink hair. So he stood up and he went through into his brother's office and said, "Come through here, I've got a fella with pink hair in here." It was unheard of at the time.'

Savile claimed a senior producer then rushed in to find out whether someone famous was in the building after spotting the Rolls-Royce parked outside. The plan had worked: 'One of the brothers turned to me,' he claimed, 'and said, "I suppose that's yours?" And I said, yes.'

A few months later, Jimmy Savile received another call, this time from an Irishman named Pat Campbell who explained that he worked for a record company. Campbell had witnessed one of the record sessions at the Mecca and explained that Warner Brothers, who had decided to release its records in the UK under licence to Decca Record Company, were looking for a new radio disc jockey to showcase their product on Radio Luxembourg.

In an era that saw the BBC operate a monopoly on domestic broadcasting, Radio Luxembourg was developing a strong following, especially among teenagers. It was billed as 'the one bright listening spot on the dial', beaming light-hearted entertainment and pop music every night of the week via a 300-kilowatt transmitter in the Grand Duchy, where, unlike Britain, commercial radio was permitted. Programmes were recorded in London and sponsored by record companies who bought airtime to showcase their newest releases.

Campbell had recommended the name of the little-known Yorkshireman to Decca boss, Sydney Beecher-Stevens, reporting that he 'had blown him away'[2] with his energy and originality. Beecher-Stevens, who would later gain infamy alongside Decca's A & R man Dick Rowe for turning down The Beatles, was in the market for a disc jockey who would be exclusive to Warner Brothers, rather than playing records on shows sponsored by a number of different labels.

Jimmy Savile arrived for his Radio Luxembourg audition at 38 Hertford Street in London sporting tartan hair. After five minutes and only three records, producer Frank Barnes stepped out of the glass box and said, 'Thanks, we've heard enough.' Two days later, Savile said he flew to New York on a two-week holiday courtesy 'of a grateful Mecca' who had recently presented him with the Manager Winter Season Gold Cup. But before he'd had a chance to fully explore the city, a cable arrived from Warner Brothers: 'Return by the weekend. Luxembourg series starting immediately.'

At the very start of a decade in which pop music was to transform British culture, and his place in it, the Radio Luxembourg gig for Decca not only sent Jimmy Savile's earnings rocketing, it consolidated his position as one of the coming men in a new industry. He might not have had a choice in the music he played, but how serendipitous it was that the very first record on his very first show, a record which also happened to be Warner Brothers' very first UK single, turned out to be 'Cathy's Clown' by The Everly Brothers. It entered the charts on 14 April 1960 at number 22 and three weeks later it was number one, where it stayed for a further six weeks.

Introducing himself with his trademark line, 'And hi there, guys and gals, welcome to the Warner Bros record show,' Jimmy Savile's voice was unlike anything that had been heard before. He was a massive hit.

'The reason I sounded different to everyone else was that I was the only DJ in the whole world who stood up,' he said. 'I knew that your voice sounds different and I was used to standing up behind all the gear in the dancehalls. All I asked for was a music stand to put a list of the records on . . . My urgency came across. I'd gesticulate and wave my arms around. I'd talk to the people rather than spout words.'

In May, less than a month after his first show for Radio Luxembourg and with the listenership for his slot having more than quadrupled, Jimmy Savile's television career began in earnest. His speculative visit to the Black brothers in Newcastle had paid off and he'd been chosen to present a new, weekly pop music show on Tyne Tees aimed at teenagers. *Young At Heart*, co-hosted by 20-year-old singer Valerie Masters, ran for eight weeks and added another £100 a week to his salary.

He was now on a roll. He was given additional shows on Radio Luxembourg, and after three months was presenting no fewer than five different half-hour pop programmes every week, travelling to London on Thursdays, his day off, and recording them in quick succession.

The most famous of all was the *Teen and Twenty Disc Club*, which went out on Tuesdays at 10.30 p.m. and Wednesdays at 10 p.m. It quickly became one of the highest-rated shows on the station and its success spawned a club offering individually numbered membership cards and a bracelet with a charm in the shape of a record. On one side was engraved the letters 'TTDC', on the other 'Dig Pop'.

Alan Simpson remembered Jimmy Savile signing his TTDC membership card on a visit to the Wakefield Locarno: 'Everyone wanted to be in a club at that time and that signed card was huge for me at school.' Even the pre-teens were encouraged to join in the fun; the 'Under the Bedclothes Club' saw the show's host urging them to put their transistor radios under the sheets so they could follow the show after bedtime.

'As kids, it was the music we wanted to hear,' said Simpson. 'Most DJs were public schoolboys from the south. Jimmy Savile wasn't. He was a working-class lad from the north who had catchphrases and gimmicks.'

In January 1961, Savile scored his greatest coup to date by flying to Los Angeles to present a gold disc to Elvis Presley on behalf of Decca. The singer was filming the closing scenes to *Wild in the Country*, and his visitor arrived late and was forced to battle through security at the studios of 20th Century Fox. Waiting for him inside was Colonel Tom Parker, complete with pink nylon coat, bowler hat and cigar.

When he got back to Britain, Savile gave an interview to the *New Musical Express*, 'I was the first d-j to be photographed with Elvis, an honour of which I'm particularly proud,' he told the reporter. He paid for the photographs to be blown up and placed on a large board outside the Mecca Locarno.

'Sure enough,' recalled Alan Simpson, 'it was in all the papers: Jimmy and the King. That's when he had his break. It showed his ability to think on his feet. Savile was the greatest PR man I ever met.' As well as the giant photo on the front step of the Mecca, he also sold copies through his Radio Luxembourg shows and donated some of the proceeds to the National Playing Fields Association. The organisation's patron was the Duke of Edinburgh.

As Savile explained to me many years later, '[Prince Philip] was a bit impressed with the style of it and we've been pals ever since.'

*

Tony Calder was 18 when he first met Jimmy Savile in the corridors of Decca Records. It was 1961, and the young man who would go on to co-manage The Rolling Stones with Andrew Loog Oldham, was a precocious sales and marketing trainee at the time. He told me he had just stormed out of a meeting when he bumped into the DJ. He has never forgotten what he said to him: '"Come with me to Leeds for the weekend. I'll make sure you get laid."'

Calder says they drove north in Savile's Rolls-Royce, arriving on a Saturday morning to find the city centre 'packed with kids'. When Calder then witnessed the scenes in the Mecca, with teenagers bopping and jiving to the new music from America, he recalls thinking to himself, 'Fuck that, I'm having some of this.' But it wasn't only the music, and the way Jimmy Savile blended records together to produce such an effect on the crowd, that appealed to the youngster.

As Calder explains: 'At one point, [Jimmy] said, "See that girl over there, you're going home with her. But you've got to kick her out by nine o'clock in the morning." I said, "Yeah, OK. Why?" And he said, "Because you're going to have another one coming at 10 o'clock." I said, "Yeah, right."'

Savile had what Calder describes as a 'shag pad' in Leeds; almost certainly the grace and favour flat supplied by Mecca: 'Three or four bedrooms and beds with people shagging in them all night long,' he says. 'There were queues of girls outside waiting to get shagged. He'd share them out. They'd do as they were told.'

Calder describes these girls as Savile's 'followers'. 'They were his little slaves. He'd obviously shagged them all before he passed them on: "Julie, go with TC." "Julie, go with Raymond." They would. They'd be told to go off and shag a few guys before they could shag him again. "You'll like that, won't you?" "Oh yes, Jimmy." "Who's the boss?" "You are, Jimmy." "Off you go then."'

The attraction, Calder felt at the time, was that Jimmy Savile 'was the father figure'. Girls trusted him.

Jimmy Savile became Tony Calder's 'mentor' and the young man spent the next 18 months being trained as one of his DJs and playing gigs on the London circuit of Mecca venues. He even took a room at the run-down Aaland Hotel in Bloomsbury, where Savile stayed when he was in London to record his radio shows.

'[He] lived in the front room so he could check who was coming in and out,' Calder recalls. 'Some nights he'd come in because he'd been out in Leeds. He'd knock on my door and say, "Oh good, you're on your own. I'm sending [a girl] down because she's got nowhere to sleep. And he'd send this girl down and you'd have to shag her."'

At Mecca, Savile reported directly to Eric Morley, who ran the Miss Great Britain contest for the company. For one 12-week period in 1961, Calder says that both mentor and protégé were seconded to work for Morley, chaperoning beauty queens.

According to Calder, teenage girls threw themselves at Savile. 'His rule was: the younger the better. I remember he shagged one girl and he told me, "That was close. I thought she was underage. But it was her [16th] birthday."'

He insists Savile was terrified of being caught having sex with underage girls and warned him about the dangers: 'Jimmy said to me, "If you fuck underage girls you can go to jail. Sixteen is the limit." . . . If a girl had her 16th birthday he was over the moon.'

According to Calder, Savile couldn't get enough sex: 'Shagging . . . was not just a night-time pastime, if it was available there and then it was, "I'll shag it now" – he never took precautions.' Instead, he boasted about his fail-safe technique. When it was put to him that he must have illegitimate children all over the country, Savile's response to his young protégé was blunt: 'Maybe, but if I don't know about them I don't care about them, and I don't want to care about them.'

Tony Calder likens the Jimmy Savile of this period to 'the Pied Piper'. He says he was 'leading them down the path and getting a blowjob on the way. It was a great life for him.

'All he was doing was going out to clubs, playing music. He had a second hand Roller and the money started to come in. And when it started, it came in like an avalanche. He was playing all over the country, doing guest appearances. He had a phenomenal place in Leeds [the Mecca Locarno]. He was king of the castle.'

By the early 1960s, Jimmy Savile might have been forgiven for feeling untouchable. With a series of hit Radio Luxembourg shows, a budding television career, a packed dancehall and a fleet of cars scattered around Leeds, life seemed sweet. But while all this was going on in the glare of publicity, it is clear he was conscious of the need to keep his other activities away from prying eyes.

Calder remembers being at the table one evening as a senior police officer was wined and dined. 'We'd go out on a Saturday night somewhere near Leeds, maybe Wakefield, and I remember going to see a jazz act. [Savile] didn't go there to hear the music, he went there because the police would all turn up and they'd have dinner. It was the only time he ever bought anything other than fucking chicken and chips.

'This guy would drink, and the one thing Jimmy hated was paying for somebody to drink alcohol. But he'd pay for it. I asked him why he was paying for it and he said, 'I'm paying for it because he's the chief of police and he's my friend and I've got to be a friend.'

Calder also remembers Savile being warned about his behaviour. '[The police officer said] "You've got to cut it out," whatever it was,' to which Jimmy 'was taken aback.' Once one police chief retired or moved on, Calder says, Savile would move on to wooing the next: 'He wasn't stupid. Whatever he was doing he was covering his back.'

Savile also began building his reputation for doing charity work, which functioned as an extra layer of insurance against those now questioning him. In 1961, Charles Hullighan, the chief porter at Leeds General Infirmary, invited the local celebrity to help out with the launch of the hospital's radio station. Savile accepted the invitation, offered his services as a volunteer porter for a few days and began what would be a lifelong association with the institution that just 15 years earlier had told him he would never again be able to walk without sticks.

When I asked Tony Calder what he thought of Savile at the time, he denies that it ever crossed his mind to analyse him. But he does say that he believes the mining accident cast a pall over his existence. 'Something affected him and he wouldn't talk about it to me. Something went wrong. Not just physically but psychologically. It affected his whole way of living, what happened down that mine. His whole outlook, his austerity, came from having a life-threatening situation. He didn't want to die. He wanted to live. The fear of what happened down that mine fucked him up for his whole life . . . I think whatever happened . . . put him behind the 8-ball, it dictated the strangeness of his life.

'We'd be sitting having a meal and something would come over him and I'd ask him what was wrong. He'd say, "I'll be alright in a minute. It's hard to explain. I was in the mine and there was an accident." And then he'd change the subject and start chatting up some bird: "How old are you?" "Sixteen." "Fucking beautiful. And does your mum and dad know you're out on the town?" "Oh yeah, yeah, they're OK." "Have you ever been to Leeds?" "No." "Would you like to go to Leeds for the weekend?" "OK." "So ring your parents and tell them you're going with Jimmy Savile to Leeds for the weekend." And they would. And they'd come for the weekend and he'd give them the train fare home. There was nothing that any girl who had been shagged could complain about,' Calder maintains. 'They got fed, they got a train ticket home and there's another five bob for a taxi from the station. He wasn't over generous. He would never pay for it. He'd never, ever fucking pay.'

Their relationship began to falter in 1962, Calder says, when some men joined Jimmy Savile's entourage 'who made him look very unattractive'.

In *God'll Fix It*, Savile opened the chapter titled 'How Do I Cope with Sex?' with the following thought: 'The word "sex" is like the word "love". It means differing things to different people. Sex at its worst is corruption, as when young people might be corrupted to provide sex.'

It now reads like a discussion Jimmy Savile had with himself. His line about sex meaning 'differing things to different people' sounds like the justification he'd settled on for the corruption he spoke of in the very next breath. Calder describes how Savile would pass girls round, and make them have sex with his acolytes before he'd go with them again. Some of these girls might have been willing, but Savile still exploited his status, from the moment he talked them into his flat, his office or into his car for the trip to Leeds, right through to the moment he cast them aside after satisfying his needs.

In the same chapter, he went on to talk about how sex, like drugs, could cause people to kill each other, as well as being the source of 'great remorse, great guilt'. As a single man who had enjoyed more than his share of sexual encounters, he insisted that his rule was never 'make love to anyone if it causes them distress'. It doesn't sound like he was convinced, as evidenced by his closing thought on the matter: 'Whether it's okay to God we'll just have to wait and see.'[3]

From my first visit to Leeds, when I had been frisked in the foyer of his flat by Inspector Mick Starkey of the West Yorkshire Police, Savile made it plain to me that his inner circle included what he described as 'high-ranking police officers'. Policemen were among the regulars at the Friday Morning Club, the weekly coffee morning Savile hosted at his flat. So how close was the relationship?

'Obviously if you run a public place you are hand in glove to the authorities,' he said. 'If anything goes wrong you want the police to come and sort it out. Therefore you are friendly with coppers because it's us versus them on the outside. We've always had a relationship with them and that still goes on.

'Now I've got a different policy,' he added. 'Today, as you know, tabloids and magazines are always sniffing, looking for this, that or the other. In my case, they say, "No one can be that good, there's got to be something somewhere." How do I beat 'em?'

He was laughing now, so much so that he struggled to get his words out.

'Every one of my places has a middle-aged woman cleaner and you can't hide anything from a middle-aged woman cleaner. If I was into the white powders or the pornography or anything like that, they would find it. And of course, when the coppers come in, I don't keep a safe or a drawer that's locked.

'A cleaner comes in, has a little look around when she is on her own, if only to get a flavour of her client. I've had all mine for years and years and years, and they are all knocked out that I never keep anything locked up. They can go in drawers and all sorts; you can't keep anything from a lady cleaner.'

I couldn't see how his middle-aged cleaners related to my original question, but that didn't seem to matter to Jimmy Savile. 'So whenever anybody from the tabloids rings up with something,' he continued, 'I tell 'em that instead of talking to me, why don't I arrange for them to have a chat with one of my lady cleaners. It knocks their story for shit.'

I asked him why he thought people thought bad things about him; why the rumours persisted, even though he had done so much for charity.

'It's the standards of journalism that have gone down,' he replied, leaning back in his chair and examining the glowing embers of his cigar. 'What the tabloids have done is make uninteresting things interesting. A lot of the stuff they write is quite uninteresting. It doesn't matter whether so and so has copped off with someone else's wife. They have educated the public to find that quite interesting.'

It wasn't a direct answer so I decided to see if he would tell me how such rumours made him feel. 'It doesn't bother me in the slightest,' he proclaimed. 'Not at all. I have a phrase when someone puts a story in a tabloid about underage sex; I say, "It would be a lot worse if it was true." They say, "Are you saying it's not true?" I say, "I'm not saying nothing, but it would be a lot worse if it was true." Of course it's not bastard true.'

So where did these rumours come from? Was it because he was at Radio 1 at the same time as Jonathan King, who was later convicted of sex with minors?

'Editors and feature journalists are quite happy if they've got something to destroy,' he said. 'They are anarchists.'

He went on to tell a story about a female reporter who once phoned him up to tell him she had been asked to join him on a cruise on the *Canberra*. She was sent as a honey trap.

'The dumb bastard editor hadn't asked me whether she knew me,' Savile cackled. 'I told her she shouldn't tell him and that she could come with me on the *Canberra*. She did and she had the time of her life, putting herself about a bit with all the young officers. She ate with me every night and people were thinking, "What the fuck is he doing with a darling bird like that?"

'And when she went back, she told her editor that she tried everything but I was as clean as a whistle. He said, "Good, I quite liked that Jimmy Savile anyway."'

People came up to him every day, he said, to say they had been at school with him, or their fathers had worked with him, or that he used to go out with their sisters and had got them into trouble. 'You don't argue with them,' Savile said. 'They like to pull you down from whatever height they put you at. It makes them feel much higher.'

He let out a loud sigh and picked something out from between his teeth. 'I'm getting past the stage of tales being told about me now.'

M ark Williams-Thomas looks and dresses like an off-duty policeman. He is a big man with a serious manner that's not hard to imagine in the environment of a police station interview room. Between 1989 and 2000 he served with Surrey Police in child protection, CID, as a family liaison officer and then in a dedicated paedophile unit.

'It was very clear [to me] the focus on policing was very much around interfamilial abuse,' he explains, 'and not on stranger or detached abuse from, say, the schoolteacher or the vicar,' he told me. I decided to focus on that and as a result started to generate some high-profile arrests and information.'

He says it was his interview with one of Jonathan King's victims that sparked the major Surrey Police investigation into the pop impresario. In 2001 King was convicted of one charge of buggery, one of attempted buggery and four charges of indecent assault on five boys aged fourteen to sixteen. In sentencing him to seven years in prison, Judge David Paget QC said, 'You used your fame and success to attract adolescent and impressionable boys. You then abused the trust they and their parents placed in you.'[1]

Williams-Thomas had left the police force by this time. 'I just got to a point where I needed a challenge,' he says. 'I needed something different. I had done everything I wanted to do. In terms of policing, I didn't want to go into firearms, I didn't want to do traffic, I didn't want to work in drugs. Child protection and major crimes [such as] murders and kidnaps were my area of expertise but it can be pretty soul destroying. All you tend to deal with is the worst ends of everybody's lives.'

He also admits the bureaucratic aspects of the job made him uncomfortable; one former colleague told him he was a 'nightmare to manage'.[2] Williams-Thomas has been quite open about the fact he would talk openly to journalists about cases, and professionally share information if he believed it was in the public interest and could benefit the investigation.[3]

On leaving the police, Williams-Thomas set up his own child protection and risk management consultancy. He also completed an MA in criminology at Birmingham University after meeting Professor David Wilson while working on *Murder Prevention*, a Channel Five series inspired by the real-life Homicide Prevention Unit within the Metropolitan Police. He would also work as a crime adviser on TV police dramas, including the long-running BBC series *Waking the Dead*, and appeared as a pundit on Sky News, commenting on high-profile criminal investigations, including the disappearance of Madeleine McCann.

As a result of his police background Williams-Thomas started to get more work in the media. In 2005 he presented the ITV miniseries *To Catch a Predator*, an exposé of chat-room paedophiles. He then went on to work with Meirion Jones on a *Newsnight* report into how an Irish paedophile priest was able to escape justice.

In the summer of 2011, while the pair worked together on research at Interpol, Jones quizzed Williams-Thomas about whether he had heard anything about Jimmy Savile during his years as a police officer. 'He was a TV celebrity who presented *Jim'll Fix It*, and someone I grew up with,' says Williams-Thomas. 'I didn't know him for anything else. He dressed in tracksuits and always had a cigar – yes, he was a strange eccentric. Did I have any other views about him? No – he was just on TV.'

Jones was surprised, and recounted what he had seen at Duncroft, and found in online forums. He then outlined how he'd like to pursue a potential investigation. The one major obstacle that existed was Jimmy Savile himself. Any such story would be a legal minefield.

On 4 November, just less than a week after Savile's death, Williams-Thomas emailed Meirion Jones to say he wanted to be involved. His experience, skills as a researcher and years of service with Surrey Police made him a valuable asset. 'We put £500 in the budget for him to look at all the evidence and come to an assessment for us,' Jones explained.[4] While Williams-Thomas did assist Meirion Jones and *Newsnight*, he says he did not get paid for the work he did.

Jones had done a number of stories about paedophiles in the past, but could not claim to be an expert on child abuse, and nor could Liz MacKean. 'You want somebody who is a child protection professional,' he explained, 'and who has dealt with these sorts of abusers . . . like Jonathan King, to go through that stuff and give you an assessment.'

Confirming that Surrey Police had investigated Jimmy Savile was vital in terms of corroborating the claims of the former Duncroft girls. Williams-Thomas advised that if they could ascertain Surrey Police had submitted a file to the Crown Prosecution Service it would demonstrate the allegations had been taken seriously. That, Jones insists, was the story in a nutshell: the fact Jimmy Savile had been the subject of a police investigation into historic child sex abuse.

Williams-Thomas's contacts would also be useful at a time when one tabloid newspaper seemed to have been given a head start on the scoop, and had already begun contacting some of the women.

He tested the water by making inquiries with a number of different forces before additional information from the women speaking to the *Newsnight* team revealed the name of a female police officer from Kingston Road police station in Staines. This officer was said to have interviewed the women as part of Surrey Police's investigation.

In addition to seeking confirmation from Surrey Police that there had been an investigation, Williams-Thomas was required to assess the evidence, which now included Jimmy Savile's activities beyond the walls of Duncroft. His behaviour at the BBC, at Stoke Mandeville Hospital and the Haut de la Garenne children's home in Jersey was in play, and Williams-Thomas made a professional estimate that they were now looking at a predatory paedophile who had offended at institutions all over the country.

On 25 November, he phoned Meirion Jones to say that he had got what they were looking for: he had received off-the-record confirmation that Surrey Police did investigate Jimmy Savile about sexual abuse of minors, and girls from Duncroft were interviewed as part of their inquiry.

In the rough early drafts of the script, Williams-Thomas's expert testimony to camera was seen as an essential component of the package. 'He's absolutely key to "Is this man a paedophile or not? Is he behaving like other paedophiles?"' said Jones.[5] There were also discussions about Williams-Thomas appearing in the *Newsnight* studio to offer his analysis immediately after the film was shown. It proved to be the closest *Newsnight* got to getting its investigation to air. Williams-Thomas was never interviewed.

When it became clear to Meirion Jones and Liz MacKean that the Jimmy Savile story was dead in the water, they agreed to let Williams-Thomas take it on.

'I went to the ITV lawyer and I went to the exec producers and the commissioner and we all had a meeting,' he recalls. 'We started to talk about it and I said, "Look, this is still early stages. There is clearly something there, but I don't know what it is yet . . ." An awful lot of people were making a lot about a letter from Surrey Police [but] right from the very beginning I said this letter was a red herring. The story was Savile is an abuser, not whether or not the authorities failed in their process.'

There was no formal commission but ITV's Factual and Current Affairs creative director, Alex Gardiner, supplied funding to develop the programme.[6] 'It is fair to say there was nervousness,' says Williams-Thomas of ITV's attitude. 'You know, this was a big broadcaster and they were very conscious how that could be perceived. But I also have to say there wasn't a single person . . . that didn't feel that we needed to do something.'

He teamed up with Lesley Gardiner, an experienced producer, and from the outset it was agreed that 'Project DJ' would be conducted in utmost secrecy. 'I ran it as though it was a criminal investigation,' says Williams-Thomas, 'and on the basis that I didn't want anyone else to know what was going on.'[7] The other clear policy agreed on at the outset was any victims who were filmed or interviewed would appear in the final programme.

While the starting point was Duncroft and some of the evidence already unearthed by the *Newsnight* investigation and online, Williams-Thomas says he was conscious of the need to broaden the search. 'If it was Duncroft alone we'd never have been able to make the programme. [The Duncroft girls] were the most vulnerable in society and as a result of that, they're the most preyed on. We've seen that with the Rochdale case [a group of men convicted in 2012 of sex trafficking of under-age girls]; people don't believe them, they don't listen to them and, of course, as a result of that they're rich pickings. We had to weigh that up with the reality of the public's perspective . . . So in order to have their stories told, we had to support them by going elsewhere.'

Newsnight's deputy editor Liz Gibbons had assumed Mark Williams-Thomas was the source of the leak that led to the February 2012 newspaper stories,[8] a charge he categorically denies. He argues it was not in his interest, given he was by now conducting a top secret investigation himself. Whatever the truth, the stories worked in his favour because they prompted Sue Thompson, a newsroom assistant at BBC Leeds in the 1970s, to make contact with *Newsnight*.

In her email, Thompson explained she had occasionally worked on a regional television programme called *Jimmy Savile's Yorkshire Speakeasy*. In 1978, she 'inadvertently walked into [Savile's] dressing room' and witnessed Savile molesting 'a young girl perhaps 13 or 14 years old'. She then gave a particularly sickening detail about the girl that cannot be revealed as it could help to identify her.

'I have never mentioned this to anyone before,' Thompson signed off, 'but felt compelled to write of my experience after reading the [newspaper] article.'[9]

Jones forwarded the information to Williams-Thomas, although he suspected someone would beat him to the story.

Eight months later, Sue Thompson became the first witness to speak on camera in the ITV *Exposure* documentary that decimated the ramparts of Jimmy Savile's mythology.

*

When asked whether ITV set any editorial bars that needed to be cleared for his film to make it to air, Williams-Thomas insists it did not. 'We set our own bar in terms of how many victims we needed in order to tell the story,' he says. 'We were constantly juggling it in terms of, is four enough? Is five enough? Six? Seven? But what we were also very clear on is that actually we needed to give them enough time to tell their stories in 49 minutes.'

Working closely with Gardiner, Williams-Thomas began widening the net. The key to finding victims, he explains, was to delve into the places Jimmy Savile had worked. 'Once we looked at Duncroft and that was basically finished . . . we focused on Leeds, we looked at Manchester, the Top Ten Club, the Mecca discos, and then *Top of the Pops* and *Clunk Click* . . . We started to try to get into those networks and groups of people. The focus was his routes and access to children.'

He recalls the first interview as being a pivotal moment and maintains he approached it with the same mindset as when quizzing a key witness as a police officer. 'I am very careful when I interview people,' he says. 'I use a whole range of techniques to see whether or not what they are telling me is truthful. I have to say that I came away the first time with the strong feeling that there was more to it. It was a gut feeling.'

Over the following months, they scoured the country for witnesses and victims. Those they found were spoken to on the phone or in person. Williams-Thomas says he was in direct contact with around twenty victims, most of whom refused to go on the record. His experience in this particular field of police work, however, taught him that he needed to give these women the space to make up their own minds. Of those who were prepared to talk, some were given guarantees their identities would be concealed.

What Williams-Thomas discovered in the course of his research was that victims and witnesses still felt a 'genuine fear' about coming forward due to Jimmy Savile's connections. '[It was] a contributing factor to why they had remained silent for so long,' he insists. 'It is why it was such a difficult process to slowly coax these people, to give them the confidence that we [would] do them justice.' After the experience of the failed police investigation and then the canned *Newsnight* report, he says, many within the Duncroft community remained deeply sceptical.

Gradually, though, a pattern began to emerge, one that Williams-Thomas recognised from his work in child protection. '[Savile] is classic in regards to a predatory sex offender who has the access and opportunity to offend,' he argues. 'Those are the two fundamental areas. Had he not had the access and opportunity to offend, he may not have offended to the degree that he did. But this is a man whose life [was] dedicated to doing things around and for children and as a result his predilection for children was fulfilled every time.'

He also found a compelling degree of consistency in the way Jimmy Savile approached girls and then inflicted his abuse. 'I have to say I believe the allegations,' he told me in late September 2012, a couple of days before the *Exposure* documentary aired on ITV. 'You can dismiss one, you can dismiss two but when you start to build them up and the way they talk about the offences against them . . . and the fact they don't know each other, it gives huge credibility to their accounts.'

From the twenty victim accounts, it was decided to film interviews with five women: two from Duncroft, one who was abused at Stoke Mandeville and two at *Top of the Pops*. The latter proved to be a turning point for Williams-Thomas, who recalls one particular interview on a Friday evening.

'Savile's offending behaviour before that was horrendous,' he says, 'but it didn't get to the level whereby I started to understand him as an offender. Up until that stage he was more distant . . . But when [one of the *Top of the Pops* victims] talked about the force that he used, the power that he used, the violence that he used, the coercion that he used, that for me was the point when I [concluded], "This is a really nasty offender, and this guy has offended against an awful lot of people."'

One of the women from *Top of the Pops* revealed Jimmy Savile had raped her in his motor caravan outside BBC Television Centre. The other said he had sex with her on a number of occasions in his BBC dressing room. She was 15 years old at the time.

'There were different groups,' Williams-Thomas says of the witnesses and victims from *Top of the Pops*. 'Some of them knew each other because they might have occasionally bumped into each other through Savile, but they were a bit distant from each other. We needed independence; we needed to separate Duncroft from Stoke Mandeville from *Top of the Pops*. It got to the position whereby the more independence we had, the stronger the individual allegations from the victims and witnesses were,' he explains.

Williams-Thomas is convinced Jimmy Savile was protected by his celebrity status. 'He was untouchable in the era in which these things happened, and because of that he gained greater and greater confidence. The reality is that if you do something wrong in front of somebody and you know that you won't get picked up for it, you'll do it again and again. Nobody ever picked him up, from what we found out, and therefore he grew in confidence and arrogance. [He thought] If nobody is going to report me or stop me from doing it, I will just carry on.'

Despite the progress they'd made with 'Project DJ', both Williams-Thomas and Gardiner remained acutely aware of the possibility the investigation could blow up in their faces, and the public could turn against them and ITV for sullying the reputation of a national hero. They were 'taking on an icon'. 'I said to Lesley, this is going to be the hardest project we've ever done but I also said if we get it right, it has the ability make a big difference.'

The next key step was to validate victim testimonies. 'We went into individuals' backgrounds,' Williams-Thomas says, 'and substantiated [evidence] to such a degree that we validated them far, far beyond any police investigation would do; to the degree whereby we would date things through photographs, looking at bricks on walls, things in the background.'

It was just as well because while ITV remained supportive, News Director Michael Jermey advised the film would only proceed to broadcast if the evidence could be used if Savile were still alive.[10]

PART THREE

Jimmy Savile's last will and testament was in probate when Georgina Ray's lawyers contacted the executors of his estate. They said their client would be taking a DNA test in an attempt to prove she was his daughter. If conclusive, it would pave the way for a possible claim under the Inheritance Act of 1975. As the only child of the late Jimmy Savile, albeit a father she never met, Georgina Ray could make the argument that she was entitled to the entire estate.

Jimmy Savile was worth £7.8 million at the time of his death. He had £4.3 million in his bank accounts, a £2.5 million property portfolio made up of flats in London, Leeds, Scarborough and Bournemouth, plus a cottage in Glencoe in the Scottish Highlands. He was also estimated to have a further £1 million in assets.

Other than the £600,000 he placed in a trust to be shared among six people, and the £18,000 to be divided equally between a further eighteen friends, he made provision for all of the proceeds from his estate to go into the Jimmy Savile Charitable Trust, which was set up to help 'poorly people in hospital beds'. The trust showed a balance of £3.6 million, soon to be increased by the proceeds from an auction of all his remaining belongings.

In late June 2012, details about the auction of his belongings were released. The sale comprised 550 lots; a museum of Jimmy Savile's life, one that he had diligently curated and stored over the course of 84 years. His flats were packed with curios, mementos and tat; on the last occasion I stayed with him in Leeds I had almost been buried under an avalanche of platform-soled boots and colourful outfits when opening a cupboard in his spare room.

The sale was set for late July and was to be held at Savile's Hall in Leeds, a conference and exhibition centre at the Royal Armouries Museum that had been renamed in his honour in 2007. Standout items from the sale were put on display at Dreweatts auctioneers in London before transferring to Leeds. They included his red chair from *Jim'll Fix It*; the yellow BMW Isetta bubble car he bought himself while appearing at the Top Ten Club in Manchester in 1965 (and once used to collect the Duke of Edinburgh from Aylesbury Railway Station); his 18-carat gold and diamond encrusted Rolex Oyster watch; his 9-carat gold bracelet featuring 55 brilliant-cut diamonds; and his 6.7 litre silver Rolls-Royce Corniche, one of a limited edition of 56 'last of line' Corniches built at the company's plant in Crewe.

But beyond headline-friendly lots such as these, the sheer size and scope of the sale spoke of his extraordinary need to be surrounded by the inanimate articles of his legend. This is what he'd talked about: the things that don't live. The hundreds of items represented so many bricks in the wall.

The auction of these 500 and more items was a final chance for Jimmy Savile to burnish his myth, and Georgina Ray was anathema to everything the collection represented. As the doors of Savile's Hall opened onto the museum of his life and times, there was no place for a 41-year-old, blonde divorcée from Cannock. DNA analysis on cigar butts, a hairbrush and bedding from the flats in Leeds and Scarborough had failed to produce samples that matched her own.[1] Ray was said to be 'crestfallen' and her solicitor Richard Egan responded by highlighting his 'serious misgivings' about 'anomalies and inconsistencies', including the fact analysts had not been able to find a single strand of Savile's bleached blond hair on the hairbrush.[2]

For Georgina Ray, the auction might have been the closest she ever came to gaining an understanding of the man she believed to be her father. For there, among the shell suits, the vests, running shorts and medals, the endless boxes of cigars, the jewellery and the Disc Jockey of the Year awards, were more revealing artefacts from a life still being celebrated, by the wider public at least, as one of giving, goodness and grace.

An Oscar Egg lightweight 10-gear racing cycle with turquoise frame, leather saddle and his original 'Express Tour of Britain' entry tag, along with his original rider number, 48, from the race; a deerstalker hat with accompanying black and white photograph of Oscar 'The Duke' Savile during his days as a race commentator; an engraved cigarette box given to him when he left the Mecca Locarno for Ilford in 1955; the Mecca Dancing gold cup; unopened parcels of *Teen and Twenty Disc Club* circular medallions; a patchwork shirt by Lord John of Carnaby Street with accompanying photographs of Savile on a hospital visit with his mother; the red satin padded bedspread with gold 'JS' monogram he used to cover the single bed in the Duchess's room in Scarborough; snaps of Savile with brides and flirting with nurses, and Savile with his brother Johnnie; the reproduction of a signed photograph of Winston Churchill; the suit, shirt, tie and white slip-on shoes he wore when he stood alongside Prince Charles and Princess Diana as they opened the National Spinal Injuries Centre at Stoke Mandeville in 1983; the race numbers and medals from his two decades of marathon running, an era in which he tried to control one addiction through another; the leather upholstered armchair and matching footstool from which he held court in his Roundhay Park penthouse.

More interesting were the associations some of the items disclosed. A whole section of the sale was devoted to 'The Royal Family', which was a revelation given he had taken pride in refusing to talk about his relationships with them during his later years. There were thirty-five lots in total, among them numerous gifts and cards from Prince Charles, Princess Diana, Prince Andrew and Sarah Ferguson: a pair of silver and blue enamel cufflinks by Asprey & Garrard, given as an 80th birthday present by Prince Charles, as well as a pair of commemorative American cowboy boots. There were Christmas cards from Charles and Diana;

Prince Charles, Princess Diana and their sons; Prince Charles and his sons; and Prince Charles and the Duchess of Cornwall, signed off with 'kindest regards', 'warmest good wishes' and 'affectionate greetings'. They were souvenirs from his journey to the very centre of the establishment that gave away nothing of what he had done when he got there.

Then there were the other gifts and tokens of esteem: the signed sketches by Rolf Harris; a Brazil nut mounted on a plinth from the patients at Broadmoor; a white onyx table lighter engraved 'To Jimmy Savile from his friends at the Fraud Squad'; a Metropolitan Police helmet inscribed in blue ballpoint pen 'To Jimmy Saville [sic] from Marylebone Police Station'; the plaques and presentation pieces from forces all over Britain; the engraved drill sergeant's swagger stick from the senior non-commissioned officers' mess at the Royal Marine Commando Training Centre at Lympstone, and a bronze statue from the sergeants' mess; a stainless steel tray engraved 'To Jimmy Savile OBE. With thanks for a great walk Easter Monday, 1976. From Aquila Youth Centre Jersey'.

Before the sale, I was contacted by Luke Lucas, a trustee of both Jimmy Savile's charitable trusts. He had known Savile for 42 years, worked for him full-time for the first seven years and described him as his 'best friend', although he refused point blank to talk about him. 'I was involved in everything, believe me, and if I wanted to tell the 42 years of stories it would need to be a very thick book,' he said. 'Thicker than the Old Testament.'

He told me a bit about Savile's attitudes towards his relations, and discussed the ongoing Georgina Ray situation. In a subsequent call, Lucas informed me that boxes of Jimmy Savile's private papers were to be deposited with Leeds University where it was hoped they would be held as a Jimmy Savile archive. He said the papers revealed the true picture of his friend's place in, and value to, the establishment. He also insisted access would be impossible until claims on the estate had been settled.

On 30 July 2012, that prospect moved a step closer with the sale of his belongings at Savile's Hall. The first lot, his Highland suit complete with Lochaber tartan kilt, went under the hammer at 10.30 a.m. and sold for £280. The tone for the day, however, was set with the second item, an ash shepherd's crook-type walking stick with a plaque engraved 'James Savile OBE'. The stick sold for £500 against a guide price of £50–£80. From that point on, almost every item in the sale obliterated its estimate.

The 2002 Rolls-Royce Corniche convertible with personalised 'JS 247' number plate went for £130,000, almost twice its guide price. The three-wheel bubble car fetched £22,000, bought by Angela Swift, the managing director of a care home company who said it would be parked inside a residential home in Barnsley. 'Many of the residents have dementia so this will hopefully provide them with some nostalgic memories,' said Swift, who also bought a gold Nike tracksuit for £500, four times its guide price.[3]

Roger Bodley, another of Savile's trustees and a former radiologist at Stoke Mandeville Hospital, bought a Highland sword and shield presented to the star in 1973 when he was named chieftain of Lochaber's Highland games. Bodley said it would be returned to the Glencoe cottage that the trustees were now planning to turn into a Scottish retreat for the disabled.

A former patient at Stoke Mandeville, George Ridgeon, spent £350 on some marathon medals. He had travelled from Gloucester in his wheelchair. 'It wasn't easy but I had to be here,' he said. 'I want something to remember my old friend by.' He was even more pleased to be presented his items by a 'pretty girl' because, he explained, 'just like Jim, I've got an eye for the ladies.'[4]

Towards the end of the sale, an original *Jim'll Fix It* badge went for a staggering £2,000. After following the sale all day, I bought a Stetson hat that Savile told me Elvis Presley had given him, and a bag of assorted medals and trinkets. I knew what was coming and this was the final farewell.

After nearly 13 hours, the last item was sold: Jimmy Savile's favourite ashtray and a Romeo y Julieta cigar that prompted one bidder to pay £140. The team of auctioneers had worked in relay, hundreds of people had attended and many thousands more followed the auction online. Every single one of the items went, apart from a certificate for an honorary doctorate awarded by Bedfordshire University that was withdrawn. The organisers had said they hoped to make around £200,000 for the Jimmy Savile Charitable Trust. The final total was over £320,000.

His life had been celebrated again, and sold off for charity: the last positive publicity Jimmy Savile would ever generate. It was, indeed, good while it lasted.

24. THE ONLY PUNTER YOU CAN
RECOGNISE FROM THE BACK

I t was late and we had just finished dinner at one of Jimmy Savile's favourite Scarborough eateries, a short walk up the Esplanade from his Wessex Court flat. He was on to his second large vodka of the evening and his tongue had loosened. All evening he had been joking with a young waitress who, he discovered, hailed from Fort William, near to Lochaber where he had been honorary chieftain of the Highland games for over 30 years.

Savile had a 'team' at Fort William, just as he did in Scarborough and Leeds, and at Stoke Mandeville and Broadmoor. They were people who were impressed by him and would attend to his needs when he was around. At that point, I hadn't found out whether he had a similar team in London for those rare occasions when he stayed at his small attic apartment on Regent's Park Crescent.

He always told me that when it came to the royal family he had taken the oath of *omertà*, which was apt given that he was prone to referring to himself as 'the Godfather'. However, on this particular evening he'd already touched on his friendship with the Duke of Edinburgh and was just beginning to tell me a story about Earl Louis Mountbatten when a woman, whom I'd guessed at being in her sixties, leaned over from the neighbouring table and, in a posh voice, informed Savile how very unhappy she was about the quality of her meal.

'Did you know a fella was following you?' he barked back, prodding a fork in the direction of a man I presumed to be her husband. 'I told him he'd get in trouble for that, what with you being underage.'

The woman did not seem to understand that this was intended as a joke or that Savile was clearly not interested in discussing the merits of the restaurant. 'It was the most awful dinner,' she blundered on regardless. 'The duck was off.'

'It was probably dead,' deadpanned Savile, who informed her that he'd played safe by having the salmon.

The woman tried a different tack, announcing that the last time she had met him it was in this same restaurant about five years ago.

'And I found your earring down the back of my sofa,' he replied without a flicker of a smile.

This lopsided exchange continued for some minutes – her oblivious to his indifference, him responding with sour-faced innuendo – until the woman reiterated that her duck was off and Savile once again countered with a reference to it probably having something to do with it being dead for so long.

'How long are you in Scarborough for?' she asked.

'About 5ft 10,' he replied, 'unless I get run over and I'll be about 7ft 6.'

The woman finally admitted defeat, settled her dispute with the restaurant and left with her husband, who had said nothing throughout. 'People are a pain in the arse,' muttered Savile. 'These sort of people will dine out on that story.'

Commotion over, we returned to our conversation and he told me about a television producer who marvelled at his ability to fit in anywhere. 'I love people coming up to me,' he added, contradicting what he had just said about the woman. 'If you're on TV you have to accept the responsibility, just like I had the responsibility for looking after my people in the dancehalls, even though they didn't know I was really doing that. People can't become second-class citizens once you come off TV. I belong to the people out there.'

Did people ever pick on him, or try it on, because he was odd? 'No, there was nothing to pick on. They thought I was a bit freaky but they couldn't tell me why. It was because I was odd. You can't really have a go at odd because there's nothing to have a go at. It's just odd. If you're disabled or you've got an encephalitic head where it's twice the size, people will have a go at you because it's a recognisable thing. Odd is not a recognisable thing. Odd means you just don't fit in. Odd is a description on its own which is indefinable. There's nothing wrong with it, it's a state that some people are in.'

When did he first realise that he was odd? 'Very early on. It doesn't mean handicapped, it just means odd.'

He called the Scottish waitress over, relayed the complaints from the next table, and ordered another large vodka. When she'd gone he talked a little about his older sister Marjory who had raised 14 children, and then about one of his nephews who had worked out that they had 420 traceable relatives alive in Britain. 'The way I look at it is that I had two brothers who were in the war and they never knew whether they would ever see home again. I could have any number of nephews and nieces out there. Do me a fucking favour.'

The conversation was jumping around and the subject it alighted on next was children. 'I hate kids,' he trumpeted, not for the first time. It was a standard line he used but not one that I necessarily believed. Only that morning I had witnessed him talking sweetly to a little girl who was waiting for her grandparents at the front door to his block of flats.

'I'm very good with them because I hate them,' he continued. 'They know I'm not some yucky adult. I like to confuse them because they don't know where they are then. Then they start to fall in love with you because they want to be with you. Nobody confuses kids like I do; they try to understand them and reason with them. I think all kids should be eaten at birth.'

A man came over to the table and was greeted with a joke: 'How do you turn a cat into a dog? Pour petrol on it, set fire to it and watch it go "woof".' The man laughed and shook his head. 'By God, you'll never meet a character like him,' he said, looking at me but motioning towards Savile. 'He's had a wonderful life.'

Savile wasn't finished: 'This copper says to this geezer, "When did you realise your wife was dead?" The geezer said, "I dunno. The sex was the same but the dishes kept piling up in the kitchen."' I tried vainly to summon a laugh but was saved by the waitress returning with the drink. Savile asked her for a doggie bag.

On the short walk back to the flat he talked about how he was a 'complete phenomenon'. He was wearing one of his thick, quilted sports coats and a woolly hat, which was prudent as it was now freezing cold. 'I'm still the only punter you can recognise from the back. If it all fell out tomorrow,' he said, referring to his hair, 'I wouldn't give a shit. It's never been dyed. I just bleach it and take all the natural colour out of it. This is natural hair.'

I asked him about the jewellery, and where the idea for the all the 'jangle jangle' had come from. The artist Harland Miller once wrote that Jimmy Savile had been the originator of the bling style adopted by American rappers.

'Deals,' hooted Savile. 'I like to do deals. There's eighteen hundred diamonds in the Rolex. They are all identically cut. The necklace is a gift from the president of South Africa. He came over and saw *Jim'll Fix It* and said that I was the 'wishbone of England' so he got this golden wishbone made up for me. The other one is from the Goldsmiths' Association of Britain.' He pulled out a pendant from beneath his jacket and tried to show me a tiny cigar, training shoe, *Jim'll Fix It* badge and record, although it was too dark to see properly.

'The thumb ring is another one from the Goldsmiths' Association when I got my knighthood. I told them that in the olden days knights used to get a thumb ring so they sent someone down to the British Library for a week to pore over books. The diamonds in that are another story.' He then launched into a rather confusing anecdote about meeting a diamond dealer in a restaurant who told him one of the stones in his thumb ring was chipped.

'Then he looked at the Rolex,' explained Savile, 'and nearly shot his load. It's a very unique piece; there's only two in the world. Mike Tyson had the other one but I reckon one of his birds has got it now.' The story finished with Savile getting a diamond in each corner of his thumb ring, for nothing. 'What can you do?' he said. 'It's not my fault.'

Back at the flat, he flicked through the TV channels before settling on a station playing classical music. He then told me that his cars were not for driving: 'They're for posing.' He said that he liked talking to 'young guys' who knew he had a Ferrari and a Rolls-Royce and yet knew he still lounged around in a shell suit. 'It's part of the charismatic package,' he offered. 'I don't have to do anything, I just have to be. I'm like a piece of soap in the bath; you can see it but when you try to get hold of it it's gone.'

It was clear that something Savile had said in the restaurant was bothering him, because he suddenly veered back onto the subject of children. 'I have no time for them but I don't hate them,' he explained. 'A single man at my age with his hair this colour . . . ' he laughed lugubriously. 'If I told everyone how much I loved children, I would finish up like Michael fucking Jackson. It's better to say I hate 'em and they should all be eaten at birth because it stops the stories dead, even for the tabloids. I don't want the tabloids to think I am a lover of children.'

In the space of a few hours he had joked with a man about getting in trouble for being caught with underage girls, and told me how he liked to confuse children into falling in love with him. Now, he was effectively conceding that his appearance, work with children and the absence of normal adult relationships in his life made him look suspect. But he was not interested in such variables, the values of which only he truly knew. Jimmy Savile's prime consideration was in controlling the outcome of the equation.

In May 1962, Jimmy Savile's career as a Mecca dancehall manager came to an end. He was not sacked for being caught with his fingers in the till or for being found in a compromising position with an underage girl. In fact, he was promoted and given his own office in the company's Southwark Street headquarters in London.

He was by now making more in his one day off than he was in the six doing his regular job as one of the company's area managers. Offers were flooding in from companies looking to capitalise on his kudos, and as he was possessed of an inquiring mind and an unquenchable appetite for making money, Mecca correctly surmised that Jimmy Savile was not going to be able to resist such temptations for much longer.

Faced with losing his star, Carl Heimann made another canny business decision by appealing to Savile's ego and bringing him further into the fold, even if it was on a part-time basis that would mean he'd be free to pursue his outside interests. But this was no token offering, because as an associate director he would be paid £50 a week and put in charge of music and DJ policy at Mecca's 46 ballrooms nationwide.

Savile celebrated his promotion by ordering a brand new Rolls-Royce from Jack Barclay's in London. He went to collect it in person wearing a pair of fur slippers. According to a newspaper report, the vehicle was fitted with a 'record player, radio, fridge and a shillelagh, the reason for the latter being in the dance hall business, possession of a blunt instrument is nine tenths of mob law.'[1]

Along with the millions now listening to his shows on Radio Luxembourg, Savile's elevated position within the Mecca organisation confirmed his new status as one of the most influential pop music tastemakers in the country.

Thick smog enveloped the capital that summer, but high above the gloom various stars were moving into alignment. A group of scowling young blues aficionados calling themselves The Rolling Stones took to the stage for their debut appearance at the Marquee Club in London. Shortly afterwards, at a Horticultural Society dance in the north-west, a drummer named Ringo Starr, formerly of Rory Storm and The Hurricanes, performed for the first time with his new group, a Liverpudlian beat combo named The Beatles.

British pop music was beginning to generate a momentum of its own, rather than relying on hits imported from the States, coinciding with seismic changes taking place in a society where young people felt increasingly empowered. Yet the country was still to shake off the last vestiges of the postwar era. Harold Macmillan's Conservative government was one based on the same old school tie cliques that had ruled for decades, and was therefore naturally suspicious of a phenomenon that in time would become known as 'youth culture'.

At the Decca studios in London, another, less noteworthy footnote was being written in the history of British pop music. In what the *New Musical Express* described as 'a hush hush session',[2] Jimmy Savile recorded 'his debut disc', a cover of the novelty record 'Ahab the Arab'.

This session was not to remain a secret for long. 'Disc Jockey in Sheik's Clothing' sang the headline above a story in the *Daily Mirror*.[3] According to the reporter, 'Mr James Savile, the most extraordinary disc-jockey in this spinning business, peeled off a oncer from a roll of £200 to buy me half a bitter and said: "Do I need any more noughts on the bank balance?"' The story went on to say that Savile had six bodyguards 'to watch over him, his business affairs and his bank balance'. Royalties from the record were to be donated to the Little Sisters of the Poor.

Cutting a disc was just one of many moneymaking schemes on his mind as the new decade started to take shape. He set up Jimmy Savile Limited and decided that his various business interests would be best served by a move back to Manchester. A sparsely furnished studio flat on Great Cheetham Street in Salford was found and he moved in with the bare minimum of belongings.

In Manchester, his operations were initially focused on the Upper Broughton Assembly Rooms, a first-floor dancehall with a sprung dance floor, and a pair of coloured fountains that spouted in time with the music. The venue was a short distance from his new digs, and familiar to him from his days at the Plaza, being located in the same block as the Whisky a Go Go, one of his favourite after-hours haunts. Posters and newspaper ads for the Jimmy Savile Disc Club duly appeared around the city.

Savile moved into a one-bedroom flat in a crumbling building. Two floors in the Victorian mansion block were derelict and the rear of the premises lay in ruins, covered in weeds high enough to conceal snoozing tramps and, Savile recognised, his Roller and new Jaguar E-Type. He agreed to pay the £1.50 a week rent, and turned the living room into his bedroom. He decided to paint the whole place black. Savile's reasoning was that with one red light bulb and one white there would be enough light to read by but not enough to see the grime and decay. Not altogether surprisingly, the residence was christened the 'Black Pad'.

Despite the fact he surrounded himself with teenage girls, partly because they gravitated towards him and provided an effective disguise for his own age, and partly because he could dominate them, Jimmy Savile still seemed to enjoy keeping people guessing about his sexual orientation. The crazy attire, the dyed hair and the conspicuous lack of a regular woman in his life gave rise to gossip. In his mind, though, any publicity was a good thing. His attitude was therefore, 'If they're talking about it, let 'em think.'

Penny-Ann Roles met Savile when she was a teenager working at the Three Coins coffee bar in Fountain Street. It was a long, dark and smoky cellar that was packed out with youngsters dancing to local bands, and a venue that Savile went on to part own. She remembers the furious reaction from her father when Manchester's most famous disc jockey dropped her home one evening in his Rolls-Royce.

'On a Sunday night he used to take a few of us to a restaurant, an Indian place in the curry centre of Manchester,' she says. 'We used to go there for a curry and he would park his Rolls Royce up. Afterwards, he would take us home with the roof down on his car, and we'd all be singing our heads off.' She remembers there were three or four girls that Savile took out regularly but insists he never tried it on with her. 'I never saw him in a relationship with anyone,' she maintains. 'Between you and I, I don't know whether he was gay.'

Other teenage girls in the area could confirm this was not the case. Pam Batty had first encountered Jimmy Savile at the Plaza. 'He used to get a coffee and come and sit with us,' she recalls. 'He was a real ladies' man. He was a charmer. A lot of people thought he was gay but nothing could be further from the truth. I don't think he was in any way, shape or form that way inclined.'

She says Jimmy Savile paid her and a friend to listen to demo tapes he was sent: 'We used to pick them up or he'd drop them off at the house or he'd pick us up and we'd go and listen to them.' Pam was 18 and an apprentice hairdresser at the time, and she also insists Savile never tried anything with her.

Pam's friend, who was younger, did get into a relationship with him, however. 'They just seemed to click,' Pam says. 'She was quite an attractive girl and obviously he thought that.'

Pam Batty says they knew Jimmy Savile was a good deal older than them, but not how much older. She also confirms that the relationship with her friend was sexual and that she sometimes stayed with Savile at the Black Pad. 'When it all fizzled out, she was quite upset,' recalls Pam. 'Obviously Jimmy wasn't; he was just Jimmy. He just carried on.'

Jeff Dexter was another young person who discovered the truth about Jimmy Savile's sex drive. Dexter had first entered Savile's orbit when he appeared as a teenage dancing prodigy at London's Lyceum Ballroom. Despite looking young for his age, Dexter was street-wise and ambitious and went on to work alongside Tony Calder in promoting pop records and DJ'ing for Mecca. 'He looked like someone off the ballroom circuit, like a ballroom manager,' he says of Savile. 'But he had three watches on, that was one thing I remember.'

Dexter was just 16 when he was hired to appear with Jimmy Savile, who was by then 36, at the *Daily Mail* Boys & Girls Exhibition at Olympia in December of 1962. The teenager was to give lessons on new dances such as the Twist and the Madison on a miniature dance floor, while the Radio Luxembourg star spun records. Other attractions at the two-week show included a sports arena, the world's biggest model railway and a scale model of the recently launched Telstar satellite.

Many years later, and some time before Jimmy Savile's death, Dexter described Jimmy Savile to me as a 'pervert' and commented that they would 'lock him up and throw away the key' if anyone found out what went on behind the scenes at Olympia. Shortly after the *Exposure* documentary on ITV, I asked Dexter about that comment and whether he witnessed anything that chimed with what was being reported about Jimmy Savile. His answer was brief: 'Yep.'

But, he added, 'All those girls, young and old, threw themselves on Jimmy. It was there for the taking . . . None of them complained, otherwise he would have been locked up years ago . . . I was 16 years old and [the girls] were my age. And the fact I'm with Jimmy Savile and I'm on stage in this ballroom set-up, to a lot of girls who come from out of town, you are fair game. So I was fair game and Jimmy was fair game at the time as well.'

Another source said: 'He didn't go looking for [girls]. They turned up. He was a pop star. When you're in that business they're always there in front of you. There were so many around. The Sixties were the sex years. All the girls wanted to try sex and all the boys wanted to be into sex. Everyone was at it everywhere like rabbits.'

'Girls chatted to us,' the source maintained. 'We were harmless because we weren't chasing anybody. We were safer than the others and by that I mean the men who were trying to trap them and marry them. We were great at consoling girls when they'd fallen out with other boys. We liked to console them.'

If Jimmy Savile was addicted to sex, as Tony Calder suggests, it was quick, emotionally detached liaisons that he sought. And in pliable teenagers, he found partners that he could control and manipulate without the prospect of having to confront the emotional void at his core. Money, his other great obsession, provided a further layer of protection.

At the start of the New Year, he set off on a tour billed as 'Johnny & The Hurricanes and The Juke Box Doubles'. It was a curious concept, combining a popular singing act with what can only be described as an early incarnation of *Stars in Their Eyes* with lookalikes performing songs in the style of Elvis Presley, Adam Faith, Gene Vincent and The Shadows. The 18-date schedule began at the Gaumont State in Kilburn and finished at the Nelson Imperial, just in time for the release of Jimmy Savile's follow-up single 'The Bossa Nova'.

While he was off touring the country, The Beatles arrived in Manchester to play two dates, at the El Rio and The Three Coins, venues owned by local promoter Danny Betesh. A month later, the group released their debut LP, *Please Please Me*, and by May were top of the singles charts with 'From Me To You'.

The album followed an identical trajectory, and on the day it reached number 1, a newspaper advertisement appeared for Jimmy Savile's next big engagement: a new weekly pop music column. 'Great news for the "with it" brigade,' trumpeted the copy. 'The *People* has signed up disc-jockey, super showman Jimmy "Luxembourg" Savile to write brutally and bluntly about records.'

Jimmy Savile was now moving smoothly through the gears. He regaled the paper with how he had built up a £20,000-a-year income 'by outrageous showmanship and brilliant tycoonery'. He was travelling almost constantly between Leeds, Manchester and London and working 'at a furious pace from 10.30 a.m. to 3 a.m., on six days a week'. On the seventh, he said, he took his beloved mum out.

In a summer that witnessed Secretary of State for War John Profumo resign over his affair with Christine Keeler, £2.3 million stolen in the Great Train Robbery in Buckinghamshire and Pauline Reade's disappearance on her way to a dance in Manchester, the first victim of what would later be known as the Moors Murders, Jimmy Savile's moneymaking bandwagon rolled into Great Yarmouth where he was compère for a seasonal showcase at the Royal Aquarium. The main attraction was teenage singing sensation Helen Shapiro, who had first topped the charts as a 14-year-old. Among those lower down on the bill were Roy Castle and an upcoming comedian by the name of Ronnie Corbett.

Savile was driven to those weekend gigs on the coast in his E-Type Jaguar, insisting on travelling in slippers and sleeping most of the way. He didn't want to spend his wages on a hotel so stayed in a caravan that belonged to a friend.

After the shows, he did not have to go looking for female company because local girls queued up to speak to him or get his autograph. The result was a steady stream of visitors to his temporary digs.

When he wasn't working, sleeping or having sex, Savile was consumed by a desire to stay fit. He would regularly round up various acolytes and run for miles, often late at night. On other occasions, he would get on his bike and cycle over the Pennines to Leeds to see the Duchess.

This was a period of pandemonium and change, driven largely by the meteoric rise of The Beatles and the slew of home-grown beat groups that trailed in their wake. Teenage girls screamed through live performances, fainting and wetting themselves with excitement, and chased the Fab Four and anyone associated with them, in and out of venues up and down the country.

The phenomenon was described as 'Beatlemania' for the first time in a story published in the *Daily Mirror* on 15 October 1963. Three days later, Savile received the news that Bill Benny had been found dead in a flat in Rusholme. Benny had taken part in a wrestling bout at the Free Trade Hall after which his business partner Vic Lewis visited him in the dressing rooms. They had headed to the Cabaret Club for dinner before Lewis retired to his hotel and 'Bill took a girl back to his flat to continue his partying'.[4] Lewis received the news at seven o'clock next morning. 'I was stunned,' he wrote in his memoirs.

Three days later, the heavens opened on Benny's funeral in Manchester. Lewis remembered how people came from all over Britain, while Savile's recollections centred on how he stole the show. 'There are no flowers or decorations on the coffin at a Jewish funeral,' he explained at our final meeting. 'I turned up with a massive wreath and put it right on top of his coffin . . . Nobody said a word, nobody objected. The king thing was that I was the meanest man in Manchester, so I stood by the coffin and put a cigar on the lid so he could have a smoke on the way over. There wasn't a dry eye in the house.'

Benny's heart had given out while being fellated. The girl had been found trapped underneath his dead body. Within hours, though, Jimmy Savile had arrived at the flat where Benny's body was found. But why he felt the need to be in Bill Benny's flat so soon after his death, how he got in there and what he might have been looking for will likely remain a mystery.

If not his keen morbid fascination, one possible explanation is that Savile was recovering paperwork from a deal that had seen Bill Benny buy the failing Hulme Hippodrome theatre from the James Brennan cinema circuit for £35,000 in November 1960,[5] before selling it to Mecca for £50,000 just sixteen months later.[6] This 43 per cent profit was turned without any renovations being done, and no mention of Benny's name being made in the sale.

Could it have been a moneymaking scam cooked up by Benny and Savile, Mecca's man on the ground in Manchester?

26. A CROSS BETWEEN A BEATLE AND AN ALDWYCH FARCE CURATE

The story of Bill Benny's death is significant not only because he was Jimmy Savile's friend but also because of its direct link to his next career spin-off. Savile told me that the reason he became a wrestler was because Benny invited him to referee a benefit contest for a grappler who had died soon after a bout. He claimed to have refused, prompting Benny to call him a 'miserable bastard'. But Savile wasn't backing out, he insisted. He wanted to fight.

He had employed a number of wrestlers as bouncers at his dancehalls and been introduced via Benny to the many former grapplers who worked in and around Manchester's club scene. After surprising Benny with his willingness to climb between the ropes, six weeks were spent training at a local gym with Bert Jacobs, who would go on to coach Britain's wrestlers at the 1964 Olympic Games in Tokyo. The all-male, physical world of wrestling was one that Jimmy Savile felt at home in. It was useful to him in terms of recruiting minders and bouncers, but also for again being able to showcase his physical prowess.

The charity bout was to be staged at the Devonshire Sporting Club in Broughton, a venue previously owned by Bill Benny. The opponent was 'Gentleman' Jim Lewis, the undefeated welterweight champion of the world who, according to Savile, had 'a temper as long as my thumb'.

On Sunday, 15 December 1963, readers of Jimmy Savile's 'Pop-Talking' column in the *People* got the exclusive low-down on his grappling debut. 'The joint was packed tight, about a thousand people,' he wrote, before recounting how he spent seven rounds 'in the air flying in one direction or the other.'

Lewis took the lead with a body slam in round three before Savile equalised with a forward roll double Nelson in the fourth. 'Two quick body slams in the seventh' ultimately clinched the contest for the more experienced man. Savile broke a toe but described it as 'about the best experience of my life'.

It seems like too much of a coincidence that a benefit event in aid of a wrestler who had died after a bout should take place at Bill Benny's club just a few weeks after Benny's own death in identical circumstances. So why was Jimmy Savile so adamant that it was Benny who had invited him to fight and not that it was Benny he was fighting for?

In October 1963, seven days before Benny's death, two boys, aged 11 and 14, appeared at Salford Juvenile Court where they pleaded guilty to stealing a £152 watch from Jimmy Savile's flat. The 14-year-old was put on probation for two years, the 11-year-old was fined £10.[1] No mention was made of whether they broke into his flat or were invited inside.

Fifteen months after Savile's death, a joint report by the Metropolitan Police and the NSPCC recorded that 13 people had come forward to make allegations of being sexually assaulted by the disc jockey and dancehall impresario in the period to the end of 1963. One, a 10-year-old boy, was said to have spotted him outside a hotel, asked for an autograph and been assaulted by penetration.

In March 2013, a review by Her Majesty's Inspectorate of Constabulary (HMIC) into allegations and intelligence material concerning Jimmy Savile reported that, also in 1963, a male victim in Cheshire reported an allegation of rape by Jimmy Savile to his local police officer the day after it occurred. He was told to 'forget about it' and 'move on'. The officer did not make a report of the allegation and, consequently, an investigation was not undertaken.[2]

For all the carnage being wrought in secret – at his flat, in dark corridors and in dressing rooms – Jimmy Savile was doing an extremely effective job of masking the compulsive side to his nature. Wrestling gave him another physical outlet but, like his work as an increasingly high-profile DJ, it also offered the promise of contact with those he preyed on.

As he began to acquire the riches he'd always craved, the next career milestone on his journey to national stardom was approaching. In the summer of 1963, ITV launched a new weekly pop programme aimed at teenagers. Filmed in London and presented by Dusty Springfield, Keith Fordyce and the teenage Cathy McGowan, *Ready Steady Go*'s combination of mimed performances, interviews and a studio audience of gyrating young hipsters proved to be catnip to the nation's teens. '[It] was doing amazing things,' said Bill Cotton, then the BBC's assistant head of Light Entertainment.[3] 'A lot of people were being affected by it.'

Among them was the incongruous figure of Tom Sloan, the BBC's head of Light Entertainment. Sloan was a disciple of Sir John Reith, the BBC's first director general, a famously autocratic leader who insisted the corporation's purpose was to educate, inform and entertain. While the pop world was anathema to Sloan, he could not stand by and let ITV dominate. His response was to task Bill Cotton with making a rival show. Cotton quickly decided it should be distinct from its competitor by being based on the charts. It was a simple but clever plan as the charts were now dominated by British acts.

Cotton's first choice as producer was Johnnie Stewart who had produced *Jukebox Jury* and a wide range of other music-related programming for the BBC. A long series of planning meetings followed. At one of these meetings, a producer named T. Leslie Jackson suggested Jimmy Savile as a possible presenter of the new show, chiefly on the say-so of his teenage son. The idea was shot down immediately and Jackson went home that evening to inform his son, Paul, that Savile 'would never work on the BBC'.[4]

Nearly 40 years later, Paul Jackson, who went on to become a BBC producer himself, recalled what his father had said that evening: 'Savile was thought to be dodgy, there was a feeling he was heavy, you didn't cross him, he was a heavy dude.'

Stewart had other ideas. But first he would have to overcome the opposition of Tom Sloan. When Stewart had announced he wanted to use Savile on *Juke Box Jury*, Sloane told him, 'I don't want that man on television'. Stewart's reply was telling, given Savile's long career and history of offending at the BBC: 'Sorry baby, but that man is box office.'⁵

Stewart wasn't the only figure at the BBC who believed in Jimmy Savile. An ally was found in the shape of Barney Colehan, a producer who had worked on *The Good Old Days* and would go on to produce *It's a Knockout*. Colehan believed the new show should adapt Radio Luxembourg's successful *Teen and Twenty Disc Club* format for television and, after some debate, Bill Cotton was finally persuaded that Jimmy Savile should be called in to make a pilot.

It was Stewart who came up with the title of the new show: *Top of the Pops*. His vision included using a quartet of Radio Luxembourg DJs as rotating presenters. Sloan and Cotton were comfortable with Alan Freeman, Pete Murray and reigning *Melody Maker* DJ of the Year David Jacobs. Jimmy Savile, however, remained a problem. 'The BBC thought he was a bit strange alright,' said Bill Cotton. 'They didn't know quite what to make of him. He seemed to me to be a kind of 20th century clown.'⁶

But Jimmy Savile wasn't the only aspect of the new show that made the BBC establishment jumpy. The wider moral panic over pop music and the effect it was having on the nation's teens was a determining factor in the decision to broadcast the new show from the BBC's northern studios. It was agreed that a converted church on Dickenson Road in Manchester was a far safer place to house these young 'undesirables' than the corporation's sparkling new Television Centre in west London.

The MP Edward Heath had seemed to speak for a generation when he grumbled about not being able to understand what The Beatles were talking about. The axis of popular music had shifted, as Jimmy Savile discovered in December 1963 when he attended the opening night of The Beatles' Christmas Show at the Gaumont Theatre in Bradford. Comparing the noise from the audience to standing 'on the starting grid at Silverstone Grand Prix car race with 30 Formula One cars revving like mad', he told me that he went to the rear of the auditorium to see whether it was possible to hear the music. Spotting his blond hair in the distance, Paul McCartney dedicated a song to 'Jimmy Savile at the back', sparking a charge from frenzied fans who believed they might be able to pursue their quarry all the way to The Beatles' dressing rooms.

The next day, Savile dropped in for tea 'with the lads' at the Empire Theatre in Liverpool only to emerge to find the building besieged by fans. Thirty police officers were required to hold back the crowds, and a borrowed car was commandeered for the group's guest to make his getaway.

He told me The Beatles of that time reminded him of 'four university students that had just graduated'. He then looked up at the picture on the wall of his living room which showed him sat between John, Paul, Ringo and George with all five of them pretending to be asleep. 'They were quite special but also quite funny,' he said. 'When you are on top of the tree like that you become more defensive than funny.'

'We knew Jimmy and we worked with him, he was a DJ, an MC on some of the shows,' confirmed Paul McCartney.[7] On one occasion in the group's early days, they offered Savile a lift in their van across the Pennines after playing a gig in Yorkshire.

'He told us all these stories about his wartime exploits, how he had been buying chewing gum and nylons and all that, and selling them,' McCartney said. 'He had all sorts of stuff going on. He was the older hustler guy, and we were very amused by these stories because he was a great entertainer, but we dropped him off at his place outside his house and we said, "Can we come in for a coffee?" and he said, "Oh, no, not tonight lads."

'When he'd gone we thought, "Why doesn't he let us in? What is it, because most people would have let us in that we gave a lift to?" So we always thought there was something a little bit suspect.'

McCartney added they were different times. '[In] that post-war boom, girls and guys, it was a much more open scene . . . free love and the Pill had just come in, so it was a completely different scene. The other aspect, of course, is that we – though not quite Jimmy – were of the age of the girls.' In December 1963 Paul McCartney was 21; Jimmy Savile was 35.

'We were all young,' McCartney continued. 'So if you're now talking about a 17-, 18-year-old boy with a 15-year-old girl, we all knew that was illegal. We knew it and it was like, "No". But the closer we were in age, of course, the less it seemed to matter. We knew with under-16s it was illegal, so we didn't do it.'

McCartney insisted they always tried to be certain when it came to girls. 'We couldn't always be sure but there was a definite no-no involved in underage kids,' he said. 'Hey, listen, we didn't have to worry. There were plenty of over-16-year-olds.'

Liverpool's finest were still riding high at the top of the charts on New Year's Day 1964 as Jimmy Savile introduced the very first episode of *Top of the Pops*. It was a new show for a new era in which beat groups, led by The Beatles, would dominate the charts on both sides of the Atlantic. The powers at the BBC were less convinced, commissioning an initial run of just six weeks.

Savile spent the build-up to the first show working closely with Johnnie Stewart in trying to 'guesstimate' what the chart would look like on Wednesday 1 January. It was a crucial calculation; the charts were released at 8.30 a.m. on a Tuesday morning, leaving little over 24 hours to have a line-up in place to film. Typically, Savile claimed to have correctly predicted eight positions out of the first Top 10.

'Everyone's nerves were sticking out like porcupine quills,'[8] he recalled of the day of the first broadcast. All bar one person, that is, for in the very next breath Jimmy Savile claimed to be as relaxed and confident as ever. In fact, he had spent the previous evening in London at the *Sunday People*'s New Year's Ball, before catching the 4.20 a.m. train to Manchester.

The Rolling Stones, who Savile had promoted extensively on his Radio Luxembourg show, rolled up at the Dickenson Road studios in their pink VW tour van. They were at number 13 in the charts with 'I Want to Be Your Man'. The Hollies, at number 17 with

'Stay', spent the hours before transmission moaning about the chaos masquerading as rehearsals. 'It was ramshackle,' confirmed Keith Richards, 'like people were making it up as they went along. Jimmy Savile's energy kept it all together. He kept popping in and out, going "All right boys, all right? He energized the whole thing before the show went out."'[9]

At 6.36 p.m., the red studio light switched to 'live' and the cameras zoomed in on Jimmy Savile. He was dressed in a sober black shirt and seated at a desk in front of a large illuminated board showing the week's chart. Unlike the other presenters on the show, he did not have 'disc maid' Denise Sampey sitting beside him to put the pick-up arm on the record as the cue for the camera to fade up to the band miming on stage. As an experienced dancehall DJ, Savile argued this is what he did every night of the week.

The Rolling Stones opened the show, followed by studio 'performances' from Dusty Springfield ('I Only Want to Be With You'), The Dave Clark Five ('Glad All Over'), the Hollies ('Stay') and Swinging Blue Jeans ('Hippy Hippy Shake'). In between were pre-recorded items with Cliff Richard with The Shadows and Freddie and The Dreamers. The finale arrived with the week's number 1 single, 'I Want to Hold Your Hand' by The Beatles. As the group were on tour in America the song was played over a montage of news clips.

'Man I lost a lot of flesh . . . because a first ever show of a series can be murder,' Savile reflected in the *Sunday People* the following week. Not that much it seems: on leaving the studios on Dickinson Road, he said he dropped into the Three Coins on Fountain Street before catching the 11.55 p.m. train back to London, arriving at 7.15 a.m. the next morning. From there, he went straight to Radio Luxembourg to 'record five shows and four commercials'. In other words: business as usual.

Top of the Pops quickly confounded the sceptics within the BBC, although there were plenty of dissenting voices among the letters from viewers: 'What an odd looking individual,' remarked a solicitor of the first show's host, while others described Jimmy

Savile variously as 'a cross between a Beatle and an Aldwych farce curate'; 'like a Presbyterian minister'; and 'mutton dressed as lamb'. The most vitriolic comments came from a retired naval officer who wrote, 'Really horrific. It ought to have an X certificate. And there was Mr Savile presiding over the orgy like a Puritan clergyman resurrected from his own churchyard.'[10]

Jimmy Savile presented the show once a month for the first three years of its long lifespan. He was the only one of the four presenters who wasn't briefed in advance on his links by Johnnie Stewart, the only one not to require the services of the 'disc maid' and the only one not to wear a suit. 'I wore what I used to wear in the dance-halls, which was teenage clothes,' explained the man who had not been a teenager for 16 years when the first show went out.

I t was my first visit to see Jimmy Savile in the Scarborough flat he bought for his mother, and he had extended me the 'honour' of sleeping in the room he kept as a shrine to her.

In her room, the narrow single bed was adorned with a pink bedspread bearing his initials in a large gold shield. Above the bedhead was an amateurish pencil drawing of the only woman that he ever loved. I knew from Louis Theroux's documentary that her laundered clothes were hanging in the slim wardrobe on the far side of the room, sheathed in polythene to keep them fresh. On a small dressing table with a mirror stood a white crucifix and a framed picture of Savile sitting at the feet of the Duchess. She was in an armchair, knitting happily. He was in a cut-off robe and white slippers leafing through what looked like fan mail.

After a night of deep slumber, interrupted only by a strange dream about someone lying on the floor next to the bed, I rose to find Savile in his armchair, looking out to sea. The room was heavy with the aroma of cigar smoke. On the low coffee table was an iced biscuit with a glazed cherry on top. It was, he explained, a 'Scarborough breakfast'. Anything more substantial was unlikely for a man who refused to have cookers in his flats because they would give women the wrong idea. And the wrong idea, as he always insisted, would only lead to 'brain damage'.

We talked about Elvis Presley, who he met on two visits to the United States. 'His devastating quality was that he was shy,' said Savile. 'Of course, any bird will tell you that if you get a good looking kid who's shy that brings out the 100 per cent predator in all women. They are so used to people like me and you being wide-heads, full of SOS – Same Old Shit – they feel comfortable with the shy ones.' It was the second time Savile had told me he thought we were alike. He was trying to reel me in.

I asked him whether there was ever a point when he thought he was falling in love. Rather than answer the question, he began telling me a familiar story about his process of deduction in the dancehalls, one that invariably meant he was left with at least 10 girls to choose from on any given night. Thankfully, before he could continue down the same well-trodden path, another thought occurred to him. 'I didn't think it was fair to tell one of them that they were the one,' he said. 'I knew I couldn't stick with it. Girls weren't the same in those days. They didn't phone you up in tears. Brain damage didn't come in for another 10 or 15 years.'

He was off and running now. 'In the late Fifties, early Sixties, there was no booze, no drugs and you had a roomful of people where you could have a conversation with any one of them. Because you weren't supposed to get your leg over that was the salient point why people wanted to do it. Girls weren't supposed to get screwed so that's why they wanted to get screwed. Lads did it because there was a big element of you're not supposed to do it.'

He took a deep puff on his cigar. 'The exciting time was when it wasn't safe and you weren't supposed to do it. There was no brain damage about it. There were no floods of tears next day.'

Jimmy Savile was 81 by this time. I asked him whether he was 'still active'. 'Yes, oh yes. I'm active in a sort of non-pushy way because there are enough people in the eight different places that I live. When I'm in town I'll get a phone call and someone will come over and see me. I don't need to be pushy. Never did.'

More than three years later, we were sitting in the same room. He had talked about the period after the war when 'everybody was confused, nobody had a job and shops didn't sell anything because nobody had any money to buy anything'. He had then segued straight into 'Flower Power', which confused me. I could not imagine

Jimmy Savile as a hippy – he was too driven, too opportunistic and too much of a capitalist. Free was a word he feared and loathed.

Once he'd finished his point I asked him when he thought sex became such a salacious topic in society. 'It was only when the tabloids started going lower orders with tits and bums that it started,' he muttered. 'What are tits and bums for? Sex. So the whole thing drifted that way and then you've got shame and then you've got divorces and then you've got big divorce settlements and things like that. So the whole thing built into a structure. It wasn't an overnight thing. But the sex thing was almost overnight because girls objected to being used as dustbins when they got the pill.'

But surely the pill gave women a greater sense of sexual liberation? 'It changed things overnight,' he argued. 'It must have reduced the sex practice by a good eighty per cent.' I tried not to smirk; 'sex practice' was just about the most functional description I had heard. He would not have noticed anyway because he was staring ahead, seemingly addressing the horizon. 'Women all of a sudden became terribly independent,' he continued, 'and they weren't going to be used as an ashtray, and quite rightly so.'

I told him I had recently seen *Nowhere Boy*, the feature film about John Lennon's adolescence. In that there seemed to be plenty of casual sex around the time Lennon formed The Quarrymen and was playing skiffle at garden fetes.

'I've had all that down the years,' said Savile. 'Girls wanted to be like that, not because they wanted the fella; they wanted to be like that because they wanted to be like that. The end product – the fella – was less important than the concept. They would wait outside the stage door of a theatre for hours and it was the waiting that they wanted. If a fella came out and said, "Right, I want three of you to come in for sex – you, you and you" they would have been terribly shocked. That wasn't what they were there for. It was the doing of it that was the thing, not so much the end product. The important bit was being with the crowd and waiting outside.'

He explained that the first time a crowd had screamed at a 'pop star' was in the 1940s in the narrow cul-de-sac leading to the Savoy Hotel. 'Johnny Ray was there and all these women were blocking the front of the hotel. This mobbing thing had never happened before. He went up onto a balcony and waved at the crowd and they all went away. Then it turned into mass hysteria with The Beatles.

'I worked with The Beatles on their Christmas Show and the copper said, "Jimmy, if you're not in the theatre by 1 p.m. we cannot guarantee you getting in at all." They weren't on until half past six at night – that's where that picture was taken.' He pointed to the same photograph of him with The Beatles as he had on his wall in Leeds. I realised it was not the only duplicate image on display. I wondered how many times such artefacts had been used as prompts, or props, for his stories.

'They did two shows a night,' he continued. 'I had to do a sketch with them . . . but it didn't work so we didn't do it . . . It was the waiting outside that was the thing, you see. There was this peculiar club of waiting outside and it wasn't the salivating at the thought of being taken in hand by one of The Beatles because that couldn't happen. It was the being there and being in the crowd outside.' It sounded like he was protesting too much – painting a convenient tableau of the times.

'I knew girls who would fantasise over the Cliffs of this world but would be quite happy to go and get a bit of leg over with their boyfriend,' he said. 'I was sitting with Cliff once in his dressing room and this kid walked in, lamped him and walked back out again . . . There was a perfectly logical explanation: his girlfriend was besotted with Cliff and he had to sit with her while she was doing all this carrying on. So before he left the theatre he decided he was going to go back stage and give him a clump. She was quite happy with her boyfriend but she fantasised over Cliff.'

'And what did you do?' I asked.

'Well, I restrained him and handed him over to the authorities.' Jimmy Savile squeezed out another of his low, slow and malevolent laughs. 'It was all good fun. The whole thing was enormous, enormous fun. It wasn't serious and it wasn't vicious and it wasn't wicked and it wasn't bad or taking liberties with people you shouldn't take liberties with. Nothing like that. It was a dead straight pull time.'

28. OUT OF THE MOUTHS OF BABES AND SUCKLINGS

Jimmy Savile returned to Leeds each week to call on his mother. On one such visit in the early 1960s he found her shivering in front of the electric fire, wrapped in shawls and with her feet up on the chair. 'She looked dreadful,' he told me. We were sitting in the flat that he bought her on the Esplanade at Scarborough, and in which he still kept her bedroom as a shrine more than 30 years after her death.

Savile explained how he paid for his mother to spend a few weeks convalescing with the Little Sisters of the Poor in the home on the opposite side of Consort Terrace. 'The money it cost me per week to look after her was what I would have spent on a night out,' he said, 'and I suddenly realised, "Holy shit, that's what money can do for you. It really can save your life."'

From that moment on, he claimed money only represented what it could be used for to help his mother: 'I made sure that she had whatever she needed,' he said.

After her illness, he told me she complained about living alone in Leeds: 'So I said to her, "Right, find yourself somewhere to live."' When she was still moaning a few months later, he said he put her in the car and drove to Scarborough. At this point, he got up and went to the window and pointed down at the pavement: 'I parked out there where I used to fasten my cycle to the railings,' he said.

Scarborough held fond memories from his outings as a child and, later, his cycling excursions from Leeds to the coast. 'I got out, leaving her in the motor so I could have a look at the spectacular view,' he went on. 'And as I turned round to get in the car

I looked up and there was a block of flats. I rang the bell and asked whether any of them were for sale. [A woman] told me one was for rent on the ground floor for seven pound a week. I said, "I'll have it." That was the Monday and the Duchess moved in on the Thursday.' Not long afterwards, he moved her upstairs after buying what he described as 'the king flat because it has views all the way round and a balcony'.

Later that day, as we stood on that same balcony looking out to sea, he told me another story about his mother and Scarborough. 'I had a caravan on the cliff tops,' he said, pointing south over the headland towards Filey. 'When the Duchess was alive it didn't do – and I had too much respect – to take girls back. If there were any assignations or dates we would drive down to the caravan five miles away.

'The kids and the young people on the caravan site would recognise whatever car I turned up in. One day they ran up, and I got out with a girl, and this kid asked, "Who's she?" I told them she was my sister. When I came out half an hour later, this same kid said, "She's not your sister." I told her she was but he had seen me laid on top of her. He had peeped in through the curtains. Rumbled in the caravan,' he hooted. 'Out of the mouths of babes and sucklings.'

Scarborough's seafront was to provide easy pickings for Jimmy Savile, something he alluded to in his autobiography. One stormy night in early 1965,[1] he had driven his E-Type Jaguar down to the front because, as he described it, he wanted to look at the waves crashing over the front. Suddenly, out of the storm, a young girl banged on the window of the car. He said he opened the door, pulled her in and closed the door again before the next wave crashed over the bonnet.

'The inside of an E-Type is not over capacious,' he wrote, 'and just now seemed to be full of wet body, long black hair, legs and bikini panties.' He explained the girl had been sitting in a nearby car with her parents when she saw him go through the barrier. She had run along the sea road after him. 'And here she was,' he marvelled. 'Such a start had to mean a good night.'[2]

Savile reported that he reversed the car 500 yards whereupon the girl told her parents that she was going for a drive with her new friend. He then added, 'Should the reader feel that her folks appear unconcerned, you would not believe the stories I might tell you about some parents.' He wrote these words in 1974 when he was coming up to his 48th birthday.

His account described how they drove around for a while, talking and smoking until 'steam started to come out' of his ears. Realising that a two-seater sports car was not conducive to what he had in mind, 'a diabolical plan formed within'. Taking her to the Scarborough flat, he wrote, 'was out of the question because the Duchess was in residence' so he headed instead to a garage where he kept his convertible Rolls-Royce. The car, he added with relish, had fold-back seats and, 'seeing as I'd saved her from a watery grave she was duly appreciative'. The girl was dropped back at her parents' house at 4 a.m.

He told readers of his newspaper column that he'd agreed to speak to the girl on the phone the following week. But when he called her, she said it would not work out because, in her words, 'You've got too much money, and I love you.'[3] In his autobiography, he embellished the story still further by stating that the girl left town that week 'to work away', although he received Christmas cards from her for some years to come.

Nothing about it rings true: the reasons the girl gave for not seeing him again despite what she felt for him, the convenient detail that she moved away soon afterwards, or the coda that he'd treated her so well that she remained in touch via cards at Christmas.

It is a story that shows how comfortable Jimmy Savile felt about putting his secrets out there for all to see. Perhaps he enjoyed the thrill: the allusion to the girl's age in the reference to her being accompanied by her parents; the fact she was of an age where she needed their consent to go off with him; his caveat that it was the girl, not him, who suggested they go off in his car. But most importantly, by writing about it in a national newspaper the very next week, Jimmy Savile's version of events – his alibi – was safely recorded in print.

Just a couple of months later, in May 1965, he decided to treat his mother to a trip to London. He put her up at the Hilton while he preferred to stay in a shabby hotel on Hunter Street. It was owned by Bill Mills, the proprietor of his previous London base, the Aaland Hotel. He'd had to move out of the Aaland in March, along with the 'young pop artists' occupying the other 13 rooms because the building on Coram Street was due for demolition. As Mills explained, 'We were told before Christmas that we would have to go, but I let the kids stay on for as long as I could.'[4]

'My Jimmy is more comfortable here than being in the Dorchester,'[5] Agnes Savile told a reporter while sipping on a cup of tea at his new digs just off Russell Square. 'He doesn't like the big hard atmosphere of the big hotels,' she added. Was this anything to do with his penchant for bringing young girls back at all hours of the morning?

It was the first time Jimmy Savile's mother had been interviewed by a national newspaper, and what she said offers a rare insight into their unusual relationship. 'My Jimmy is just an ordinary sort of chap,' she insisted. 'I know some people are outraged by him, but really he is playing to the public. It's all an act. I know, I'm his mother.

'He has always wanted me to have the very best', she went on. 'He's given me a picture postcard flat at Scarborough overlooking the sea, put a taxi at my disposal so I needn't walk anywhere, and an open credit account at any shop. Nothing is too much trouble for elderly people or youngsters, he helps them as much as he can.'

Agnes Savile spoke of how her youngest son had helped women and old people off the trams in Leeds as a child. 'Now he opens church fetes and functions,' she said. 'Yes, he does it free . . .' In fact, she said he did too much for charities: 'He never seems to have any time to relax,' she added. 'Even if he gets into a train he is signing autographs.'

The lack of girlfriend or any apparent romance in her son's life was clearly being noted by this time because the reporter's final question to Agnes Savile was whether she would like him to marry. 'Yes, but in the entertainment world it is a great hazard,' she replied. 'In Manchester, three or four thousand teenagers attend his record sessions; it must be a very understanding wife who would put up with all the adulation he gets. I have never heard him say he wanted to get married. But I hope he does one day when he retires for in the entertainment world there is no happiness at all.'

In the Duchess's 'king flat' in Wessex Court on Scarborough's Esplanade, I probed Jimmy Savile about his relationship with his mother. He was adamant there was 'no tactile affection'[6] during his childhood, and that he had to learn how to enjoy her. It wasn't love but friendship, he said.

I wanted to know how their relationship evolved in the years following his father's death, and how it developed to the point where he once described it as 'living through her proxy'. The first thing he told me was, 'She was ruthless.'

It's an assessment that Tony Calder, who met Agnes Savile when he went to stay with Savile in the Mecca house in Leeds, agrees with. He describes her as 'domineering', and Savile's devotion was such that it got 'to the point where it was embarrassing'.

'He'd get up on a Sunday morning in that dirty fucking house – his shagging house in Leeds. His mum lived round the corner. He'd walk round and see her, and they'd go to church.' Savile, Calder recalled, would be 'kissing her hand coming out of the church. He had his arm around her like she was his girlfriend. It was a bit sad.

'You could see that he'd never have a serious relationship with another woman while his mother was alive because she wouldn't approve of it,' he says. 'That was his whole take on it: "I'm shagging like crazy because she doesn't know about it and I see her on Sunday to go to church and I see her in the week when I've bought things for her."'

When Calder chided Savile for the fact he'd never be famous beyond the shores of Britain, he replied that he didn't care because it would be too far away from his mother. '"Mother": she was always "Mother",' Calder recalls. 'Or "the Duchess". She wasn't very pleasant to many of the people with him and she treated me like one of the ponces around her son.'

Another source has warmer memories of Agnes. He too confirms her youngest son was in thrall to her. 'He loved her to death. But the Duchess was the boss . . . [when he visited her] he had to behave himself. He couldn't be smart. He became a different Jim. "Now Jimmy, I want you to sort this out, go down to the shop for me and this window needs fixing." It was all that.'

A young Mancunian DJ named Dave Eager became Jimmy's unofficial assistant at the top Ten Club. 'All [Jimmy] ever said about his childhood to me,' says Eager, 'was that his mother and him always had a relationship where it was constantly on test.'

Eager recounted how such conversations played out: '"What are you buying me for my birthday, Jim?" "What do you think I'm buying you? A set of Pyrex dishes." "What?" "Somebody like you at your age should be in the kitchen cooking food. So Pyrex dishes is what you're having." "No, I'm not." "Yes, you are." His mother, because of her nature, would never, ever ask Jim for money. So there was always this little game.' Eager states Agnes treated her son 'like a little boy. He never grew up in her eyes.'

Another constant in their relationship, it seems, was Agnes's sense of disapproval. According to another of Agnes's visitors: 'She'd go, "I don't know how he dares go out dressed like that." . . . She'd tell me stories about when he was little, like he used to wear a big hat when [they] went to the shops. The stories were from when she had control of him and now he was out of her control.'

Agnes would regularly moan about him, often when he was within earshot: '"He doesn't come anymore. He used to come and see me every night but now I don't hear from him for a week sometimes."' Eager describes such exchanges as a test of how much control Agnes still exerted.

The more he provided, the tighter her grip on him. 'She had a lurking suspicion that I would come unstuck sooner or later,' Savile wrote in his autobiography.[7] He also said she never watched him on television or congratulated him on his achievements, and lived in constant fear of the police knocking at the door: 'She thought I was stealing all the money,' he said.[8]

And yet, Jimmy Savile's mother became his most regular and conspicuous companion. 'Bit by bit she turned into a terrific sort of pal,' he told me. 'I found that me teaming round with her – I used to take her to functions and awards dinners; she was only five foot tall and had this golden hair – well, people loved it.' They went on holidays together to the Imperial Hotel in Torquay, where Agnes enjoyed playing the one-armed bandits in amusement arcades, and Rome to visit the Vatican. Bizarrely, Savile maintained she had 'the energy of a teenager and could pleasure all night as often as the opportunity arose'.[9]

In 1991, Jimmy Savile told Anthony Clare that he realised he could have a better time 'teaming' about with his mother because a conventional girlfriend would give him 'brain damage'.[10] With the Duchess he could have a meal or take off somewhere with no strings attached. They had a great time together; a time, Savile insisted, 'you couldn't have . . . with a girl'. When Clare asked him why, he replied, 'Well, because a girl would be a different kettle of fish, because a girl is more of a partnership. As against the Duchess – she brought me up for the first part of her life and I brought her up for the second part of her life.'

Over the course of his life, Jimmy Savile offered many reasons for why he never married. He claimed that his peripatetic lifestyle legislated against it. He argued there were just too many girls. He said it was because he had never been in love. They are very possibly true, although his preference for girls under the legal age of consent was surely a more conspicuous obstacle. It is also tempting to speculate that the certain knowledge he had to provide for his mother, to ensure above all else that she would never want for anything again, left an emotional void in his life.

Dave Eager recalls one particular conversation in the 1960s. They were discussing relationships and Savile said, 'You could meet somebody, think, "You look beautiful" now and . . . have a great relationship. But if they had a stroke would you be prepared to look after them for the rest of your life? If the answer is you're not sure, you're not giving them 100 per cent commitment.' Eager says that years later Savile confirmed this was exactly how he felt about marriage.

'That's why he had his mother living with him,' Eager says. '[Savile said] "I don't want to think there's nobody looking after her. She's my mum." And that's what he meant about family. That's why he got involved with all the charities because they were his family. He was giving to them and getting back emotion.'

In the aftermath of the revelations about Jimmy Savile, Jeff Dexter said he believed Jimmy was a victim himself. I have wondered this myself and suggested to Dexter that Savile could have been abused as a child. 'He never had a proper girlfriend,' he replied. 'He loved his mother. He should have really been in care. Instead he created millions and millions of pounds of charity for lots of other people because he really didn't know who the fuck he was.'

Not long after his difficult encounter with Jimmy Savile for the *In the Psychiatrist's Chair* series, Anthony Clare wrote a newspaper article about the hold powerful mothers can have over their sons: 'The denigrating, rejecting mother can breed in her son a view of women as controlling and castrating that survives into adult life and affects and contaminates his relationship with women. Such a son may spend a lifetime taking revenge or trying to win the approval that eluded him in childhood. Either way, it is the women in his life who will bear the brunt.'[11]

Savile preferred to see it another way: '[The Duchess] doesn't nag me to get married and settle down, but in any case there is no question of it. If I fell into the arms of some other woman, I wouldn't be able to look after my Mum so well, and that wouldn't be fair.'[12]

With its limited capacity, the Upper Broughton Assembly Rooms was only ever going to be a staging post until something bigger came along. Fate intervened just 12 days after the first episode of *Top of the Pops* when the building was gutted by fire. Everyone was forced to flee the building, including 40 people preparing for a wedding party on the floor below. A night porter had to be plucked from the roof by firemen.

Savile had already moved on. The Belle Vue complex was Manchester's self-proclaimed 'Showground to the World', containing myriad attractions including hotels, pubs and theatres, zoological gardens, a fairground and a speedway stadium. It also boasted Europe's largest ballroom, the New Elizabethan. Sam Mason was its general manager, and hired Savile to bring his crowd-pulling skills to Sunday nights at his vast venue.

Savile went to take a look around. He was not overly impressed by what they saw. Belle Vue's team of joiners were instructed to build a revolving stage tiered like a wedding cake, with a DJ box flanked by two specially commissioned 6ft by 4ft speakers containing huge bass bins. When the stage revolved, the guest groups would appear from the other side.

Forty years later, Savile told me that he regarded Mason's invitation to fill the 3,500-capacity dancehall as a challenge: 'I'd never do anything from a purely egotistical point of view,' he maintained. 'I'd do it for money, I'd do it to get a crowd going for a charity do, yes.' He took on Belle Vue, he explained, 'just to see if the brain still worked'.

Posters and newspaper advertisements for the new-look Top Ten Club promised 'Fabulous Top Recording Groups and Artistes' plus 'Top international DJ Jimmy Savile with his unique Sound Power Disc Deck'. Curiously, Savile was pictured alongside holding a small chimpanzee from the zoo. 'It's a Gas! It's a Ball! It's Like Crazy Man!' screamed the text, and the teenagers of Manchester seemed to concur.

On Sunday evenings, the Top Ten Club's star attraction pulled up either in his Rolls-Royce, E-Type or bubble car, which would be parked outside the entrance for the young patrons to gawp at. And when the stage revolved bringing him to the front, he signalled his entrance by blowing on a hunting horn. A conspicuous adornment to the specially commissioned DJ box was a framed picture of Savile shaking hands with Elvis Presley.

Alan Leeke remembers his first visit to the Top Ten Club in 1963. He was living with his parents in Gorton, just a 10-minute walk from the venue. '[It] was membership only to get round the Sunday laws at the time,' he says. 'You had to be 16 to go but lots of people, myself included, altered the date of birth on the membership card. It was only typed on. I was probably 15 when I started going.' He describes the clientele as 'completely teenage'.

Leeke recalls that Savile came on last, after the featured band had played, and that none of the other DJs were allowed to play records from the current Top 20. Leeke also says he witnessed Jimmy Savile regularly going off with girls from the Top Ten Club in his car, either before he went on stage or after he came off. 'He'd go off and come back 20 minutes later or half an hour later. He always had girls from their mid to late teens, from what I could see.' Leeke says it was well known that Jimmy Savile liked them young.

When I ask how he thinks he got away with it, Leeke replies, 'Because a lot of the girls thought they were the only ones that it happened to. I think they realised afterwards it wasn't, but by then it was too late to say anything . . . [Savile] loved them. That was his attitude. The more he could get the better he liked it.'

As a young man, Leeke admits to being 'star struck' by the famous DJ, and reveals he was among a group of youngsters invited back to the Black Pad one night after the ballroom closed.

Another visitor confirmed there was a steady stream of people coming to the flat: 'Girls came round to the pad to have a coffee and a tea and a chat. They'd stay for a while . . . and then they'd go away smiling having enjoyed themselves.'

He went on to say that when Savile wasn't working or doing gigs at dancehalls, girls would start arriving from lunchtime. 'Then when they'd gone another group would come round at four o'clock. And they'd have a nice time and go away. And then at about six o'clock, another couple of girls would come round for a cup of tea. And they'd go away smiling. It was nice, friendly things.'

I asked what was meant by 'nice friendly things'. The reply? 'Tea and friendliness.' When I asked what sort of girls Jimmy went for, the answer was: 'I think Jim preferred girly girls rather than smart girls. When the girls lost the giggle, it's gone; that sort of girl. Girls who are prepared to do a cartwheel and jump and dance and have a giggle and a laugh. Not the ones that go to work and be dead straight and sensible. He liked fun girls, show girls.'

In 1964, Jimmy Savile was advertising his taste for teenage girls in his weekly newspaper column. There were numerous mentions of 'Miss Twinkle', otherwise known as Lynn Ripley, who was only 16 and dating Dec Cluskey of The Bachelors when she entered the charts in November that year with 'Terry', a teenage tragedy song recorded for Decca about the death of a boyfriend in a motorcycle crash. The record was banned by the BBC who considered it to be in bad taste. Savile wrote about 'Miss Twinkle' calling round, most probably to the Aaland Hotel, and seemed to be very interested in the state of her love life.

As well as being Savile's reliable hunting ground for teenage girls, the Top Ten Club was also where the BBC recruited youngsters for the studio audience of *Top of the Pops*. Cecil Korer was an assistant producer on the show who although only 29, looked considerably older; so much so that he wore a wig during recordings to disguise his balding head among all the dancing youngsters. One of Korer's duties was to go talent spotting on Sundays at Belle Vue and hand out tickets for the next week's show.

'The audience were always young teenagers, from 13 up to 16 or 17,' confirms Stanley Dorfman, who directed *Top of the Pops* once a fortnight from the show's inception in January 1964. 'Kids were dying to be on it . . . If they were dancers and were attractive, obviously they got on.'

Dorfman remembers Jimmy Savile for being 'absolutely brilliant' as a presenter. 'He was totally outgoing, he had the kids right away. They adored him because he talked like them and he knew about the music and he was always funny.'

Part of the attraction, Dorfman believes, was they knew Savile was on friendly terms with many of their idols. He shared a table with The Beatles and Brian Epstein at Mecca's prestigious Carl-Alan Awards at the Empire Ballroom, Leicester Square, and as compère of the first *NME* Poll Winners Party, he introduced the Fab Four to Wembley's packed Empire Pool. Bounding onto the stage in a light suit, dark glasses and a variety of hats, the zany, platinum-haired DJ told screaming fans, 'Nowhere in the whole wide world has such a concert been assembled.' It was a claim supported by the line-up: The Beatles, Manfred Mann, The Tremeloes, Cliff Richard, Billy J. Kramer, Freddy and The Dreamers, Kathy Kirby, Gerry and The Pacemakers and The Rolling Stones.

The Stones were riding high in the charts at the time with 'Not Fade Away', their first big hit. After championing the group to the doubting bosses at Decca, Savile had set about applying a positive spin to five young men being portrayed as the antithesis of the clean-cut 'Mop Tops'.

He told me that he had witnessed the 'mini riots' at some of the Stones' early gigs and reckoned they played on their reputation for trouble. 'They were the sort of group that almost promoted it,' Savile said. 'It went with the territory but at the height of the rioting, if you parked outside Mick Jagger's house you would see him at 11 o'clock in the morning going down the road to the Queen's Club with a tennis bag and tennis gear. It was all part of the game.'

That summer, shortly after Savile's newspaper column prediction had come to pass that 'It's All Over Now' would give the Stones their first number 1 record, the group were booked to play at the Top Ten Club at Belle Vue.

The band flew in from a short tour of northern Europe and their reputation seemed to follow them. According to those who were there, the atmosphere that night in the New Elizabethan Ballroom was febrile, and not even Savile's team of infamous doormen could stop fights breaking out across the venue. At one point, the police were called in to restore order. Jimmy Savile stood at the front of the revolving stage playing records to try to relieve the tension.

It was then, he said, that one of his disc jockeys informed him The Stones were refusing to go on. Instructing the DJ to take over, Savile went to the back of the revolving stage to find out what the problem was. It transpired that The Stones' instruments had got lost in transit and they were refusing to use those belonging to the support group.

Savile's response was characteristically blunt: he pointed to where three of his largest minders were standing and growled, 'You've got the time it takes this stage to revolve to make your mind up . . . If you're not going to play you're going to be unconscious because my minders are going to chin all of you.' All except drummer Charlie Watts, that is. Savile claimed that Watts looked him up and down before speaking. 'You would, wouldn't you?' he said. 'No danger,' replied Savile. 'And I'll throw you to the fucking audience. I guarantee you that.'

Left with no choice, The Rolling Stones grabbed the instruments on offer and climbed onto the revolving stage. Meanwhile, Jimmy Savile took up a position on the top tier from where he could keep an eye on the group, his dancehall and, most importantly, savour his victory. 'I would have had the bastards chinned and slung to the crowd,' he told me. 'If they'd lived or died, it wouldn't have mattered to me.'

Bill Wyman confirms the story is true: 'Eventually, after prolonged arguments, we agreed (or were forced!) to go on stage by Jimmy Savile, the compere, and the management', he wrote in his memoirs.[1]

Jimmy Savile was quite prepared to use violence, whether real or threatened. Todd Slaughter was a teenage Elvis Presley fanatic who had met Savile in Great Yarmouth in the summer of 1963. They had stayed in touch, and the following spring Slaughter visited London to appear on *The Teen and Twenty Disc Club* to promote his 'Elvis via Telstar' campaign which, it was hoped, would culminate in a live concert being beamed to Europe using the new satellite.

On his way to see Savile at the Aaland Hotel, Slaughter says he was pounced on by 'a bunch of ne'er-do-wells'. Help was at hand. 'Jimmy appeared,' he says, 'and went up to one and put his hand at the side of his face and plunged his thumb into the guy's eye socket. What spurted out was horrific.'

Jimmy Savile was named *Melody Maker*'s Disc Jockey of the Year in September 1964, and took his mother along to the gala lunch at the Savoy Hotel as his special guest. In deposing the suave, well-spoken and smartly dressed David Jacobs, this strangely-attired, working-class son of Yorkshire had struck an early blow for 'the classless society' that Labour leader Harold Wilson would outline on becoming prime minister less than a month later.

Not everyone was pleased, it seemed: 'Although disc jockey Jimmy Savile may be "with it" I think it is ridiculous of him to keep his age secret,' wrote Miss B.F. Tilehurst in a letter published in the *Daily Mirror*. 'It is obvious he hasn't been a teenager for at least fifteen years. As for that silly hair . . . get it cut!'

The truth was that Jimmy Savile was now closing in on his 38th birthday, making him much older than almost everyone in the pop world he now ruled. John Lennon was 24, Paul McCartney was 22, Mick Jagger and Keith Richards were 21. When she made her *Top of the Pops* debut in February 1964, Cilla Black was just 20. 'To me,' said Black, 'Jimmy Savile seemed like an old man even then.'[2]

Perhaps it was his age that explained why Savile viewed the pop business differently to those caught up in its maelstrom. His newspaper columns were ripe with allusions to what he clearly considered to be the most important aspect of this new industry.

After returning from his second trip to California to see Elvis Presley in April 1964, he pondered on Colonel Tom Parker, 'the cash brain behind Elvis'[3] and marvelled at how together they were making £40,000 a week. On other occasions, he talked about sitting in the leather chairs at Isow's restaurant in the West End and watching the 'the big brains' at work while ruminating on how a 'star can make £1,000 a week, but if a theatre is a sell-out, a promoter can make £1,000 a night'. When quantifying the growing popularity of The Rolling Stones, he referred not to record sales but the fact they were 'grossing five or six hundred pounds a week'. To Jimmy Savile, pop music was nothing but business.

His own wealth remained his most reliable source of copy, though, whether in writing about taking delivery of a new Rolls-Royce, insuring himself for a £1 million before taking a helicopter flight to open a night club in Rhyl or spending £250 on a pair of 'black jewelled mink shoes'. In December 1964, a profile in the *Daily Sketch* described him as crouching by the gas fire 'like a beatnik hitch-hiker who had just borrowed enough money to pay for a night's kip in [an] obscure hotel'.[4] And yet, as the article reported, Jimmy Savile was now making £40,000 a year for himself and another £46,000 for charity.

His moneymaking enterprises now included appearing in films (*Ferry Across the Mersey*) and fronting TV specials for foreign markets (*Pop Gear*). After the success of his debut bout in

Manchester, he was snapped up on a lucrative five-year contract by wrestling promoter George Rel.

In the dilapidated flat in Manchester where Savile carried on living, however, there was little more than a kettle and a single ring for heating baked beans. If anyone drove him south to London, they were made to sleep on the floor of his 18-shilling-a-night room at the Aaland Hotel.

Savile's star continued to rise and his banner year was capped when he was hired as compère of The Beatles' 1964 Christmas Show at Hammersmith Odeon. He told me the building was under permanent siege from screaming fans, and that he passed the hours before the curtain went up by helping young girls to spend some priceless seconds with their heroes. 'I finished up all week running up and down stairs like a flippin' yo-yo with deserving causes until the Fab Four started to call me Dr Dogood,' he said.

It was a label he liked, and corresponded with how he determined the world should see him as. Although he continued to exhibit a perverse pride in his tight-fistedness, especially when it came to his own living arrangements, Jimmy Savile was becoming increasingly well known for his charity work; the do-gooding somehow counterbalancing what he was demanding and taking from the young people who looked up to him. His increasingly high-profile acts of spontaneous kindness to help others, he claimed, influenced how he came to organise his perpetual motion lifestyle.

'I came to a crossroads,' Savile said. 'I found I was making enough money out of one or two days of work to live like a millionaire. What do you do in this situation? Do you turn into a money grabber? Or do you see if there is anybody to be helped along the way? I chose the latter path.'[5]

But like the many facets of Jimmy Savile's existence, the reality wasn't quite as simple as that. While he undoubtedly generated very significant sums for a variety of good causes over the course of his life, he was and remained a money grabber to his core. And if his charitable deeds were designed to salve a guilty conscience, there is evidence he knew he had to raise a lot to balance the ledger.

In early October 2012, a woman came forward to reveal that Jimmy Savile raped her in his hotel near Russell Square in 1964. She was a 16-year-old virgin at the time.

The woman said they had first met when she appeared on his Radio Luxembourg show to talk about her Elvis Presley fan club. Savile was due to fly out to America soon afterwards to pay his second visit to 'the King', and he asked the girl for a picture of herself that he could take and show to her idol.

According to the woman, who did not want to reveal her identity, on returning from the States, Savile phoned her house and told her that he had a present for her from Elvis. She was understandably thrilled and recalled walking to the London hotel where Savile was staying. She said he met her in his pyjamas. He then took her into his room, pinned her to the wall and started kissing her. The woman said she pleaded for him to stop. He whispered, 'You're an angel,'[6] before pushing her onto the bed and raping her.

The woman, who said she weighed just six and a half stone at the time, said, 'I couldn't stop him. I was telling him it hurt. I was holding my body so tight to try to stop him, but he was so heavy, he was too strong. Afterwards, he said to me, "You're alright now," as if he'd done me a favour.' Savile then got dressed and went out to dinner with a friend, offering her some badges from *Kissin' Cousins*, Elvis Presley's new film, before he left.

The girl returned by train to the family home in Essex, and after missing her next two periods, the awful realisation dawned that she was pregnant. She says she tried, and failed, to induce a miscarriage. Not long afterwards, her parents confronted her. 'They knew it was Jimmy because he called the house the same week to speak to me,' she said. 'My mum told him I was pregnant and he said, "It's not possible." Those were his words. He didn't call again.'[7]

The woman recalled her father wept when he realised what had happened, and that she was taken one Sunday morning to a local GP who performed an illegal abortion. It cost £150, money that she had to borrow from her grandmother. She said she went through the ordeal without painkillers, and went on to suffer a series of miscarriages in her twenties.

Not long after this story was published, the Metropolitan Police announced it had discovered an intelligence record held by its Paedophile Unit, also dating from 1964. The first entry on the record related to a house on Battersea Bridge Road in London that was inhabited by four older girls and a youth, possibly a homosexual. It stated absconders from Duncroft Approved School used the house.

A second entry contained the notes 'Absconders' and 'Vice Ring' and mentioned three 'coloured' men who were charged with living on the immoral earnings of two girls identified as having absconded from Duncroft. One of the men was given a prison sentence of two years, one failed to appear at the Central Criminal Court on 5 November 1964 and the third was found not guilty. In the ledger, Jimmy Savile was recorded as being a regular visitor to the house.[8]

*T*ime magazine's cover story on 15 April 1966 anointed London as 'The Swinging City'. Postwar austerity felt like a fading memory, affluence and individuality were changing the face of society, and old class divisions were dissolving amid the influx of young people from the provinces to the capital. From John Lennon and Paul McCartney to Mick Jagger and Keith Richards; Michael Caine to Terence Stamp; Jean Shrimpton to Twiggy, the icons of this new age were young, British and, for the most part, working class.

The country also had its youngest prime minister for 70 years, a pipe-smoking Yorkshireman by the name of Harold Wilson. But another son of the West Ridings was determined to defy the ageing process, picking up Disc Jockey of the Year awards in numerous polls while protesting to newspaper reporters that he was still only 17. The truth is Jimmy Savile was fast approaching 40.

'He never struck me as being that old,' says Stephen Hayes, who joined the Manchester City Police as a cadet in 1963 and went on to work in A Division, based at the Bootle Street station in the city centre. He recalls the centre of Manchester, where the city's thriving nightlife unfolded, as being an area 'full of old warehouse properties . . . separated by a web of narrow entries and alleyways . . . the type of dark alleys you'd use to film a Jack the Ripper movie'. He says that 'as the evening's entertainment turned steamy, the doorways became occupied with couples . . . having sex under the cover of darkness, making good use of the stone steps to adjust for height and optimum penetration without the knee ligaments collapsing, or a disc slipping out of place'.[1] He adds that police officers, even those on duty, were as likely to be found indulging as civilians.

Later, as a plain-clothes officer, Hayes says he was one of a small group of police officers who paid social visits to Savile at his flat. 'One of the lads used to be a bit closer to him than the rest of us,' he explains. It would seem to confirm what Tony Calder says about Savile going out of his way to cultivate close relationships with police officers wherever he was.

'We used to tag on for the girly element,' adds Hayes. When I asked him what he meant by 'girly element', Hayes confirmed Savile always had girls in his flat, although he was adamant they were above the age of consent. Of the three or four police officers that went at any one time, some would disappear off into another room with them. He also says one of the officers was from the drug squad and would sometimes take along cannabis which he would smoke with Savile at these social meetings.

'[The officer Savile was close to] used to go wherever [Savile] was, wherever he was appearing,' replies Hayes. 'We all did really. It was part of the social life; let's go and have a laugh at Savile, sort of thing. It wasn't gigs; we'd just turn up anywhere and everywhere where drugs were likely to be. In those days, there was very little serious hard stuff. It was always speed, especially purple hearts, and the cannabis.'

I ask Hayes why they were in Savile's flat, and what they were doing. 'It was a case of "What shall we do?"' he says. 'Let's go and look at Savile, that sort of thing. It wasn't laid on, it was just there and there were girls in the place. They never struck me as children. They were like 18 or 20, I'd have thought . . . It was no big deal, Savile was just another mug to go and visit and take advantage of. Nobody had really heard of paedophiles.'

When the crumbling house in Manchester was made the subject of a compulsory purchase order, Savile hung in long enough to make sure of being offered an alternative by the council. In his case, and despite the fact he could afford a mansion if he wanted one, it was an £8 a week council flat on Bury New Road in Salford.

Alan Leeke, who first came across Savile at the Top Ten Club, was by this time working as a junior reporter on a local newspaper. He visited the one-bedroom, penthouse apartment, having been sent to write a story on Ascot Court's famous new resident. He says he arrived to find Savile sitting in darkness.

Leeke had got to know Savile through *Top of the Pops* while it was recorded at the converted church on Dickenson Road in Rusholme. 'I had an entry pass to go in any time,' he says. 'I saw him there and would talk to him about various things. He used to introduce me to the various pop acts that were on: Charlie [Watts] of The Rolling Stones, The Bachelors and Cilla Black.'

On another occasion, Leeke arranged to write a news item on Jimmy Savile and his many cars, which were being kept in a garage off Great Ancoats Street. When he went round to arrange a time for some photographs to be taken, he again found the flat in darkness. 'Both times I went there the curtains were always closed,' Leeke confirms. 'Not a lot of furniture; a few records on the wall in frames, not very comfortable.'

He recalls that on his second visit Savile was wearing a tracksuit. Soon after he arrived, he says, a girl turned up. 'She was 16-ish and wearing a miniskirt,' he says. 'She went straight into the bedroom and [Savile] followed her. He said to me, "I'll be back shortly."' The young reporter was left to sit alone in the darkened front room.

'Then [Savile] came out of the bedroom and shouted, "Are you still there?"' says Leeke. 'I said, "Yes", and stood up and went into the corridor where the other room was.' Leeke recalls the kitchen was at the far end of the corridor. 'I was stood in the corridor and could see straight into the kitchen. And that's when he proceeded to wash himself off in the kitchen sink.'

Given that Jimmy Savile regularly entertained police officers and plied them with teenage girls, it is perhaps not surprising that he felt empowered enough to advertise to a journalist that he was having sex with teenagers, albeit a young journalist who he knew and felt confident was too overawed to say anything. But the fact that Savile then exhibited the contempt he felt for these girls by washing his penis in the kitchen sink in front of that journalist speaks volumes about how he viewed sex as a cold, emotionless act. It also demonstrates his technique for avoiding censure, one that worked by making those who witnessed his behaviour feel a sense of complicity in it.

The girl, Leeke says, eventually came back into the sitting room. 'I thought to myself, "He's not going to want me here." So I made my excuses and said to him that I'd see him on Sunday at the Top Ten Club when we'd sort out arranging to take some photos of the cars. And that was it.'

Alan Leeke says he subsequently went out with three girls who had all had sexual relationships with Jimmy Savile. They were aged between 16 and 17 at the time, and each said the sex was always quick, and took place in his car or in his flat.

'One or two of the girls told me [washing himself off] was something he did [after sex],' Leeke adds. 'But the more I think about it now, I wonder whether that was all set up, what with me being a member of the press. Just to set it up to show a member of the press that he could do that.'

In October 2012, Mary (not her real name), a grandmother of four, recounted how Jimmy Savile had taken her virginity in 1966. She was 15 at the time, flat chested and just entering puberty. She said that she'd developed a crush on the DJ after attending the Top Ten Club, and sent him a drawing she had done of him. When she didn't get a reply, she approached him in person one Sunday evening at Belle Vue.

'I said I was the girl who sent the picture and was sorry not to hear from him,' Mary said. 'He looked me up and down and said, "I didn't know what you looked like then." We exchanged telephone numbers and he started to call me. He invited me to his flat in Higher Broughton, on the border of Manchester and Salford.'

She maintained her parents thought little of their 15-year-old daughter being dated by a man approaching 40.

On the day he took her virginity, Mary recalled going to Piccadilly station in Manchester to change out of her school uniform before catching a bus to his flat. 'He was lying in bed, with his clothes on, waiting for me,' she said. 'He was disappointed I'd changed out of my uniform and asked me to put it back on, so I did.

'He beckoned me to the bed. I was still clothed, but he was all over me. When he got on top and I felt him start to slip his penis in, I said "No, no", but he said it was OK, it was only his thumb. He said we wouldn't go all the way until I was 16, but he was having sex with me. I thought I loved him and I wanted to please him.'

On two occasions, Mary claimed Savile's friends watched while he had sex with her. Another time, he took a call from his mother while he was having sex with her. 'He kept on talking to her for quite a few minutes, but never stopped having sex,' she said. 'Even as a naive girl, I felt humiliated.'

She claimed to have visited Savile's flat frequently, and on each occasion they had sex. Afterwards, he might occasionally offer her a cup of tea before giving her the bus fare home.

Mary said her parents were taken in and charmed by Jimmy Savile. One evening she recalled he drove her home for dinner. 'We arrived in his Rolls-Royce, having just had sex at his flat. My dad was thrilled, guiding the Rolls into the driveway, enjoying the looks from the neighbours. Jimmy leapt out and kissed my mother's hand. But as we stepped through the dining-room door, he couldn't resist touching me between the legs.'

On another occasion, she wrote to a friend to tell her how Jimmy Savile had taken her to bed. The girl's mother intercepted the letter and contacted Mary's parents. Mary said her father refused to believe that Jimmy Savile would behave in such a manner. She also said that Jimmy Savile dumped her when she turned 18.

So, far from being a dirty secret that Jimmy Savile strove to conceal, his desire to have sex with teenage girls, and the frequency with which he was able to satisfy this desire, had mutated into an expression of power.

Alan Leeke says he discovered one of the girls he knew had fallen pregnant and given birth to Savile's child in 1967. 'She had the child adopted,' he explains. 'She got over it, they always do. I haven't seen that girl for 30-odd years now and I would imagine it's something that would still remain in her memory.'

He says Savile had dumped the girl on finding out, telling her he couldn't possibly have made her pregnant because he was sterile. 'I knew the girl and I knew that what she was telling me was true,' Leeke insists. 'She wasn't the type to make these things up.' He says the girl's father went looking for Jimmy Savile on two occasions. Both times he was armed with a shotgun.

Dave Eager was in his late teens when he first encountered Jimmy Savile. He was studying to become a teacher and playing part-time in a band when Savile offered him part-time employment, first as a DJ at the Top Ten Club and then as his de facto assistant.

I met Dave Eager for the first time in London, shortly after the first stories about the shelved *Newsnight* investigation had appeared in the newspapers. Jimmy Savile's exposure as a prolific sex offender was still some months off. Eager was, and has remained, adamant that he saw nothing in Savile's behaviour that gave him cause for concern.

In our first conversation he told me how in the late 1960s, Savile paid him the handsome sum of £10 a week to sift through the hundreds of letters he received. 'I used to come back to Manchester every Saturday to collect his mail,' Eager said. 'It got to the stage where, I can't remember how much it was, but I could sign cheques up to a certain amount.'

I put it to Eager that Jimmy Savile must have trusted him to give him access not only to his mail but his chequebook, and that trust was something that went against Savile's very nature. In a convoluted manner, Eager then seemed to inadvertently suggest that evidence of his behaviour was beginning to emerge, even then: 'He said, "What it is Dave, is I love my women, but if you ever fall out with somebody you're never quite sure if it's going to be a problem. So, with a guy, I've got no problems."'

Because he was taking care of much of Savile's administration, Eager knew that he stayed in the Adrian Hotel on Hunter Street when he was in London. He also knew that when girls came to visit him at the hotel, Savile insisted they were taken home afterwards in a car. 'He used the same firm,' said Eager.

At the end of each month, Eager said he would see the bill listing the times that the cars had been sent. 'I said, "Jim, you've had a lot—" "Shut up and sign the bill," [said Savile]. We used to have a joke about it but it proved to me that he always looked after the ladies to make sure they went home safely . . . Everything was done with absolute courtesy.'

When I referred to the allegations that had begun to surface in the reporting of the axed *Newsnight* investigation, Eager said that Savile was always wary of being 'set up' by a newspaper, but was not surprised that stories were now coming out about him. 'If somebody 25 years later says, "Jimmy came to my house and Jimmy stayed the night and, by the way, I was only 14," Jim would say, "Well I did know her but that was in 1976 when she was 18" . . . How do you start proving something 30 years later? I think Jim was always concerned. I don't believe he did anything wrong but he was always concerned that someone might be prepared to say something for money.'

Ten months later, and in the full glare of the unfolding scandal, Dave Eager restated that he'd seen and heard nothing, and expressed his horror at the lurid revelations in the press. Among other things, he also admitted to me that he was privy to Jimmy Savile's pathological fear of sexually transmitted diseases. 'The one thing Jimmy always did, and told me he did, was he had a routine with TCP,' he explained. 'Everyone who knew him would know that. He wouldn't say, "I've had a girl." He'd say, "TCP tonight!" You don't know if he was joking or serious. It was always

TCP. He was absolutely fastidious about that; it was his code word.'

According to 'Giving Victims a Voice', the joint Metropolitan Police Service and NSPCC report into allegations of sexual abuse made against Jimmy Savile to officers working on Operation Yewtree, the peak years of his offending took place in the 10 years from 1966. And in the year that England's place at the centre of the universe was sealed with victory in the World Cup final at Wembley, Jimmy Savile was everywhere, it seemed.

Rolling in cash thanks to his Radio Luxembourg shows, *Top of the Pops* appearances and DJ gigs up and down the country, he took to generating further publicity via various madcap stunts. He ran from London to Brighton to win a £100 bet, and donated the money to the Little Sisters of the Poor. He worked a seven-hour shift in a Welsh coalmine with his brother Vince to raise money to buy a guide dog. He competed in the Latrigg Fell Race, continued to wrestle professionally at halls across Britain and completed a Royal Marines endurance march across Dartmoor. After the latter, Savile remarked that he hoped it would encourage teenagers to walk long distances to help charities.

Jimmy Savile's relationship with the Royal Marines extended to his final act, when his coffin was carried into St Anne's Cathedral in Leeds on the shoulders of a regimental guard of honour. It was through the Royal Marines that he established a rapport with Lord Louis Mountbatten that in turn established the bridgehead for his long and close affiliation with the royal family. The association with one of Britain's crack fighting forces began with his desire to physically prove himself and then developed as he resolved to complete every element of Royal Marine training, earning himself in the process an honorary Green Beret.

'I invited three Marine Commando N.C.O.s to *Top of the Pops* last week, two of them photographers,' he wrote in his newspaper column after completing his first run, in which he beat his brother

Vince, a serving naval officer at the time. 'And seeing as they're used to snapshots of strong men doing strong things, to see them taking pictures of all those miniskirts was a good laugh. They didn't even mind lying on the floor in their best suits for the best pictures.'[2]

On other occasions, he wrote about how teenagers should spend a compulsory four weeks working in a hospital so they could see another side of life, and about the Manchester taxi run to Blackpool with his 'family of 200 blind or crippled children'. Savile and his other brother, Johnnie, organised a fund-raising concert at the Royal Albert Hall for the victims of the Aberfan disaster in Wales, the proceeds from which they planned to hand out from his car. It was not to pass without incident, however: 'I refuse to hand over the money to the Mayor of Merthyr Tydfil,' Johnnie Savile told one newspaper. 'There has been so much arguing about it.'[3]

Meanwhile Jimmy Savile, further embellishing his standing as a philanthropist, was using his newspaper column to publicise the talks he gave to gatherings of Catholic priests and nuns. He spoke on the topic of teenagers.

On one occasion, he was invited to speak to a group of nuns who taught at schools in Lancashire. The event was organised by a Jesuit priest, Father George Giarchi, who Savile had worked with on a series of 'pop missions for teenagers'.[4]

'Children want the chance to respect people,' Savile told the sisters. 'They know they've got to have authority, and that there must be a penalty when they do wrong.' He explained that teenagers were '80 per cent don't knows, 10 per cent "right" people and 10 per cent hard cases', and advised the nuns to concentrate on the 80 per cent because 'It's better to save a load of the could-be's, than waste time on the ones born to be double villains.' As a parting shot he said that he would pray for them, adding 'and I hope you'll pray for me'. He naturally failed to mention his own special focus on those teenagers that could not be saved.

Dave Eager told me he remembered accompanying Savile to some of Father Giarchi's 'preach-in' events, which were aimed squarely at the young. 'He was a character,' Eager said of the priest. 'It was all anti-drugs, anti-underage sex, live the Catholic life, that sort of thing.' I tried on more than one occasion to contact George Giarchi, who left the clergy in the 1970s, for comment, but got no reply.

'[The clergy] had never heard anything like it,' Savile said after their first appearance together. 'I was honest with them. I told them all about sex and drugs and the dangers. I didn't mince words. And they believed me.'[5]

So did Guy Marsden, Jimmy Savile's nephew. One of 14 children raised by Savile's older sister Marjory, Marsden is now a father of four and grandfather of ten. He works as a roofer in Leeds.

Marsden told me that he decided to run away in his early teens having been 'in and out of trouble with the law'. He hitchhiked to London with three friends where, he explained, they stayed for around five weeks. It was the first of a number of such trips that took place over an 18-month period.

On their first trip in 1967, Marsden recalled they were hanging around Euston Station. 'Unbeknown to us then . . . it's like a pick-up point,' he said. A man approached them, asked what they were doing and offered to buy them food. Marsden said he and his friends accompanied the man to a nearby flat.

After a few days at the stranger's flat, Guy Marsden's uncle mysteriously appeared. 'I half hid, I half ran because I thought, "I'm properly going to get bashed,"' he said of seeing Jimmy Savile walk into the room. 'But it weren't. It were a more casual thing – "You better come with me." And then I thought I were probably still in trouble. We all went; we stuck together.'

Marsden claimed that 'Uncle Jimmy' moved the runaways into a house. Over the ensuing weeks, he also took the boys to a number of parties. There were no women at these soirees, only men and children. Marsden maintained that he realised immediately what sort of parties they were.

One of the houses, he described as being particularly memorable: 'The big feature of it were, when you went in, the swimming pool . . .' he explained. 'It were a room with a big swimming pool and it were so inviting. Everybody used it and were diving into it. It had lights in it; it was lit up. It was unbelievable . . . All you wanted to do was stay there for ever.' Marsden said he believes the house belonged to a famous pop impresario of the time.

'What happened were if the parties run through, at some time you'd fall asleep through [the] night or early morning. And then, next day when you woke up, you still had the run of wherever you were.' If another party was being held, he said, the boys would be put in the car and taken there. He claimed some parties would continue for days and across a number of locations.

Marsden told me that he remembered the children in attendance. He said they were aged between six and ten, and from time to time they were led into rooms with adult males. Noises could be heard coming from inside, he said. 'None of these kids were stressed. It was as though they were really, really enjoying what they were doing. That's the sad part really.'

He went on to name a number of celebrities that he encountered at these events but insisted he never saw his uncle Jimmy go into a room with any of the children.

Marsden is adamant he wasn't abused and that only one of his three friends 'went behind the door' with a man. He now thinks he knows why they were there: 'Someone must have had an idea that we would [be] a good intermediary for these kids. We were all young and slapping each other and messing about . . . and kids relate to things like that, so they'd come to us. It might have stressed them if there were only adult men.'

He went on to tell me their stay in London came to an end when one of his friends was caught stealing money. It was at this point that Marsden said he first met 'Uncle John': 'I hated him because he were taking us away from all we loved down in London. But . . . we were getting the boot anyway. We couldn't be trusted.' He maintained it was Johnnie, Jimmy Savile's older brother, who ordered them back to Leeds.

Guy Marsden and his friends made further trips to London and he says that each time they fell back into the same scene. Known to the police in Leeds, he claims he told them about what he'd experienced in the capital. 'I might have said it three times in all the times I was picked up,' he told me. The response? 'Shut up yer knob.'

Marjory Marsden, Guy's mother, idolised her youngest brother, thanks in no small part to the fact he would occasionally turn up at the Seacroft estate in Leeds carrying a colour television or a new telephone under his arm. As a result, the Marsdens were one of the first families on the estate to own either. But according to Guy, his father, Herbert Marsden, 'couldn't stand [Jimmy Savile], he absolutely hated him . . . hated him with a vengeance'.

When I asked him whether he ever discussed with his uncle what had gone on in London, Marsden insisted there was an unspoken agreement that nothing would ever be said. He also told me he was sent to Borstal at the age 16, and believes Jimmy Savile was responsible. 'Apparently one of the people who were meant to be defending me . . . it turned out they were quite good friends. And [Jimmy Savile] said to the judge, "I think [a custodial sentence] will do him the world of good" . . . He made it seem like the reason I were in prison was because of him.'

In later life, Jimmy Savile would boast about the calibre of his contacts within the legal profession to police officers investigating allegations against him regarding historic sex offences.

Otley had been largely untouched by the decade of change. The hills that enclosed this sleepy market town at the gateway to the Yorkshire Dales seemed to act as a buffer to the seismic activity going on beyond. But as chairman of the town's urban district council in 1967, Mayor Ronnie Duncan was determined to bring a flavour of the Swinging Sixties to town.

Duncan was a big noise locally, the fifth generation of his family to run William Ackroyd and Company, a textile company established in 1836 that had once employed the majority of Otley's adult population. As mayor and head of the council, he wanted to do something different with the town's gala social event, the annual Civic Ball.

He told the local newspaper that by rebranding what had traditionally been a staid affair, and calling it a 'Pop Civic Ball', he hoped to appeal to 'the young and young-in-heart amongst our townspeople'.[1] The event, which was to be held in a marquee on the grounds of the local rugby club on Friday, 6 October, would feature live music supplied by Chris Barber and his jazz band supported by local outfits, The Mouldy Warp and Ellison's Hog Line. It would also have a celebrity guest of honour.

Knowing that Jimmy Savile was well-known in Otley thanks to his cycling and his early DJ engagement in the Wharfedale Café in the town centre, Duncan decided to write to the star of radio and television and invite him along as his 'chief guest'. He also recruited an old friend of Agnes Savile, who was also a regular visitor to Otley, to make contact to see if she could apply some gentle persuasion.

Jimmy Savile didn't bother writing a letter of reply; he simply scribbled his thoughts on Duncan's letter and sent it back to him, using the same envelope. 'He responded to say yes, he would like to come,' Duncan told me, although further research proved the deal wasn't quite as simple as he said. In fact, Jimmy Savile outlined a set of six conditions for the councillor, as reported in the local newspaper:[2]

1. Make sure that my normal fee of £200 goes to an Otley charity – [Duncan's] Answer: The £200 fee will go to an Otley charity. Ta very much indeed.
2. I wish to sleep the night on the Chevin, in a tent, which you will organise, plus sleeping bag and large torch – Answer: I will personally organise a tent on the Chevin, plus sleeping bag and large torch, for you to sleep overnight, and moreover will hold you to it.
3. A guard of honour of six young ladies – in another tent of course – to keep me safe – Answer: I'll organise the guard of honour of six young ladies but I won't be held to their compliance, or your safety!
4. A trip round Otley hospital the next lunchtime (Saturday) – Answer: The Matron is delighted by your suggestion of a visit on Saturday and I look forward to accompanying you.
5. The presentation of some Otley honour – framed drawing or painting of Otley – Answer: I shall organise a framed drawing or painting of Otley for you, and I am exploring the possibility of conferring upon you the Freedom of the New Market Conveniences.
6. Some cigars and matches – Answer: I'm stocking up with cigars and matches – bring outsize ashtray.

If Jimmy Savile's demands for girls were barefaced, what's also notable was his insistence on being given access to the local hospital. According to Liz Dux, a lawyer representing scores of Jimmy Savile's victims, it became one of his regular conditions for making personal appearances in the decades that followed: 'Whenever he arrived at a new place that he hadn't been to before, he'd ask where the hospital was.'

In his autobiography, Savile boasted that his unusual demands ensured that the tickets to the Otley ball sold out in record time: 'My ultimatum of "no tents, no girls, no me" meant the council had to go through with it,' he wrote.[3] He also claimed that a notice for female volunteers brought in 'well over a hundred young lady applicants'.

Council records show that the 12 members of Otley District Council met on Monday, 11 September 1967 and Duncan referred to arrangements that had been made both for the Pop Civic Ball and 'for the reception and convenience of his official guests',[4] which presumably covered Savile and the six young women he'd demanded as his fee.

'Some of the members only then realized what they were doing,' claimed Savile in his book, ignoring the fact he wasn't present at the meeting. '[They said] "We can't have a council meeting to decide which six of our girls sleep with this man."' He maintained the council members were 'more bewildered than outraged', yet claimed half of them still got up and left the meeting.

Ronnie Duncan remembered it rather differently: 'Some of the blue-haired Tories were not exactly in favour of having a Pop Civic Ball but their distaste was levelled at me and not at Jimmy Savile.'

Six girls were finally selected: Andrea Barber, Alma Lucas, Lynn Mitchell, Ann Simpson, Catherine Spence and Jennifer Woodhead. When I asked Duncan how old they were, he replied: 'I don't think we are talking about sub-teenage. I imagine they were all over the age of 16 but I have no reason to know.'

It is clear from a local newspaper article, however, that there was considerable unease in Otley over the event, and Jimmy Savile's demands. In the build-up, the BBC Home Service sent a reporter to interview John Herdman, the chairman of the Pop Ball committee. In a subsequent newspaper article, Herdman admitted, 'the interview touched on some topical and controversial points'.[5]

Ronnie Duncan did not attend the Pop Civic Ball for the simple reason that he was getting married on the same day. Jimmy Savile arrived wearing a Union Jack blazer, strings of beads round his neck and a sou'wester on his head. He also had a friend in tow.

Jimmy Corrigan was king of Scarborough's seafront amusement arcades and a member of Savile's informal running club in the North Yorkshire seaside town. When we spoke, however, Duncan was adamant the Jimmy Corrigan in question was James Lord Corrigan, owner of the recently opened Batley Variety Club and a string of bingo halls around Yorkshire. The two men not only shared a name; they were first cousins.

On the night of the Civic Ball, the six young women were kitted out in identical patterned shift dresses. As Jimmy Savile recalled, 'They looked good enough to eat.'

According to Savile's account, one of the girls' fathers arrived and 'hauled her off home. She protested loudly but dad would have none of this preposterous situation.' Corrigan, who Savile described as his 'millionaire pal', clearly couldn't believe his luck: 'When he saw the crumpet his eyes shot out a mile and his total conversation for the evening was an incredulous "Are we kipping with them?"'[6]

Jimmy Savile was not required to do anything at the ball other than bide his time. At the end of the night, he recounted how he, Jimmy Corrigan and the five remaining girls were driven up to the Chevin, a local beauty spot overlooking the town, where two tents were waiting for them in a clearing in the trees. 'Needless to say,' he added with a sickening inevitability, 'the girls' tent fell over and we all had to finish up together.'

Savile's account of the night was typically upbeat: 'Dawn came and with it the council chairman and his cars. It was seven totally exhausted campers that fell back down the hill to a breakfast we couldn't eat because we had laughed too much.'

The photograph in the following week's paper tells a different story. Jimmy Savile and Jimmy Corrigan are pictured with the six girls. Only Andrea Barber appears to be laughing. It looks like she has just said something to Lynn Mitchell, who unlike the forced smiles worn by the other girls, looks decidedly grim-faced.

'To my knowledge [Jimmy] behaved perfectly sensibly,' protested Duncan, who said he was impressed with the way Savile conducted himself on the hospital visit the following day. 'The revelations that have come upon us since then are an amazement to all of us, I think . . . I had got no suspicions of any sort that he'd be taking advantage of the girls. My view was here is a man who has got nothing to sell but himself, and therefore what he wished for in terms of publicity and newsworthy comment is the price that I'm paying.'

I put it to Ronnie Duncan that six girls was a highly unusual payment for a personal appearance. 'I just thought it was one of his gimmicks, you know, that would make good publicity for him,' he replied. 'I saw absolutely nothing sinister in it. Maybe I should have done but I didn't.' He also maintained there were no complaints from any of those who camped on the Chevin.

I was able to track down and speak to one of the women who stayed on the hillside with Jimmy Savile and Jimmy Corrigan that night, although she asked not to be identified. Her account is rather different from Duncan's.

She was 17 at the time, and insists she was not the youngest of the six girls selected. Moreover, she also claims there was no selection process, as most of the girls were the daughters of, or known to, local councillors and prominent local businessman. Indeed it was Andrea Barber's father, who ran the tobacconist's shop in town where Jimmy Savile bought his cigars, who forbade his daughter from going.

She also told me the Jimmy Corrigan in question was a good deal younger than Jimmy Savile, making it highly unlikely that it was James Lord Corrigan of Batley Variety Club fame, despite Duncan's insistence. Jimmy Corrigan of Batley was born in 1925, making him a year older than Jimmy Savile. He was also known throughout his life as James rather than Jimmy. Jimmy Corrigan of Scarborough, on the other hand, was born in 1939, putting him in his late twenties at the time of the ball.

Perhaps most significant is the revelation that they did not in fact spend the whole night on the hillside. And this was not due to one of the tents collapsing, but because it was attacked by a group of local youths.

The woman recalled it was bitterly cold when the girls got into their sleeping bags in the separate tent that had been set up for them in the clearing. It was at this point, in the early hours of the morning, that Jimmy Savile, who had been plying them with vodka all night but not drinking himself, came in and 'tried it on' with each of the girls.

Although the woman refused to elaborate on what had happened on the grounds she didn't think it fair on the others in the tent that night, she did describe Jimmy Savile as 'a disgusting old man' and 'a pervert'.

Her version of events was that they 'were saved' when youths from the rugby club shot out the paraffin lamps with air rifles. 'They had followed us up there,' she said. She described the girls huddling in the tent while a fight broke out between Savile and the youths. '[Savile] was violent, really nasty once he turned,' she added.

When I asked her about the newspaper photograph taken the next day, she sighed. 'I was just thinking, "Get me out of this shit." I was out of my depth. It was horrible.'

If Jimmy Savile was confident enough by 1967 to ask local government officials for payment in girls, it was possibly because he had recently dodged a bullet. According to George Tremlett, who worked weekend shifts on the news desk at the *People* from 1961 to 1968, the newspaper's crack team of reporters carried out an investigation into Jimmy Savile.

When I asked Tremlett whether it was an investigation into Jimmy Savile's preference for underage girls, he replied: 'Without a shadow of a doubt. And it was specific. They had names. The standard practice with the *People* . . . was everything had to be evidenced with statements that needed to be agreed by lawyers and so on. That was standard drill.'

The *People*, then a broadsheet, was a paper with a pioneering reputation in the field of investigative journalism.[7] In the 1950s it had broken the story of the Messina brothers' prostitution ring in Soho, which Hugh Cudlipp, editorial director of the rival *Daily Mirror* and *Sunday Pictorial*, described as 'the most courageous exposure of its kind'.

So why did the *People*'s findings never see the light of day? Editor Sam Campbell had hired Jimmy Savile as a columnist in a bid to attract a younger readership, chiefly on the advice of his daughter who listened religiously to his Radio Luxembourg shows. She was a boarder at Roedean School in Sussex at the time, and like millions of other teenagers across Britain, listening to *The Teen and Twenty Disc Club* was a guilty pleasure, one that was best enjoyed, at Savile's behest, 'under the bedclothes'.

'The reason that he spiked it was that Jimmy Savile wrote a weekly column for the paper,' claimed Tremlett. 'I was about eight or ten feet from the [Campbell's] desk because he used to sit in the same room as the editorial staff. I was there when somebody walked past me to the desk and they were told that [the story] was killed. They walked back and grumbled. It wasn't what I would call a rebellious grumble; people expected the editor to edit the paper, and Sam Campbell was one of the great Fleet Street figures.'

In 1966, Sam Campbell died suddenly from a heart attack, aged 58. In January 1972, shortly after Jimmy Savile had been awarded an OBE in the New Year's honours list, the second instalment of a major four-part series was published in the *People*. Its banner headline screamed: 'Me and My 3,000 Birds – At last! Jimmy Savile's own story'.[8]

Representatives of all Britain's main political parties attended the press conference, at which each declared his support for a campaign sparked by five company secretaries working in the head office of Colt Ventilation and Heating Ltd in Surbiton. The women had offered to work one Saturday morning a month for no extra pay, profits or overtime.

This gesture was made against the grim backdrop of a stalling economy, compounded by an increasing deficit in the balance of trade, a damaging spate of strikes, the six-day war in the Middle East, a devalued currency and rising bank rates. What had spurred the secretaries to act was a letter written to *The Times* by the Conservative MP John Boyd-Carpenter in which he had suggested Britain could alleviate the economic stagnation being experienced under Harold Wilson's Labour government if those 'in responsible positions' set such an example.

The initiative taken by the women at Colt snowballed to the extent that by 5 January 1968, when the MPs from both sides of the House convened, it had become a national effort. Operating under the slogan 'I'm Backing Britain', companies from all over Britain signed up, thousands of Union Jack lapel badges were produced, and ordinary citizens even began to send money to the Treasury to reduce the national debt. The Duke of Edinburgh was sufficiently impressed to send a telegram of encouragement.[1]

Jimmy Savile had nothing to offer the drive to increase exports – his fame was a uniquely British phenomenon – but he had no intention of missing out on what he saw as an opportunity for easy publicity. After offering his services as a volunteer porter at Leeds General Infirmary, where he already recorded inserts for the hospital radio station, he ensured the newspapers were on hand to record his first day on the job. By giving nine days over a two-month period, he told them, he calculated he was contributing the equivalent of £1,600.

One paper reported that he turned up in his Rolls-Royce Silver Shadow and wore a white porter's jacket over a Union Jack waist-coat. Another described him as a 'Plain man's philosopher, everybody's friend, nobody's fool' before revealing 'He chatted up, charmed, kissed, saluted, or hailed anything that moved.'[2] Sir Donald Kaberry, MP for North-West Leeds and chairman of the hospital governors, said, 'He will be treated as an ordinary worker.'[3] Mr E.N. Hill, the assistant house governor, was more effusive; claiming his effect on the patients was 'quite magical'.[4]

Jimmy Savile insisted this was no publicity stunt. Instead, he saw himself as a figure around whom Britain could rally. As he told readers of the *People* the very next Sunday: 'There's bags and bags of spirit . . . in this country. I know as I see it all over. What is needed is a Winston Churchill to gather it all up, point it in the right direction and . . . Boom! All those clouds lined with devaluation and unemployment would blow away, and quickly.'[5]

As an example of the sort of pluck that might yet save the UK from financial ruin, he cited Jimmy Corrigan, his friend from Scarborough. Clearly, the Pop Civic Ball in Otley was still on his mind because he revealed he had outlined similar terms for a charity event in Bingley, only this time he and Corrigan would sleep in a tree house in Shipley Glen. The conditions? 'As usual, my wages of fun bodyguards – six local girls.'[6]

An outbreak of foot and mouth disease foiled the plan, and the girls were spared the fate that befell their counterparts in Otley. Instead, Savile and Corrigan spent the night on a raft in the middle of a river in flood. 'My pal could have bought the town,' he wrote, 'but he wouldn't have dreamt of backing out just because everything wasn't sweet. That's what I call spirit.'[7]

On that same Sunday, Michael Parkinson commented on Jimmy Savile's burgeoning persona, one that now amounted to more than being a fast-talking, bizarrely dressed figure of fun. In a *Sunday Times Magazine* special edition on Yorkshire, Parkinson's profile, headlined 'Honest Jim', described an enigma, albeit one with a shrewd head for business and a rare social conscience. In it, Savile aptly summarised his place in society: 'To most people I am a question mark.' It was a status that never changed.

The interview took place in the studios of Radio Luxembourg, and at one point Parkinson reported a telephone call coming through from Leeds General Infirmary. Savile claimed the call was from a dying 11-year-old boy who wanted a chat as a birthday treat. Such calls were a regular occurrence, the producer of the show told Parkinson, who went on to describe the DJ, TV star and charity fund-raiser as, 'Savile the Social Worker'.

At the end of the piece, Savile offered his own reasons for why he was able to do what he did, although it better explains how he was given such access to the sick and vulnerable: 'I think the majority of people like me and I think they like me because they know I'm honest.'[8]

Even once the allegations about his erstwhile friend had surfaced, Dave Eager still maintained that hospitals offered Savile the sort of unconditional emotional engagement that was lacking in the rest of his life. 'When he was starting in the hospital wards, he said to me, 'Dave, how could I possibly stop doing it? If you wheel somebody down to the theatre and they ask whether you'll be there when they come round, it gives me something to look forward to.'

Eager also recalled the pull was even stronger when Savile knew the patient was dying. 'He'd know when somebody had not got long to live,' Eager confirmed. 'They'd look at him and say, "Jim, can I ask you something? When I die, can you wheel me down to the mortuary?" He'd say, "If that is showing someone love and respect, and they'd like that, there's no way I won't be there to wheel them down because that is the promise I've made."'

What's more likely is that hospitals provided Jimmy Savile with both a captive audience and easy pickings. Where better to satisfy his longing for adulation, especially at a time when his age was beginning to show and his allure as a frontline pop star was fading, than in an environment where everyone was confined to a bed? And in being required at the most vulnerable, precarious moments in the lives of some of those people, he was enabled, both in terms of the ready access he was afforded and in the way those charged with patient care could be manipulated. It was a devastating mix, and one that he intuitively grasped.

Jimmy Savile's standing as a volunteer and fund-raiser for the sick, the disabled, the old and the young grew apace. In 1968, a patient at Broadmoor high-security psychiatric hospital wrote to him, asking whether he would open a fete for the hospital's League of Friends. A gift was sent with the invitation: a Brazil nut set on a wooden plinth. Underneath, on a silver plate, was inscribed the legend: 'NUTTERS INC – Jimmy Savile.'

'I dropped a line back saying I would only go if the boss asks me,' Savile told me at our first meeting. 'I got a letter from the boss so I went. I had an immediate affinity with the place.' It was the start of an association with the Berkshire hospital that would continue for decades.

It did not take long for Jimmy Savile to progress from pushing old ladies in wheelchairs at Leeds General Infirmary to being invited into the operating theatre to witness heart surgery. 'There in front of me was life with a capital L,' he wrote, 'and my life can never be the same after such an experience.' When the patient came round from the anaesthetic, he celebrated by going off to 'a dance at the nurses' home'.[9]

In May, by which time the 'I'm Backing Britain' campaign had wound down amid widespread apathy and press criticism, Savile was invited to spend a week in Dublin, Belfast and Cork at the request of Lady Valerie Goulding who admitted approaching him about helping her to raise money for the new Central Remedial Clinic with 'some trepidation'. Savile took along his mother and his white Rolls-Royce and was responsible for raising around £3,000. And according to the *Irish Times*, he bestowed 'a kiss on every adult female whom he chanced upon'.[10]

Later that summer, he led 500 teenagers on a sponsored walk to pay for the Margaret Sinclair Centre in Rosewell, played football in a half Rangers, half Celtic jersey for St Joseph's Hospital and gave a sermon at a teenagers' mass in Tunbridge Wells. In 1968 alone, he claimed to have raised £58,000 for 'backstreet charities'.[11] 'My conscience is clear,' he said. 'I've taken a lot I know, but I've given a lot as well.'

Jimmy Savile set his course for the centre of the British establishment with the 'I'm Backing Britain' campaign. It won him kudos and respect, which allied to his apparently selfless desire to help those less fortunate than himself, made people begin to reappraise a man who up until that point had divided opinion. His stature was growing within the BBC as well, a fact underlined with the news that he had been signed up by Radio 1.

The BBC's new station for pop music had been launched in a bid to fill the void left by pirate radio. By the time the government moved to outlaw them, the pirates, led by stations such as Radio Caroline and Radio London, and operating from rusting ships or disused sea forts in international waters, had changed the listening habits of the nation. It was in response to this demographic shift that the BBC decided to reorganise its radio output, ditching the Home, Light and Third Programmes in favour of four national networks, complemented by a chain of local stations.

As the controller for Radios 1 and 2, Robin Scott's first task was to assemble a team of DJs and presenters on a tight budget. His second task was to assuage fears within the corporation. Many on Scott's roster of disc jockeys had only recently come ashore, and there was consternation about these wildcards broadcasting on the BBC without the safety net of pre-approved scripts.

As Jeremy Paxman put it to the Pollard inquiry, the BBC had been 'aloof from popular culture for so long. Pirate radio comes along and all these people in metaphorical cardigans suddenly have to deal with an influx . . . of people from a very, very different culture. And they never got control of them.'[12]

Dawn broke on this brave new world at 7 a.m. on Saturday, 30 September 1967 as Tony Blackburn, formerly of Radio London's pirate ship MV *Galaxy*, welcomed listeners 'to the exciting new sound of Radio 1' before cueing in 'Flowers in the Rain' by The Move.

Like Blackburn, many of the names on Radio 1's first roster of DJs had built their followings on the pirate airwaves: Kenny Everett, John Peel, Ed 'Stewpot' Stewart, Chris Denning and Emperor Rosko, to name a few. 'They have invaded the corridors of the BBC,' thundered the *Daily Mail*. 'What Radio 1 is doing is to introduce a new and potentially vicious competition among the men who make up the new disc-jockey team. They have been given short contracts and great deal of weeding out is yet to be done.'

Alongside the edgier pirate DJs who doubtless gave the retired Lord Reith palpitations were a cadre of more familiar names: Pete Murray, Alan Freeman, David Jacobs and Jimmy Young, as well as a new talent imported from Ireland, Terry Wogan. But despite being named DJ of the Year by numerous publications over the preceding three years, Jimmy Savile was not recruited for the launch of the new pop station. 'I think they don't want me because I earn three times as much as the other jocks,' he said at the time.[13]

That all changed with one phone call from Robin Scott. A show that played records between pre-recorded interviews with ordinary people Jimmy Savile met on his forays around the country was scheduled to start on Radio 1 on Sunday, 2 June. Its host celebrated by ordering himself a £13,500 Rolls-Royce with 22-carat gold handles, and negotiated a boot full of Green Shield stamps into the bargain. He later claimed his deal with the BBC included being bought a brand new Roller each year.[14]

Johnny Beerling, who produced *Blackburn's Breakfast Show* in the early days and would go on to become Radio 1's controller, saw the timing of the move as significant. 'Jimmy had never wanted to be just another DJ on the station and was canny enough to wait . . . to see how it was doing before he joined. [He] was also shrewd enough to realise there was more mileage in joining as a solo turn than at the same time as all the others.'[15]

Four decades on, Jimmy Savile admitted as much to me: 'There was Tony Blackburn, DLT, the guy who got the sack with the helicopter and the beard [Noel Edmonds]. They were all characters, household names and we were all friends. But we were also in fierce competition with each other. I was the man who never tried. I used to float in and float out, never went to any parties and never once went to the BBC Club. That marked you as a double oddity.'

Jimmy Savile was spending less and less time in Manchester by this stage. *Savile's Travels*, his new show on Radio 1, was predicated on his increasingly nomadic lifestyle, while *Top of the Pops* required him to be in London more and, it seems, still provided a ready source of teenage girls. On the band's first appearance on the show, Status Quo's 18-year-old frontman Francis Rossi was invited to Savile's dressing room with the words, 'Come and see me tarts. Some fucking tarts we've got in.'[16]

The average age of the studio audience at *Top of the Pops* rose following the move to London, but girls under the age of 18 still found it easy to get in. Now in colour, the show became a weekly window onto the latest fashions. 'I like clothes that show what a girl is really about,' remarked producer Johnnie Stewart. Asked whether that included see-through blouses, he replied, 'There's nothing wrong with them, and I'd let the girls in, but I would make sure they didn't get in shot.'[17]

Stanley Dorfman, Stewart's co-producer and director, insists that he never saw Jimmy Savile with a girl at *Top of the Pops*. He also says Savile rarely, if ever, joined the stars, producers and members of dance troupe Pan's People in the BBC bar afterwards. 'He was an absolute enigma,' says Dorfman. 'It was like he'd come in every week playing the part of Jimmy Savile. I had no indication of what he was like at home and I didn't bother to find out.'

*

In November, Savile completed the next stage of his Marine Commando training at Lympstone in Devon, carrying 35lbs of equipment over a nine-mile course in less than 90 minutes. He was also photographed with his arms round the two 'dolly birds' chosen as the hostesses on his new BBC1 game show, *Quiz Bingo*. The format saw teams drawn from hospital staffs all over Britain. The armed forces, the BBC, the NHS, the Catholic Church; Jimmy Savile's tentacles were spreading into all corners of British society.

An indication of his acceptance within rarefied circles was to be found in the suit decorated in bananas he wore on one episode of *Top of the Pops*. At the time, he was 'chaperoning' Hillary 'Gussy' van Geest, the debutante heiress to a banana fortune. His journey to the centre of the establishment was well under way.

Dave Eager, who worked as his personal assistant, said this was also a time when Jimmy Savile began to change. 'One of the things he always said to me about this business is, "The most liked person is also the most hated because it's worth hating something that other people like . . . This is why you are always good news for a newspaper. You've got to be aware . . . that the more you become known, the more you become part of the establishment, the more you're going to get people hating you."'

33. EINS, ZWEI, DREI IN THE SKY

Today's shell suit was blue with solid blocks of red on the jacket and flashes of white and green on the sleeves. He was wearing a pair of glasses I hadn't seen before: the old NHS-style in tortoiseshell.

The electric fire was on and Savile had classical music playing from his favourite satellite channel. A fresh cigar was smoking between his fingers while in the distance, above the boxy houses nestled on the slope overlooking the arcades and chip shops that stretched along the half-moon of the pleasure beach, a squall broke across Scarborough.

Whenever I stayed with him, the mornings were a time for reflection; it was a still, meditative, contemplative state he seemed to have perfected over the many years he had spent alone.

I sat down on the velour-covered sofa with its taupe and tan chevrons. Above the fireplace hung a large photograph of the *Queen Mary* cruise liner passing behind Scarborough's white-washed lighthouse.

I wanted to know about the mysterious powers of hypnotism he claimed to possess. The pitch and cadence of his voice, a voice that became the standard-issue impersonation for just about every British citizen born before 1980, occasionally induced a drowsiness in me, especially if subjected to it for long stretches at a time. After a few hours listening to his pulsing drone – and occasionally being scolded for interjecting with a question or a request for clarification – I invariably found myself needing a break.

Often we'd sit in silence, and if it was after six in the evening he'd pour himself a generous tumbler of scotch. He told me he'd never touched a drop until after his heart bypass in 1997, maybe because alcohol made him more apt to make the sort of throw-away comments that revealed more about the real Jimmy Savile than any of his vertiginously tall stories.

So when did he first realise he had powers? 'I was in the Isle of Man doing a disc jockey thing in Douglas,' he replied. 'And in the hotel I was staying at, because I was the star DJ at the time, the waitress came across and said – er – er – what's his name now?' He groped for the name of the hypnotist he claimed had recognised his powers. I knew the name, and reminded him: it was Josef Karma.

'Josef Karma. Yes, he was doing a one-man show at the Royal. So Josef comes over to my table. And I said to him, "That's a fascinating game is that." And he said, "You can do what I can't do Jim." And I said, "What's that?" "You can do mass hypnosis. You probably don't know you're doing it but you know the effect you've got on people. You know what you can do but you don't know how it comes or what it's called. You can do mass hypnosis and I can't."'

Savile claimed that Karma had offered to teach him about hypnosis, and they worked together for a few weeks before he started to hypnotise people under his tutor's guidance. He said he found that he could do it quite easily.

'So when I came back to Leeds after the six weeks, I found . . .' he paused for a moment to relight his cigar, 'a hypnotherapy clinic. They'd get patients in and let me hypnotise them and try to sort them out, and I learned various techniques. I don't use it very often.'

He cackled and looked straight out to sea.

'There was one classic occasion in A & E at Leeds General Infirmary. This kid, about 12 years old, was in a cubicle having a massive asthma attack. I knew it weren't an asthma attack because when he saw me I could see the light of recognition in his eyes. So I went in and said "Hello" and he couldn't breathe. I gave him the

'*Eins, zwei, drei* in the sky*", and he stopped breathing like that.'
Savile snapped his finger.

'The doctor and staff nurse had the needle and all the gear and
the doctor said, "Ah Jim, you're doing your black magic again.
You know we don't like that."'

If he was telling the truth, it illustrated the extent to which he
was able to penetrate hospital departments. I knew he volunteered
in the casualty department at the hospital in Leeds, but was
unaware his duties extended beyond wheeling patients as a porter.
What he was telling me he was given a free rein to wander in and
out of cubicles, and was free to touch as well as speak to the sick
and injured.

'I once found a geezer who was in a car crash,' he went on. 'I was
in the ambulance and I jumped down and walked out and there was
this fella, still in the driving seat. His windscreen had smashed and
shards of glass had gone into his eyeball. These shards were sticking
out of his eyeball. He was in a bit of a state so I did the "*Eins, zwei,
drei* in the sky*" – and I told him to hold still and not close his eyes.
The ambulance men came and they said, "Uh, Jimmy Savile!"'

His voice lowered, and his eyes closed as he recalled how he
warned the paramedics of what they were about to see: 'Shards of
glass in the eye, just take him out but don't say anything to him. I
whispered in his ear that he was going to be OK now and that
everything would be alright.'

Despite his appearance and unsettling manner, Jimmy Savile
succeeded in soothing the nation into believing that, in his hands,
everything would be alright.

In the months after his former friend's reputation had been
reduced to smoking ruins, Dave Eager phoned me in a state of panic.
He told me Savile had sent him to check out the venue in the Isle of
Man before signing the contract for the summer season. Eager had
met Josef Karma and known of Savile's interest in hypnosis. He was
now terrified that he too had been hypnotised; blinded to what was
happening right under his nose.

As the 1960s drew to a close, Jimmy Savile could reflect on the heights he'd scaled, the riches he'd accumulated and the view from his newly elevated position within both the BBC and society at large. And yet he cannot have been anything other than acutely aware of the appalling duality of his existence. On the one hand, the plaudits for his charity work and the promotions gained on the back of his audience-winning ability as a broadcaster; on the other, the almost total disregard for the risks to his reputation and the wreckage wrought by his darkest impulses and actions.

The popularity of his Radio 1 show, *Savile's Travels*, and the changes afoot within the station only accelerated the pace of his ascent and frequency of his offending. In February 1969, Douglas Muggeridge, the 40-year-old nephew of Malcolm Muggeridge, the celebrated author and jouranlist who had become an outspoken critic of the permissive age, succeeded Robin Scott as controller of Radios 1 and 2. In his four years as head of Overseas Talks and Features, Douglas Muggeridge had described Bush House as 'like a mini NATO',[1] with 40 different nationalities working in perfect harmony. According to Johnny Beerling, Muggeridge was 'much straighter' than Scott and wanted more 'public service' alongside the 'pop stuff'.[2]

'I like pop music,' insisted Savile's new boss when news broke of his appointment. 'I have this sort of sympathy with what it's trying to do, as part of a social revolution.'[3] It did not sound like a glowing endorsement of the infant Radio 1's *raison d'être*, although Muggeridge went on to say his plans were to expand on the 'tremendous success' of the station – and that would mean further opportunity for one of its biggest stars.

Savile's Travels was a vehicle for promoting the brand of Jimmy Savile. It was predicated on constant movement and bringing its host into contact with ordinary people. In doing so, it provided a showcase for his extraordinary lifestyle as he variously got lost up Ben Nevis in a snowstorm while testing camping equipment, ran up the stairs of the Post Office Tower for charity or pushed a 13-year-old girl in a wheelchair the 24 miles from Watford to London to raise money for sick and handicapped children. The format established Jimmy Savile not so much as a man of the people, but *the* man of the people.

His world was now viewed through the prisms of publicity and profit. In pursuing seemingly philanthropic goals he still succeeded in advertising how much he was making. No chance was missed. A personal appearance to open a new extension of a Halifax biscuit factory allowed him to broadcast the fact he was donating his fee to charity. 'I suppose the tax people could be awkward and say that as I did the job, it was my fee,' he said. 'But I don't think they'll mind. They know it's difficult for stars to help charity. I don't get the needle to the taxman – we have a very good relationship.'[4]

He was a blur of perpetual motion, and ordered a custom-built motor home to facilitate his criss-crossing of Britain. 'I want to live the life of a gipsy,' he proclaimed on unveiling the £6,500 Mercedes Devon Conversions with its large double bed at the back, upholstery in red, gold tassels for looping back the curtains and a stained glass dividing door. It would provide his primary lodgings, and, more importantly, make him more elusive than ever. With its bed and guarantee of privacy, it was a vehicle built for purpose. As he said at the time, 'There is no end of uses to a motor caravan.'[5]

'They never knew where I went,' he told me of his bosses at the BBC. 'I used to park it outside Broadcasting House. People couldn't believe it. For about four years I parked on a piece of dirt around the back of King's Cross station.'

While the summer of 1969 saw rioting in the streets around the old family home off Burley Road in Leeds, Jimmy Savile was having the time of his life. He became the first civilian to be presented with a Marine Commando Green Beret. Shortly afterwards, he stripped to the waist and cavorted on a float with a 20-year-old carnival queen at the Battle of Flowers parade in Jersey. His mother rode in a car behind, holding aloft a card with the message: 'I'm watching you Jimmy'.[6] If Agnes Savile knew nothing of what her son was up to, their relationship was used to create the impermeable veneer of innocent fun that became his trademark.

In late September, Savile was asked to compère Radio 1's very first talk show, *Speakeasy*. Produced by Reverend Roy Trevivian of the BBC's Religious Broadcasting department, the 45-minute, Saturday afternoon discussion programme was designed, according to the *Radio Times*, to address 'what really matters to teenagers today'. As the nation's oldest teenager, Jimmy Savile would be required to interview experts and guests in between playing hit records and fielding questions from the studio audience of youngsters.

The novelist John Braine was one of the panel guests for an early show that tackled the subject of nudity. In admitting he liked looking at naked women, but still believed that 'short skirts and transparent blouses were the engines of the devil',[7] Braine epitomised the gulf between the old and young in a society that was in a state of flux. Other topics for shows included teenage marriage, drugs and alcohol.

In October, a *Speakeasy* on censorship played the controversial record, 'Je t'aime, moi non plus' by Jane Birkin and Serge Gainsbourg. The single had been banned by the BBC and described by the Vatican as 'obscene'. Afterwards, producer Roy Trevivian said he agreed with the ban. Jimmy Savile had different ideas, however. 'To my mind the words are completely innocent,' he said. 'It's just the heavy breathing that gives rise to certain thoughts.'[8]

In another programme discussing the issue of birth control, Savile said something that would have stung the girl Alan Leeke knew in Manchester, or the young secretary raped in London: 'I have never given anyone a kid in my life and I am sure that if I was having it off and the Pope said I had committed a sin by not producing offspring, I would say I'd wait to appear before Our Lord because I don't think he'd be that unreasonable.'[9]

Trevivian, a Methodist minister turned Anglican clergyman, was a brilliant but troubled character. 'He was a quite extraordinary person,' says Reverend Colin Semper of the man he succeeded as the show's producer. 'He was a really dynamic presence in religious broadcasting, but he drank quite a bit.'

An obituary for Trevivian bears this out: 'The work of a producer-cum-performer perfectly fitted one side of his character, but left the damaged side cruelly exposed,' it said. 'The years of total abstinence required of him by Methodism were more than made up for in Broadcasting House bars.'[10]

Despite Trevivian's drinking and bouts of melancholy, *Speakeasy* quickly built a reputation for attracting high-profile guests. In the build-up to the 1970 general election, Defence Minister Denis Healey and Conservative party chairman Anthony Barber both appeared in a bid to appeal to young voters. In January 1971, Enoch Powell faced Jimmy Savile's inimitable brand of questioning: 'Now Enoch, what do you think about the permissive society at the moment?'. 'Now Enoch, you've got two lovely girls and well, if they'd been lads instead of girls, what do you think about pre-marital sex?'

Bosses at the BBC were won over by Jimmy Savile's ability to act as a bridge between generations and social classes. So much so that he was the controversial choice to present a BBC2 show, *Ten Years of What?*, that looked back on the 1960s. And rather than falling flat, as some critics within the BBC predicted, he earned fresh acclaim for the way he approached interviews with heavyweights such as Cardinal Heenan, the Archbishop of Westminster, Enoch Powell, Malcolm Muggeridge and Arnold Schlesinger, former aide to President Kennedy.

As a profile piece in the respected magazine the *Listener* later suggested, 'The way he conducted himself in BBC TV's review of the decade ... persuaded many of those within television, who had dismissed him as a mere fairground huckster, that he had a keen understanding of current affairs; and in *Speakeasy*, his capacity to grasp the most esoteric of subjects and conduct discussions with some high-powered intellects betokens an active brain under the cloth and bells'.[11]

In August 1970, Jimmy Savile was invited by the BBC to sit on watchdog panels that advised on programmes and policy. 'I'm very pleased about it,' he said. 'The governors realise that even though I have straw on the outside of my head, it doesn't mean there's straw inside it too.'[12]

That same summer, Jill (not her real name) was a newly married 19-year-old living in Brighton. She told me about one day receiving an unexpected visit from a man driving a Rolls-Royce. The man told her he was Jimmy Savile's chauffeur, and his boss, who was making a personal appearance at Worthing Town Hall, wanted to meet her. Jill had been a member of Savile's fan club and had written to the disc jockey two years earlier.[13] She agreed to go.

When Savile spotted her, she said, he put his arm round her waist and frogmarched her to his motor caravan, locking the door behind them once she was inside. 'He was standing up, and it was weird. He said to me, "Oh you're a beautiful little dolly bird" and I just sat there and thought, "Is this a compliment?" I wasn't sure. He said, "I'd like to lock you up in my cupboard and take you with me everywhere I go", and I sort of just looked at him and thought, "What is happening here?" Then he said, "I could buy the house next door to your house and I'd be very happy." He kept saying, "I'm the strongest man in England" and I remember I just looked at him and thought, "This guy's a nutter." Then it happened so fast; he was on top of me. I was back on the bed and Jimmy Savile was on top of me. It was literally a fight. He was trying to rape me.'

'He shoved my hand in his trousers. He had an erection,' she says. His hands, meanwhile, were exploring under her skirt. According to Jill, Savile demanded to know whether she was on the pill. When she replied she was not, he got angry and shouted, 'Why not?'[14]

After twenty minutes of struggle, Jill managed to pull herself free. As she headed for the door, Savile asked whether she wanted to be a dancer on *Top of the Pops* and said she could take something from the motor caravan as a souvenir. She took a small crucifix with a deer at the foot. She still had it when she reported the attack to Sussex Police in 2007, and when she recounted her story for a second time to a Crown Prosecution lawyer in 2012.[15]

'Such an ectoplasm exists around [Savile],' wrote Philip Norman in the *Guardian* in the summer of 1971, 'that it has become difficult to perceive the actual man at all . . . He and the BBC are now one, and what a beast with two backs and several wigs that makes.'[16]

Norman's tirade broadened into a wider attack on what he saw as the insidious effect of Radio 1 on the nation's intellectual health: 'Savile and Young and Blackburn – how like the names on a death roll they sound – are in fact part of a life that will not change: a power stronger than government, more insidious than filth, and as permanent as the Inland Revenue.'

Although he was never able to laugh at himself – the wilfully bizarre appearance, the nonsensical catchphrases and the espousing of bizarre philosophies on life were all protective layers, and ones he managed – Jimmy Savile could afford to let such criticisms ride. The truth is that his burnished reputation, one that he had fashioned himself as an everyman saint, was now blinding all but his victims and those, like Norman, who were repelled by his very being.

And how appropriate that this elevation should be celebrated in the first month of the new decade with an appearance on *This is*

Your Life, after Eamonn Andrews surprised him by stepping out of an inspection parade of Royal Marines.

Jimmy Savile had discovered that people would do pretty much anything for him because of what he did for charity. 'People leap about, yes they do, they leap about if I want something,' he confessed.[17] On a wheelchair push from Rochester to Bromley in Kent, he revealed that he wrote to the organiser with his now customary demands: 'Find me a blonde teenage bird who lives in a house with a drive so that I can park outside so she can wake me in the morning with tea at eight o'clock.' 'They leapt about,' he said. And in the morning? 'Knock, knock.'

Charles Hullighan, head porter at Leeds General Infirmary, enthused in a newspaper interview about Savile's work at the hospital. 'At present most of Jimmy's work is in Casualty,' he said. 'He arrives at midday and stays till five the following morning. Sometimes he comes and works on the busiest nights in Casualty – Saturdays. Sometimes he goes on ambulance duty.

'If you really want to know what Jimmy gets out of working in the Infirmary,' added Hullighan, 'I think it is for the relaxation of meeting people. People are his life. You have to see him handling them to realise how deeply he is involved.'[18]

What Hullighan got out of it is another matter entirely. In 1972, he was made company secretary of the firm that dealt with Jimmy Savile's earnings. He was paid a monthly salary and contributions towards a pension, sums that enabled him to own homes in Leeds and Scarborough. Exactly what he earned is not known, but the *Telegraph* reported that in 1981 he shared in directors' pay of £91,500, the equivalent of more than £300,000 today.[19]

At Broadmoor, Jimmy Savile had awarded himself the title of 'Honorary Assistant Entertainments Officer'. He began organising concerts on Thursday evenings and a regular disco night. 'I am the hospital's contact with show business,' he explained of his role. 'I don't work at Broadmoor as I do in Leeds Infirmary. It is not that sort of place. But I have access to all the wings and I visit to talk to patients. Chat, as you know, is a form of therapy, so I can be of help.'[20] The same method was working at Britain's highest security mental hospital.

In March 1971, soon after accepting a Carl-Alan disc jockey of the year award from Prince Charles, Jimmy Savile set out on his greatest physical test to date: an 876-mile walk from John O'Groats to Land's End. His *Savile's Travels* motor caravan followed behind, the driving shared by the Manchester taxi driver he had bought his first Rolls-Royce from, a young businessman from Hull, his brother Vince and the transport manager from Broadmoor Hospital, another hospital employee who had been sucked in and who, like others, would be named as a beneficiary in his will.

Thirty-one days later, a 33-strong Royal Marines band, helicopters and a crowd of hundreds joined him for the last two miles of his epic trek. 'A fantastic fact is that I've never been alone for one hour since leaving John O'Groats,' he wrote in his newspaper column the next week. 'I've wheeled cripples along in wheelchairs who didn't want to be left out . . . I've pushed prams with assorted babies in. I've slowed down to a shuffle with a 90-year-old lady gripping my arm and sped fleet-footed downhill . . . with an entire youth club tailing out behind like Halley's Comet.'[21]

Walking among his flock, shepherd's staff in hand, Jimmy Savile's conviction that he was a 'chosen one' had transmogrified into something altogether more terrifying. A self-appointed Messiah figure was now among us.

PART FOUR

After completing his length-of-Britain walk, Jimmy Savile rewarded himself with a short break before starting work on *Savile's Yorkshire Travels*, a new television series for BBC North. More likely is that he was lying low after the body of 15-year-old Claire McAlpine was discovered by her mother, on the floor, next to her bed in the family home on Bushey Hill Lane, Watford. Empty sleeping pill bottles and a red leatherette diary with a tiny lock and key were found nearby.

The girl's mother, Vera McAlpine, claimed the diary revealed her adopted daughter had been having sex with BBC disc jockeys she met through *Top of the Pops* after appearing as one of the show's dancing 'dolly birds' under the stage name Samantha Claire.

As the *News of the World* reported, 'The diary told of one radio disc jockey who took Samantha to his home for the night and gave her a pill which made her feel she was "floating on a cloud" It told of another DJ who asked the teenager back to his sumptuously furnished home and about whom passages in the diary so shocked her mother that she immediately contacted the BBC.' [1]

Claire McAlpine's suicide was the second controversy to hit the show in a short space of time. Since 14 February 1971, the BBC had been reeling from seven consecutive weeks of stories published by the *News of the World*. They were exposés that promised to lift 'the lid off the BBC and the glamorous world of the disc-jockey'. [2] Payola – cash payments to obtain plugs for records and appearances of bands on TV shows – was the first scandal. It was one that the BBC hoped would die down after it launched a half-hearted investigation into bribery and made a token dismissal or two. It was wrong.

The revelations contained damaging details on the use of call girls and sex parties as inducements to 'well known BBC celebrities', the deceit of producers and DJs in pushing records in which they had a financial interest, the rigging of the pop charts and female record pluggers 'working on a bed-for-plugs basis'.

'There are only two ways to get air-play . . . money and sex,' claimed one promotions man in the first instalment of the paper's sensational scoop. And with the BBC enjoying a monopoly on airplay for pop music in the post-pirate era, the result was 'a Klondike-style rush from the record industry'.

If payola was the name given to the scandal that engulfed the BBC, the five-month investigation by a team of the *News of the World*'s reporters went a good deal further than the murky practices involved with promoting new records.

Jimmy Savile managed to stay out of the story, other than for a quote he gave in early January when the allegations first surfaced: 'Pluggers and payola people never bother me,' he said. 'What could they give me that I haven't got already?'[3] It was true that *Savile's Travels* was not regarded as a prime target for the pluggers; at the Tuesday morning 'surgeries' in the Radio 1 Club offices on the fourth floor of Egton House, the holy grail was getting records approved by the producers of shows presented by Tony Blackburn, Tony Brandon, Dave Lee Travis, Terry Wogan and Jimmy Young.

More pertinently, Jimmy Savile was not someone who particularly liked his fellow disc jockeys. He was therefore unlikely to have been caught rolling around the floor with them in a pot-fuelled orgy at a plugger's flat.

Things became more uncomfortable, however, when the investigation moved on to *Top of the Pops*, and specifically the activities of one of Savile's good friends, the show's in-house photographer Harry Goodwin. The pair had known each other since before the programme's launch, from their days of knocking around together with Bill Benny in Manchester. 'We had the best of times; we were very close and loved arguing the point together,' Goodwin recalled many years later. 'We would argue about who was the better with women.'

Undercover reporters listened in as Goodwin boasted of taking pornographic pictures of young girls on *Top of the Pops* and showing 'blue movies' in his locked dressing room for production staff. When an 'internationally famous British male star' offered to buy one of the films, Goodwin refused, saying, 'You are not having it because – [another famous TV star] is one of my best customers and he has not seen this yet. He will go mad when he sees this.'[4]

Goodwin claimed he was 'shopped' and went on to relate how three CID officers and a security officer at the BBC 'inquired into the matter'. He said, 'They went through every locker – they were all wrenched open – and they never found nothing.' More telling is that he admitted he was tipped off 'by friends'.[5]

Stanley Dorfman confirms that *Top of the Pops* had been the subject of a police investigation in the late 1960s after allegations were made that underage girls were being exploited in the dressing rooms before and after shows. 'There was a rumour,' he explained before admitting members of staff were interviewed.[6] 'The police came to inquire and we had them in the office for a week,' he says. 'Nothing came of it and they went away.'

In Goodwin's taped conversation with the *News of the World*, he talked of girls in the studio audience posing for 'porny' photographs, and recounted a liaison between a male member of a pop group and a girl dancer. 'The people who see that show don't know what's happened [behind the scenes],' he bragged to the undercover reporter. 'I think they should start the cameras in the dressing rooms.' Less than two weeks after the story ran, Claire McAlpine was dead.

Vera McAlpine told the *News of the World* how she had read Claire's diary a month before her daughter took her own life. She had been horrified to discover entries containing accounts of Claire spending the night with two BBC DJs, one with a show on Radio 1 and the other a presenter on *Top of the Pops*, and had banned her daughter from ever appearing on the show again. Of the *Top of the Pops* presenter mentioned in the diary entries, she said, 'Some of the passages were so shocking that I would rather not repeat them . . . But the police know what they said.'

She went on to recount how she had phoned the BBC to tell them about the second DJ. 'I gave them the man's name,' she said. 'I asked if they realised [Claire] was a child of 15, and I said something had to be done about it to save other girls from the same sort of thing. I demanded to speak to "the man right at the top" but they said quite abruptly that this was impossible.'

Sometime later, Vera McAlpine said she did finally receive a call from the BBC. It was explained to her that the DJ in question had been spoken to and had flatly denied the allegation so there was nothing more to be done. The BBC did not interview Vera McAlpine or her daughter, who had appeared on *Top of the Pops* on four occasions. Neither, she said, did the BBC contact the police: 'They simply shrugged it off as though nothing had happened.'[7]

There are two small but potentially significant details in what Vera McAlpine told a reporter from the Press Association. The first is one of the disc jockeys had offered Samantha a 'contract which would make her famous'. The second was her daughter had taken part in two television programmes in Yorkshire.[8]

After her death, two of Samantha's friends came forward to recount their own experiences on *Top of the Pops*. Donna Scruff was just 13 and yet had appeared as a dancer in the audience on three occasions. 'We are supposed to be 15,' she said, 'but most of the girls are much younger and lie simply to get in.'[9]

She spoke of how Claire, or 'Samantha' as she was known to them, told people she was 23, and her only goal was to be on television. If that meant sleeping with a disc jockey, so be it. Donna Scruff also recalled that Claire was invited back to the *Top of the Pops* presenter's dressing room and had subsequently gone out with him on a couple of occasions. Of the other man mentioned in Claire McAlpine's diary, Scruff said he was a disc jockey who picked her up after a broadcast of *The Rosko Show* on Radio 1, before taking her back to his flat. They'd had sex, but only once; he'd made her do the washing-up while he watched boxing on television.

Samantha had told her that two other girls, both aged 15, also went to the flat from the show, a detail corroborated by 14-year-old Janine Hartwell. 'I know a group of 15-year-old girls who slept with him after his shows,' she said of the DJ in question.

Vera McAlpine's lament is indicative of the prevailing attitudes at the time. 'I now realise I should have telephoned the police,' she said, 'but I thought they would be more severe with my daughter than they would be with the pop stars.'[10]

Officers with Hertfordshire Police took possession of Claire McAlpine's diary, before passing it on to Detective Chief Superintendent Richard Booker of Scotland Yard. Booker had been chosen to lead the wider investigation into activities at the BBC.

Lord Hill, chairman of the BBC Governors, launched his own private inquiry, headed by Brian Neill, a highly respected QC. The heavily redacted results of his investigation were not publicly revealed until some 42 years later.

On 5 April 1971, the BBC announced plans to introduce a minimum age limit for girl dancers in the audience of *Top of the Pops*, a system of adult chaperones and a requirement for written permission from the girls' parents. The corporation's official reaction to the death of Claire McAlpine was typically non-committal: 'This would seem to be a matter for the police and the coroner's court and the BBC has no comment to make.'[11]

It is interesting to note that it was Jimmy Savile, one of two regular presenters of *Top of the Pops*, who decided to comment on these measures the very next day. In fact, he spoke to a number of newspapers, indicating that the BBC had put him forward as a spokesman.

Savile protested the show was 'remarkably free of seductions and drug taking but there are lots of dates made by everybody'. After seven years presenting *Top of the Pops*, he claimed, 'I have lots of girlfriends. I've visited their homes and count their parents as friends too.'[12] It was a textbook alibi from a man who had perfected the art of seducing parents before abusing their children.

He went on to liken *Top of the Pops* to a 'high class discotheque' saying that 'with 250 people involved you could always find scandal if you dug deeply enough'. He insisted he could not remember Claire McAlpine, despite the fact she had danced on a show he presented and his admission that he had 'an eye for a pretty girl'. He said he was 'upset' and hoped the inquest would reveal any association with the programme, before stating his understanding that there was a minimum age of 16 for girls in the audience. 'But it's not surprising if anybody gets in who is younger,' he added. 'Who knows these days if a girl is 14 or 17?'

In fact, Jimmy Savile seems to have treated Claire McAlpine's death as an affront. He appeared on the popular magazine programme *Pebble Mill*, surrounded by teenage girls, and spoke of the high standards governing everybody who worked on *Top of the Pops*. Then, on the eve of the inquest into Claire McAlpine's death, 'bachelor disc jockey Jimmy Savile', as he was billed in the *Daily Express*, went further still. 'Many a time I have dated a good looking girl I have met on the show,' he confessed. 'But what I say to them is "Ask your folks if I can come round for tea." I much prefer being with a family, with a pretty girl in the centre, than a session in the back of my car. For one thing, you can't see how pretty the girl is in the back of my car.'[13]

What's staggering is how little Jimmy Savile tried to conceal what he was doing. Even in a culture that had been altered, if not transformed, by the sexual revolution, albeit a culture that still celebrated the leery comedy of Benny Hill and his ilk, it's impossible not to be shocked by the fact that one of its biggest stars could openly talk about charming a girl's parents before molesting her in the back of his car. That Savile then spelt out exactly how and where he did this, is even more astonishing.

'My dressing room at *Top of the Pops* is a weekly meeting place of 20 to 30 people,' Savile went on. 'Half of them are teenagers, the other half are parents. The parents are not there to chaperone their daughters. They are there because they are as interested in me as their children are.'

He said there was 'a popular misconception' that young girls were only interested in sex. 'Well,' he joked, '19 and 20-year-olds with some experience of the world may look at me as a sexual object. But the younger ones, the 14 to 16-year-olds, don't even think about sex. In fact they would be most offended if you suggested anything sexual to them.'

To the *Daily Mirror*, he explained, 'I've met young crumpet that would knock your eyes out. Fourteen-year-old girls with bodies on 'em like Gina Lollobrigida. I love 'em, but not in the going to bed sense.' He claimed that girls went to 'great lengths' to find out where he lived and often camped out on his doorstep. 'Once,' he declared, 'a big sack arrived at my home with "A present for Jimmy" marked on it. Well there was this chick inside it. She was just seventeen. We had a cup of tea together and whiled away an hour together chatting.'[14]

So here was Jimmy Savile putting it all out there once again, ensuring his unorthodox, high-wire alibi was released into the public domain, while simultaneously reminding the nation of what a trustworthy, family-friendly figure he was. It was becoming dogma, an insurance policy: admit to just about everything, even his modus operandi – charming the parents, taking girls for a ride in his car, having teenagers in his flat. It was now a game, a twisted thrill. Nobody was going to touch him; he was worth too much to the BBC, and too much to the needy of the nation.

One can only speculate at how Vera and David McAlpine felt as they prepared for the inquest and read quotes such as these in the morning papers. More hurtful was the postscript to one of stories which suggested detectives were now considering the possibility their daughter was a fantasist.

On 7 April, nine days after Claire McAlpine's death, coroner Marcus Goodman recorded a 'suicide' verdict. A police constable read out the last entry in Claire's diary from the morning of 29 March. 'I can't take it anymore, I am just a dreamer and none of my dreams will ever come true.' The 15-year-old had swallowed two bottles of her mother's sleeping pills and eaten bread to keep them down.

At the inquest, she was described as being 'in a world of her own'[15] and effectively dismissed.

More than 40 years on, the diary is unaccounted for, although Claire's half-brother Mark Ufland insists Jimmy Savile was one of those named in its pages. 'Savile was the one who was mentioned primarily,' he says.[16] 'As far as I know, Jimmy Savile was interviewed as a witness. The diary was dismissed as delusional. It was the word of a 15-year-old with emotional problems against the word of the BBC.'[17]

According to a BBC source spoken to by the *Telegraph*, James Crocker, a solicitor on Brian Neill's inquiry team, questioned Jimmy Savile. At the interview, Savile refused to cooperate and was said to have mocked the entire process.

'Savile came before Crocker but just made fun of him,' the BBC source explained. 'He sent Crocker up, and Crocker complained bitterly to the BBC. He went to the head of the BBC's legal team, Richard Marshall, who had set up the inquiry, but there was nothing he could do about it. This all remained private within the BBC.'[18] Internal BBC correspondence from the time demonstrates that the decision not to make the report public went right to the top: Director General Sir Charles Curran wrote to BBC Chairman Lord Hill to recommend as much.

In 2013, a Freedom of Information request finally brought into the light of day the 64-page document completed by Brian Neill QC in 1972, albeit with vast swathes redacted. In it, Neill acknowledged that *Top of the Pops* presented 'certain problems in that it introduces into the labyrinthine TV Centre a substantial number of teenage girls' before urging the BBC to issue 'clear guidelines' as to who was to be ultimately responsible for the behaviour and control of 'audiences of this kind'.

Bill Cotton, who had become the BBC's head of Light Entertainment after the death of Tom Sloan in 1970, was interviewed and appears to have succeeded in persuading Neill that instances of immorality on the show were rare. 'The girl [Claire McAlpine] had come to see [Cotton] on several occasions,' the report states, 'and had invented stories for the purpose of getting access to him. He said she seemed to him in a sort of fantasy world but that she had not made any sexual advances of any kind.'[19]

It is tempting to speculate what specifics those 'invented stories' Cotton spoke of might have contained. What is clear, though, is that Jimmy Savile's boss at the BBC was not prepared to listen to anything that might possibly tarnish one of his brightest stars. It was just as Savile had figured. He had picked his target carefully, and covered his tracks with ruthless efficiency.

Later, in another of the non-redacted passages from the Neill report, an executive makes a point of praising Jimmy Savile at a BBC management board meeting for offering an 'effective defence' of Top of the Pops.[20] For the BBC, this was all that mattered. And Jimmy Savile recognised as much.

By March 1972, less than a year after Claire McAlpine's death, he evidently felt comfortable enough to take a reporter from the Weekly News into his dressing room at Top of the Pops. It was described as being 'full of girls'[21]. They included four girls from Halifax that Savile had met 'during church discussions', a 'lonely' American he encountered on Speakeasy, a Scottish girl he met through Belfort Hospital in Fort William and a young TV actress who was playing a schoolgirl when Savile first noticed her as a 16-year-old. She had walked across the Top of the Pops studio floor wearing a 'lurex crochet suit'. Savile stopped her, recorded an interview for Savile's Travels and then wined and dined the girl's parents that night. According to the paper, he had become 'a friend of the family' who 'pops up to their Ipswich home whenever he has the time'.

Jimmy Savile's response to escaping unscathed from the payola scandal and the suicide of Claire McAlpine was to throw himself more conspicuously than ever into his charity work. He was photographed with a crew of Scarborough lifeboat men ahead of a major national walk to raise money for the RNLI, spent a week touring the country for the National Association of Youth Clubs and led a crowd of 30,000 in the fourth annual walk for the Central Remedial Clinic in Dublin. At the end, he was reported to have 'delighted the crowd by stripping to the waist and flinging his shorts into a screaming throng'.[1]

In the autumn of 1971, a journalist tracked Savile down to his motor caravan, parked as usual in a seedy area by a refuse tip close to King's Cross station. 'I tramp around the country like a grey timber wolf,' he explained, after being served tea from a transport café by his driver. 'I'm a wild animal, aware of the world and its surroundings and aware of my own needs.'[2] He then boasted of having raised £60,000 for charity that year with the intention of making £100,000 by the time he was done.

He talked of the two days a week he worked as a volunteer porter at Leeds General Infirmary and of the similar role he performed at Stoke Mandeville where he also had a key role with the hospital's League of Friends. Then there was his title of 'Honorary Assistant Entertainments Officer' at Broadmoor, with a secondment to Rampton, its sister hospital in Nottinghamshire. Just a couple of months earlier, he had taken 10 patients and a number of staff from Rampton on a coach trip to Scarborough.

It is noteworthy that the article commented on the fact that some people 'put his charity work down to publicity, tax-loss, a guilty conscience or all three'. Naturally Savile shrugged such doubts off: '"I'm a good Catholic," he said. "I go to church whenever I can and I talk to God. Sometimes I ask God if I am doing the right thing; if I should continue helping where I can."'

David Winter was a BBC producer who occasionally filled in for Roy Trevivian on *Speakeasy*, and later became head of Religious Broadcasting. 'I once listened bemused as Savile expiated at length in the BBC canteen on the reasons why St Peter wouldn't dare bar him from heaven,' he said. "What do you mean he's led an immoral life?" God would say to him. "Have you any idea how much money he's raised for charity? Or how many hours he'd put in as a porter at that hospital? Get them doors opened now, and quick!"'[3]

Now a Church of England priest and a columnist for the *Church Times*, Winter recalled trying to tell Jimmy Savile that religion didn't quite work like that. 'It's a million miles from the Christian concepts of sin and grace,' he said. 'Savile, a practising Roman Catholic, was in fact echoing a whiff of a medieval idea – supererogation. I do more good than is strictly required in order to offset faults and sins – mine, or other people's.'[4]

The BBC sacked Roy Trevivian in 1972. As producer of the *Thought for the Day* programme he had allowed a speaker to launch an attack on Prime Minister Edward Heath's handling of the escalating problems in Northern Ireland. When added to his drinking and occasional outbursts, it was judged the time was right to let him go. Producing duties on *Speakeasy* were largely taken over by Reverend Colin Semper, then head of Religious Broadcasting for BBC Radio.

In light of the scandal, I asked Semper how he viewed Jimmy Savile's relationship with his faith. 'That's a very, very difficult question,' he replied. 'He had a kind of delight in saying that he went to church. But the going to church was not in any way a community thing. It always seemed to me that he was in and out.

It was episodic in a way . . . His faith might have been abundant to him but the coherence of it was very difficult for me to understand.'

Another aspect of Savile's life that Semper found hard to fathom was his relationship with his mother. 'My success has extended her life,' Savile told one newspaper,[6] before explaining how it was impossible for him to fall in love while she remained his responsibility. 'There was a kind of exclusivity to it, there really was,' Semper offered of his bond with the Duchess. 'I don't think I ever had a conversation with him where he didn't quote her or talk about her or say he was going to see her.'

By the end of 1971, Jimmy Savile was being described as 'the spearhead of [the BBC's] Christian attack'.[7] He was chosen to present the *Top of the Pops* leading up to the Queen's Speech on Christmas Day, and on Boxing Day, two hours were put aside to allow him to tell the story of his life. 'Jimmy Savile is the BBC's not so secret Christmas formula,' stated the *Sunday Times*, 'with new added RELIGION.'

Savile had also been invited to join Lord Longford's 52-strong commission of inquiry into pornography, which had been inspired by Mary Whitehouse's campaign to clean up the British media. Longford was determined to challenge claims that Soho's red light area and the proliferation of adult magazines did no harm to the moral fabric of the nation. Jimmy Savile joined high court judges, clergymen, psychiatrists, professors, and, bizarrely, Cliff Richard on the commission. He described it as a 'worthy and well-meaning attempt to sanctify Sodom before it's too late'.[8]

On the first day of 1972, Jimmy Savile's stealthy progress towards the centre of the establishment was recognised when he was named in the Queen's New Year's honours list. The award of an OBE was in recognition of the many thousands of pounds he had raised for charity and his tireless work for hospitals.

He said that he opened the letter from Prime Minister Harold Wilson late one night in Leeds and was so excited he phoned his brother Vince before driving to Leeds General Infirmary in his van. 'Somebody had just died,' he told me. 'An old lady of 80 . . . so I'm pushing her from the ward to the fridge and it brought everything back to square one.'

A stretcher-bearer at Leeds General Infirmary was asked to comment on the news and said, 'They often say he's a bit of a twit. Us, we think he's a bit of a bloody saint.'[9] Such an endorsement might have had something to do with the fact he was offering porters free holidays in the caravans he kept on the coastlines of North Yorkshire, Dorset and Devon.

Jimmy Savile was now openly boasting about being able to 'claim Lords, Ladies, Earls, Ministers, Cardinals and branches of the royal family as friends and acquaintances'.[10]

In the first instalment of a major newspaper series on his life, he talked of his days as a black market operator in Leeds and marvelled at how far he had come. 'Little did I think, in those super, starving days, that I would finish up dropping cigar ash on the Queen Mother's carpet,' he said before regaling readers with how he had taken the opportunity to sit on the throne at St James's Palace, or 'that perfect Princess Alexandra's husband would bash his head on a cupboard in the infamous *Savile's Travels* caravan.'

His use of the word 'infamous' was another hint at what was really going on behind the scenes. Dennis Garbutt was employed as the driver of Savile's motor caravan at the time. His wife Lucy told a newspaper that Dennis, who now suffers from dementia, was a patient in Leeds General Infirmary when Savile offered him the job. She said he lasted a year before quitting in disgust.

'Savile would say to him, "Go and get a cup of tea, Den", and that was his way of saying he wanted to be alone and it was obvious why,' Lucy Garbutt said.[11] 'Den would then go to the pictures or just walk the streets for a while. [He] knew what was going on and we regret not doing anything about it at the time. He said Savile would have girls wherever he went.'

She reported that her husband told her how Savile routinely lured young girls onto the double mattress at the back of the motor caravan.

'I couldn't say how many, it was all over the country every time they stopped,' she continued. '[Dennis] said, "These girls are barely older than our daughter", who was 12 at the time. When he stopped he would have young girls . . . I really regret it now but Den always said he had nothing to prove it, he just knew what was going on.'

In the second newspaper instalment of his life story, Jimmy Savile wrote at length about spending the night with six girls in a caravan. 'About a thousand arms and legs pinned me to the bed,' he claimed, describing the scene as looking like 'a cross between a double-X sex film and multi-legged octopus.'[12]

He then described the 'pandemonium' when knocking was heard at the door of the caravan the next morning. One of the girls rose naked and looked out of the window to see her mother and father outside. In his autobiography, Savile admitted, 'Escape was uppermost in my mind.' But after rapidly getting dressed, he called them in and then bluffed that he had been there half an hour without being offered any breakfast. 'Heaven be praised, the parents stood for it,' he added.[13]

This anecdote was followed by another: 'It was only a little later that fine summer day when trouble loomed again.'[14] Savile then described walking along the beach with two minders when a girl wearing a one-piece swimsuit spotted him. He said she looked 'good enough to eat'. The girl invited him to meet her parents and explained they were staying in a caravan.

Savile wrote that he left his minders with the parents and went back to the caravan with the girl. Inside, he reported the temperature was 'nearly 100 degrees' so he sunk into a chair 'wringing wet with the heat and temptation'. Just as the girl began changing out of her swimming costume, the parents returned.

By putting it in print, Jimmy Savile was, in effect, performing the same mind trick on the readers of his autobiography as he did on the parents of the youngsters he went on to abuse, having first charmed them from the protective clutches of their parents.

Dee Coles experienced this brazen approach in the summer of 1972, when she was a 14-year-old enjoying a holiday with her mother on the island of Jersey. Jimmy Savile had his motor caravan parked in the car park of the hotel where they were staying.

Forty years later, Coles told ITV News that Jimmy Savile didn't seem like a stranger because he was on television so often. She produced photographs of the star with his arms wrapped round her outside the vehicle.

Coles and her friend accepted Savile's invitation to step inside. It was only when he locked the door of his motor caravan behind them, she explained, that she felt what she describes as 'immense panic'. The two girls were made to perform sex acts on the man described as the BBC's religious 'spearhead'.

Just like Jill in Worthing, Dee Coles's hands were thrust down the front of Jimmy Savile's trousers. 'It was my first introduction to the male body,' she recalled, 'so the whole thing was just an incredible shock. After it happened, he tried to get us back in the van a second time, and my memory is that for me it was the end of the holiday. I just didn't go near him or the van or see [the other girl] again.'[15]

When she looks at those photos, Dee Coles thinks back to what a young 14-year-old she was. 'I think 14-year-olds in the Seventies just were', she says. 'There was no way any of my friends or I wore make-up or got dressed up to go out on the town. We were quite naïve. It's always going to be a shock to anyone being sexually abused but the innocence just disappears as soon as something like that happens.'

'It saddens me greatly to think that so many other children suffered sexual abuse from Jimmy Savile. As a 14-year-old you don't have the thought that it might be happening to anyone else.'[16]

And still the public face of Jimmy Savile remained blemish-free. The same motor caravan in which he had abused so many young people was parked outside Buckingham Palace when the Queen Mother presented him with an OBE. Accompanying him on his trip to the palace were his mother and a porter from the X-ray department at Leeds General Infirmary.

Afterwards, he cavorted for photographers and film crews and began signing autographs, with the addition of its three new letters.

Six months later, Lord Longford published his report on pornography. It concluded that young people were 'particularly vulnerable to the sex exploiters' influence, and need special protection'. It also defined pornography as that which 'exploits and dehumanises sex, so that human beings are treated as things and women in particular are sex objects'.[17] Jimmy Savile didn't utter a word throughout his time on the commission.

I t was Valentine's Day and I was standing, as per Jimmy Savile's instructions, outside the Thai Rose massage parlour on Marylebone High Street. I didn't know it at the time, but he was watching me. He was laughing and pointing with his pals in Ossie's Café, the greasy spoon next door. It was one of his regular haunts when he was staying at his London pied-à-terre close to Broadcasting House.

I was working on my third major magazine profile piece on Jimmy Savile and he had offered to provide 'some colour', which explained why I was standing in a light drizzle outside a dubious-looking establishment on a busy street in central London. As the rain became heavier, Savile eventually poked his head out of the door of the café. 'Now then,' he croaked, still pretending to be doubled up with the hilarity of it all. 'You're going to catch your death of cold out there.'

Four years after our first interview, I now believed that Jimmy Savile enjoyed the fact that I knew so much about him, or had at least amassed a wealth of material. It pandered to an ego of quite vast proportions; an ego he consistently denied possessing. This story, I had told him in advance, was to be different. I did not want to hear the same old tales – 'The Not Again Child', 'The Pirate of the Dancehall', 'The Fun' and 'The Brain Damage'. I wanted to write a piece about the hidden Jimmy Savile; the man of influence with unlikely connections and hitherto unseen reserves of power. First, though, there was the small matter of breakfast. He ordered a cup of tea and two fried eggs on white bread.

Savile's teeth were a mess, a collection of jagged talons chipped into random shapes and differing shades of grey and yellow. I had watched him eat on a number of occasions and it wasn't a spectacle I enjoyed. With egg yolk dripping from his lips, I concentrated on my own breakfast and tried not to look up.

He seemed particularly happy with himself on this particular morning, specifically about his choice of venues for this latest article: a greasy spoon café, the Athenaeum Club where he was a member, and back to his flat in Leeds, where once again he had suggested I should stay overnight.

As we ate, I told him I was in the midst of organising a charity event and would appreciate his advice. His response was a lengthy monologue about how he got everyone from the governor of the Bank of England to the Duke of Edinburgh working for him in the drive to build a new National Spinal Injuries Centre at Stoke Mandeville. 'You've got to be a bit of a conman to make it work,' he concluded.

This was just a prelude to what I really wanted to find out about, namely the circles he'd mixed in over the years, and specifically his relationship with Lord Louis Mountbatten, the Duke of Edinburgh's favourite uncle and a man many believed to be the power behind the House of Windsor. First, though, I had to listen to a 10-minute account of how he earned his Royal Marine Commando Green Beret. As he unfurled his story, I was aware of customers coming in and out, waiters shimmying from behind the counter, and the coffee machine gurgling, spitting and coughing.

'That was when I first met Lord Louis,' Savile said, and I snapped back to attention. 'He was the commandant general. It was the attraction of opposites. He had not the faintest idea of who I was or what I did. All he knew was that I was a freak with long hair. He wanted to know what this long-haired geezer was doing with this crack fighting corps.'

According to Savile, Mountbatten had been the man who sanctioned his entry into 'the Firm', the term he regularly used to describe the royal family. 'Whenever it came to doing anything, he

[Mountbatten] would say, "I'll cut the ribbon but get Savile down. He can do the speeches. He does it better than me." Coming from Lord Louis, and he was the favourite uncle of the Prince of Wales, it meant I hooked up with the Prince of Wales. It was the respect that Lord Louis had for me. It meant what was good enough for Lord Louis was good enough for him. That's how I got to know all these people. Lord Louis was the governor.'

Savile recounted how he had once gone to open the new sergeants' mess at the Marine Commando training base at Lympstone. 'Lord Louis was going to come down and open it,' he said. 'But he said, "I'll cut the ribbon but get Savile down here to make the speeches."'

Before I could press him, he caromed off into a convoluted story about how the Marines had raised the money for five 'amazing crystal chandeliers' for the new mess. 'Being a sniffer-abouter,' he said, 'I realised the press were going to take them to the cleaners for spending fifteen grand on five crystal chandeliers.'

Eventually, he got round to explaining that Mountbatten had officially opened the new mess before handing over to him to deal with the press. Savile said his deft handling of potentially tricky questions about the expensive new fixtures had greatly impressed the last viceroy of India, former sea lord and ex-head of the British armed forces, and that, he added, was enough to seal his entry into the establishment's innermost circles.

Such details were revealed only by knowing which stones to look under, but it was tiring, time-consuming work. We had a long way to go so I decided to move onto more familiar ground. Was Savile, as he liked to put it, still 'birding'?

'Yes, yes,' he blathered. 'But you have to adapt. One of the things that I had to adapt to some years ago was the fact of being older. This year I'm 81.' He pointed out 'two birds' that had come into Ossie's Café while we had been sitting at our table. I hadn't noticed either of them looking our way. 'I've got to adapt because at 81 I can't go pulling. It's obscene,' he said. He paused for a moment and looked out at the rain-lashed street. Then he repeated the point in case I hadn't quite got it: 'It's obscene.'

'I don't go to clubs, you see, because once you've been the boss you don't take kindly to being a punter. It wouldn't do for me to go in and start putting myself about a bit. There's not even a word for a guy of 81 trying to pull a younger woman.' He stopped again for a moment to chew on a corner of toast. 'It's obscene,' he said for the third time in 20 seconds.

The rain stopped as suddenly as it started. Jimmy Savile slurped on his mug of tea and brightened as quickly as the weather: 'If they hit me on the head and bundled me into the boot of a car and had their wicked way with me in a lay-by, I won't object. You've just got to adapt at not being able to do it.'

Released in March 2013, the report by Nottinghamshire Healthcare NHS Trust Forensic Division on Jimmy Savile's trips to Scarborough in 1971 and 1972 with patients from Rampton Psychiatric Hospital is a disconcerting document. This is not due to the revelations it contains, but because of what is not said, and the language used throughout.

In August 1971, Jimmy Savile organised and led a coach trip for 10 patients and members of staff to Scarborough during which, the report states, 'they visited an ice-cream parlour, went on a boat trip, had tea with the Lord Mayor, met some Scarborough officials and The Duchess'.[1] Note how an inquiry by a mental health institution into a serial paedophile's activities with psychiatric patients in its care refers to Agnes Savile.

The Lord Mayor of Scarborough in 1971 was Councillor Peter Jaconelli, otherwise known as the town's 'Ice Cream King'. Born in Glasgow and raised as a strict Roman Catholic, Jaconelli had lived in the North Yorkshire seaside town since the age of seven when his father moved the family business south in a bid to grab a slice of the lucrative seaside trade.

Jaconelli had trained as an opera singer but his destiny was dollops of ice cream sold to the day-trippers and holidaymakers who flocked to the town in summer. He had married Anna, an Italian woman who worked at a Leeds wafer factory with his sister, in 1960, and over time, set about successfully branching out into restaurants and establishing nationwide distribution for his ice cream and desserts.

Tipping the scales at 21 stone and boasting a 50-inch waistline, Jaconelli was nothing if not an advertisement for his wares. During his first year as mayor he earned a place in *The Guinness Book of Records*, downing 512 oysters in 48 minutes and 42 seconds on national television. He also featured on an episode of *Savile's Travels*, going head to head on the mat at his Ippon judo club with the show's host and his great friend.

Jaconelli founded the judo club in Scarborough in 1955 and, despite his huge girth and waddling gait, claimed to be a black belt. Boys that attended the club say that he wasn't anything of the sort, although they report he did enjoy practising a particular throw that involved him pressing his groin into his young sparring partners. It transpires that Peter Jaconelli was well known for more than being the wealthy businessman and prominent local politician who appeared on the town's tourism posters sporting a knotted handkerchief on his head.

Scarborough seafront was a magnet for young people, especially runaways and strays, and Jaconelli's ice-cream parlour on the front employed scores of them over the years. Its proprietor was rumoured to be a member of a group of older men known locally as 'The Club'. It was a set that was said to include Jimmy Savile and his old pal and running mate, the amusement arcade owner Jimmy Corrigan, now dead. Some allege The Club's members attended sex parties for which local youngsters were procured.

In February 2013, a former member of the Ippon judo club and teenage employee at Jaconelli's ice-cream parlour wrote to the chief executive officer of Scarborough Borough Council to demand the former mayor be stripped of his title of Alderman of the Borough. The letter, published on the independent local news website Real Whitby, stated that Jaconelli, who died in 1999 having served almost 30 years on the town's council, 'was a predatory paedophile who preyed on local children'.[2] Councillor Geoff Evans supported the claim, confirming that Jaconelli sexually abused children, and propositioned him as a 14-year-old. Evans went further, suggesting that Jaconelli only escaped prosecution because of his 'political connections with the Conservative Party and the police'.

In late September 1972, Jimmy Savile organised a second trip for patients from Rampton to Scarborough. This time twelve patients and nine staff joined him on a special train from Retford. The official report, which is brief to the point of being cursory, states, 'During this trip, patients visited the amusements, the zoo and met The Duchess again.'

Jimmy Savile had by now been given his own lodgings at Broadmoor – a disused attic above two offices – and his own set of keys.[3] Each week after recording *Top of the Pops*, he drove to the maximum-security psychiatric hospital in Berkshire, let himself in and then sat with the patients to watch the show. He claimed that one wall in the TV room was decorated entirely with his photographs, something that baffled visiting MPs and 'bigwigs'.[4]

Rampton was opened in 1912 as an overflow for patients from Broadmoor, and as at its sister hospital, one of four 'special hospitals' in the UK, Savile claimed, '[the staff and patients] stand for me the same'.[5] He described how when he visited, 'the sub-normal patients come and hang off me like presents off a Christmas tree. I gather up great armfuls of them. I have got a great way with sub-normals.'[6]

In a newspaper article, Savile publicly commended Rampton's nurses for being 'only too ready for unpaid off-duty trips if it helps its sub-normal'[7] before going on to recount how in September 1972 they had visited the zoo, owned by one of his friends, an amusement arcade owned by Jimmy Corrigan, and a seafood café owned by Peter Jaconelli. The latter was specially emptied for the occasion and is where Agnes Savile joined the party.

A couple of months later, Savile again waxed lyrical about the patients he was given access to at the two high-security hospitals: 'They are people of incredible tenderness and affection,' he wrote. 'They can sit by you and stroke your face with a tenderness you could write beautiful poetry about. Then along can come an electric storm in the brain and the same hand that strokes you can grip you like iron. But they are essentially innocent, and when I say that I love them, the mothers of these boys know exactly what I mean.'

It is not too far-fetched to expect the police in Scarborough to have been informed that Jimmy Savile was escorting patients from a secure psychiatric hospital to the town, and details supplied of their itinerary. Yet when the allegations against Savile spewed forth in late September and October 2012, North Yorkshire Police stated it had 'carried out extensive searches of force records which did not reveal a local connection'. This despite the fact Jimmy Savile had not only been interviewed and photographed on numerous occasions at the residence he'd owned in the town since the 1960s, but had been awarded the Freedom of the Borough of Scarborough in 2005, before being buried in a local cemetery after one of the most highly publicised funerals in memory, one that had seen his funeral cortège proceed along the Foreshore in front of crowds marshalled by members of the North Yorkshire Police.

Despite being tissue thin on detail, the Rampton report does reveal a little about Jimmy Savile's access at the hospital. 'Two retired members of staff have confirmed JS did enter the secure area at least on three occasions and gave assurance that JS was escorted by staff at all times, had no keys and was not left alone with any patients,' stated the two-page document instigated by Dr Mike Harris, Rampton's executive director of Forensic Services and chief officer for High Security Care, in response to a Freedom of Information Act request. 'They re-iterated that during these visits JS was treated like any other professional visitor.'

Of course, Jimmy Savile – or JS, as the report insisted on calling him throughout – was not any other professional visitor. In fact, he wasn't a professional visitor at all.

The report concluded, 'JS had contact with some patients at Rampton Hospital' but 'no evidence has been found in any documents reviewed or during discussions with retired staff that anything untoward took place involving patients.'

No mention was made of the period in which he had his motor caravan parked in the hospital's grounds, or the fact he was seen heading to and from the vehicle with a number of different females.

As for the level of access he was given at Broadmoor, in October 2012 a spokesman for West London NHS Trust, which has managed the hospital since 2001, stated the allegations relating to Jimmy Savile were from 'a time when Broadmoor was a separate, somewhat isolated organisation'.[8] The very next day, the *Guardian* reported a Department of Health spokesman as saying, 'it is far from clear why any such role [at Broadmoor] would have required possession . . . of a set of keys. We need to establish how he came to have them and on what basis.'[9] Both questions were among the terms of reference for the investigation launched by the Secretary of State for Health and overseen by Kate Lampard. It remains to be seen whether the report includes details of the 1977 outing from Broadmoor he led to Bournemouth, which included lunch at his nightclub, the Maison Royale.

On the Sunday his account of the Rampton trips to Scarborough was published in the *Sunday People*, Jimmy Savile was to be found in the resort town on the south coast. He had just done a deal to take over a nightclub complex in Bournemouth and was staying in the flat he had secured as part of the package. He told me his plan was to move the Duchess into it so that he could keep an eye on her. It never came to fruition: a telephone call from a friend informed him that his mother had died quite suddenly while staying the night at his sister's house in Filey. Agnes Savile was less than a month short of her 86th birthday.

In the following day's *Yorkshire Evening Post*, Savile paid tribute to his 'beloved Duchess': 'She was entirely trustful of me in my showbiz life, and I have never known her to reprimand me,' he explained. 'If I took some dolly-bird home she would give her the "hard eye" look-over before accepting her and making a real friend of her. But I think she was glad I did not marry. We were so close.

She never even hinted to me about getting married, and I had no inclinations. Ours was a complete association.'[10]

After a post-mortem, the Duchess's body was placed in a coffin in the front room of her daughter Christina's house on Welford Road in Filey. Jimmy Savile sat in a chair next to the casket and hardly moved, later describing the period as 'the best five days of my life'.[11]

'We hadn't put her away yet and there she was lying around, so to me they were good times,' he told Anthony Clare twenty years later. 'Once upon a time I had to share her with other people. We had marvellous times. But when she was dead she was all mine, for me.'[12] When Agnes Savile's body was transferred to Leeds, and the house belonging to her daughter, Joan, Jimmy Savile rode in the front of the hearse.

A requiem mass was arranged for the following Monday at St Anne's Cathedral in Leeds, followed by a funeral service at Killingbeck Cemetery. In his autobiography, Savile wrote, 'as I fixed things for the final personal appearance of the Duchess it gave me the exact feeling that I was actually fixing to bury my own body. In some ways I was.'[13]

On the day before the funeral, Savile wrote in his newspaper column about how his mother stuck 'like a warm thought in the minds of 50 million people'. He claimed that a 'big business house' was planning to use her for a TV commercial because audience research had demonstrated she had 88 per cent 'instant name recognition without a picture'.[14]

When Vince Savile had died, Agnes gave their youngest son his wedding ring. Jimmy Savile was now desperate to add his mother's ring to his little finger. His older sister Christina claimed the ring but after being awoken one night by a burning sensation on the finger she was wearing the ring, she conceded that their mother wanted him to have it.

Dozens of floral tributes were arranged on the steps of the cathedral to greet the cortège of six vehicles transporting members of the Savile family. Jimmy Savile again decided to travel in the hearse with the coffin, dressed in a black fur coat and dark rimmed spectacles. Vince and Johnnie Savile, along with two of their brothers-in-law, carried the tiny casket to the high altar, where Jimmy Savile knelt down alone before it.

Four hundred people heard the requiem mass celebrated by Father William Kilgallon and Father Dennis O'Connell, who had befriended Agnes through the Margaret Sinclair Centre. Later, Jimmy Savile's colleagues on the night ambulance shift at Leeds General Infirmary volunteered as a guard of honour at the cemetery. Savile later claimed that 'official groups' were also sent to the funeral by the 'Irish government and Scotland Yard',[15] which, if true, further reveals the degree to which his influence now spread.

Having dominated the funeral with his antics, Jimmy Savile also dictated the appearance of his mother's final resting place. The marble tomb he had designed was huge and costly, with the words 'The Duchess' in big letters and her real name below. He was the only beneficiary of her will, being left £106.

The divisions within the Savile family were hinted at a week later, when Johnnie Savile was pictured in a newspaper picking rotting wallpaper from the damp-infested walls of his basement flat in Clapham, south London. The headline above the story read 'Life with the Other Savile'. 'I refuse to ask Jimmy for help,' explained the 53-year-old rep of a printing firm and father of two, who revealed that he had joined a local squatters' group.[16]

'[Johnnie Savile] could play my uncle Jimmy like nobody,' Guy Marsden told me. '[He'd say,] "I'm your brother and you don't give me owt and all I'm going to do is go on t'radio and tell everyone." And my uncle Jimmy would cough up . . . he couldn't beat him.' Sure enough, the newspaper report mentioned that Jimmy Savile had agreed to give a donation to the squatters' group when his brother was offered a house.

Jimmy Savile climbed the ladder of a scaffold tower and on reaching the platform at the top, spread his arms wide and soaked up the acclaim. Below, 20,000 sun-baked teenagers from all across Ulster cheered their approval. A chain-link fence shimmered in the distance. It had been erected by the Royal Marines and marked a different sort of dividing line to the one these young people were used to, enclosing the makeshift arena laid out on the disused airfield at Nutts Corner.

Beyond the fence stood hundred of officers from the Royal Ulster Constabulary, backed by troops of the British army. The forces of law and order, or oppression and fear depending on which side of the sectarian divide you came from, maintained a watchful if twitchy presence. At this moment in time, however, the temporary fence represented a line between young and old. Youngsters from opposite sides of an increasingly bitter sectarian divide had come together to walk and to witness a pop festival, and now they were in the hands of a higher authority; a man describing himself as the 'Pied Piper of Peace'.

As the cheers eventually subsided, Savile addressed his captive audience from his high vantage point beside the stage. 'You have proved that the teenagers of Northern Ireland see more then violence in life,'[1] he blared, as a sea of clapping hands rippled before him. 'This is the greatest day of my life so far.'

Fifty-one bombs had exploded across Northern Ireland and the British mainland in the previous year alone, killing 29 people and injuring hundreds more. In February 1972, the IRA claimed responsibility for an explosive device that went off at Aldershot Barracks, killing six female ancillary workers and a Roman Catholic padre. It was thought to have been planted as retaliation for the Bloody Sunday massacre of 14 civilians, seven of them teenagers, carried out by British troops in the Bogside area of Derry just a month before. On 14 April, 24 separate Provisional IRA bombs went off at points across the province, and gunfire was exchanged between gunmen and the security forces. On one single Friday in July, 'Bloody Friday', 22 bombs exploded in a 74-minute period, killing nine and injuring 130.

In the summer of 1973, the Northern Ireland Association of Youth Clubs, the only interdenominational youth organisation for both sexes in Ulster, decided to contact Jimmy Savile. As vice-president of the National Association of Youth Clubs in Britain and a regular visitor to Ireland through his work with the Central Remedial Clinic, he was deemed the perfect choice to lead an eight-mile sponsored walk to raise money for a new youth centre in Belfast. Security forces advised Savile that he could be a target for IRA snipers but he was having none of it. The chain-link fence he said, would keep him safe, 'not from bullets but from birds'.[2]

The walk began in the village of Mullusk, with Savile dressed in a bright yellow tracksuit and setting a brisk jogging pace from the front. Three helicopters whirred overhead, while soldiers and police officers mingled with the crowds that lined the route. 'It was most moving to see women weeping as we passed,' recalled Savile, who explained his grandparents had been born in Belfast, so this was like 'coming home'.[3]

Afterwards, reporters jostled to get a word from the colourful emissary from the mainland. He told them there were times when 'a man has to stand up and be counted'[4] before offering his blueprint for peace. 'The growing generation in Ulster have to ask themselves whether they want to appreciate the beauty of life, or smash their surroundings, shoot one another and plant bombs then run away like cowards,' he said. 'If that's really their idea of a good time, then we've got no hope.

'I feel I've succeeded if the kids here have had a better time with me than among the troubles clamouring for their attention. Maybe at the end they will decide they have been wasting their lives fighting instead of having a ball.'[5] There were no more IRA bombs in 1973.

Jimmy Savile was still a good decade away from being at the height of his powers, and the apex of his influence, yet here he was remodelling himself as a platinum-haired peace envoy. There was now no limit in his mind to what he could achieve.

Since his mother's death, he had been the subject of another BBC documentary, *The Life of Jimmy Savile*, which he had narrated himself. It was presented as a montage of a fast-moving life: cycling from Land's End to John O'Groats, volunteering his services at Broadmoor and Stoke Mandeville, and talking seriously about his charity work and religion. Amid his cod philosophising, he'd also revealed things about himself: 'I'm not homosexual,' he said, 'I like girls – but I've never got around to marrying anyone.'[6]

He enjoyed keeping the press guessing, and relished deceiving them over the prospect this marital status might be about to change thanks to a fabricated affair with Polly James, the 25-year-old former singer from Pickettywitch. 'I'm a normal sort of chap. I've fancied her for three years. It's just taken me this long to make up her mind that I mean it,'[7] he said. Six weeks later, Polly James, who was in the process of launching her solo career, announced that Jimmy Savile was too old and she'd gone back to her ex-boyfriend. Former band members have since claimed that there was no relationship, and it was a 'a set up for publicity'[8] designed to promote the band's new single.

In late December, at a gala evening attended by captains of industry at London's Talk of the Town club, the Variety Club of Great Britain named Jimmy Savile its Showbusiness Personality of the Year. After accepting the award and basking in the acclaim of his peers, he left for Broadmoor to do an overnight shift.

Jimmy Savile was now seen as a man who could communicate with the population at large. The Department of Environment hired him to front a £750,000 campaign on the importance of wearing car seatbelts. Its slogan, 'Clunk Click', became the title of his new Saturday evening chat show on BBC1.

Clunk Click started its eight-week run in May, with Jimmy Savile promising anything but the usual format. 'It will be about people and places with which the average TV viewer would not normally have any contact,' he said. 'It seems to me that there are so many people doing such valuable jobs who have never been heard of. Why not give them a chance to speak?'

He insisted that nothing on the show would contravene what he described as 'the social code', before adding, 'Say what you like about the pop scene but I have never done anything which I believe would corrupt anyone.'⁹

The show's producer was Roger Ordish, who first met Jimmy Savile when he was employed as an occasional director on *Top of the Pops*. Ordish's first impressions had not been particularly favourable: '[It was] his unapproachability,' he recalled soon after the slew of stories about Jimmy Savile's offending behaviour began to emerge. 'We weren't actually communicating.'

There was nevertheless something about Ordish that Bill Cotton instinctively felt made him 'the right man for Savile', and he despatched the producer to Broadcasting House to meet him. Ordish would end up working with for the next 21 years.

The reviews of the new show were not unanimously positive. 'The candid serenity of [Savile's] face rebukes the cynical but does not prevent us from feeling like hospitalised invalids who are being visited against their will,' wrote Peter Black in the *Daily Mail*.¹⁰

As this suggests, Jimmy Savile was now as famous nationally for his charity work as he was for his TV and radio appearances. He spoke regularly of his role at Stoke Mandeville Hospital, and launched a scheme to build an £8,000 luxury recreation lounge at its National Spinal Injuries Centre, housed in a series of antiquated Nissen huts.

He also revealed why he so enjoyed working in the hospital's mortuary department. 'I find I've got an aptitude for dead people,' he said. 'When I'm holding somebody that has just died I'm filled with a tremendous love and envy. They've left behind their problems, they've made the journey. If somebody were to tell me tonight I wouldn't wake up in the morning it would fill me with tremendous joy. Sometimes I can't wait.'[11]

In September 1973, soon after his triumphant march through Belfast, Jimmy Savile was offered an improved two-year contract with BBC Radio 1. *Savile's Travels* would be extended to two hours and he would be paid around £15,000 a year for his two shows. By delivering big audiences for a station that was still regarded as an upstart organisation by higher powers at the BBC, Savile was deemed to be more than worth his pay rise.

Before putting the deal on the table, however, Douglas Muggeridge, the controller of Radio 1 and 2, first needed to put his mind at ease. He'd heard rumours about Jimmy Savile, and specifically what went on during the making of *Savile's Travels*.

Rodney Collins was 23 years old at the time, and had been employed as the network's publicity officer since April 1971. He had got to know and like Muggeridge during his stints on music papers, and his job involved advising the controller on the public image of the networks and the people it employed. Collins described his boss as being 'open to ideas, open to challenges and open to accepting new broadcasters'.

Of the DJs on Radio 1, Collins stated that Jimmy Savile stood out, describing him as 'a different animal to everyone else'. Unlike those who had come over from the old Light Program or those recruited from the pirate stations, Savile had already made his name, which meant, in his words, that *Savile's Travels* and *Speakeasy* were 'very much moulded around what [he] believed he could bring to Radio 1'. In fact, Collins doubted whether the programmes 'would have continued with any other presenter'.

Collins said Jimmy Savile differed from his colleagues in other ways, too. 'I had a home number for absolutely everybody apart from Jimmy Savile,' he reported. 'If I wanted [him], I either had to leave a message for the producer's office or it was Leeds Infirmary. Savile was his own man.'

He admitted that 'rumours about disc jockeys came through all the time', although they were not exclusively about sex. It was, therefore, fairly routine for Muggeridge to ask him to inspect what was being heard on the grapevine. On this occasion, and as the fallout from payola and Claire McAlpine's death saw Radio 1 'zigzagging all over the place', Muggeridge asked Collins to make inquiries with a number of leading newspaper editors about whether they had heard the rumours about Jimmy Savile 'entertaining' young girls in the *Savile's Travels* motor caravan. More importantly, he was to ascertain whether they were planning to pursue them in print.

'I spoke to four journalists,' Collins explained. What they told him was yes, they had heard the stories but they were not planning to run with them. This was due, they said, to Jimmy Savile's exceptional popularity and the work he did for charity. Two days later, Collins verbally reported the news back to Muggeridge.

One question remains: where did Douglas Muggeridge hear the rumour? 'He never told me and I never asked,' Collins replied.

Andy Kershaw maintains rumours about Jimmy Savile were still rife by the time he joined Radio 1 in 1985: 'At the end of one appearance, one of Savile's producers – so went the legend – was sitting on the rear step of the vehicle while Savile had his way with a young member of the audience within. Then a little old lady came up the road. "Where's Jimmy?" she asked. "Er. He's gone already, I'm afraid," the producer lied. The vehicle by this stage was bouncing on its axles. "Oh dear. Well, please will you give him this from me?" And she handed over a jar of marmalade. "I made it myself," she explained. "It's for Jimmy. To thank him for everything he's doing for the young people."'[12]

What else he was doing was, of course, becoming apparent to the young people at Duncroft Approved School in Staines. There, his favourite girls would be taken for a drive in his Rolls-Royce and soon enough, he'd have their hands down his trousers, his tongue in their mouths and his fingers in their knickers. He told them he'd be able to tell if they were virgins.

Jimmy Savile's modus operandi was to test the girls out in order to convince himself they wouldn't say anything. He'd offer them money in a post office account, jobs at his nightclub complex in Bournemouth or trips to the BBC. In return he'd demand oral sex – 'Jimmy specials' as he'd call them. If they looked like being sick, he'd fling open the car door and make sure they vomited outside.

He'd remind them that if they refused to cooperate they would ruin things for the other girls; there would be no more visits, no more free cigarettes and no more minibus trips to the BBC where they got to mingle with his famous 'friends'. Worse, he'd tell them he'd ensure everyone knew who was responsible.

Jimmy Savile knew exactly what he was doing, as one former Duncroft girl explained: '[He] did it in such a way that he always covered himself. You knew it was your word against his and you would never be believed . . . he manipulated situations . . . we were vulnerable and in need of love and attention.'[13]

40. THE ONLY THING YOU CAN EXPECT FROM PIGS

Over the course of the four years I had been interviewing Jimmy Savile, we had established an unlikely rapport; unlikely, given he was adamant he didn't need or have friends, and I had spent a large chunk of my teens and twenties warning anyone who would listen that Jimmy Savile was an 'Agent of Satan'.

If we were at one of his various homes he would inevitably ease himself into a reclining chair and a fresh Cuban cigar would be lit as a symbolic cutting of the ribbon on the talks. Talks is probably the wrong word, because I would be expected to initiate a line of questioning before listening in respectful silence as he laid the brick of one anecdote on top of another, gradually disappearing behind the wall of his own mythology. He selected stories as I imagined he picked records during the Fifties and early Sixties.

By 2008, he was but an occasional presence in the papers. There had been a recent story about the West Yorkshire Police using his voice on 'talking signs' that were being trialled on lamp posts in the Hyde Park, Headingley and Woodhouse areas of Leeds. The signs were designed to warn students about the risks of burglary. There had not been much else.

Publicity of a different kind was on his mind during this particular meeting in Leeds, specifically the *Sun*'s coverage of an abuse scandal that had broken over the Haut de la Garenne children's home in Jersey. Jimmy Savile had first visited the home in the early 1970s to open a fete. It was the period in which the worst offences were alleged to have taken place.

A black and white photograph had emerged of Savile at the home. In it, he was wearing a tight-fitting tracksuit with large, square-framed sunglasses that looked like they were on upside down. He was on his haunches, surrounded by a big group of children. At the edge of the group a boy of about eight was holding up a giant badge saying 'Jim Fixed It for Us'. *Jim'll Fix It* did not begin until 1975, which therefore suggests he was a visitor to Haut de la Garenne over a number of years.

When confronted by a reporter about the picture, Savile's kneejerk reaction was to deny he had ever visited Haut de la Garenne. Two days later, though, he admitted he'd made a mistake. While there was a shortage of new facts to report, the *Sun* kept using the picture of Jimmy Savile with those poor, unfortunate children as a motif for a case without leads; an emblem of an island's assumed shame.

The phone rang suddenly and Savile picked up. 'Morning . . . Have we heard from our friends? . . . Really? . . . Right. Right . . . You tell me what you want to do and I'll do it,' he chortled, before his face settled into a grim smile.

'I see . . . Right, now then, does your pal think we've got a good chance if we go for this or what? . . . Yeah . . . Yes . . . No . . . Right . . . Yeah . . . Right . . . Yes. Is that possible or not? . . . Good, send that off . . . You'll need your counsel fella to tell me in the morning whether we've got a chance . . . Right, so the bottom line is that you've got a press release there and he'll tell me in the morning whether we have a go and if we do have a go, you release that in the morning and we'll have a go . . . Right . . . So you'll let me know in the morning . . . Good . . . Ta ra.'

Savile put the phone down. 'That's the lawyers,' he said. 'They've got a reply from the *Sun* saying they don't think they've hurt me at all. They're going to put a press release out but the counsel are going to tell me in the morning what chance of success we have. If it's 70 per cent or over, we'll have a go; if it's less than 70 per cent we'll just go to the press complaints and it's just a slap on the wrist. That's our plan for tomorrow morning.'

He showed me a copy of the letter his lawyers had been instructed to send to the paper and reiterated how much money he had made over the years by taking or threatening legal action against tabloids. And yet, by this point, I had not found a single story that implicated Jimmy Savile in a scandal, let alone one that had resulted in a legal windfall.

I asked him how he was meant to remember where he had been on any given day thirty-five years ago. 'Thirty-eight years ago,' he snapped. 'I was there for half an hour.'

Perhaps realising that he had revealed how much he did remember, he softened. 'A load of bollocks. Anyway, the thing is, they know what they're doing. They want to get away without a slap and if goes to the press complaints they'll see that as a victory.' Thirty-eight years ago would have put his visit at 1970. The photograph, which featured a *Jim'll Fix It* badge, could not have been taken before 1975. It appears that Jimmy Savile, who was a regular visitor to Jersey, was calling on the children of Haut de la Garenne for five years at least.

Savile remarked that it was easy to write about a murder or a rape. 'The difficult stories are good news stories . . . With a murder or a rape all you've got to do is get a name, a date, a time and a place. Then you speak to someone next door and you can be done in half an hour. You're home and dry.'

I put it to him that he had spent the best part of 50 years in the media spotlight and yet had never been the victim of so much as a kiss and tell. Why, given this apparently spotless record, were the tabloids now hunting him?

'How the hell should I know?' he grunted. 'The only thing you can expect from pigs is shit.'

D espite the lukewarm reviews, a second 13-week run of *Clunk Click* was commissioned, beginning in February 1974. The show was a product of its time and it allowed Jimmy Savile to embellish his reputation as an incorrigible flirt. Nothing was thought of the fact he walked onto the set at the top of one programme and regaled the audience with how one group of 'young ladies' on the beanbags had tried to rip his trousers off. Or that later in the same show, after interviewing Pan's People, the scantily clad, all-female dance troupe from *Top of the Pops*, he introduced a video sequence in which he chased them around a tree like a grotesque, groping Benny Hill.

In another episode, girls from Duncroft Approved School were to be found sitting on the beanbags. The star guest that week was Gary Glitter. 'Do young ladies go to great lengths to get next to you, as it were?' Savile asked the glam rocker.

'Yeah, and I go to great lengths to get next to them,' leered Glitter, real name Paul Gadd. He then peered into the darkness: 'I'm having a look round the audience now to see if there's anyone I fancy.'

Savile guffawed and pointed over to the teenagers on the beanbags. 'We always line our artists up,' he said. It was after this episode of *Clunk Click* that Keri claims she encountered Gary Glitter in Jimmy Savile's dressing room.[1]

Another former Duncroft girl alleges that Savile offered cash incentives to sit on the beanbags at *Clunk Click*. BBC files released following a Freedom of Information Act request contain evidence that if he did bribe his victims, he made sure to claim the money back. The following passage is taken from a letter to Jimmy Savile from the BBC's Contracts and Finance department, dated 18 April 1974: 'We understand from London that during the above programme [*Clunk Click*] you dispersed £10 each to the following young people'.[2] The three names are redacted; the money was reimbursed.

Roger Ordish, the show's producer, admitted he had heard the rumours that Jimmy Savile 'was interested in young females' but remains adamant that he never witnessed anything that made him suspicious or gave him cause for concern. 'How this could have happened in a dressing room, I don't quite know,' he protested. 'There wasn't time for that sort of thing. He turned up at two and if he wasn't in his dressing room he'd be in the studio rehearsing. If he was in his dressing room, he'd be with me or a researcher or with wardrobe or with people from the press.'

The newspaper columnist Jean Rook was one of Jimmy Savile's more regular and vocal critics, which might explain why he made a point of inviting her on to the show. In the article she wrote about the experience, Rook painted a rather different picture of scenes in his dressing room at *Clunk Click*: 'He moves everywhere in a throng of worshipping spastics, and for all I know, even lepers. His dressing room at the Beeb is crammed with every sick, lame, down-at-heel youngster who wants to get near enough to The Master to touch the hem of his long blond hair.'

Rook pressed Savile on his constant publicity seeking, to which he responded: 'What good would it do these handicapped kids? Why should I need to see another picture of myself in the papers, except that it could raise another £2,000 for charity?' He maintained nothing mattered 'as long as I'm trying to do the right thing by these kids and The Governor Upstairs'.

Rook concluded by reporting being up close and personal with Jimmy Savile left her feeling 'slightly sick'. She likened it to being 'too close for too long to the ceiling of the Sistine Chapel'.[3] It is clear from reading a letter Rook wrote to Savile in 1984, however, that her opinion of him changed over time. Describing herself as 'your loving and ill organised friend', she explained how 'overwhelmed' she was by his 'royal doings at Stoke Mandeville and the Royal Variety Show', before adding, 'nobody in the world but you could have got away with it and yet made it look so easy and natural that the royals were bound to go along with you.'

I put it to Roger Ordish that Jimmy Savile had developed a Messiah complex. 'He did, you're absolutely right,' Ordish responded. 'We used to laugh at him a bit, particularly when [we went to see him] in the radio studio. He'd bring along these rather pathetic hangers-on – they'd be disabled or blind or emotionally disturbed. I used to say that these people just wanted to touch the hem of his raiment. It was like that.'

Savile's popularity continued to grow. He was someone the major political parties clearly viewed as a potential vote-winner, and in the run-up to the snap election called for late February 1974, he appeared in party political broadcasts by both the Conservatives and the Liberals.

When pressed about where his allegiance lay, Savile replied: 'I'm an individual, you see, so for an individual really there's only the Conservative Party, because that's the freedom touch, isn't it?'[4] He revealed he'd only spoken out for the Liberals because his brother Johnnie was standing as the party's candidate in Battersea North.

It is remarkable to reflect on the fact that the endorsement of a long-haired disc jockey represented currency in political circles of the time. A confidential Whitehall report commented on his appointment as honorary assistant entertainments officer at Broadmoor, while among a series of recommendations sent to ministers by civil servants within the Hospital Advisory Service, mentions were made of the work Jimmy Savile was doing at the maximum-security institution. They included his fund-raising for a new minibus and disco equipment for his Thursday evening sessions with patients.

'Apart from the undoubted pleasure the hospital gains from having him around, he has pioneered outings for patients and has overcome opposition from outside and inside the hospital to these ventures,' stated the report. 'His energy, enthusiasm, sincerity and devotion to Broadmoor and its patients and staff are infectious and he performs the function of an unofficial but very successful public-relations officer outside the hospital, which can only be of great benefit for Broadmoor as a whole.' Health Minister David Owen and Secretary of State for Health Barbara Castle were among the recipients.[5]

Jimmy Savile was happy to put his name to just about anything, as long as the terms were agreeable. He was the well-paid and familiar face of the government's seat belt campaign, the next phase of which was designed to shock the public by showing him talking to a brain-damaged victim of a road accident. He persuaded a construction firm to build a patients' lounge at Stoke Mandeville in return for a 10-minute personal appearance at the Ideal Home Show at Olympia, and made £10,000 for charity while advertising Daz and Fairy Liquid. He was also awarded the Commando Medal for his fund-raising for the Royal Marine Museum, found time to devote four days to doing a series of sponsored walks in Dublin and Belfast, and began writing his autobiography in a series of exercise books, a task that earned him a handsome advance of £15,000. For every penny he made for charity, though, there was some form of personal remuneration: publicity, payment in kind or kickbacks via sponsorship deals.

It was a peculiar form of alchemy. Joan Bakewell identified it in August 1974, in one of the first heavyweight newspaper profiles to be published about Jimmy Savile. 'Today [he] is famous simply for being famous',[6] she wrote. '[He] seems to have created a fantasy life. The reality of his own life is the acting out and living out of that fantasy.'

As part of her research, Bakewell spoke to some of the people who worked with Savile. 'He certainly likes the hero worship he gets from young girls,' commented one.

The piece went on to reveal some of the questions being asked about Jimmy Savile at the time. One concerned his insatiable hunger for publicity. Bakewell reported that he worked hard 'at keeping his fame bright with a series of publicity stunts. These things are never done entirely for their own sake: each feat is sponsored for some good cause, usually, and with full media fanfare.'

Bakewell chaired a religious quiz show that Savile appeared on, and commented on how he had been in a rush to get away afterwards. 'I should make the hospital by one a.m.,' he told her. 'They don't start dying till two.'

When she inquired whether anyone had ever tried to take him for a ride, Savile replied that if they had, it had taught him a valuable lesson: 'If you help people in a little way they will thank you. In a big way, they won't. And if you set out to help people in bulk they'll kill you. Martin Luther King, Mahatma Gandhi, John Kennedy and the good one of them all, Jesus Christ. You must never look for a reward. There isn't any.'

If Jimmy Savile now bracketed himself alongside some of the greatest figures in history, he also alluded to his basest instincts. 'I'm no saint. I want it to be known I'm a great crumpet man,' he told a reporter from the *News of the World*. He reckoned wealth no longer guaranteed success when it came to seducing girls: 'I'll be out on a charity walk and I'll say to a girl, "I'll call tomorrow and take you out in the Rolls! Often that will make her run up the nearest tree in fright."'[7]

Like so many others who knew and worked with him, Dave Eager claimed that he never witnessed Jimmy doing 'anything untoward'. But when I outlined the allegations made by former Duncroft girls, Eager did recall a comment Savile once made: 'He [said] to me, "You've always got to be careful with your image. I've been going to a school and I've been taking kids for a ride in my Rolls-Royce, and I've got to be careful not to do that again."'

Such discretion was in short supply in Savile's autobiography, which was published in the autumn of 1974. The headline splashed across two pages of the *People* as part of a major serialisation blared, 'Why I Never Married – I can have my pick of 25 dollies any night'. Below, Savile regaled readers with how 'in my game the girls abound like summer flowers'.

He talked about one lucky escape when an attractive teenage girl knocked on the door of his flat in Manchester. 'Normally such manna would be consumed,' he confirmed before explaining that on this occasion, and by sheer luck, he had gone out and left the girl on the step. A short distance from his flat, he was pulled over by a police car. The officer told him the girl who had just gone into his block was an absconder. Savile denied all knowledge of her. 'Lucky boy',[8] replied the officer before driving off to collect the runaway.

The reference to 'his block' suggests the girl had gone to his 10th-floor flat in Ascot Court on Bury New Road, while the 'Lucky boy' remark from the police officer indicates that he was known for keeping such company. That he was confident enough to play the situation for laughs not only in his autobiography but also in a national newspaper only confirms that Jimmy Savile felt untouchable.

Three days after the extract ran, a journalist asked Savile why his extraordinarily prolific love life wasn't plastered all over the papers. 'Perhaps that's just because it's all so normal,' he lied. 'What is the worth of a tale of a two-hour seduction? By what stretch of the imagination could that be considered news?'[9]

Bob Bevan had just returned from a trip to Belgium with Jimmy Savile when the book serialisation began. As the PR man for ferry company Townsend Thoresen, Bevan had contacted Ted Beston, the producer on *Savile's Travels*, to propose a stay in a holiday village owned by the company during which it was hoped they could record some material for the show. Savile duly wrote back, inviting Bevan for a meeting in his studio at the BBC.

'When I entered the basement studio it was full of people,' wrote Bevan. 'Most were handicapped, some were in wheelchairs, and others were just hangers-on.' Savile told Bevan of his relationship with P&O and about how he had just come back from another free cruise to Gibraltar. Then, once the studio had emptied, Bevan was furnished with further details: 'Jimmy boasted how he kept [the Gibraltar minister of tourism] waiting on the quay while he seduced a girl in his cabin. He left nothing to the imagination.'

Savile agreed to the trip to Belgium on certain conditions: one, that he could take a Rolls-Royce, a driver and a few friends, and two, he would not be required to spend a penny of his own money. Bevan recalled the 'friends' Savile took were 'an attractive girl' and 'another guy called Bob'.

The former, he remembered as 'a well-spoken, bluestocking charity worker' who Jimmy Savile proceeded to have noisy sex with in his chalet. 'To my mind, he didn't have a great deal of respect for women,' said Bevan, who stayed in the next door chalet and heard everything through the wall. 'He used them for his own ends and would be fairly indiscreet.'[10]

The other member of the party was almost certainly Bob Brooksby, who Bevan described as 'a member of Jimmy's entourage and a feature of his life'.

Brooksby worked for an advertising agency called the London Press Exchange, although his primary purpose was acting as Jimmy Savile's fixer. In 1972, while working for Wilkinson Sword, he had been spotted passing a brown envelope to Bob Monkhouse, then the presenter of the TV game show *The Golden Shot*. When a Wilkinson Sword item appeared among the prizes on the following week's show, ATV's production controller suspected collusion. Monkhouse was called in and fired.

Brooksby had won favour with Savile by organising the design and construction of the special performing chair he sat in for *Clunk Click*, a prototype of the chair later immortalised on *Jim'll Fix It*. In time, Brooksby would become instrumental in setting up the sponsorship deals and payments in kind that greased Savile's wheels, confounded the taxman and ensured he evaded censure from the BBC. Savile would describe Brooksby as 'Uncle Bob' and as one of his 'honorary personal assistants'.

'Bob kept a little eye on Jim,' recalled Janet Cope. 'Jim used to ring Bob if a Procter & Gamble or some such rang wanting him to do something. Jim always used the same phrase: What's in the bin?

In other words, how much money were they going to pay him. I used to pass these messages on to Bob Brooksby or Harold Gruber, Jim's accountant.'

The next major milestone in Jimmy Savile's career would see him go into business with Brooksby, lining their pockets on the back of children's dreams.

42. A PARTICULARLY RELIGIOUS MOMENT

The programme that transformed Jimmy Savile from a star into a national institution came about as the result of a chance meeting in a corridor at the BBC. At least that's the way Jimmy Savile always told it. 'Bill Cotton said to me, "Listen, you've been fixing it for people all your life. Why don't we do a programme where we fix it for people on film?" [I said] "Yeah, alright then. We'll call it *Jim'll Fix It*." He said, "Jim Will Fix It?" I said, "No, J-I-M, apostrophe, double L. *Jim'll Fix It*. It comes easily off the tongue." And that was it. That's how it started. We didn't do a pilot. Straight in – bang! Twenty years.'

Bruce Forsyth's *Generation Game* and *That's Life* were both examples of popular contemporary British television programmes that hinged on the participation of the general public. Their success helped pave the way for a trial 10-week series of the BBC's new wish-fulfilment show in the summer of 1975. As its host, Jimmy Savile was invited to appear on the early evening news magazine show *Nationwide* to explain what the new programme was about and, more importantly, to appeal for letters.

The response was huge. For three months, producer Roger Ordish and his production team sifted through bulging mailbags to whittle the 9,000 letters down to a longlist of 200 requests. It was agreed that wherever possible, 'Fix It' items would be filmed in the studio in front of a live audience. The new show was given a Saturday evening slot starting in early June.

For the title sequence of *Jim'll Fix It*, it was decided to film Jimmy Savile leading a train of children round Shepherd's Bush in the style of a modern day Pied Piper. Roger Ordish recalled a very specific memory from that day: 'We stopped somewhere and there was a mother and daughter leaning out of a top window. '[Jimmy said to the mother] "Who's that with you? Is it your sister?" . . . She said, "No, it's my daughter." He asked her how old she was and the daughter said 16. Jim turned to us and said, "Legal! Legal!"'

The Osmonds were at the peak of their popularity in the summer of 1975, and the family pop group were the subject of many hundreds of letters written by adoring fans. Fortunately for the makers of *Jim'll Fix It*, The Osmonds were in the UK to film a series for the BBC over two intensive weeks at the Television Theatre on Shepherds Bush Green. The recording of the first episode of *Jim'll Fix It* was scheduled for the same venue on the group's one day off.

In a major coup for Roger Ordish, America's favourite toothy, singing Mormons agreed to take part, filming an item in which Jimmy Savile appeared at the stage door and invited in three teenage girls who had been waiting in the rain for a glimpse of their idols. After sitting them down on the set and asking them what they'd been doing, Savile asked them to turn round. The trio of bedraggled 15-year-old girls were stunned to find The Osmonds lined up and ready to play.

It was the highlight of an opening episode that also included studio segments with a young girl dancing with Pan's People and, bizarrely, Jimmy Savile's erstwhile girlfriend, Gussy van Geest, learning how to apply clown make-up. *Jim'll Fix It* badges were hung round the necks of a boy who got his wish to drive a train and a girl who attempted to start the Channel tunnel with mechanical diggers on Ramsgate beach. But for Bill Cotton, the BBC's head of Light Entertainment, the most memorable item of them all was the very first 'Fix It': a girl called Mhairi Read who swam with dolphins at Windsor Safari Park. 'As I watched it,' Cotton said, 'I thought, "We have a hit show here."'[1]

The sheer scale of *Jim'll Fix It*'s success took everyone by surprise, not least its host. The viewing figures started high and then just kept on climbing. Added to that, as Ordish recounted,

'The feel-good factor engendered by the programme was considered very high, particularly by advertisers.'

The result was payola. In the first season, a boy who wanted to steer a ship was filmed at the helm of a Townsend Thoresen ferry. 'Yet more massive publicity,' confirmed Bob Bevan, the company's PR man at the time. 'As we were getting quite closely linked with Jim, our advertising agency decided it would be a good idea if he featured in our TV commercials.' A fee of £10,000 was agreed with Savile for a single day's filming.[2]

'[Jimmy] was very, very good at that,' Ordish conceded. 'He was quite brilliant, in fact. One time we [covered] the introduction of the 125 train and we had Sir Peter Parker, the head of British Rail, come to the studio to give the badge. Jim did the "SOS" [Same Old Shit] to him and he finished doing several years of TV commercials for British Rail. It netted him a fortune.'

I asked Ordish whether Jimmy Savile ever pulled rank and insisted that a company he was associated with or being paid by was featured over another. 'Not directly,' he replied. 'But he'd be very clever and say, "I'll only be able to film those links for the compilation programme [while I'm] on a cruise liner." He'd know he could then say he was on a P&O cruise liner or Cunard.'

Not everyone was so smitten with the new show, though. Having savaged *Clunk Click*, the *Mail*'s TV critic had clearly not mellowed on the subject of Jimmy Savile: '[His] personality worries many people, making them feel as an antique dealer might when forced to sit on a genuine, simulated plastic Hepplewhite chair, complete with a cushion that makes rude noises.'[3]

In a separate article, the psychiatrist and children's author Catherine Storr described *Jim'll Fix It* as 'intolerably patronising' and 'an insult to the dignity possessed by a child in his natural environment'.[4]

From the outset, Ordish recognised that the format for *Jim'll Fix It* placed Jimmy Savile outside his own natural environment. He reasoned that the show's host was 'never really comfortable with children'. But rather than being a problem, this was something Ordish used it to his advantage: 'I tried to structure the programme so that he really didn't have much to do, just being this mystery figure in the middle of it all. I don't think *Jim'll Fix It* would have worked with anyone else, say a showbiz person or a comedian. It wouldn't have been this strange, aloof character. I think he would have loved to have been a *mafiosi*.'

'Jim hated children,' Janet Cope told me. 'He made no bones about that; he called them "little brats". They were a nuisance and annoying to him. He used to watch people cooing over a pram and he'd give me this look.'

As an aside, Ordish also revealed that his young daughter couldn't stand Jimmy Savile: 'She couldn't bear him talking to her. He spooked her, I think.' She was not the only one.

After the massive viewing figures for series one, a *Jim'll Fix It* Christmas Special was duly commissioned. The highlight was to be a film of nine-year-old Gary Merrie from Liverpool who had written in requesting to visit the place where baby Jesus was born. It was a rare example of a 'Fix It' item in which Jimmy Savile appeared, chiefly because he arranged it to coincide with a 10-day trip he'd been invited on by the Friends of Israel Educational Trust.

In the days after Savile's death, John Levy, who organised the trip to the Holy Land, described him as 'a real philosemite'[5] who was generous in his fund-raising for the Women's International Zionist Organisation and the British Friends of the Laniado Hospital in Netanya.

Savile had once boasted to the *Jewish Telegraph* newspaper that the Friends of Israel connection and the filming for *Jim'll Fix It* were merely a cover for the real purpose of his visit. He claimed he had been invited by Israeli president Ephraim Katzir to advise on matters of national security.

When I asked him about the purpose of his trip, Savile chuckled. 'It's a professional secret,' he said, before confirming he was dealing with 'the president and the entire cabinet of the Israeli government'. On another occasion, he said that he 'went over and did a favour for the Israeli prime minister'. On his return, he received a gift from the Israeli embassy in London.

It sounds outlandish, even if one of Savile's friends, a Jewish businessman from Manchester, swore that the reason for his trip to the Middle East was to sound out a possible meeting between Israel's prime minister Menachem Begin and Egyptian president Anwar Sadat. Savile was chosen, the man said, because of his Jewish connections and his friendship with Gladys Cottrell, the mother of Sadat's wife, Jehan.[6]

Jimmy Savile did meet officials during his ten days in Israel, including General Moshe Dayan, Israel's hero of the Six Day War. At a reception in Jerusalem hosted by the city's mayor Teddy Kollek, he also met President Ephraim Katzir. He told me he arrived at the function wearing a pink suit with short sleeves. 'I was such a freak that nobody wanted to talk to me,' he said.

The president was guided around and introduced to guests. 'He didn't know who the fuck I was,' Savile claimed before describing how offended he'd been that Katzir kept looking over his shoulder during their brief chat. When the President asked him how he was enjoying Israel, Savile took his chance: 'I said, "I'm very disappointed because you've all forgotten how to be Jewish and that's why everybody is taking you to the cleaners."'

Now that he had Katzir's undivided attention, Savile said he decided to give him chapter and verse: 'You won the Six Day War, you took all that land, you give it all back and you give the only oil well in the area back and now you're paying the Egyptians for the oil that you had.' He claimed Israel's President asked him to step into another room whereupon he invited the strange Englishman with the white hair and the short-sleeved pink suit to repeat what he had just said to his colleagues in the Knesset.

'Send a car for me in the morning,' Savile replied. The next day, he insisted the cabinet was called in and 'they did what I suggested and it worked out 100 per cent successful'.

'That is a typical example of how everything got twisted,' scoffed Ordish, who was on the trip to produce the segment for

Jim'll Fix It. 'He said that to other people in my presence, surely knowing that I knew that was not what happened. We met the president of Israel but the president of Israel is not a powerful person, he's a figurehead. It's the prime minister who is the important one. They way he talked about it made it sound like he was mediating between Palestine and Israel.'

Ordish put it down to Savile's rampant 'egotism'. 'He'd never tell a story in which he'd have a red face or look foolish. Everything was always a triumph. That's how he saw his life progressing.'

So the idea of Jimmy Savile being a secret peace envoy was what he himself described as 'SOS – Same Old Shit'? 'It certainly was,' Ordish replied.

Whether or not he had any part in the historic 1977 meeting between Begin and Sadat – and he did later claim to have attended the Egyptian embassy in June 1975 to discuss 'a VIP invitation to meet President Sadat in Cairo'[7] – something truly momentous happened on Jimmy Savile's trip to the Holy Land.

Colin Semper, who was also on the trip to produce a discussion programme for *Speakeasy*, recalled Savile telling him how the image of Jesus wandering in the wilderness held enormous significance for him. 'He got totally obsessed by the desert,' Semper said of their time in Israel. 'Whilst I was visiting the shrines, the churches, the mosques, the ruins, he was refusing to enter the tourist spots; he preferred the wilderness.'[8]

In *God'll Fix It*, a series of conversations between Savile and Semper about Savile's relationship with God, the chapter titled 'Have I Had Any Religious Experiences?' contains Jimmy Savile's recollections of being alone in the wilderness by the Dead Sea, 'at the place where the Good Samaritan looked after the chap who had been set upon by the robbers'.[9] He described his experience in this place as 'a particularly religious moment'.

He talked about setting off early in order to be able to stand alone. 'I was mightily pleased at that moment,' he said. 'I was able to be in the same area where Jesus Christ had walked and lived and worked out his mental application to the world. That gave me a chance to work out my mental application to the world in exactly the same way as he did. I weighed up form as he must have weighed up form; and I came to certain decisions.'

Given what else was happening in his private life, it is telling that Jimmy Savile likened it to 'totting up the score of life'. He said that he tried to see whether he had 'gone right' or 'gone wrong', concluding that while he might have gone wrong in 'specific instances', overall he felt he was going in the right direction. 'I was wobbling about in between the white lines a little bit and sometimes crossing over the line,' he admitted, 'but coming back, as it were.'

During his time alone in the wilderness he said he 'felt God very close by me'.

While in Israel, Jimmy Savile caroused in the lively university town Be'er Sheva, camped near the Sea of Galilee and recorded an episode of *Speakeasy* at a kibbutz. On another occasion, he dragged the camera crew to the Judean hills because he wanted to be filmed with John Levy and his friends walking from Jerusalem to Bethlehem.

'I wanted a staff,' Savile said, 'and saw this branch on a tree, which looked to me just as I imagine Jesus's staff. I tore it off and used it myself.'[10] The walking aid wasn't the only connection he felt with the Son of God; Jimmy Savile also grew a beard for the first time in his life.

So did he really see himself as a Messiah figure? Ordish thought he did. Semper, though, was less convinced: 'He talked a lot about his work in hospitals in a way that he thought he had a pastoral gift towards people, and especially people who were ill,' said the reverend. 'Whether he described it as messianic, I'm not so sure. I think he did have a kind of exaggerated self-worth – "I can do this, I can do that". He did that quite a lot.'

When I asked Semper how he now felt about Savile, he audibly exhaled. He described him as tactfully as he could, calling him 'an enormously complex character' and 'a ruined person'. When pushed to clarify what he meant by ruined, Semper replied, 'His proclivities overpowered his undoubted intelligence.'

According to the joint report published by the Metropolitan Police and the NSPCC in January 2013, the years 1974 and 1975 mark the nadir of Jimmy Savile's offending, with allegations of fifteen sexual assaults recorded for both years.

'He was extremely proud if not boastful about what he could do physically,' recalled Colin Semper, the producer of Jimmy Savile's *Speakeasy* show for Radio 1. 'He talked about it a lot. I'm sure that was partly him bolstering himself against the onset of old age.'

As he neared 50, and the end of his latest test of physical endurance – a 12-day run from Land's End to London in January 1976 – Savile offered up his own explanation of why he pushed himself so hard, and so publicly. 'It's about discipline,' he said. 'It takes discipline to run 30 miles a day, and when I get back to London I will apply that same discipline to my work.'[1]

The 291-mile slog was undertaken to raise £1,000 for disabled people, although it certainly generated plenty more than that for Savile, thanks again to the work of Bob Brooksby. Following behind him all the way was a motor caravan emblazoned with 'You're Tea-rific', the slogan of the British Tea Council. His running gear carried the same branding. 'Uncle Bob doesn't work for me but he organises a lot of things for me,' explained the man who had become an expert at making charity pay. 'So he gets a lot of the spin-offs.'[2]

The Tea Council promotion covered Jimmy Savile's expenses and more in return for the exposure he guaranteed. The arrangement eventually stretched to providing a specially adapted Range Rover with a bed in the back – in effect a smaller version of the *Savile's Travels* caravan that had been the scene of so many assaults.

Brooksby, who admitted that he worked on deals for Savile on everything from cars and furniture to clothes and food, offered his own brief clarification of how the relationship worked: 'A lot of my business involves publicity deals [Savile] helps with. We both make out of it. And I lose all his incidental expenses among my accounts.' Brooksby had even furnished Savile's London flat close to Regent's Park.

Fix It Promotions, the company they established in May 1977, would made money hand over fist, cashing in on the bankability of *Jim'll Fix It* and the feel-good factor Roger Ordish spoke of. Savile went on to appear in advertising campaigns for children's shoes, tyre companies and insurance brokers, the latter being a neat fit given what he told one newspaper about his financial problems.

'The trouble is, you cannot have more than £15,000 in any one society,' he bragged, ignoring the fact that millions were unemployed at the time. 'We brusque and dour North Countrymen don't like stocks and shares. We prefer to put our money into building societies. I also buy whopping great insurance policies.'[3]

Sometimes, he didn't have to do anything at all. On one occasion, Brooksby claimed to have been sent a box containing £3,000 in notes, accompanied by a note from an unnamed woman saying she wanted to buy Jimmy Savile a watch for Christmas. Brooksby spent the money on an 18-carat gold Rolex encrusted with 80 diamonds. In return, the star offered up his old watch as a raffle prize and appealed for the woman to contact his business manager so that he could 'take her for a trip round London in a charity ambulance and give her a cup of tea'.[4]

But the discipline Savile spoke of in relation to his latest, heavily endorsed sponsored run was not only required for the extraction of revenue from any given situation. It is now evident Savile needed to apply it in keeping a tighter rein on his sexual appetites. *Jim'll Fix It* had pulled in more than 15 million viewers a week in its first season, and in doing so had made its host an icon for daydreaming children everywhere. Allied to the growing fanfare for his charity work, he now had a lot more to lose from bad publicity or, worse, exposure.

'I'm wondering . . . [if he] suddenly saw, particularly with *Jim'll Fix It*, that there was this immense respectability coming to him, this saintliness,' reflected Roger Ordish. 'Maybe he thought, "One day, I'll get a knighthood so maybe I should mend my ways or at least be a damn sight more careful about how I do these things."'

As always, managing this vast deceit remained a high-wire act, albeit one that Jimmy Savile appeared to be enjoying. When Lord Justice Lawton sat on an Appeals Court hearing for a 17-year-old part-time disc jockey who had been given a detention order, he offered the opinion that such work could result in 'indulging in occasions for sin'. An enterprising reporter contacted well-known radio DJs such as David Hamilton, Tony Prince and Nicky Horne, who all took the opportunity to hit back. But not Jimmy Savile. 'The geezer's 100 per cent right,' he said. 'If you get into clubs and places like that you are coming up against all sorts of temptations – drugs and under-aged birds and things. This is the 1976 temptation. Some of us go down and some of us don't – it's the responsibility of the person involved.'[5]

This was classic Savile, rebuffing allegations with a nod to what he was up to away from prying eyes – smoking cannabis with police officers, coercing underage girls into sex, lulling parents and hospital workers into a trance of compliance – while reinforcing his newly earned credentials as a pillar of society.

That same month, at a Scarborough conference for Young Conservatives, he took another step closer to the inner circles of power after being introduced, in her hotel suite, to Margaret Thatcher, who had recently been installed as leader of the opposition. Savile took his opportunity to make an impression by gallantly clearing the suite when it became clear Thatcher wanted to go to bed. It was a gesture that sowed the seeds for a long and close relationship, the next stage of which was to see her grant him an exclusive one-hour interview for *Speakeasy*, followed by an item for *Jim'll Fix It* in which two girls got to ask her questions in her office at the Houses of Parliament.

In March, the *Listener*, the BBC-produced magazine designed to provide 'a medium for intelligent reception of broadcast programmes', ran a profile piece that further endorsed Jimmy Savile's new stature. On the one hand it celebrated the 'amazing ability of the BBC to absorb, contain and afford expression to the most eccentric and wayward of talents, while remaining true to itself, particularly in the case of Jimmy Savile, OBE'. On the other it pinpointed the 'curious form of media-inspired solipsism that allows [Savile] to disappear so effectively as a private citizen'.

The most revealing words come in the profile's concluding paragraph: '[Jimmy Savile] has graduated from disc-jockey to "personality", and now, he just has to be. He serves on advisory hospital boards and rubs shoulders with royalty – a member of the establishment, in fact.'[6]

His halo was being buffed and polished: a second series of *Jim'll Fix It*; a gold medal from the Grand Order of the Knights of Malta, a Catholic charitable organisation; and the announcement that he would once again be marching for peace in Belfast, this time alongside Betty Williams and Mairead Corrigan, the women who had sparked a spontaneous movement in Ulster after Corrigan's sister lost three children in a confrontation between two IRA operatives and members of the British army. The march, in November 1976, would see Jimmy Savile lead more than 10,000 teenagers from both sides of the sectarian divide from Ormeau Embankment in east Belfast to Crawfordsburn Country Park in County Down.

Entranced by his own omnipotence, Savile took it upon himself to berate the Labour government for its 90 per cent tax bracket on the highest earners in society, shortly before revealing some of the deals that allowed him to play the Inland Revenue like a fiddle. But in the course of his now habitual grandstanding about the size of his personal wealth, he made an uncharacteristically sloppy mistake by reminding Salford Council he was still paying just £10 a week in rent on the flat at Ascot Court on Bury New Road, and using it on only a handful of occasions each year.

'No, I don't feel guilty about having a council flat while others are homeless,' he barked, having just boasted about owning a nightclub complex in Bournemouth, the Maison Royale, that had been valued at over £1 million. 'I do a fair bit for charity.'[7]

Days later, as he prepared to celebrate his 50th birthday, Savile opened the papers to discover that his throwaway comment about the council flat had blown up in his face. 'Morally, he shouldn't think twice about remaining in the property,' said a spokesman for Shelter, the homeless charity. His Ascot Court neighbours were equally dismissive. At a time when there were more than 6,000 people on Salford's housing list, the council's housing committee chairman described the situation as 'deplorable'.[8]

Dave Eager told me that Savile was incandescent. '[He] rang me up and said, "Go to the caretaker, get the keys and take all my personal possessions out of the flat." He told Salford Council they could have the flat back with all the furniture. The idea that a Labour councillor should try to get a story on his back when he'd done nothing wrong, and not even have the courtesy of speaking to him first, well, he found it objectionable. He said he didn't want anything more to do with Salford.'

If there was one thing Jimmy Savile hated more than being parted from his money, it was being publicly embarrassed. His response was to attempt to spin the story back onto a more favourable trajectory by insisting he would leave his furniture and television, as long as the flat went to a needy couple. It didn't work. He only had himself to blame.

Soon after moving his belongings out of the 10th-floor apartment in Salford, Jimmy Savile also sold the old family house on Consort Terrace in Leeds.

As Colin Semper said, Jimmy Savile's natural intelligence (a Mensa test, completed at Broadmoor Hospital under the supervision of a consultant psychiatrist, awarded him an IQ of 150, putting him in the top one per cent in the country) was occasionally hostage to the darker forces at work in his nature. But in the baking hot summer of the Silver Jubilee year, and the 12 months that followed, such considerable mental power was not sufficient to prevent him from making a series of atypical, and potentially costly slip-ups.

The first came in July. Soon after being interviewed by a newspaper while surrounded by teenage girls in his dressing room at *Top of the Pops*, Jimmy Savile went to stay at Henlow Grange health farm in Bedfordshire. He said it was in preparation for a world record bid on the number of Channel crossings in a day, a stunt that would earn £10,000 for Action Research for the Crippled Child, and doubtless more in advertising kickbacks from the Hovercraft company.

At Henlow Grange, Savile met a 16-year-old trainee beautician named Julie Ball. She said he charmed her and drove her home where he signed autographs for local children and sat up late talking with her family. The very next night, he took the teenage girl to see a play in Letchworth. She said they had to leave early because of the commotion he caused.

On the drive home, Julie Ball reported they cruised around country lanes until Jimmy Savile found a quiet lay-by. 'He put soft romantic music on the stereo,' she said. 'We sat and talked. Then he climbed into the passenger seat beside me . . . We kissed and cuddled for half an hour and he kept on saying, "This is special." He was very passionate.'

The 16-year-old told the *News of the World* that she thought she was in love with the star of *Jim'll Fix It* and *Top of the Pops*, but admitted that 'it's too early to talk of plans of any kind'.[9]

When the newspaper put Julie's claims to Jimmy Savile, he didn't flinch. 'Yes, I took her for a spin in my car. It was, I thought, a treat for her after the kindness her family had shown me. But no way did we stop for a kiss and a cuddle.' He insisted Julie's mother had contacted him to explain that a freelance journalist had offered her daughter £50 for the story, and he'd advised her to take it: 'Julie is a very pretty girl and this is her moment of glory. When

I found out what was being said I didn't want to leap about and say, "That's not true." It wasn't hurting me and I suppose it was doing something for the girl.'

Daphne Ball believed her daughter's account of her evening with Jimmy Savile, although she didn't seem particularly worried about what had happened. 'After meeting Jimmy I trusted him and liked him,' she said.

Julie, though, was distraught to learn what the man she had fallen in love with had to say about their tryst. 'He must be trying to preserve his image,' she said.

It is another textbook example of Jimmy Savile's approach: the subtle grooming of the parents, the ride in the Rolls-Royce, the sweet nothings and then the decisive move to claim what he'd wanted from the outset. Then, as he had done in numerous other situations, he rode it out. He even managed to twist the first and only kiss and tell story to appear about him by making the nation feel complicit through sharing what he had been up to with a girl barely above the age of consent.

No more was said about Julie Ball in the days, weeks and months that followed. But it turns out she was not the only object of Jimmy Savile's lust during his week at the health farm.

Claire (not her real name) was an 18-year-old chambermaid at Henlow Grange. She told a newspaper that Savile asked her to serve him breakfast in his room. Lewd comments about her breasts quickly escalated into groping her until one day she opened his door to find him lying naked on the bed with an erection. 'I felt disgusted and humiliated,' said Claire. 'I tried everything not to be sent back to his room again.'

Two weeks after the Julie Ball story, Savile let his guard slip once again. After breaking his ankle in a charity walk for Belford Hospital in the Scottish Highlands, he was on crutches as he hobbled onto the Mallaig to Glasgow train. At Queen Street station he was met by an 18-year-old model who he described as having become 'a very close friend'[10] over the course of the previous three years.

'She is probably the most beautiful of the people who are around to meet me when I travel to their part of the world,' Savile said of the girl. 'If I was contemplating marriage, I would hope it would be to a girl like her.' There was no comment about the fact that his 'friendship' had started when the girl was just 15.

There was no comment either about the fact Jimmy Savile was appearing in a series of newspaper advertisements for Start-rite shoes at the time. The campaign consisted of a full-page photo of the wide-eyed pillar of the establishment holding up an infant's sandal. The slogan above the picture read: '"They're No. 1 for school, gals!" Jimmy Savile OBE.'

In 1977, Janie Jones was released from prison. Three years earlier she had been found guilty on seven charges of controlling prostitutes and four charges of attempting to pervert the course of justice at London's Old Bailey. She had also faced charges of blackmail but been cleared. The madam and former pop singer had spent 200 days on remand and been refused bail on 13 occasions. She was sentenced to seven years imprisonment.

At her first Old Bailey trial, Jones had been found not guilty of offering sexual favours to disc jockeys as an inducement to play records. Her part in organising sex parties for President Records in her Kensington flat had nevertheless provided some of the most salacious detail in the payola scandal, the sordid affair exposed by the *News of the World* that had eventually forced Jimmy Savile into defending his own reputation and that of the BBC.

Jones served three years in Holloway where she became friendly with the Moors murderer Myra Hindley, who convinced her the killings of five children were the sole responsibility of her lover, Ian Brady. On her release, Jones became an outspoken supporter of Hindley, arguing she was a reformed woman and should be granted an early release.

It was around this time that she claims to have received a strange summons from Jimmy Savile who had been the DJ at the New

Elizabethan Ballroom, one of Brady and Hindley's favourite Manchester haunts before their arrest. 'He was bragging that he had met Ian Brady,' said Jones. 'He said it was disgraceful that I was siding with Hindley against [him].'[11]

Savile could have conceivably met Brady in Manchester or during one of his occasional visits to various maximum-security prisons, although it's understood the psychopath spent much of his time in solitary confinement. But on what possible grounds could he defend the sadistic Moors murderer?

Perhaps his experiences at Broadmoor had turned Jimmy Savile into a more understanding individual but it's more likely, in my opinion, that he recognised something of himself in a man who had manipulated and dominated others, and who possessed the same blend of charm, narcissism and utter lack of empathy and remorse for what he had done.

But sticking up for Ian Brady wasn't all that was on Jimmy Savile's mind in that meeting, as Janie Jones recalled. He was particularly fascinated by the parties she held at which women dressed as schoolgirls. '[Savile] just kept saying that he could not understand why people went on about 13-year-old girls because they were "gagging" for it,' she said. 'I told him that anybody who wants to go with a 13-year-old is a paedophile.'

I n 1977, a 12-year-old girl went into Stoke Mandeville Hospital to have her tonsils removed. Now in her late forties, she recalls that rather than being in a bed alongside other children, she was put on a geriatric ward.

The woman first reported her experiences to officers working on Operation Yewtree, and this is the subsequent statement she made to a former police child protection officer employed by Slater & Gordon, the firm representing scores of Jimmy Savile's other victims. Liz Dux, a specialist child abuse lawyer with the firm, employed the services of the child protection expert because, in her words, 'She was able to say straight away whether she believed they [those making allegations] were telling the truth, because she knows the sort of things that victims remember.'

I feel it is appropriate, with her permission, to let this woman's account speak for itself.

'I remember being bored and asking one of the nurses if I could go into the day room to watch television. I imagine she was glad to agree because I had been making a nuisance of myself on the ward. The nurse directed me to a day room which was a short walk down the corridor. I was wearing a flimsy homemade nightdress that came down to my knees, with a dressing gown over the top. I was a very slight build and my hair was in two pigtails.

'As I went through the ward door on my way to the day room I saw a skinny man wearing a long coat. He was also wearing brown tracksuit-style trousers. By this I mean the trousers that he was wearing had no buttons or a zip. He had white to blond shoulder-length hair and was wearing heavy rings and a gold chain around his neck. He was smoking a cigar. I didn't recognise the man at the time.

'The man asked me, "Where are you going?". I recall that it was difficult for me to talk because my throat was sore. I said in a very croaky voice, "To the television room". The man said, "I'll show you" and he walked me down the corridor. I can't recall what the man said but he was friendly and I felt comfortable in his company.

'I recall that as we walked along the corridor the man opened a door which led to a room that contained a mop and bucket. Looking back, I realise that it must have been a cleaning cupboard. The man gave a short laugh and closed the door without going in. Almost immediately afterwards we arrived at the day room.

'As we arrived at the day room an elderly man was leaving and I saw that he nodded an acknowledgement to the man who was accompanying me. The day room was a small room with a black and white television, which was stood on a low wooden table. There were a number of identical chairs in the room and an armchair. I went and sat on one of the chairs. The man said to me, "Have you got a boyfriend?" I didn't answer because although I had boys who were friends, I didn't understand the concept of a boyfriend.

'The man then leant down in front of me and positioned his body so that he was between my legs. I remember that he had a distinctive muggy odour. The man was gentle, almost caring. As he pushed my legs apart I saw that he had pulled down his trousers, not all the way but sufficiently to expose his penis. I recall that his penis had a distasteful smell. He then manoeuvred himself forward and as I remained seated he inserted his penis into my vagina.

'I didn't feel threatened by what he was doing to the point that I recall touching his cheek with the palm of my right hand. His cheek felt very clammy. The man's penis was only in me for a short time. He then made a groaning noise and ejaculated. He withdrew his penis and then pulled up his trousers. His semen had gone all over the seat I was sitting on and over the inside of my thighs. He then wiped me and the chair with the front of his white coat. Having done so, he stood up and without saying anything walked out of the room. The door to the room had been open throughout what had happened.

'I have a distinct memory of getting off the chair and going to the doorway of the day room and watching the man as he walked down the corridor. I watched him until I lost sight of him when he went through some double doors at the end of the corridor.

'What happened just seemed surreal. I was in shock and unable to put into context what had happened. I felt disorientated and walked back to the ward. I seem to remember initially I couldn't find my way and went to a couple of other wards before I found mine. I hadn't been gone very long. The whole thing happened very quickly, probably no more than 15 minutes.

'As I went back to the ward I said to the nurse who had given me directions to the day room, "Your porter hurt me". And the nurse said, "Where?" I couldn't tell her so pointed to the area of my vagina. She said, "Don't say anything, I'll get into trouble."

'Having received this response I just went and sat on my bed. It was difficult to describe how I felt. I understood what had happened and that it was wrong and I felt strongly that I wanted people to know. I waited for the nurse who I had just told to become involved with a patient and I went over to her desk and got a pen. I tore out two pages of a bible, which was in my bedside unit. The pen I had taken didn't work so I returned to the nurse's station and got a pencil. I wrote on one of the torn out pages, "To the doctor. Your porter hurt me. Please ring my Dad."

The woman said she then wrote down the address and telephone number for her father.

'I then signed the page,' she continued, 'and I posted the sheet of paper in a letterbox that was situated in the corridor beyond my ward. I remember reading the word "letterbox". The box was red and it was high up. I remember I had difficulty stretching up to post the page. I thought at the time I was posting the note to the doctors at the hospital.

'The very same night of the rape I was in bed after the lights had been turned out. Although the ward was dark there was a partial light. I was half asleep when the same porter who had assaulted me earlier in the day came to my ward. This was the first time that I'd ever seen him on the ward. He was wearing the same clothes as he'd worn earlier.

'I saw him walk straight to my bed as if he knew exactly where I was. I was frightened and I pulled the covers over my head. I could smell the same muggy odour that I'd smelled on him earlier in the day. The man stood to the left of my bed and without saying anything thrust one of his hands under the covers and positioned it between my legs. Although he didn't insert his fingers he rubbed it on my vagina. I heard him make a sound as if he was enjoying what he was doing. He touched me in this way for only seconds; probably 10 to 20 seconds. I remember that his movements were rushed.

'Again, I was really shocked by what was happening and didn't know how to respond. I kept my head under the covers throughout. Just as suddenly as he had appeared he removed his hand and walked away from my bedside.

'As he walked away I peeked my head out from under the covers and saw that he'd walked over to the bed of an elderly lady. As I watched him, I saw him literally jump on top of the woman so he was lying face down on top of her. As he did this, I heard a nurse shout, "You shouldn't be in here, Jimmy." I saw that he got off the lady and walked out of the ward. Nothing further was said.

'The next day when I woke up, I noticed the woman who occupied the bed opposite me had gone and I didn't see her again. As a result of being assaulted by the porter on a second occasion I decided I wanted to make sure that the doctors were aware of how the porter was behaving, so I wrote a second note, again on a page torn from the bible in my bedside unit. I wrote exactly the same message as I had done the day before and posted the note in the same letterbox.

'Later during the course of that day I decided to try and find the porter. I don't know what I intended to do. I left the ward and I made my way to the corridor, which led off the day room, the same corridor I'd watched the porter walk down after he'd raped me. I walked down the corridor myself and through the double doors I'd seen him go through.

'I went into a bar where people were wearing white coats. I thought they were all doctors. They were sitting at tables, drinking and smoking. As I walked into the room one of the men said, "You shouldn't be in here," and he escorted me out. I couldn't see if the porter who had assaulted me was in the bar or not. I went back to my ward and didn't say anything further to the staff about either of the incidents, and I cannot remember anything more of my stay in hospital.

'When I was about 14 years old I was watching television and I saw the porter who had assaulted me in hospital. I recognised his voice to begin with. The picture on our television was of poor quality and quite distorted. I was amazed to see the man was the porter from the hospital. I was sure of it because I recognised him visually and his mannerisms. His voice was very distinctive. I couldn't understand why the porter from the hospital was on television.

'In time I came to know that the porter was Jimmy Savile but I remained confused at that stage about the situation.'

Other than the utterly brazen and callous nature of Savile's attack on the girl, the most shocking aspect of her account is the clear-eyed recollection of telling a nurse on the ward what had just been done to her, and her attempts to notify other members of the hospital staff.

Since Savile's death and the dam wall breaking on his secret life of offending, it has become blindingly obvious it wasn't such a secret life after all. At Stoke Mandeville, and at the other hospitals where he invested the bulk of his time, it seems that his behaviour was, if not well known, then at the very least discussed among members of staff.

In October 2012, in the immediate fallout from the scandal, Buckinghamshire Healthcare NHS Trust stated it was 'shocked' to hear of the allegations about Jimmy Savile, adding, 'We are unaware of any record or reports of inappropriate behaviour of this nature during Jimmy's work with the trust.'[1]

In the late Seventies, John Lindsay was working as a detective constable with Thames Valley Police. He claimed it was then that a young female nurse at Stoke Mandeville told him staff were concerned about Jimmy Savile's conduct during hospital visits.

'[The nurse] said to me at the time they didn't like Savile because he was touching little girls in hospital, not necessarily in a sexual way, but touching them and they were unhappy about the way he was going on,' Lindsay said. 'They told the little girls who were in hospital to stay in bed and give the impression they were asleep.'[2]

Lindsay reported the allegations to a senior colleague who brushed them off: 'Jimmy Savile is a high-profile man,' the senior officer is reported to have said. 'He must be OK. He could not be doing anything irregular. Don't worry about it.' Nothing more was done and, Lindsay argued, there was little else he could do.

As a patient at Stoke Mandeville, Rebecca Owen recounts that she overheard nurses talking about how Jimmy Savile picked his targets: 'It was an air of resignation that you had to put up with it,' she said. 'There was some sort of ironic chatter between the nurses about who would be the lucky one to go off to his room. And then, as one of the nurses was leaving or passing by my bed, she leant over and said the best thing you can do is stay in bed until he's gone and pretend to be asleep.'[3]

Such assaults were taking place from the very start of Savile's long association with Stoke Mandeville. A visitor to the hospital, who was nine at the time, claims Savile fondled him in his Rolls-Royce at a fund-raising event for the hospital in the very early 1970s. In 1971, Caroline Moore, who was paralysed from the chest down, was a 13-year-old patient at Stoke Mandeville when she says Savile attacked her in a corridor.

'I was quite shy and lonely,' recalled Moore. 'I don't remember him saying anything to me but he leant down and I was excited because I thought he was going to give me a wee peck on the cheek. But he took my face in his hands and rammed – and that is the only way I can describe it – he rammed his tongue right down the back of my throat, to the point where it almost made me gag . . . Afterwards he just walked off as if nothing had happened.'[4]

Another female patient reported a similar assault on her taking place in the late 1980s. She was in bed recovering from an operation at the time.

Like Liz Dux's anonymous client, Caroline Moore tried telling people what had happened to her. 'I told my family at the time: they didn't take it seriously because he was such a high-profile character,' she said.

In the same period that Detective Constable Lindsay informed his superior what he'd been told by a nurse at Stoke Mandeville, Samantha Dearan recounts how as an 11-year-old Savile repeatedly groped her during Catholic mass at the hospital's chapel. The Dearan family worshipped at the chapel, and Samantha was regularly asked to carry round the collection plate.

'Savile used to stand in the separate little room during mass,' she explained, 'and I had to go in there to get the offering plate while the service was going on. It was horrible; I used to hate it. I knew what was going to happen before I walked through the door. I just tried to get in and out as quickly as possible. It was so blatant it made you even more afraid to say anything. I thought it was my fault.'[5]

Samantha Dearan said the assaults continued for three or four years, and that Savile liked to keep the door open so he could see the priest. She believes he got a thrill out of it. 'Eventually,' she admits, 'I stopped going to church because of him.'

It wasn't only at Stoke Mandeville that Savile exploited his status as a famous benefactor to secure access to unsuspecting and largely defenceless patients. At Leeds General Infirmary, where he had hoodwinked the board of governors with his voluntary work and then bought the loyalty of the porters with his offers of free holidays in the caravans he kept dotted around the British coastline, he was acting with a similar level of impunity. And again, he was encouraged that nobody appeared to want to stop him.

In May 1972, June Thornton, a nurse from York, was admitted to the hospital for an operation on her spine. As she lay in bed, she recollects seeing Jimmy Savile approaching a young female patient on the same ward.

'At the bottom of the ward, sat in a high-backed chair with arms, was a young woman,' recounted Thornton. 'It being a neuro ward, I think she had brain damage; she was sat there, not on this planet, bless her. Then Jimmy Savile came in and kissed her. I thought at the time he was a relative but then he kissed her neck and started rubbing his hands down her arms, and he started to molest her. There wasn't a thing I could do about it because I was laid flat on my back.[6]

'When a nurse eventually came in, I mentioned Jimmy Savile and pointed over to the girl and said, "If he comes anywhere near me I'll scream the place down."' Thornton said the nurse merely shrugged her shoulders.[7]

Another former patient at the hospital claims Savile touched her inappropriately in a lift after she had undergone spinal surgery in 1973. 'I felt too frightened to report it because everyone thought he was a saint,' she said.[8]

In the same year, Beth, then a sixteen-year-old who lived at home with her parents in a village near York, was admitted to Leeds General Infirmary with a suspected nervous breakdown. She told me she was treated at the hospital for a period of three months. Towards the end of this period she recalled sitting on her bed in the middle of a 'big, long ward' when Jimmy Savile, who she had seen around from time to time, came over to chat.

'Come with me,' she remembers him saying, and he took her to a newsagent just outside the hospital whereupon he instructed the shopkeeper to give her whatever she wanted. 'He swept his hand – magazines, sweets, everything,' Beth said. Soon after she

YOUR PORTER HURT ME

returned to her bed, a pile of items appeared. 'I thought I was the chosen one,' she reflected. 'I now realise he was grooming me.'

The very next day, Beth was again sitting on her bed when she says Jimmy Savile sent for her. 'A porter in a white coat came to pick me up from the ward. He took me through these corridors until we were in a sort of underpass under the LGI.' Off a corridor leading from the service area was a small office. 'The porter said nothing,' she maintained, 'he just knocked and opened the door.' Inside, Jimmy Savile was stood, leaning on a wall.

'He pulled me to him and started kissing me,' explained Beth, who remembers wearing a cheesecloth dress she had made for her stay in hospital. 'He had one hand on my right thigh and the other on my left breast. His tongue was in my mouth.' She insisted Savile said nothing, other than asking her one question: 'Are you on the pill?' When Beth said no, she told me he put his hand over hers and forced her to masturbate him. She said he was wearing tracksuit-style trousers, which were down around his ankles by this point. He did not wear underwear.

'It all happened so fast,' Beth explained. 'When he'd finished, he said, "You've got to go now," and knocked on the door.' Outside the office was waiting a different man, who was dressed in a white T-shirt rather than a white porter's jacket. This second man took her back to the ward. Beth says that when she tried to tell a nurse what had happened, she only got as far as mentioning Jimmy Savile's name before the group of nurses laughed and walked away.

'It was tried and tested,' she said of the manner in which she was groomed, taken from the ward and assaulted. 'No words were spoken, the knock on the office door, the different men to take me there and back to the ward.' She claims not to have seen Savile again before being discharged. When she told her parents, she said her father refused to believe her. Her mother said she felt most people would feel the same as her father.

But it wasn't only patients Savile preyed on, it seems. An account posted to an online Leeds forum[9] on the day his death was

335

announced suggests that he had keys to nurses' accommodation at Leeds General Infirmary.

The author claimed his ex-wife was a student nurse at the hospital in the early 1970s. As a volunteer porter, Savile would enter 'when the girls would be in various states of undress' or regularly went 'into the shower room at the end of the girls' shifts to "clean".' According to the post, complaints were made to the board of the hospital but nothing was done.

'The girls in my fiancées' [sic] room were really getting scared of him, so one evening me and another of the girls' boyfriends sneaked into their room after the girls came off duty. [Savile] used his master key to "accidentally" walk in – and me and the lad were in his face. He went white and ran out.'

The man recounted how Savile returned minutes later with security guards. He warned the girls that if anything was said, they would lose their jobs.

The same source claimed that six months later he and a friend got into a fight with Savile after he groped and then slapped the man's girlfriend at the student nurse's Christmas ball at Leeds Polytechnic. His account stated Savile had tried to press charges but there were too many witnesses. The incident was hushed up, as was Savile's attempted rape of another student nurse.

Leeds Teaching Hospitals NHS Trust, which has managed Leeds General Infirmary and St James's University Hospital since 1998, has consistently denied having 'any record of complaints about Jimmy Savile's behaviour made during the time he was a volunteer and charity supporter at Leeds General Infirmary or at any of our other hospitals'.[10] That said, it confirmed records dating back to the 1980s and beyond were difficult to search 'due to the change in governance structures.'

Liz Dux, who represents 27 clients, both male and female, who were abused while in the care of the National Health Service, says Savile's attacks on patients at hospitals in Leeds included forcing children to masturbate him and digital penetration. These offences took place from the late 1960s to the mid 1970s.

Beth told me that she saw Jimmy Savile at Leeds General Infirmary in the final years of his life. 'He was walking quickly flanked by two police officers,' she said. 'He had the air of a very important man. I remember thinking how pretentious it looked.'

The attempts by Savile's victims to report him are a recurring theme, Dux confirms. 'We had a body of people saying, "Yes, I did tell someone and they didn't believe me so what was I supposed to do?"'

British society rose as one to salute the saint in its midst. In June 1978, Bob Brooksby chauffeured Jimmy Savile to the Dorchester Hotel where members of the royal family and stars of show business rose to give a standing ovation as he walked into the banqueting hall for a special Variety Club luncheon.

Angus Ogilvy, husband of Princess Alexandra and president of the National Association of Youth Clubs, which Jimmy Savile had raised funds for, was the first to get up to speak: 'He has done more than perhaps anyone else to make the lives of unfortunate people happier than they might ever have been,'[1] said Ogilvy.

Savile talked of how he had felt 'great friendship from the off' with Ogilvy and his wife, socialising with them at the NAYC headquarters on Devonshire Street in London and at any number of gala events. Princess Alexandra was a patron of a hostel for girls in care: 'At this place I'm a cross between a term-time boyfriend and a fixer of special trips out,' he added.[2]

It sounds uncannily like the role he created for himself at Duncroft, where their paths certainly crossed at a garden party in May 1974. The Queen's cousin was a patron of the mental health charity MIND, and on that occasion she greeted Jimmy Savile with a level of enthusiasm and familiarity that is said to have shocked the school's main governor, Lady Montagu Norman.

Bill Cotton, by then controller of BBC1, was the next to pay tribute in the Dorchester's banqueting hall: 'Jim Callaghan might be Prime Minister and Jimmy Carter President of the United States, but when you say *Jim'll Fix It* everybody knows who you mean.'³ Jimmy Savile nodded and waved, drinking in the acclaim. He was seated between Lord Louis Mountbatten and Sir Billy Butlin, two men representative of the social poles he now spanned.

The Christmas cards from members of the royal family and the ease with which Savile was able to get a 13-year-old girl inside Buckingham Palace during a royal reception – something he boasted about on Michael Parkinson's chat show – underlined how, through Mountbatten's patronage, he had become a firm favourite in royal circles.

'Royalty are surrounded by people who don't know how to deal with it,' he explained of the fascination he seemed to hold for them. 'I have a freshness of approach which they obviously find to their liking . . . I have a natural good fun way of going on and we have a laugh. They don't get too many laughs. Some people have said I'm a court jester. I know I have freak value.'⁴

'He was terribly pleased to know famous people, particularly the royal family,' Roger Ordish recounted. 'I remember we once did something with Angus Ogilvy, who was toe in the water with royalty. We were filming and he didn't even introduce me. I thought that was a bit strange. It was almost as though he was jealous: "They're going to know me, they're not going to know you, sunshine."'

With viewing figures of over 16 million and thousands of letters arriving each week, *Jim'll Fix It* was causing its star to make some uncomfortable readjustments. 'He said it's the worst thing he ever did,' recalled a friend. 'He said it ruined him . . . He said, "Wherever I go in the world anyone under 20 calls me Jim'll . . . Jimmy Savile is dead." He never got to be Jimmy Savile again.'

Ordish confirmed the reality was someway removed from the popular perception of Jimmy Savile as the nation's Santa Claus. 'For someone who was so calculating about his own image, and so ambitious for himself, he occasionally said things that jarred and were, frankly, out of order,' he said. 'He sort of hoped no one was listening.'

When I asked *Jim'll Fix It*'s producer to give me an example of the odd comments Jimmy Savile sometimes made, he recounted a conversation with Gill Stribling-Wright, one of the researchers on the show. 'Jim was talking about some very beautiful woman on the programme and Gill said to him, "Do you fancy her?" He said, "Oh no, much too old." [The woman] was only 25, or something like that. He then said, "Walnut, walnut."'

Ordish explained 'walnut' was Jimmy Savile's reference to the woman's clitoris. It's no surprise to learn members of the production team described *Jim'll Fix It*'s host as 'weird'.

And yet despite making such remarks to young women working on the show, he was strangely puritanical when it came to what he allowed on *Jim'll Fix It*. 'We did an air-sea rescue thing that involved some girls,' Ordish explained. 'These girls pushed their teacher into the sea, obviously knowing that the air-sea rescue was coming, but I remember Jim asking me how I was going to do it. He didn't want it to be disrespectful.'

Ordish believes the incredible viewing figures for the show – it even topped ITV's *Coronation Street* in some weeks – forced Savile to look at himself and make some tough choices: 'I suppose [he] was thinking, "I better go straight here."'

Just not quite yet, it seemed. Jimmy Savile's mutually beneficial relationship with P&O came to an end that summer when he was thrown off the company's flagship, the luxury liner SS *Canberra*, after complaints from the parents of a 14-year-old girl. The girl in question was not the only teenager he attempted to lure into his cabin on that cruise, as Jane (not her real name), then 16, testified.

The star approached Jane and a friend and promised them autographs if they followed him back to his first-class quarters. They were taken inside whereupon he immediately began taking off his trousers. Jane said he begged her for a cuddle before pulling her onto his bed.

'He was very forceful and wrapped himself right around me,' she recounted. 'It was quite frightening. At one point he slipped out of his pants and started rubbing himself up against me. I could feel that he was excited.' Jane now believes that if her friend, who took photographs of the incident, had not been present she would have been forced to have sex with Jimmy Savile.

A few days later, Jimmy Savile was summoned to the captain's day room. Complaints had been made to a ship's officer before the *Canberra*'s captain heard as the parents of a 14-year-old girl described how the 51-year-old celebrity had pursued their daughter around the ship.

Savile denied everything. 'But the more I quizzed him,' said the captain, who refuses to be named, 'the more convinced I became that he was lying. He was a shifty sort of chap whose eyes darted all over the place. The parents, who were not travelling first class, were very decent, ordinary people who were scandalised by Savile's unwanted attention to their daughter.

'I told him he disgusted me and I wanted him off my ship when we reached Gibraltar. I detailed an officer to make sure he remained in his cabin until we reached the Rock. He was to take all his meals in his cabin and was not allowed to leave it under any circumstances short of shipwreck.'[5]

Brian Hitchen, the former newspaper editor, confirmed that he heard the story about Jimmy Savile's expulsion from the *Canberra* all those years ago. So why did he not report it? 'Two reasons,' he replied. 'In those days newspapers did not write "nasty" stories about celebrities unless the famous had been handsomely paid for their often fairly tame revelations. The second reason is because Britain's libel laws too often help make those like Savile untouchable.'[6]

Having escaped public condemnation for his shocking behaviour at sea, the next stage in Jimmy Savile's unlikely metamorphosis took place a year later with the publication of *God'll Fix It*, a slim volume that outlined his views on faith. In his preface to the series of interviews contained within, Reverend Colin Semper had some interesting things to say about the man he produced on *Speakeasy* for four years.

He described him as a 'mystery man' and 'difficult to know', and asked, 'Who is this blond-haired eccentric who can help a prostitute with a problem on the same day as he introduces *Songs of Praise*?' Semper had no answers, as such, but was convinced Savile was genuine. Why? 'Because however clever you are, if you are not genuine, you will be found out.'

Semper likened Savile to a wizard: 'You never know what kind of answer you're going to get. Usually the answers are off-beat, they can sound crazy but I have come to think that it could be a brave and glorious madness.'[7]

The book itself is extraordinary, and as close as Jimmy Savile ever came to a mea culpa. As well as illuminating his twisted view of the world, it also revealed how he justified his actions.

In the chapter titled 'How Do I See Jesus of Nazareth?', he talked about how every human body was unique. 'Nature makes one body of a woman, say, into that of a nymphomaniac, or that of a man into a very hot sex outfit. You can't expect all of these to behave in the same way. God's suggestions, the suggestions of Jesus, are therefore different for different people.'[8]

In the very next chapter, he again bracketed himself alongside Martin Luther King, Mahatma Gandhi and Jesus Christ himself for the way he was occasionally vilified for his very public good works. He said he was aware that the more he did, the more likely it was that he would find that someone would want to kill him.

In the chapter 'What Happens When I Die?' he discussed his work in the mortuaries of Stoke Mandeville and Leeds General Infirmary, and how 'the imperfect chemical envelope' of the body changes in death. He stated his belief that those who had 'surrendered' themselves to evil in life would be 'surrendered to the forces of evil' in the afterlife, and said death was something he was looking forward to 'with quite considerable excitement'.[9]

The most significant confessions, however, came towards the end of the book. In 'Am I Saved?' he admitted being an 'abuser of things, and bodies, and people' and recounted how he took troublemakers in his dancehall downstairs to the boiler room whereupon they'd be tied up and gagged. After everyone else had gone home, his minders would beat them.

He also acknowledged that he took advantage of women: 'That shows you that the forces of evil are causing me to do something which, on reflection, I would rather not have done,' he argued. 'I am frail like everyone else.'

It was but a minor concession before he outlined how he weighed his actions. 'I often wonder if [God] works a debit side and a credit side, or whether a debit is a debit full stop. I think I'm in credit but I would hate to think that I could commit all sorts of sins just because I might have a credit balance.'[10]

'He saw the fund-raising as part of his credit side,' agreed Semper. 'The more he could get, the more bonus points he'd have in the Kingdom of God.'

Jimmy Savile expanded on the theme of credit and debit in the chapter 'What Shall I Say at the Pearly Gates and at the Judgement Table?' He explained how he would argue with St Peter if he pointed out all the sins he had committed, and argue that it was the machine of [his] body' that had caused him to do such things.[11]

'It could be that the person arriving at the judgement seat had been given a body prone to excesses because the glands dictated that he should be more than was really normal,' he said. 'The temptation could also be towards sexual excess in a girl – and I have known many – who has been born a nymphomaniac. She can't resist a man who runs his finger down her arm . . . She might not really want to be possessed by that man, but her body – and this is a medical fact – finds great difficulty in resisting.'[12]

It is a telling passage, and one that for once affords a view beyond the high walls of Jimmy Savile's assiduously constructed façade. It also suggests that his access to the psychiatrists at Broadmoor had helped him to arrive at some kind of understanding of, and explanation for, that which he believed his own glands 'dictated'. Conveniently, he decided that such people should be forgiven because they were more 'unlucky than bad'.

And yet, in a discussion on how he coped with sex, he once again demonstrated his unerring ability to reference the very core of his depravity, even in the process of delivering his lessons on life: 'Sex at its worst is corruption,' he said, 'as when young people might be corrupted to provide sex.'[13] Sex, was fine, he maintained, as long as it didn't 'cause distress'.

'That awful book,' sighed Reverend Colin Semper when I asked him for his reflections on a specific line he'd written in the preface to *God'll Fix It*: '[Jimmy] worked at being a character, almost as if to say, "They'll never catch me out."' Semper agreed it has taken on a very different complexion in light of what we now know.

'[Savile] liked to be outlandish and then he'd sort of cover it up,' he said. 'He was a kind of chameleon, really. He flitted from place to place and took on the foliage of the place. It was a strange, strange business really.'

Thirty-five years on, he acknowledged that Jimmy Savile was trying to balance out what he had done; that he was mitigating for it in some way before moving forward and, in his mind at least, trying to atone for his sins. I put it to Semper that what Jimmy wrote indicates he could have been in no doubt that what he was doing was wrong. 'I think he did too,' Semper said quietly. 'I think he definitely knew.'

Despite rising public fears about children being at risk from predatory adults and a shift in emphasis in childcare away from solving and containing the problem of delinquency and towards the protection of the most vulnerable members of society, in April 1978, the National Council for Civil Liberties stated that two of its affiliated groups, the Paedophile Information Exchange and Paedophile Action for Liberation, should be allowed to campaign for an abolition of the age of consent.

Jim Callaghan's Labour government was planning to reform the law at the time and the Protection of Children Bill proposed to tighten the rules on child pornography by outlawing indecent images of children under the age of 16. The NCCL's response was to advocate reducing the age of consent to 14, arguing 'childhood sexual experiences, willingly engaged in, with an adult result in no identifiable damage'. It claimed children would suffer more from having to recount their experiences in court.

In 1976, the NCCL had filed a submission to a parliamentary committee arguing that the new law could lead to 'damaging and absurd prosecutions'. Two years later a letter written by the NCCL's legal officer, a young lawyer named Harriet Harman, in official response to the bill, argued that pornographic photos or films of children should not be classified as 'indecent' unless it could be proven that the child had suffered. The NCCL's suggested amendment placed the onus of proof on the prosecution.

In its official submission, the NCCL stated, 'Although this harm may be of a somewhat speculative nature, where participation falls short of physical assault, it is none-the-less justifiable to restrain activities by photographers which involve placing children under the age of 14 (or, arguably, 16) in sexual situations.

'We suggest that the term "indecent" be qualified as follows: A photograph or film shall not for this purpose be considered indecent (a) by reason only that the model is in a state of undress (whether complete or partial); (b) unless it is proved or is to be inferred from the photograph or film that the making of the photograph or film might reasonably be expected to have caused the model physical harm or pronounced psychological or emotional disorder.'

The Protection of Children Act was passed on 20 July 1978. It was the last major child protection legislation for eleven years.

PART FIVE

Mark Williams-Thomas had five of Jimmy Savile's victims on film, as well as others who had witnessed his offending behaviour. What he did not have, though, was a final part to his hour-long documentary. He needed expert, independent analysis of the evidence and it came with the contribution of Ian Glenn QC. After watching the filmed interviews, Glenn said it was his opinion that Williams-Thomas had enough for Jimmy Savile to be arrested were he still alive.

The next step, Williams-Thomas decided, was to show the material to Esther Rantzen, the television presenter and founder of Childline, the child protection charity. Rantzen held her head in her hands when she saw it. 'I think it was incredibly powerful,' says Williams-Thomas. 'Rantzen's was a very genuine response. The evidence, when you looked at it all together, was compelling.'

Executive producer Alex Gardiner, commissioning editor Ian Squires and ITV's director of television Peter Fincham were all well aware of the risks involved in the exposé of a national hero and stayed closely involved throughout the process, reviewing new interviews as they were completed. Williams-Thomas maintains that while they remained supportive throughout, there was no input in terms of how the investigation was managed: 'I was left with Lesley [Gardiner] and between the two of us we built it and put it together.'

On 7 September, a three-page letter from Williams-Thomas and Gardiner arrived at the office of George Entwistle, who was about to take over as director general of the BBC. The letter set out the allegations against Jimmy Savile made in ITV's forthcoming *Exposure* documentary as they related to the BBC, and posed a number of questions.

Paul Mylrea, the BBC's director of Public Affairs, told the Pollard inquiry that the legal team initially drove the corporation's response to the letter. 'They were beginning to examine what there was on record, whether there was anything – any knowledge of Savile,' he said. What is apparent, though, is that lines of communication within the BBC had already started to break down. Panic was setting in.[1]

Four days later, Stephen Mitchell, the deputy director of BBC News, collared Meirion Jones and raised the Savile issue. Mitchell said there had been no management interference in the decision not to proceed with the *Newsnight* story. When Jones began to outline why he believed pulling the story would have grave consequences for the BBC he recalls Mitchell shutting him down.

The official BBC line on what it was that *Newsnight* had been investigating was now taking shape. When the website Digital Spy ran a story on how similar the BBC's investigation was to the one in ITV's upcoming documentary, the BBC press office moved to set the record straight. 'We [the BBC] were pursuing a particular angle related to the CPS/Police which we were unable to substantiate and which was therefore not broadcast.'[2]

The very next day, some nine days after receiving the letter from Williams-Thomas and Gardiner, Julian Payne, the BBC's head of press, finally sent a reply. It stated the *Newsnight* investigation was abandoned for 'editorial reasons' and quoted exactly the same rationale about the CPS and the police.

Lesley Gardiner was furious about the time it had taken for the BBC to respond. '[It] was almost dismissive in terms of what they were going to do about it,' remembers Williams-Thomas. 'I think that was a significant point. [The situation] was aggravated, of course, by the fact that they . . . then issued a very different statement. That was only because it was massively in the media eye. It raises the question of what they thought. Did they think it was just going to go away?'

On 28 September, five days before the ITV documentary was scheduled to be broadcast, and amid widespread reporting of the allegations it contained, the BBC issued a second statement: 'While the BBC condemns any behaviour of the type alleged in the strongest terms, in the absence of evidence of any kind found at the BBC that corroborates the allegations that have been made it is simply not possible for the corporation to take any further action.'[3]

Newsnight's editor, Peter Rippon, added his voice to the denials coming out of the BBC. 'It is absolutely untrue that the *Newsnight* investigation was dropped for anything other than editorial reasons. We have been very clear from the start that the piece was not broadcast because the story we were pursuing could not be substantiated. To say otherwise is false and very damaging to the BBC and individuals. The notion that internal pressure was applied appears to be a malicious rumour.'[4]

In an email to Rippon, Meirion Jones expressed his concern at his editor's attempt to 'rewrite history'.[5] He pointed out that if there was to be an investigation – by the BBC Trust or the House of Commons Culture and Media Committee – 'we have to be honest'.

Jones continued: 'You made the decision that we had enough to TX [transmit] once we had confirmation that the police had investigated [Savile] – on top of the victim interviews we had already done . . . I don't know what happened to change your mind and I thought that was a bizarre decision but I accepted that you decided to drop the story for Editorial Reasons because ultimately you are the Editor and it is up to you to make those calls.'

Rippon drafted a response that he emailed to Stephen Mitchell for approval. The email was never sent to Jones. Instead, they met face-to-face. Rippon contends that it was at this meeting that Jones told him that Surrey Police had interviewed all the women they had spoken to. Both Meirion Jones and Liz MacKean maintain they were consistently transparent about the fact that Keri was not part of the police investigation and therefore *Newsnight* had more than Surrey Police did when the CPS made its decision.

As the pressure on the BBC continued to mount, questions were now being asked in the press about whether information had been withheld from the police. Meanwhile the chain of internal communication within the BBC only seemed to grow. The BBC press office advised, wrongly, that a response should emphasise that the information provided by Keri was already known to the police.

Williams-Thomas remembers the week before transmission as being one of the most stressful of his life. 'It was probably the closest I've been to having a nervous breakdown,' he admits. 'We were about to expose an individual who was highly regarded and respected and who had been a national institution. And ultimately, it was down to Lesley and I. We were responsible for this and for looking after the five people who were about to go on national TV. That is a big, big commitment.'

The first wave of press coverage about the imminent *Exposure* film contained some strong criticism. Roger Foster, Savile's nephew and one of the organisers of his three-day funeral, said he was 'sad and disgusted'. He voiced his fear that the allegations would have a negative effect on his uncle's charity legacy. 'The guy hasn't been dead for a year and they're bringing up these stories,' he said. 'I just don't understand the motives behind this.'

'His family came out and said that it was a disgrace,' says Williams-Thomas. 'So I was in the firing line from that. I was in the firing line for ITV, I was the face of the programme.' It was upsetting, but he says he tried to ignore it. 'I was very determined that what I was doing was right. I wanted to give a voice to those five people. I knew there would be other victims out there and I was hoping they would come forward. I never knew it would be as many as did come forward but I always hoped that there would be some other people that had the confidence to [do that].'

In the period leading up to the documentary being aired, Williams-Thomas sat at home with his eldest daughter listening to a particularly vociferous phone-in show on Radio Leeds. 'My phone was ringing all morning,' he remembers. 'My agent was calling me saying "Radio Leeds are after you." I thought, I'm just not talking. So they did this phone-in and people were saying [they were] trying to get hold of Mark Williams-Thomas and he's not returning their calls.'

Williams-Thomas has three children. His eldest daughter was 17 at the time. 'I remember [her] saying, "What you've done is right." You know what, that is quite a strong thing to say.' His 13-year-old daughter, also 'got it', he says. '[She said] it was the right thing to do to expose an individual like that.'

At five minutes past five on the afternoon of 2 October, Peter Rippon responded to internal pressure within the BBC by publishing a blog post outlining his reasons for not broadcasting *Newsnight*'s report on Jimmy Savile. Helen Boaden, Stephen Mitchell, the Corporate and News PR departments and the BBC's head of Corporate and Public Affairs were all involved in tweaks made to the original briefing document Mitchell had instructed Rippon to prepare. The office of Director General George Entwistle was also kept in the loop.

In the final, approved text, Rippon denied there had been a 'BBC cover-up' and that *Newsnight* had 'deliberately withheld information from the police'. However, he did nail his colours firmly to the mast by claiming, 'if we could establish some sort of institutional failure we would have a much stronger story'. He restated the line that the CPS decision not to proceed was based on a lack of evidence rather than Jimmy Savile's age, and that it was the crucial factor in persuading him 'not to publish'.[6]

Within an hour, Jeremy Paxman, *Newsnight*'s most senior presenter, emailed Rippon with his own thoughts. He said the blog post did not answer all the accusations laid against the programme, adding, 'I think we make a problem for ourselves by running away from this story.'[7] He outlined five points of serious concern and asked Rippon to reconsider doing something on the story. In one of a series of subsequent emails, Rippon argued that not covering the story was 'the least worse option'.[8]

Amid the deluge of newspaper stories and the spiralling sense of confusion at the BBC, the trustees of one of Jimmy Savile's charitable funds released a statement of their own: 'We are conscious of the dedication and effort that Sir Jimmy made throughout his lifetime to charity. He raised more than £40 million for good causes, giving away 90 per cent of his income. The broadcast of such serious allegations, which by their very nature will be one-sided, may impact on the charitable trust and its endeavours.'[9]

Williams-Thomas and Gardiner were still in the editing suite on the morning of 3 October. Their documentary was to be broadcast later that evening. By now, the media tide had turned firmly in their favour, and a dozen victims of Jimmy Savile were now telling their stories in papers and on news bulletins across Britain. 'It was a real change,' Williams-Thomas acknowledges. 'We then had the media onside.'

Even the BBC had finally bowed to the pressure, announcing its Investigations Unit would assist police inquiries into its former star, a man who was now being posthumously rebranded as Public Enemy Number 1.

The former Surrey Police officer at the centre of the growing storm spent the rest of the afternoon doing interviews. Williams-Thomas was tired and surviving on shredded nerves. He agreed to stay on at ITV headquarters until the early evening in case any further changes were required to the programme, but was adamant that he wanted to watch the documentary at home with his family.

He remembers trying to grab a couple of hours' sleep at a London hotel. 'It was still frantic,' he says. 'My phone was ringing non-stop . . . I must have got half an hour because I was just exhausted.'

The walls had been breached and beyond lay the ugly truth Jimmy Savile had spent his life trying to conceal.

The new decade began with Britain's first female prime minister in residence at 10 Downing Street. Jimmy Savile had been keen to capitalise on the promise of his early contacts with Margaret Thatcher, who he had hosted on a visit to Stoke Mandeville in December 1977. He even claimed a share of the credit for her election triumph. When they had filmed a segment for *Jim'll Fix It* at the Houses of Parliament, she'd asked him to fix it for her to become PM.

After the election of 3 May 1979 had swept the Tories into power and Thatcher into office, he said Downing Street staff had followed up to secure her the spoils. 'Her secretary rang to say she was rather upset because I hadn't been round to give her her badge. 'I reported to Downing Street a few days later and presented [it].'[1]

Savile 'bumped into' Thatcher again soon afterwards, during the Conservative Party conference at Blackpool. He was in the process of completing 'Jim's Daily Dozen', a month-long series of sponsored runs through towns across Britain, sponsored, thanks to Brooksby, by Hoover and Procter & Gamble. Savile told the prime minister that he would like some of the money raised to go to a charity of her choice.

He was wooing her, and it was working.

Mrs Thatcher would present a cheque for £10,000 to the NSPCC, courtesy of Jimmy Savile, at a luncheon at Downing Street on 6 February 1980. As his host heaped praise and photographers snapped away happily, Savile squirmed with faux embarrassment. It was merely the prelude to the serious business of his visit. He needed something back from the prime minister, especially having agreed to spare her government's blushes by leading the campaign to build a new National Spinal Injuries Centre at Stoke Mandeville Hospital.

The wooden Nissen huts housing the unit since 1944 had been badly damaged in a series of winter storms. Five ceilings had collapsed, seriously jeopardising the centre's ability to treat the 750 inpatients and 2,000 outpatients it saw each year. When no NHS funding was forthcoming for repairs, the country's leading spinal injury facility faced up to the prospect of imminent closure. Staff and patients staged a sit-in protest that generated column inches in the newspapers but little else. Time was running out.

The situation at Stoke Mandeville dominated the meeting Jimmy Savile orchestrated with Dr Gerard Vaughan, minister of state for Health. Over tea and cake at the House of Commons, Vaughan outlined the new government's thinking on the National Health Service, a philosophy which ordained that special projects such as rebuilding work at hospitals, even such urgent work as that required at Stoke Mandeville, would need to be supported by voluntary contributions, in line with the cuts in public expenditure Prime Minister Thatcher was implementing across the board. Vaughan suggested this meant they had a problem. 'Not really,' replied Savile, and they struck a deal.[2]

Jimmy Savile would lead a campaign to rebuild the spinal injuries unit at Stoke Mandeville using private money and donations. In other words, it was to be a pioneering example of the type of 'partnership' between government and the public that the prime minister was so keen to promote.

'Jim needed high profile institutions,' explained Janet Cope, who had worked at Stoke Mandeville Hospital since she was fifteen. 'The spinal injuries centre was world famous, it was unique. It pioneered the treatment of the paralysed. Broadmoor was the first hospital for the criminally insane; Leeds General Infirmary was on his doorstep and a huge teaching hospital. Little local hospitals were no good to him. They were not high profile enough.

He needed something that would smack you in the face. Stoke Mandeville was very, very high profile and it brought Jim fame and us money.'

Jimmy Savile launched the campaign in late January at a press conference at Church House, Westminster. The target, he said, was between six and ten million pounds. He maintained he was unconcerned about those who said it was the responsibility of the NHS, and therefore the government, to find the money.

'This is the way they used to build hospitals years ago,' he said, 'and it's not that bad a way to build a hospital in these straitened times.' He went on to explain that a £5 donation would pay for a brick, £50,000 would provide a bed and £250,000 would fund a ward.[3]

Afterwards, Vaughan pledged the government's support for the appeal. 'This is a unit we must sustain, look after and develop,' he told the assembled reporters. 'There is a public responsibility to see that these people get the kind of care they deserve.' When asked what backing the government would give, Vaughan replied, 'There's a limited amount of money available in this country for health care. If we want more, we have to look outside the NHS.' According to the Spinal Injuries Association, he did at least offer assurances that government money would pay for the running costs of the new centre.

Savile rounded off proceedings by asking for the first donation to the new fund. On hand was Douglas McMinns, a retired businessman from Buckinghamshire who handed over a cheque for £150,000. As Vaughan posed outside with the cheque and two young paraplegics from Stoke Mandeville, Jimmy Savile reiterated that he was very happy to support the government's controversial stance.

The very next day, an editorial in the *Daily Mail* began banging the drum: 'Those like Mr Savile, who tirelessly take the hat round for this country's hospitals, do a wonderful job,' it boomed. 'The *Daily Mail* is wholly in favour of a financially beleaguered National Health Service tapping as much as it can from the charitable impulses of the public.'[4]

Despite the economic malaise afflicting Britain, the response was instantaneous. A spray paint company pledged to donate a penny for every can sold that year. Ski Yoghurt offered £100,000. Quaker Oats offered £200 a mile for Savile to run a marathon around Ben Nevis. BUPA sponsored an entire ward. Meanwhile, all over the country ordinary people found unusual ways of raising money, from sitting in baths of baked beans to donating money left by the tooth fairy. Cheques and postal orders flooded into the Spinal Injury Centre offices at Stoke Mandeville, where members of staff suddenly found themselves pressed into action as campaign organisers.

At the Downing Street luncheon, Jimmy Savile had pressed the prime minister on the subject of tax deduction for charitable donations. Not, in this case, to enhance his own bank balance, but because it would significantly facilitate the success of the campaign. Thatcher had told Savile that she considered the existing arrangements a 'considerable disincentive to those who are contemplating charitable donations'.[5]

A week after his visit to Downing Street, Savile sat in his small flat on Park Crescent, a short walk from Broadcasting House, and began penning a letter: 'Dear Prime Minister, I waited a week before writing to thank you for my lunch invitation because I had such a superb time and I didn't want to be too effusive. My girl patients pretended to be madly jealous + wanted to know what you wore + what you ate. All the paralysed lads called me "Sir James" all week. They all love you. Me too!! Jimmy Savile OBE.' He signed off with three kisses.

The roadmap had been unfurled and the destination was now clear: a knighthood.

This fawning letter was not the first piece of correspondence on the matter of the premier's lunch with Jimmy Savile. A confidential memo sent on the afternoon of the event from Mike Pattison, Thatcher's private secretary, to Martin Hall of the Treasury, and also copied to Gerard Vaughan's office at the Department of Health, requested the chancellor's clarification on the seven-year covenant system.

Two weeks later, a note from the Treasury revealed that the chancellor had already decided that the next Finance Bill would reduce the time necessary for charitable covenants to qualify for tax relief from seven years to four. 'We cannot even hint at this to Jimmy Savile at present,' Pattison wrote in his memo to the prime minister. 'We have to treat it as a Budget secret. Would you like to write to Jimmy promising to take it up personally as in the attached draft [of a letter]? We will then give you a follow-up letter when the Budget has been announced.'[6]

Jimmy Savile was moving in rarefied circles. In May 1980, following his annual sponsored walk in aid of the Central Remedial Clinic in Dublin, he sat down for a meeting with Charles Haughey, the newly elected Irish prime minister. Haughey had requested the meeting through Lady Valerie Goulding, the aristocratic founder of the clinic. In the early 1970s, the two had worked closely when Haughey was head of the clinic's fund-raising committee.

Afterwards, in a note written on Central Remedial Clinic headed paper, Lady Goulding repeated a suggestion made by Ireland's most senior politician at the time, stating Savile 'could be a good mediator as he really is very well in with Mrs Thatcher and members of the opposition as well.'[7] In subsequent years, Savile became a regular visitor to Haughey's home in Abbeville, Kinsealy.

As well as his direct line to the prime minister, he admitted to frequently calling in to Buckingham Palace: 'Yes, I can call them up there and go round for a chat, but I can't say any more than that,' he told one reporter.[8]

Years later, he was more forthcoming with me about the extent of his relationship with the royal family, and how he put it to use in persuading Victor Matthews, construction magnate and proprietor of the *Daily Express*, to come on board with the bid to rebuild the facilities at Stoke Mandeville.

'I know exactly what I can do and what I can't do,' Savile said of his royal associations over breakfast at Ossie's Café in Marylebone. 'What I did with [Matthews] was give him an out. I said to him, if you come across anybody that can help us or get involved, let me know. I left his office and phoned the palace. I got the Duke of Edinburgh's secretary to write a letter to him saying, "I understand you are going to help Jimmy Savile build Stoke Mandeville Hospital. This is a wonderful thing and will be much appreciated by the country. Philip."

'When I went round . . . to see the Duke of Edinburgh, he said, "The letter: it's gone." He said to me, "Do you know the geezer?" And I said, "No, never met him before in my life."'

Savile told me he'd received a telephone call the very next day. Matthews told him that he'd got the letter and realised Savile had 'put an arm up his back'. Matthews put it to Savile that he had dictated the letter. It was an accusation he didn't deny. As he recalled, Matthews then asked him, 'Why are you so honest?' To which he replied: 'I'm always honest with the people I deal with.' He claimed Matthews then said, 'Who says you've got a deal?' Savile replied, 'Prince Philip.'

Matthews knew he'd been manipulated and asked Savile what it was that he wanted. 'Your building company, the *Daily Express* and the London *Evening Standard* [also owned by Matthews],' came the reply. The deal was struck.

'What was in it for him?' Savile asked rhetorically, having polished off his eggs on toast. 'Well, he was still a mister at the time. I'm not saying what I did was get him a title or anything like that but he finished up in the House of Lords.' A dedicated Thatcherite, Matthews was indeed awarded a peerage by the prime minister towards the end of 1980. The fact he also owned the Cunard Line, and therefore the QE2, was an added bonus for Jimmy Savile, given that he was now persona non grata with P&O.

On 6 March, Gerard Vaughan updated the prime minister on the progress of the fund-raising campaign: 'Jimmy Savile has made an excellent start,' he wrote. 'The fund is approaching £300,000, largely from small donations which are coming in well. He and I, with the Department, have also established a number of potential sources of more major finance; and (though he is keeping this confidential at this stage) Victor Matthews has promised him full involvement – of the Express newspapers and, even more important, of the building components of the Trafalgar Group (Trollope and Colls and Cementation).'

The extent of Savile's blossoming relationship with Prince Charles became clearer in the same note sent by Gerard Vaughan to the prime minister: 'Even more encouraging, though again confidential at this stage, Jimmy Savile tells me that the Prince of Wales has agreed to be Patron of the Appeal.'[9]

The relationship with Prince Charles was sanctioned and fostered by the Duke of Edinburgh who viewed Jimmy Savile as someone who might be useful for his eldest son when it came to the common touch. Savile had met Charles and talked with him at various events but now he joined a circle of unofficial advisers to the heir to the throne, chiefly because of their shared interest in disabled charities. Charles had visited Stoke Mandeville in 1977, where he met and talked with the Spinal Injuries Centre founder, Dr Ludwig Guttman. His relationship with Savile blossomed over the following years, to the point where Princess Diana would describe the disc jockey and fund-raiser as her husband's 'mentor'.

Donations to Jimmy Savile's Stoke Mandeville Appeal topped the £1 million mark within eight weeks. Readers of the *Daily Express*, which threw its weight behind the campaign, received an 'I Fixed It for Jim' lapel badge and car sticker when they filled out and returned a donation coupon in the newspaper. From teenage schoolgirls doing a sponsored swim to nurses donating their lunch money, penniless housewives sending in Green Shield stamps to Borstal boys walking from London to Nottingham, it was a campaign that seemed to capture the imagination within every strata of society. And there on the news and in the papers, on the nation's lapels and in its car windows, was the face of Jimmy Savile.

The enthusiasm for the Stoke Mandeville campaign marked the opening of an era of national charity appeals.

'People who are disabled are not like us,' Savile pointed out as the money kept pouring in. 'They can enrich our lives far more than we enrich theirs. I might be doing something for them – but they do an even better thing for me.' They most certainly were, for inadvertently they were making him bulletproof.

The drive to rebuild the spinal unit at Stoke Mandeville was not the only multi-million pound campaign that Jimmy Savile lent his face to in the early part of 1980. He was also the man chosen to front the most lucrative account in British advertising.

After 30 years of steady decline, British Rail had become a national joke, and a bad one at that. Blighted by a series of industrial disputes and offering a service lampooned for late or cancelled trains, not to mention famously terrible sandwiches, BR was responsible for the sour taste familiar to the millions that used it. Under the leadership of Peter Parker, who was made chairman in 1976, a plan was hatched to revive Britain's love affair with high-speed trains. The first step was the introduction of the Inter-City 125, with the first sets going into service in the autumn of that year.

The battle to win the BR account was fiercely fought, with six of the country's leading advertising agencies in the running. Peter Marsh of Allen, Brady & Marsh understood that he needed to make an impact with his initial pitch. His answer was to keep a delegation of British Rail officials waiting in a deliberately filthy waiting room at his company's offices. Only at the point when they were ready to walk out did Marsh, dressed in full BR uniform, put his head round the door and remind them that this was what their customers experienced on a daily basis.

If Marsh had grabbed their attention, he still needed to nail the final stage of the pitch to secure the account. Recognising that an experienced presenter would be required to effectively relay the mass of information he wanted to get across, he set his researchers to work on producing a statement that underlined the personality chosen believed in an integrated, publicly owned rail service that offered customer value and was committed to modernisation. A number of presenters were called in to do a filmed audition, including Terry Wogan and Jimmy Savile, who claimed to travel in excess of 30,000 miles each year by train. The taped candidate statements were then played to members of the public who were asked for their reactions. 'Everybody endorsed [the one] with Jimmy Savile,'[10] said Marsh.

But when the results were fed to Peter Parker, BR's chairman was unconvinced. He said that he wanted more research done. 'We're a bit like a doctor, Peter,' Marsh replied. 'We don't have to love our patients to give them the correct advice. Because of the robustness of the results we cannot other than recommend [Jimmy Savile] without any reservation.'

The decision was made. Marsh was hired and Britain's national rail network was about to be rebranded via the exhortations of a man the public seemed to trust above all others.

'I sort it all out myself,' bragged Savile when asked how much he was earning from the TV and billboard adverts that became ubiquitous from March 1980. 'British Rail come and say, "Will you do the job for £x?" "Ridiculous, I answer, make it £3x, and go away and think about it." They go away, cogitate and usually we sort out a figure that is closer to my idea than theirs.'[11]

'I didn't like him very much,' admitted Marsh, 'but I didn't have to. When he delivered his words he was brilliant. When you are a professional, you have to deal with people you wouldn't choose to go to the opera with.'

The Jimmy Savile seen in the ads was a new and unfamiliar one; Allen, Brady & Marsh briefed him meticulously on his clothes and hair, two components of his image that had never previously been up for discussion. The result was a suited, freshly shorn figure that looked like he meant business. And that business, all £6 million of it, was proclaiming 'This is the age of the train.' It was a slogan, like the man who delivered it, which became a part of the fabric of British life.

It seems inconceivable at a time when vast swathes of the public regarded Jimmy Savile as the one of the most trusted and admired men in Britain; a time when he had the ear of senior members of the royal family and the nation's most powerful political figures; a time when he was the mouthpiece of national concerns; when the *Jim'll Fix It* Christmas special drew 22 million viewers, that he should also be the subject of serious allegations reported to police forces at opposite ends of England.

The first related to Detective Constable John Lindsay's conversation with a more senior officer at Thames Valley Police. More shocking still is the revelation that in 1980, as Jimmy Savile was being feted by the prime minister and calling in favours from the Duke of Edinburgh, he was summoned by West Yorkshire Police to provide a cast of his teeth.

Bite marks had been found on the bodies of two victims of the Yorkshire Ripper, the serial killer then believed to be responsible for the murders of 11 women. The third victim, Irene Richardson, a prostitute from the Leeds suburb of Chapeltown, had been found near the Roundhay Park flat Jimmy Savile had only recently moved into.

Former detective John Stainthorpe spent 40 years with the West Yorkshire Police and was involved in the massive manhunt to bring the killer to justice. 'When the Ripper was really active one of the suspects put forward by members of the public was Jimmy Savile,'[12] he confirmed. He remembers the tip-off being supplied anonymously.

Dr Mace Joffe, a Harley Street dentist, was contacted to take the mould. Dr Joffe is now dead, although a friend insisted he'd revealed that the police said Jimmy Savile was a suspect because he was known for using prostitutes in and around Leeds.

And yet the public face remained as inscrutable and as blemish-free as ever. His policy on what made it into *Jim'll Fix It* bordered on the puritanical: 'I was very firm in telling the BBC what I didn't want,' he explained. 'Violence, lavatory jokes, sex and such like can go in all the other shows that want them.'[13]

48. ALL SORTS OF TROUBLE

'Ah ha, is that the fearless reporter, he who wields the sword of truth? The famous journalist scourge of all wrongdoers?' It was how Jimmy Savile liked to open our telephone conversations. He had called to tell me there were reporters wanting to speak to him about the feature I had written in the June 2008 edition of *Esquire* magazine. It was a long and detailed piece, based on three lengthy interviews, two in London and one overnighter hosted at his flat in Leeds.

'Jim the Fixer', as the feature was headlined, was my third big Jimmy Savile story to be published in five years. In that time, he'd accommodated me, pricked my curiosity and seemingly accepted that I was one of the only journalists who wanted to know more. I was also a source of publicity, the oxygen of which he had found to be in short supply in his old age.

On my previous visits to Leeds and Scarborough, Savile had told me all about his six-decade reign of brilliance. He was not kidding when he referred to himself as 'the Godfather' and his observance of the code of *omertà* was anything but a joke. He had spent a lifetime drawing attention to himself without ever really revealing who, or what he really was. At our first meeting he told me, 'I am the man what knows everything but says nothing. I get things done but I work deep cover.' On that occasion, he was referring to his peculiar relationship with the royal family.

For the *Esquire* story, he again enjoyed the challenge of saying a lot but revealing little. What he gave me, though, was revelatory enough for the *Sunday Times* and the *Mail on Sunday* to devote column inches to exploring the veracity of his claims. Could Sir Jimmy Savile, octogenarian celebrity relic, really be one of the best-connected men in Britain? Neither paper could find anyone to disprove my findings, although Paul Merton and Ian Hislop still had fun at his expense on the following week's *Have I Got News For You?*

'Now then, you've got me in all sorts of trouble,' announced Savile flatly from the other end of the line. He hadn't seen a copy of the magazine yet and I wasn't sure whether he had caught the previous Friday's episode of the show. For a split second I was wrong-footed. A low, tobacco-coated cackle confirmed he was as laid back about life as he always claimed to be. For the time being, Jimmy Savile was news again and that was just fine by him.

He asked me how I'd been and I told him I had split up with a girlfriend. I was knee deep in boxes and self-pity, and about to temporarily move out of the flat we had bought together and into a concrete shed at the bottom of a friend's garden. 'It could be worse,' snapped Savile. 'You could be with me at Stoke Mandeville, looking at a knockout teenage girl who's just been told she's never going to walk again.'

This was typical, I thought: no-nonsense Yorkshire logic deployed to obliterate all emotional obstacles in its path. He was obviously at Stoke Mandeville Hospital in Buckinghamshire, doing his rounds at the National Spinal Injuries Centre, a facility part funded and still owned by his charitable trust. I knew he spent a couple of nights at the hospital most weeks and tried to imagine what he'd been doing that day. I wanted to see him in his Stoke Mandeville environment.

'Or you could have the *Sun* knocking on your door because you've been carrying on with underage girls.'

This conversational sucker punch caught me unawares, and by the time I had properly absorbed what he'd just said, Savile had performed another of his deft sidesteps. He announced he was about to embark on a 16-day cruise of the Mediterranean on board the *QE2*, a liner he'd boasted about travelling on more than

30 times. I heard a rustling of paper before he reeled off a list of dates and scheduled shore visits. And then, in his staccato for emphasis way, he added, 'So, why-don't-you-phone-my-man-at-Cunard-and-say . . . you-are-coming-to-interview-me?'

And with that, he fixed it.

I woke with a dry mouth and a pulsing headache from too much to drink the night before. I had spent the evening alone in a beach-front bar in Cadiz, wondering what the hell I was doing there and why I was about to embark on a short cruise with a man I'd spent so much of my life obsessing over.

A feeling of dread had settled in the pit of my stomach. There was no magazine commission this time, only his promise of a 'nice break' and 'a bit of fun'. A bit of fun, in this case, that would involve four days at sea with an aged bachelor in a shell suit. After all this time carrying him around in my head, all the time wondering about him and trying to find out who he was, this, I felt sure, was the beginning of the end.

Light poured through the window of my budget hotel room. I showered, got dressed and headed downstairs where the duty manager called me a taxi. As we reached the port nestling beneath the ramparts of the historic old town, Cunard's iconic flagship reflected the morning sunlight. Viewed from a distance, the ship seemed to dwarf the cranes and the brightly coloured containers stacked in the depot alongside. Up close, the long shadow cast by her vast hull offered shade to the column of OAPs waddling back along the quayside.

Cadiz was the last overseas stop on the ship's farewell cruise of the Mediterranean. Six months from now the QE2's 39-year, globe-crossing story would end in Dubai, where £200 million of Saudi money was waiting to be spent on transforming her into a luxury, floating hotel.

I paid the taxi driver and pulled my travel bag to the bottom of the gangplank where a white uniformed ship's officer ticked my name off a list. On stepping aboard, I was led through a series of red-carpeted corridors to cabin 1077 on 1 Deck. 'So you're the famous journalist,' said the woman officer as she opened the door and handed me the keys. 'We've been expecting you.' The words had come straight from the lips of Jimmy Savile.

Inside, the decor reminded me of his flats in Leeds and Scarborough: familiar deep reds and purples in the carpet, bedspread and curtains, offset by dark wood in the cabinets and wardrobes. It even had a similar aroma, the cabins of the *QE2* being among the last indoor areas in the English-speaking world where it was permissible to smoke. Savile, I'd been told, was in cabin 2044 so I picked up the phone and called. There was no answer.

Lying on the bed was a printed programme of the day. Afternoon activities included 'low impact aerobics on 7 Deck, C stairway', 'darts competition with Cruise Staff in The Golden Lion Pub', 'Afternoon Tea with Pianist Frankie in the Queens Room' and, at 5 p.m., a 'Sailaway Party!' where passengers could enjoy the 'live sounds of our Caribbean Band ChangeZ' at the Funnel Bar on the sun deck. Tonight's dress code was 'semi formal – jacket and tie for gentlemen, cocktail dress or trouser suit for ladies'. I unpacked my bag and went for a wander.

By lunchtime, I had still not found him. On the pool deck, the early afternoon sun had begun baking the bald heads and bingo wings resident in the deckchairs. Up a flight of metal stairs, a metal balcony afforded a view onto a gently perspiring congregation of mahogany-tanned torsos and food-filled bellies below. Inside, snaking lines of silver-haired passengers pushed trays between food stations offering cold meats, salads, and a whole rotunda of desserts at the Lido Restaurant's all-day buffet. I kept on searching, climbing another set of stairs to the boat deck and heading back inside, past the Royal Promenade shopping area with its Harrods concession.

Further on and down another flight of stairs, a large rectangular display case dominated the wall at one end of an expansive landing. Inside it were scores of photographs, suspended at different distances from the glass. Black and white and colour pictures captured the great, the good and the glamorous enjoying what looked like glitzy nights and lazy days at sea. I stopped for a while and looked at them until my eyes relaxed and the faces dissolved into a gently vibrating blur: Nelson Mandela, David Niven, Princess Margaret, Paul Newman, Bing Crosby, Richard Burton, Elizabeth Taylor, Princess Margaret, a platinum-wigged Mr Punch. My vision snapped back into focus and inevitably, he was there: Jimmy Savile, gurning at me from bottom right of the cabinet. And there again, middle left, just along from Les Dawson. And again, top right. And there, through a doorway to my left, he was again, only this time it really was him.

He was sitting at a table in the corner of the Golden Lion pub, talking to a couple who I estimated to be in their thirties, which made them comfortably the youngest passengers I had seen in my hours on board. He was in familiar pose, leaning back in his chair; foot up on a barstool, right elbow cocked and a cigar smouldering between gilded fingers. Wisps of bleached white hair escaped from underneath a backwards-facing baseball cap and he was wearing his pink, John Lennon-style glasses. A black tracksuit top unzipped to the waist revealed his bare chest and stomach. Beneath his matching tracksuit trousers, unlaced white running shoes, no socks. Like the decor of the QE2, his look was largely unchanged by the decades.

'Well now,' he said on spotting me. He rose slightly and shook my hand with just enough vigour to rattle the thick, S-shaped links on the chunkiest of his gold bracelets. 'Let me introduce my friend, the famous, fearless reporter and frequenter of some of London's finest massage parlours.' It was typical Savile. In the past, he had answered my mobile phone and explained I was in the capable hands of a busty masseuse. The couple were from Birmingham, and after nearly two weeks on board they appeared to be on familiar enough terms with Savile to realise that this is what he was like.

I asked him how the cruise had been so far. 'An endless round of ceaseless pleasure,' he said before getting to his feet and suggesting we go for a tour.

Progress was painfully slow because Savile liked, in his words to 'spread pleasure'. It was how he described his 'duties' on board. First he clasped the hand of a lady with a backcombed mist of blue-tinted hair before kissing it theatrically, clutching his heart and emitting his catchphrase yodel of pleasure. Then he interrupted a game of Scrabble to tell an American couple that he played in Chinese because that way nobody knew if he was cheating. They did not seem to know who he was but played along with him anyway. A few metres later he told three giggling women from Scotland that I was from the *Sun* and on the lookout for new topless models for Page Three.

We walked down a corridor and he told me how he'd been teasing the girl who worked in the gift shop. He'd told her he was shoplifting lighters and took me there to prove it. 'I'm a thief, always have been,' he said to the girl at the till. She was not British and could only summon a wan smile.

On the way out, he stopped an English couple who appeared to be in their late sixties. Motioning to the wife, he warned the husband he was being stalked by an underage girl. 'I wanted you to know,' he said conspiratorially, 'because you could get into trouble for that.' They told him he was 'incorrigible' and hurried past. Jimmy Savile chuckled to himself and shuffled on.

It was like Tourette's of the soul.

I n February 1981, an industrial tribunal heard a divisional nursing officer at Springfield Psychiatric Hospital allege that Johnnie Savile had sexually assaulted a female patient. Jimmy Savile's 61-year-old brother had been employed as the hospital's entertainments officer for six years before being sacked for gross misconduct in April 1980.

As nursing officer John Edwards explained, Mr Savile had been 'larking about' and 'miming to a record'[1] in his office when he lifted the woman's smock and began touching her stomach and breasts. The 37-year-old woman, it transpired, had been admitted to the south London hospital following a drug overdose. Edwards said he did not know of any other complaints against Johnnie Savile, although another former patient subsequently came forward to tell me how he had raped her in his office at Springfield.

Johnnie Savile denied the accusations. 'I was worried the case might affect Jimmy, but why should I hide in a corner just because I'm his brother,' he had said on the first day of the tribunal two months earlier. 'In the end I spoke to Jimmy and he just said, "Go ahead and fight it."'[2] The two brothers did not speak again for eight years.

Dave Eager revealed that on one occasion Johnnie Savile tried to sell a story to the papers about his younger brother. Eager said he could not remember what the story was about, although he did remember what Jimmy had done about it when the *News of the World* phoned him up for a quote: 'Dave, learn a lesson,' he said. 'When they rang me, if I'd said, "No Comment", they'd have got a comment. So when they rang me, I said "It will take more than the *News of the World* to come between me and the love that I have for my brother." He then put the phone down.'

Eager did not like Johnnie Savile. 'He was pretending to be Jimmy,' he recalled. 'Jim did things by psychology, he'd try to weigh you up. You knew he'd done the calculation with what would work – the kissing up the hand and all that. Obviously he got it wrong sometimes. But Johnnie Savile just did it because he felt he could. He'd lech onto people. He'd bowl up to you and make out like he knew you. [He] would say, "I'm Jimmy Savile's brother," and he was there in your face the whole time.'

On one occasion Savile sent Johnnie away with Eager on a foreign trip with underprivileged children from a home in Manchester. Eager said Johnnie Savile turned up at the airport wearing a T-shirt with 'I'm Jimmy Savile's brother' emblazoned on the front. They went to Mamaia in Romania. Although Eager claimed not to remember when the trip took place or the name of the Manchester children's home, he did recall that the home was subsequently embroiled in a scandal.

In 2014, the Department of Education announced it was launching an inquiry into Jimmy Savile's activities at schools and children's homes. Among the institutions listed was Broome House in Manchester. Ronald Hall, a former warden of Broome House, was Assistant Director of Manchester Social Services when he was arrested by Manchester detectives in 2001. He was jailed for 11 years for 21 counts of sexual and physical abuse. His deputy at Broome House, Ian Gray, was given a 14-year sentence for serious sexual offences.[3]

Soon after Education Secretary Michael Gove commissioned the inquiry, a former resident at Broome House told the *Manchester Evening News*[4] how Ronald Hall had driven him from the home and delivered him to Jimmy Savile at Piccadilly Station. He said Savile plied him with alcohol and he woke up on the floor of his flat in Salford. He also stated that Savile visited Broome House on a number of further occasions.

Despite the unwelcome publicity surrounding Johnnie Savile's dismissal, and the feud it sparked, it was never going to be enough to derail the runaway locomotive of Jimmy Savile's popularity. 'If there's going to be any salvation it starts with us,' was his rallying cry as the Stoke Mandeville total neared £5 million. 'No sitting around waiting for a skint Government to plug the leaks. No point in writing to papers to complain how best to spend the nation's housekeeping money.'[5]

As well as his fund-raising work and a new series of *Jim'll Fix It*, Savile also managed to fit in monthly presenting duties on *Top of the Pops* and his new show on Radio 1. *Savile's Travels* and *Speakeasy* were no more, replaced first by the *Double Top Ten Show* on a Sunday afternoon, and then by *Jimmy Savile's Old Record Club*.

He referred to his studio at Broadcasting House 'The Surgery' because of the waifs, strays and unfortunates who flocked to bask in his aura. 'Anybody looking strange who turns up gets sent down to me,' said Savile. 'It's the same when I do the Fix It show.'[6]

Paul Gambaccini had worked as a DJ on Radio 1 since 1973 and he'd heard the rumours about his bizarre colleague very early on. The scenes in 'The Surgery' only served to fuel such talk, he said. 'The expression I came to associate with Savile's sexual partners,' said Gambaccini, 'was either one used by production assistants or one I made up to summarise their reports: "underage sub-normals". He targeted the institutionalised, the hospitalised – and this was known. Why did Jimmy go to hospitals? That's where the patients were.'[7]

Gambaccini said that paedophilia was considered 'so far beyond the pale' at the time that people simply didn't believe it happened.

Speculation was also rife, Gambaccini added, that Jimmy Savile's well-publicised fondness for working in hospital mortuaries was in fact a cover for his necrophilia. Certainly, Savile had never been reticent about advertising his interest in death. 'I find I've got a great aptitude for dead people,'[8] he told one reporter in 1972. In his autobiography, published two years later, he spoke with pride about laying out the remains of an old man who had burned to death,[9] and of wheeling bodies away from the geriatric ward at Stoke Mandeville.[10]

'I just happen not to freak out,' he said of why he chose to wheel corpses to 'the fridge'. 'To be with somebody when they've just gone to heaven is an honour and one of the most fulfilling jobs. I take great care of them . . . If it's an old person, I'll be thinking that what I'd like to do is to take a photocopy of all the things they have known. If it's a young person, I think to myself: you may have missed a lot of good times but sure as anything, you've missed a lot of grief.'[11]

But still there was no apparent appetite for examining the murkier aspects of Jimmy Savile's life, not least while he was all-powerful within the BBC, working unofficially for the royals and leading the charge to build a hospital unit for the nation, a project undertaken on the behalf of a reluctant but grateful government.

In January 1981, he met with Thatcher again, this time to show her the architect's plans for the National Spinal Injuries Centre. He took the opportunity to press her for some form of financial contribution from the government, as a gesture of good-will and in recognition of the sums raised by members of the public. The prime minister remained non-committal, although documents show that the Department of Health and Social Security were keen that she did not commit NHS funds to the campaign.[12]

Two months later, during a lunch at Chequers, Jimmy Savile again asked her for government support, making another cheeky request while he was it: inviting the prime minister to appear on *Jim'll Fix It*.

In a handwritten memo to her private secretary, Mrs Thatcher relayed that she had promised her guest that she would get a 'government contribution', and a figure of £1 million was discussed. Savile wrote to Thatcher, stating that they would be grateful for any sum and there was no hurry. Equally, he would understand if no money was to be made available.

When asked by officials how much she had promised, Thatcher said she would discuss it with Patrick Jenkin, then Health and Social Security secretary. The prime minister was more decisive on the matter of *Jim'll Fix It*, however, telling her guest that she would not be accepting his invitation.

Jimmy Savile's standing within the establishment can perhaps be gauged by looking at a single day in July 1981. Having spent the morning at Ascot organising the Prince of Wales's showjumping activities for the Stoke Mandeville appeal, he passed the evening with Margaret and Denis Thatcher. They attended a fund-raising performance of *Anyone for Denis?* at the Whitehall Theatre before repairing to 10 Downing Street. At one point in their conversation, Margaret Thatcher had told Jimmy Savile of her 'deep worry' about the violence erupting in inner-city areas of London, Birmingham, Leeds, Liverpool and Sheffield.

Later, as they sat with their shoes off and their feet up, Savile suggested a contest for schools in the troubled areas that would divert attention away from violence and towards raising more funds for Stoke Mandeville. As a prize, he proposed the prime minister throw a party at either Number 10 or Chequers for selected pupils from each school. Thatcher said she would think about the idea.

She spent the next day touring Toxteth, scene of some of the worst disorder.[13] 'I admire the lady enormously,' Jimmy Savile told reporters. 'She's a worker.'[14]

It's my belief that one of the keys to understanding the mutual attraction between Jimmy Savile and Margaret Thatcher were both outsiders, and recognised this truth in each other. He was the brusque, uneducated northerner who had broken down the doors of the BBC and trampled the old Reithian order underfoot. She was from a similarly unfashionable background and yet made it to the top of the male-dominated political establishment. Both were prepared to do what it took, and neither seemed to care what anyone thought of them.

Savile went on to reveal the government had given him the use of a 'courtesy room' at Admiralty House for entertaining leading businessman for the Stoke Mandeville campaign. The talk, led privately by Prime Minister Thatcher, was when, rather than if, he was awarded a knighthood.

He didn't have to wait long. In October 1981, the Vatican awarded Jimmy Savile the title of Knight Commander of St Gregory in recognition of his work for charity. In a private ceremony at the Apostolic Delegation in Wimbledon, Papal Nuncio Archbishop Bruno Heim, presented him with a medal. 'It's diplomatical [sic],' Savile told me. 'They were given the recommendation and assured I wouldn't let the side down.'

A month later, Savile sat next to the Duke of Edinburgh at a special meal at Stoke Mandeville Hospital. His Royal Highness had laid the foundation stone for the new National Spinal Injuries Centre, and been shown around the site by a man who ignored protocol by addressing him as 'Boss'.

As the year drew to a close, Jimmy Savile learned that his courting of the prime minister had been successful. Norman Fowler had replaced Jenkin as DHSS secretary in a cabinet reshuffle and a note to Thatcher dated 30 December 1981 states: 'Mr Fowler has agreed to make available half a million to £1m for the Stoke Mandeville Appeal and he agrees you [Thatcher] should announce this tomorrow.' According to the documents, the government decided to release the money as the International Year of Disabled People was coming to an end and because it wanted 'to show our interest in the disabled has not ended'.

Fowler successfully argued that the figure should be £500,000, with an equal amount going to other causes. The cash injection nevertheless took the Stoke Mandeville fund to around £6.5million. 'I hope this will be an impetus to the appeal, and that the target will be reached very soon,' said Thatcher. 'It must not just be one year when we put a spotlight on the disabled, and then do nothing after that.'

'It is a good job I was sitting down – otherwise I would have fallen over with surprise,' gasped Jimmy Savile, playing along with the stage-managed announcement.[15] He then posed for photographers alongside Norman Fowler, clutching a giant cardboard cheque for £500,000 made out to 'Jimmy Savile Stoke Mandeville Appeal'. Jimmy Savile would be invited to spend Christmas at Chequers with the Thatchers.

Direct channels were now being opened to the very sources of power. As one of the highest-profile entrants in the inaugural London Marathon in the late spring of 1981, Savile had written to the Queen after the Lord Chamberlain, Lord Maclean, ruled that the following year's race would not be routed up the Mall in front of Buckingham Palace. In February 1982 it was announced that the Queen had decided to overrule the decision.[16]

Jimmy Savile was still dressed in his running gear when he met Pope John Paul II during his historic tour of Great Britain in the summer of 1982. He attended the papal mass at Westminster Cathedral before running the four miles to Southwark to help out at a service for the sick.

'The Pope didn't have the faintest idea who I was when he met me,' he explained one day in Scarborough. Savile went on to say he had given the Pope a blessing on behalf of Our Lady because, in his words 'he was looking tired'.

A year earlier, Pope John Paul II had survived an assassination attempt after being shot at point blank range: 'I told him to get some sleep and that he would wake up with the strength of 20 men,' said Savile pointing to a black and white photo on his wall of the Pope stopping to talk to him on his way out of Southwark Cathedral. The Pope gave Savile a Rosary which he kept permanently in his briefcase.

'Within a day I had him bang at it,' Savile gurgled. 'He used to say to Cardinal Hume, "Is the blond one here today?"' Savile also bragged to me about being on stage for the papal visit to York, where 190,000 pilgrims flocked to the racecourse on the Bank Holiday Monday. 'They wanted somebody who could go on and tell the people what to do if they fainted or whatever. So there are all these people waiting for the Pope, and then I came on. Well, you can imagine . . . the last person they expect to walk onto the fucking stage is me. You could hear a pin drop. I walked up to the microphone and said, "I am not He . . . but He will be here in a minute." Then I walked off one side and he [the Pope] walked on the other.'

He claimed to have a 'rapport' with the Pope. 'It gave me no problem addressing a quarter of a million people, no problem at all.' Father Jim O'Keefe, who was handling press for the York leg of the papal tour, confirms Jimmy Savile did make an announcement on stage but did not introduce Pope John Paul II.

As someone who professed to be a devout Catholic, I asked him how it felt to meet God's representative on earth. 'He was a punter,' Savile muttered. 'So am I. So are you. So are the people out there. We're all the same, we're all equal.'

He applied the same philosophy to his meetings with men at the opposite end of the spiritual spectrum. Peter Sutcliffe was the man convicted of the string of murders for which Savile himself had been briefly considered a suspect. The star of TV and radio had offered his services as an intermediary should the killer make contact with the police during the manhunt.

The serial killer dubbed the Yorkshire Ripper was arrested on 2 January 1981, and sentenced to life imprisonment after being found guilty of thirteen counts of murder and seven counts of attempted murder. He was incarcerated in Parkhurst, the maximum-security prison on the Isle of Wight.

Savile was invited to Parkhurst as a guest of the governor, John Sandy, in February 1982. Thirty prisoners joined him on a sponsored jog inside the perimeter fence in aid of the Stoke Mandeville fund. It was, he claimed, his third visit to the prison.

'Peter was one of the many guys I said hello to,' Savile said. 'I spoke to him for several minutes each time . . . [He] was part of the very relaxed atmosphere in there . . . I told a few jokes and Peter and everyone else was in high good humour. They were all terribly friendly.'[17]

If psychopaths and serial killers remain a source of macabre fascination in the wider culture, for Jimmy Savile they represented something altogether different. One night at his flat in Leeds he told me how the only television programmes he watched were documentaries about dark, powerful men; figures such as Adolf Hitler or mafia bosses. He had already tried explaining to me why he felt so compelled to visit Fort Breendonk in Belgium, the site of a Nazi concentration camp, and had spoken at length of his long-held desire to understand those who had been committed to Broadmoor, and how they were treated.

Peter Sutcliffe became the most notorious of Broadmoor's patients when he was transferred to the hospital in March 1984. Savile spoke of the killer being 'ordinary', on one occasion even describing him as being 'as good as gold'. I wondered then, as I wonder now, whether Jimmy Savile studied psychopaths and killers because he wanted to understand more about himself. And by becoming part of the apparatus that treated such people, did he hope to learn how they were identified, diagnosed and treated by the system? Such knowledge would ensure he'd never end up in the same predicament.

The first cracks began to appear in the spring of 1983, although few knew where to look for them. As Jimmy Savile, presenter of two of Britain's most popular television programmes, the face of British Rail and a man with the ear of those in power, prepared himself for the crowning achievement of his life, the opening of a brand new National Spinal Injuries Centre at Stoke Mandeville Hospital, a project he had started, funded and managed himself, trouble was brewing. Serious trouble.

Savile believed he was untouchable, and yet on one occasion he did talk about the biggest mistake he ever made. During his time on *Jim'll Fix It* and *Top of the Pops* he told Alison Bellamy, the journalist who wrote the family-endorsed biography, about being invited by a junior school in Leeds to give a talk to the children. A few days later, he said that two girls from the school, aged around 10 or 11, rang the doorbell of his flat in Leeds. He let them in and insisted they had a look around, and they then stayed for a chat and a cup of tea.

One of the girls told her father. 'He flipped, calling me a pervert and all sorts, and rang up the *News of the World*,' Savile explained to Bellamy.[1] Savile said photographers were stationed outside his gates for the next six months.

In the report on Operation Newgreen, the West Yorkshire Police's attempt to investigate itself over its relationship with Jimmy Savile, a former officer recalled that officers from the Police Women's Unit regularly visited Savile to see if he had information about missing girls.

At our very first meeting, Savile had recounted with some relish how the tabloids had tried to put the squeeze on him. After seeing them off, he said he met one of the editors at a function many years later. '[The editor] said to me, "I've got to tell you something. We put you in the washing machine. Every conceivable angle we explored. We had people parked outside your house. We knew where you went. You didn't even blink. Not once."' The spin Jimmy Savile put on it was that it earned him the 'total respect of Fleet Street'.

More revealing, though, is the reaction of the father of one of the girls he invited into his flat. Although the dates of this incident appear to be lost, it must have taken place sometime after the mid 1970s when Jimmy Savile moved into his flat at Lake View Court. He would have been an idol for schoolchildren, thanks to his work on television and radio, so unless the schoolgirl had reported something untoward about her visit, or unless he had heard the rumours of Jimmy Savile's proclivities on the Yorkshire grapevine, there would appear to have been little immediate cause for concern.

'Paedophile' was not a term that was commonly used or understood at the time, and while children were warned about talking to or accepting things from strangers, Jimmy Savile was familiar to just about every child in Britain. He was undeniably strange but a stranger to no one with a television set or radio. In 1985, he was even asked to put his name to *Stranger Danger*, a book warning children of the perils of talking to adults they didn't know.

It is tempting to speculate whether the incident Savile spoke of to Alison Bellamy throws a potentially revealing new light on the series of interviews that ran in the *Sun* in April 1983. 'Everyone knows he works long hours at Leeds Infirmary, Stoke Mandeville Hospital and Broadmoor Hospital for the Criminally Insane,' ran the introduction to the series on day one. 'But there is another side to the 55-year-old disc jockey. A dark side never revealed before.'

The headline above the opening double-page instalment read 'MY VIOLENT WORLD, BY JIM THE GODFATHER'.[2] And underneath: 'How I fixed it the night I wanted someone beaten up.'

What followed lifted the lid on what the paper described as the 'ruthless, calculating Jimmy Savile. A man who engineered his own rise to the top with cold precision. A man who is not scared of violence.' It was a side to Savile that was totally at odds with the man that kids clamoured to be with, parents admired and the most powerful in society were happy to be associated with.

On the day the stories first appeared, Savile talked with evident pride about how in his dancehall days he instructed his bouncers to deal with a 'geezer lying on the pavement looking up the girls' skirts as they came in'. He said quite matter-of-factly that he instructed them to kick the man's head in. He then went on to say how he dealt with one of his staff he discovered had been ripping him off. The man's clothes were dumped on the pavement outside the flat Jimmy had arranged for him. 'When you are the Godfather you can't have your troops getting out of action,' he added menacingly.

The revelations continued in the same vein with a story about a guy who had tried to steal his girl when his back was turned. Savile told the girl to accept the man's dinner invitation, order the most expensive dish on the menu and then complain of a headache and leave. His Rolls-Royce would be waiting for her outside the restaurant. The next day, Savile confronted the man in front of the rest of the staff: 'He thought he was going to have his legs broken – it wouldn't be anything unusual. But what I did to him [by humiliating him in front of everyone else] was more damaging.'

The portrait of a cold, conniving figure was embellished still further when he admitted, with a certain chilling thrill, that he never lost his temper: 'I don't allow myself the luxury of personal feelings,' he said. 'It's the same with my ladies.' He said that making love was 'non-emotional' and that he was never less than 'logical and mechanical in my dealings with women.'[3]

The story in the next day's edition attempted to get to the bottom of how Savile had maintained his 'Mr Clean' reputation, despite the repeated boasting about how prolific his love life had been. 'I like girls,' he began. 'Plenty of them. Before I go out, I write my telephone number half a dozen times on bits of paper and put them in my pocket.'[4]

These admissions hinted not only at his addiction to sex, but also the psychopathic level of detachment he felt towards those he inflicted himself on.

'I have a busy sex life – as long as the circumstances are right and it's not hurting anyone. It has got to be a natural progression – not just an animal rushing about, a farmyard rutting.' The caveats had by now become conversational ticks – 'as long as the circumstances are right and it's not hurting anyone'. It was also not the first time he had likened himself to an animal when discussing sex. Previously he had described himself as a wolf.

Then, towards the end, came the most revealing passage of all, albeit wrapped in the now customary film of indignant denial. 'I never ever take advantage of a fan,' he maintained. 'If a girl asks me for an autograph I don't say, "You're nice, come home with me for three days."'

'Fans can be very emotional,' he explained. 'If some girl travels a hundred miles and turns up on my doorstep, I never invite her in and make love to her. I don't care about my good name or bad name, but it would confuse her brain if I made love to her, and it wouldn't be fair.' Was he thinking about the girls at Duncroft and on *Top of the Pops*, or even Claire McAlpine when he said this? Or was the memory of the schoolgirls from Leeds still so fresh that he felt compelled to serve up an unsolicited denial of precisely what he had been doing?

'Parents can trust their 17-year-old daughters with me. They could come and spend the night at my flat if they were stuck for somewhere to stay, and I'd never take advantage. I'm careful who I make love to.' And then, as a final coda to the piece: 'I'm very careful to stick to the rules with my girls.'

Paul Gambaccini has his own very clear theory on these newspaper interviews and their odd timing, given the glow of public approval that Jimmy Savile basked in. Speaking on national television on the day before ITV's *Exposure* documentary finally obliterated his former Radio 1 colleague's reputation, Gambaccini recalled hearing that Jimmy Savile was about to be exposed by the press. He said Savile had quickly arranged an interview with a rival tabloid that effectively put a stop to the negative article.

'On another occasion,' Gambaccini said, 'and this cuts to the chase of the whole matter, he was called and he said, "Well you could run that story, but if you do there goes the funds that come in to Stoke Mandeville. Do you want to be responsible for the drying up of the charity donations?" And they backed down.'

Kelvin Mackenzie, editor of the *Sun* at the time, categorically denies that the paper backed down from exposing Jimmy Savile as a sex predator and child abuser for fear he would pull the plug on his support for Stoke Mandeville. 'If we had the story I can assure you we would have fucking printed it,' he told me in no uncertain terms.[7]

Admitting that the truth about Jimmy Savile had been 'a massive shock', even for someone who had edited the *Sun* for 13 years, Mackenzie agreed the stories in his paper could have been a smokescreen. 'He was a seriously devious bloke, that much is clear,' he said. 'Who's to say that he knew a paper had the story of what he was up to, and it was in the background, and he put out these revelatory stories to deflect attention from them.'

This, after all, was a series of stories that ran firmly counter to the popular perception of the star as a do-gooding eccentric, popular figure of fun and lay saint. But why, when the Prince and Princess of Wales, who were still enjoying the flush of public approval, were set to cut the ribbon on a project the nation had participated in, did Jimmy Savile see fit to hammer huge dents in his own pristine public image?

Dave Eager said Savile told him that he put out the stories to divert unwanted attention from one of his high-profile colleagues at Radio 1. But this makes little sense given how remote Jimmy Savile kept himself from the colleagues he only ever saw as rivals.

Gambaccini's recollections are much more plausible, especially when one considers that Jimmy Savile did, in fact, put out a concurrent series of stories with a rival tabloid to counteract the negative spin of the *Sun*'s revelations. On the day when the *Sun* led with 'How I Pick up Girls on the Marathon', Savile was also pictured in the *Daily Star* with an infant female, a patient from Stoke Mandeville, under the headline 'THE REAL GIRLS IN MY LIFE'.

The rival story opened with the following passage: '"Hang on a minute," says Jimmy Savile, "I promised this bird I would give her a ring." In his tiny flat near London's Regent's Park he sits back, large cigar stuck rakishly in his mouth, and reaches for the phone. But despite the snappy language, this is no romantic call. The girl is in her teens, lives in Devon and has an inoperable brain tumour.'

The interviewer went on to say that although Savile did not deny that he was 'a bit of a ladies' man' in his earlier days, 'there is no doubt who the most important girls in his life are today.'

Savile even had the temerity to discuss the revelations being published in the *Sun*. 'Listen, I'm not surprised I'm a target for the "nudge-nudge" brigade but I've got no skeletons in my cupboard and some people can't stand that. They think, "Look at him, unmarried and with his money – there must be something. But there isn't, no more than the average person."' It was a hugely risky strategy, whether he was shielding the truth about himself or someone that he might have leverage on in the future.

According to Gambaccini, Jimmy Savile played the tabloids 'like a Stradivarius' in order to keep his years of abusing behaviour secret. 'He had an imperial personality in show business,' he said. 'I'm not talking about his personal life. You just didn't mess with Jim. He was the governor.'

Certainly, his spinning of the *Sun* revelations represented an audacious piece of crisis management. He gave the *Daily Star* enough to make himself seem believable, and human, but then pulled it all back to what he wanted everybody to concentrate on in the first place: his tireless work for charity. He freely admitted that in his early days there were girls and groupies camped outside his home. He didn't deny that he had enjoyed them. 'But that's all changed now,' he insisted. 'Ever since I started my hospital and charity work, it all stopped. People began to look at me differently.'

And then, in his time-honoured method of nipping potentially damaging revelations in the bud – in this case possibly the concerns being expressed by nurses at Stoke Mandeville – he shared an anecdote with the *Star*'s readers designed to demonstrate his big heart. In fact, all it revealed was the level of access and the total freedom afforded him by the hospital he had become synonymous with.

It concerned a young female patient who was paralysed after jumping off a building. She had become depressed so Savile went over and talked to her. He said, 'Listen, I've got to tell you that I fancy you and I'm here for the weekend. If I can spring you off the ward, will you come and watch TV with me in my motor caravan? But I've got to warn you – the caravan only has a bed in it.'[8]

He explained that the girl was so 'slaughtered by the effrontery of this' that she agreed. She got herself dressed up, he bought her flowers and chocolates and they spent four hours watching television in his vehicle. 'Now can you imagine what the muckrakers would have made of that story if it had got out?' said Savile, a look of incredulity on his face.

It was out in the open now, and whether or not anything happened in the motor caravan, he had done what he always did in times of possible trouble: he got his story into print first. And who would dare to believe anything otherwise when a man as important, as famous and as powerful as Jimmy Savile had been prepared to talk about it in the first place?

The day afterwards, Jimmy gave a less colourful version of the same story to the *Sun*. He'd survived. He'd stared down a potentially ruinous exposé, spun the negative press to his advantage and then ultimately spiked the *Sun* with a better story for a tabloid rival. It was a high-risk strategy, but not one that was undertaken without checks and balances being in place. Jimmy Savile knew full well that his standing within the establishment, coupled with the vast fund of goodwill he had built up over the three years it had taken him to build a new Spinal Injuries Centre, were persuasive countermeasures for whatever the tabloids now knew about him, or indeed had known for a very long time. A cartoon published in the *Sun* soon afterwards[9] seemed to confirm as much. In it, Jimmy Savile is dressed as a gangster, wearing a black shirt, pinstripe jacket and Fedora. A machine gun is slung over the back of his chair. Margaret Thatcher is standing before him, showing him pictures of Labour Party leader Michael Foot, NUM leader Arthur Scargill, and opposition politicians Denis Healey, Tony Benn and David Steel. The caption underneath reads: 'Bump off this lot and I'll see you get a knighthood.'

British Rail underlined his standing in society when it decided to extend his £80,000 a year advertising contract. 'We carried out market research surveys among a cross-section of the public to see if their view of Jimmy Savile had altered,' said BR spokesman David Ewart in the aftermath of the *Sun*'s week of salacious stories. 'There had been no drop in his credibility.'[10]

As for his own reflections on the episode, Jimmy Savile appeared to be interested in nothing but reasserting his vice-like grip on proceedings. 'Nothing appears without me helping to organise it,' he said of the less than flattering newspaper coverage.

But if the public still loved him, doubts were beginning to surface within Whitehall. Margaret Thatcher had been lobbying senior civil servant Robert Armstrong, chairman of the Honours Committee, stating her firm belief that Jimmy Savile should be awarded a knighthood for his services to Stoke Mandeville. Indeed, she had put his name forward for the first time in November 1981, well before the National Spinal Injuries Centre had even been completed. It was decided then, and a year later when Thatcher tried again, that it would be better to wait.

Soon after the revelations in the *Sun*, Prime Minister Thatcher went in to bat for Jimmy Savile for a third time. However, in a climate in which the threat of AIDS was causing widespread consternation, the claims about his promiscuous sex life, allied with the thuggish aspects of his dancehall career, meant it was again decided that it would be wise to consider him for a future list.

There were no such reservations within the royal family, though. In late July, the 120-bed National Spinal Injuries Centre welcomed its first new patient. A few days later, on 3 August, Jimmy Savile stood on the front steps with Prince Charles and Princess Diana alongside for the official opening.

His stock was similarly high with the Catholic Church; in December, Cardinal Basil Hume, Roman Catholic Archbishop of Westminster, proposed Jimmy Savile for membership at the prestigious Athenaeum Club. The club, founded in 1824 as a 'meeting place of men who enjoy the life of the mind', is situated in a grand Georgian house on Pall Mall with pillars at its entrance, a sweeping staircase and superb library. At lunchtime, its dining room resembles a Who's Who of the British establishment, with former prime ministers rubbing shoulders with bishops, artists and professors. A spokesman for Cardinal Hume said, 'He is a great admirer of what Jimmy has done for young people and Stoke Mandeville and is delighted to help in this matter.'[11]

For the second year in a row, Margaret Thatcher invited Savile to Chequers for New Year's Day drinks and lunch.

I asked Jimmy Savile whether he was sad that this was the last time he'd cruise on the *QE2*. 'No, no, no. It's all marvellous,' he said before reminding me that he didn't have feelings, because he was 'odd'.

He'd decided that he wanted a cup of tea so we headed back to the Lido restaurant where he grabbed a cup and saucer and helped himself to a small pile of crab sticks. We settled on a quiet table near the window. After all the performance of the last hour or so he said he wanted some peace.

Between noisy slurps of his tea that stained the white crab flesh coagulating around his teeth, he asked me about the coverage of my *Esquire* story in the papers. I mentioned the double-page spread in the *Daily Mail*. 'A dirty, greasy paper,' he hissed before adding there were two people the tabloids wanted more than anyone else, 'Me and Cliff.'

We were soon on the move again, returning outside to sit in the sun at a table near the pool. Shore leave was nearly over and in the next hour we were set to leave Cadiz, bound for Southampton. The conversation was stop-start, thanks mainly to Savile barking 'Morning!' at each and every passer-by. An elderly English woman pointed out that it was now the afternoon, to which he replied: 'Why tell the truth when you can get away with a lie?' He shot me a glance and there was a flicker of a grin: 'SOS. Same Old Shit.'

A young woman with Down's syndrome seemed keen to attract his attention from a neighbouring table. Savile got up and went over to where she was sitting. He told her to budge up so he could sit down next to her. He took her hand and the young woman lit up. 'I've heard you've got another fella on board,' Savile deadpanned. She laughed and held his hand tighter. He then turned to the young woman's mother. 'She's two-timing me, I knew it.'

I had not before seen how he behaved in the company of the people he had so famously spent much of his life and his fortune helping – the mentally and physically disabled, young offenders, the sick, the old and the vulnerable. He seemed warm and genuine, and the young woman's parents were delighted.

Before long we were on the move again. This time, we headed towards his cabin, which even from outside was identifiable by its stale smell of cigars. Savile fished the key out of his tracksuit pocket and unlocked the door. There was no suitcase, just a small rucksack on a chair next to the bed. He explained he had a suit in the wardrobe for formal evenings and otherwise he would make do with one tracksuit, two T-shirts, one pair of shorts, two pairs of pants and two pairs of socks which would be worn and then washed in the sink, allowed to dry overnight and then worn again. Next to the television were two boxes of cigars and a couple of bottles of duty-free whiskey.

I produced a copy of *Esquire* from my bag and he sank into one of the two armchairs, plucked a cigar from one of the boxes and lit up. He soon found the feature, adorned with a full-page portrait photograph that had been taken outside the grand pillars of the Athenaeum Club. He looked unfamiliar in the picture, wearing a dark suit, red tie and his knight of the realm medal attached to a gold chain around his neck.

After a brief scan of the pages, he chuckled to himself and put the magazine down. He didn't want to talk, and turned on the television instead, selecting 'Bridge Cam' from the menu of channels. It was what it said: a camera mounted on the bridge of the ship which, for now, was showing an unchanging view of the port of Cadiz. The pictures were accompanied by classical music that, said Savile, was 'perfect'.

I asked him about the day the picture was taken. He had come to London to collect a medal from Prime Minister Gordon Brown at 10 Downing Street in recognition of his efforts as a Bevin Boy miner in the final months of World War II. He didn't want to talk about the event and immediately changed the subject, asking me about 'the state of my romance'. I described the glorified shed I had moved into. 'Well, there you go,' he replied, eyes still fixed on the unchanging picture on the television. 'Remember, this is all about R & R. Sunshine. Food. Good kip. A bit of fun.'

He seemed happy to sit there in silence, other than for the gentle strains of classical music coming from the telly. I wasn't sure what to do so I asked him if he really loved the music during his early days as the world's first dancehall disc jockey, or whether in fact it was the power that he enjoyed, the power to make people dance. 'No,' he corrected. 'It wasn't about the music or the power, it was about opportunity.'

There would be plenty of time to talk, he said. Savile picked up the phone and called the bridge to ask if the captain would permit us to come up and watch us sail away from the best seat in the house. 'You will ask him though, won't you, Deborah?' he enquired of the captain's secretary. 'You know what a stickler for protocol I am.'

Permission granted, we headed off again, along the length of the ship and up to the bridge where we met Deborah, who made a fuss of him. Captain Perkins was a large, plump man in white uniform. Savile had the copy of *Esquire* under his arm and though he had still not read the piece, he proudly showed off the picture. The captain then told a rather awkward story about the Radio 1 road show coming to his home town when he was a kid and Jimmy requesting two young virgins to spend the night with him. Savile's face betrayed nothing. He closed the magazine, bowed slightly and shook the captain's hand, thanking him for his kindness in allowing us to be on the bridge at this important time.

We moved outside to observe the sudden buzz of activity as the massive mooring chains were pulled aboard while a small flotilla of pilot boats mustered to guide out us out of the harbour. It was a clear, bright evening, one that held the promise of a memorable sunset, and Captain Perkins had us set on a westerly course across the Bay of Cadiz.

Jimmy Savile looked straight ahead and muttered to no one in particular that Perkins had his facts wrong about the road show. He said he could not be bothered correcting all the inaccuracies he heard about himself. 'They think it's true, and that's all that counts,' he said. 'But in actual fact it's all a load of old bollocks.'

Once beyond the harbour, the wind freshened. I walked Savile back to his cabin where he slumped in his chair and yawned. I suggested leaving him so that he could read the article in peace. He knew I was intrigued by him, but the *Esquire* story was no hagiography. I had again referred to how he liked to brag and posited the possibility that he could be a fantasist. The smooth passage of the next few hundred nautical miles depended not on his reaction to these opinions – he had heard far worse in his time – but to my admission that he scared me as a child. I decided to tell him before he read it for himself.

'You're not the only one,' he muttered. A low, menacing laugh vibrated quietly behind his cigar.

52. I AM THE BOSS – IT'S AS SIMPLE AS THAT

After nineteen years of service, Jimmy Savile was axed from Radio 1. Controller Johnny Beerling, who wanted to reshape the network to appeal to the younger end of the market, recalled he had come to an agreement with Savile in the first half of 1987, although the news was not released until later. 'I knew if word got out the press would have a field day so it was important to keep it confidential until I had secured a replacement,' said Beerling.[1]

Savile wanted to control the news of his departure in the same way he controlled every aspect of his existence. He initially suggested that his exit should be dressed up as his own magnanimous decision to move aside in order to give a younger man his opportunity, in keeping with Radio 1's latest social action campaign on youth unemployment. The news leaked before that, though, and Beerling was forced to grovel, telling the press, 'it is unthinkable that we would want Mr Savile to go'.[2]

Sure enough though, in September Jimmy Savile was photographed with his replacement, 26-year-old DJ Nicky Campbell. As chairman of the Hands Across Britain campaign which highlighted the chronic level of unemployment in the country, Savile explained how it had been his choice to step down: 'I said to the Controller of Radio 1: "How about we find a new guy to give him the same sort of start in showbusiness that I had?"' Beerling duly described it as a 'noble gesture . . . just typical of him'.[3]

A year later, another story broke, this one about Jimmy Savile's latest, and most extraordinary, career move. Again, it came about after secret talks over a number of months with senior officials at the Department of Health.

Alan Franey knew Jimmy Savile from the ten years he spent working as an administrator at Leeds General Infirmary. He had gone on to become deputy secretary at the National Institute of Biological Standards and Control, which was the job he held when in 1987 he was approached about a 'six-week secondment period to Broadmoor Hospital as part of a task-force'.

Franey was invited to a meeting at the Athenaeum Club that was attended by a number of Health Service officials and Jimmy Savile, whom he had become friendly with through the LGI and then via Savile's informal Leeds running club. It was at this meeting at the Athenaeum that Franey was 'persuaded that a move to Broadmoor . . . would be a very good career step'.[4]

Franey has acknowledged that he would have not have been interviewed for the post unless Jimmy Savile had put his name forward.[5] He maintains his subsequent appointments as Broadmoor's General Manager and Chief Executive were on his 'own merits', and that he heard no allegations made against Jimmy Savile while he was in charge.[6]

In late August 1988, the Department of Health announced that the management board of Broadmoor special hospital, with which it shared the responsibility of running the 520-bed high-security facility in Berkshire, had been suspended. It was to be replaced with a six-man task force, which would take over the running of the hospital until a new general manager was appointed. The change was part of a wider restructuring programme in management, operation and policy at the special hospitals (the others being Park Lane and Moss Side in Liverpool and Rampton in Nottinghamshire). The most eye-catching aspect of this change was that a member of the new Broadmoor task force was none other than Jimmy Savile.

At the time, Broadmoor, which by now housed Peter Sutcliffe and gangland boss Ronnie Kray, was at the centre of a damaging industrial dispute with the Prison Officers' Association, the union to which the bulk of the hospital's nursing staff had been affiliated since the 1940s. A daytime overtime ban resulted in patients being left in seclusion for long periods, and there was also dissatisfaction over the shortage of staff housing. 'This has nothing to do with the dispute, which is nothing that can't be solved,' insisted Savile of his appointment to the new task force. 'In any family there is a fall-out here and there.'[7]

Although the Department of Health wanted to adopt a low-key approach to the upheavals at the hospital, the news was leaked by the mental health charity MIND. It believed the changes were being made in secret to pre-empt the publication of a highly critical special report by the Hospital Advisory Service on the state of the special hospitals. The report, which had already been submitted to the Department of Health, was thought to find serious fault with Broadmoor's management, its nurses and the lack of care that had led to many patients becoming institutionalised.

Although the Department of Health denied the allegation, and remained reluctant to confirm the composition of the task force, the make-up of the six-man team was revealed. Dr Louis Warnants of the Department of Health would take over temporarily as Broadmoor's medical director, Dr John Tait would take over the role of Chief Nursing Officer, and Professor Michael Morgan would become the hospital's administrator. They would be joined by senior civil servant Clifford Graham; an assistant secretary at the Department of Health Dr Donald Dick; and Jimmy Savile, Broadmoor's honorary assistant entertainments officer for the past 20 years. 'It is logical . . . that I should be on the task force,' said Savile, 'because I know my way round the hospital.'[8]

A few days later, Savile outlined how he would approach this latest challenge within the Health Service. Describing the task force as 'an advisory body with teeth', he restated his knack of getting things done. 'Others have the knack of talking, or sitting on committees,' he said. 'But I make things happen.'[9]

Savile went on to reveal his manifesto for change: the introduction of smaller wards, private rooms instead of the Victorian-style dormitories, individual therapy for patients and a flexible time-table. As for his methods: 'I will adopt the long, steady, undramatic role which avoids the whizz-kid approach. My main objective is the curing of every single patient in the hospital so that they can be released into the community.' He then added, 'Curing for me means the containment or stabilisation of the patient: trying to make sure he won't commit the same offence again.' Jimmy Savile was given a new office close to Broadmoor's red brick perimeter wall.

While Jimmy Savile was talking like he was the man in charge, the Department of Health moved quickly to assert that its under-secretary Clifford Graham was in fact chairman of the new task force. This had no effect whatsoever. 'He is chairman of the special health board,' Savile corrected, 'and I am the chairman of the task force. We work together.'[10]

An entire government department and a senior civil servant were never going to be enough to derail Jimmy Savile. 'I have lived here for 20 years,' he announced, 'by seniority I must know more than anybody else. Because I live here I call myself the chairman of the task force. Technically, I could be anything. I live here, I am the boss; it's as simple as that. That's why the Department of Health would not dream of telling me what to do, they say, OK Jim, it's all yours.'

Savile did concede that certain civil servants would 'be going potty'[11] about the fact he had been handed the responsibility for rescuing the 125-year-old hospital from administrative meltdown, but claimed that he didn't care one jot. His rapport with the prime minister and with Edwina Currie, the junior health minister who ratified his appointment, was such that he felt confident enough to make a public promise: 'I can't fail.'

So how did Jimmy Savile come to be appointed to such an impor-tant job at a secure facility that had become demonised by the press for the killers, rapists and psychopaths it housed? And what was the nature of Jimmy Savile's role at Broadmoor in the years before he came to describe himself as 'the boss'?

Broadmoor occupies an area of 53 acres on a high ridge offering panoramic views across the Berkshire countryside. Its series of high red brick blocks with narrow arched windows were designed by Sir Joshua Jebb and overlook terraced gardens and administrative buildings and, beyond an internal wall, staff houses, a social club and games field. Block 6 was where the most disturbed and dangerous patients were detained, many of them having recently arrived from court and facing up to the consequences of their crimes. Other blocks were home to older patients, those with behavioural disorders or men who were deemed to pose a reduced risk. Women were housed separately.

In 1949, Broadmoor was taken over by the Department of Health. It was run by the Board of Control, while admissions and discharges continued to come under the jurisdiction of the Home Office. Ten years later, it was reclassified as a special hospital under the new Mental Health Act, and designated for individuals in need of 'treatment under conditions of special security on account of their dangerous, violent or criminal propensities'.

The novelist Patrick McGrath lived at Broadmoor from the age of seven when his father, the Glaswegian forensic psychiatrist Dr Pat McGrath, was appointed as the medical superintendent at Broadmoor Lunatic Asylum, as it was then known. In 1957, the family moved into a red brick villa a few yards from the main gate, and McGrath says his father was already acutely aware of what he had inherited: an overcrowded, failing institution, one in which some patients were forced to sleep in corridors, a staff who saw themselves as prison wardens, and only two psychiatrists – Dr McGrath and one other – to attend to the 800 mentally ill men and women in their care.

Pat McGrath was an able and fearless administrator, one who bridled whenever Broadmoor was incorrectly referred to as a prison. He was forced to wrestle with the complex problems caused by the inertia in Whitehall, his masters at the Department of Health and the Home Office, and the vested interests of an entrenched old guard at the hospital, many of whom were members of families in which jobs, and houses, had been handed down over generations.

As members of the Prison Officers' Union, nurses dressed like warders in their uniforms and peaked caps. The emphasis at Broadmoor was on security, and the philosophy was custodial rather than therapeutic. As one study of the special hospitals remarked: 'As a union, in the short term, [the Prison Officers' Union] delivered; but simultaneously and almost inevitably they transmitted through their organisation the prevailing attitude of the prisons: detention, restraint, toughness, a "macho" culture where the biggest and most violent patient (or prisoner) would be brought into submission.'[12]

Dr Pat McGrath discovered that he was on a hiding to nothing. A combination of the stigma attached to mental illness, the widely held reluctance to entertain notions of rehabilitation, and an old boys' network among a staff that enjoyed higher pay than other nurses and promotions based on service rather than merit, created a culture in which doctors and other professionals were viewed with suspicion, or characterised as 'soft'. Procedures were painfully slow due to the duplication involved in reporting to two government departments, while the prospect of negative press coverage remained a constant deterrent to change.

An example of the latter was the case of Graham Young, 'the teacup poisoner', who was released from Broadmoor in 1971. Young went on to poison around 70 more people, ensuring the decision to free him sparked intense, vociferous and widespread criticism. Young was eventually sent to Parkhurst, where he eventually died.

Life for the staff working within the walls was what McGrath's son describes as 'a proper, old established English community'. As superintendent, his father set out to reduce the potential for confrontation with the vested interest groups he worked with, and made a point of being accessible during evenings spent in the social club. It was here that Patrick McGrath recalled first meeting Jimmy Savile in or around 1970.

'I walked in the door and there, at the far end of the bar on a padded sofa-type seat with my mum and dad, was a very incongruous figure, instantly recognisable with his platinum blond hair and the cigar as the extroverted figure we were all familiar with from *Top of the Pops*,' he said. 'What I remember from that encounter was that he was behaving like one would expect him to behave. He was loud and making a big fuss of my dad.

'My dad hated that sort of thing but [Savile] was saying what a great man my father was. I had the feeling my father was tolerating his presence because it probably meant that the hospital would get some favourable publicity as a result. He thought it was a bit of waste of time and I think he instinctively disliked the character of Jimmy Savile.'

Whatever the private views held by Broadmoor's bespectacled chief superintendent, in an interview for the 1972 documentary *The World of Jimmy Savile*, Pat McGrath Snr talked of how Savile would arrive in the middle of the night and sit beside the beds of patients who couldn't sleep. He described Savile as 'unselfconscious' and his interest as 'very real', and commended the fact that he helped many of Broadmoor's long-stay patients to 'feel a connection with the outside world'.

McGrath's son looks back now and believes the opportunities for Jimmy Savile's offending would have been greatly restricted in an environment where patients were kept under close surveillance and heavy gates were locked every few yards. He did say, though, that the hospital's famous visitor once offered his younger sister a ride in his Rolls-Royce. She was in her early teens at the time, and McGrath clearly remembered his father's response: 'Over my dead body.'

But as McGrath remarked, his father was also convinced that 'whatever helped break down institutional isolation contributed to rehabilitation'.[13] It explains why he was so enthusiastic about encouraging work experience, cultural excursions and family visits for patients. It also might explain why against his better judgement he was willing to tolerate Jimmy Savile, who soon began organising pop concerts and weekly disco nights at Broadmoor, as well as bringing guests with him when he arrived on a Wednesday evening after recording *Top of the Pops*. On one occasion, he arrived accompanied by two members of Pan's People.

Within 18 months or so of Jimmy Savile arriving at Broadmoor on the invitation of members of 'NUTTERS INC', as per the plaque that he kept as a memento, he was claiming that his work at the hospital differed from the role he performed at Leeds General Infirmary. 'It's not that sort of place,'[14] he said of the Berkshire hospital, although it is significant that he was already boasting about having access to all the wings inside Broadmoor.

In those early days, he would park his motor caravan in the grounds, just as he did on his visits to Rampton. Rumours quickly started circulating among the staff. In October 2012, the daughter of a principal nursing officer told one newspaper that Savile took 'trusted patients' out for rides in his car and 'liked to have his way' with young women visiting relatives. She said he would stand at the main gate 'in his swimming trunks, gold chain and sunglasses' and entice them into his motor home.[15]

Naomi (not her real name) met Jimmy Savile as a teenager. Her mother was a journalist for a local paper who covered Savile's regular visits to the hospital. In 1975, Savile invited Naomi and a friend to watch an episode of *Top of the Pops* being recorded at Television Centre in London. Savile then asked her parents whether Naomi could come to watch him at work on his radio show at Broadcasting House. They agreed, chiefly because they considered him to be a family friend but also because their daughter was keen on becoming an actress and they hoped that he might offer her some assistance.

The teenage girl travelled alone from Surrey and met Savile at his London flat. After the show, they returned to the flat where Naomi claimed he lunged at her and forced his tongue down her throat. When he asked her whether she was enjoying it, the girl said she was not. 'I think the only reason he stopped when I told him to was because he was worried about my mother and father knowing,' said Naomi. She told her mother what had happened but said she didn't seem to grasp how serious it was.

Former psychiatric nurse Richard Harrison maintains his colleagues were deeply suspicious of Savile because 'paedophiles gravitated towards him'.[16] Another member of staff reported seeing Savile taking a girl of less than 16 to his flat in the grounds, having picked her up at the annual Crowthorne Festival.

By 1978, Broadmoor had been 'modernised and liberalised', as Patrick McGrath recalls. Block 6 had become Monmouth House, the women's block had been renamed York House and the most dangerous patients were now housed in Norfolk House. New clinical paradigms were being discussed which led to the nursing staff becoming more militant in their response to change.

Jimmy Savile had not only been given his own small house on the estate, but the use of the hospital's transport manager, Don Bennett, who claimed the Department of Health gave him double the amount of annual leave so he could chauffeur Savile wherever he needed to go. More significant still is that Savile was now in possession of his own set of keys, claiming that he was allowed to come and go from Broadmoor 'without let or hindrance'.

Savile once recalled Dr Pat McGrath asking him why he liked visiting Broadmoor. The answer to the question, he insisted, had come to him only that morning. 'I had arrived at twenty past two . . . I drove into the Broadmoor estate and saw the great wooden sign which proclaims "Broadmoor Hospital. Strictly private. No admittance". But I have the entitlement to drive past that sign, to go in and out. That puts me in an incredibly privileged position.'[17]

Entitlement and privilege: these are key words in understanding how Jimmy Savile was given a free rein at the hospitals he frequented.

Dr Pat McGrath retired in 1981. The role of medical superintendent was divided up among a three-man management team consisting of the medical director, chief nursing officer and administrator. No single figure had any managerial authority over the other two, allowing the Prison Officers' Association to fill in the managerial vacuum. By 1988 Broadmoor, as the most prominent of Britain's four special hospitals, had become an outpost cut off from the NHS and the criminal justice system. 'Utopian indulgences would not bring about change,' wrote Charles Kaye and Alan Franey, two men who were to be deeply involved in the new order that emerged from the chaos. 'Deep-rooted attitudes and practices were established realities, thriving on neglect and indifference . . . In a very real sense the country had the special hospitals it had helped to create.'[18]

Edwina Currie recalls a meeting with Jimmy Savile in Leeds in the month of his appointment to the Broadmoor task force. The special hospitals were her responsibility under the auspices of the then health secretary Kenneth Clarke. In her diaries, Currie described Savile's thoughts on the regime at the Victorian hospital as being 'intriguing'.

During their meeting, Savile told her he had discovered millions of pounds missing from budgets. He also highlighted poor use of the hospital's housing stock, which was monopolised by local families with long associations with Broadmoor. Savile said he suspected some members of staff were inflating their salaries and told Currie he had threatened to pass on information to the tabloid newspapers about any individuals who caused trouble.

Currie believes Savile blackmailed staff in order to stop the Prison Officers' Association calling a potentially ruinous strike. She said his methods included, 'going into the office, checking employment records of staff he was targeting and establishing that some of them were up to no good, such as claiming overtime to the tune of £800 a week. He checked accommodation records and found some people occupying them were nothing to do with the hospital but were relatives of staff. I have no doubt that he used a degree of arm-twisting and blackmail to get the staff to do what he wanted. 'That also suggests to my suspicious mind a modus operandi for other places.'[19]

It is now Currie's view that Savile 'was finding stuff he could hold over the staff so that if anybody challenged him and said, what are doing in those girls' rooms, he could say, "Don't you challenge me. I know you have been overpaying yourself, I know you have been fiddling the books." And that would mean that people would be much more reluctant to out him or to take any complaints any further.'[20]

She claims that she never liked Jimmy Savile but it should be pointed out that her diary entry at the time – 'Attaboy!' – sounded an altogether enthusiastic note about the methods he employed.

Not surprisingly, the staff at Broadmoor took an instant dislike to Jimmy Savile, with some describing how he would walk into secure areas detaining the most dangerous patients in the UK and laugh off their warnings.[21] Richard Harrison, who joined Broadmoor as a psychiatric nurse in 1974 and worked there for 30 years, says he and many of his colleagues considered him 'as a man with a severe personality order and a liking for children'.

Within a month of assuming control, Savile was at loggerheads with Broadmoor's 600-strong branch of the Prison Officers' Association. George Temple, chairman of the POA Broadmoor branch, accused the task force of doing 'a hatchet job', insisting 'they have virtually told around fifteen of our senior nurse managers, people with years of experience, that if they don't fit in with the new regime they will have to go'.[22]

Savile denied the accusations, presumably having threatened those who refused to step into line with exposure in the newspapers. In a subsequent television interview, he reiterated his hard-line stance: those who did not like planned management changes should consider finding a job elsewhere.

Alan Franey arrived at Broadmoor in October 1988, becoming the seventh member of the task force. He did so in the immediate aftermath of the damning report by the Health Advisory Service Inspectorate. 'Time is running out for Broadmoor,' stated the report, before shedding light on 'an inward looking institution with some very doubtful methods of dealing with disturbed behaviour'.

The picture it painted was of a regime run on 'suspicion and fear rather than trust' in which there was 'scant regard for human dignity'. Patients were 'infantilised' and their rights viewed as a 'necessary nuisance'. Another of the report's findings highlighted how 'the suppression of heterosexual activity has created a situation where homosexuality is implicitly tolerated'.[23] Edwina Currie set Franey a target of six weeks to draw up an action plan to implement the 200 and more recommendations contained within the report.

Fortunately for Franey, he had a major ally in Jimmy Savile, who had already begun ringing around building societies to ask for special mortgage terms for staff. He had also contacted the contractors that built the NSIC at Stoke Mandeville in a bid to solve the chronic delays and overspend in the hospital's planned building works. He was free to do as he pleased. When asked whether the prime minister had a say in his appointment, Savile replied, 'Shall we say, if she had been asked I am sure she would not have objected.'[24]

In Savile's eyes, his close ties with Thatcher made him a formidable if not invincible opponent for anyone stupid enough to stand in his way. Her former private secretary Robin Butler had by this time become head of the Home Civil Service and succeeded Sir Robert Armstrong as chairman of the Honours Committee. Thatcher again lobbied for her friend to be knighted, but the outcome was the same: 'Under the headings Benefactions, we have again considered the name of Mr Jimmy Savile, whom you have of course considered on previous occasions. We have concluded that he should not be recommended.' Butler referred Thatcher to his predecessor's correspondence on the matter before again outlining his reasons for turning Savile down.

'Mr Savile's latest help to the DHSS has been over Broadmoor. None of us would want to denigrate his many services. But my committee and I still fear that his manner of life – on his own confession – has been such that a high award for him would be an unhelpful signal when we are still having to grapple with an AIDS problem which threatens to intensify; and that a knighthood for him would not benefit the honours system in the eyes of the public.'[25]

It possibly explains why in early December 1988 the prime minister was so keen to pose for photographers with Jimmy Savile on the front steps of Downing Street. He was there on the pretence of handing over two cheques for £10,000 after conveniently discovering (again) that he had £20,000 left over from his latest fund-raising efforts. 'I thought if I got the Prime Minister to hand over the money [which went to the Multiple Sclerosis Society and Riding for the Disabled] she would get more recognition than me,' he said.[26] It was an example of toadying and crass opportunism but effective nonetheless. Looked at another way, it was simply a further down payment on the knighthood, which Thatcher now seemed to crave as much as Savile did.

Less than a month later, it was announced that Jimmy Savile had successfully negotiated with the Home Office and the Department of Health for the movement of 60 patients from Broadmoor, the biggest transfer in the hospital's 125-year history. 'We are looking at each case to consider whether there is a more suitable place for them than Broadmoor,' explained Clifford Graham. 'It is a gradual process of making [the hospital] more caring without lessening the security.'[27]

The Health Advisory Service and MIND both voiced their support for the move, while Professor Michael Morgan, the hospital's temporary administrator, paid tribute to Jimmy Savile's unique brand of leadership: 'Since Jim has taken over, it has enabled me to do things more quickly and taken away a lot of bureaucracy,' he said.

Two of the 60 patients to be moved had been sent to Broadmoor for murders, something the tabloid press in particular was up in arms about. 'Jim Fixes It for 60 Psychos to Go Free' screamed the headline in the *News of the World,* followed the next day by 'STORM AS JIM FIXES IT FOR 60 PSYCHOS' in the *Sun.* Jimmy Savile wasted no time in instigating legal proceedings against both papers, for which he received substantial libel damages.

The tabloids were not the only ones to express their concerns about Savile's radical new broom. 'He's just a frontman,' grumbled one member of staff, speaking on behalf of colleagues who feared they were being softened up for major job cuts and changes of working practice. 'It's who he knows not what he knows.'[28]

It was a fair assessment. Thanks in part to the support he now enjoyed from Downing Street, Highgrove House and Whitehall, Jimmy Savile was able to act with impunity. He had one friend, Alan Franey, on the task force, and had his sights set on getting other members of his inner circle involved in the future. Answering only to Clifford Graham, who remained a staunch admirer, and Edwina Currie's replacement, junior minister Roger Freeman, who was no match for a man who had his opponents running scared, it is little wonder that Savile felt confident enough to pose for a newspaper clutching his set of keys to Broadmoor.

Having bragged about how the government had brought him in following his success at Stoke Mandeville, Savile, Thatcher's 'man on the ground', showed the press around the hospital's new wing, newly completed below budget and scheduled for opening in spring 1989. It represented the blueprint for a new Broadmoor that would house far fewer patients. But Savile wasn't finished there: 'I am asking the Government to give me a halfway house to run,' he explained. 'It will provide all the finishing touches to help our patients get rehabilitated.'[29] He added that he hoped to help patients prepare for life on the outside by falling in love, even if sex was still off the agenda within the confines of the hospital. 'All guys together or all girls together isn't very healthy. We have got to give our patients some reason to want to be rehabilitated. And falling in love is one of the strongest.'

Senior civil servants, the press and the unions were all now powerless to stop Jimmy Savile from doing as he pleased – even if the former did, at least, succeed in delaying his knighthood. 'Nobody can be frightened of me,' Savile protested. 'It would be beneath anybody's dignity to be frightened of someone dressed like this . . . It is a kind of smokescreen but it is not a gimmick.'[30]

53. 50 MILLION, GIVE OR TAKE A FEW QUID

We were half way across the Bay of Biscay and silence reigned in Jimmy Savile's cabin. Go on, I told myself, say it. So I did. 'I want to write a book about you.'

I knew what his response would be because I had suggested it before. In Scarborough, he had told me about how a tabloid journalist once called him up in the early Seventies and said that because his paper had more cuttings on him than on anyone else, he was going to write a biography. Savile's response was: 'No thanks.' Instead, he wrote *As It Happens* longhand in a series of exercise books. He said he even negotiated his own publishing deal, before editing and proofing the book himself.

Nobody would be allowed to apply a different spin to his well-rehearsed version of events. 'No!' The tone was always firm and final. 'If anyone is going to write a book it's going to be me. Otherwise I'd have to spend the rest of my life explaining how they'd got it all wrong.' Subject closed.

Around the time Jimmy was writing *As It Happens*, he was also running a nightclub complex in Bournemouth. On his trip to Downing Street to collect his Bevin Boy medal from Prime Minister Gordon Brown, he stopped off to have his photo taken outside the Athenaeum Club. While he was doing that, I chatted to his driver, a tall, well-built man who appeared to be in his mid-50s. His name was Luke Lucas.

Savile later told me that Lucas had been sleeping rough under Bournemouth pier when he walked into the Maison Royale nightclub and asked for a job, something that Lucas insists is not true.

On that morning in central London Lucas explained he began working for Savile in Bournemouth and never stopped. He was a trustee of both Savile's charitable trusts and clearly a member of one of Savile's teams, the small groups of people he could call on in the places he variously called home.

I decided to ask Lucas about how Savile had been handed the reins of the Maison Royale. Savile had told me that the owners had called him out of the blue and made an offer he 'could not refuse'. Three years later, when his consultancy deal came to an end, he claimed to have spectacularly transformed the fortunes of the failing venture.

It was not exactly how Lucas remembered it, though. Instead, he shook his head and commented what a sad story it was: the owner of the Maison Royale being found dead in his swimming pool a couple of weeks after Jimmy took over.

I began to wonder whether perhaps the great secret lurking behind the impenetrable façade of Jimmy Savile was that he had been responsible for a death, or worse still, he had killed someone himself. The way he talked about the summary justice meted out to those who caused trouble in his dancehalls, of his pride in having former *Sonderkommandos* under his command, and now the troubling image of a body in a swimming pool all contributed to the darkening cloud of doubt in my mind.

Some time later I asked Savile about what Lucas had said. He didn't blink: 'He fell on his sword, poor bastard.'

He quickly changed the subject, insisting that Luke Lucas was one of the few people who listened to his advice and acted on it. 'Now he's a multi-millionaire and head of one of the biggest security firms in the country,' said Savile, looking smug. He told me again about how he had turned around the fortunes of the Bournemouth complex before getting out after three years. When I asked why, he said it was because the directors thought they could make more money without him. 'Six weeks later the place was completely empty.' Beyond the cigar, a low cackle swilled in the back of his throat.

I asked Savile what sort of boss he thought he was. 'Iron fist in a velvet glove. I could stroke your cheek but I could also knock your block off.' I did not doubt that he was, and certainly had been, a hard bastard. 'Ah ha, but I was a clever fighter,' he replied. 'I knew all the big villains but they knew never to mess with me.'

Then he was off again, veering into a story about a businessman he knew who made washing machines. This man came to seek Savile's advice about an offer for a big money takeover of his company. The advice wasn't heeded and the businessman ended up broke. 'Some people collect butterflies. Some people collect Georgian brooches. I collect money,' Savile sighed.

So how much was he worth? 'Fifty million, give or take a few quid.'

Since Jimmy Savile's death, I have tried to get Luke Lucas to elaborate on his relationship with Savile but he has consistently refused to comment about his friend. 'I did not discuss Jim at the height of his popularity,' he says, 'and nor will I now.'

I f the opening of the National Spinal Injuries Centre represented Jimmy Savile's greatest triumph, the moment that he reached the apex of his fame and popularity, it also left a void. The charity appeal closed immediately after the centre opened, even though donations continued to pour into the coffers of the Jimmy Savile Stoke Mandeville Hospital Trust. It left the man who had led the campaign casting around for alternative ways to expend his considerable energies.

His response was to fill the hole with physical exercise. The importance that long-distance running assumed in Savile's day-to-day existence cannot be underestimated. Having cycled and wrestled competitively, and pushed himself beyond normal limits in earning an honorary Green Beret, he was still consumed by the need to distance himself from the sickly child and bed-bound invalid of his distant past. Running began as a hobby but turned into an obsession, to the extent that one journalist theorised that in 'its movement and essential isolation, he has found the true expression of his personality'.[1]

In 1983 Jimmy Savile ran two full marathons and five half marathons or shorter distance races. In 1984, this increased to five full marathons and four half marathons. A year later, by which time he was approaching his 59th birthday, he completed no fewer than nine full marathons and nine half marathons. In 1986, he took part in the London Marathon for the sixth straight year and managed an additional 13 half marathons. By 1987, the drive to prove himself and keep old age at bay was manifested in five full marathons and 13 half marathons. 'He's addicted, and it's getting worse,' said Janet Rowe, his secretary at Stoke Mandeville.[2]

In training, Savile regularly clocked up over 100 miles each month, with his daily mileage being recorded faithfully in his notebooks. The ad hoc running club of friends and acquaintances joined him on weekend slogs up the Yorkshire Dales and at the big events where they acted as his 'minders'. Members of this club included Jimmy Corrigan and Alan Franey.

Sometimes Savile's thirst for physical exercise was such that he'd jog on the spot while home alone watching television. On other occasions, he'd think nothing of setting off on a 10-mile run to a favourite transport café with only the money for a cup of tea in his pocket. He'd then run the 10 miles back again.

He relished the belief that people continued to underestimate him, and savoured the feeling of bloody-minded pride when he proved them wrong. The pay was good too; he charged upwards of £10,000 to wear a company's logo on his running vest because he knew that the cameras would be on him whenever he was in the field.

But this neurotic hammering of the tarmac was about more than simply cash and egotism. For someone who had publicly railed against the damage caused by drink and drugs, despite what one member of the Manchester City Police says about his fondness for cannabis in the Sixties, in running Jimmy Savile finally discovered his own narcotic of choice: 'It's an amazing feeling and once you've tasted it nothing else will do,' he said before the 1986 London Marathon, '. . . the excitement of that fantastic fitness feeling . . . is a powerful drug. Withdrawal symptoms are acute.'[3]

He was interested enough to attend a private medical lecture on the impact all this exercise was having on his physiology. There, he learned how the body's receptors produced tiny quantities of opiates when pain and fatigue set in. His conclusion was 'all marathon runners are junkies', and after three or four hours of pounding the roads 'we are all drugged up to the eyeballs because our receptors in the areas of pain have demanded this self-manufactured anaesthetic'.[4]

After fixing it for the 1986 race to be routed up the Mall, Jimmy Savile was rewarded with a lifetime entry into the London Marathon. He became a regular feature of the television coverage, waggling his cigar at the start and the finish, grinding ever forward surrounded by a phalanx of running pals, and waving to the crowds who cheered him every step of the way. After finishing the 1986 race he even popped into the palace for a shower and a cup of tea with the Queen. 'This man Savile has the keys to so many doors,' said marathon organiser John Disley, shaking his head in wonder. 'I just don't know how he does it.'[5]

A year later, Jimmy Savile offered a rare glimpse into his mindset as he dragged his ageing body around the 26.2-mile course. 'At times I feel like strangling every other competitor in the race,' he confessed. 'I mean really, truly murdering them. You hate them for being there, you hate yourself for being there, you hate the organisers, the marshals, the spectators, the whole damn shooting match. It happens because your body chemistry gets in a mess because of the fatigue. Then as soon as you cross the finish line, choirs of angels start to sing in your head. You are in love with the world and everyone in it. You weep and laugh at the same time. You want to throw your arms around strangers and hug them.'[6]

He was in no fit state to do anything of the sort after crossing the finishing line at Westminster Bridge in 1987. On completing the course in three hours and forty-two minutes, a full half an hour faster than his previous year's time, witnesses reported that Savile 'was completely out of it – he did not know where he was'.[7] He'd had to be carried along by his minders for the last few miles of the race. It turned out that he had fallen asleep on the roof of his London flat a few days before, and was suffering from sunstroke.

The narrow focus he now applied to his running was, though, much more than a last-ditch attempt to preserve his fading youth. It was, in effect, a safety valve – and one that seemed to be having the desired effect. After the prolific nature of his offending in the Seventies, the number of alleged offences dating from the early 1980s suggests that he was gradually bringing his deviant behaviour under control: two in 1983, and one each in 1984 and 1985.[8] Sadly, it was but a blip.

Jim'll Fix It celebrated its 10th anniversary in 1985. Along with his Sunday afternoon radio show and sporadic appearances on *Top of the Pops*, it ensured Jimmy Savile remained a familiar landmark in the cultural landscape of Britain. That said, his profile was most definitely diminishing.

The contract for advertising British Rail, a deal that had earned him around half a million pounds, was not renewed as the business was divided up between a number of different agencies. Jim O'Brien, BR's joint managing director, said the 'Age of the Train' had done a great deal to raise the image of rail travel but it made people think the railways were in 'a state of decline'. The same could be said for the man to whom Sir Peter Parker awarded a gold ticket, allowing him to travel first class on any route on the network.

Savile could be quietly satisfied that among those that really mattered he was now regarded as something more than simply an oddball entertainer. He was moving into the final, most powerful stage of his career, assuming the guise of an elder statesman. At a gathering of Health Service officials at Highgrove House, Prince Charles introduced him as 'my health adviser, Jimmy Savile'.[9]

Stoke Mandeville, where he stayed overnight and had a small suite of rooms, became the nearest thing he had to an office. He felt no compunction about voicing his opposition when his former allies within the Health Service published proposals to charge hospital charities for the use of NHS staff in administering fund-raising schemes. When a shortage of nurses resulted in the closure of beds at the centre he had built and continued to fund through his trust, Savile reacted by subsidising a recruitment drive. No decision, other than medical, was taken at the NSIC at Stoke Mandeville without his say-so. If a new piece of equipment was required, Jimmy Savile signed the cheque.

He even revealed the appeal had allowed him to foster closer relations with the police. When officers were informed of conmen masquerading as fund-raisers, they informed Jimmy Savile and waited for his decision on what to do next. 'The law came to me because they didn't want to bring problems to my charity,' he explained. 'They were very pleased when I gave them my answer ... "Nick [them] now."'[10] Among the hundreds of items in the auction of his belongings in the summer of 2012 was an ornamental lighter with the inscription: 'To Jimmy Savile. From all his friends at the Fraud Squad.'

The Spinal Injuries Centre that he referred to as 'Jimmy Savile's country club', assumed a more significant place in his world. Rather than being another medal on his lapel, or the biggest trophy in his cabinet, Stoke Mandeville was a place he could go to replenish himself. 'I can't just cut it off like a guillotine,'[11] he admitted after the frenetic period of the fund-raising had passed. 'It's not a bad thing to spend a weekend surrounded by lovely patients who've got plenty of time to talk.'[12]

On another occasion he talked about 'what a great scene' Stoke Mandeville represented: 'Just right for an old dance hall manager like me, who's used to being up all hours ... Where else can you find a captive audience of 1,000 people in need of a laugh and a joke?'[13]

Savile particularly liked to prowl the wards at night, looking for sleepless patients who would provide such a captive audience. Janet Cope told me that although he was disliked in the main hospital, Savile would regularly wander down to the gynaecological ward. 'He would say "I'm going down to see my ladies ...".' He thought it was a laugh because bearing in mind what they'd all had done, they couldn't have children. Jim hated children.' For his part, Savile insisted that his only motivation was to 'take away some of the pain'.

In October 1984, that pain arrived courtesy of the Provisional IRA. Five people were killed and thirty-one injured when a bomb detonated at Brighton's Grand Hotel during the Conservative Party conference. The device went off at 3 a.m.; its target was the prime minister. Thatcher escaped unhurt but one of her closest allies, Trade and Industry Minister Norman Tebbit, was carried from the rubble on a stretcher having fallen through four floors of the ruined building. His wife Margaret, who was in bed alongside him at the time of the explosion, was paralysed in the fall. They were both taken to Stoke Mandeville.

Nearly 30 years after the blast that changed their lives, and seven months on from the allegations that destroyed Jimmy Savile's reputation, Tebbit shared his recollections of the man he had told to 'bugger off' because he made him laugh so much that his broken ribs were hurting. 'I've got no doubt Jimmy Savile was a very odd fellow, and I'm pretty sure he was in breach of the law on a number of matters,' said Lord Tebbit. 'But I do not know that it's possible, 40 years on, to do justice in the sense of knowing just how many of those allegations are complete and true. Jimmy did a great deal of good, as well as wrong. And in anybody's life, you have to look at both sides of the ledger.'

Tebbit admitted that he always had 'worries about Jimmy'. When asked what he suspected Savile might have been up to in his private life, he replied, 'I would not have been surprised to find he was having homosexual relationships with young people.' His wife confirmed that she felt he 'had a homosexual air about him'.[14]

The Tebbits were not alone in harbouring such doubts. Thatcher was determined her friend, a man who embodied her thinking on how the NHS should be financed and who averted the potential embarrassment of the country's main spinal injuries unit being forced to close, should be rewarded. In the summer of 1984, she refocused her attention on securing him a knighthood in the Queen's birthday honours list. Once again she was left disappointed.

In a letter dated 1 November and addressed to Thatcher's private secretary Robin Butler, Sir Robert Armstrong reiterated the 'continuing misgivings' of the committee, explaining this time that their view 'had shifted'.

'I acknowledge both the value of his work at Stoke Mandeville and the new public awareness of what has been done. But we remain worried. It is not just the interview and reports in the *Sun* and elsewhere in the spring of 1983, though they would, I feel, be quickly recalled. Fears have been expressed that Mr Savile might not be able to refrain from exploiting a knighthood in a way which brought the honours system into disrepute.'[15] Perhaps of greater significance is the fact that Armstrong added, 'The lapse of time has served only to strengthen the doubts'; doubts, he said, that 'were strongly felt'.

Thatcher was not to be deterred, and yet the response was the same in 1985. When a further request was then turned down in November of 1986,[16] Thatcher's new private secretary, Nigel Wicks, wrote to Armstrong on her behalf, stressing she was 'most disappointed' with the decision. 'She wonders how many more times his name is to be pushed aside, especially in view of all the great work he has done for Stoke Mandeville. She would therefore like you to consider further the inclusion of his name in this list.'

For all those who expressed misgivings about Jimmy Savile, or who privately recoiled at the way he talked about his sex life, kissed up the arms of young female patients, whispered suggestions in their ears, and worse, they were outnumbered by those at the National Spinal Injuries Centre who remained devoted to their main bene-factor. Dr Isaac Nuseibeh, a consultant spinal surgeon at the NSIC, had known Savile since 1973 and confessed that when he first met him he thought his interest 'was a gimmick – to help himself'. Nuseibeh's opinion had changed, though, to the extent that he waxed lyrical about the happiness he spread, describing him as 'a super humanitarian'.[17]

In 1987, Jimmy Savile paid for a seven-year-old Palestinian boy who had been shot and injured in a Beirut refugee camp to be flown to Stoke Mandeville for treatment. He also fixed it for Princess Diana to visit the hospital to unveil a £750,000 body scanner paid for by his trust. When Diana arrived, he opened his tracksuit to reveal a T-shirt bearing the slogan 'For Sale', at which she roared with laughter before giving him a playful slap. 'Princess Diana was fond of Jim,' recalls Janet Cope. 'She'd walk round the wards and then go off for a private chat with him.'[18] It was during these chats that Savile is understood to have nurtured Diana's interest in the work being done at the centre.

Cope also told me that Diana wrote to Savile regularly. When I asked her what the letters said, she replied they were 'along the lines of "it was so lovely to talk to you, I feel so much better now. Thank you for your advice, I know where you are when I need you."'

Jimmy Savile was sufficiently confident in his standing with senior royals to dispense with protocol. He greeted Prince Philip with his familiar, 'Hello, boss' at a Variety Club of Great Britain luncheon, before making him laugh by revealing he had a cigar tucked in his sock. It was something Prince Philip affectionately referred to in his speech.

'It could be misconstrued if I said he was a great friend,' Savile confessed, 'but there is no doubt that we have a great rapport. The rapport is the attraction of opposites and we have amazing fun together.'[19] Savile also discussed his unusually close relationship with the prime minister, alluding to the secret of his success with those in positions of power. 'Instinct means I behave differently with different people,' he said. 'If I am having a bit of fun with people at the top end of the scale, I'm always careful not to get into any bother. I'm also a specialist in minding my own business.'

Having assumed the role of unofficial court jester to the House of Windsor, he drew guffaws from the Queen Mother and Princess Diana when he greeted them at the 1984 Royal Variety Performance dressed as a theatre doorman. On another occasion he theatrically laid down a coat, Walter Raleigh-style, for the Duchess of Kent when she visited a hospice in York. The stunt backfired when her limo ran over the item of clothing. It was the duchess who later presented him with an honorary doctorate of law at Leeds University.

In July 1985, the special relationship he enjoyed with Prince Charles and his wife was thrown into relief by his success in persuading Princess Diana to make an appearance on a two-hour *Drugwatch* television marathon as part of the 'Just Say No' campaign. 'I put it to them that this anti-drugs campaign is a tremendous thing and I was sure the Princess would want to get involved with it,' he said after being spotted leaving the royal residence. 'I was keen that the Prince and Princess should be associated with the programme. For some reason even the more bizarre elements of the teenage world – the punks and the drug addicts – respect them 100 per cent.'[20]

Savile's influence on Prince Charles was such that during a short tour of the north-east in early 1986, he talked the heir to the throne into changing his schedule in order to drop in on the Harton and Westoe Colliery Welfare Club in South Shields for a game of dominoes with the locals. 'I know the club because I used to stay with old uncles and aunties in the South Shields area,' said Savile. 'I am absolutely delighted that he has taken up my suggestion.'[21]

And yet even as his influence continued to grow and expand into new areas, there were hints at what lay beneath. Viewed with the benefit of hindsight, they resemble a series of red flags planted across the landscape of his life.

On the day that *Jim'll Fix It* celebrated a decade as one of Britain's best-loved television shows, the *Sun* ran an interview with the man who had become legendary for making children's dreams come true. The headline above the piece read: 'Kids? I Don't Actually Like Them.'[22]

It is noteworthy, given how he had told Alison Bellamy about the threats from the father of a Leeds schoolgirl he allowed into his penthouse, that the interview should begin with Jimmy Savile talking about how he would not let children through the door. 'Never, ever,' he asserted. 'I'd feel very uncomfortable . . . They may idolise me but they're not coming into my gaff. A lot of them also say, "Fix it for me to ride in your car." Now I'll go along with that so long as they have their mum or their dad with them. Otherwise, no way. I'm a realist, I've seen the trouble other people have got themselves into through no fault of their own. I'm not going the same way. You just can't take the risk. The ordinary person might. But if Jimmy Savile is involved, it's headlines.'

Viewed in the light of what we now know, it's tempting to venture that the incident with the father of the Leeds schoolgirl was still fresh in his mind. This was also the time he put his name to the *Stranger Danger* book.

'I've got nothing to hide,' he reiterated. 'I don't read smut and I don't like it. But the older I get the more advisable it is to have a policy. I mean, people look at you and say: "What's under that stone?" Most people believe something is there, I'm saying they would all be disappointed.'

On collecting his honorary doctorate, Savile addressed a group of final year law students at Leeds University, and again offered an oblique reference to what might be hidden beneath the stone. He spoke on the subject of success, and it is clear that his narrow escape was still playing on his mind. 'There are two ways of winning,' he began. 'One is to win by getting to the top rungs of whatever you choose, but the other is not to lose. Let me explain. You can be quite clever at what you do but if, say, you're tempted early on to act outside the law and you get caught by this Big Brother society of ours with computer records storing our slip-ups for ever, one little incident could mean disaster for years.' He claimed that money was 'the oil that stops life rubbing up against you. It protects you.'[23]

Jimmy Savile had little to fear from computer records, it seems. During the 1980s, a young girl is understood to have reported Jimmy Savile for sexually assaulting her in his motor caravan in a BBC car park. She made the allegation to officers at Hammersmith and Fulham police station. An officer from Scotland Yard's Juvenile Bureau was subsequently detailed to look into the matter but no evidence was found that would support a prosecution. The Metropolitan Police insist 'no trace of a police file has been found despite extensive efforts'.[24] The investigating officer is now dead.

In 1986, a 19-year-old woman entered a police station in Southport and made a complaint about historic sexual abuse by Jimmy Savile and others. She told officers of Merseyside Police that a family friend, who worked as a cameraman at the BBC and had abused her at his home, was responsible for introducing her to Jimmy Savile at BBC Television headquarters in west London. She was nine years old at the time.

'I can remember him taking me to see Savile in a room with a table, a mirror, a wardrobe and a couple of chairs,' said Alice (not her real name). 'The cameraman called him Uncle Jim. Savile sat in this high-backed chair and he asked me to sit on his knee while he signed my luminous pink autograph book. I was wearing a pink dress with my hair in pigtails.' She claimed he sat her 'right back on his body' before molesting her.

'The cameraman was in the room at the time but he didn't do anything,' she maintained. 'He took me to see Savile another two or three times and then left the room. I can remember he was bony and he stank.' Over the next two years, Alice said she was taken to the BBC on a weekly basis and sexually assaulted by more than 30 men.

She also says the abuse has wrecked her life, leading to mental health problems, suicide attempts and her five children being taken into care. Merseyside Police, for its part, insists the report was dealt with 'appropriately'. Again, nothing was done.

I n late 1989, Jimmy Savile welcomed journalists into his office at Broadmoor Hospital. He was able to look back with pride on how he had put a cap on soaring building costs. 'What we needed was a strong hand to take the decisions no one wanted to take, someone who didn't understand everyone else's rules, and that was me,' he explained. He'd even managed to get another of his own men on to the hospital's new management board, a body he described as 'a highly intelligent reference library'.

The management boards had been established as another element of Clifford Graham's new blueprint. 'It's a team of eight experts,' Savile explained. It included a GP, a forensic psychiatrist, a local architect and, in his words, 'a multi-millionaire owner of a security company'.[1] The latter is how Savile always described Luke Lucas, although Lucas maintains he was 'not a member of Broadmoor Hospital Management'.

While the prime minister still struggled to get Jimmy Savile's name on the shortlist submitted by the Honours Committee for the Queen's approval, there is little doubt that once she succeeded it would be accepted without a second thought. His relationship with the royals, and particularly Prince Charles and Princess Diana, became deeper and more intimate during the time he was seconded by the government to fix the mess at Broadmoor.

In 1987, Jimmy Savile had persuaded Charles to attend a ceremony for carers in London. A year later, he sat in the Prince of Wales's private office making calls to television producers inviting them to a cocktail evening hosted by the prince at Kensington Palace as a thanks for their contribution to a recent charity telethon. In November that year, Jimmy Savile was a guest at Charles's 40th birthday party.

'He played the fool to our big-eared Prince's Lear,' recounted one St James's Palace aide in the days before the funeral in Leeds. 'He could speak the truth to power with impunity. His own version of the truth, of course, but from all I could see it was usually pretty good sense. And because he wasn't guilty of having a posh accent, an Oxbridge degree or a suit, his words were received as from the oracle itself.'[2]

Cracks had started to appear in the royal marriage. Charles had become increasingly snappy with his wife while Diana's unhappiness and sense of isolation manifested itself in an eating disorder. When Sarah Ferguson's romance blossomed with Prince Andrew, Diana was repeatedly told that she should be 'more like Fergie'.

In May 1989, Jimmy Savile made an unexpected appearance at Prince Charles's offices. Sarah Goodall, who had joined the staff a year earlier, recalls him licking up the arm of one of the Lady Clerks. When Goodall later asked another member of staff what Savile was doing there, she was told he was 'working with [Princess Diana] on a project for Stoke Mandeville'. She claims her jaw hit the floor when it was explained to her that he was 'also trying to patch things up between the Boss and the Bossette. He arranged for them to meet in Dyfed in Wales so they could comfort flood victims together in public. Their Royal Highnesses weren't speaking at the time, so to bring them together was quite a feat.'[3]

In a recorded telephone conversation the following New Year's Eve, Princess Diana poured her heart out to a friend, James Gilbey, about the state of her relationship with her husband and his family. She also made a startling admission about the role Jimmy Savile now played in their lives.

When the conversation turned to her sister-in-law, Diana revealed: 'Jimmy Savile phoned me up yesterday, and he said. "I'm just ringing up, my girl, to tell you that His Nibs has asked me to come and help out the redhead, and I'm just letting you know, so that you don't find out through her or him; and I hope it's alright by you."' By late 1989, Sarah Ferguson had begun attracting rather too many negative headlines.

This brief exchange disclosed a side of Jimmy Savile not normally seen: deferential, keen to please. It also seems to confirm what Roger Ordish said about the change that came over him when in the company of social superiors.

Diana explained to Gilbey that she had replied: 'Jimmy, you do what you like.'

When Gilbey asked what Savile had meant, Diana replied: 'Sort her out. He said, "you can't change a lame duck, but I've got to talk to her, 'cause that's the boss's orders, and I've got to carry them out. But I want you to know that you're my number one girl".' Diana confirmed that by 'His Nibs' Savile meant Prince Charles. 'Does he get on well with him?' asked Gilbey. 'Sort of mentor,' replied Diana.

I questioned Jimmy Savile about this conversation, and his relationships with Prince Charles, Princess Diana, Prince Andrew and Sarah Ferguson during our days together in Leeds in 2008. 'I was helping [Sarah Ferguson] not get publicity, rather than to get publicity,' he admitted. 'To cool things down. It was one of those; it was all part of my odd ways of going on. The thing about me is I get things done. They tippled that I can get things done, and that I work "deep cover" . . . People don't realise I'm deep cover until it's too late.'

In 1990, as the divisions deepened within the royal household, Jimmy Savile was asked to attempt his latest and most audacious rescue bid. Dickie Arbiter, a press spokesman for the Queen, had been employed by Prince Charles since 1988 to handle his media relations. 'Savile was brought in by an aide as a sort of "Jim'll Fix It" to fix the state of the marriage, but of course it didn't work,' said Arbiter. 'His role was informal, ad hoc. He would just roll in and roll out again.'[4]

Arbiter's opinion was Savile 'was a pretty ghastly man'.

But it was not only marriage guidance that Jimmy Savile was sought out for. He also advised Prince Charles on key appointments to his staff. When his private secretary Sir John Riddell decided to return to the City, Charles asked Savile to meet with one of the candidates suggested as his successor. After consultation with Savile and Richard Aylard, Major-General Sir Christopher Airy was appointed private secretary and treasurer to the Prince and Princess of Wales.

Aylard, a man Charles's authorised biographer Jonathan Dimbleby described as 'having become his most trusted lieutenant',[5] expressed doubts about Airy. And yet he was still appointed. Jimmy Savile's opinion clearly carried considerable weight.

During our time together on the QE2, Savile revealed that he regularly played jokes on Princess Diana. Of the Duke of Edinburgh, all he would offer was, 'He thinks I'm very odd, as does Prince Charles.' Janet Cope confirmed to me that Prince Charles used to phone Savile regularly at Stoke Mandeville.

All three sent telegrams of congratulation when Jimmy Savile's name finally made it onto the Queen's birthday honours list in the late summer of 1990, as did Prince Andrew. The Duchess of York sent a homemade card while Angus Ogilvy sent his warmest wishes in a handwritten letter. It was the last list that Margaret Thatcher made recommendations for before she was forced to resign. And it was her letter that informed Jimmy Savile that they had succeeded in getting him the knighthood they both desired.

Savile claimed he was lying in bed in his London flat when the envelope dropped through the door. He said that he was so excited that he signed the acceptance form, jumped in a taxi and delivered it in person to Downing Street. His feelings of exhilaration, anticipation and relief continued to build until the news could be announced some five weeks later.

Roger Ordish said he knew in advance, and claimed it was the closest he ever got to seeing the real Jimmy Savile. 'I was very pleased,' he recalled. 'We were walking up the street back to the Portland Place flat and he said, "I shouldn't be telling you this, but

I've got a knighthood. You're not to say anything." I was very touched to be trusted. I didn't even tell my wife.'

After being shown the letter from Thatcher and the telegrams from the various royals, Lynn Barber, the respected broadsheet journalist, asked Jimmy Savile why he thought it had taken so long. He replied, 'I would imagine I unsettled the establishment because the establishment would say, "Yes, Jimmy's a good chap but a bit strange . . ." And I think maybe in the past I suffered from the vulgarity of success. Because if you're successful in what you do you can become a pain in the neck to a lot of people, especially if you're doing it in a volunteer manner, right?'[6]

It was an uncannily accurate assessment of the discussions that had taken place over a number of years between the prime minister's office and the Honours Committee.

But what he said next, in response to Barber's question about the tabloid rumour mill, is one of the most illuminating things that ever passed his lips. 'I had a lively couple of years with the tabloids sniffing about, asking round the corner shops – everything – thinking there must be something the authorities knew that they didn't. Whereas in actual fact I've got to be the most boring geezer in the world because I ain't got no past, no nothing. And so, if nothing else, it was a ginormous relief when I got the knighthood, because it got me off the hook.'

It was an extraordinary comment. He could have declared that it was a huge honour and stated how humbled he felt. But instead, he talked of the Queen giving him 'this tremendous responsibility' and about the overwhelming sense of relief that came with it.

To her credit, Barber went on to press Savile about the rumours that he liked 'little girls'. She reported he responded with a flurry of patter. Then, when he'd got his bearings, he reverted to the line he had used time and time again: that teenagers only flocked around him because he got to meet their idols.

When she then asked him about sex, he likened it to going to the bathroom, adding, 'I've never been one to explain to people what I do when I go the bathroom and I'm not a kiss-and-tell punter. All

I can say is that I've never got anybody into any trouble; I've never knowingly upset anybody'.

He reiterated that there was no room in his life for love: 'I don't have girlfriends because it's not fair, the same as I don't have plants because I'd never be back to water them, and I don't have cats and dogs, and I don't have kids because I'd never be there to see them.' It was an elucidation that had become another brick in the wall.

Barber's was the first of a series of major profiles in the lead-up to his investiture. Shortly afterwards, he was interviewed at Stoke Mandeville where he was photographed in his spartan living quarters. He again talked about why he had never married: 'I have such a marvellous lifestyle, I have knock-out relationships here and I can bugger off when I want, which is not the stuff relationships are made of.' Janet Rowe, his secretary at the hospital, told the journalist, 'You'll never find out what the true Jimmy Savile is like because he's so complex. It's very difficult to get him to open up.'[7]

The music magazine Q tried, but again he stonewalled. Only this time he let slip that his well-practised ripostes to questions about relationships, marriage and the dark rumours that now swirled about him were in fact a tactic. 'As far as skeletons are concerned, I must be the most boring punter in the world because I haven't got any. I'm totally boring,' he said for the umpteenth time. 'It knackers everybody. There are no skeletons and I've got knighted so that proves it, doesn't it?'[8]

In late October, he was interviewed at the flat he'd been given at Broadmoor. He talked about the work being done at the hospital and the new, softer image it was trying to project, underlining again that its patients were mad rather than bad. 'A true psychopath really enjoys what he's doing,' he said. 'We don't have anyone like that here.'

If Jimmy Savile had learned anything at Broadmoor he might have grasped the black irony underscoring this statement. For delivering it was a man who exhibited so many of the behavioural traits on the psychopathy checklist Robert Hare devised to identify those who committed crimes: the slippery charm; the mask worn to conceal his true self from others; the low cunning and willingness to manipulate; the absence of normal human emotions; the lack of empathy; the sexual promiscuity; the inability to admit mistakes; the fear of commitment; the ability to evade capture; and, most importantly, the repeated attacks on the vulnerable. Of course, Jimmy Savile would not have been able to see this, due to the grandiose self-image that made him incapable of understanding how others might perceive him.

Savile went on to defend those who had committed awful crimes while wracked with mental illness, arguing 'There's no point asking about that dark night . . . when something terrible happened because it wasn't really them doing it. It was someone else using their body.'[9] It was the same rationale he used for his own sexual desire in *God'll Fix It*.

One wonders what Avril Harris must have thought when Jimmy was pontificating about his gypsy lifestyle precluding anything more lasting than a fling. She had been just 13 when Jimmy Savile and his friends used to whistle at her from the Mecca flat in Leeds. She said she bumped into him again in her twenties, when he would chat her up and try to take her back to his flat. She resisted but described him as 'an eagle pursuing a mouse'. In the summer of 1990, they finally became lovers. She was 46; he was 64.

The relationship did not last, mainly due to Savile's long absences and her suspicions that he was with other women. It was, in fairness, just as he always said. But Avril Harris's most vivid memory of Jimmy Savile was from the night before he was knighted at Buckingham Palace. 'He was sitting on the bed naked, and he began softly crying,' she said. 'I joined him and hugged him closely. He became quite emotional about what an important moment it was.'[10]

The next morning, as he set off for the palace, Savile announced that this was the start of a new chapter. 'There's the old established business of Jimmy Savile, disc jockey, who can be had for £10,000,' he quipped. 'And there's Sir James Savile who comes a lot more expensive.'[11] He took as his guest Clifford Graham, the man who had rubber stamped his appointment to the Broadmoor Hospital task force. As the sword touched his shoulder and he was instructed to arise, Sir James could reflect that Jimmy was indeed now off the hook.

Not long afterwards, *This Is Your Life* took the unprecedented step of surprising the same unsuspecting star for a second time. But time, rather than Jimmy Savile, it was the newly titled Sir James Savile OBE who was to be honoured, although there was dissent over the decision among members of the production staff.

Roy Bottomley was the chief scriptwriter on *This Is Your Life*, and a former news reporter on the *Daily Sketch*. According to Norman Giller, a fellow scriptwriter on the show, Bottomley refused point-blank to work on the Savile tribute. 'I'm not going to write it,' Giller remembered his colleague saying, 'The man's notorious.' Bottomley then explained how former Fleet Street colleagues had been trying for years to find evidence that Savile 'molested underage girls'.[12]

Jimmy Savile's eldest sister Mary arrived from Australia to join her other five siblings, including Johnnie, with whom he was now reconciled. She was followed through the famous doorway by former Mecca chairman Eric Morley; the wrestler Big Daddy; disc jockeys Tony Blackburn and Dave Cash. Leeds General Infirmary head porter Charles Hullighan, a director of Jimmy Savile Ltd, spoke fondly of how they secured 'plunder' from their visits to companies in and around Leeds. Former *Top of the Pops* colleague David Jacobs reminisced about the long-haired upstart from up north. Bill Wyman, recently married to Mandy Smith, who he had started dating when she was just 13, paid tribute to how Jimmy had been one of the first to support The Rolling Stones.

And still they came: members of the Royal Marines; patients and staff from Stoke Mandeville; Janet, his secretary, who explained how Savile now planned to build a children's hospital in Peterborough. *Jim'll Fix It* producer Roger Ordish; the boxer Frank Bruno; Alan Franey, Jimmy Corrigan and members of his running club who jogged onto the set in their marathon gear.

Among those already seated were the magician Paul Daniels and Peter Jaconelli, former mayor of Scarborough.[13]

Towards the end of the show, host Michael Aspel read out a message from a special contributor: 'Jimmy, I and millions more salute you. God bless. Margaret Thatcher.' Off the hook indeed.

t was my last full day on the *QE2*. I woke up with a hacking cough and decided to go for a wander. There was no sign of Jimmy Savile and we had made no firm plans to meet. We were both ready to get off now; last night he'd told me he was looking forward to getting home. For him, home meant a couple of days at a high-security psychiatric hospital in Berkshire before heading the short distance to Stoke Mandeville, the second of his three-pronged circuit of hospitals. 'You're totally knacked by the last two days of a cruise,' he'd confided while puffing on a cigar in the bar.

When I found him, near the scruffy golf net located midway up the terrace of decks at the rear of the ship, he was looking bedraggled. His hair was wild and he'd worn the same black shell suit every day of the cruise. He had been performing pretty much non-stop for two weeks. He was still at it though, telling a story I'd heard already on a couple of occasions to two old boys wearing trousers pulled high onto the foothills of their bellies. He was regaling them with how he'd poured two bottles of vodka into the water urn and that's why everyone was legless. They were not legless of course, but the men still laughed. Savile asked whether they fancied a glass and they guffawed. The stories seemed to be sapping his energy.

'Have you enjoyed your cruise, Jim?' asked one of the men. 'Horrible,' deadpanned Savile. 'Too much sunshine, too many loose women.'

I picked out a sun lounger from the rows arranged neatly on the deck, and kicked off my flip-flops. After a few minutes, Savile spotted me. He came over, sitting on the corner of the next lounger along. The sun was starting to burn so he unzipped his black shell suit top to reveal a blue T-shirt bearing the legend 'All I want is world peace' and then in smaller writing underneath, ' . . . and a bit of leg-over and chips'.

He then pulled off his tracksuit trousers. Underneath he was wearing a pair of scoop-legged nylon running shorts, the type worn on *Superstars* in the 1980s. From the front the shorts were cut in a shape that reminded me of the upside down, half-moon leather sheath worn by Tarzan, only these were in a metallic blue. His legs were lean and largely hairless; he was in good shape for an 81-year-old.

We talked about his John O'Groats to Land's End walk in 1971. 'Thirty one days, 932 miles,' said Jimmy, who liked to boil his achievements down to bald figures.

I then asked him about Sally, a woman we had spent some time with during the evenings on the ship. She was recovering from leukaemia, having lost two previous husbands to cancer. I'd never before seen how he behaved around women he liked – and I reckoned he liked her. I'd watched him carrying on and doing his act, pretending he was having heart palpitations or asking a giggling victim back to his cabin for a massage. But Sally was not the type to giggle and play along. She was too sophisticated for that, plus she seemed fond of him: curious, too.

Would he see Sally again? 'Doubt it,' he said without a flicker. 'I've done her a favour because she's had a tough time. And she's done me a favour because she's with me.' He explained what he meant, referencing the rather tipsy young woman who had stumbled up to him in the bar a couple of evenings back and asked whether she could sit on his lap.

'When that Scotch girl, who is done up to the nines every evening, comes over and starts carrying on with me, I've got Sally with me so her old man doesn't get the hump. Otherwise, it would be all meetings are off, including Uttoxeter.' I nodded but said nothing. 'They're all brain damage,' muttered Savile.

Looking back, he was acknowledging that Sally was being used as a cover. How many times had he used women like this? At the time, I seriously doubted whether the man in the bar feared his wife, who was probably in her mid-thirties, was in any imminent danger of being whisked off her feet by an octogenarian with bleached white hair and a penchant for polyester.

Savile got up and moved off to stand in a shaded corner by the top of the stairs. The shorts, which were shorter than I first feared, were becoming alarmingly translucent thanks to the sun pouring through a porthole behind him. I really did not want to see an outline of what lay beneath.

This ensemble was completed by white towelling sports socks pulled up to the lower calf and a green knotted handkerchief on his head. It was like a Chapman brothers' reimagining of a post-card caricature from the golden days of the British seaside.

'Morning,' bleeped Savile as two women pulled themselves up the stairs. One of the women checked her watch: 'But it's the afternoon now Jimmy,' she said. He looked straight ahead: 'Why tell the truth when you can get away with a lie.'

Jimmy Savile kept on running: the London Marathon and eight fun runs and half marathons in 1988; the London Marathon and a further nine shorter distance races in 1989; the London Marathon and no fewer than thirteen half marathons or fun runs in 1990.

But the fanatical pursuit of endorphins produced by exercise was not enough, not even allied to his commitments at Broadmoor, which became less pressing after the appointment of Franey and the new hospital board, and his ongoing radio and TV work. The report published in 2013 by the Metropolitan Police and the NSPCC recorded allegations against Jimmy Savile of 19 sexual assaults in the years between 1986 and 1990: six at the BBC, three at Stoke Mandeville and ten in other locations.[1]

He needed a focus; something that would enable him to do deals, raise money and shore up his reputation. The next multi-million pound project, he decided, was to be a new children's hospital in Peterborough, where the locally based travel company Thomas Cook had given him a flat after hiring him as a highly paid business consultant. Like other big businesses, it saw Jimmy Savile as a man who could open many doors along the corridors of power.

'It will be much more than just a hospital,' Savile explained of the 60-bed facility he planned to create on a green field site next to the existing Edith Cavell Hospital. 'It will be somewhere that children will enjoy going to . . . When I built Stoke Mandeville, I told the architects I wanted a stately home with a hospital inside. This time I want a magic castle with a hospital inside.'[2]

He'd sketched out his plans on a scrap of paper during the wedding reception for his long-suffering secretary Janet Rowe (now Janet Cope), before giving them to the Fitzroy Robinson Partnership, the firm of architects that designed the National Spinal Injuries Centre. Savile said that he was putting in £50,000 of his own money and hoped Thomas Cook would contribute to the tune of a further £1 million. Chief executive Peter Middleton certainly sounded enthusiastic: '[I] told him that Thomas Cook would support it if he got if off the ground.'[3]

Jimmy Savile was confident that he could make it happen. After all, he had just persuaded Hitachi and the Japanese government to sell him a £2 million magnetic resonance imaging system for considerably less than half price, and talked Princess Diana into dropping into Stoke Mandeville for the machine's unveiling.

His role as a trusted confidant and adviser to the royals was reaffirmed in early June 1991 when Prince William was rushed to hospital with a depressed fracture of the skull after a schoolmate caught him with a glancing blow while swinging a golf club. Diana travelled with her oldest son in the ambulance while Prince Charles followed behind in his Aston Martin. Later that evening, as the second in line to the throne underwent surgery, Charles took the decision to honour an existing engagement by going to the opera.

Dave Eager remembers the day of the accident clearly. He was in London on business and had phoned Jimmy, as per usual. On this occasion, though, Savile sounded different. Eager was told to get to the flat on Park Crescent as soon as he possibly could. 'So I got round there and he opened the door . . . in the full morning suit, the royal insignia, the royal crest, everything,' said Eager. 'He was dressed in the full Monty as a knight.'

When Eager asked what was going on, Savile replied that he had received a call from Prince Charles, who had been due to present the Duke of Edinburgh Awards as his father was away. According to Eager, when Prince William sustained his injuries, 'Prince Charles said to Jim, "I am sure the people receiving [the] awards, providing it's all done at Buckingham Palace, will be just as thrilled to have them presented by Sir James Savile, so please will you represent me and Prince Philip?"'

He said Savile was desperate for someone to witness him being picked up in the royal car, dressed in the full regalia. 'You are one of the few people who can look at me and say, this guy from 22 Consort Terrace has finally achieved something,' he told Eager. 'You know what it means to me to be dressed up like this. Stay and watch me.' Eager did as he was told: 'The car came up and we waved each other goodbye,' he said. 'I felt so proud of him.'

Although there were to be no further Christmas lunches at Chequers now that his friend Margaret Thatcher had gone, Jimmy Savile's name still carried weight within the Department of Health. Having cajoled Bovis into offering to build the buildings of the new children's hospital at cost price, and secured commitments of £2 million from the European Community, as well as the promise of a further £1 million from Thomas Cook, Savile was invited to Downing Street to brief ministers on the plans. He claimed to have raised a further £1 million himself but was still some £5 million short of his target.

'The only problem I have at the moment is with my conscience,' he explained. 'In the middle of a recession I don't feel I can go as strong getting money from the public as I did with Stoke Mandeville. I've got £3–4,000,000 worth of promises but you can't ask companies to pay up when they've got their backs to the wall.'[4]

Three days after his talks with government ministers, Jimmy Savile's influence within the royal family was laid bare in a story published in the *Sunday Times*. Under the headline 'Truce', royal author and journalist Andrew Morton, a man trusted by Princess Diana and her inner circle, described the 'DJ, television personality, indefatigable charity worker and obsessive marathon runner' as 'an unlikely royal peacemaker'.[5]

Morton revealed how Princess Diana had sought Jimmy Savile out for a 'little homespun advice' after being angered and upset by a story in a rival newspaper highlighting the parlous state of her marriage. Princess Diana had celebrated her 30th birthday alone, and anonymous sources close to the Prince of Wales briefed the press in defence of his decision to stay at Highgrove rather than join his wife in London.

In the *Daily Mail* story that had so offended Diana, royal correspondent Nigel Dempster wrote, 'Charles's friends believe that [she] is much more adept at projecting her image and as a result has generally had a more sympathetic press. Perhaps this is why Charles's friends are trying to redress matters. They were determined that the other side of the story should come out.'

According to Morton, 'It was the fiercest of the thunderstorms to break over a royal relationship entrapped in a summer of discontent.'

On the day after Diana's birthday, Jimmy Savile spoke to both Charles and Diana in an attempt to pour oil on troubled waters. '[His] opinions carry weight in both camps,' wrote Morton, whose sources are acknowledged as having been impeccable. 'As the unofficial court jester, he articulates opinions that courtiers can only think.' By the end of the week, an uneasy truce had been declared.

Janet Cope told me her boss was 'in and out of Kensington Palace' in this period: 'Diana was on the phone to him quite a lot.' Dave Eager recalled what Savile told him about his approach with the royals. 'Jim would say, quite clearly, that Charles was born into an era when the media expanded so fast there wasn't time for somebody who was focused on something else to realise how the media was developing and affecting their lives. He had a lot of sympathy for the way Charles was not treated very well by the media. They didn't understand the life that Charles was brought up in. Jim empathised with Charles and highly respected him. He said to me, "There are certain people in life where you believe what they are saying, and they believe what you are saying. And Charles, when he says something, you believe that you are getting it straight from the heart." That's why he respected him.'

Ken Wharfe, Diana's former protection officer, has his own take on the ministrations of this unlikeliest of advisers. '[He] used to just turn up at Kensington Palace and at functions. When Diana was carrying out an engagement around the country he would just turn up out of the blue like it was the Jimmy Savile visit rather than the Princess Diana visit. I don't think Diana was a great fan of his in the way that the Prince of Wales was.'[6]

That said, Savile was able to convince Diana to visit Peterborough in 1991 to take part in the 150th anniversary celebrations for Thomas Cook. He also got her interested in the work done at Broadmoor, and offered her sanctuary there on days when she needed time out of the spotlight.

A week or so after representing Prince Charles and his father, Jimmy Savile was back on royal duty. By day, he entertained Norma Major, Barbara Bush and other wives of G7 summit leaders during a visit to Stoke Mandeville, taking the opportunity to kiss up the arm of America's first lady. By night, he swapped his shell suit for something more formal for the gala reception at Buckingham Palace.

A few years later, Bunny Lewis, the showbusiness manager and record producer who interviewed Savile for national newspapers in his early days and became a close friend, offered his own opinion on why he was so valued by royalty: 'I don't think it's what he sees himself but they see him as. In the past they have considered and accepted his advice very seriously, and indeed benefitted from it . . . I think he has tried very hard to make them more human.'[7]

Jimmy Savile tried to do the same with some of the more infamous patients at Broadmoor Hospital. In 1991, Frank Bruno, the British heavyweight boxer, was at a crossroads in his life and career. He had lost successive world title fights when he first encountered the TV star and charity worker.

'I had just finished my third pantomime season when Sir Jimmy took me to one side. He said: "Francis, young man," – he always calls me Francis – "I want to ask you a very serious question and your answer could change your life. Do you want to be remembered as a pantomime fairy or as a champion boxer." It was then I decided to give my all to becoming world champion.'[8]

It was during the period Savile was mentoring Bruno – encouraging him to join him on charity runs and hospital visits – that he took the heavyweight boxer to Broadmoor for the opening of a new gymnasium. On a tour of the secure ward, he turned to his guest and said, 'I want you to meet this gentleman.' He introduced Bruno to a bearded man dressed in a garish shell suit who was leaning against a window ledge. The two chatted for a few minutes.

Bruno asked the man whether he would be using the new fitness equipment and joked that he could do with losing a few pounds. The man replied that fitness wasn't his thing and asked the fighter, who had recently lost to Mike Tyson, when he was going to be making a comeback. At this point, Jimmy Savile jumped in: 'He's fighting me next week,' he said. The patient replied in that case Frank Bruno had 'no chance'.[9]

'I didn't know he who was,' says Bruno of the man. 'Afterwards Savile asked, "Do you know who you met?"'

Speaking after the exposure of a man he liked and respected enough to have appeared as a friend on *This Is Your Life* and attended his funeral, Bruno told one newspaper: 'I was in Broadmoor to open a gym, not to meet a man who killed 13 women. Savile planned it. It was not a nice thing to do to me. If I had known it was the Ripper, I'd have tried to get out of it. It was a scary feeling.'

A photographer was on hand to capture the moment Frank Bruno shook hands with Peter Sutcliffe. And there, standing a couple of paces back, was Jimmy Savile clutching a cigar. 'I didn't know a photographer was taking pictures,' insisted Bruno. 'When the photo came out I rang Savile and said, "What was that all about?" He apologised but by then it was too late. That picture has hounded me. I want to say sorry to every victim's family and anyone that was upset.'[10]

*

Even now he had the trappings of a man who had been accepted into the establishment, Jimmy Savile could not escape the insidious whispers that continued to swarm around him. In truth, he did not help himself, as his radio interview with the consultant psychiatrist Anthony Clare demonstrated.

The exchange, recorded for the Radio 4 series *In the Psychiatrist's Chair*, was a heated one, and Clare emerged from it bloodied and bruised, reporting he found some of the things Savile had said to be 'disturbing'.[11]

Clare was surprised to find his subject had 'a certain dislike for people' and held some interesting opinions on the subjects of sharing and sacrifice. 'He seemed to show no interest in them at all,' he said. 'Considering the work he has done and his public persona he appears to be at odds with himself.'

The interview is enthralling, and appears to exemplify what Jimmy Savile had previously said about psychiatrists, namely 'We should burn shrinks. Burn the bastards.'[12] It was a startling comment given his long association with Broadmoor Hospital and his promotion of work done in the field of mental health. 'If a psychiatrist would think that I was strange,' Savile said, 'it would take me absolutely no effort at all to completely unsettle him and maybe show that he himself needed some treatment.'

Savile certainly tried to unsettle Anthony Clare, and as a result the interview was a study in defensiveness and obfuscation. It opened with Clare asking why he agreed to the interview given his opinion on psychiatrists. Savile said he found it hard to say no.

Clare then asked him whether he ever got depressed before quizzing him on his childhood. It did not take long for the dominant and recurring themes to materialise: the supremacy of money in his list of priorities, his total absence of feelings, a complete unwillingness to open up.

In explaining why he had bought seventeen brand new Rolls-Royce motor cars over the course of his life, Savile said, 'If a

scandal comes up . . . or the people go off you, you're finished.'
With a brand new Rolls-Royce in the garage, and everything in his
life paid for, he could then 'go and be very unhappy in the south of
France, covered in shame and sunshine and mad birds with bikinis
on for a long time because there was a new Rolls-Royce there and
a new this and new that.'[13]

Clare was clearly intrigued by Savile's stated fear of being ruined
by a scandal, and pressed him to explain more. 'In actual fact
today the concern has been taken away,' he replied. 'In the old
days, we'll say ten years ago, many people were ruined in my game
by scandals that never existed . . . Today it's not like that at all,
because today we can actually sue people who tell lies.'[14]

Savile explained the recent libel victories of Jeffrey Archer and
Koo Stark had made his life a lot more comfortable.

They discussed his mother before segueing into a prickly
exchange on marriage, relationships and children. 'A kid with me
is on trial, like I'm on trial with the kid,'[15] explained the host of
one of the most iconic children's shows in British television history.
'We get on like a house on fire but there's no yukky nonsense
about it and I've got no paternal feelings.'

On the subject of charity, Savile confessed that he was more
interested in the process of making money than the people who
would benefit from it. On matters of faith, he restated his need
only to know that he was going in 'the right direction'.

After more thrust and parry, Clare tried changing tack: 'The
key feature of your lifestyle is your control of it . . . Nobody makes
demands on your lifestyle. Such demands made are demands that
you have in a sense accepted.'[16]

'If anybody makes demands they don't make them twice pal,'
Savile replied, 'because they get the sack after the first time.'

The conversation kept returning to Savile's childhood and his
refusal to acknowledge the place of emotion in his life. He described
'ultimate freedom', to which Clare responded by asking if he was
conscious of things such freedom offered that needed to be resisted.

'It would be easy to be corrupted by many things, when you've got ultimate freedom,' answered Savile, 'especially when you've got clout. I could be corrupted. I'd like to think that up to press I've managed to stay like I was.'[17]

'It is only in the cracks and crevices of the conversation that doubts lurk,' wrote Clare a year later, citing Savile's relationship with his mother and his insistence on maintaining emotional independence from the rest of the human race as the marks of someone with 'powerful reasons to shun intimacy'.

Of his 'morbid preoccupation with death' – the desire to work in hospital mortuary departments, the days he spent in a room with his dead mother – Clare posited that people with 'a distaste for emotions, who place great value on predictability and control, who see life as incorrigibly messy and death as a frozen model of perfection, are half in love with death. The dead don't let you down, don't make demands, don't limit your freedom.'

The psychiatrist concluded that Jimmy Savile was a 'calculating materialist' with no need for people. 'He could cope with people needing him,' Clare said, 'as long as they are satisfied with the things he is prepared and able to give them – in most instances material things, and in no instance himself.'[18]

Savile's mortal fear of being embarrassed or exposed was something that Roger Ordish recognises. 'His extraordinary attitude to the press was not, "Oh, how nice. Here's someone who is going to give me some publicity and do a nice story about me." It was, "You're not going to catch me out." He was so much on the defensive that it often ended up as meaningless gobbledygook.'

Not long after the interview with Anthony Clare, Jimmy Savile began spinning. '[Clare] only asked me about feelings about people, love, getting married and having children. He was slightly overawed by me because I employ consultant psychiatrists at Broadmoor. He should have broadened the issue.'[19]

The interviewer on this occasion, Angela Levin, asked him whether he was a psychopath. 'I know psychopaths. I've seen them at Broadmoor,' Savile replied, contradicting what he had previously said about the patients at the hospital. 'They have no emotion in

relation to human life. But I love certain things. Nature moves me
. . . I just don't have those feelings with another human being.' It
sounded uncannily like the dictionary definition of a psychopath.

Levin probed him about how he felt when journalists made
insinuations about his private life. His answer, given the open
nature of the question, was again revealing. 'If anybody categorically said to me, "Do you associate with little girls?" I would say,
"No, I don't." I never have done and I have no kinky desire to go
that route. The people who know me know that the last type of
people I gravitate to are children.'

Jimmy Savile was 67 and his powers were waning. Despite the
fanfare in the media, including his appearance at an Anglia TV
telethon and the backing of the local evening paper, his plans to
build a 55-bed children's hospital in Peterborough disguised as a
fantasy castle with turrets and flagpoles came to nothing.

Detailed plans were submitted to Peterborough City Council,
and in May 1991, Peter Lee, director of Planning and Environmental
Health at the Town Hall wrote back, stating, 'The City Council is
not opposed to the proposed development but does have reservations about the design philosophy employed. Whilst it is recognised
the unconventional design is intended to ease the concerns of children who attend the hospital, it is considered the proposed scheme
will lie uncomfortably with the existing Edith Cavell Hospital.'

Savile was not the sort of person to give up easily, or to take no
for an answer, so why did a campaign announced on national
television fizzle out so quietly? The official reason given was the
downturn in the economy and expenditure cuts forced on Thomas
Cook by its owner Midland Bank. But could it have been that
rather than easing the concerns of children, somebody in a position of authority found out that giving Jimmy Savile his own
children's hospital, one that he vowed to be at constantly, would
have achieved the exact opposite? With the appeal fund standing
at just short of £500,000, the decision was made to redirect the
funds to a children's medical charity in the city. Janet Cope, a

staunch defender of Jimmy Savile's reputation, has no doubts about why the appeal foundered. 'It's simple,' she said. 'People had got appeal fatigue.'

It wasn't the only high-profile aspect of his life that was under threat. After 19 years, so too was *Jim'll Fix It*. Recently appointed BBC1 controller, Alan Yentob, had arrived wielding a new broom.

'He wants to quit at the top,' said a BBC spokesman when it was announced that the series filmed in 1993 would be the programme's last. It echoed the manner of the stage-managed exit from Radio 1. Will Wyatt, managing director of BBC Television, was quick to pay tribute: 'Jimmy Savile has been one of the stalwarts of our entertainments programming for more than a quarter of a century . . . We owe a great debt to Jimmy for all his BBC work and wish him well for the future.'[20]

Savile admitted he had no immediate plans for the future, other than buying a new motor home and travelling round the country. A couple of weeks later, however, he served up the truth about why he had quit the show that had turned him into one of Britain's biggest stars. 'Along comes Jack the Lad,' he said, referring to Yentob, 'and if he sacks a small show, he's only a small manager. But if he sacks a big one like mine, he's a big manager. Instinct tells me to quit while I'm at the top. It shows supreme survival confidence.'[21]

He'd always said he wanted to be 'loaded with nothing to do'. Now it was Jimmy Savile's turn to have his wish come true.

t was 7.45 p.m. and we were in Jimmy Savile's cabin. The *QE2* was a short distance off Land's End. He told me to take a seat as there was something he wanted to do. Reaching over to the shelf below his cabin porthole, he located a bottle of champagne from among the cigar boxes and bottles of scotch, and presented it to me. He wanted to know whether I thought it had 'been worth the trouble'. It had. He'd been both generous and kind but when I tried to articulate my gratitude he would hear none of it.

'On a cruise there's nothing to complain about,' he said, 'and complaining is part of the fabric of our lives. Not being able to complain leaves a void. But, you see, I don't need to switch off. I come on a cruise because it's a ceaseless round of pleasure and fun. When you get off you go cold turkey for about three months.'

Satisfied he'd made his point, he began again with the life coaching, suggesting I should think outside the box more and try 'to make a few quid'. He wanted to see me do well. Maybe an American magazine would be interested in the story of a cruise on the *QE2* with Jimmy Savile. The truth was, his fame was contained within the borders of the small group of islands that would soon be in view.

He asked whether I'd thought about working in TV – he reckoned I'd be good. 'They' – there was disdain in his tone – 'only want to talk about celebrities.' He said it had always been thus and to prove his point he told a story about getting slung off Michael Parkinson's chat show with Michael Palin. He was 'a giggler', recalled Savile of the Monty Python star. 'Once he starts he can't bleedin' stop.'

Palin and Savile had done their one-on-ones with the host when the third guest, Donald Sinden, came on. 'An awful twat, he was so boring. They all lie,' he said, referring to actors. 'That's what they do.'

Savile recalled pretending to doze off. The audience started laughing, which then set Michael Palin off. 'Parkinson lost it,' he chortled. 'He asked us to leave the set. So we did. We went and sat in the front row with these two birds. Well that was it, the place was in uproar.'

Eventually, Savile and Michael Palin were called back onto the sofa. 'We took these two birds with us.' He remembered Parkinson was seething by this stage. He said the chat show host told them both they would never be invited on his show again.

'You've got to go through the turbulent times,' announced Savile, slamming shut his filing cabinet of celebrity anecdotes and reverting back to the tutorial. 'It's like the flu, you get over it and then one day you'll wake up happy, and then you'll be knacked. Why? You'll be confused.'

I asked him whether he was speaking from experience. Had he ever been confused? 'No, because I was different – always have been.'

I left with the bottle of champagne. 'If you cop for the Lido I'll come in a bit later and do my state visit,' he said. 'It always generates a bit of heat.' He was now repeating himself word for word. I couldn't help but wonder whether he was going senile.

We dined in separate restaurants that evening. I sat on my own in the Caronia restaurant while Savile ate alone in the more upmarket Britannia Grill.

Later, as the sun waned and bathed the English Channel in a glorious mauve, I looked across the room at the elderly couples engaged in conversation and wondered what Jimmy Savile thought about when he glanced up from his food and saw couples that had been married for 50 years and more.

I felt a twinge of sadness about leaving him. There had been chinks of insight, as well as moments of genuine warmth. But I'd also had my fill. I'd already told myself that I would be among the first off this floating waiting room when it docked at Southampton.

After trailing in Savile's wake, listening to him bid passers-by 'Good morning', no matter what time of day it was; wrestling with my discomfort as he continually warned old men about the dangers of being caught with underage girls, in this case their elderly wives; and pontificating about everything from marriage to the death toll in the Western Straits during World War II, I was ready for the firmer footing of normal life.

For Jimmy Savile, normal life meant being collected on the quayside by his driver from Broadmoor Hospital, before being whisked off to the high-security hospital in Berkshire to begin the round of constant touring all over again. Broadmoor, Stoke Mandeville and Leeds General Infirmary were about the only places where he still felt wanted; needed, even. After the weeks at sea it was back to the hospital beds, locked wards and wheelchairs: the captive audiences.

PART SIX

Jimmy Savile opened his eyes to find himself in an unfamiliar room festooned in flowers. There was a long and angry gash in his chest. 'I thought I was lying in a coffin in a chapel of rest,'[1] he said. It was a bed at Killingbeck Hospital in Leeds, 36 hours after he had undergone quadruple heart bypass surgery. Having put if off for 37 years, he'd finally had to take out another insurance policy, one that would turn out to buy him fourteen more.

He was first informed the arteries pumping blood to his heart were closing in 1970, but for nearly four decades refused to do anything about the congenital defect that went on to kill his mother and two of his sisters. He said the experience of working in hospital operating theatres and witnessing the side effects of anaesthetics was the reson he was so reticent. In 1993, when a different cardiologist had informed him that he only had days to live, he'd still not felt moved to act: 'Something inside me told me it wasn't the right time.'

Two things changed his mind. The first was a television programme about a Leeds-based cardiologist, Dr Alistair Hall, who had devised a drug from snake venom that was being used successfully in the treatment of heart conditions. The second was the sudden death of his sister Christina in Malta.

'In the months leading up to that point I had been forced to think about my health problems more and more often,' he explained. 'My stamina was decreasing, and part way through runs or uphill climbs I'd be out of breath and often unable to complete them. I knew something was wrong and my body was letting me know it was getting worse.'

He contacted Hall and arranged a visit to Killingbeck Hospital where he underwent a series of tests. Hall's radical new treatment was not a suitable course of therapy in his case but a relationship nevertheless developed between the two men, and Savile decided to put himself in the young consultant's hands.

He only told one friend, his old cycling pal Dave Dalmour, that he was going into hospital, and even then he didn't say what it was for. They had stopped off en route at one of his favourite cafés for a bacon sandwich washed down with a cigar.

When the time came to be wheeled down to the operating theatre, Jimmy Savile maintained the façade of supreme confidence: cracking jokes with the porters as he went. But the truth was he was scared. He insisted on wearing his Royal Marines Green Beret before the surgery, and instructed Hall to place it back on his head before he woke up.

The operation took three hours, and was conducted by the surgeon Kevin Watterson who was assisted by Hall. After being put under, Savile was wired up to heart and lung machines and his chest was opened along the breastbone using a circular saw. Three incisions were made in his left leg, through which a vein was removed. This vein was then cut into four pieces and stitched onto the arteries at the point of the blockages.

Afterwards, he was taken back to the ward where he was attached to an ECG machine and ventilator. He was not taken to the high dependency unit because it was thought he might disturb the other patients. It proved to be a wise decision. 'The first thing I remember when I came round,' he said, 'was a nurse leaning over me with her ear to my mouth and asking if I was alright,'[2] And Savile's first reaction to discovering that he had made it and was still alive? He reached up and grabbed the nurse's breast. The incident was duly hushed up.

Within five days he started exercising and after six was allowed to go home. He left the hospital in running shorts and cap, waving to the battery of press photographers and film crews waiting outside. Dave Dalmour picked him up in the Rolls-Royce and they stopped off at the same café for a bacon sandwich on the way back to the flat overlooking Roundhay Park. When news broke of his operation, messages from well-wishers had flooded into the hospital. They included personal calls from Prince Charles and Princess Diana.

Being sawn in half, as he liked to describe it, was perhaps the most serious setback of his retirement, but it was by no means the only one. Indeed, Jimmy Savile's twilight years were to be plagued by problems of his own making.

In 1994, three years earlier, two former pupils at Duncroft School had gone to the *Sunday Mirror* with their accounts of being sexually assaulted by the star in the 1970s. Paul Connew, the newspaper's editor at the time, said he believed the women. But he decided not to publish because they both insisted on remaining anonymous and he feared losing a costly defamation case. 'A star-struck jury would have been impressed by Savile's protestations and the fact that we were actually not producing two frightened women in the witness box,'[3] he told a lecture audience in London in the summer of 2013.

'In truth, at the time, post-Maxwell, the *Sunday Mirror* had limited resources [and] we were having to lose staff,' Connew continued. 'We just didn't have the resources or the evidence to mount an investigation. You couldn't [use] a child of the age that Savile was seen to prefer and you couldn't find a journalist who would fit that bill.'

There is no question that Jimmy Savile would have sued. In his dotage, his lawyers were kept increasingly busy firing off letters to those their client saw as launching attacks on his reputation, challenging his control or conspiring to bring about his downfall.

The Christmas after the *Sunday Mirror* had thought better of exposing him, Biddle & Co. send a strongly worded letter to the BBC to explain that their client was seeking 'substantial damages' after Chris Morris announced Jimmy Savile's death on his Radio 1 show. Six months earlier, the satirist had read out a similar spoof obituary for Michael Heseltine.

The publicity surrounding Savile's heart operation stirred the deeply unpleasant memories carried by the woman, now in her early thirties, who he had raped in the television room at Stoke Mandeville when she was 12 years old.

'As I matured I came to know that Savile was a national hero,' she said, 'someone who was held in high esteem by society. And this sickened me. During the summer of 1997, I was going through a low period following the death of my father and I began to dwell on what Savile had done to me. I therefore decided that I wanted to speak out,' she says.

She wrote a letter to Savile's secretary Janet Cope: 'Dear Janet. In 1977 Jimmy Savile raped me.' She included her telephone number, mobile number and address. 'I took the letter by hand to Stoke Mandeville Hospital,' she said, 'and I asked where Savile's office was. I was given the directions and I went to the office. No one was there so I put the letter in what I believed to be his secretary's in-tray. I was very disappointed not to receive a response.'

After a week, the woman decided to try again, writing a second letter identical to the first. Once more, she took the letter by hand to the hospital and left it in an in-tray in Savile's office. 'Again I received no response to the letter,' she reported.

Finally, she decided to send a letter to Savile himself. The letter started with the words, 'You raped me in 1977', and again she provided her name, telephone number and home address. This time, the woman chose a framed picture of a dog and a cat and pushed the letter into the back of the frame. She then wrapped it up to make it look like a present, and took it to the same office. 'On this occasion,' she recalled, 'there was a lady sitting in the office when I arrived. I told her I had a present for Savile and she told me to put it on a filing cabinet that was situated next to a fax machine.'

There was no response. 'I feel very let down by Janet Rowe [who had remarried by this time and become Janet Cope],' said the woman. 'I felt sure she, as his secretary, would have read my letters.' (In 2012, the woman maintains she Googled the name Janet Rowe and saw a photograph of Savile's secretary: 'This was indeed the woman I spoke to on the third occasion that I visited his office at Stoke Mandeville Hospital.')

Janet Cope confirmed to me that she answered all mail addressed to Jimmy Savile at Stoke Mandeville Hospital. She said there were 'a lot of crank letters but we just chucked them in the bin'. Most were begging letters, she insisted, and she maintained that she never saw anything sinister or that gave her cause for concern.

When I repeated the allegation made by the woman who says she was raped as a 12-year-old, and asked whether Cope had any recollection of such a letter, she replied, 'No, none whatsoever.' I then asked her whether if she had, she would have dismissed it as a crank letter. 'I can't even imagine what I would do . . . in that position,' Cope replied. 'Instinct would be to tear it up and chuck it away because it was a crank. But I never received anything like that, ever.'

Cope refuses to believe that Jimmy Savile was guilty of the hundreds of allegations made against him, even though she was forced to write a letter of her own, this one containing a grovelling apology to the man she had idolised and served so loyally. In 1999, Jimmy Savile had instructed Biddle & Co., his firm of solicitors, to seek damages from his former secretary following an interview she had given to a national newspaper in which she'd expressed her dismay and deep sadness at being unceremoniously sacked after 28 years of loyal service.[4]

Since first meeting Savile at Stoke Mandeville in 1971, Cope had come to regard herself as a cross between surrogate mother and wife. As well as dealing with all his correspondence, which increased dramatically during the campaign to build the National Spinal Injuries Centre, she made herself available on the phone to him every day. She'd cleaned his quarters at the hospital, done his laundry and regularly invited him to her home for his favourite meal of minced beef and mashed potatoes. He rarely thanked her for these acts of quiet generosity, but she put up with his thoughtlessness all the same. She liked to joke that with them, it was a case of 'till death do us part'.

Speaking to the newspaper reporter in her fastidiously neat bungalow, Cope recalled how Jimmy Savile had become 'the man in her life' after her first husband died of cancer. When she married for a second time in 1990, Savile had given her away and even paid for the reception. But then quite suddenly, in early 1999, he terminated the relationship in the most callous manner.

Cope had retired from the NHS two years earlier and been made a member of staff on the Jimmy Savile Stoke Mandeville Hospital Trust. 'He was having a lunch meeting with consultants and a new trustee,' she said of the day she found out her services were no longer required. 'The connecting door to his room was open. I'd taken in some sandwiches and sat on the sofa. Jimmy put his feet up on the desk and declared, 'I'm going to take it easy now. I'm letting these new people take over.' Then, motioning at Cope, Savile had said, 'And she's out.'

Other than for taking the uncharacteristic step of standing up to him over his decision to sack two maintenance men, Cope claimed to have no understanding of why he had suddenly cut her adrift. She said that she never saw him again. She heard from his solicitors though, who called seeking a full retraction and apology for what their client considered to be 'false and damaging allegations'.

Mavis Price from Leeds General Infirmary, the wife of the consultant cardiologist who first diagnosed Jimmy Savile's heart problems, subsequently took over the day-to-day administration of his life.

Just over two weeks after Jimmy Savile emerged from his heart operation, Princess Diana was killed in a car crash in Paris. He was invited to the funeral service at Westminster Abbey but was too weak to attend.

In our final interview, I asked Savile again about his relationships with the royals. 'What you've got to realise is how many books have been written about them by people who don't really know them,' he said. 'Paul Burrell and people like that.' I put it to him that having worked as Diana's butler for ten years, Burrell must have surely known her better than most.

'Yes, he did,' said Savile, suddenly changing his tune. 'I helped him get out of his court case.' In 2002, Burrell was charged with the theft of items belonging to the Princess of Wales but the trial collapsed when it emerged the Queen had spoken to him and a public interest immunity certificate was presented to the court. 'That was something else,' smiled Savile, leaning back in his chair, eyes tightly closed as if mentally picturing the next brick being laid on the wall.

'Nobody could get him off the hook. The entire world had him on the hook. He fell out with [Diana's] trustees . . . Paul was very upset about this and because he was so upset, he was a danger, you see. So they invented this thing that he'd half-inched some of her gear, which he hadn't.' (In April 2014, Janet Cope showed me a 1998 letter from Paul Burrell in which Diana's former butler said how much he was looking forward to 'spending some quality time with Jimmy. I need some sound and wise advice from him as he always knows the right answer.')

Savile pointed to my tape recorder and told me to turn it off. It was the only time in all our meetings that he requested me to do this. He then proceeded to explain how he'd collected all the soft toys that had been left by mourners at the gates of Kensington Palace. He'd taken them away and had them laundered. He said they were now in bags at his lock-up at Stoke Mandeville Hospital. It's a story that Janet Cope insists was exaggerated.

He then went on to tell me a little about the time in 1999 when Prince Charles came for lunch at the three-bedroomed cottage he'd recently bought near Glencoe. Savile said he first clapped eyes on the building when he'd cycled through the Highland glen during World War II. More than half a century later, he bought it, paying the previous owner, the celebrated mountaineer Hamish MacInnes, £125,000 for the privilege.

When Savile learned the Prince of Wales was to visit the area and present a minibus to a mountain rescue team, he issued his invitation. His friend, Julie Ferguson, was asked to source local salmon, lamb and a bottle of Laphroaig whisky, which he knew the prince liked.

Special Branch arrived ahead of the prince to conduct a sweep of the building, before Jimmy Savile greeted his special guest. He was wearing a kilt of Lochaber tartan, a green military-style shirt and his Royal Marines Green Beret. Ferguson and two friends acted as waitresses, each in monogrammed aprons bearing the letters 'H', 'R' and 'H' respectively – a special touch Savile was especially pleased with. They served Savile and his guest the lamb and the salmon, which, Ferguson later revealed, had been obtained from a local poacher.

Savile paused for a moment to dig out a photograph of him and Prince Charles in the local post office, a photo opportunity that a royal aide confirms Savile orchestrated. 'He'd never been in a post office in his life so I took him to where I drew my pension,' Savile chuckled. '[Charles] said, "Does this happen very often?" And I said, "Yeah, every week."'

I asked him whether it was true that he had been a mentor to Charles, as his first wife had once said. 'Yes,' he replied. 'But the new mentor has taken over now, you see: Camilla. I'm quite pleased not to be the mentor and I'm quite happy to be a friend because it's less restricting.'

Did he see anything of Prince William and Prince Harry? 'No,' said Savile. 'They know me and know of me, and they know that I occupy a very strange place in the life of their mother and the life of their father. And what they can't work out is why I'm so different. I don't bother with them, I keep my distance, but they know if push comes to shove that I could be as useful to them as I was to their mum and to their dad.'

So it was just as Louis Mountbatten had said: 'If there's a problem, Jim can fix it'? 'Yes, yes,' he replied.

What he could not seem to fix, however, were the persistent rumours that continued to dog every interview and now threatened to eclipse the standing he had acquired as a philanthropist, businessman and friend to the nation.

In late 1999, filming began on a one-off documentary which followed the filmmaker and journalist Louis Theroux as he attempted to prise off Jimmy Savile's famously protective outer shield and get to the real man underneath. Theroux is celebrated for his ability to get his subjects to reveal themselves, but with Savile, who he visited in Leeds, Glencoe and Broadmoor (although the footage from the latter did not make it into the final edit), he found it impossible to get his quarry to admit to anything beyond his inherent oddness.

When Louis Met Jimmy went out on the evening of 13 April 2000 and became an instant talking point for everyone who saw it. It has been voted one of the 50 best British documentaries of all time, chiefly because of the memorable way it depicts what Anthony Clare had discovered nine years earlier: namely that Jimmy Savile took pride in making it impossible to see beyond the towering walls of his self-constructed mythology.

'We can talk about anything,' proclaimed Savile at the outset. 'You'll find out how tricky I am.' The duelling with Theroux was an exercise in control, and one that he seemed to relish. But as the filmmaker fought against the fast-running tide of Savile's word-for-word repetition of stories he had told thousands of times to thousands of different people, what emerged was a picture of a man who simply refused to open up for anyone.

'I was always aware he was someone with secrets and I think he enjoyed having those secrets,' Theroux told me. 'I think he enjoyed being perceived as someone with secrets. He wanted it known that he had secrets because he knew that intrigued people. He was constantly dropping dark hints that there was more to him than you knew.'

Theroux recalled one evening they spent together in Leeds which was not recorded for posterity. 'I was trying to get that little morsel of something that might lead me to some greater under-standing,' he said. 'As a conversational opener I asked him whether he had been following the Myra Hindley story. I think she was dying of cancer at the time. He just said, "I am the Myra Hindley story." And he left it at that. I didn't even want to gratify that with a follow-up question because I knew he would just shut it down. But it was a typical Jimmy-ism where, I now think, he was suggesting that he either knew her better than anyone or that he embodied the darker impulses that she had acted out.'

In the face of Theroux's dogged refusal to give up, Savile at one point hissed, 'You can make it as negative as you like. See you in court. I'll take a few quid off you the same as I'll take a few quid off anybody.'

Towards the end of the documentary, as they drove back from Scotland to Leeds, Theroux asked Savile about the rumours he had sex with underage girls, and pressed him on why he insisted he hated children. 'We live in a very funny world,' he reasoned, 'and it's easier for me as a single man to say, "I don't like children" because that puts a lot of salacious tabloid people off the hunt.'

Theroux responded by asking him whether this was a form of self-defence against accusations that he was a paedophile.

'How do they know if I am or not?' Savile shot back. 'How does anybody know whether I am?' He stated again this was his policy, nothing was going to change it, and that 'it worked like a dream'.

After the film came out, Savile tried to laugh it off, describing it as 'an exposé with nothing to expose'.[5] While privately he might have been thrilled at having won the duel with his interrogator, he cannot fail to have been concerned about the light the film had shown him in.

For now, despite his royal connections and continued fund-raising activities – as patron of the Leeds Institute for Minimally Invasive Technology; supporting a DNA library to explore genetic links to heart disease; backing a Centre for Adolescent Rehabilitation run by an old contact from the Royal Marines; giving £40,000 to fund research into MRSA at Hope Hospital, Manchester – it was the background noise of speculation and gossip that seemed to concern those who still deemed Jimmy Savile worthy of press coverage. And the documentary had done nothing to silence the whispers.

His rebuttals continued in a similar vein, although he occasionally came up with new ways to deflect the accusations. 'A girl said to me last year, "You take chances – newspapers would love to know about this",'[6] he told one reporter about a tryst in his van. 'I told [the girl] I'd be considered the luckiest bloke in the world to pull a darling bird like her, but she'd be the one explaining what she was doing with an old geezer. She said, "No wonder no one's written about you. You clever bastard!"' It was stock Savile: flirting with the truth enough to make his story sound plausible and yet still managing to turn it into a testament to his enduring potency and brilliance.

When asked what type of girl he went for, he replied: 'It could be a gymnast or a girl of 18 or 19 I run with who's got a terrific working body, and if it's got nice running shorts on, that's even more tasty.' He was approaching his 75th birthday by this time, and still referring to a woman as 'it'.

In old age, Savile came across as an increasingly paranoid figure; one who appeared to be acutely aware of the prospects of his world crashing down around him. When it came to discussing one of his favourite subjects – money – he highlighted the financial provisions he had made for such an eventuality: savings in the form of income-paying policies rather than cash. Less cash meant less chance of being extorted,[7] and as we shall see, the threat of blackmail was a very real one in his twilight years, particularly as those he had abused as children grew up and confronted what he had done to them.

As the clouds gathered ahead of the catastrophic weather system that would sweep away everything he had built, the denials continued to pour out of his mouth. 'I couldn't tolerate the idea of being thought a paedophile, because it is sickening to me,' he said on one occasion. 'But as a single fella you can be anything to anyone, so they could stick you with it. If they haven't written about it, it's because I'm patently not one . . . If I saw a little kid looking at a lovely big boat in a toy shop window, once I might have gone in and bought it for him, but I'd never do that now. If I saw a friend's child in a terrible storm, I would drive past rather than give them a lift. And if I was seen too much in schools, for example, it might be a bit strange, and they'd be right to tag you.'[8]

His protestations were now beginning to start from a position of guilt and work backwards towards an alibi; he said he didn't have a computer in any of his homes because he might be suspected of downloading pornography. 'I prefer to stamp out the smouldering before the flames start,' he said. In other interviews, he again trotted out the line about how boring he was: 'I don't do drugs, booze or underage sex . . . People get the wrong idea because people have had the wrong idea forever.'

He was so well acquainted with the accusations that he was issuing his denials before they had even been made. He was also making threats, as a reporter on the *Bucks Free Herald* newspaper found out in 2000 on being summoned to Savile's office at Stoke Mandeville following the death of a local man who was known to the hospital's most famous volunteer. Savile had heard the man had died after being mugged in the street, and was raging when the journalist arrived.[9]

'I want you to tell me what happened with [name of the dead man]. If you hear that someone has done this then I want you to tell me who straight away. I want to know names and I can have them waking up in hospital with every bone in their body broken. All I have to do is call my friends in the IRA. They'll have someone waking up in hospital the next morning eating their breakfast through a f***ing straw.

'I know the IRA, men from the IRA, and you don't need to ask these guys twice,' he spat. 'I'm serious. Don't f***ing think I'm not serious. I can get them done – just with a phone call. That's all it takes, young man. If someone has done this to [man's name] that makes them my enemy. And you don't want to be my enemy.'

As his fame and currency diminished, Jimmy Savile gradually retreated into a lonely netherworld of conjecture and ridicule; a fading figure with no place in, nor love for, the modern world and onto which a nation could project its mockery and fears. In July 2004, the *Radio Times* voted him 'Britain's Greatest TV Oddball'. Also on the list was Stuart Hall.

A year later, Savile was offered a now rare payday, this time as 'the face' of Velcro. He was a curious choice as brand ambassador given nothing had ever stuck to him. In January 2006, he picked up a six-figure cheque for making a cameo appearance on *Celebrity Big Brother*, emerging as a surprise fairy godfather to housemates that included Jodie Marsh, Pete Burns, Chantelle Houghton, George Galloway and Michael Barrymore.

'When he went into the *Big Brother* house it was striking to see him in a context where he was around people who were bigger or more famous than he was,' said Louis Theroux. 'In an odd way, he was actually quite shy. Because he was a control freak you could see that sometimes he was a bit vulnerable and at sea in situations where there were more important people around than him.'

After his brief stint in the house, Savile came out publicly in support of Barrymore, the comedian whose career had nosedived after a partygoer had been discovered dead in his swimming pool. 'He's a lad who is OK, a very pleasant guy,' Savile said. 'But he got into choppy water and that can destroy people's confidence. He's on tenterhooks as he doesn't know if anyone's going to have a go at him.'[10] He knew how Barrymore felt. Unlike the hapless comedian and game show host, though, Jimmy Savile had refused to stay even one night in the *Big Brother* house. Why? His mortal fear of being 'banged up'.

In June 2006, it was announced that *Top of the Pops* was to be axed. As host of the very first show in 1964, Jimmy Savile was invited back to co-present the last. In breaks between filming, the report on Operation Yewtree stated, he sexually assaulted a member of the studio audience, a teenage girl. It was the last allegation recorded against him.

He was fast approaching his 80th birthday, a milestone that was marked by Prince Charles with a gift of a box of Cuban cigars and a pair of Asprey cufflinks bearing his fleur-de-lys crest. On the card, the heir to the throne wrote, 'Nobody will ever know what you have done for this country Jimmy. This is to go some way in thanking you for that.'[11]

*C*elebrity Big Brother turned out to be a bad move for Jimmy Savile. His appearances over two days and the resulting coverage in the newspapers were enough to provoke one woman in her early forties to act on the memories of her time at Duncroft Approved School in the late 1970s. They were memories she had been turning over in her head for some time.

'It's really sad that someone can work all their life for charity and everyone's like, "He's such a wonderful person", and there's silly old [me] sitting at home and she knows he's not a wonderful person,'[1] she said of her decision to pick up the phone and contact Childline. 'He does paedo stuff under the guise of charity, it's almost like he's above the law, untouchable.'

On getting through to the child protection charity, the woman told the voice at the other end of the line that she had witnessed Jimmy Savile indecently assaulting a fellow Duncroft resident who she believed was 14 at the time. She was advised to contact the authorities, so she telephoned Dorset Police on 11 May 2007 to recount the same story about the star of *Jim'll Fix It* and *Top of the Pops* sitting among the girls in the television room one evening, grabbing the hand of her friend and forcing it down onto his crotch.

The matter was duly reported to Surrey Police, the force covering the area for Duncroft, and on 13 May 2007, a female Detective Constable on the Surrey Public Protection Investigation Unit contacted the woman. The policewoman was informed by the woman that her friend had previously told her about Jimmy Savile's advances, and they had agreed a code word that would be

used if he did it again. At the time, there was a television advertisement for Vesta Curry containing the catchphrase 'Oooh, beef
biryani'. They settled on this as the signal because it was a running
joke among the girls and it would not attract attention. When she
heard her friend suddenly say, 'Oooh, beef biryani' on the evening
in question, she looked over to see Jimmy Savile take her hand.
'He was squeezing it,' the woman said, 'so then she would have
been squeezing his testicles and his penis.'[2]

The woman also said she had heard things from other girls and
witnessed the arrival of large boxes of chocolates for Savile's
favourites. She explained that Duncroft's staff had a high regard
for their famous visitor.

The Surrey Police investigation was codenamed 'Operation
Ornament', and four days later contact was made with the head
office of Dr Barnado's, the organisation that ran Duncroft when
the incident was alleged to have taken place. Surrey Police wanted
to find out whether the charitable organisation knew of any other
allegations and which other girls had been in residence between
1977 and 1979.

On 21 May, the Detective Constable and a female colleague
from Surrey Police visited the woman who made the original
complaint at her home. Four pages of written notes were taken.

A period of nearly five months elapsed before an address was
found for the woman it was claimed had been assaulted. When a
letter was finally sent to her, it explained Surrey Police were investigating 'allegations of a historic nature that have [sic] alleged to
have taken place at Duncroft Children's Home in Staines in the
1970s'[3] It requested that she get in touch. No reply was forthcoming. In fact the victim was furious that her erstwhile friend
had started a process she wanted no part of.

On 16 November 2007, the same female DC paid a 'cold call'
on the woman's house. There was nobody in so she left a card. A
few hours later, the woman called. Since receiving the letter, she
explained, she had been thinking it over. She then asked whether
the investigation concerned a well-known person. When the police

officer asked whom she had in mind, the woman replied: 'Jimmy Savile.'

An account of the incident was taken down over the phone in which the woman said he had taken her hand and moved it onto his groin and manipulated it until he got an erection. He had also invited her to go for a ride in his car. Two days later, she said, a box of chocolates arrived for her at Duncroft. She thought the incident must have taken place in 1978, when she was either 14 or 15.

She claimed not to remember the girl who had made the complaint, and had not been in touch with her since leaving Duncroft. She also insisted she did not want to make a statement and was angry at being named.[4] Four months later, she was still asserting that she did not want to be involved if the investigation was 'just in relation to her.'[5]

The corroboration of the original witness's account, however, prompted a review of the investigation. As Surrey Police describe it, there was an 'early recognition of the sensitivity surrounding the persons involved and the need for information security to prevent "leaks" to the media and subsequent compromise to the investigation and credibility of witnesses'.[6] On 18 December 2007, Jimmy Savile was registered as a suspect on the Surrey Police computer system and linked to the investigation.[7]

A little over a month later, West Yorkshire Police unveiled their campaign to fight crime in the Hyde Park, Headingley and Woodhouse areas of Leeds. Talking signs were attached to lamp-posts from which the voice of Jimmy Savile warned students about the risks of not keeping property securely locked up. 'We had the idea of using a well-known voice,' explained Chief Inspector Mark Busley, 'and Jimmy Savile was asked because he is a well-known Leeds person.'[8]

Jimmy Savile was indeed a 'well-known Leeds person', particularly with the West Yorkshire Police. Four serving and retired officers were regulars at the weekly 'Friday Morning Club' meetings he held in his flat.[9]

The signs were still in use in the student areas of Leeds four months later, when an email was sent from the anti-corruption team at Surrey Police to their counterparts in West Yorkshire, informing them that they were investigating Jimmy Savile and to request any intelligence relating to him. It was now almost a year since Operation Ornament had been launched.

The reason for using this back channel, it has been claimed, was the senior investigating officer's concern that the investigation remained confidential. A week later, Surrey received an intelligence report, the only one West Yorkshire Police claimed to hold on Jimmy Savile. It related to an incident when a female student had jokingly stolen his pink-lensed spectacles one night at the Queens Hotel. It was an incident that Savile made hay from in the newspapers.

Back in Surrey, the task of tracing the other Duncroft girls identified by Barnado's took over a year. But before they were contacted, there was a significant development. Another woman, Jill from Worthing, had reported a separate indecent assault by Jimmy Savile dating back to July 1970. Jill told officers from Sussex Police how she had been collected by his chauffeur and taken in his Rolls-Royce to Worthing where Savile's motor caravan was parked. After inviting her inside, he pushed her down onto a bed, grabbed her hand and thrust it onto his groin.

Jill emigrated not long after the incident. But on moving back to Britain with her husband, she had grown increasingly agitated by the sight of Jimmy Savile on television and in the media.

In 2007, and by now divorced, she decided to write a letter to the *Sun*. In November that year, as Surrey Police began widening the remit of Operation Ornament, a reporter from the newspaper arrived to interview her, explaining that 'a lot of others'[10] had not been so lucky and managed to escape as she did. Jill was advised that if she were to make a complaint to the police, others would follow; however she decided she was not willing to go through with it.

A little less than four months later, in March of 2008, the same female reporter returned. Jill was told that the paper now had new information that Jimmy Savile may have been connected to the disgraced Haut de la Garenne children's home in Jersey. But unless she was willing to report her allegation to the police there was little that could be done. She was convinced this time and rang Sussex Police to tell them what Jimmy Savile had done to her 38 years earlier.

Jill was visited that evening by a detective sergeant and a detective constable who explained what they would need in order to 'pursue an allegation':[11] she would have to contact her ex-husband, who she had told of the incident at the time, as well as her former workmates, who had laughed when she informed them what had happened in Jimmy Savile's motor caravan parked in broad daylight near Worthing Town Hall. The police officers added that the complaint would need to be corroborated, and warned that while they believed her story, few others would. They also said Jimmy Savile would have expensive lawyers who would make 'mincemeat' of her.[12]

The day afterwards, Jill, who was approaching 60 at the time, texted the reporter from the *Sun* to tell her she was unwilling to cooperate with a police investigation. She duly contacted the Sussex Police officers to tell them she had decided against making a formal complaint, insisting she wanted to 'let sleeping dogs lie'.[13] The bottom line was that she was not prepared to be the sole supporter of a possible prosecution.

In early April, Sussex Police learned of what Surrey Police were doing after having made a confidential request for intelligence that might impact on their investigation into Jimmy Savile through the Impact Nominal Index (INI) computer database. Officers from the two forces spoke and swapped notes on the fact that the victim in each case did not wish to proceed.

Nine days later, an entry on the Sussex Police crime report confirmed that a prosecution was unlikely: 'The checks conducted have been time consuming and taking [sic] me away from other priority cases in the CID office,' wrote one of the officers. 'With a clearly reluctant witness and difficulties corroborating her claims from other sources I feel these papers should be filed.'[14] The matter was not referred to the Crown Prosecution Service, although a copy of the crime report was faxed to Surrey Police.

At a review meeting in North Surrey, the deputy senior investigating officer concluded that the *modus operandi* of the incident in Sussex, allied to the fact that the accounts of both informant and victim in the Duncroft case were sufficiently similar, amounted to 'further corroboration'.

On 19 May, one of the former Duncroft girls identified from the Barnardo's list responded to the letter sent by the Detective Constable from Surrey Police. She did not claim to be a victim but asked whether the person being investigated was Jimmy Savile. A day later, the same woman phoned back to reveal that another woman, who was not at Duncroft, had been indecently assaulted by Jimmy Savile at Stoke Mandeville Hospital in the early 1970s. It was now also known that the incidents were being discussed openly on the Duncroft area of the Friends Reunited website.

The DC contacted the woman in question and was told what had happened to her during a visit to Stoke Mandeville Hospital in or around 1973. On that occasion, Jimmy Savile had been larking about, climbing up a flagpole in the hospital's grounds. As she left, he asked her for a kiss but rather than a friendly peck on the cheek he instead forced his tongue into her mouth. The girl was 14 at the time. She agreed to provide a written statement but also stated she was not interested in taking the matter further.

A further meeting was called at Walton police station in which advice was taken from the senior investigating officer on Operation Arundel, the investigation by Surrey Police into historic sexual abuse that stemmed from the successful prosecution of Jonathan King, Jimmy Savile's friend from Decca Records and his colleague on *Top of the Pops*. Caution was urged; there must be no allegations of 'trawling' for witnesses or victims.

Initially, only those former Duncroft girls identified from the list by the witness and victim of the alleged assault would be contacted, and even then they would be provided with limited information so there could be no claim they had been prompted. This decision was soon overturned when it became apparent that more former Duncroft residents should be sought out to ensure no witnesses were missed.

It was also resolved that a meeting should be held with a lawyer from the Crown Prosecution Service in light of the fact the first victim did not want to make an allegation. The deputy senior investigating officer then decided that at this stage statements should not be taken from anyone other than the two victims: the girl from the television room at Duncroft and the girl assaulted at Stoke Mandeville. Crucially, neither was to be told that other victims had come forward.

Eight days later, the senior officer in the North Surrey Child Protection team based at Walton police station and the detective chief inspector met with senior staff at Surrey Children's Services to 'agree a plan on safeguarding and information security'.[15]

Nearly seven months on from her first conversation with the police, the woman who was assaulted in the television room at Duncroft was still refusing to give a tape-recorded account of what had happened. She did, however, consent to the female DC taking notes. The jottings included such phrases as 'Everyone was all over him. Girls got excited. Staff thought he was God. Not supervised' and 'Teenage girls. Thought funny. Seen on TV "dirty old pervert".'[16] The women reiterated that she wanted nothing more to do with the investigation as her family was going through a difficult period.

A few days later, on 9 June, Surrey Police put the file onto the computerised police system for dealing with major crimes.

Fourteen of the twenty-three women identified by Surrey Police as being at Duncroft at the time the incident took place were spoken to, plus the Stoke Mandeville victim. The same DC conducted a two-hour recorded conversation with the witness who first reported the assault at Duncroft, explaining that hers was the only complaint. In fact, she was fully aware of two further incidents by this stage.[17]

In a meeting on 15 July between the senior investigating officer, his deputy and the reviewing lawyer from the Crown Prosecution Service, the lawyer's advice was recorded as follows: 'There was no case to proceed as the incidents were relatively minor and they were so long ago there would be grounds for an abuse of process argument.'[18]

But within 24 hours, the scope of the investigation widened still further when another former Duncroft girl, one who had left in September 1977, made contact with Surrey Police. She would go on to give a recorded account in which she recalled how Jimmy Savile would visit the school and ask the girls to comb his hair and massage his neck. On one occasion Margaret Jones, Duncroft's principal, instructed her to take Savile to Norman Lodge, the pre-release hostel on the grounds that housed a small number of girls aged between 16 and 18. She was told to make him tea.

According to the woman, Jimmy Savile knew that she wanted to become a nurse when she left Duncroft. 'He then shocked me by suggesting that if I performed a certain act on him he could guarantee a job when I qualified at Stoke Mandeville.'[19] He assured her that a blowjob wouldn't be a problem as he could simply slip down his tracksuit bottoms.

Her response, she said, was to make an excuse and hide in the lavatories until he had gone. It landed her in trouble. While her claim did not technically constitute an offence, as she was over 16 at the time and no contact was initiated, she was adamant that the interviewing officer did not ask whether she was prepared to give evidence if Jimmy Savile was prosecuted, although the police officer's recollection is different.[20]

By mid August, a meeting of senior Surrey officers had settled on an eight-point rationale for why Jimmy Savile should be interviewed, whatever the final outcome from the CPS. Shortly afterwards, the Detective Constable was instructed to prepare a report for the Crown Prosecution Service. The file, on which its advice would be given, was to be delivered personally to the reviewing lawyer.

It marked the end of the most intensive period of the investigation, although the 15 months it had taken to get to this point certainly seem to have contributed to the crucial discrepancies that appeared in the file that was handed to the lawyer on 22 January 2009. At that meeting, the CPS lawyer advised the female police officer to read copies of Jimmy Savile's books to see if any mention was made of charities or children's homes. She did, but clearly failed to notice the reference on page 150 of *As It Happens* to Princess Alexandra and her patronage of a 'hostel for girls in care'. It was an establishment in which Jimmy Savile described himself as a 'cross between a term-time boyfriend and a fixer of special trips out'.

In late March 2009, the same Surrey Detective Constable met with the senior crown prosecutor and was advised that no further action should be taken. The lawyer then recommended that a senior officer should meet with Jimmy Savile to apprise him of the details of the allegations and the subsequent investigations.

A little over two months passed before the senior officer in the North Surrey Child Protection team sent a letter to Savile via recorded delivery. It was a request for him to make contact.

Savile telephoned the very next day whereupon he was informed of the allegations that had been made against him. His response was not one of shock or horror. Instead, he coolly explained that he had a 'West Yorkshire Inspector who usually deals with this sort of thing'.[1] A loose arrangement was made for a meeting with Surrey Police officers the next time he visited either Stoke Mandeville or Broadmoor.

Five days passed, and then a call came through to the Surrey Police control room. It was from a West Yorkshire Police Inspector, who stated he was the Force Incident Manager based in the control room at a police station in Leeds. He explained that Jimmy Savile was a personal friend and that he had lost the letter from the senior officer at Walton police station.

Not only did the Inspector pass on his friend's phone number, he also offered up a key detail to the officer in the Surrey Police control room, namely that Jimmy Savile got 'so many of these types of complaints'.[2]

The call was unusual to say the least: a senior officer from one force helping to arrange a meeting with detectives from another on behalf of a friend who was to be questioned over serious allegations of indecent assault. After taking the call, the officer in the Surrey control room contacted the senior investigating officer on the case to relay what the West Yorkshire Police Inspector had said.

Two days later, that senior investigating officer sent an email to the head of Child Protection at West Yorkshire Police. In addition to intelligence reports on the progress of the investigation that had been promised in an earlier communication, reference was made to the unusual call from the WYP Inspector. Clearly, the officer's mention of his friend being regularly subjected to such serious allegations had registered with those in Surrey. 'There may be nothing in this,' wrote the Surrey Police detective in the email to the Detective Chief Inspector at West Yorkshire, 'but if there have been other allegations against [Savile] then they should really be recorded to build up an intelligence picture.'[3]

The reply from West Yorkshire stated that the Detective Chief Inspector had brought the matter to the attention of the Inspector's head of department. West Yorkshire Police later claimed the Inspector was 'given words of advice regarding his contact with Surrey in line with existing force policy'.[4] WYP also relayed to Surrey that its Head of Crime had been notified of the investigation into Jimmy Savile so that the command team could be briefed.

The intelligence report detailing the Surrey Police investigation was sent and duly uploaded by West Yorkshire Police to its computerised intelligence system. It was recorded in such a way that access was restricted, meaning that it was not shared across departments. According to the West Yorkshire Police, the decision was made by a supervisor within the Force Intelligence Unit 'in line with correct procedures to ensure the Surrey investigation was not compromised'.[5]

It was almost a year late. The Surrey Police Senior Investigating Officer had first spoken to the acting head of the Child Protection Unit at West Yorkshire Police in July 2008 when it had been agreed the intelligence report containing the allegations against Savile would be sent to the WYP. Yet according to the WYP, there was no trace of the information on its files. The trainee detective chief inspector who was acting head of the Child Protection Unit at the time, recalled the telephone conversation but 'could not recollect the information being sent by Surrey Police'. This is odd given it concerned one of the best known men in Leeds.[6] Stranger still, West Yorkshire Police have found no reason to question why no attempt was made to chase it up.

When a further telephone conversation between Surrey Police and Jimmy Savile failed to fix a time and a place for the interview, and nothing more was heard from him for nearly three months, the Detective Constable from Surrey eventually decided to follow up with a second letter. It was sent on 24 September, and telephone arrangements were finally made for Jimmy Savile to be interviewed under caution at Stoke Mandeville Hospital.

Savile's delaying tactics and use of an intermediary from his home police force had worked because the interview would take place on 'home turf': his private office at a facility he had built amid huge public fanfare, rather than an interview room in a police station. Savile had set the parameters for the interview before it had even begun. Or as the March 2013 report by Her Majesty's Inspectorate of Constabulary put it, 'The way in which the interview was arranged was Savile-led, rather than police led.'[7] The interview took place on 1 October 2009 and lasted for precisely 56 minutes. Joining Savile in his private office were the two female officers from Surrey police who had worked on the case as well as an unnamed trustee of the Jimmy Savile Stoke Mandeville Charitable Trust who he had asked to attend. As Surrey Police have reported, 'It is not clear in what capacity this male was present as there is no indication that Savile required an appropriate adult and he was not acting as a legal representative.'[8]

It has subsequently been established that other trustees knew about the interview but the hospital authorities were not informed.[9]

From the outset, Savile, who identified himself as James Wilson Savile (missing out Vincent, one of the middle names that appears on his birth certificate) was in belligerent mood, very possibly encouraged by the deferential approach adopted by the police officers who first asked whether it was OK for them to call him 'Jimmy', and then thanked him for his kindness in seeing them.

Savile confirmed his date of birth and began his denials before a proper question had been asked: 'That makes me 83,' he stated, 'and proud that in 83 years I've never, ever done anything wrong . . . That doesn't mean to say that in my business you don't get accused of just about everything because people are looking for a bit of blackmail or the papers are looking for a story . . . but if you gotta clear conscience, which I have, everything's okay.'[10]

The response? 'Lovely, thank you.' The tone was set.

When the police officers explained to the unnamed man that the purpose of him being there was to advise Savile, to observe whether or not the interview was being conducted fairly and to facilitate communication, he replied: 'I understand and if Jim wanted my opinion I would say not to answer any questions without first speaking to a solicitor, but that's entirely up to him of course.' It was the only thing he did say.

'I'm quite happy to answer questions, because if you've done nothing wrong then you're ok,' Savile added. 'If somebody alleges you've done something . . . I've had so much of it in 50 years, it started in the 1950s and it's always either someone looking for a few quid, or a story for the paper.'

It was explained to him that this was an out of custody interview and the mandatory caution was read out to remind him he did not have to say anything but it may harm his defence if he did not mention when questioned something which he later relied on in court. The same officer then proceeded to recount the three main allegations, two made by women who were residents at Duncroft School in the late 1970s and one from Stoke Mandeville. As she did so, Savile repeatedly barked, 'Out of the question'.

When the policewoman had finished, Savile offered his own recollections of Duncroft, which he described as a 'posh borstal'. The passage pertaining to how he came to be at the school in the first place has been redacted by Surrey Police, although it now seems clear, through an information officer's inadvertent admission, that the interview transcript was sent to Buckingham Palace for approval, and that the blacked out passage in question makes reference to Princess Alexandra, the Queen's cousin and a visitor to Duncroft.[10]

Savile was asked about his charity work, which he described as being done at some personal cost: 'You can see the friendly way that I am,' he said, 'and all of a sudden somebody turns round and bites your leg, and it's the same at Leeds Infirmary, it's the same here [Stoke Mandeville].'

Suddenly, and without prompting, he changed tack. 'When you're doing *Top of the Pops* and Radio One, what you don't do, is assault women,' he said. 'They assault you, that's for sure, and you don't have to because you've got plenty of girls about.'

Jimmy Savile had taken charge of proceedings, regaling his interrogators with tales of his charity and television work; rolling out the same old stories in exactly the words he'd used in countless newspaper and television interviews over the decades. 'I take this sort of thing very, very seriously,' he warned them at one point, and referenced 'his policy'. It was something he promised to come back to later.

Thirty-plus years on, his recall of Duncroft was impressive, although he denied ever being in a common room with a television in it, going as far as to say that he never even saw a television at the school. He also denied ever having a 'one to one' with either a girl or member of staff. 'No, never,' he said. 'You never do that in lock-ups . . . for fifty years I've had a set of keys at Broadmoor, but I never forget the rules, never forget the rules. You can if you want but you finish up dead.'

When the Surrey Police officers moved on to the first allegation – the report that in the TV room at Duncroft he had taken a girl's hand and placed it on his crotch – Savile replied: 'I can specifically say that that's not my nature and it never happened and it is a fabrication. Why on earth anybody would want a fabrication I don't know, probably cos it's coming up for Christmas and they're looking for a few quid off a newspaper.'

When he was then told what the woman had said, Savile scoffed: 'It's starting to sound like the Mad Hatter's tea party, this.'

The blunt denials continued on through the perfunctory questioning over the second allegation of his offending at Duncroft: 'Out of the question,' he snapped. 'No, not at all.' 'Never, never, never.'

One of his more revealing answers came from a question he was asked about how old he remembered the girls being at Duncroft. He answered with a question: 'How old is a girl when she gets nicked, and finished up in court, and finished up with a custodial sentence? It would be sixteen, nineteen . . . so you didn't really bother whether they were sixteen, what the hell they were, because they all seemed like adults, and they all acted liked adults.'

'So did you ever ask any girl at Duncroft to perform a sexual act?' asked the police officer.

'Never.'

'Did you specifically go to Duncroft knowing it was an all girls place to receive sexual gratification?'

'No, out of the question. That is a complete flight of fancy, and fantasy . . . '

'Did you ever use your TV or radio status to request this?'

'No, not at all, never. Never done that in my life.'

After again denying all three allegations investigated by Surrey Police, Savile decided it was time to have his say: 'We showbiz people get accused of just about everything. One of the reasons is people are looking for money, and they will try blackmail, and they will write letters saying that if you don't send us money I will say you have done this and you have done that . . . there is a group of people who just like causing trouble, because we get plenty of that anyway . . . that's why I have up in Yorkshire, where I live in Leeds, a collection of senior police persons, who come to see me socially, but I give them all my weirdo letters, and they take them back to the station.'

Without pausing for breath or even considering the wisdom of going into more detail with two investigating police officers, he

477

described one such letter from a girl in Devon. He said he gave it to the 'girls', meaning the staff at the hospital. Then he confessed to receiving another letter from a consultant doctor about a patient, presumably at a hospital where he had been accused of carrying out an assault. Savile said he handed that letter to the staff, too. 'My girls here were furious,' he claimed.

It seems unfathomable now that two police officers, who had listened to a number of women recount how Jimmy Savile behaved at Duncroft School, didn't press him on what allegations these letters contained.

'Wearing my Broadmoor hat, I don't find it amazing at all,' he continued unchallenged, 'because people do strange things . . . even doctors don't know why they do it . . . you've got to be prepared that they will do it, and ever since being on TV and radio and stuff like that, there's always been people who think that you're an easy touch for a few quid.'

The police officers wanted Savile to return to the 'policy' he had mentioned earlier in the interview, but first they asked about his relationships with police officers in Yorkshire, and the fact he passed such letters on to them.

'One of the reasons I do that is things happen to people like me that don't happen to normal people,' he explained. 'And just in case anything happened to somebody like me then the lads would be able to sift through all this weirdo stuff and maybe find some-body that they . . . '

'Okay,' interjected the police officer, 'so your expectation in handing the letters to them is that they're going to investigate them?'

'No, no, not investigate them, no. Not going to do anything with them, but if anything happens to me . . . '

'Store them on your behalf then?'

'Well yeah, but they don't keep them very long. They pass them round the office and everybody has a laugh just like the girls here did when we got the thing from the consultant.'

He was being quite open about the fact that he'd received threat-ening letters in the past. He claimed they had not been investigated, however. 'If I got an instinct that it was a bit dodgy then the forensics are just round the corner at [Wetherby] and so I can get them looked at as a favour, cos I know the people in there.'

Finally – finally – Jimmy Savile returned to the 'policy', the phrase he had dropped so ominously at the beginning of the interview. 'I take these things very seriously,' he reiterated before recounting how he had successfully sued five newspapers. 'Not one of them wanted to finish up in court with me,' he warned, 'so they all settled out of court.'

Buoyed by the ease with which he'd swatted away their questions, Savile decided it was now time to issue a threat. 'Now this to me,' he said, 'is exactly one of those things, so I've already told my legal people that somebody were going to come and talk to me, and they've got a copy of your letter . . .'. He then added, 'if it doesn't disappear for any reason, then my policy will swing into action . . .

'I have an LLD, that's a Doctor of Laws,' he boasted, 'not an honorary one but a real one. That gives me friends. If I was going to sue anyone, we would not go to a local court, we would go to the Old Bailey cos my people can put time in the Old Bailey . . . So my legal people are ready and waiting. All we need is a name and an address and then the due process would start . . . obviously if I'm prepared to take somebody to court and put them in front of a judge then there can't be much wrong with my policy of behaviour because I've never done anybody any harm in my entire life . . . I have no need to chase girls, there are thousands of them on *Top of the Pops*, thousands on Radio One. No need to take liberties with them.'

It was a tried and tested form of defence. 'In fact, from a newspaper point of view I'm very boring . . . I don't drink no booze, no drugs, no kinky carryings on, don't go to brothels or anything like that . . . . But because I take everything seriously I've alerted my legal team and they may be doing business. And if we do, then you ladies,' he said, motioning to the two Surrey Police officers, 'will finish up at the Old Bailey as well because we will be wanting you there as witnesses.

'Nobody ever seems to want to go that far,' he warned. 'I'm known in the trade as litigiousness [sic] which means to say I'm willing to pull people into court straight away, no messing thank you.'

And still he was allowed to go on, uninterrupted and undeterred by the two police officers in the room. He described how he brushed away women who tried to blackmail him like 'midges' before again underlining his status, and the ramifications of taking legal action against him. 'I own this hospital,' he said. 'NHS run it, I own it . . . If I wasn't here they wouldn't get the quarter of a million pound a year that they need to keep it going. There's nobody these days of that calibre that can do that.'

'Okay,' said one of the Surrey Police officers at last. 'So Jimmy, is there anything you want to add . . .'

'No, not at all,' he snapped. 'It's complete fantasy, it really, really is . . . neither thing was at a place where you get away with what they said . . . and I wouldn't want to in the first place anyway. Complete fantasy.'

It was 11.40 a.m. when the interview was called to a halt. It had been an utterly one-sided affair, one politely described by the statutory body responsible for inspecting the police forces of England and Wales, as 'ineffective'.[12]

On 28 October 2009, three days before Jimmy Savile celebrated his 83rd birthday, the same female Detective Constable who had interviewed the victim and witness of the indecent assault in the television room at Duncroft, the victim of the indecent assault at Stoke Mandeville and the teenager who was propositioned at Norman Lodge at Duncroft sent letters to each informing them 'the CPS has decided no further police action on this cases'.[13]

Not only were Savile's assertions in the interview allowed to pass entirely uncontested, but no checks were subsequently made on his whereabouts at the relevant times or the number of occasions he had visited Duncroft. Neither were his revelations about the close relationships he enjoyed with police officers in Leeds relayed to senior officers at West Yorkshire Police.

The investigation had foundered due to serious and inherent flaws. As Her Majesty's Inspectorate of Constabulary concluded in 2013, 'By regarding each victim in isolation, Surrey Police did not alert victims to the existence of each other – and therein presented themselves with an insurmountable obstacle.'[14] The report by the Department of Public Prosecutions said much the same, although it did at least adopt a more sympathetic tone. 'It would have been proper to give each (at least once she had given her initial account) the reassurance of knowing she was not alone.'[15]

Less than a month after Operation Ornament was wrapped up, and only six weeks after Jimmy Savile had faced down two Surrey police officers from his private rooms at Stoke Mandeville, I paid him a visit in Scarborough.

I had started the process of widening the search for the real man behind the façade, tracking down and speaking to people who had grown up in Leeds in the 1930s, finding former Bevin Boys, interviewing cyclists who remembered him from his days as Oscar 'The Duke' Savile and wrestlers who recalled his bizarre outings between the ropes. I wanted to demonstrate to him that I was no longer content with merely listening to the same old stories, often word for word, and was serious about trying to prise off the mask to see what, if anything, lay beneath. I figured that I had nothing to lose: if he was angered by my desire to explore beyond his clearly defined account of events, I would simply press on regardless.

I knew that Jimmy Savile was supremely controlling and accepted it would be necessary to work in wide concentric circles, picking off those who he was unlikely to still be in contact with but might still offer nuggets of information that would ring true. It was a relief that he seemed to be flattered by the lengths I had gone to, although there were of course the now customary admonishments for pulling him up on facts or quizzing about detail. At last, between the long tracts of familiar anecdote, there were glimpses of fresh insight.

On the Friday evening, we spent an hour or two talking about his cycling career, and touched also on the period he spent in the mines, a time that he seemed happy to leave enveloped in a fog of uncertainty.

The following morning was spent down on the Foreshore and then discussing his wrestling days in a café around the corner from the flat on the Esplanade. I knew the reasons he gave for taking up wrestling, and was conscious of the fact he would never admit it was part of a wider longing to be acknowledged as a formidable physical specimen. What I didn't know was why he decided to quit after what he insisted was a career spanning 107 fights.

'Perfectly logical,' he snapped. 'I stopped because I started trying to get hold of 20 million quid for Stoke Mandeville Hospital. I couldn't afford to be damaged. You know what I said about quitting while you're ahead; well I stopped fighting there and then. Quit while you're ahead.'

It did not quite tally with what the flamboyant, blond-haired wrestler Adrian Street had told me. He'd said he'd given Savile such a hiding in his last bout that he never wanted to return. 'Wrestlers in general resented Savile being allowed in the business, especially those who were told to lose to him by stupid, greedy promoters who thought that his celebrity would fill their arenas,' Street explained. 'It wasn't that he was ever capable of stealing their thunder. He wanted to wrestle as a publicity stunt and to try to prove he was a tough guy – which I proved him not to be.'

There was no way Jimmy Savile would ever admit to weakness or tell a story against himself, so I steered the conversation onto Broadmoor. I began to ask him about being appointed to the task force by Edwina Currie, junior health minister at the time.

'No,' he interrupted, before I had even finished my question. 'I was appointed by someone far more powerful than that. It was the top civil service boss. They ran Broadmoor and that will reflect on these real hierarchies. I started off with a collection of very senior civil servants and they all wanted Broadmoor out of trouble. 'I'll get it out of trouble for you,' I said. 'All you have to do is leave me alone.'

I put it to him that he must have been very highly thought of in the NHS at that time. 'I don't know about that,' he said, and began spluttering with laughter. 'Highly feared more like.'

He went on to outline his thoughts on mental health; that the Broadmoor patients, for that's what they were, could not be blamed for their crimes. They required treatment not punishment. That was not something that would ever be recognised, I suggested, while it continued to be a place that was demonised by the tabloids.

'That's their game,' he spat. 'You can't blame a lion for jumping on something and eating 'em. You can't blame a tabloid for demonising something, because it's what it does. All you hope is they don't want to demonise you. They demonise anybody they decide to demonise. Like, what's his name . . . The comedian kid where the kid got pegged in his pool . . . '

Michael Barrymore?

'They demonised him. Michael said to me one day, "The papers will never be happy until I'm dead. They're trying to kill me now. They're nearly succeeding, I tell you." Michael never committed any crime in his whole life. Alright, he was associated with something but nobody could say you've done this or you've done that.'

He then went on to talk about Gary Glitter.

'Now Gary, all that he's done is taken his computer into PC World to get it repaired. They went into his hard drive and found all these dodgy pictures and they told the police and the police think, "A famous person? Oh my goodness, we'll have them." But Gary has not tried to sell 'em or show them in public. They were for his own gratification and whether that's right or wrong is of course up to him as a person. They didn't do anything wrong but they are then demonised. And of course, if you were to say to a couple, "Gary Glitter, what's he done wrong?" They would say, "Oh, nothing, he's just sat at home watching these dodgy films."'

I was stunned and immediately challenged him, reminding Savile that Gary Glitter had faced child sex offences in south-east Asia.

'And are you telling me that some evil person didn't stick two little birds into him?' he retorted. 'He was like that but he wasn't public with it and he didn't do anything. I'm not trying to defend him but the facts are the facts. A person can get demonised and do nothing because the papers will decide to demonise them.'

He told me about how in the 1950s, two policeman came into his dancehall and informed him that he had been reported going in and out of public toilets in Leeds: 'I said, "Is that right? Well now then," I said, "How long have you been checking toilets? That must be a terrific job. Do you have to have a bath when you get home because you stink of piss and shite? Do you have to do an eight-hour shift in a toilet?"

'And when they realised they weren't getting anywhere they got up and left. They were trying to demonise me, do you understand? Me particularly, I can't remember the last time I used a public toilet. Years and years and years ago. It doesn't do for someone looking like me to be seen coming out of a public toilet. Someone might come out and say, "I've just had a piss next to Jimmy Savile" and in a week that will have turned into something else. What I do is open toilets. I've opened a toilet at the Flying Pizza in Leeds. There's a big plaque on the wall that says "Opened by Jimmy Savile". I do odd things like that but people are always ready to demonise you and it first started in my case in the Fifties.

And still he wasn't finished: 'I know traffic wardens who delight in getting a result. I know clampers who delight in seeing something they can clamp. They quite like the idea of making somebody's life awkward. Jobs like that attract a certain type of person. I've got my Broadmoor hat on because I know people do strange things. The world is full of some quite odd people. I understand them because it's my business.'

In light of the startling defence he had just offered on behalf of Gary Glitter, I asked him whether he thought the conviction of Jonathan King was an example of the demonisation that he talked of.

'Yes, yes, perfect example,' he said. 'It wasn't as vicious in Jonathan King's days as it was with Barrymore and Gary Glitter. The world is more vicious now and the tabloids have got a list of people that they think they might have a chance of shafting. So there's always somebody on the lookout for something.' In a typical non sequitur he began rambling on about Richard Nixon trying to find dirt on a political opponent. Nothing was found: 'So Nixon said, "Oh well, we'll just have to give him something to deny." That's just as good as shooting somebody between the eyes.'

On the *QE2*, he had made a throwaway comment that the two people the tabloids wanted more than anyone else were Jimmy Savile and Cliff Richard. 'Even now the tabloids would pay a fortune for something on Cliff or on me,' he said, 'albeit we are not as frontline as we were. His choice is to spend his life in the sunshine. My choice is to spend my life at Leeds Infirmary or Stoke Mandeville. We are not frontline entertainers but we're still a name. Cliff? He's single, he's successful, he's got a few quid, he's got a clean, wholesome image, there's nothing on him.'

He stared into the middle distance. The record button on my tape machine clicked up to signify the cassette had finished. We sat in silence.

Anecdotally at least, Jimmy Savile was well known to police officers in Leeds for a very long time. He'd alluded to as much in his autobiography when referencing the female police officer 'dissuaded' from bringing charges against him for harbouring a teenage runaway. She had done so, he wrote, because 'it was well known that were I to go I would probably take half the station with me'.

This claim tallies with Tony Calder's accounts of Savile actively cultivating relationships with senior officers in the 1960s, and sitting at a restaurant table while one warned Savile to 'cut it out' – whatever 'it' might have been. There were also the stories that Savile himself told about his various brushes with his local police force: sending officers packing when they had questioned him over hanging around public toilets in Leeds; getting his knuckles rapped for being over-zealous with troublemakers at the Mecca dancehall; warning them their teenage daughters were better off with him than the other 'slags and scumbags'. 'We've always had a relationship with [the police],' Savile told me in Scarborough in 2006, 'and that still goes on.'

In October 2012, soon after the revelations about his offending first came to light, stories began to emerge about his connections with the police, particularly those in Leeds. A spokesman for the West Yorkshire Police countered by stating the force had not conducted any historic investigations into Jimmy Savile, and of the many calls being received from his victims in the West Yorkshire area, 'none . . . alleged any failure by police to investigate previously'.

The only intelligence the West Yorkshire Police held on Savile concerned a report on his 'mugging' following a gala awards night in the Queens Hotel in Leeds in 2008. An inebriated young woman had pinched his favourite round-framed, pink spectacles from his nose as a joke. Sensing some coverage, Savile reported the theft to the papers and local television news, giving the same quote to all: 'If she is caught I will ask the bench to give 100 hours community service – as a carer in my flat.' He got the glasses back but the home help was not forthcoming.

The police spokesman went on to say that Savile had supported some West Yorkshire police campaigns in the past, but none in recent years, and the force had no knowledge of its officers attending Savile's flat in a social capacity although they were free to do what they wished when off duty.[1]

Both of these latter statements were misleading at best. As recently as 2008, West Yorkshire Police had launched a campaign encouraging the public to supply information about handlers of stolen property. It was organised in conjunction with the Leeds District Community Safety Partnership, a multi-agency public, private and voluntary partnership focused on reducing crime and disorder, and the decision was made to use a local celebrity in the media launch. Jimmy Savile was chosen. In the same year, the same partnership used a recording of Savile's voice for its 'talking street signs' campaign, which gave residents advice about crime prevention.

Furthermore, for more than 20 years, serving and retired police officers had been among those attending Savile's so-called Friday Morning Club meetings at his penthouse flat.

Those who regularly gathered on the leatherette sofas in Savile's front room included local businessmen, a retired doctor, a wealthy pharmacist, a local hairdresser, a café owner and pals from his dancehall and marathon days.

Joe Baker knew Jimmy Savile longer than any of these men, having first met him at St Anne's Elementary School in the 1930s. As a founder member of the club, Baker recalled how Savile would 'hold court' and enjoy the admiring glances when the phone rang and he could announce it was Princess Diana calling for a chat. 'We always thought he saw himself as one of the mafia,' Baker told *The Times* in October 2012. 'Any problem that arose, he used to say, "My people will take care of it." Now we are wondering who "my people" were.'[2]

Another regular, a company director who refused to be named, confirmed that Savile, 'liked to give the impression of being some sort of Godfather, sitting menacingly at the centre of his web'.[3]

Baker remembers around a dozen people attending each week, of which he says three quarters were usually serving or retired police officers. According to the West Yorkshire Police, however, only eight of its men were ever present at these weekly socials: four on a single occasion, and four as regulars. Of the latter, two are known to be Inspector Mick Starkey, now retired and formerly the Force Incident Manager based in the control room at Killingbeck Police station in Leeds, and Sergeant Matthew Appleyard, who is stationed at Wetherby police station.

Mick Starkey joined the force in the mid Seventies and within a short period was seconded onto the Yorkshire Ripper enquiry. Following this unusually rapid promotion, he spent most of the remainder of his three-decade career as a plain-clothes detective.

One retired West Yorkshire Police inspector, who served alongside Starkey in the Chapeltown division in the mid 1980s, recalls that his colleague was among a group of officers who made regular trips to visit Jimmy Savile. He maintains it was common knowledge at Chapeltown Police Station that Savile was visited by Starkey and other colleagues, and that it was accepted as the norm. 'I didn't really ask questions about it,' he said.[4]

'One morning they set off in a police car, there were about three or four of them. It was as if they were all going there for some reason. They were all on duty and in uniform. I knew [Savile] had a relationship with the police, and that is not unusual as a high-profile person. But whether [he] would see that in terms of protecting himself, I don't really know.'

Savile described Starkey as his 'bodyguard' and the burly inspector had appeared in the local papers talking about how he regularly drove his famous friend across the Yorkshire Dales in his Rolls-Royce Corniche.

'He was a part of my life as I grew up,' Starkey explained in the days after Savile's death. 'He was a distant figure associated with *Top of the Pops*, Pan's People and everything that was trendy. I never thought for a minute that in later life, as a serving police officer, I would meet him professionally or that subsequently we would become close friends.'[5]

At the wake following the requiem mass for Jimmy Savile, I spotted Mick Starkey sitting at a table with a number of men in their late fifties and sixties. He seemed suspicious at first, but when I reminded him how he had frisked me in the foyer of Savile's Roundhay Park flat some seven years before, he invited me to sit down and join him and the other members of the Friday Morning Club for a drink.

Only Starkey seemed willing to talk, however; the others did not want to know. He told me he thought Savile was lonely towards the end of his life, and talked a bit about driving him out onto the moors to the tiny railway station where his father had once worked, or to Dunnies Café in Otley and country pubs. He said that Savile expressed regret that he couldn't go into pubs and simply blend in.

When I mentioned the Ripper manhunt, and the fact that the body of one of the victims, Irene Richardson, was found in Roundhay Park close to Savile's flat, Starkey laughed and explained how Savile enjoyed the commotion and getting his breakfast off the police in the mornings.

More interesting still was what Starkey said – or didn't say – about the secret Jimmy Savile, the one seen only by members of the inner circle, including, presumably, those who attended his weekly coffee mornings. Although I didn't ask, Starkey said he thought Savile was 'asexual'. The answer arriving before the question was a reminder to me of the times I had spent interviewing Savile, and clearly of the considerable time Starkey had spent in his company. He had picked up on some Savile's habits and phrases, such as the next one that came out of his mouth: 'You know what the big secret about Jimmy Savile is, don't you? There was no secret.'

Almost exactly a year after this brief encounter with Starkey in a bar in Leeds city centre, and a month after the West Yorkshire Police had issued its inaccurate statement, Theresa May, the home secretary, commissioned a review by Her Majesty's Inspectorate of Constabulary. She instructed it to 'explicitly concentrate' on establishing 'which police forces received reports and/or allegations in respect of Jimmy Savile' before the launch of Operation Yewtree, and whether those allegations were 'robustly investigated and if there were any police failings in so doing'.

Little over a month later, West Yorkshire Police conducted an initial review of the Friday Morning Club. It found that officers on neighbourhood patrols had attended the meetings, which consisted of nothing more salacious than 'Savile and his friends sitting drinking tea and discussing current events'.[6] In the report it submitted to the HMIC, it stated, 'No evidence of impropriety by the officers who had attended Savile's home address was found.'[7]

The HMIC made enquiries of all 43 police forces in England and Wales but when its report was published in March 2013, records disclosed only five allegations of sexual assault being recorded by police against Savile between 1955 and 2009. Only three police forces on the mainland had investigated him in his lifetime: the Met in 2003, Surrey between 2007 and 2009, and Sussex in 2008. (In 2009, the State of Jersey Police had deemed there to be insufficient evidence to proceed after a man came forward to claim Savile had sexually assaulted him as a child at the Haut de Garenne home.) 'The results are stark,' stated the HMIC in its introduction to 'Mistakes were made', a survey of the systemic failings of police forces across Britain.

Given the prolific nature of his offending over such a long period of time, it is deeply concerning that the enquiry succeeded in uncovering only three new pieces of intelligence relating to Jimmy Savile. The first was the paper ledger created by the Metropolitan

Police Service Paedophile Unit in 1964, in which the DJ was mentioned as visiting a house in Battersea where absconders from Duncroft School were known to reside.

The second was an anonymous letter sent to the Vice Squad at New Scotland Yard in 1998 by someone who claimed to be 'closely involved' with Savile. The letter stated Savile was a homosexual and a 'deeply committed paedophile', and related how Savile had been 'extremely angry and frightened' after being threatened with blackmail by a rent boy. So much so that he'd changed his telephone number.

The third new piece of intelligence was a 2003 crime report by the Metropolitan Police following a complaint by a woman who claimed Jimmy Savile had sexually assaulted her during filming of *Top of the Pops* in 1973. The woman told officers she would not support a prosecution, but would reconsider if others came forward.

As the police force area in which Jimmy Savile lived throughout his life, West Yorkshire Police should have received details, and had records on its systems, of not only the intelligence reports generated by Surrey Police and Sussex Police in the course of their recent investigations, but also the 1964 paper ledger, the computerised record of the anonymous letter sent to the Vice Squad at New Scotland Yard in 1998, and the 2003 crime report by the Metropolitan Police.

West Yorkshire Police reported that it was initially unable to retrieve any of these records.

While HMIC's findings variously laid blame at the door of the Metropolitan Police Service for categorising the 1998 letter and the 2003 report in such a way that access to both was restricted (due in both instances to Savile's celebrity status), and with Surrey and Sussex for being unable 'to move beyond the reluctance of victims to support a prosecution', and for their failure to inform victims that 'others like them existed',[8] the most acute discomfort was felt by senior officers at WYP force headquarters in Wakefield.

The issues identified read like a catalogue of ineptitude, negligence and possibly worse. They included, not surprisingly, the call made by the West Yorkshire Police Inspector (unnamed in the report) to offer his assistance with arrangements for Savile's interview by Surrey Police, and the comments Savile made in that interview about his close relationships with senior police officers, including the passing on of 'weirdo' letters. HMIC felt these 'clearly suggested police officers in West Yorkshire may have been inappropriately close to Savile'.[9]

It was also pointed out that more than forty of Savile's victims from West Yorkshire had come forward to Operation Yewtree, along with two former West Yorkshire Police officers who stated they had been aware of Savile's 'contact with young girls'.[10]

Prior to the report's publication, an exchange of correspondence had led to a meeting between the West Yorkshire Police and officers from HMIC. At this meeting, the topics for discussion included the knowledge or otherwise of intelligence reports sent by the Metropolitan Police in 1964 and 1998; the seemingly total absence of information and intelligence on Savile on WYP systems; the information received that WYP officers had been told to patrol near to Savile's home address; Savile's involvement in the Yorkshire Ripper enquiry; and the need to obtain relevant information on Savile from current police officers and staff.

The officers from HMIC finished by reiterating its determination to understand the relationship between the force and Jimmy Savile.

John Parkinson, the then chief constable of West Yorkshire Police, referred the matters to the Independent Police Complaints Commission (IPCC) and announced that the force would conduct its own internal enquiry, with a view to publishing a report. To all intents and purposes, Jimmy Savile's home police force would be investigating itself.

On 12 February, West Yorkshire Police admitted that it now believed it had in fact received an electronic copy of the 1998 letter but was still trying to identify the material. Further entries had been found in the form of four crime reports with Savile as the victim.

Crucially, as we shall see, a West Yorkshire control room report was also unearthed that expressed concern for Savile's welfare.[11] A day later, a letter from the IPCC requested that the force record as a conduct matter the action of retired Inspector Mick Starkey.

By May 2014, some seven months later, a spokesman for the IPCC could not tell me when the findings of the independent investigation (the most serious of its type) would be published.

64. TWO 16-YEAR-OLD GIRLS FROM THE UKRAINE

Late on a dark, wet November night on the coast of north-east Yorkshire, the proprietor of Café Fish, one of Jimmy Savile's favourite Scarborough restaurants, joined us in the bar area. Savile was wrapped up in a thick jacket, and a furry Arctic cap with earflaps was pulled down over his forehead. He'd told me earlier in the day that he was suffering from angina. He suddenly looked very old.

The proprietor was a large man who perspired gently beneath a white short-sleeved shirt. He seemed excited to see Savile and made a fuss about telling us all about which fish had been freshly caught that day. I suspected he was upping his game because the local celebrity was in.

Savile settled on the lobster. The memories from the *QE2* of the white crab flesh stuck to his jagged teeth, coupled with the volume of cigar smoke I'd inhaled over the course of the day, made me nauseous for a moment. Struggling to speak, I put myself in the proprietor's hands. He deliberated theatrically before making his choice, and then brought the chef out from the kitchen to confirm the wisdom of his selection. Savile sat quietly, brooding beneath his layers. I sensed he was less than impressed with all the fuss that was being made.

We were offered a complimentary drink each; 'Good old fashioned Scarborough hospitality,' said the proprietor. Savile had a large scotch – his second of the evening. I went for a large glass of the house red, hoping it would settle my stomach. The proprietor went behind the small bar to fix himself a drink before rejoining us to recount some of the times his famous guest had been in. Savile stared ahead, occasionally nodding. He said nothing.

Suddenly, the door flew open and a woman burst in looking wet and wind-lashed. The proprietor was called away. 'Two weeks ago she was like an obedient dog,' muttered Savile, jutting his chin at the woman. 'Now she's got him right at it.' He settled back into the banquette and took another loud slurp at his whisky.

A few minutes later, we were joined in the small bar area by a group of couples, all talking loudly and laughing. They looked to be in their late thirties and early forties, so a chance encounter with Jimmy Savile represented a big deal. He seemed happy to chat, though it was standard fare to those who had heard it all before: 'Indestructible,' when asked how he was; 'Ah, but you didn't remember a stamped addressed envelope,' when they asked him why he'd never replied to the letters they'd written to him on *Jim'll Fix It*.

Our drinks were nearly done. A waiter approached to ask whether we needed anything. 'Two 19-year-old girls from the Ukraine, please,' said Savile without a flicker. Our table was ready. He signed an autograph on a napkin for one of the men in the party and shuffled through to where the tables were set.

The only other people in the dining area were two elderly women who were tucking into their main courses at a small table next to a window. The rain streaked the glass, blurring the red brake lights of traffic moving up the hill outside. We were shown to a table for four in a corner of the room. I sat down opposite Savile but he motioned for me to move because he wanted to put his feet up on the chair next to mine. We ended up sitting diagonally across from each other. Another round of drinks was ordered.

For some reason, the conversation began with global warming and as usual, Savile was uninterested in any opinion other than his own. Whatever argument I put forward or comment I offered, he seemed intent on contradicting it. Experience had taught me that this was how he could be at this time of day. He'd had a drink now and I believed him when he said he rarely, if ever, touched a drop during his heyday. It clearly affected him now.

I had seen him in this sort of mood with Louis Theroux; it was as if he wanted to remind himself of his superior intelligence.

The conversation then switched onto 'flag birds', his system of ensuring that none of the disc jockeys he employed in his dance-halls ended up falling out over girls. They had women throwing themselves at them, he said, and the way his system worked was that every lad was allowed one 'flag bird', which meant that none of the other lads could make a move on her. As soon as he switched his flag bird, the previous one would be fair game. He said it worked a treat.

The starters arrived and Savile was now working up a head of steam, rattling on about how stupid the Romans were for inventing marriage. I was bored; I had heard his views on 'brain damage' and the fact he did not want to be responsible for a 'living thing' on for too many occasions.

The arrival of the main courses seemed like an appropriate junction at which to change the direction of the conversation, if such a one-sided discussion could be described as such. So I asked him whether he ever got angry. I had seen what I considered to be anger flush through him earlier in the day when he launched into his diatribe about Gary Glitter and the tabloids.

'Never.'

It was like he said, there was no room in his life for normal human emotions. There never had been. He did admit, though, that he occasionally got annoyed with himself for bumping into things. He was 83 years old but still living his life on his own terms; bowing to nobody, changing for nobody. I wondered whether he was beginning to fray mentally.

'Do you know what I do when that happens?' he asked me, smiling for the first time in the evening. I shook my head.

'I say to myself, 'Jimmy, you – stupid – fucking – CUNT.'

The last four words of the sentence were delivered in a growling crescendo, climaxing with the word 'cunt' being spat with such force that I noticed the shoulders of the women at the other table rise involuntarily. There was an eerie silence in the room, not even the clink of cutlery.

Hearing the commotion, the waiter rushed over to check that everything was OK. He asked whether there was anything else we needed. 'Two 16-year-old girls from the Ukraine,' said Savile, shaving three years off his previous answer, before craning forward to shovel another hunk of lobster into his mouth. He looked up and his lips stretched into the same thin grimace that I had first witnessed in the lift going up to his penthouse flat in Leeds.

Little more was said that evening. On returning to his flat, I left him sitting in his front room, electric fire blazing, and went to bed. This time I wasn't billeted in the Duchess's room, but in a tatty box room opposite the bathroom. The next morning I woke early, packed and left. I never saw Jimmy Savile again.

Four months later, at a graduation ceremony in St Mary's Church, Luton, he was given an honorary degree from the University of Bedfordshire in recognition of his work for the National Spinal Injuries Centre at Stoke Mandeville Hospital.[1]

65. THE LAST GREAT GIMMICK

Death was one of Jimmy Savile's favourite subjects. He talked to me about it on many occasions, beginning at our very first meeting in Leeds in 2004. He was 77 at the time and we were sitting in the flat where his body would be discovered some seven and a half years later.

I asked him whether death was something he feared. 'No,' he replied firmly, as a thick coil of cigar smoke unspooled around his head. 'For 25 years as a voluntary hospital porter I had to put the lately deceased away in their boxes. I got quite used to death.' He then explained he'd been comfortable with death ever since the nuns in the old people's home opposite his childhood home had invited him to say goodbye to the recently departed.

Later during that first interview, he also told me about visiting the site of a former Nazi concentration camp near Brussels. 'As a student of people I had to go on my own and wander about just to pick up the vibes,' he said. 'I thought it was an amazing experience. I came out with absolutely no answers but I didn't go there looking for answers. I went there to pick up the vibes.'

In *The World of Jimmy Savile*, the 1972 film that offered him a platform for his bizarre views, he had tried to explain what his faith meant to him. 'My own God, in that he's moulded to my own image a bit – he suits me,' he said while perched on a spindly exercise bike. 'I believe in God, because if for nothing else it's a good gamble.

'If we went through life thinking if when we die, we rot and that's it, well that's alright. But it's much nicer to go through life with a faith that when we do die we go on to an even better life. Therefore it follows logically that if you try to live life through a decent code, it's a hope that when the time comes you go off, for want of a better word, to a life hereafter, a heaven. So from a gamble point of view, it's a good thing.'

In *God'll Fix It*, in the chapter 'What Happens When I Die?', Savile used the death of his mother as the pretext for a further nugget of what he liked to call 'JS wisdom': 'Be nervous about death with the nervousness of excitement . . . Death is a great adventure, a wonderful journey, the last great gimmick.'

I was reminded again of what Professor Anthony Clare had pointed out 20 years previously, 'People with a distaste for emotions, who place great value on predictability and control, who see life as incorrigibly messy and death as a frozen model of perfection, are half in love with death.'

I also thought again of the time in Scarborough when he'd described the sense of calm he felt when faced with the prospect of imminent death during a publicity stunt with the Police Air Arm flight display team. 'It's all a bit of fun,' he had concluded as we ambled past the amusement arcades and chip shops on Scarborough's sea front. 'All of a sudden you climb out of the aircraft and think, "Gonna die. Didn't die. Very good" . . . It didn't bother me because I'm a bit odd. One minute you're here, the next minute you're not.'

It would not be the last time we discussed death – his own and other people's – and yet looking back I am still struck by what he said in closing on that very first occasion we spoke: 'How you die is quite important.' And given what he wrote about his hopes for the final reckoning, that the debit column of his carnal sins would be weighed against the credit of his good works, it is surely telling he was found with his fingers crossed.

The first text arrived at 2.20 p.m. on 29 October, and within minutes my phone was bleeping with fresh messages. Jimmy Savile, just two days short of his 85th birthday, had been found dead in his flat in Leeds.

In the days that followed, a sense of Jimmy Savile's stature as a national icon began to emerge through stories in local papers up and down Britain. In Buckinghamshire, David Griffiths, general manager of the National Spinal Injuries Centre at Stoke Mandeville Hospital, spoke of the birthday party the staff had planned for their chief patron, while Paul Smith, executive director at the Spinal Injuries Association, told the local BBC News about the influence he wielded at the hospital and how 'a great many spinal injury people really do owe him a debt'.[1]

In Crowthorne, Councillor Jim Finnie remembered the times when he had sat with Savile on the board at Broadmoor. 'He supported the wellbeing of its patients and its staff,' offered a spokesperson for the trust that now runs the hospital. 'He was instrumental in developing and opening the hospital's first gym, which was well used and appreciated by our patients.'[2]

In Peterborough, Nigel Hards, who worked for Thomas Cook when Savile was its highly paid consultant in the early 1990s, and had been involved in the fund-raising campaign to build a new children's hospital in Peterborough, a plan that mysteriously fizzled out, talked of 'a very complex character' who established a charity road race, a children's medical charity and brought his friend Princess Diana to the city. He also recounted how Savile liked working at the mortuary at Stoke Mandeville Hospital, 'because he thought it would be easier for loved ones if he was there when they came in'.[3]

Scarborough businessman James Corrigan, whose late father had owned an amusement arcade on the seafront and accompanied Savile on midnight runs along the seafront and to the Otley Civic Call, told his local paper how he'd grown up knowing Savile as a close family friend. 'He came to every Christmas dinner at our house from before I was born until last year,' he explained, 'with the exception of three times when he got a better offer. One of those was when Margaret Thatcher invited him to go to Chequers.'[4]

Corrigan added that Savile regularly brought guests to these family get-togethers, including on one occasion Mairead Corrigan who was awarded the Nobel Peace Prize in 1976 for her efforts to end the violence in Northern Ireland. 'Savile was the strangest thing anyone could inherit,' he said, 'and I inherited him from my father.'

Cardinal Keith O'Brien, Britain's most senior Catholic clergyman, thanked Savile for the 25 years he had been a patron of Across, a charity that takes seriously ill or disabled pilgrims to Lourdes, and explained their long friendship had developed through Jimmy's mother.[5]

Other stories were of a more personal nature. Two elderly women from Pocklington shared fond memories of him from their time as land workers in the early 1950s. In Manchester, he was recalled attending a bat mitzvah resplendent in a silver suit. In Stourbridge, gym owner Jim Charles cast his memory back to when Jimmy Savile was president of the National Amateur Body Building Association. The role required him to hand out medals to winners at the Mr Universe competition, including, on one occasion, to an unknown called Arnold Schwarzenegger. 'He took us to Park Lane to a fashionable restaurant and then went to the loo and left us to pay the bill,' said Charles.[6]

Curiously, given that his fame was a uniquely British phenomenon, Jimmy Savile's death made headlines in far-flung corners of the world. The *New York Times* reported how he served up 'patter that in its manic opacity verged on Dada' and described him as a 'puckish man' who was responsible for 'a torrent of claims, some true, some false and others occupying the vast limbo of credibility between them'.[7]

Towards the end the week I telephoned Howard Silverman, who I had met briefly when out with Savile in Leeds. Silverman, who was a regular at the Friday Morning Club meetings, told me he had visited his friend in the week before he died, as had Professor Alistair Hall, a cardio specialist at Leeds General Infirmary who Savile once invited me to dinner with at the Flying Pizza in Headingley. Silverman confirmed he was found in bed in a shell suit, which was how he would have wanted it.

Five weeks before he died, Savile had gone on a cruise on the *Queen Elizabeth* for its maiden voyage around Britain. Luke Lucas, Savile's long-time friend, colleague and a trustee of both the charities that bore his name, accompanied him. Savile had been taken ill and was forced to leave the ship in Liverpool. He was admitted to hospital where he was diagnosed with pneumonia. Alistair Hall later revealed that four of his major organs were failing.[8]

In the week before he died, Jimmy Savile checked himself out of hospital and returned to his home, where he gave his final interview to Alison Bellamy of the *Yorkshire Evening Post* and had his portrait taken: a gaunt, hollow-eyed figure wreathed in cigar smoke and a dark green Lacoste tracksuit.

Two quotes in particular jumped out from that last interview. First, Savile said he thought people were getting 'a bit bored of his old stories' and then, after Bellamy talked about her children, he allowed a rare crack of light to shine through: 'That is something I have missed out on, kids and grandkids,' he said. 'I'll never know what it's like.'[9]

Never once in all our meetings, or in any interviews I'd read, had Jimmy Savile ever expressed doubt about his own brilliance or admitted even a passing interest in commitment of any kind. It sounded like he knew his time had come.

Mick Starkey took him for a drive on the Dales, and to buy some cigars from his tobacconist in Otley. 'He was very tired but we had a long chat and he reminisced about his life,' said Starkey. 'I'm sure he knew the end was near.'[10] Alan Franey, who had Savile to thank for his entrée to Broadmoor and claimed to know him 'probably as well as anybody', phoned and found his old running mate 'very tired and short of breath'. He described Savile as being mentally alert but resigned to his fate. 'I'm coming to the end of the tunnel,' he'd said.[11]

Even the Friday Morning Club meeting was cancelled, Savile informing his regulars that he was 'in bed and on strike'. Later that evening, Alistair Hall called round to the flat to make one last effort to get him to return to hospital.

The next morning, Roddy Ferguson, the husband of the woman Savile had befriended as a 15-year-old and who had helped serve lunch to Prince Charles in Glencoe, tried calling. There was no answer. When his niece Amanda McKenna did the same, she contacted the caretaker of the flats and asked him to go in and check. Alan Hepworth, the caretaker, found Jimmy Savile's lifeless body in his bed.[12]

Alistair Hall was called out to take care of the formalities. The cause of death, it later emerged, was cardiac arrest, heart failure, ischaemic disease and renal failure.[13]

Silverman sounded mildly exasperated at some of the coverage in the national press that painted his friend – the best man at his wedding, no less – as a loner. He was also frustrated by the fact that, as he described it, 'the inner circle is becoming the outer circle', a less than subtle reference to the manner in which Jimmy Savile's grand finale was being organised.

There had been a limit to what I had been able to find out about Savile's family up to that point. The last of his siblings had died in 1997 and he became irritable when asked to talk about them. I had listened to him taking calls from their numerous offspring, and heard him say that he didn't view his nephews and nieces any differently from anyone else who crossed his path.

It was therefore fascinating to now see his relatives emerge. Roger Foster, his 66-year-old nephew, had taken on the role as Savile family spokesman. He told the press that his uncle had hoped to be buried alongside his mother and father at Killingbeck Cemetery in Leeds, but had discovered some years before that the plot was full. Instead, he would be laid to rest on a hilltop overlooking the sea at Scarborough.

'We have found a beautiful spot in Woodlands Cemetery where you can see North Bay, South Bay, Scarborough Castle and even the seaside flat that he bought for his mum,'[14] added his niece Amanda McKenna. For the time being, she said, his flat would be left exactly as her 'Uncle Jimmy' had left it, even down to the last cigar he smoked, half finished in the ashtray.

In the Rhondda Valley, Vivian Savile, another nephew, told the story of his famous uncle's visit in 1964: 'I remember we were at home and there were hundreds of children climbing over the wall to get a glimpse of him . . . Nothing like it had ever been seen in Porth before.'[15]Accompanying the article was a black and white photo of Savile standing with his eldest brother Vince and his sister-in-law Sadie. The teenage Vivian, clad in full Teddy boy regalia, lurked at the shoulder of his peroxide-haired uncle, a look of sly pride playing across his features.

Towards the end of the week, Foster revealed that his uncle Jimmy would be buried in a gold coffin that, in accordance with his final wishes, would be lowered into the ground at a 45-degree angle 'so he could see the sea.' The last great gimmick indeed.

My attempts to track the course of Jimmy Savile's existence had become all consuming, providing reliable dinner party entertainment for those who liked to remind me of my failure to make significant progress towards any meaningful discovery.

I told myself that he was like the central character in the Woody Allen film *Zelig*, possessed of an uncanny knack of popping up at key and unlikely points in time. I naively believed that Jimmy Savile's story might work as an alternative history of popular culture in postwar Britain, with his progress across its landscape illuminating some dark and forgotten corners. It was also, I said to anyone who was still prepared listen, a story about our childhoods – and how darkly prophetic that turned out to be.

I hoped too that the journey might also end in some kind of understanding of how he'd come to assume such a central place in my life.

I had always planned to confront him in a final climactic encounter with what I hoped would be the truth. But like Conrad's Kurtz, he was supremely controlling, which meant there was no prospect of speaking to anyone on the inside without it getting back to him and the line of enquiry being shut down. I also knew that anyone he would allow me to speak to would only spin the lines he'd been feeding so relentlessly and for so long.

If he had succeeded in drawing me in and knocking some of the sharp edges off my suspicions, I can confidently say he never did quite manage to turn me.

Even after the days and nights I'd spent with him, the kindness he'd seemed to show me and his consistent denials about there being a secret beyond what you saw, there was never any doubt in my mind that arriving at the real Jimmy Savile would entail a journey into the heart of darkness. Hence the title I'd planned for my book, and now its opening chapter: 'Apocalypse Now Then'.

I just hadn't figured on him dying when he did, at a point when I had advanced only a short distance upstream. He had always threatened to live forever and his immortality – secured, I suspected, via some Faustian pact – was something I had taken for granted. So when the news broke, I felt not only sad but angry. Angry he had robbed me.

Jimmy Savile's three-day funeral was marked with a combination of the solemnity usually reserved for departed statesmen and the tawdry showmanship that had been his hallmark. I arrived in Leeds on the afternoon of Tuesday, 8 November to find the city cowering under dank, grey skies. Three satellite TV trucks were parked on the short ramp leading from the station and camera crews lined the pavement in front of the Queens Hotel.

Inside, amid the brown marble, patterned carpet and twinkling chandeliers of the hotel's public bar, his American-style coffin, finished in a brushed gold satin, had been put on display. On a small table nearby were arranged a single white candle, a crucifix, a framed black and white photograph of Savile with his thumbs up, his two *This is Your Life* books and a glass ashtray containing two cigars. One, half-smoked, was the last he ever enjoyed.

Pockets of people, many elderly or in wheelchairs, took photos of the coffin on their mobile phones and traded stories of when they met Jimmy Savile and how he had touched their lives. Single flowers and small bouquets had been left on tables to either side, many bearing cards. One thanked him for all the good times and was signed by a member of *The Teen and Twenty Disc Club*. Another card was made out to 'The Boss' and signed from 'Tich – Manchester Team 1962–66'.

As people came and went, I heard about how he helped one man get into the army; met others on jogging circuits of Roundhay Park; wheeled a child into Leeds General Infirmary; joked with cyclists on club runs across the Yorkshire Dales; wished diners happy birthday in local restaurants; chatted with fellow marathon runners and sat at the bedsides of the recently paralysed. I was also told how he lusted after younger sisters and invited lads up to the manager's office at his dancehall to dish out packets of cigarettes.

One elderly woman came in alone and tenderly stroked the portrait printed on card and displayed on an easel. She explained quietly that she had her photo taken with him when he came to wrestle in Lincolnshire in the late 1960s. She insisted he'd been 'an absolute gentleman'.

A short walk up the hill from the Queens Hotel brought me to the city's Victorian Quarter with its trio of sparkling arcades. Restored in recent years and now home to some of the most fashionable shops and boutiques in Leeds, it was the site of the old Mecca Locarno. Now, some half a century on, the Mecca's elaborate trio of marble and faience arches, and its miniature balcony above, provided the façade for a branch of Reiss.

West of the city centre, set amid a dull hinterland between the university campus and a swathe of uninspiring business hotels, office buildings and council housing, was the street Jimmy Savile grew up on. Opposite number 22 Consort Terrace, an unremarkable four-storey terraced house near the top of an incline, a modern, dark-bricked housing development occupied the space where once he'd skulked through the corridors of the St Joseph's Home for the Aged.

The next morning, Professor Alistair Hall stopped in City Square to look across to the Queens Hotel where crowds watched at a respectful distance as the gold coffin was loaded into the hearse for its final tour of the city. I had met Alistair and his colleague Professor Mohan Sivananthan, a consultant cardiologist, over dinner a few years earlier.

Hall told me how his relationship with Savile had blossomed and about the financial support he had given to research projects he and Sivananthan had undertaken in the field of heart disease. We walked up the hill together and he explained that having done well for the decade following his operation, the last four years had witnessed a steady decline in Savile's health. He also spoke of how Princess Diana had called when he was in hospital for his heart operation.

On the approach to the cathedral, thousands of people waited behind temporary barriers, while a scrum of photographers and camera crews jostled near the steps. Grey-haired men who appeared to be wearing the regalia of Freemasonry showed mourners to their seats.

I sat down next to a man with medals on his blazer. He introduced himself as John Bailey, or Bill, as Savile used to call him. I'd seen him in black and white photographs at Savile's flat, accompanying the platinum-haired disc jockey under nets and over walls and through ponds during his bid to become the first civilian to receive an honorary Green Beret from the Royal Marines. Savile was to be buried with his Green Beret in one hand. Bailey smiled at the memories: 'People forget he was 39 when he started the commando training course and 42 when he finished it,' he said.

The sound of applause from outside signalled the arrival of the hearse, followed by a lone chant of 'Jimmy, Jimmy'. The congregation rose.

As I listened to the eulogies, I experienced a range of emotions: sadness; a conflict over my persistent doubts, fuelled by what I had started to hear from people who worked with or knew him from his dancehall days, people who vouched for the fact he liked girls young but argued that it was a different time, different place; uncertainty about what the future held. I was torn between the eccentric old man whose life was being celebrated here and all around the country, and the shapes now beginning to emerge from the shadows.

At the end of the service, a curious-looking figure rose to his feet and shouted for everyone to clap. He had a mop of rust-coloured hair and was wearing black tracksuit trousers and a mustard-coloured sweatshirt bearing the legend 'Jimmy's Eager Helper'. A *Jim'll Fix It* badge hung from his neck. It was Dave Eager, one of Savile's protégés and his 'personal assistant' from the 1960s. Outside, meanwhile, reporters surrounded Frank Bruno and the former Radio 1 DJ Mike Read. They were the only 'celebrities' to attend.

British seaside resorts in winter project a peculiar sense of foreboding, and on this particular November morning, the atmosphere in Scarborough was as leaden as the skies. From the Grand Hotel, the vast sandstone typewriter that serves as a reminder of to the town's Victorian heyday, a small crowd was visible on the corner of the Esplanade, gathered in front of the flat Jimmy Savile bought for his mother.

Below on the Foreshore, beyond the flashing lights and bleeps of the amusement arcades, the billboard running around the front of the Futurist Theatre (forthcoming attractions: Ken Dodd, Cannon and Ball and the Chuckle Brothers) bore a simple message: 'Goodbye Jimmy'.

I walked north towards the harbour, past the lifeboat station, the rock shops and chip bars, tracing the route I had taken with Savile on previous visits. Outside the Ivy House Café, a free bus was waiting to take mourners to Woodlands Cemetery. It was clear that after the turn-out in Leeds, Scarborough's farewell was to be a more low-key affair. The bus left before the cortège had rounded the corner, and did so with only six of its fifty-two seats occupied.

The only other people on the top deck were two women who sat at the front. As we trundled along Marine Drive and away from the town centre, they chatted excitedly about the photographs they wanted to take of the coffin. The bus stopped at the railway station but nobody else got on.

Climbing out of the town, we passed Scarborough Hospital before alighting at the end of the tree-lined driveway leading to the cemetery. Inside, police officers and marshals in fluorescent bibs patrolled the perimeter of a cordon erected for the 200 or so people that had gathered to watch. The grave had been dug on a slope and in front of a stand of tall trees. There was no view of the sea, only the faint outline of Scarborough Castle in the gloom.

Once the funeral vehicles arrived and the seven-foot gold casket was lifted out and placed on a platform above the grave, Father Martin Kelly of the Diocese of Leeds made an address that was broadcast over loudspeakers, followed by a short reading by Amanda McKenna, Savile's niece. Then, when the undertakers took their positions on either side of the coffin, the press photographers and gaggle of curious onlookers surged forward, snapping away as it was lowered into the ground.

Finally, as Father Kelly concluded his Hail Mary, the clouds parted for the first time in three days to reveal the briefest glimpse of blue skies beyond.

Like Savile at the site of the former concentration camp, I had picked up the vibes. On the way in, I had noticed a pub near the gates of the cemetery. It was called The Duchess, and on the pavement outside a blackboard invited mourners to 'celebrate Jimmy with us'.

He'd always said his only wish in life was to have a telephone to heaven so that he could talk to his mother. In death, there was nothing more for me to do than sit and drink in a pub that could have been named after the only woman he loved.

Operation Newgreen, as the West Yorkshire Police enquiry was named, took four months to complete. Its review staff included an investigation team of 14 detective constables. More than 200 people were spoken to and 400 inquiries conducted in the course of over 3,000 working hours.[1] In May 2013, Assistant Chief Constable Ingrid Lee wrote in her foreword that she hoped it would show 'the open and transparent nature of its review'.

The reality was somewhat different. The Newgreen report reads not as a genuine bid to understand and learn from mistakes that were made, but as a study in defensive self-justification and the redirection of blame. In many passages, it is characterised by a tone of barely concealed exasperation. This despite 76 crimes involving 68 victims having been reported in the West Yorkshire area relating to Jimmy Savile in little more than seven months; among them, eight incidents of rape: four on males, four on females.[2]

Assistant Chief Constable Lee conceded that 'it was important for the public to know the scale and nature of West Yorkshire Police officers' involvement with Savile during his lifetime', and said to that end West Yorkshire Police had 'committed resources' to search for the truth and to 'separate myth and rumour from fact'.[3] Information, she claimed, was sought from every serving police officer and staff member, including where possible, those who had retired from the force.

Then, without issuing any form of apology to those who had felt unable to report Savile's crimes in the past, or weren't listened to when they did, she played straight into detailing the positive steps WYP had made in its tackling of sexual abuse.

According to the report, the West Yorkshire Police cannot categorically say whether it or its predecessors ever received information on the 1964 ledger uncovered in the files of the Metropolitan Police's Paedophile Unit. What is known is that the handwritten ledger lay undiscovered for decades.

Before computerised intelligence systems became commonplace in the 1980s and 1990s, retention of intelligence was not co-ordinated nationally. The system used by the West Riding Police, which preceded the formation of the modern West Yorkshire constabulary, was typical: each division had its own collator's office responsible for the collation and action of intelligence linked to crimes. It was a system based on paper cards in which, as the Newgreen report pointed out, 'the decision making process [about whether or not to record a specific piece of intelligence] was at times subjective'.[4] When the force introduced computer-based intelligence recording in 1992 and 1993, not all the historic information on these paper cards was converted.

By rights, though, intelligence should have been 'owned' by the collator's office in the area where the person resided. Information about Jimmy Savile should therefore have been forwarded to Leeds. The Newgreen report stated that when its officers examined the 1964 ledger there was 'no information contained within it that relates to West Yorkshire nor any entry regarding its communication to WYP'. This appears to have been enough for them.

The case of the anonymous letter dated 13 July 1998 and sent to the Vice Squad at Scotland Yard is far more troubling. The letter begins with the line, 'I supply here information which if looked into by one of your officers will yield a secret life not unlike that of [name redacted]. I can not [sic] give you my name as I am too closely involved and do not wish to be in the limelight and have the finger pointed at myself.'[5] It went on to explode the myth of Savile's charity work, and described his homosexuality as 'an open secret with those who know'.

The letter also said Savile had been recently involved with a 'young rent boy', to whom he gave his telephone number in Leeds. This number was subsequently changed because Savile received 'threatening calls from the rent boy, who was going to go to the press and expose his paedophilia, if he did not give him more money'. The letter contended Savile was 'very angry and frightened' at the time. Furthermore, it said Savile kept pornography at one of his houses before outlining further details about his regular activities in Leeds.

'He thinks he is untouchable because of the people he mixes with,' the letter continued. '. . . There are many more things I could tell you but they are trivial in comparison with the main issue.' The letter closes with a warning that now appears remarkably prescient: 'When JIMMY SAVILE falls, and sooner or later he will, a lot of well-known personalities and past politicians will fall with him.'

This uncorroborated piece of intelligence was processed and forwarded to both the Met's Organised Crime Group Paedophilia Unit and the West Yorkshire Police Force Intelligence Bureau. And yet it was never properly investigated, despite the obvious lines of enquiry into Jimmy Savile, including the fact he had changed his telephone number because of a blackmail attempt and, not least, the allegations he was a practising paedophile.

A full audit of all West Yorkshire Police systems failed to confirm that it was still in possession of what could, and should, have been a vital piece of intelligence.

The review team for Operation Newgreen tracked down and spoke with the detective constable at the Met who is thought to have handled the letter and created the initial intelligence report. The officer insisted that he remembered receiving the information, entering it into a master ledger and then faxing it to West Yorkshire Police.

While working in the Clubs and Vice Team at the Met in the 1980s and 1990s, the same officer also recalled receiving a number of other similar letters about Jimmy Savile, which he believed to be written by the same author. He said he submitted the letters to another unit within the Met and also sent a number of them to West Yorkshire Police. He maintained it was common knowledge among his colleagues that Savile was a paedophile, adding that at some point in 1989 he believed an officer within the same team was investigating him.

Further enquiries by the Newgreen team identified another former police officer who had worked within the WYP Force Intelligence Bureau on the specialist sexual offences intelligence desk during the time the anonymous letter was supposed to have been received. This officer recalled receiving information relating to Jimmy Savile 'in or around 1998 but could not remember the specific content of the report or who had sent it'.[6]

When this officer was spoken to again, he remembered the 'information may have included some discussion around conducting a joint investigation into Savile involving WYP and a number of forces,'[7] although he was said to be unable to specify which. He recalled the information had been sent from New Scotland Yard's Paedophile Unit, with whom he had a 'good working relationship'.

And this is where the picture becomes murky. According to Operation Newgreen, for some inexplicable reason the West Yorkshire Police officer 'did not record the information on any WYP computerised system'. Instead, he brought the information to the attention of his second line manager [listed in the report as Detective Inspector Z]'. He said that D/Insp Z 'took the information from him and when [he] later asked what was happening with it, [he] was told that it was in hand'. Detective Inspector Z died in 2002.[8]

Neil Wilby, who runs a whistle-blowing website that exposes corruption and miscarriages of justice within the West Yorkshire Police, is not altogether surprised. 'I think when Savile's name was typed onto the police system, there was probably something that flashed up and said that all enquiries were to be turned over to a specific officer that acted as his liaison . . . It seems to me that there was some sort of barrier preventing the normal process of officers within that police force.' Could that specific officer have been the unnamed, mysterious and now dead Detective Inspector Z?

In its report, West Yorkshire Police made little effort to conceal its eagerness to cast doubt on the accounts of both the officer at the Met and its own officer who worked on the specialist sexual offences intelligence desk. Nothing was found, it stated, when searches were done to locate the additional anonymous letters the Met officer spoke of, and nor were details uncovered of an investigation into Jimmy Savile in 1989. West Yorkshire Police went as far as identifying a further 24 officers who worked alongside the detective constable in question and 'all of those spoken with cannot remember having seen or heard any intelligence relating to Savile'.[9]

But despite such protestations, it appears that Savile's predilections and offending behaviour were known about well beyond the Clubs and Vice team at Scotland Yard. Of the 35 serving and retired West Yorkshire Police officers who came forward with information (a number just big enough to confer credibility), one, a former member of Leeds Vice Squad, said he believed his unit had conducted an investigation into Savile in the early 1980s which involved allegations of assault on two girls.

In countering the claim, the WYP stated that it had traced a number of officers working in Vice and none could recall such an investigation. The retired officer was clearly sticking to his story, however, as the matter has been voluntarily referred to the Independent Police Complaints Commission.

Another former WYP officer who offered information to Newgreen served with the force in the late 1960s and early 1970s, and recalled accompanying a member of the Police Women's Unit (a female-only unit that dealt with incidents involving women and children) to Savile's flat to look for a female reported missing by her parents. The retired officer said this was 'a regular enquiry by the Police Women's Unit' because girls – in his words, 'not children as such, but teenagers around 16/17 years and upwards' – regularly attended Savile's club on Mill Hill in Leeds.

This is the only mention I have ever seen of such a club, and again, no police records of these visits would appear to exist. If nothing else, the account demonstrates at the very least that Savile was known in police circles for associating with teenage girls.

Of the four retired West Yorkshire Police officers who had contacted Operation Yewtree after its launch in October 2012, two had information about rumours that circulated about Jimmy Savile. One said he was known in the early 1960s for taking young girls to his barge in Leeds for parties, while the other said he was renowned for being a 'pervert'. Doubts were cast on the veracity of these claims, too.

But in trying to answer every allegation, the report succeeded only in undoing itself. The Met Police officer spoken to by Newgreen did not work on Scotland Yard's Paedophile Unit and therefore was not in contact with the WYP detective constable who recalled receiving the intelligence on Savile. As the report conceded, this 'brings into question whether the information being referred to by both officers is one and the same'.[10] It also raises the very real possibility that the 1998 letter was not the only piece of intelligence to have mysteriously disappeared.

Jimmy Savile had no qualms about covering his tracks. He was open with the Surrey Police officers about the type of letters he received, and the fact he had trusted police officers to whom he could turn in times of trouble. It was a tried and trusted tactic on his part: placing evidence right under the noses of the police because it was the least obvious place to look.

But while the West Yorkshire Police's report on Operation Newgreen could not conceal its embarrassment over the cosy relationship Savile enjoyed with some of its officers – despite its claim that 'Much of the conjecture has been fuelled by Savile himself'[11] – it did try to nail the perception that he exploited these connections to evade arrest.

At the beginning of the section on the Friday Morning Club, the Newgreen report stated that 'rather than rely on the accounts provided by the police officers due to their perceived close relationship with Savile, the review placed a great emphasis on identifying all of the people who attended the FMC. The intention,' it said, 'was to bring a degree of independence to this important issue and once and for all establish what happened at the FMC.'[12] Sadly, this degree of independence did not extend to naming the police officers who visited Jimmy Savile in his flat.

Sergeant Matthew Appleyard was first questioned in December 2012. He is said to have explained that he first met Savile while working as a community officer in the Roundhay Park area. He was invited in for a coffee and accepted. In its defence, WYP pointed out that at the time officers were being encouraged to have 'more interaction with the community'. But Appleyard became a regular at the Friday morning meetings, even going into Savile's flat for a coffee when he wasn't there. He denied that anything occurred that compromised his position as a serving officer.

It then emerged that Savile had spoken in his Surrey Police interview of handing 'weirdo' letters to 'senior police people', and that the letters were either destroyed or kept in case anything happened to him. Savile also named a West Yorkshire Police Inspector, who other officers attending the meetings identified as being responsible for inviting them. But not one of the officers recalled seeing or hearing about letters that involved 'any accusations of sexual assault or any other crime committed by Savile'.[13]

There was one letter, however, that the Inspector talked about in his interview, albeit without 'being able to provide any detail'.[14] This was not the usual begging letter or lame request for support for a charitable cause. This message contained threats of violence and, according to the Inspector, it caused Savile considerable concern. So much so that it was read out in front of other members of the Friday Morning Club who advised it should be preserved for fingerprints and reported to the police.

The Inspector contended that the local detective chief inspector at the time was informed about the letter by one of the other WYP officers at the meeting. Curiously, none of the other police officers present recalled notifying the DCI, and only one could remember a conversation about such a letter. As for the DCI in question, he claimed no knowledge of investigating threats to Jimmy Savile or being made aware of any threatening letter.

What the DCI did recall, though, was attending Jimmy Savile's flat at the request of the local divisional commander. He was there, he said, to provide 'crime advice to Savile after he had expressed concern for his safety'.[15] Somewhat predictably, the WYP's 'extensive enquiries' failed to establish whether this was one and the same incident, and it reported 'no other people have any recollection of the matter'.

At this point in the 59-page document, there was no mention of the West Yorkshire control room report, the same one HMIC stated 'expressed concern for Savile's welfare', or what the early part of the Newgreen report referred to as a 'communication log relating to a friend of Savile'.[16] Given that Inspector Mick Starkey managed the Killingbeck police station control room, and is under investigation over the claims he made the call to Surrey Police, there would appear to be reasonable grounds to question whether it was Starkey who put in this separate call on his friend's behalf.

But if this was the case, why did he decide to bypass the local detective chief inspector and go straight to the top of the chain of command instead?

Neil Wilby has his own theory: 'Either with the force's knowledge or without, there seems to have been a process undertaken of cleansing the paper files and any electronic traces of documents or records that pertain to Savile. There's been a disinfecting process here. If anybody comes along, they are not finding anything at all.'

The destruction of evidence from the five-year Yorkshire Ripper enquiry would appear to be a case in point, even if West Yorkshire Police describes it as a quite normal procedure. What now remains of the 151,000 'actions' raised, the 158,000 vehicle enquiries and the 31,000 statements taken are just 198 boxes containing key exhibits, the prosecution file and the list of people spoken to. These are listed on the enquiry's nominal index card system.

The Newgreen review uncovered four index cards relating to Jimmy Savile. From the paucity of information preserved on his place in Britain's biggest ever murder investigation, the report stated that it 'was not possible to establish the relevance of the reference numbers'. One card did reveal, however, that Jimmy Savile offered his services as a go-between should the Ripper wish to make contact with the police.

Neil Wilby's views on Operation Newgreen and the report that followed are unequivocal. 'If you look at the substance and the content and the overall intention . . . it wasn't going to get to the truth. It wasn't going to find anything out, it wasn't going to get to the bottom of things.'

The chairman of the West Yorkshire Police Federation, Jon Christopher, seemed to agree, highlighting the fact nothing was written down because of who Savile was. 'At the time Jimmy Savile was a very large character in Leeds,' he said, 'and certainly some officers may well have been duped. It could have been seen as a bit of kudos for someone to be seen to have a relationship with someone as prominent as him.'[17]

As cracks appeared in the credibility of the Newgreen report in the days following the publication of the Newgreen report, it emerged that four of Savile's victims, rather than as the report indicated, had been five years old when Savile had attacked them.

There were a few concessions. Among them was an admission that the long-standing relationship between Jimmy Savile and WYP was over-reliant on his 'personal friendships' with serving officers. But this was a relationship that went further than simple coffee mornings at his flat. He had fronted local campaigns on behalf of the police. He had been a lunch guest of the chief constable at Millgarth police station. He had opened a climbing wall at the notorious Killingbeck police station in 1995, after which a plaque was mounted to commemorate the event; in 1998 he'd been the guest speaker at an officers' mess dinner, talking about how policing in Leeds had changed before being driven home by the assistant chief constable.

He had also been invited by police officers to attend open days (2008) and made financial contributions to a variety of charitable causes linked to the WYP.

What's more, Jimmy Savile had repeatedly offered the use of his flat for the policing of large events such as pop concerts in Roundhay Park, a ruse he employed to befriend police officers. Some of those officers went on to attend his weekly get-togethers where they drank tea, coffee and sometimes something stronger, and thought they were putting the world to rights. And where sometimes they listened to Savile mocking those who wrote him begging letters. They did all this because he'd seduced them.

After claiming to have spoken to more than forty people who attended the Friday Morning Club or knew of its existence, West Yorkshire Police stated it had found no evidence of any police impropriety or misconduct.

So why did it not include in its findings the details of a conversation overheard by one company director who attended Savile's weekly get-togethers? In October 2013 the man, who wanted to remain anonymous, explained to a national newspaper that he specifically recalled overhearing Savile talking to Mick Starkey at the end of one Friday morning meeting.

'Jim said something to him [Starkey] about getting in touch with Surrey Police because they were trying to contact him. He never said what it was about, but he had lost their names and numbers. He thought Mick would be able to contact them more easily because he had access to the right numbers. Jim said he was going away on business so he wouldn't have time to do it, but he could meet up with them at Stoke Mandeville.'[18]

The businessman claimed detectives from Operation Newgreen interviewed him for more than two hours, and that he told them about this conversation. He also said the interview was witnessed by his daughter. But no mention was made of the conversation in the West Yorkshire Police report.

When Assistant Chief Constable Ingrid Lee spoke to the BBC after the report was published, she stated, 'The people engaged with Jimmy Savile [didn't know] that actually there were these allegations against him.'[19] This is hard to believe if indeed Mick Starkey did make a phone call to Surrey Police.

The revelation that the Newgreen report's authors did not deem it necessary to include the testimony of one of the Friday Morning Club regulars followed hard on the heels of another story that made a mockery of Ingrid Lee's promise of transparency. As a former Leeds police constable, speaking under an assumed name, told the *Mirror*, 'there wasn't a copper in Leeds who didn't know Savile was a pervert'.[20]

In 1965, the officer recounted coming across Savile's Rolls-Royce while patrolling on his bike at night in an area near Roundhay Golf Club. At first he suspected the car, which was parked in a secluded spot in a lay-by, had been stolen. As he approached the vehicle, however, he noticed the lights were on inside.

'[Savile] was in the driver's seat and next to him was a very young female. He was a famous local figure,' said the retired officer, who was in his early twenties at the time. 'I was quite impressed it was him. I said, "What are you doing Jimmy? What's the matter?" He replied, "I'm waiting for midnight. It's her 16th birthday tomorrow."'

He said that Savile then gave him a wink. 'I checked my watch and saw it was 11.45 p.m. There was just 15 minutes to go and he seemed quite anxious. I looked over to [the girl] and asked if she was okay, and she just smiled at me but didn't say anything. She was definitely young. She looked around 15.' At this point, he recalled Savile looked up at him and told him to 'piss off', adding, 'If you want to keep your job I suggest you get on your bike and fuck off.'

Later, when the rookie officer relayed the incident to his sergeant, he was told to drop it: 'He's got friends in high places,' the sergeant warned. '"If you know what's good for you, you'll leave it there." ... He was so well-connected, he was like a superstar ... the police were in the palm of his hand.'

By October 2013, two years on from Savile's death, Operation Newgreen appeared to be fatally holed. After concluding a review into an entirely unrelated conduct matter concerning Assistant Chief Constable Ingrid Lee, for which she was exonerated, the chief constable of Avon and Somerset, Nick Gargan, expressed his views in a letter to his counterpart Mark Gilmore in West Yorkshire: 'It seems clear to me that Operation Newgreen does not have the look and feel of an independent report,' he wrote. 'As I turned from one page to the next, I saw example after example of the author putting the case for West Yorkshire Police. At times this case was put with some force and emotion and more than a hint of exasperation with other bodies.

'In that respect, Operation Newgreen was unsuccessful if it was its intention to give an impression of independent assurance: it may even have had the effect of strengthening suspicion that West Yorkshire Police was at the very least being defensive.'[21]

And at the very most? Chief Constable Gargan did not deem it necessary to convey his thoughts.

I f the report on Operation Newgreen did little to persuade the public that West Yorkshire Police had been as transparent as Assistant Constable Ingrid Lee promised, at least it acknowledged Jimmy Savile had a relationship with his local police force in Leeds. In Scarborough, the other town in which he spent the greatest part of his time, Savile appeared to have been airbrushed out in same way the plaques and signs bearing his name were removed once his reputation had been reduced to dust.

Tim Hicks and Nigel Ward, reporters on the independent local news website Real Whitby, began digging in October 2012. Initially, their curiosity was pricked by a series of newspaper stories about Savile's alleged connection with a 2003 police investigation into a paedophile ring operating around seafront arcades in Scarborough in the 1980s.

The first newspaper story[1] claimed 'senior police officers . . . had concerns that Jimmy Savile may have been involved' and that a number of paedophiles were operating in Scarborough, 'including a man who abused children at his caravan overlooking the seaside resort'. Jimmy Savile had told me about the caravan he'd kept a few miles down the coast from Scarborough, and how he'd taken girls there. He'd said the same to Louis Theroux.

A second story followed that claimed police had named Jimmy Savile as being part of the ring, which also numbered 'two prominent businessmen', Peter Jaconelli and Jimmy Corrigan Snr.[2] Hicks and Ward began investigating who, if anyone, knew, and if so, what they knew and when.

Savile, Corrigan and Jaconelli were prominent figures in Scarborough. Jimmy Corrigan, the friend who accompanied Savile to the Otley Pop Civic Ball in the 1960s, was the town's most famous amusement arcade owner. Peter Jaconelli was a former mayor, councillor and poster-boy for Scarborough; a millionaire who owned an ice cream business and a restaurant on the Foreshore. Corrigan's amusement arcade and Jaconelli's ice cream parlour were both on the itinerary for the outing Savile led for patients from Rampton Psychiatric Hospital in 1972.

Two women came forward as the allegations about Savile multiplied. Both claimed he had sexually abused them in Scarborough, one in the late 1960s and the other in the late 1980s. A further two women, neither of whom is thought to have been abused, contacted the local paper in Scarborough independently to recount how they had been interviewed by police officers working on the 2003 investigation, and, more pertinently, questioned about Savile, Jaconelli and Corrigan. The *Express* reported North Yorkshire Police's claim that it had 'no record of an investigation' into Jimmy Savile, as well as its request for the women to make contact.[3]

The 2003 investigation was in fact extensive enough for intelligence to be uploaded to the Home Office Large Major Enquiry System [HOLMES]. The technology is used in major inquiries that generate large volumes of intelligence and witness evidence. The investigation ultimately led to the conviction of two men for sex offences, although one was later cleared on appeal.

According to the original article in the *Express*, during the trial 'Savile's name was the hot topic of conversation'.[4] A statement on the North Yorkshire Police website, however, told a different story, namely that after carrying out 'extensive searches of force records' no 'local connection'[5] in relation to Jimmy Savile had been revealed. This statement has subsequently been removed and retracted.

It was this assertion, however, that ensured North Yorkshire Police was not included in Her Majesty's Inspectorate of

Constabulary (HMIC) review, commissioned by the Home Secretary in November 2012 to 'assess police knowledge of and response to the historical allegations made against Jimmy Savile, and potentially into similar allegations against other individuals'.

In presenting the findings of that review to Parliament, Home Secretary Theresa May's recorded that 'In particular, I asked that [it] establish clearly which forces received reports or allegations in respect of Savile and related individuals prior to the launch of Operation Yewtree . . . For each of those forces, I asked HMIC to review the extent to which the allegations were robustly investigated and whether there were any police failings in doing so.'[6]

HMIC's report, published on 12 March 2013, made it clear, the Home Secretary said, 'that failures by police forces, particularly in respect to the quality of investigations and the sharing of intelligence, enabled Savile to act with impunity for over five decades. It is also clear from the report that Savile could and should have been apprehended earlier . . . '

The report's author, HM Inspector of Constabulary Drusilla Sharpling, has confirmed that it was the lack of intelligence, or 'local connection', that explains why North Yorkshire did not figure in her investigation. This lack of intelligence also ensured Peter Jaconelli was not investigated under the terms of Operation Yewtree's Strand 2 of 'other individuals associated with Savile'.

Allegations about Jaconelli being a paedophile were made by a number of individuals and first published on Real Whitby in February 2013, a month before the publication of HMIC's report. They prompted more witnesses and victims to come forward with similar claims against the lascivious former mayor and close associate of Jimmy Savile.

Hicks and Ward were convinced that North Yorkshire Police had knowledge about Jaconelli's behaviour, and if this could be proved there was a good chance it also knew about Jimmy Savile's. From October 2012 onwards, the information Real Whitby uncovered was consistently passed on to officers from Operation Yewtree, who then passed it on to North Yorkshire Police.

Following the publication of HMIC's report, Tim Hicks, who had by this time been interviewed by a Detective Constable and Detective Sergeant from Operation Yewtree, wrote to Drusilla Sharpling, outlining the statements made by the two witnesses to Jaconelli's offending. Hicks detailed Jaconelli's close connection with Savile and the fact both witnesses claimed the police were aware of his offending. He received no reply.

Less than a month later, Hicks and Ward were informed that all matters relating to Savile's activities in Scarborough were now being forwarded to North Yorkshire Police. Despite assurances from Scarborough Borough Council that the details of the two witnesses who had come forward with allegations about Jaconelli had been passed on to the police, neither had been contacted by the NYP.

The widespread criticism of West Yorkshire Police's report on Operation Newgreen prompted Hicks and Ward to redouble their efforts. A series of Freedom of Information Requests were submitted to North Yorkshire Police in a bid to ascertain whether any of its officers had attended Savile's Friday Morning Club meetings. Having developed witnesses who testified to Jaconelli's offending behaviour and vouched that the local police knew about it, Real Whitby felt confident in publishing its most serious claim to date: 'North Yorkshire Police Force Intelligence Bureau failed to pass on the intelligence they undoubtedly had about Savile and his associate Jaconelli, to the Surrey investigation [2007–09].' It was, Hicks contended, a failure that significantly diminished the chances of a prosecution being launched.

Hicks also voiced his fears on Real Whitby that the North Yorkshire Police would be allowed to 'investigate and exonerate itself'[7] in the same way as its counterparts in West Yorkshire. He wrote to Detective Chief Inspector Orchard of Operation Yewtree requesting 'any investigation into Savile in North Yorkshire must now include the Jaconelli paedophile ring first exposed by the *Sunday Express* . . . ' He also recommended the North Yorkshire investigation be 'conducted by another force or by the IPCC, to ensure an impartial investigation and avoid the lack of confidence over the recent West Yorkshire Police investigation'.

Based on the information it received from Real Whitby, the Independent Police Complaints Commission. It wrote to the Chief Constable of North Yorkshire Police directing him to consider whether there were any conduct matters that should be the subject of a referral. Nine days later, on May 29, Assistant Chief Constable Sue Cross of North Yorkshire Police replied with the findings of an internal inquiry.

'The research that has been conducted clearly indicates that Savile was not shown as a "Nominal" either in his own right or in connection with anybody else on any North Yorkshire Police systems,' wrote Cross.[8] 'The available information clearly shows that there was no intelligence held on North Yorkshire Police systems in respect of Savile in his own right (or in respect of his alleged associations with others) which would have required investigative or enforcement action by North Yorkshire Police . . .'

The report by Cross went on to dismiss all the specific allegations made by Real Whitby. Had, as Hicks suggested, North Yorkshire Police questioned witnesses about Jimmy Savile as part of its 2003 investigation into the seafront paedophile ring? 'The available information indicates that the material investigation was conducted using the HOLMES facility,' reported Cross, 'and that Savile is not recorded in the HOLMES system in any form.'

She also denied any North Yorkshire Police officers had attended the weekly socials in Savile's flat in Leeds.

What her letter to the IPCC did reveal, though, was that in September 2008 Jimmy Savile was invited by the North Yorkshire Police to join the Chief Constable as guest of honour at an awards ceremony held at Selby Abbey. A NYP vehicle and driver were sent to collect him from his home in Leeds. Cross described the Community Idol scheme as a 'project intended to encourage positive behaviour amongst young people'. By this date, the police's Impact Nominal Index system would have included intelligence reports uploaded by Surrey Police in 2007 and Sussex Police in

2008; intelligence that would have shown Jimmy Savile as being anything but an appropriate choice to hand out prizes to young people.

Five days later after Cross had given North Yorkshire Police a clean bill of health with regard to its prior knowledge of Jimmy Savile's offending, or that of his friends and associates, Hicks was informed by the IPCC that North Yorkshire would not be investigating Real Whitby's allegations. He was told the concerns that he'd raised were 'not eligible' to be recorded as a police complaint because he did not 'fit the definition of a complainant under the Police Reforms Act 2002'.

Hicks and Ward refused to give up. By September 2013, they had found more witnesses to, and victims of, Jaconelli's offending in Scarborough. One, who wished to remain anonymous, recalled how in 1968, as a fifteen-year-old, he had been lewdly propositioned for sexual favours by Jaconelli outside his shop. When he refused, Jaconelli openly mocked the teenager in front of passers-by.

'I told my parents and my father took me to the police station where I made a statement,' the man told Real Whitby. 'The police officer I spoke to said he believed me and was aware of similar allegations against Peter Jaconelli. However, he said Jaconelli was a Town Councillor, I believe a County Councillor, Judo club owner, business man and all round pillar of society. I was a school boy!'

With North Yorkshire Police still to comment or interview the witnesses and victims unearthed by Real Whitby, Hicks decided to write an open letter. It was emailed to North Yorkshire Police and Crime Commissioner Julia Mulligan and Chief Constable Dave Jones, and published on the Real Whitby website. Hicks highlighted what he considered to be the two 'critical' failings by North Yorkshire Police: the first was its failure 'to arrest Jaconelli . . . which would have surely led them to wind up the vice ring he led in Scarborough, including Savile'; the second was 'the apparent failure by the Force Intelligence Bureau to pass on intelligence

North Yorkshire Police had undoubtedly developed on Savile during the 2003 paedophile investigation'. Again, there was no reply.

On 1 November, North Yorkshire Police was officially exonerated by the IPCC of any blame for its failure to detect Savile while he was alive. 'I am now able to let you know we have completed the review of all the evidence and material relating to the late Jimmy Savile,' wrote Moir Stewart, the IPCC's Director of Investigations, 'and we have decided to take no further action with regard to your force.'[9] Further Real Whitby emails to the IPCC and North Yorkshire Police went unanswered although at least the Metropolitan Police deigned to reply: an officer working on Operation Yewtree reiterated to Hicks that all communications to him would be automatically forwarded to North Yorkshire.

The cycle of request, allegation and silence was finally broken when the BBC's regional documentary programme *Inside Out* picked up on the story. By this stage, Real Whitby had received a letter from Scarborough Borough Council threatening legal action over its claims of a cover-up due to Jaconelli's status as a prominent former Councillor.[10]

On the evening of 10 February 2014, *Inside Out* broadcast its report. It contained interviews with some of the witnesses to Jaconelli's abuse, and a succession of 'no comments' from the police and Scarborough Borough Council. More damaging to the police than its failure to respond to the series of questions posed by the BBC, however, was the revelation that it had failed to contact or interview any of the witnesses who had by now made allegations against Jaconelli. Contrary to what Moir Stewart had said, North Yorkshire Police were shown to be ignoring evidence, evidence it did not even have to go out and find. And yet, as its statement made clear, the IPCC still stood by its decision not to take any further action.

It was now evident to the North Yorkshire Police that the matter was not now simply going to disappear. A statement published on its website immediately after the *Inside Out* report was televised, said NYP was 'considering the content of the programme, its effect on previous matters and the potential need for any future investigative work that would best serve the interests of those directly affected'.[11] Those who took part in the programme, and 'who were the subject of direct contact with the late Mr Jaconelli' were invited to get in touch.

Sensing a decisive shift, Real Whitby's reporters once again articulated their concerns to Drusilla Sharpling, and it was only then that the HMIC reversed its decision and instructed North Yorkshire Police to conduct further investigations.

While North Yorkshire Police's third internal enquiry was under way, a process that took six weeks rather than the nine days spent compiling the report delivered by Assistant Chief Constable Sue Cross, Tim Hicks again contacted Operation Yewtree. He stated his belief that the evidence in the *Inside Out* programme it contained proved the integrity of Yewtree had been compromised. The reply from a Metropolitan Police Detective Inspector on the Operation Yewtree team was perfunctory to say the least, notifying Hicks that allegations concerning Jimmy Savile and Peter Jaconelli did 'not fall within the jurisdiction of the Metropolitan Police to investigate'.

Hicks was again advised to direct new information to North Yorkshire Police and told that the Metropolitan Police would no longer correspond with him. This, despite the fact the Metropolitan Police was the lead force on Operation Yewtree, of which the second strand concerned 'other individuals associated with Savile'. Individuals, surely, like the late Peter Jaconelli.

What the review of all North Yorkshire Police systems to 'ascertain if there was any recorded information in relation to Savile, Jaconelli and their known associates and friends, in respect of any reported offending found was enough for a further statement to be issued.

On 3 April 2014, as a result of its third internal enquiry, North Yorkshire Police announced it had voluntarily referred itself to the

Independent Police Complaints Commission over the way in which the force recorded and responded to 'reports it received against two men regarding child sex abuse'.[12] It went on to say that the referral specifically related to how 'North Yorkshire responded to an allegation it received over a decade ago about Jimmy Savile . . . '

The NYP statement also referenced 'several allegations made recently about Savile's friend, Scarborough resident Peter Jaconelli, who died in 1999'. It confirmed that had Jaconelli been alive today he would have been interviewed under caution and 'a file of the evidence would have been submitted for consideration by the Crown Prosecution Service'.

Chief Constable Dave Jones did not specify in which year the Savile allegation was recorded but the reference to 'over a decade ago' would appear to point to the 2003 paedophile ring investigation, as consistently argued by Real Whitby. Either way, this was information that could and should have been relayed to Surrey Police when a request for information about Jimmy Savile was made in 2007, and to Sussex Police when it did likewise in 2008.

North Yorkshire Police added that it would look at whether information it held on record had been 'comprehensively disclosed to Her Majesty's Inspector of Contabulary (HMIC) when it, and other police forces, were asked to do so in December 2012 and again in May 2013'.

Two and a half years after his death, and more than ten years after first interviewing him in his penthouse flat in Leeds, my journey ended in the spring of 2014 in a garage in Aylesbury. It belonged to Janet Cope, a woman who refuses to believe the allegations levelled against Jimmy Savile, who she served with such devotion, and who sacked her so suddenly and unceremoniously some 15 years before.

We had spent a couple of hours in her pristine bungalow, looking through boxes of letters and photo albums and talking about the past. Janet Cope had told me about her decades working at the National Spinal Injuries Centre at Stoke Mandeville Hospital, and about how she had organised the sit-in that led to Savile taking on the task of building a new centre from the ground up. The campaign, which became a national cause célèbre, had, she recounted, been the busiest and very possibly the happiest time of her life, and she was not prepared for her abiding sense of achievement to be crushed under the debris from the ruined reputation of the man who led it.

'It's been destroyed, all of it,' she said quietly, turning over photographs of her and Savile mugging for the camera with her campaign colleagues in the office, or as dignitaries were led around the site as the foundations were laid and the buildings rose from the dirt. 'It's unfair. He can't answer back so it's up to me and others to defend him. If I'd have seen him doing anything wrong I would have challenged him. He knew that.'

In the envelopes and boxes were letters and invitations from Downing Street and Buckingham Palace, and photos that recorded visits from Margaret Thatcher, Sarah Ferguson, Barbara Bush and the wives of the G7 leaders. There was a table plan from the Duke of Edinburgh's visit in 1981, with a detailed minute-by-minute breakdown of his itinerary, and a letter thanking them for his subsequent visit three years later.

Jimmy Savile had wounded Janet Cope; she explained she had cried for weeks after he told her she was no longer needed. But even after the threatening letter she received from his legal advisers, even after he had forbidden her from returning to Stoke Mandeville, and even after the way he had exerted control over her for nearly thirty years, she remained steadfast in her denial of all that has since been said about a man she insisted had taught her so much.

In the garage were more boxes containing yellowing news-papers, photo albums and a dog-eared contacts book, the one that Janet Cope kept for Jimmy Savile and used to manage his life. In it were numbers for Downing Street, ministers and embassies; for Highgrove, Buckingham Palace and Balmoral; for hospitals, hospices and schools; for Peter Jaconelli, too.

A survey of Britain in the light of what we now know of Jimmy Savile reveals a landscape littered with the fragments of shattered memories and splintered reputations. The most conspicuous frag-ments have fallen from some of Britain's biggest institutions – the National Health Service, the BBC and the police, but the rubble is scattered far and wide. It includes the names of those arrested and charged by Operation Yewtree, even those who have been cleared. Buried within it too is the public's trust in the judgement of leading figures in government, the Church and the royal family, as well as, surely, the private guilt of those who chose not to see, not to ask and not to speak out.

For some, like Janet Cope and others who invested themselves in Jimmy Savile and what he asked of them, and even Roger Ordish, who explained how for so long he had enjoyed watching the reactions of those he told what he had done in his career, the past must now resemble a hall of mirrors. What was once taken for granted, and celebrated, is now so distorted and grotesque it is almost impossible to process. The same applies to Dave Eager, who wore a sweatshirt bearing the words 'Jimmy's Eager Helper' to the Requiem Mass in Leeds, and got to his feet to call for Savile's coffin to be clapped from the cathedral.

I can only imagine what it must feel like to have the floor fall away from under your feet, and everything you believed in be dismissed as a lie. But what cannot be ignored is the gulf between their interpretations of the past and what is now understood about the man who beguiled them and so many others.

'The universal abhorrence at Jimmy Savile's predatory career is a rare moment of self-revelation,'[1] declared an editorial in the *Guardian* the day after the joint report by the Metropolitan Police and the NSPCC was published in January 2013. Hundreds of victims had come forward in the aftermath of ITV's *Exposure* documentary, of which 450 made allegations of sexual abuse relating to Jimmy Savile. Across the 28 police areas in England and Wales, it was recorded that he had committed 214 criminal offences over a period of more than fifty years. Eighty-two per cent of those involved were females, of whom the majority were aged between 13 and 16. There were 31 allegations of rape, of which more than half were committed on minors.

'This whole sordid affair has shown the tragic consequences of what happens when vulnerability collides with power,' said Metropolitan Police Commander Peter Spindler.[2] 'He exploited his celebrity status, he traded on the currency of celebrity to get almost unprecedented access to our institutions, to our hospitals, to our schools. And there he took advantage of the most vulnerable in society, adults and children, though sadly primarily children, for his own sexual gratification.'

On the same day, Keir Starmer QC, the director of public prosecutions, published the conclusions of an internal Crown Prosecution Service review carried out by Alison Levitt QC into the Surrey and Sussex police investigations of 2007 and 2008. He described its findings as 'profound' and apologised for the part the CPS had played in failing those women who reported Jimmy Savile when he was alive. Starmer also stated his conviction that whole-sale changes were needed in the way authorities deal with victims of abuse.

The CPS report showed that Savile could have been prosecuted over three allegations of sexual abuse if police had handled the complainants differently. Starmer also acknowledged that the police and the CPS were likely to have dropped many sexual assault complaints in the past because the victims were treated with a 'degree of caution which is not generally justified'.[3]

'In my view, these cases do not simply reflect errors of judgment by individual officers or prosecutors on the facts before them,' he declared. 'If that were the case, they would, in many respects, be easier to deal with. These were errors of judgment by experienced and committed police officers and a prosecuting lawyer acting in good faith and attempting to apply the correct principles.'

It is the opinion of Liz Dux, the lawyer representing more than seventy of Savile's victims, that the impact of Savile's six decades of abuse is unprecedented. 'Nothing has touched the country the way that this has,' she argues. 'His celebrity status is one part of it, but I think also it's because people from all walks of life were affected, both male and female. If it's a care home, like the poor kids in Jersey, people might think it doesn't really affect them. And if it's the Church, they might think it was not unexpected. But here was someone who was an everyday part of our lives. He was part of our generation's childhood. And because his victims were from everywhere in the country, and from every type of social class, and the fact his offending was just indiscriminate, the combination of those things has really marked a watershed.'

Watershed is the word Starmer also used, and it's appropriate when assessing the surge in the reporting of historic child abuse cases since the Savile scandal burst like a sore. Across the country, rape charities and helplines have been inundated with calls; Greater Manchester Police witnessed a 121 per cent increase in such allegations in the period between November 2012 and April 2013,[4] while Kent Police confirmed a 211 per cent rise. In total, 1,204 historic child abuse claims were made to police forces across the UK in the same period, an increase of 70 per cent. It is a black irony that the pull on resources has contributed to the arrest rate actually falling.[5]

By Spring 2014, more than thirty separate investigations were still ongoing at NHS institutions that Savile came into contact with, while Education Secretary Michael Gove instructed further inquiries be undertaken into his dealings with 21 schools and children's homes across England. Whatever is found and disclosed, the sheer number is testament to the extent he was able to penetrate society and the fixtures that hold it together.

Sources close to Dame Janet Smith's independent review into culture and practices at the BBC during the time Jimmy Savile worked there suggest her report will show he could have abused as many as 1,000 young people in the corporation's dressing rooms and studios, and while travelling the country under its banner. Smith has used the same methodology she employed in the inquiry into serial killer Harold Shipman, where rather than the fifteen murders he was convicted of it was established the true figure was probably closer to 250.

At two of the hospitals he was most closely linked with, Stoke Mandeville and Broadmoor, Savile used his power and status to bully staff into acquiescence, and his victims into silence. At Stoke Mandeville, those who challenged him were reminded he could turn off the funding tap at any minute. Janet Cope confirmed to me that she had witnessed him being 'lethal to other people, and I mean lethal'. She also said he was 'good at threatening people. It is how he got such a lot done.'

At Broadmoor, the blackmail used on recalcitrant members of the Prison Officers' Association was of a blunter variety. He was given offices and accommodation at both hospitals, a luxury he was also afforded at Leeds General Infirmary.

'I saw his behaviour change from making a request to making a demand for anything he wanted,' said Christine McFarlane, former director of nursing and patient care at Stoke Mandeville.[6]

'This happened as his power and fame for raising money for the spinal unit grew. He did change, and latterly was not the nice person that everyone knew at the beginning.'

McFarlane spoke of the freedom Savile had 'to walk wherever he wanted' and also how he hated to be challenged. 'He was Jimmy Savile, nobody argued with him,' she said. 'There was a fine balance for them [staff] to reach in not upsetting Jimmy to the point where he was likely to walk away or try to take his money away.'

So how did he get away with it, and for so long? Commander Spindler coined a phrase that, at first glance, appeared to absolve those who either failed to see or turned a blind eye to what was taking place on their watch. It also provides comfort to those who prefer to view the past through rose-tinted spectacles like the ones Jimmy Savile used to wear. 'It's a question for British society to answer,' Spindler said. 'We are talking about six decades of abuse. We do need to set this in the context of society at the time . . . but we were all taken in. You could say he groomed a nation.'

I now look back and wonder if he was grooming me, offering up all that access, taking me for lunch and fixing it for me to join him on the QE2 in return for a legacy he wanted me to secure in print; a legacy he surely knew was destined to end up like his gravestone – smashed to smithereens, ground down and deposited as landfill. Why else would he have chosen as his epitaph 'It was good while it lasted'?

The journalist, novelist and playwright Andrew O'Hagan believes to an extent we were all complicit; that we get the celebrities we deserve. In a memorable essay in the *London Review of Books*,[7] he identified the period in which Savile acquired his fame as a time when the cult of personality suddenly eclipsed all other considerations, and the power of celebrity, as we know it today, was unleashed.

'And so,' wrote O'Hagan, 'you open Pandora's box to find the seedy ingredients of British populism. It's not just names, or performers and acts, it's an ethos. Why is British light entertainment so often based on the sexualisation of people too young to cope? And why is it that we have a press so keen to feed off it? Is it to cover the fact, via some kind of willed outrage, that the culture itself is largely paedophile in its commercial and entertainment excitements?

'The public made Jimmy Savile,' he concluded. 'It loved him. It knighted him. The Prince of Wales accorded him special rights and the authorities at Broadmoor gave him his own set of keys. A whole entertainment structure was built to house him and make him feel secure. That's no one's fault: entertainment, like literature, thrives on weirdos, and Savile entered a culture made not only to tolerate his oddness but to find it refreshing.'

Here was a man, after all, who blithely put his hand up the skirts of teenage girls as they jostled and smiled coyly for the cameras during the links on *Top of the Pops*, and who asked for, and got, six local 'dolly birds' as payment for a personal appearance at a provincial ball. This was a man whose idea of a treat for young hospital patients was to take them to the motor caravan he was allowed to park in the grounds, and who laid on girls for visiting police officers. And he was doing it in an era when children were being murdered and buried on the Moors around Manchester, The Rolling Stones were writing lyrics telling a fifteen-year-old girl they didn't want to see her ID,[8] and Gary Puckett & The Union Gap were warning, 'Better run girl, you're much too young girl'.[9]

By the time his lustre as a teenage idol began to fade, Savile had remade himself as a trusted if unlikely establishment figure. He was feted by administrators, aristocrats and royalty, and viewed as a vote winner by politicians looking to connect with the young or bask in the glow he acquired from his charity works. Prime Minister Thatcher, whose blushes he spared by rebuilding the nation's leading specialist spinal injuries unit, recognised in this outsider something of herself. She later described him as a shining example of the 'enterprise Britain' she envisaged when she took office. Prince Charles, who sought his common touch and counsel, and Princess Diana, who valued his advice and soothing words, were similarly charmed and enthralled.

There are those who recall the Jimmy Savile of the late 1950s, and remember even then that he 'liked them young'. In that world, they argue, it was nothing out of the ordinary. By the time societal attitudes began to change, however, and systems were put in place to ensure regional police forces could more effectively share information with each other, Savile's offending had all but stopped. By then, of course, he was Sir Jimmy Savile, safely entrenched at the centre of concentric, defensive rings of influence. And instead of walking round ballrooms flanked by heavies, calculating how many girls he would be able to pick from, he was free to stroll through ministry corridors and hospitals, confident in the knowledge that he had too much power, too much sway, to be challenged.

He engineered opportunity through an act of mass deception, one that saw him create a seemingly virtuous circle in which his fame and connections were harnessed to help those in need. In return, he accepted society's gratitude and the kudos that came with it. It was a mechanism of the most venal kind. A cunning calibration of his celebrity, popularity and good works for the nation being enough to blind even those close enough to see through it.

'These people couldn't have coped, couldn't have spoken out, because their whole lives would have been totally collapsed at the time,' says Caroline Moore of his victims. She was one of them; he abused her while she sat in a wheelchair at Stoke Mandeville.

His was the perfect cover. His victims were generally young, vulnerable and unsuspecting. Some were on the margins of society, meaning their testimonies would never breach the ramparts of a reputation that was national in scale. It was so preposterously easy, so matter of fact, that it never seemed to occur to anyone that despite his weird appearance and the sinister things he said and did, Jimmy Savile might possibly be up to no good.

The endless drip of salacious headlines and the spiralling numbers of alleged victims have had a desensitising effect, but the scale of his deceit and depths of his depravity have lost none of their power to shock. 'It was just so opportunistic, and it was so prolific, it's like it happened every single day of his life,' remarks Liz Dux, who has specialised in abuse cases for more than fifteen years. 'I've never seen abuse like this where every opportunity he had to be with someone, he would assault them. He didn't even try to hide anything. It was just so blatant that you just cannot believe he got away with it for so long.'

Over a period of forty years, police forces up and down the country dismissed or buried reports about Jimmy Savile, while his willingness to engage lawyers and the popularity he enjoyed persuaded newspapers from going to print with the information they had. Even in death he seemed to exert this same power, as the BBC, which had failed to act on reports and rumours about him in the past, spiked the *Newsnight* story that would have exposed him, and avoided much of the internecine chaos that followed.

It is also true that Jimmy Savile led a life designed to avoid detection. He travelled constantly, living on the road for much of the period in which his offending was at its most prolific. Many of the people who counted themselves as his friends knew very little about what he did or the 'teams' he kept in other towns. He never let anyone get close enough to see what really lay beneath, not even the women who claimed to be his girlfriends in later years. As the curator of his own myth, his stories were woven into a tapestry so elaborate I'm sure he even believed what he'd created by the end.

The cost of his unmasking has not only been reckoned in financial terms. The £2 million spent on concluding the part of Operation Yewtree that related to Savile, and the £5.3 million spent by the BBC on its three different inquiries up until March 2013,[10] pale into insignificance when weighed against the toll his abuse has taken on the individuals he deemed to be helpless.

There are others who suffered indirectly. From those who acted in good faith in assisting his fund-raising efforts, and who must now wonder what they inadvertently helped him to do, through to those like his nephew Vivian, who hero-worshipped him and died of a broken heart less than two weeks after the revelations about his uncle emerged; to his horrified friends, some of whom have received counselling[10], through to the three men who committed suicide in the wake of the revelations, the collateral damage has been widespread and indiscriminate.

Of those who took their own lives, one had Jimmy Savile to thank for landing a job as DJ in the 1960s, and attended both his funeral in Leeds and burial in Scarborough. The police claimed they were not investigating the man, although a newspaper had made enquiries. His body lay undiscovered in his Doncaster flat for two weeks.[11]

Another was a clergyman said to be so anxious about the police investigation spreading to Cornwall he left a suicide note in his home before throwing himself into the sea at Trevone.[12] The third was the least lamented: David Smith, a convicted paedophile who was employed by the BBC as a chauffeur and who is thought to have driven Savile in the 1980s. He was found dead in his Lewisham home on the morning he was due to stand trial on two counts of indecent assault, two of indecency and a fifth charge of rape involving a 12-year-old boy, crimes that were reported as part of the Savile inquiry.

Alan Collins, a solicitor with a Manchester law firm representing scores of Savile's victims, spoke of his clients' anger at being denied the chance to see Smith face justice. 'Victims often take a great deal of time to psychologically prepare themselves to come forward and confront their abusers,' he said. 'They have a desire to be vindicated.'[13]

Of course, there is no hope of that with the victims of Jimmy Savile's abuse. 'The scars of those attacks are deep, and they do remain,' confirms Dee Coles, who was a teenager when she was attacked by Savile in his motor caravan in Jersey.[14] Of those who gave evidence to Kate Lampard's NHS Inquiry, and were asked to do so at the hospitals where they were abused, some are now reported to be suffering from post-traumatic stress disorder.

'We are definitely making life better for victims of abuse,' maintains Liz Dux, 'but it has come at a cost to some of these victims and that's why I feel so passionately about the [compensation cases against the Savile estate, the BBC, the NHS, and other organisations].' Dux explains that her clients fall into two camps: those who have been emotionally destroyed and those who have managed to channel their anger and are now campaigning for something to be done. 'Until their own cases are resolved they are just not going to get closure. A lot of them had parked it away, then opened it out and got no help once they had. They now need to be able to deal with it and move on.'

Keir Starmer, who stepped down as director of public prosecutions on 1 November 2013, is clear on what should be done. 'The time has come to change the law and close a gap that's been there for a very long time,' he told *Panorama*. 'I think there should be a mandatory reporting provision . . . a clear, direct law that everybody understands . . . Since the Savile scandal some steps have been taken to assist victims through the difficult process of reporting abuse and the criminal trial process, but now the government needs to act in a more positive way to make sure the silence that surrounded Savile and allowed his horrific abuse to go unreported can never happen again. We are now calling on the government to introduce legislation whereby those in regulated activities who have direct knowledge of abuse and fail to do the right thing and report it will face prosecution.'

He had just watched the recorded testimony of one of Savile's victims, the girl who was raped as a 12-year-old after being led to the television room at Stoke Mandeville Hospital. 'If there had been a compulsion to report the abuse at the time victims may have been spared their ordeals,' Starmer said. The recently established National Crime Agency has asked the government to consider the proposals.

Such a law might have protected that girl in 1977, and her life might have turned out differently. As she said in her interview with the child protection expert retained by Slater & Gordon, 'Being raped by Savile whilst in hospital has had a profound effect on my life. It has reinforced the feeling with me that I am a victim. I have come to see myself as someone who was born to be abused. Subsequently I have felt that I was responsible for Savile's attack because I had not struggled or resisted in any way. I felt even worse because I had put my hand on his cheek as he was raping me, something I couldn't explain to myself. The rape left me feeling ashamed and dirty, as though I was different and less deserving than my peers.

Throughout her adult life she says she has felt like she has 'some kind of label' that identifies her as a victim to men with whom she has come into contact. 'This has led me to being abused and mistreated by men over and over again,' she said. 'I have never had a healthy loving relationship. Every man I have been with has either abused me emotionally or physically and I can't help but feel that I was conditioned to expect that sort of treatment.

'I have not wanted to be a victim and have fought very hard to move forward . . . I have struggled with depression and feel that my capacity to deal with life has been undermined by my past. I have no resilience and have hit rock bottom every time I have to deal with one of life's blows. I have made several suicide attempts in my life.'

The man responsible for such carnage never faced trial. He is the same man I spent years interviewing, dining out with and accompanying across oceans; and many more years before that talking about and becoming convinced of the sickness at his core. I had nothing more than his self-proclaimed oddness, his bizarre appearance and his warped philosophy on which to base those assumptions. And yet somehow, he managed to throw me off balance. Then, as with others, he disarmed me and charmed me with his kaleidoscopic account of what seemed to have been an extraordinary life.

Now, in the unforgiving light of his exposure, the claims I once made about him now don't seem so wild after all.

Was he sexually abused as a child, as many abusers were? It's impossible to say, although it was something that seemed to run in his family: his older brother Johnnie lost his job over claims he sexually assaulted a patient in a mental hospital, and in March 2014 it emerged that his nephew, the son of his sister Joan, was sentenced to four years in prison in 1986 for sexually assaulting a 14-year-old girl.[11]

What he told me about never having been a child can, I believe, only have informed his inability or unwillingness to have normal relationships, while also contributing to his need to surround himself with people much younger than himself. And what of that formative experience on the train when he claimed an older woman thrust her hand down his trousers and took what she wanted? It was an act of cold compulsion that he seems to have replayed and inflicted over and over again.

In hindsight, I wish I had pressed him more on his attitudes on sex, particularly in light of the strange things he said and wrote. I can at least be satisfied I asked him about the rumours on every occasion we talked.

For a while, I had wondered whether his secret might have been murder – particularly in light of what I'd been told about the owner of the Maison Royale in Bournemouth – but I found nothing concrete to support that theory. It would have made his constant shifting and obdurate refusal to allow anyone into his confidence that much easier to understand.

The reality is he was never going to give up that which he'd guarded so jealously and for so long; the things he knew would lead to his certain fall. Added to this, experience had taught there was no real appetite for pursuing him. He had been seen to do too much good, and he knew too many powerful people for that to happen. The contacts book shown to me by Janet Cope was his insurance. It was just one of so many policies he took out.

Another was his faith, which might explain why a man who did so many terrible things also resolved to do so much good, or at least wanted to be seen to be doing so. 'He always told me the scales would always balance,' Cope recalled, although Reverend Colin Semper is sure that Jimmy Savile knew in his heart that what he was doing was wrong, and that the tireless fund-raising was a doomed attempt to pay off his debt.

In the ten years since I pushed on the front door of Lake View Court and sat with a feeling of nervous anticipation as he descended in the lift, my feelings about Jimmy Savile have been twisted and tested and bent out of shape until they've broken into pieces. Did I choose him or did he choose me? I'm still unsure. As with all who encountered him, other than those who were subjected to the appalling reality of what he was, Jimmy Savile stayed out of reach; a plume of acrid smoke that billowed and dispersed before any sense could be made of it.

Ultimately, the truth is where it always was. All that remains is rotting in a concrete-encased coffin, buried at an angle in an unmarked spot on a North Yorkshire hillside.

ENDNOTES

CHAPTER 1

1 Roger Bodley, speaking in the foreword of the catalogue for Dreweatts' auction of Jimmy Savile's possessions
2 *Independent on Sunday*, 30 October 2011; *Sunday Times*, 30 October 2011, *Sunday Telegraph*, 30 October 2011
3 *Mail Online*, 20 September 2012
4 BBC News Glasgow and West Scotland, 3 October 2012
5 *Daily Express*, 9 October 2012
6 *The Times*, 10 October 2012
7 ITV *Daybreak*, 9 October 2012
8 *Daily Telegraph*, 9 October 2012
9 *Daily Mirror*, 10 October 2012

CHAPTER 3

1 *Yorkshire Post*, 8 November 1972
2 *The Times*, 23 December 1989
3 Jimmy Savile, *As It Happens* (Barrie & Jenkins, 1974), p. 2
4 *Reveille*, 23 May 1970
5 *Sunday Times Magazine*, 2 August 1992
6 Savile, *As It Happens*, p. 1
7 *Daily Mail*, 3 January 2004
8 *Sunday Times Magazine*, 2 August 1992
9 Anthony Clare, *In the Psychiatrist's Chair* (Heinemann, 1992), p. 249
10 Alison Bellamy, *How's About That Then?* (Great Northern Books, 2012), p. 24
11 *The Times*, 23 December 1989
12 *Sunday Times Magazine*, 23 May, 1982
13 *Sunday Times Magazine*, 2 August 1992
14 *The Times*, 23 December 1989
15 *Independent on Sunday*, 22 July, 1990
16 Clare, *In the Psychiatrist's Chair*, p. 241

CHAPTER 4

1 'Psychotherapy in Prisons and Corrective Institutions [Abridged]', *Proceedings of the Royal Society of Medicine*, 8 December 1953
2 'Anna Raccoon' blog, 23 October 2012
3 'Swallow Falls Softly' posted on www.careleavers.org.uk, 30 November 2011
4 'Anna Raccoon' blog, 23 October 2012
5 *Mail Online*, 2 November 2012
6 *Mail Online*, 2 November 2012

7 Pollard Review Report, 18 December 2012, p. 44
8 Kat Ward, *Keri Karin – the Shocking True Story Continued* ... (self-published, 2012), p. 56
9 Ibid.
10 Pollard Review Report, 15, p. 105
11 Pollard Review Report, Appendix 12/009
12 Pollard Review Report, p. 32
13 Pollard Review Report, p. 32
14 Transcript from Nick Vaughan-Barratt interview with the Pollard Inquiry, 29 November 2012, pp. 25–26
15 Pollard Review Report, 25, p. 107
16 Pollard Review Report, 34, p. 110

CHAPTER 5

1 Savile, *As It Happens*, pp. 4 and 6
2 Ibid., pp. 138–139
3 Ibid., p. 138

CHAPTER 7

1 *Yorkshire Evening Post*, 1 November 2011
2 Ibid.
3 Pollard Review Report, 18, p. 47
4 Pollard Review Report, 21 & 22, pp. 48–49
5 Liz MacKean interview to Pollard Review, p. 34
6 Ibid., p. 37
7 Pollard Review Report, 31, p. 51
8 Pollard Review Report, 32, p. 52
9 Liz MacKean interview to Pollard Review, pp. 12–13

CHAPTER 8

1 Savile, *As It Happens*, p. 11
2 Savile, *As It Happens*, p. 12
3 Ibid., *As It Happens*, p. 13
4 *Sunday Times*, 2 August 1992
5 Savile, *As It Happens*, p. 15
6 *Newcastle Journal*, 13 November 1999
7 Savile, *As It Happens*, p. 23
8 Ibid., p. 24
9 Ibid., p. 25
10 *Daily Mail*, 30 July 1994
11 *Sun*, 23 January 1978
12 *Sun*, 2 April 1984
13 *People*, 6 September 1981, 13 August 1980
14 *Daily Telegraph*, 26 March 2008

CHAPTER 9

1 Pollard Review Report, 49, p. 55
2 Pollard Review Report, 23 (a), p. 26
3 Helen Boaden Pollard Inquiry interview transcript, 20 November 2012, p. 19

4 Pollard Review Report, 67, p. 62
5 Pollard Review Report, 67–68, pp. 61–62
6 Helen Boaden Pollard Inquiry interview transcript, 20 November 2012, p. 25
7 Helen Boaden Pollard Inquiry interview transcript, 20 November 2012, p. 28
8 Pollard Review Report, 80, p. 65
9 Pollard Review Report, 88, p. 67
10 Pollard Review Report, 21, pp. 48–49
11 Pollard Review Report, 92, p. 69
12 Pollard Review Report, 100, pp. 72–73
13 Pollard Review Report, 112, p. 77
14 Pollard Review Report, 141, p. 85
15 Pollard Review Report, 128–137, pp. 82–84
16 Pollard Review Report, 128, p. 82
17 Pollard Review Report, 133, p. 83
18 Pollard Review 141 & 148, pp. 85 & 87
19 Pollard Review Report, 144, p. 86
20 Pollard Review Report, 162–163, p. 90
21 Pollard Review Report, 167, p. 91
22 Meirion Jones interview with Pollard Review, Part 1, p. 67

CHAPTER 10

1 *Sunday Times Magazine*, 2 August 1992
2 Savile, *As It Happens*, p. 25
3 *Sun*, 23 January 1978
4 *Reveille*, 15 March 1962
5 Savile, *As It Happens*, p. 29
6 Full transcript of Jimmy Savile interview conducted by Frank Broughton for *Last Night a DJ Saved My Life* (Headline, 2003)
7 Broughton interview transcript
8 *Wharfedale Observer*, 3 November 2011
9 Ibid.
10 Broughton interview transcript

CHAPTER 11

1 *Mail on Sunday*, 6 November, 2011
2 *Sunday Mirror*, 6 November 2011
3 Ibid.
4 *Daily Mail*, 3 December 2011
5 *Yorkshire Evening Post*, 8 November 2011
6 *People*, 18 December 2011
7 *This Morning*, 15 June 2012
8 Pollard Review Report, 4 & 5, pp. 116–117
9 *Daily Mail*, 19 October 2012
10 Pollard Review Report, 9, p. 118
11 Ibid., p. 118
12 Ibid., p. 118
13 Pollard Review Report, 11, pp. 118–119
14 Pollard Review Report, 7, p. 117
15 'Jimmy Savile Scandal: the Pollard Tape in Full', *Daily Telegraph*, 11 December 2013

16 Peter Oborne – *Daily Telegraph* Blogs – 27 November 2013
17 Pollard Review Report, 54, p. 34
18 Pollard Review Report, 17, p. 139

CHAPTER 12

1 Jackie 'Mr TV' Pallo, *You Grunt, I'll Groan* (Futura, 1985), p. 5

CHAPTER 13

1 *Daily Express*, 24 August 1951
2 Savile, *As It Happens*

CHAPTER 14

1 Pollard Review Report, 15, p. 119
2 Pollard Review Report, 17, p. 120
3 Pollard Review Report, 19, p. 121
4 Pollard Review Report, 28, p. 123
5 Pollard Review Report, 35, p. 125
6 Bellamy, *How's About That Then?*, pp. 236–237
7 *Yorkshire Evening Post*, 12 March, 2012

CHAPTER 16

1 *Wharfedale Observer*, 3 November 2011
2 Savile, *As It Happens*, p. 32
3 West Yorkshire Police – Operation Newgreen, p. 37, 7.38
4 *Sunday People*, 29 March, 1964
5 Eric Morley, *The 'Miss World' Story*, (Angley Books, 1967) p. 95
6 *Sunday People*, 29 March 1964
7 Broughton interview transcript
8 Savile, *As It Happens*, p. 34
9 Mark Willerton, *No Secret Anymore: The Real Kathy Kirby* (Matador, 2013), p. 14
10 *Daily Express*, 24 March 2013
11 *Sunday People*, 22 December, 1963
12 Savile, *God'll Fix It*, p. 38

CHAPTER 17

1 Dave Haslam, *Manchester, England* (Fourth Estate, 1999), p. 89
2 Ian Skidmore, *Forgive Us Our Press Passes* revised edition (Revel Barker, 2008), p. 181
3 George Melly, *Owning Up: The Trilogy* (Penguin, 2000), p. 450
4 *Guardian*, 4 April 2000

CHAPTER 19

1 Bellamy, *How's About That Then?*, p. 157
2 Savile, *As It Happens*, p. 51
3 *Daily Telegraph*, 13 October 2012

CHAPTER 20

1 *Daily Mirror*, 4 August 2013
2 Alan Bailey, *208 It Was Great: An Affectionate Anecdotal Journey Between 1958 and 1975* (Alan Bailey, 2008) p. 104
3 Savile, *God'll Fix It*, p. 58

CHAPTER 22

1 *Guardian*, 21 November 2001
2 *Sunday Times*, 9 December 2012
3 *Guardian*, 24 February 2013
4 Pollard Review interview transcripts. Meirion Jones, 12 November 2012, pp. 80–81
5 *Guardian*, 26 February 2013
6 *Guardian*, 24 February 2013
7 Pollard Review Report, Appendix 12, 12/051, A3/011
8 Pollard Review Report, Appendix 12, 12/122, A4/223
9 Pollard Review interview transcripts. Meirion Jones, 12 November 2012, p. 142
10 *Guardian*, 26 February 2013

CHAPTER 23

1 *Sun*, 15 July 2012
2 *Sun*, 16 July 2012
3 *Daily Mail*, 30 July 2012
4 *Daily Mail*, 30 July 2012

CHAPTER 25

1 *Reveille*, 9 August 1962
2 *New Musical Express*, 20 July 1962
3 *Daily Mirror*, 9 August 1962
4 Vic Lewis and Tony Barrow, *Music and Maiden Overs* (Chatto & Windus, 1987) p. 118
5 *Guardian*, 5 November 1960
6 *Guardian*, 22 March 1962

CHAPTER 26

1 'Giving Victims a Voice – Joint Report Into Sexual Allegations Made Against Jimmy Savile by the Metropolitan Police and the NSPCC' (January 2013), p. 17
2 '"Mistakes Were Made" – HMIC's review into allegations and intelligence material concerning Jimmy Savile between 1964 and 2013' (HMIC, 2013), p. 13
3 Steve Blacknell, *The Story of Top of the Pops* (Patrick Stephens Ltd, 1985), p. 16
4 *Guardian*, 2 November 2012
5 Blacknell, *The Story of Top of the Pops*, p. 20
6 Ian Gittins, *Top of the Pops: Mishaps, Miming and Music* (Ebury, 2007), p. 9

7   Blacknell, *The Story of Top of the Pops*, p. 20
8   *Independent*, 22 November, 2012
9   *Top of the Pops – 1964–2002* by Jeff Simpson (BBC Worldwide, 2002), p. 13
10 BBC TV Audience Research Reports, 1964, VR/64/11

CHAPTER 28

1   Cross-referenced with Savile's Pop Talk column in the *People*, 7 March 1965
2   Savile, *As It Happens*, pp. 141–142
3   *People*, March 7 1965
4   *Daily Sketch*, 26 March 1965
5   *Evening News*, 6 May 1965
6   Clare, *In the Psychiatrist's Chair*, p. 267
7   Savile, *As It Happens*, p. 112
8   *Daily Telegraph*, 29 October 2011
9   Savile, *As It Happens*, p. 59
10 Clare, *In the Psychiatrist's Chair*, pp. 254–255
11 *Guardian*, 6 August 1992
12 *Daily Mirror*, 15 October 1971

CHAPTER 29

1   Bill Wyman, *Stone Alone: The Story of a Rock'n'Roll Band* (Perseus, 1991), p. 252
2   Gittins, *Top of the Pops: Mishaps, Miming and Music*, p. 10
3   *People*, 19 April 1964
4   *Daily Sketch*, 7 December 1964
5   *Reveille*, 30 May 1970
6   *Daily Mail*, 3 October 2012
7   *Daily Mail*, 3 October 2012
8   'Mistakes were made', p. 19

CHAPTER 30

1   Stephen Hayes, *The Biggest Gang in Britain* (Grosvenor House Publishing, 2013), p. 16
2   *People*, 26 June 1966
3   *Daily Sketch*, 15 December 1966
4   *Daily Mirror*, 30 August 1966
5   *Sunday Times Magazine*, 14 January 1968

CHAPTER 31

1   *Wharfedale & Airedale Observer*, August 1967
2   Ibid.
3   Savile, *As It Happens*, p. 122
4   West Yorkshire Archive Service, Document ref LC/0T/1/41
5   *Wharfedale & Airedale Observer*, September 1967
6   Savile, *As It Happens*, pp. 121–122

7 Roy Greenslade, 'People Power', *British Journalism Review*, Vol. 19, No 1, 2008
8 *People*, 23 January 1972

CHAPTER 32

1 *The Times*, 13 December 1967
2 *Guardian*, 10 January 1968
3 *Daily Mail*, 10 January 1968
4 *Guardian*, 10 January 1968
5 *People*, 14 January 1968
6 Savile, *As It Happens*, p. 123
7 *People*, 14 January 1968
8 *Sunday Times Magazine*, 14 January 1968
9 *People*, 3 March 1968
10 *Irish Times*, 2 May 1968
11 *Daily Mail*, 26 October 1968
12 *Daily Mirror*, 22 February 2013
13 *Daily Sketch*, 3 September 1967
14 *Daily Sketch*, 7 June 1968
15 Johnny Beerling, *Radio 1: The Inside Scene* (Trafford Publishing, 2008), p. 51
16 *Daily Mail*, 5 November 2012
17 *Evening News*, 9 September 1968

CHAPTER 34

1 Beerling, *Radio 1: The Inside Scene*, p. 52
2 *Evening Standard*, 6 July 1965
3 *Evening Standard*, 18 December 1968
4 *Daily Mail*, 2 April 1969
5 Motor Caravanners' Club press release, 12 June 1969
6 *Daily Mail*, 3 September 1969
7 *Observer*, 28 Sept 1969
8 *People*, 19 October 1969
9 *Observer*, 18 January 1970
10 Trevor Beeson, *Priests and Prelates: The Daily Telegraph Clerical Obituaries* (Continuum Publishing Group, 2004), p. 61
11 *Listener*, 23 March 1976
12 *People*, 16 August 1970
13 *Guardian*, 11 January 2013
14 *Sun*, 2 October 2012
15 *Guardian*, 11 January 2013
16 *Guardian*, 21 July 1971
17 *Mirror Magazine*, 4 March 1970
18 *Reveille*, 30 May 1970
19 *Daily Telegraph*, 4 November 2012
20 *Reveille*, 30 May 1970
21 *People*, 4 April 1971

CHAPTER 35

1 *News of the World*, 4 April 1971
2 *News of the World*, 14 February 1971

3 *Daily Mail*, 9 January 1971
4 *News of the World*, 21 March 1971
5 *News of the World*, 21 March 1971
6 *Daily Telegraph*, 13 October 2012
7 *News of the World*, 4 April 1971
8 *Guardian*, 5 April 1971
9 *Daily Mail*, 5 April 1971
10 *Guardian*, 5 April 1971
11 *Guardian*, 5 April 1971
12 *Evening News*, 6 April 1971
13 *Daily Express*, 7 April 1971
14 *Daily Mirror*, 7 April 1971
15 *Guardian*, 8 April 1971
16 ITV News, 14 December 2012
17 *Sunday Telegraph*, 14 October 2012
18 *Daily Telegraph*, 16 October 2012
19 *Daily Telegraph*, 5 June 2013
20 *The Times*, 7 June 2013
21 *Weekly News*, March 4 1972

CHAPTER 36

1 *Irish Times*, 10 May 1971
2 *Sunday Times*, 19 December 1971
3 *Daily Mirror*, 14 October 1971
4 David Winter, *Winter's Tale: Living Through an Age of Change in Church and Media* (Lion Publishing, 2001), pp. 114–115
5 Article on www.davidwinter-author.co.uk
6 *Daily Mirror*, 15 October 1971
7 *Sunday Times*, 19 December 1971
8 *People*, 16 January 1972
9 *Sun*, 1 January 1972
10 *People*, 16 January 1972
11 *Daily Mirror*, 12 October 2012
12 *People*, 23 January 1972
13 Savile, *As It Happens*, p. 145
14 Ibid., p. 146
15 Interview with Lucy Manning, ITV News, 2 October 2012
16 BBC Radio Jersey, 3 October 2012
17 *Daily Mirror*, 20 September 1972

CHAPTER 38

1 Nottinghamshire Healthcare NHS Trust Forensic Division – Summary Report – JS Investigation, May 2013
2 'Savile associate Jaconelli finally exposed', www.real-whitby.co.uk, 14 February 2013
3 *Sunday People*, 8 October 1972
4 *Daily Mail*, 8 December 1972
5 *Sunday People*, 8 October 1972
6 *Daily Mail*, 8 December 1972
7 *Sunday People*, 8 October 1972

8 www.getreading.co.uk. 11 October 2012
9 *Guardian*, 12 October 2012
10 *Yorkshire Evening Post*, 9 October 1972
11 *Telegraph Magazine*, 9 August, 1974
12 Clare, *In the Psychiatrist's Chair*, p. 266
13 Savile, *As It Happens*, p. 115
14 *People*, 15 October 1972
15 *Sunday Magazine* (*News of the World*), 13 May 1984
16 *Evening News*, 23 October 1972

CHAPTER 39

1 *Daily Mail*, 21 September 1973
2 *Northern Daily Mail*, 24 September 1973
3 *Daily Mail* 21 September 1973
4 *Daily Express*, 24 September 1973
5 *Northern Daily Mail*, 24 September 1973
6 *Daily Mirror* 8 November 1972
7 *Daily Mirror*, 1 December 1972
8 *Daily Mail*, 26 October 2012
9 *Daily Express*, 31 March 1973
10 *Daily Mail*, 21 May 73
11 *Daily Mail*, 8 December 1972
12 *Sun*, 13 March 2013
13 Pollard Review, Appendix 12, 12/059, A3/127

CHAPTER 41

1 Pollard Review, Appendix 12, 12/023 A1/259
2 *Daily Express*, 21 February 2013
3 *Daily Express*, 24 April 1974
4 *Guardian*, 22 February 1974
5 *Daily Telegraph*, 4 November 2012
6 *Telegraph Magazine*, 9 August 1974
7 *News of the World*, 22 September, 1974
8 *Sunday People*, 13 October 1974
9 *Guardian*, 16 October 1974
10 Bob 'the Cat' Bevan, *Nearly Famous: Adventures of An After-Dinner Speaker* (Virgin, 204), pp. 131–133

CHAPTER 42

1 Roger Ordish, *The Jim'll Fix It Story* (Hodder & Stoughton, 1992), p. 15
2 Bevan, *Nearly Famous – Adventures of An After-Dinner Speaker*, p. 136
3 *Daily Mail*, 16 June 1975
4 *Listener*, 19 June 1975
5 *Jewish Chronicle Online*, 3 November 2011
6 Bellamy, *How's About That Then?*, pp. 144–145
7 *Daily Mirror*, 25 June 1977
8 Colin Semper, introduction to Savile, *God'll Fix It*, p. xii
9 Savile, *God'll Fix It*, pp. 33–34
10 *Observer Magazine*, 11 May 1981

CHAPTER 43

1 *Daily Mirror*, 30 January 1976
2 *Sun*, 27 October 1976
3 *Evening News*, 9 December 1977
4 *Sun,* 17 December 1977
5 *Daily Mirror,* 7 February 1976
6 *Listener*, 23 March 1976
7 *Sun*, 27 October 1976
8 *Northern Daily Mail*, 28 October 1976
9 *News of the World*, 17 July 1977
10 *Daily Mail*, 2 August 1977
11 *Daily Telegraph*, 20 October 2012

CHAPTER 44

1 BBC News website, 10 October 2012
2 *Guardian*, 18 July 1980
3 BBC News, Beds, Herts & Bucks, 11 October 2012
4 *Daily Mail*, 10 October 2012
5 *Sun*, 19 October 2012
6 BBC *Look North*, 10 October 2012
7 *Mirror*, 11 October 2012
8 *Mirror*, 6 October 2012
9 Twiggster: www.motforum.com, 29 October 2011
10 *Guardian* 31 October 2012

CHAPTER 45

1 *Daily Mail*, 20 June 1978
2 Savile, *As It Happens*, p. 150
3 *Daily Mail*, 20 June 1978
4 *You Magazine, Mail on Sunday*, 23 February 1992
5 *Daily Express*, 4 October 2012
6 *Daily Express*, 4 October 2012
7 Colin Semper, introduction to *God'll Fix It*, p. xv
8 Savile, *God'll Fix It* (Mowbray), p. 9335
9 Savile, *God'll Fix It* (Mowbray), p. 9
10 Ibid., pp. 21–22
11 Ibid., p. 42
12 Ibid., p. 56
13 Ibid., p. 56

CHAPTER 46

1 Pollard Review Report 57, p. 131
2 Pollard Review Report 66 & 67, p. 133
3 *Guardian*, 28 September 2012
4 *Sunday Mirror*, 30 September 2012
5 Pollard Review Report 5, p. 136
6 Pollard Review Report 38, pp. 146–147
7 Pollard Review Report 39, p. 147

8 Pollard Review Report 40, p. 148
9 *The Times*, 2 October 2012

CHAPTER 47

1 *Daily Express*, 30 December 1993
2 *Daily Express*, 17 June 1980
3 *Guardian*, 24 January 1980
4 *Daily Mail*, 25 January 1980
5 *Mail Online*, 28 December 2012
6 National Archive: Downing Street memo, 22 February 1980, Mike Pattison to Prime Minister
7 www.thejournal.ie, 28 December 2013
8 *Daily Mail*, 2 February 1980
9 *Daily Star*, 12 May 2013/National Archive: Letter headed PRIME MINISTER, March 6, 1980, and initialled G.V.
10 *Daily Star*, 12 May 2013
11 *The Age of the Train*, BBC4, 15 September 2012
12 *Daily Telegraph*, 11 October 2012
13 *Jim'll Fix It* Annual (Purnell Books, 1980)

CHAPTER 49

1 *Evening News*, 2 February 1981
2 *Daily Mail*, 9 December 1980
3 BBC News, 7 March 2007
4 *Manchester Evening News*, 7 April 2014
5 *Daily Express*, 24 December 1980
6 *Sun*, 23 February 1980
7 BBC Radio Five Live, 23 October 2012
8 *Daily Mail*, 8 December 1972
9 Savile, *As It Happens*, p. 117
10 Ibid., p. 156
11 *Daily Mail*, 8 January 1994
12 BBC News, 28 December 2012
13 *Sunday Mirror*, 19 July 1981
14 *Sunday People*, 6 September 1981
15 *Daily Express*, 2 January 1982
16 *Sun*, 3 February 1982
17 *Daily Star*, 3 September 1982

CHAPTER 50

1 Bellamy, *How's About That Then?*, p. 246
2 *Sun*, 12 April 1983
3 ibid.
4 ibid.
5 Interview on *Daybreak*, ITV1, 1 October 2012
6 *Daily Star*, 12 April 1983
7 Interview on *Daybreak*, ITV1, 1 October 2012
8 *Daily Star*, 12 April 1983

9 *Sun*, 12 April 1983
10 *Daily Mail*, 21 June 1983
11 *Daily Mail*, 20 December 1983

CHAPTER 52

1 Beerling, *Radio 1: The Inside Scene*, p. 215
2 *Evening News*, 16 July 1987
3 *Daily Mirror*, 14 September 1987
4 Charles Kaye and Alan Franey (eds), *Managing High Security Psychiatric Care* (Jessica Kingsley, 1998), pp. 34–35
5 *Exposure Update: The Jimmy Savile Investigation* – ITV
6 *Exposure Update: The Jimmy Savile Investigation* – ITV
7 *Guardian*, 30 August 1988
8 *Daily Telegraph*, 30 August 1988
9 *Sunday Times*, 4 September 1988
10 *Sunday Telegraph*, 4 September 1988
11 Kaye and Franey (eds), *Managing High Security Psychiatric Care*, p. 40
12 *Sunday Mirror*, 25 September 1988
13 *The Economist, Intelligent Life Magazine*, September/October 2012
14 *Reveille*, 30 May 1970
15 *Mail Online*, 13 October 2012
16 Channel 4 News, 31 October 2012
17 Savile, *God'll Fix It*, pp. 31–32
18 Kaye and Franey (eds), *Managing High Security Psychiatric Care*, p. 49
19 *Sunday Times*, 27 October 2013
20 *The Saturday Night Show*, RTE, 3 November 2012
21 *Mail Online*, 13 October 2012
22 *The Times*, 21 October 1988
23 Health Advisory Service Report on Broadmoor Hospital (HAS, 1988)
24 *Sunday Telegraph*, 4 September 1988
25 *Sun*, 17 July 2013
26 *Daily Express*, 10 December 1988
27 *Sunday Times*, 1 January 1988
28 *Independent* 12 January 1989
29 *Sun*, 20 January 1989
30 *Independent*, 12 January 1989

CHAPTER 54

1 *Observer*, 10 May 1987
2 Ibid.
3 *Weekend Magazine*, 16 April 1986
4 *Weekend Magazine*, 7 May 1986
5 *Sunday People*, 20 April 1986
6 *Observer*, 10 May 1987
7 *Evening News*, 13 May 1987
8 'Giving Victims a Voice', 7.14, Figure 5
9 *Vanity Fair*, 15 February 2013
10 *Daily Mirror*, 12 June 1987
11 *Sunday Times* 29 April 1984
12 *Weekend Magazine*, 6 February 1985

13 *Sunday Mirror*, 19 January 1986
14 *Guardian*, 15 June 2013
15 *Sun*, 17 July 2013
16 *Sun*, 17 July 2013
17 *Sunday People*, 13 September 1981
18 *Daily Mirror*, 6 November 2011
19 *You Magazine*, 12 May 1985
20 *Mail on Sunday*, 21 July 1985
21 *Daily Express*, 1 February 1986
22 *Sun*, 27 May 1985
23 *Weekend Magazine*, 10 October 1986
24 'Giving Victims a Voice', p. 9

CHAPTER 55

1 *Guardian*, 1 November 1989
2 *Daily Mail*, 8 November 2011
3 *The Palace Diaries: 12 Years with HRH Prince Charles* by Sarah Goodall and Nicholas Monson (Mainstream)
4 *Sunday Times*, 4 November 2012
5 Jonathan Dimbleby, *The Prince of Wales: A Biography* (Little, Brown, 1994), p. 495
6 *Independent on Sunday*, 22 July 1990
7 *Sunday Mirror Magazine*, 9 September 1990
8 *Q Magazine*, November 1990
9 *News of the World*, 21 October 1990
10 *Daily Mirror*, 10 June 2012
11 *Evening Standard*, 27 November 1990
12 Norman Giller, 'This is My Strife: How I Let Savile off the Hook', Sports Journalists Association, 5 October 2012
13 *This Is Your Life*, ITV, 13 December 1990

CHAPTER 57

1 'Giving Victims a Voice', Figure 5, p. 16
2 *Daily Express*, 20 June 1990
3 *Daily Express*, 7 November 1990
4 *Evening Standard*, 5 July 1991
5 *Sunday Times*, 7 July 1991
6 *Sunday Times*, 4 November 2012
7 *Is This Your Life?*, Thames Television, 1995
8 *Sun*, 11 March 1996
9 *Daily Mirror*, 29 September 1998
10 *Sun*, 11 November 2012
11 *Daily Telegraph*, 14 August 1991
12 *Q Magazine*, November 1990
13 Clare, *In the Psychiatrist's Chair*, p. 252
14 Ibid., p. 253
15 Ibid., p. 259
16 Ibid., p. 271
17 Ibid., p. 277
18 Ibid., pp. 242–243

19 *You Magazine, Mail on Sunday,* 23 February 1992
20 *Daily Mail,* 29 December 1993
21 *Daily Mail,* 8 January 1994

CHAPTER 59

1 *Daily Mail,* 7 October 1997
2 *Sunday Times Magazine,* 4 February 2001
3 *Press Gazette,* 15 July 2013
4 *Mail on Sunday,* 26 September 1999
5 *The Times,* 8 May 2000
6 *Sunday Times Magazine,* 4 February 2001
7 *Sunday Telegraph,* 26 December 2004
8 *Sunday Times Magazine,* 4 February 2001
9 *Daily Mirror,* 20 October 2012
10 *Daily Star,* 20 January 2006
11 *Guardian,* 29 October 2012

CHAPTER 60

1 In The Matter of the Late Jimmy Savile – Report to the Director of Public Prosecutions by Alison Levitt QC, pp. 26–27
2 Ibid., p. 23
3 Ibid., p. 44
4 Report Into Operation Ornament by Detective Superintendent Jon Savell, 11 January 2013, 3.9, p. 7
5 In The Matter of the Late Jimmy Savile, p. 31
6 Report Into Operation Ornament, 4.4, p. 12
7 Report Into Operation Ornament, 4.8, p. 12
8 BBC News, 25 January 2008
9 Report Into Operation Ornament, 8.11, p. 43
10 In The Matter of the Late Jimmy Savile, p. 14
11 Ibid., p. 15
12 Ibid., p. 17
13 Witness statement to Sussex Police, In The Matter of the Late Jimmy Savile, p. 16
14 In The Matter of the Late Jimmy Savile, pp. 47–48
15 Report Into Operation Ornament, 5.7, p. 18
16 In The Matter of the Late Jimmy Savile, p. 52
17 Ibid., p. 55
18 Ibid., p. 55
19 Ibid., p. 38
20 Levitt, pp. 40–41, points 97–99

CHAPTER 61

1 Report Into Operation Ornament, 3.21, p. 10
2 Report Into Operation Newgreen by West Yorkshire Police, 7.29, p. 34
3 Report Into Operation Ornament, 7.27, p. 28
4 Report Into Operation Newgreen, 3.9, p. 13
5 Report Into Operation Newgreen, 7.29, p. 35

6 Report Into Operation Newgreen, 7.25, p. 33
7 'Mistakes Were Made', 6.16, p. 27
8 Report Into Operation Newgreen, 7.28, p. 34
9 *Daily Telegraph*, 13 January 2013
10 Transcript of recorded interview with Jimmy Savile by officers from Surrey Police, 01/10/2009
11 *Daily Star*, 20 October 2013
12 'Mistakes Were Made', 6.16, p. 27
13 In The Matter of the Late Jimmy Savile, p. 67
14 'Mistakes Were Made', 6.16, p. 27
15 In The Matter of the Late Jimmy Savile, p. 115

CHAPTER 63

1 *The Times*, 17 October 2012
2 *The Times*, 27 October 2012
3 *Daily Mail*, 18 October 2013
4 *Daily Telegraph*, 18 October 2013
5 *Yorkshire Evening Post*, 8 November 2011
6 Operation Newgreen – West Yorkshire Police by Detective Chief Superintendent David Knopwood, 3.5, p. 12
7 Operation Newgreen – West Yorkshire Police, 3.10, p. 13
8 'Mistakes Were Made', 2.21, p. 7
9 Ibid., p. 7
10 Ibid., 10.6, p. 44
11 Ibid., 10.8, p. 44

CHAPTER 64

1 BBC News, Beds/Bucks/Herts, 7 March 2010

CHAPTER 65

1 BBC News, Beds/Berks/Herts, 30 October 2011
2 *Wokingham Times*, 2 November 2011
3 *Peterborough Telegraph*, 1 November 2011
4 *Scarborough News*, 1 November 2011
5 *Scottish Catholic Observer*, 4 November 2011
6 *Halesowen News*, 4 November 2011
7 NYTimes.com, 2 November 2011
8 Bellamy, *How's About That Then?*, p. 195
9 *Yorkshire Evening Post*, 31 October 2011
10 *Yorkshire Evening Post*, 8 November 2011
11 BBC Entertainment and Art News, 30 October 2011
12 *Daily Star*, Sunday 6 November 2011
13 Bellamy, *How's About That Then*, p. 259
14 *Mirror*, 4 November 2011
15 *www.walesonline.co.uk*; 3 November 2011

CHAPTER 66

1 Operation Newgreen – West Yorkshire Police, 6.10, p. 25
2 Operation Newgreen – West Yorkshire Police, Appendix A, p. 59
3 Operation Newgreen – West Yorkshire Police, p. 4
4 Operation Newgreen – West Yorkshire Police, 7.2, p. 26
5 'Mistakes Were Made', 5.9, p. 20
6 Operation Newgreen – West Yorkshire Police, 7.15, p. 31
7 Operation Newgreen – West Yorkshire Police, 7.16, p. 31
8 Operation Newgreen – West Yorkshire Police, 7.18, p. 32
9 Ibid.
10 Operation Newgreen – West Yorkshire Police, 7.17, p. 31
11 Operation Newgreen – West Yorkshire Police, 8.2, p. 41
12 Operation Newgreen – West Yorkshire Police, 8.4, p.41
13 Operation Newgreen – West Yorkshire Police, 8.16, p. 44
14 Operation Newgreen – West Yorkshire Police, 8.17, p. 44
15 Operation Newgreen – West Yorkshire Police, 8.19, p. 44
16 Operation Newgreen – West Yorkshire Police, 3.7, p. 12
17 *Daily Telegraph*, 10 May 2013
18 *Daily Mail*, 18 October 2013
19 *Yorkshire Post*, 10 May 2013
20 *Daily Mirror*, 17 October 2013
21 *Yorkshire Post*, 8 October 2013

CHAPTER 67

1 *Sunday Express*, 28 October 2012
2 *Daily Express*, 24 October 212
3 *Daily* Express, 23 October 2012
4 North Yorkshire Police website, 31 October 2012
5 Home Office: Written statement to Parliament: HMIC's review into allegations and intelligence material concerning Jimmy Savile
6 BBC News, 12 March 2013
7 Real Whitby – Savilegate: Operation Countryman II (2) – 15 May 2013
8 Letter from Sue Cross, T/DCC North Yorkshire Police to Director of Investigations IPCC, dated 29 May 2013
9 Letter to Tim Hicks from Rebecca Reid of IPCC, dated 4 June 2013
10 Open letter from Tim Hicks to North Yorkshire Police re Jimmy Savile and Peter Jaconelli. 20 September 2013
11 Statement by Deputy Chief Constable Tim Madgwick, North Yorkshire Police, 1 November 2013. www.northyorkshire.police.uk
12 BBC News York & North Yorkshire, 4 April 2014

CHAPTER 68

1 *Guardian*, 11 October 2013
2 *Daily Telegraph*, 11 January 2013
3 *Guardian*, 11 January 2013
4 BBC News, 6 October 2013
5 *Police Oracle*, 9 October 2013
6 ITV News Interview, 12 November 2012
7 *London Review of Books*, 8 November 2012

8 Rolling Stones 'Stray Cat Blues'
9 Gary Puckett & The Union Gap 'Young Girl'
10 *Yorkshire Evening Post*, 15 October 2013
11 *Milton Keynes Citizen*, 20 March 2014

SELECT BIBLIOGRAPHY

Bailey, Alan *208 It Was Great: An Affectionate Anecdotal Journey Between 1958 and 1975* (Alan Bailey, 2006)

Beckett, Andy *When The Lights Went Out: Britain in the Seventies* (Faber, 2009)

Beerling, Johnny *Radio 1: The Inside Scene* (Trafford Publishing, 2008)

Bellamy, Alison *How's About That Then?* (Great Northern Books, 2012)

Bennett, Alan *Untold Stories* (Faber, 2006)

Bevan, Bob *Nearly Famous: Adventures of An After-Dinner Speaker* (Virgin Books, 2003)

Blackburn, Tony *The Living Legend: An Autobiography* (W H Allen & Co, 1985)

Blacknell, Steve *The Story of Top of the Pops* (Patrick Stephens Limited, 1985)

Burrell, Paul *A Royal Duty* (Michael Joseph, 2003)

Clare, Anthony *In the Psychiatrist's Chair* (Heinemann, 1992)

Clarkson, Wensley *Hit 'em Hard: Jack Spot, King of the Underworld* (Harper Collins, 2002)

Cowley, Dr Chris *Face to Face With Evil: Conversations with Ian Brady* (Metro Publishing, 2011)

Cresswell, Janet *Ox-Bow* (Chipmunka Publishing, 2007)

Dimbleby, Jonathan *The Prince of Wales: A Biography* (Little, Brown, 1994)

Dingwall, Robert, Eekelaar, John and Murray, Topsy *The Protection of Children: State Intervention and Family Life* (Basil Blackwell, 1983)

Eggar, Robin *Tom Jones: The Biography* (Headline, 2000)

Elliott, Brian *Yorkshire Miners* (Sutton Publishing Ltd, 2004)

—— *Yorkshire Mining Veterans:In Their Own Words* (Wharncliffe Books, 2005)

Fabian, Jenny and Byrne, Johnny *Groupie* (New English Library, 1969)

Garfield, Simon *The Wrestling: The Hilarious True Story of Britain's Last Great Superheroes* (Faber, 2007)

Goodall, Sarah and Monson, Nicholas *The Palace Diaries: 12 Years with HRH Prince Charles* (Mainstream, 2007)

Ferris, Roy and Lord, Julian *Teddy Boys: A Concise History* (Milo Books, 2012)

Fraser, Derek *A History of Modern Leeds* (Manchester University Press, 1980)

Gittins, Ian *Top of the Pops: Mishaps, Miming and Music* (BBC Books, 2007)

Glinert, Ed *Manchester Compendium: A Street by Street History of England's Greatest Industrial City* (Penguin, 2009)

Greene, Sir Hugh *The Third Floor Front: A View of Broadcasting in the Sixties* (The Bodley Head, 1969)

Haslam, Dave *Manchester, England* (Fourth Estate, 1999)

Hayes, Stephen *The Biggest Gang in Britain* (Grosvenor House Publishing, 2013)

Kaye, Charles and Franey, Alan (eds) *Managing High Security Psychiatric Care* (Jessica Kingsley, 1998)

Kershaw, Andy *No Off Switch* (Virgin, 2011)

Kynaston, David *Austerity Britain 1945–51* (Bloomsbury, 2007)

Lee, Carol Ann *One of Your Own: The Life and Death of Myra Hindley* (Mainstream, 2011)

Lewis, Vic and Barrow, Tony *Music and Maiden Overs* (Chatto & Windus, 1987)

Loog Oldham, Andrew *Stoned* (Secker & Warburg, 2000)

Melly, George *Owning Up: the Trilogy* (Penguin, 2000)

Messenger, Chas *Cycling's Circus* (Pelham Books, 1971)

Moore, Charles *Margaret Thatcher: The Authorized Biography, Volume One: Not For Turning* (Allen Lane, 2013)

Morley, Eric *The 'Miss World' Story* (Angley Books, 1967)

Morton, Andrew *Diana: Her True Story* (Michael O'Mara, 1992)

Nichols, Richard *Radio Luxembourg: The Station of The Stars: An Affectionate History of 50 Years of Broadcasting* (WH Allen & Co Ltd, 1983)

Nott, James L. *Music For The: Popular Music and Dance in Interwar Britain* (Oxford University Press, 2002)

Ordish, Roger *The Jim'll Fix It Story* (Hodder & Stoughton, 1992)

—— *Jim'll Fix It Annual 1980* (Purnell Books)

—— *Jim'll Fix It Annual 1981* (Purnell Books)

Pallo, Jackie 'Mr TV' *You Grunt, I'll Groan:The Inside Story of Professional Wrestling* (Futura, 1987)

Parton, Nigel *The Politics of Child Abuse* (Macmillan, 1985)

Peel, John *Margrave of the Marshes: His Autobiography* (Bantam Press, 2005)

Preedy Bob *Live Like a Lord: James Corrigan's Amazing Story* (R. E. Preedy, 2002)

Rose, Eddie *Send In the Clowns: British Professional Wrestling 1964–1984* (Temple DPS Ltd, 2008)

Savile, Jimmy *As It Happens* (Barrie & Jenkins, 1974)

Savile, Jimmy *God'll Fix It* (Mowbrays, 1979)

Simpson, Jeff *Top of the Pops: 1964–2002* (BBC Worldwide, 2002)

Skidmore, Ian *Forgive Us Our Press Passes* (Revel Barker, 2008)

Stanford, Peter *The Outcast's Outcast: A Biography of Lord Longford* (Sutton Publishing, 2003)

Stewart, Ed *Out of the Stewpot: My Autobiography* (John Blake, 2005)

Street, Adrian *Sadist in Sequins* (Adrian Street, 2012)

Thompson, Ben (ed.) *Ban This Filth: Letters from the Mary Whitehouse Archive* (Faber, 2012)

Ward, Kat *Keri Karin – the Shocking True Story Continued …* (self-published, 2012)

Williams, Emlyn *Beyond Belief* (Pan, 1968)

Willerton, Mark *No Secret Anymore: The Real Kathy Kirby* (Matador, 2013)

Winters, David *Winter's Tale: Living Through an Age of Change in Church and Media* (Lion Publishing, 2001)

Wyman, Bill *Stone Alone: The Story of a Rock'n'Roll Band* (Perseus, 1990)

The Official Top 40 Charts (Virgin, 2009)

Top of the Pops Annual 1975 (World Distributors Limited)

Top of the Pops Annual 1976 (World Distributors Limited)

Top of the Pops Annual 1977 (World Distributors Limited)

Top of the Pops Annual 1978 (World Distributors Limited)

Top of the Pops Annual 1979 (World Distributors Limited)

Top of the Pops Annual 1980 (World Distributors Limited)

ACKNOWLEDGEMENTS

There are many people without whom this book would not have been possible. Foremost, I would like to thank Richard Milner, my editor, for having faith in it over a long period of time, and for his enduring enthusiasm and wise counsel. Also at Quercus, David North for backing the project, and Josh Ireland for his tireless and expert work on the copy.

I am lucky to have an agent such as Peter Straus at Rogers, Coleridge and White, and to have been previously represented by Hannah Westland, who believed in me, and the book in its various incarnations, when others (including me) did not.

Many have played a significant role in helping me through various aspects of the story: Meirion Jones and Liz MacKean, Mark Williams-Thomas, Liz Dux, Gerard Tubb, Tim Hicks and Nigel Ward at Real Whitby, Ross Howard, Neil Wilby at upsd. co.uk and, most significantly, all those who were willing to revisit the past and talk to me about their experiences.

My thanks also go to the very talented editors who commissioned the various long-form magazine features that serve as its foundations: Michael Hodges, David Whitehouse, Jeremy Langmead and Alex Bilmes. Gerard Greaves of the *Mail on Sunday* was also kind enough to give me the time to get it started.

Others to have contributed in a number of small but important ways include John Hopkins, Frank Broughton, Louis Barfe, Sam Parker, Toni Houghton, Richard Benson, Kester Aspden, James Brown and Michael Holden, and, of course, my parents, siblings and in-laws.

A special mention should be made of Andrew O'Hagan, whose brilliant essay, 'Light Entertainment', published in the *London*

Review of Books in November 2012, provided renewed impetus and interest in the book, and whose advice and encouragement have been invaluable. The same goes for another author I greatly admire, David Peace, whose interest and generosity provided an unexpected boost when I needed it most.

The subject matter of this book, I feel, makes a dedication inappropriate. There is, however, one person who has shown the patience, the love and the understanding that has enabled me to complete it – my beautiful wife. Thank you sweetest, for all this and more.

INDEX

Across 502
age of consent law 344–5
Airy, Major-General Sir Christopher
    424
Alexandra, Princess 338, 471, 476
Ambrose, Bert 125
Andrew, Prince 424
Appleyard, Sergeant Matthew 489,
    517
Arbiter, Dickie 423
Armstrong, Sir Robert 387, 415
As It Happens 14–15, 306—7, 407,
    471
Athenaeum Club 66–67, 282, 388,
    390, 394, 407
Aylard, Richard 424

Bailey, John 508
Baker, Joe 61, 68, 488–9
Bakewell, Joan 305–6
Ball, Julie 323–4
Barber, Andrea 238, 239–40
Barber, Anthony 257
Barber, Lynn 16, 29, 425, 426
Barrymore, Michael 461, 484
Batty, Pam 187–8
BBC (British Broadcasting
    Corporation) 272–3
  abuse of young people by Savile
    while working for 113, 165,
    167—8, 433, 536
  assists police inquiries into Savile
    354
  criticism of handling of Savile situ-
    ation 10, 93

decision not to broadcast
    Newsnight investigation into
    Savile 77–9, 90–2, 109–13,
    350–2, 540
  and *Exposure* documentary 350–1
  independent review into culture
    and practices of during time
    Savile worked at 536
  Managed Risk Programme List
    (MRPL) 55
  and Payola scandal 265–6, 297
  Savile's high standing at 272–3
  and *Top of the Pops* scandal
    266–73
Beatlemania 191
Beatles 185, 189–90, 191, 196–8,
    199, 204, 217, 221
Bedwell, Dave 105
Beecher-Stevens, Sydney 150
Beerling, Johnny 248–9, 254, 393
Bellamy, Alison 380, 503
Belle Vue complex (Manchester)
    214–16, 217
Bennett, Donald 114, 401
Benny, Bill 132–3, 137–8, 193
  death of 191–2
Bernstein, Sidney 47
Beston, Ted 307
Bevan, Bob 307–8, 312
Bevin Boys 59–68, 391, 407
Bevin Boys Association 67
Biddle & Co. 451, 453
Binks, Jack 131–2
Black, Cilla 220
Black, George and Alfred 149

Blackburn, Tony 5, 248, 249
Blake, Judith 52
Boaden, Helen 70–1, 76, 77, 78, 79, 92, 110, 353
Bodley, Roger 177
Booker, Detective Chief Superintendent Richard 269
Bottomley, Roy 428
Boy, a Girl and a Bike, A 66–7
Boyd-Carpenter, John 243
Brady, Ian 326
Braine, John 256
British Rail 362–3, 387, 413
Broadmoor 72, 246, 396–406, 426–7
  appointment of Savile to task force and power of 401, 402, 403, 405–6, 421, 483—4
  blackmailing of staff by Savile 402, 536
  Health Advisory Service Inspectorate report on 403
  industrial dispute 394–5
  management boards 421
  modernisation and liberalisation of (1978) 401
  restructuring programme and setting up of task force to manage 394–6
  Savile as 'Honorary Assistant Entertainment Manager' 260, 274, 287, 304–5
  Sutcliffe at 379
  transfer of patients from 405
Brooksby, Bob 308–9, 318, 319
Broome House (Manchester) 372
Bruno, Frank 437–8, 509
Buckinghamshire Healthcare NHS Trust 332
Burrell, Paul 455
Bush, Barbara 437
Busley, Chief Inspector Mark 465

Butler, Robin 404
Butlin, Sir Billy 339
Butlins Holiday Camps 7-Day race 102–3
Buttle, Derek 106

Café Fish (Scarborough) 495–6
Calder, Tony 152–6, 210, 487
Cameron, David 10
Campbell, Nicky 4, 56, 393
Campbell, Pat 149–50
Campbell, Sam 242
Cardus, Jim 12
Castle, Barbara 305
Castle, Roy 190
Celebrity Big Brother 461, 463
Central Remedial Clinic 246–7, 293, 359
Charles, Jim 502
Charles, Prince 4, 18, 88, 175–6, 261, 283, 361, 388, 413, 417, 418, 421–2, 423, 424, 434–5, 436–7, 451, 455–6, 461–2, 504, 538–9
Christophe, Jon 519
Churchill, Winston 47
Clare, Anthony 16, 29, 212, 213, 439–42, 500
Clarkson Brothers 43–4
Clunk Click 57, 69, 71, 295, 302–3, 308
Colehan, Barney 196
Coles, Dee 278–9, 541
Collins, Alan 541
Collins, Jeffrey 142, 144, 145–6
Collins, Rodney 296–7
Colt Ventilation and Heating Ltd 243
Connew, Paul 451
Cope, Janet (née Rowe) 85–7, 308, 313, 356, 411, 414, 416, 417, 424, 426, 434, 436, 442–3, 452–4, 532–3, 536, 544

Corbett, Ronnie 190
Corrigan, Jimmy 95, 118, 239,
    240–1, 244, 286, 321, 411,
    501–2, 523–4
Corrigan, Mairead 321, 501–2
Cotton, Bill 195, 196, 272–3, 310,
    311, 338
Cottrell, Gladys 314
Crocker, James 272
Cross, Assistant Chief Constable
    Sue 527
Crown Prosecution Service (CPS)
    73, 75–9, 79, 91–2, 109, 111,
    350, 351, 353, 470, 534–5
Curran, Sir Charles 272
Currie, Edwina 396, 402–4, 483

Daily Express 108
Daily Star 385
Dalmour, Dave 82–3, 102, 450
Dayan, General Moshe 314
Dearan, Samantha 333
Decca Record Company 149–50
Deller, Helen 91–3, 109, 110, 112
Dempster, Nigel 436
Dexter, Jeff 188–9, 213
Diana, Princess 175–6, 361, 388,
    416–18, 421, 422–3, 424, 434,
    435–6, 437, 451, 454–5, 501,
    508, 539
Dick, Dr Donald 395
Disley, John 412
Donegan, Lonnie 128
Donnelly, Jimmy 131, 133
Dorfman, Stanley 217, 249, 267
Double Top Ten Show 373
Dr Barnado's 464
Drugwatch 417–18
Duncan, Ronnie 236–7, 239, 240
Duncroft Approved School for Girls
    31–8, 50–1, 165

Savile's abuse of girls at 31, 33,
    34–6, 37, 38, 50–4, 56–7, 72,
    73, 164, 297–8, 451, 463–5,
    468–9, 470, 475–6
Dux, Liz 237, 327, 333, 336–7, 535,
    540, 541–2

Eager, Dave 211, 212, 213, 229–30,
    232–3, 245, 250, 253, 306, 322,
    371–2, 384, 434, 509, 534
Edinburgh, Duke of 152, 174, 179,
    243, 282, 360, 361, 364, 376,
    417, 424, 533
Edmonds, Noel 249
Edwards, John 371
Entwistle, George 38, 39, 70, 71,
    77, 78, 349–50, 353
Esquire 365
Evans, Chris 56
Evans, Geoff 286
Exposure documentary 8, 164–9,
    349–54, 534

Fairley, Alan 123
Ferguson, Julie 114, 456
Ferguson, Roddy 114, 504
Ferguson, Sarah see York, Duchess of
Fincham, Peter 349
Finnie, Jim 501
Fix It Promotions 319
Foster, Roger 8, 89, 90, 114–15,
    352, 504
Fowler, Norman 376–7
Francis Café (Scarborough) 95–6
Franey, Alan 394, 401, 403–4, 406,
    411, 428, 433, 503
Freeman, Alan 196
Freeman, Roger 406
Friday Morning Club 12, 102, 158,
    465, 488–9, 491, 516–17, 520,
    526

Friends of Israel Educational Trust
313

Gambaccini, Paul 373, 383–4, 385
Garbutt, Dennis 277
Garbutt, Lucy 277
Gardiner, Alex 164, 349
Gardiner, Lesley 164–5, 349, 350
Gargan, Nick 522
Gervais, Ricky 4
Giarchi, Father George 232–3
Gibbons, Liz 54–5, 70, 73, 76, 165
Gilbey, James 422, 423
Gilmore, Mark 522
'Giving Victims a Voice' report
(2013) 194, 231, 317, 433, 534
Glenn, Ian 349
Glitter, Gary 57, 69, 71, 73, 302,
484–5
God'll Fix It 15, 126, 156, 315,
341–4, 500
Goldsmiths' Association 182
Goodall, Sarah 422
Goodwin, Harry 266–7
Goslett, Miles 90–1, 92, 110–12
Goulding, Lady Valerie 246–7, 359
Gove, Michael 372, 536
Graham, Clifford 395, 396, 405,
406, 421, 427–8
Granada 135
Grand Hotel (Brighton)
bombing of by IRA (1984) 414–15
Grand Order of the Knights of
Malta 321
Gray, Ian 372
Griffiths, David 501
Guttman, Dr Ludwig 361

Hall, Professor Alistair 54, 120,
449, 450, 502, 507–8
Hall, Ronald 372

Hall, Stuart 5, 461
Hamilton, David 5
Hards, Nigel 501
Hardy, James 110
Hare, Robert 426–7
Harman, Harriet 345
Harper, Inspector Lewis 132
Harris, Avril 146, 427
Harrison, Richard 400, 403
Harry, Prince 456
Hartwell, Janine 269
Haslam, Dave 130
Haughey, Charles 359
Haut de la Garenne children's home
(Jersey) 72, 163, 299–301, 467,
491
Have I Got News For You 16, 366
Hawley, Caroline 90
Hayes, Stephen 224–5
Haymes, Dick 31
Healey, Denis 257
Heath, Edward 196
Heimann, Carl 44, 122, 123, 124,
141, 148, 184
Henlow Grange health farm 323–4
Hepworth, Alan 504
Her Majesty's Inspectorate of
Constabulary see HMIC
Herdman, John 238–9
Hicks, Tim 523, 525–6, 528–9, 530
Hill, E.N. 244
Hill, Lord 269
Hindley, Myra 325–6, 458
Hitchen, Brian 341
HMIC (Her Majesty's Inspectorate
of Constabulary) review/report
(2013) 194, 491–2, 525
Hollies, The 128, 199
Home Office Large Major Enquiry
System (HOLMES) 524, 527
Hullighan, Charles 155, 260, 428

Hulme Hippodrome 191
Humble, Janet 110
Hume, Cardinal Basil 388
Hymns, Sue 87–9, 90

Ilford Palais-de-Danse (London)
    122–3
'I'm Backing Britain' campaign
    243–4, 246, 247
In the Psychiatrist's Chair series
    213, 439–42
Inside Out 529, 529–30
IRA 292–3, 414–15, 460
Israel 313–15

Jackson, Paul 195–6
Jackson, Peter 144
Jackson, T. Leslie 195
Jacobs, Bert 193
Jacobs, David 148, 196, 219, 428
Jaconelli, Peter 95, 285–7, 523–31,
    525, 526
Jagger, Mick 218
James, Polly 294
Jermey, Michael 169
Jim'll Fix It 13–14, 310–13,
    319–20, 321, 339, 340, 364,
    413, 443
Jim'll Fix It tribute show 58, 69, 70,
    74, 109
Jimmy Savile Charitable Trust 90,
    173
Jimmy Savile Stoke Mandeville
    Hospital Trust 90, 410
Jimmy Savile's Old Record Club
    373
Jimmy Savile's Yorkshire Speakeasy
    165
Joffe, Dr Mace 364
John Paul II, Pope 377
Johnson, Joan (née Savile) 24

Jones, Chief Constable Dave 528,
    531
Jones, Janie 325–6
Jones, Margaret 31, 32, 33, 34, 35,
    37, 470
Jones, Meirion 31, 33, 34–8,
    50–1, 53–6, 58, 71, 72–3, 74,
    76–8, 79, 91–3, 110–11, 113,
    162–164, 350, 351
Jukebox Jury 148

Kaberry, Sir Donald 244
Karma, Josef 252, 253
Katzir, Ephraim 313, 314
Kaye, Charles 401
Kelly, Father Martin 510
Kent, Duchess of 417
Keri 36–8, 50–1, 52, 53, 56–8, 69,
    72, 74, 75, 77, 79, 111, 112,
    113, 302, 351, 352
Kershaw, Andy 297
Killingbeck Hospital (Leeds) 449, 450
King, Jonathan 159, 161, 468, 485–6
Kirby, Kathy 125–6
Korer, Cecil 217
Kray, Ronnie 139

Lack, Dr Christofer 32
Lawton, Lord Justice 320
Lee, Assistant Chief Constable
    Ingrid 511–12, 520–1, 522
Lee, Peter 442
Leeds 21, 41
    during Second World War 41, 43, 44
Leeds District Community Safety
    Partnership 488
Leeds General Infirmary 87, 245,
    252–3
    Savile's voluntary work at 11, 87,
    155, 244, 245–6, 253, 260, 274
    sexual assaults by Savile at 333–7

Leeds Teaching Hospitals NHS Trust 336
Leeke, Alan 215–16, 226–7, 229
Lemmon, Dennis 147
Lennon, John 203
Levin, Angela 441–2
Levitt, Alison 534
Levy, John 313, 316
Lewis, Bunny 437
Lewis, Jim 193–4
Lewis, Vic 191
Life of Jimmy Savile, The (tv documentary) 294
Lindsay, Detective Constable John 332, 364
Listener 258, 321
Little Sisters of the Poor 27, 185, 206, 231
Livingston, Hannah 51, 53, 55, 69
Lochaber's Highland games 177, 179
London Marathon 377, 410, 412, 433
Longford, Lord 276, 280
Lucas, Alma 238
Lucas, Luke 176, 407—8, 409, 421, 503
Lucas, Savile 407–8

McAlpine, Claire 265, 267–8, 271–2, 273
McAlpine, Vera 265
McCartney, Paul 197–8
McFarlane, Christine 536–7
McGrath, Dr Pat (senior) 397, 398, 399, 401
McGrath, Patrick 397, 398–9, 401
MacInnes, Hamish 455
MacKean, Liz 38, 50–5, 56, 69, 72, 73, 75–6, 77, 78–9, 87, 92, 111, 113, 163, 164, 351

McKenna, Amanda 51, 89, 90, 114, 504, 510
Mackenzie, Kelvin 384
McMinns, Douglas 357
Maison Royale 408
Manchester 133, 224
Margaret Sinclair Centre (Rosewell) 247
Marsden, Guy 233–5, 291
Marsden, Herbert 235
Marsden, Marjory (née Savile) 24, 181, 235
Marsh, Peter 362–3
Marshall, Richard 272
Marshall, Tony 143
Martin, Steve 122
Mason, Sam 214
Mastermind 48
Masters, Valerie 151
Matthews, Victor 359–60
May, Theresa 491, 525
Mecca Locarno dancehall (Leeds) 41, 120–2, 141–5
Mecca Ltd 122–4, 135
Melly, George 132
Melody Maker 219
Mepham, John 128
Merton, Paul 16
Metropolitan Police/NSPCC report ('Giving Victims a Voice') (2013) 194, 231, 317, 433, 534
Metropolitan Police 223, 419, 492, 493, 530
Middleton, Peter 434
Miller, Harland 182
Mills, Bill 209
MIND 338
Mitchell, Bruce 130, 141
Mitchell, Lynn 238, 240
Mitchell, Stephen 55, 70, 71, 73–4, 77, 79, 112, 350, 351, 353

Monkhouse, Bob 308
Moore, Caroline 332–3, 539
Moors Murders 190
Morgan, Professor Michael 395, 405
Morley, Eric 123, 153
Morphet, Robert 3–4, 5, 7
Morris, Chris 451–2
Morton, Andrew 435–6
Mountbatten, Lord Louis 231,
    282–3, 339
Muggeridge, Douglas 254–5, 296,
    297
Muggeridge, Malcolm 254
Mulligan, Julia 528
Murray, Pete 196
Mylrea, Paul 112, 350

National Association of Youth
    Clubs 338
National Council for Civil Liberties
    (NCCL) 344–5
Neill, Brian 269, 272
Newgreen, Operation 380, 511–22
News of the World 265
  investigation into *Top of the Pops*
    266–7
Newsnight investigation 50–8,
    69–79, 163–4, 350
  decision not to broadcast by BBC
    77–9, 90–2, 109–13, 350–2,
    540
  reasons given by BBC for shelving
    91–2, 353
  Sunday Mirror story on axing of
    109–10
Nicol, Sylvia 114
Nixon, Richard 486
NME Poll Winners Party 217
Norman, Lady Montagu 32, 338
Norman, Philip 259
North Yorkshire Police 288, 524–31

Northern Ireland 292–3
Northern Ireland Association of
    Youth Clubs 293
Nottinghamshire Healthcare NHS
    Trust Forensic Division 285
Nuseibeh, Dr Isaac 416

O'Brien, Cardinal Keith 502
O'Brien, Jim 413
Ogilvy, Angus 338, 339, 424
O'Hagan, Andrew 537–8
O'Keefe, Father Jim 378
Oldie 110–11, 112
Ordish, Roger 295, 303, 304,
    310–11, 312–13, 314–15, 320,
    339, 424–5, 533
Ornament, Operation 463–6
Osmonds 311
Otley Pop Civic Ball 236–41
Owen, David 305
Owen, Rebecca 332

P&O 307, 340
Paedophile Action for Liberation
    344
Paedophile Information Exchange
    344
Palin, Michael 442–3
Pallo, Jackie 96
Pan's People 302
Parker, Colonel Tom 220
Parker, Peter 362, 363
Parkhurst 378
Parkinson, John 493
Parkinson, Michael 245, 442, 444–5
Parks, Reg 122
Parsons, Tony 4
Pattison, Mike 358–9
Paxman, Jeremy 247–8, 353
Payne, Julian 350

payola scandal 265–6, 274, 297, 312, 325
People 190, 241–2
Savile's column for 190, 193—4, 242, 244
Perkins, Captain 391
Peterborough children's hospital project 433–4, 435, 442—4, 501
Petty, Douglas 103, 104, 106
Philip, Prince *see* Edinburgh, Duke of
Plaza (Manchester) 127–30
polio scare 135
Pollard inquiry 55, 57, 74, 77, 91, 247, 350
Pollard, Nick 79, 92–3
pornography
Longford's commission and report on 276, 280
Powell, Enoch 257
President Records 325
Presley, Elvis 152, 201–2, 220
Price, Mavis 114, 454
Prince of Wales Colliery (Pontefract) 60
Prison Officers' Association 394–5, 401, 402, 403, 536
Prison Officers' Union 398
Project DJ *see Exposure* documentary
Protection of Children Act (1978) 344–5
Purdew, Stephen 110
Purnell, Herbert A. 60

QE2 cruise 366–70, 389–92, 430, 442, 444–6
Quality Street Gang 133
Queen Elizabeth cruise 503
Queen Mother 417
Quiz Bingo 250

Radio 1 247–9, 254–5, 259, 354
Radio Luxembourg 149–52, 196, 242
Rampton Psychiatric Hospital 274, 285–9
Rantzen, Esther 349
Ray, Georgina 89–90, 173, 174
Ray, Johnny 204
Read, Mike 509
Ready Steady Go 195
Real Whitby website 523, 525, 526–7, 528
Reith, Sir John 195
Rel, George 221
Richard, Cliff 486
Richards, Keith 199
Richardson, Irene 364, 490
Riddell, Sir John 424
Ridgeon, George 177
Ripley, Lynn 216–17
Rippon, Peter 38, 50, 54, 55, 69, 70–1, 73–9, 91, 93, 110, 111, 112–13, 351, 353
Rochdale case 165
Roche, Bishop Arthur 6
Roles, Penny-Ann 187
Rolling Stones 185, 198–9, 217–19, 220
Rook, Jean 303–4
Rossi, Francis 249
Rowe, Dick 150
Rowe, Janet *see* Cope, Janet
Royal Marine Museum 305
Royal Marines 231–2, 250, 256, 282, 508
Russell, Ken 101–2, 103, 106, 107–8

Sadat, President Anwar 315
St Joseph's Home for the Aged 27, 247, 507

Salford Council 321–2
Sampey, Denise 199
Sandy, John 378
Savile, Agnes (mother) 20, 21–5, 28,
    40, 80–1, 209–12
  death and funeral 289–91
  relationship with son 209–13, 256
Savile, Christina (sister) 24, 290, 449
Savile Institute 54
Savile, Jimmy
  Abuse Allegations 9–10
    alleged connection with paedo-
      phile ring in Scarborough
      523–4, 527, 531
    awareness of behaviour by
      hospital staff and hushing up of
      331–2, 334, 335, 336
    on BBC premises 113, 165,
      167–8, 433, 536
    and Broome House residents 372
    denial of abuse allegations 383,
      459–60, 475–7
    Duncroft School residents 31, 33,
      34–6, 37, 38, 50–4, 56–7, 72,
      73, 164, 297–8, 451, 463–5,
      468–9, 470, 475–6
    and *Exposure* programme 164–9,
      166, 349–54, 534
    father of Leeds schoolgirl inci-
      dent 380–1, 418–19
    fear of victims in coming forward
      167
    handling of by North Yorkshire
      Police 288, 524–31
    handling of by West Yorkshire
      Police 380, 492—4, 511—22
    and Haut de la Garenne chil-
      dren's home 72, 163, 299–301
    HMIC report (2013) 194, 491–2,
      525
    at Leeds General Infirmary 333–7
    luring of girls into cabin on P&O
      cruise and expulsion from the
      Canberra by captain 340–1
    Metropolitan Police/NSPCC
      report ('Giving Victims a
      Voice') (2013) 194, 231, 317,
      433, 534
    and Newgreen Operation/Report
      511–19
    Newsnight investigation and
      decision not to broadcast by
      BBC 35, 38, 50–8, 69–79, 90–2,
      109–13, 163–4, 350–2, 353, 540
    number of offences committed 534
    and Operation Yewtree 9, 327,
      493, 525, 526, 530, 540
    People investigation 241–2
    protected by celebrity status and
      charity work 168, 297, 332,
      333, 341, 374, 384, 386–7, 539
    rape allegations 9, 168, 194,
      222–3, 371, 452–3
    rumours over interest in teenage
      girls 16, 36, 39, 145–7, 159–60,
      297
    seducing of parents before
      abusing children tactic 270–1,
      273, 324
    at Stoke Mandeville Hospital 53,
      167, 72, 327–36, 433, 452–3,
      468, 542–3
    Surrey Police investigation before
      death 52–3, 55, 69, 71, 72–3,
      75, 76–7, 78, 163–4,
      463–71, 472–81, 493
  Charity and Hospital Work 16,
    28, 155, 213, 221–3, 231, 232,
    255, 260, 274–5, 305, 338, 458
    and Broadmoor 260, 274, 287,
      289, 304—5, 394–6, 398–405,
      421, 426, 483–4

Central Remedial Clinic fund-raising 246–7

marching for peace in Belfast 321

National Spinal Injuries Centre at Stoke Mandeville campaign 72, 178, 282, 356–7, 359—62, 365—8, 373, 374–7, 380, 410, 532

Peterborough children's hospital project and failure to get off the ground 442–4, 433—4, 435, 501

and Rampton Psychiatric Hospital 285–7, 288–9

reasons for working in hospitals 245–6

sponsored walks and runs 261, 293–4, 318–19, 355, 359, 431

talks given to Catholic priests and nuns 232–3

voluntary work at Leeds General Infirmary 11, 87, 155, 244, 245–6, 253, 260, 274

voluntary work and fundraising at Stoke Mandeville Hospital 72, 85, 274, 295—6, 305, 413–14, 416

walk from John O'Groats to Land's End 261, 431

Music and Show Business Career

advertising campaigns involved in 319, 325

axed from Radio 1 393

British Rail advertising contract 362–3, 387, 413

in *Celebrity Big Brother* 461, 463

Clunk Click 57, 69, 71, 295, 302–3, 308

courting of publicity 95, 103, 107, 152, 231, 305–6

dancehall and Mecca career 48, 82–4, 120–34, 138, 141–5, 153–4, 184–5, 391, 497

diminishing of profile 413, 460–1

Disc Jockey of the Year awards 219–20, 224

first tv appearance over polio vaccination campaign 135

and government's seat belt campaign 305

hosting of Top Ten Club at Belle Vue 214–16, 218–19

Jim'll Fix It see *Jim'll Fix It*

People column 190, 193–4, 242, 244

popularity of 13, 297, 304, 373, 540

Quiz Bingo 250

and Radio 1 247–9, 254, 256–7, 296, 373

and Radio Luxembourg 149–52, 196, 242

running of nightclub complex in Bournemouth 407–8

singles recorded 185–6, 189

and *Speakeasy* radio show 256–7, 258, 275, 373

Ten Years of What? 257–8

and *This Is Your Life* 48–9, 259–60, 428–9

Top of the Pops presenter 196–200, 217, 249, 269–70, 276

tours 189

view of pop business 220

wrestling career 96, 193–4, 195, 231, 483

Young At Heart for Tyne Tees Television 151

Personal Life

age 220, 224

association with the Royal
Marines and awarded Green
Beret 231–2, 250, 256, 282,
508
and Athenaeum Club membership 388
auction of belongings (2012)
173–8, 414
autobiography *see As It Happens*
awarded Bevin Boy medal 67,
407
awards and accolades 19, 294,
321
as black market operator in
Leeds 41, 44, 277
childhood and upbringing 20–9,
543–4
cigars 18, 47, 137
and cycling 45, 66, 81, 101–8
and death of Benny 191–2
and death of father 120
death and funeral 4–7, 51–2,
231, 500–1, 504, 506–10
and death/funeral of mother
289–91
demand for girls as condition for
making an appearance at Otley
Pop Civic Ball 237–41, 244
dislike of children 181, 183, 313,
418, 458
dress style and hair 13, 86, 94,
130, 142, 143, 148, 182, 369
early jobs 42, 43–4, 45, 81
eccentricities and oddball
persona 35, 59, 62, 63, 82, 130,
142, 143, 180–1, 461
elder statesman figure 413
fear of sexually transmitted
diseases 230
feels untouchable 154, 168, 307,
380, 463, 513

finances and money 131, 189,
221, 459
fondness for working in hospital
mortuaries 373–4
frugal living 221, 226
health problems 4, 449–50
heart bypass surgery 252, 449–51
as honorary chieftain of
Lochaber's Highland Games
177, 179
honorary doctorates awarded
178, 417, 419, 498
and hypnotism 81–2, 251–3
illness when a child 22–4, 28
IQ 322
jewellery 182–3
kiss and tell story about and
response to 323–4
knighthood 48, 376, 387, 404–5,
415–16, 424–5, 427–8
lack of emotion 15, 28, 29, 43,
86, 427, 440, 441, 497
last weeks before death 503
'love child' 89–90, 173
and McAlpine's suicide 265,
267, 270, 272, 273
marathon and long-distance
running 137, 410–12, 433
meeting with Pope John Paul II
377–8
Messiah complex 261, 304, 316,
342
mining accident and back injury
65–6, 80–1, 155
mining career 59–68
motor caravan 255–6, 277–8
OBE 18, 28, 38, 48, 276–7, 279
parental background 21–2
physical exercise and fitness 190,
410–11
and politics 304

reasons for not marrying 212–13, 426

relationship with father 26

relationship with and influence on the royal family 152, 175–6, 179, 231, 282–4, 338, 339, 359–60, 361, 388, 413, 416–18, 421–4, 434, 435–7, 454–6, 538–9

relationship with mother 15, 81, 201, 206–7, 209–13, 256, 276, 289–90, 441

relationship with the police 158, 225, 413–14, 487–90, 493, 516–17, 519, 523

relationship with siblings 28–9

relationship with Sue Hymns 87–9

relationship with Thatcher 320–1, 355–6, 358, 375, 387, 404, 415, 417, 538

religion and faith 15, 275, 275–6, 315–16, 341–2, 499–500, 544–5

removal of headstone at burial site 3–4, 7–8, 10–11

Rolls-Royces 130, 184, 248, 439–40

scrap metal business 81, 120

and Second World War 40–5, 59–60

and sex 156–7, 227, 343–4, 383, 425–6

sexual activities with teenage girls 153, 154, 156, 188–9, 203, 207–8, 215–16, 226–9, 277–9

suing against detractors 451–2, 479

Sun revelations of sex life (1983) 381–7, 415–16

Theroux's documentary on 4, 16–17, 134, 201, 457–8

thuggishness employed in dance-halls 133–4, 381–2, 387, 408

tributes paid to after death 4, 56, 501–2

trip to Israel 313–16

view of death 27, 117, 342, 373–4, 441, 499–500

wealth 173, 220–1

will 90, 114–15, 173

and Yorkshire Ripper case 378, 519

Savile, Joan *see* Johnson, Joan

Savile, John Henry (brother) 24, 29

Savile, Johnnie 291, 371–2, 428, 544

Savile, Marjory (sister) *see* Marsden, Marjory

Savile, Mary (sister) 20, 24, 428

Savile, Vince (brother) 20, 24, 43

Savile, Vince (father) 20, 21, 25–6, 81, 120, 123

Savile, Vivian 505, 540–1

Savile's Travels (radio programme) 249, 254, 255, 296, 373

Savile's Yorkshire Travels 265

Scarborough 94, 95, 118

Scarborough Borough Council 286, 526, 529

Scott, Robin 247, 248, 254

Scruff, Donna 268–9

Second World War 40–5

Semper, Reverend Colin 257, 275–6, 315, 316, 318, 322, 341–2, 344, 544–5

Shapiro, Helen 190

Sharpling, Drusilla 525, 526, 530

Shepherd, Rochelle 72

Shipman, Harold 536

Silverman, Howard 502, 504

IN PLAIN SIGHT

Simpson, Alan 143–4, 145, 146, 151
Simpson, Ann 238
Simpson, Mavis 122
Sinclair, Sister Margaret 22–3, 24
Sinden, Donald 445
Sivananthan, Professor Mohan 508
Skidmore, Ian 132
skiffle 128
Slaughter, Todd 219
Sloan, Tom 195, 196
Smith, David 541
Smith, Dame Janet 536
Smith, Paul 501
Soames, Mary 47–8
South Kirkby Colliery 60, 61, 62, 68
Speakeasy (radio show) 256–7, 258, 275, 373
Spence, Catherine 238
Spindler, Commander Peter 10, 534, 537
Springfield Psychiatric Hospital 371
Squires, Ian 349
Starkey, Inspector Mick 12, 158, 489–91, 494, 503, 520–1
Starmer, Keir 534–5, 542
Starr, Ringo 185
Steel, Ian 107
Stewart, Johnnie 195, 196, 198, 249
Stewart, Moir 529
Stoke Mandeville Hospital 163, 386, 434, 536–7
National Spinal Injuries Centre campaign 72, 175, 282, 356–7, 359–62, 365–8, 373, 374–7, 380, 410, 532
Savile's fundraising and voluntary work at 72, 85, 274, 295–6, 305, 413—14, 416
sexual assaults by Savile on patients and awareness of by

staff 53, 72, 167, 327–36, 433, 452–3, 468, 542–3
Storr, Catherine 312
Stranger Danger book 381, 419
Street, Adrian 483
Stribling-Wright, Gill 339–40
Sun
interviews with Savile (1983) 381–7, 415–16
Sunday Mirror 109–10, 451
Surrey Police 78, 161–5, 463–4, 534–5
interview of Savile over abuse allegations 474–80
investigation into Savile abuse allegations 52–3, 55, 69, 71, 72–3, 75, 76–7, 78, 163–4, 463–71, 472–81, 493
Operation Arundel 468
Sussex Police 467–8, 534–5
Sutcliffe, Peter 378, 379, 438
Swale, John 83–4, 121
Swift, Angela 177

Tait, Dr John 395
Taylor, Warwick 60–1, 67–8
The Forgotten Conscripts 67
Tea Council 318
Tebbit, Norman 415
Teen and Twenty Disc Club 151
Temple, George 403
Ten Years of What? 257–8
Thatcher, Margaret 49, 374–5, 404–5
attempt at securing knighthood for Savile 376, 387, 404, 405, 415–16
and Grand Hotel bombing 414–15
relationship with Savile 320–1, 355–6, 358, 375, 387, 404, 415, 417, 538

582

Theroux, Louis 4, 16–17, 134, 201, 457–8, 461, 497, 523
This is Your Life 48–9, 259–60, 428–9
Thomas, Brian 142–3
Thomas Cook 433, 434, 435, 442, 501
Thompson, Mark 4, 77, 90, 92, 93, 111
Thompson, Sue 165–6
Thornton, June 334
Top of the Pops 167–8, 196–200, 217, 226, 249
  axing of 461
  Savile as presenter 196–200, 217, 249, 269—70, 276
  scandal over young girls being exploited 266–73
  and suicide of Claire McAlpine 265, 267–9
Top Ten Club (Belle Vue) 174, 211, 215, 217, 218
Tour of Britain cycle race (1951) 66, 84, 102, 104–8
Travis, Dave Lee 5
Tremlett, George 241
Trevivian, Reverend Roy 256, 257, 275
Tyne Tees Television 149, 151

Ufland, Mark 272
Upper Broughton Assembly Rooms 186, 214

van Geest, Hillary 'Gussy' 250, 311
Variety Club of Great Britain 294
Vaughan, Dr Gerard 356, 357, 360
Vaughan-Barratt, Nick 38–9

Wales, Prince of *see* Charles, Prince
Ward, Nigel 523, 525–6, 528

Warnants, Dr Louis 395
Warner Brothers 149, 150
Waterloo Main colliery (Leeds) 64, 68
Watterson, Kevin 450
Watts, Charlie 218–19
West Yorkshire Police
  attending of Savile's Friday Morning Club 158, 465, 488, 491, 520
  campaign to fight crime 465
  negligence over Savile allegations 492–4
  and Operation Newgreen 380, 511–22
  relationship with Savile 380, 472, 487–90, 493, 519–20, 521, 523
  and Surrey Police investigation 472–4
  and Yorkshire Ripper case 364
Wharfe, Ken 437
When Louis Met Jimmy 4, 16–17, 134, 201, 457–8
Whitehouse, Mary 276
Wicks, Nigel 416
Wilby, Neil 514–15, 518, 519
William, Prince 434, 456
Williams, Betty 321
Williams-Thomas, Mark 38, 53, 69, 71, 73, 113, 161–9, 349–50, 352–3, 354
Wilson, Professor David 162
Wilson, Don 104
Wilson, Harold 224
Wilson, Jimmy 67, 104
Windsor, Jim 21
Winter, David 275
Wogan, Terry 362
Woodhead, Jennifer 238
Woodlands Cemetery 3, 7, 10

World of Jimmy Savile, The
  (documentary) 399, 499
Wyatt, Will 443
Wyman, Bill 219, 428

Yentob, Alan 443
Yewtree, Operation 9, 327, 493,
  525, 526, 530, 533, 540

York, Duchess of 422–3, 424
Yorkshire Ripper 364, 378, 490,
  518–19
Young At Heart 151
Young, Graham 398
Younghusband, Jan 39